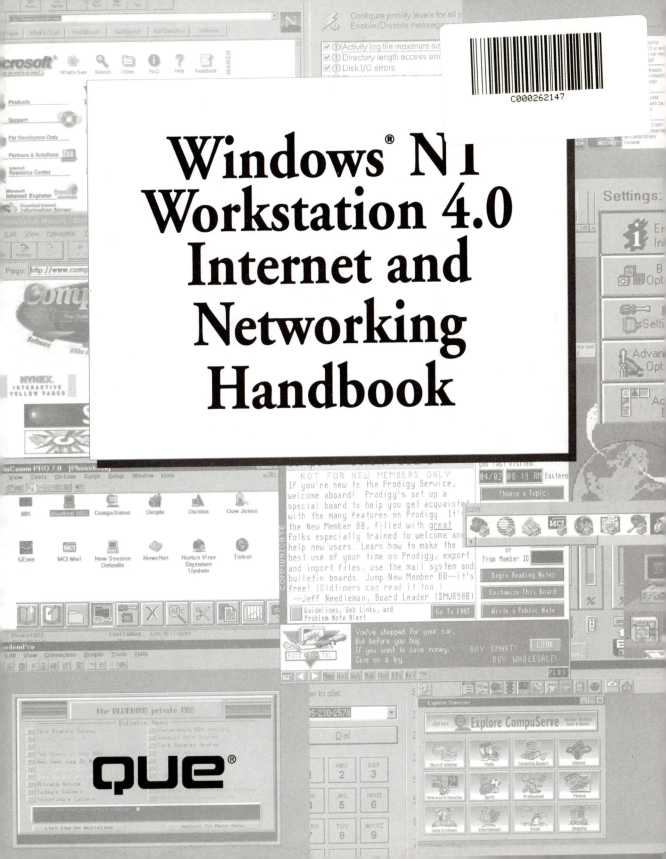

Windows® NT Workstation 4.0 Internet and Networking Handbook

que®

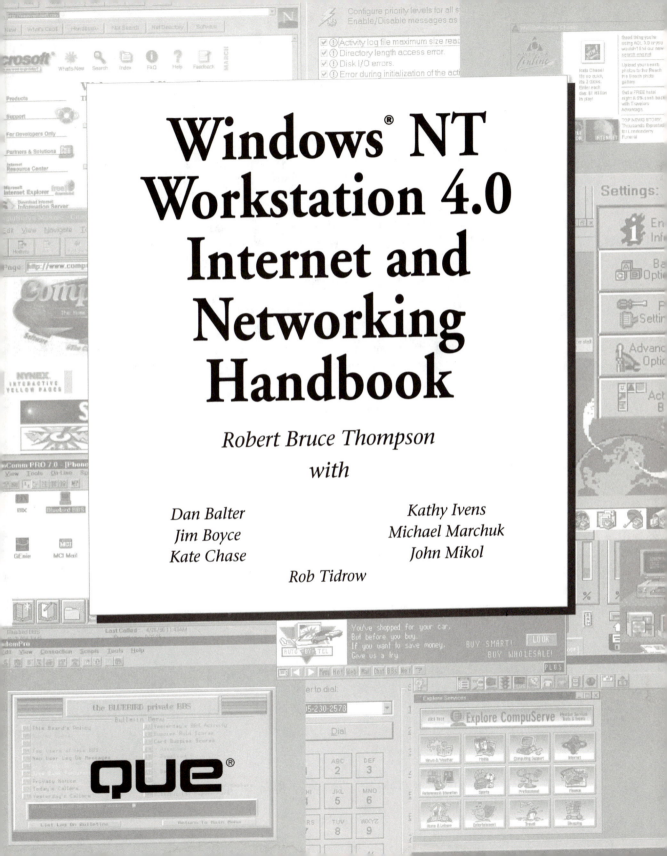

Windows® NT Workstation 4.0 Internet and Networking Handbook

Robert Bruce Thompson

with

Dan Balter
Jim Boyce
Kate Chase

Kathy Ivens
Michael Marchuk
John Mikol

Rob Tidrow

Que®

Windows NT Workstation 4.0 Internet and Networking Handbook

Library of Congress Catalog No.: 96-68990

ISBN: 0-7897-0817-5

98 97 96   6 5 4 3 2 1

Interpretation of the printing code: the rightmost double-digit number is the year of the book's printing; the rightmost single-digit number, the number of the book's printing. For example, a printing code of 96-1 shows that the first printing of the book occurred in 1996.

Screen reproductions in this book were created using Collage Plus from Inner Media, Inc., Hollis, NH.

Composed in *Stone Serif* and *MCPdigital* by Que Corporation

Credits

President
Roland Elgey

Publishing Director
Brad R. Koch

Editorial Services Director
Elizabeth Keaffaber

Managing Editor
Michael Cunningham

Director of Marketing
Lynn E. Zingraf

Acquisitions Editor
Elizabeth South

Product Director
Kevin Kloss

Production Editor
Julie A. McNamee

Editors
Elizabeth Barrett
Lisa M. Gebken
Thomas F. Hayes
Lori Lyons
Theresa Mathias
Sarah Rudy

Strategic Marketing Manager
Barry Pruett

Technical Editors
Robert Bogue
Michele Petrovsky

Technical Support Specialist
Nadeem Muhammed

Acquisitions Coordinator
Tracy Williams

Software Relations Coordinator
Patty Brooks

Editorial Assistant
Mark Kane

Book Designer
Ruth Harvey

Cover Designer
Jay Corpus

Production Team
Stephen Adams
Debra Bolhuis
DiMonique Ford
Amy Gornik
Jason Hand
Daniel Harris
Kay Hoskin
Clint Lahnen
Darlena Murray
Laura Robbins
Susan Springer

Indexer
Chris Wilcox

To my wife, Barbara, without whose help and forbearance this book never would have been written.

—RBT

About the Author

Robert Bruce Thompson is President of Triad Technology Group, Inc., a Winston-Salem, NC network consulting firm, with 24 years' experience in programming, systems analysis, microcomputers, data communications, and network administration. He is certified by Novell as a Master CNE, by IBM in Advanced Connectivity, by AT&T in Network Systems Design, and is currently working on certification as a Microsoft CSE. He specializes in network systems design, branch office networking, and the application of technology to the needs of small businesses. Mr. Thompson holds an MBA from Wake Forest University. Mr. Thompson is a contributing author for Que's *Using Windows NT Server 4.0, Special Edition* and for *Upgrading and Repairing Networks*. He can be reached via Internet mail at **thompson@ttgnet.com**.

Dan Balter is a senior partner in Marina Consulting Group, a Microsoft Solution Provider located in Thousand Oaks, California. Dan works as an independent consultant and trainer and has been involved with several different network operating systems and PC application programs throughout his 12-year career. Dan takes pride in turning complex, technical topics into easy-to-understand concepts. He has specialized in integrating tax and accounting software into networked environments. Dan is certified as a Novell NetWare Engineer (CNE) and is very close to completing his certifications both as a Microsoft Certified Systems Engineer (CSE) and a Certified Network Professional (CNP) as awarded by the international Network Professionals Association (NPA). Dan graduated from U.S.C.'s School of Business in 1983 and has been featured in over 25 personal computer training videos, including Windows NT and Windows 95, for KeyStone Learning Systems Corporation. Dan can be contacted by phone at 805-497-6100 or via the Internet at **73361.1611@compuserve.com**.

Jim Boyce, the lead author for *Windows NT, Installation and Configuration Handbook,* is a contributing editor and columnist for *WINDOWS Magazine* and a regular contributor to other computer publications. He has been involved with computers since the late 70s, and has worked with computers as a user, programmer, and systems manager in a variety of capacities. He has a wide range of experience in the DOS, Windows, and UNIX environments. Jim has authored and co-authored over two dozen books on computers and software.

Kate Chase is a writer and columnist specializing in online services and the Internet. She spent five years as a technical forum leader with AOL before merging her two careers into computer journalism. Her work appears frequently in *I-Way*, *Maximize for Windows*, *DOS World*, and other magazines, and Kate writes a regular column covering cyberspace for the *L.A. Village View*, albeit from her home on a remote mountain in England. She would like to thank Chris and Alex for their unflinching support. She can be reached via Internet e-mail at **katechase@aol.com**.

Kathy Ivens has been a computer consultant since 1984, and has authored and co-authored many books on computer subjects. She is a frequent contributor to national magazines, writing articles and reviewing software. Before becoming an expert in computing, Ms. Ivens spent many years as a television producer, where she had fun producing sports and was mildly amused producing news and entertainment programs. Preceding that career was some professional time spent as a community organizer and also as a political consultant. She still doesn't know what she wants to be when she grows up.

Michael Marchuk has been involved with the computing industry for over 17 years. Michael currently manages the development research department for a mid-sized software development firm while consulting for small businesses and writing leading-edge books for Que Publishing. Along with his bachelor's degree in Finance from the University of Illinois, he has received certification as a Netware CNE and a Compaq Advanced Systems Engineer.

John Adam Mikol is the Senior Vice President of Triad Technology Group, Inc., a Winston-Salem, NC network consulting firm. He has 15 years' experience in programming, systems analysis, data communications, Unisys mainframe administration, System V and BSD UNIX administration, VAX Cluster administration and Wide Area Network design, implementation and administration. Mr. Mikol is certified by Novell as a Master CNE, by AT&T in Network Systems Design, by Digital Equipment Corporation in DECnet, Advanced DECnet, Advanced Networking and others, and is currently working on his Microsoft CSE. He holds a BS in Computer Science from Western Carolina University.

Mr. Mikol specializes in enterprise computing, connectivity in multiple-site, multiple-platform environments, branch office networking, TCP/IP and the Internet. He is a contributing author for Que's *Using Windows NT 4.0 Server, Special Edition*. You can reach him via Internet mail at jam@ttgnet.com. Triad Technology Group, Inc. may be contacted at 910-748-9867 (voice) or 910-748-8714 (fax).

Rob Tidrow has been using computers for the past six years and has used Windows for the past four years. Mr. Tidrow is a technical writer and recently was the Manager of Product Development for New Riders Publishing, a division of Macmillan Computer Publishing. Rob is co-author of the best-selling *Windows for Non-Nerds*, and has co-authored several other books including Inside the *World Wide Web, New Riders' Official CompuServe Yellow Pages, Inside Microsoft Office Professional, Inside WordPerfect 6 for Windows, Riding the Internet Highway, Deluxe Edition*, and the *AutoCAD Student Workbook*. In the past, Mr. Tidrow created technical documentation and instructional programs for use in a variety of industrial settings. He has a degree in English from Indiana University. He resides in Indianapolis with his wife, Tammy, and two boys, Adam and Wesley. You can reach him on the Internet at **rtidrow@iquest.net**.

Acknowledgments

Until you write a book you can't appreciate how many people will be involved and the level of teamwork that is required. Although the authors may be the only names on the cover, all we really do is provide the raw material. The Editorial, Design, and Production staff at Que turn it into the finished product you are holding, and my appreciation goes to each and every one of them.

My specific thanks go to three people at Que. To Elizabeth South, Acquisitions Editor, for guiding me through the entire process, for putting up with countless phone calls and dumb questions, and for taking a chance on me in the first place. To Kevin Kloss, Product Director, for keeping the entire project on track and for offering valuable technical advice all along the way. And finally, to Patty Brooks, Operations Coordinator, for cheerfully taking on the hassles of getting evaluation copies of software from numerous vendors, often on ridiculously short notice because I didn't plan ahead. Way to go, folks.

—Robert Bruce Thompson

We'd Like to Hear from You!

As part of our continuing effort to produce books of the highest possible quality, Que would like to hear your comments. To stay competitive, we *really* want you, as a computer book reader and user, to let us know what you like or dislike most about this book or other Que products.

You can mail comments, ideas, or suggestions for improving future editions to the address below, or send us a fax at (317) 581-4663. For the online in-clined, Macmillan Computer Publishing has a forum on CompuServe (type **GO QUEBOOKS** at any prompt) through which our staff and authors are available for questions and comments. The address of our Internet site is **http://www.mcp.com** (World Wide Web).

In addition to exploring our forum, please feel free to contact me personally to discuss your opinions of this book: I'm **74201,1064** on CompuServe, and I'm **kkloss@que.mcp.com** on the Internet.

Thanks in advance—your comments will help us to continue publishing the best books available on computer topics in today's market.

Kevin Kloss
Product Development Specialist
Que Corporation
201 W. 103rd Street
Indianapolis, Indiana 46290
USA

Contents at a Glance

Contents

3 Configuring Windows NT Workstation for Communications 119

II Using Dialup Communications   153

4 Using Communications Programs   155

5 Using Commercial Online Services   207

8 Configuring Windows NT Workstation as a Network Client

337

9 Configuring Windows NT Workstation as a Network Server

373

IV Using E-Mail and Remote Access   411

10 Configuring Windows NT Messaging   413

V Using the Internet   547

13 Understanding the Internet and TCP/IP   549

15 Using Web Browsers   645

18 Building an Intranet 799

Introduction

The story of Microsoft workstation operating systems has been one of continuing advances in data communications capabilities. MS-DOS was essentially meant for stand-alone computers, offering only grudging support for data communications. Windows 3.0 and later Windows 3.1 improved somewhat on the minimal communications facilities provided by MS-DOS, but there was still a long way to go. Just ask any Novell NetWare administrator about the joys of connecting Windows 3.x to a Novell network.

With Windows 3.11 for Workgroups (WFWG), Microsoft finally started to get serious about building data communications and connectivity into their operating systems. WFWG out-of-the-box provided decent peer networking and also greatly improved support for Novell NetWare, though it still required client software supplied by Novell. WFWG also included a usable, if pedestrian, fax program and support for Microsoft mail. The first glimmer of support for the Internet also showed up in WFWG. Although WFWG did not provide TCP/IP as a standard transport, it did support a freely available Microsoft TCP/IP stack, laying the first foundation stones for Microsoft's subsequent Internet charge.

Microsoft made a quantum leap in data communications and connectivity with the introduction of Windows 95 in August, 1995. For the first time, a workstation operating system out-of-the-box provided all of the tools needed to connect to diverse network operating systems, to use Dial-Up Networking, and, via the Universal Inbox, to provide fax and electronic mail. What's more, Windows 95 made it easier than ever before to do these things. If Windows 95 was not quite yet the long sought after "universal client," it at least came closer than any previous workstation operating system.

With Windows NT Workstation 4.0, Microsoft has made another leap. Like Windows 95, Windows NT Workstation 4.0 includes all the tools you need to communicate with the world, many of which are improved over those provided in Windows 95. Unlike Windows 95, Windows NT Workstation 4.0 provides these tools in a secure, stable, rock-solid environment well-suited to corporate requirements.

As many observers have pointed out, Microsoft regards Windows 95 as a tactical product, and Windows NT as the strategic operating system. In fact, at least one observer has opined with some justification that Microsoft appears to have written Windows 95 simply to increase the number of 32-bit applications available to run on Windows NT. Although Microsoft will happily take your money for Windows 95, they'd really rather you bought Windows NT Workstation 4.0. They're right—you should.

This overall view is confirmed by the very limited penetration of Windows 95 into corporate America and the increasing interest in Windows NT. Many corporate IS departments see little benefit in deploying Windows 95 because they realize that Windows NT is where they will ultimately end up. In most corporate environments, connectivity and data communications support are one of the most important features of a workstation operating system. Windows NT Workstation 4.0 provides the best foundation for building this connectivity.

What This Book Is About

This book teaches you how to use Windows NT Workstation 4.0 to communicate with other computer systems, whether they are across the hall on a local area network or across the world on the Internet. Windows NT Workstation 4.0 completely overhauls the communications features included in earlier versions of Windows NT, and adds several new ones. In this book, we explore how to use each of these features to the best advantage.

Windows NT Workstation 4.0 Internet and Networking Handbook leads you step-by-step through the maze of understanding telecommunications facilities, installing communications hardware, and configuring communications services and clients. You will learn how to use Windows NT Workstation 4.0 to connect to remote hosts via modem, to connect to your local area network, and to access the Internet.

Most of us have met at least one "expert" who understands data communications theory perfectly, but can't configure a modem or get a workstation connected to a LAN. Theory unbacked by practical experience is next to useless. Conversely, understanding the practical applications of data communications without having a solid grounding in theory may allow you to get a lot of work done in the short term, but you'll never be able to tie it all together. Keeping this is mind, we try in this book to strike a balance between explaining the theory needed to understand data communications and the hands-on practice needed to implement data communications using Windows NT Workstation 4.0.

Who This Book Is For

If you manage Windows NT Workstation 4.0, this book is for you. It explains what you need to know to install, configure, and manage the communications services provided by Windows NT Workstation 4.0 in a business environment. You will find advice on choosing applications and utilities to supplement those provided with Windows NT Workstation 4.0, on setting up Windows NT Workstation 4.0 as a network client, and on connecting to the Internet.

If you are upgrading from Windows 3.x or Windows 95 to Windows NT Workstation 4.0, this book is also for you. In many respects, the communications services provided by Windows NT Workstation 4.0 resemble those bundled with Windows 95. The increased power and functionality of Windows NT Workstation 4.0 relative to Windows 95 allows many of these services to be expanded and enhanced. This book shows you how to take advantage of the improved communications services provided by Windows NT Workstation 4.0.

If you are running Windows NT 3.5x, this book is also for you. Although Windows NT 3.5x itself provides powerful communications features, these features have been completely overhauled in the upgrade to version 4.0. With the shift to the Windows 95 GUI, the 4.0 upgrade increases ease-of-use across the board. It also improves on the core functionality and power of many communications features. This book teaches you how to maximize the benefit of the communications features provided by Windows NT Workstation 4.0.

And finally, if you are already using Windows NT Workstation 4.0, this book is for you. It will teach you how to get the most from the tools you already have and how to choose additional tools to build on the communications power of Windows NT Workstation 4.0.

How This Book Is Structured

Windows NT Workstation 4.0 Internet and Networking Handbook is divided into six sections including appendixes. We begin by covering the fundamentals you need to understand to use data communications productively, including understanding communications services, selecting and installing communications hardware, and configuring Windows NT Workstation 4.0 for communications.

We then examine traditional asynchronous dialup communications, including selecting a communications program, connecting to commercial online services and setting up a bulletin board system. From here, we proceed to local area networks, covering what you need to know to build and maintain a LAN. After that, we examine some of the specialized communications services provided by Windows NT Workstation 4.0, including e-mail and remote access. Finally, we delve into the Internet, first explaining the theoretical background you need to understand the Internet, and later examining how to use Windows NT Workstation 4.0 both to access Internet services provided by others and to provide Internet services of your own.

The following sections explain briefly which topics are covered, chapter by chapter.

Part I: Getting Started

Part I contains three chapters that explain basic data communications concepts, the services and facilities used to communicate data, and the Windows NT Workstation communications environment.

Chapter 1, "Understanding Communications Basics," begins by explaining the fundamental concepts of data communications. It also describes the various types of data communications and introduces the variety of services that can be accessed using communications. Finally, it provides an overview of the communications facilities built into Windows NT Workstation.

Chapter 2, "Understanding Communications Services and Hardware," goes on to give you the essential information you need to understand communications facilities and services and the hardware used to connect them. This chapter focuses on using communications facilities and services provided by the telephone company, as opposed to LAN connections. If you've ever wondered exactly how Frame Relay differs from ATM or how fast a T3 connection is, here's where you'll find that information.

Chapter 3, "Configuring Windows NT Workstation for Communications," completes the Getting Started section by showing you how to install and configure the computer hardware and the operating system to get the most from the communications capabilities built in to Windows NT Workstation.

Part II: Using Dialup Communications

In Part II, we move on to traditional dialup asynchronous communications. Just a few years ago, local area networks were rare and few people had even heard of the Internet. When you talked about data communications, you were talking about dialup asynchronous connections. Today, LANs and the Internet get most of the attention, and the dialup connection has become just one of the many ways of communicating data. A niche remains for asynchronous dialup communications, however, and we examine that niche in this section.

Chapter 4, "Using Communications Programs," explores the world of traditional general purpose communications programs. This chapter discusses the features that are most important in a general purpose communications program, explains why they are important, and goes on to examine terminal emulation and file transfer protocols in some detail. We look at the HyperTerminal communications applet bundled with Windows NT Workstation 4.0, which is all many people will need. For those with more demanding requirements, we look at three of the best general purpose communications programs available in ProComm Plus, QModem Pro, and WinComm Pro.

Chapter 5, "Using Commercial Online Services," introduces the "Big Two" commercial online services: America Online and CompuServe. We look at the troubled Prodigy service, which was recently sold at a huge loss by Sears and IBM to a group of investors. Lastly, we look at The Microsoft Network, originally conceived as a competitor to AOL and CompuServe, but now recast by Microsoft primarily as an Internet access provider.

Chapter 6, "Setting Up a Bulletin Board System," covers installing and running a BBS in a business environment. For many businesses, a BBS provides an efficient and inexpensive way to keep in contact with customers and support their outside sales forces. Windows NT Workstation 4.0 is an excellent platform for operating a BBS, and we show you how to use it to bring up a bulletin board system of your own.

Part III: Using Local Area Networking

Part III introduces the subject of the local area network (LAN). More data travels on LANs than on all other data communications services combined, and Windows NT Workstation 4.0 fits superbly into the LAN environment, both as a client workstation and as a server for a small LAN.

Chapter 7, "Building a Network Infrastructure," teaches you everything you need to know to select and install the hardware and cabling needed to support a local area network of your own. It also explores bridges, routers, gateways, and the other components needed to support wide area networking and connections to the Internet.

Chapter 8, "Configuring Windows NT Workstation as a Network Client," explains how to set up Windows NT Workstation 4.0 as a client on local area networks running Windows NT Server and Novell NetWare. It also covers configuring Windows NT Workstation 4.0 TCP/IP for connecting to UNIX hosts and to the Internet.

Chapter 9, "Configuring Windows NT Workstation as a Network Server," explains how to use Windows NT Workstation 4.0 as the core of a small local area network. If your situation demands a bit more than a simple peer LAN, but you can't justify installing a full-blown server-based network running Windows NT Server or NetWare, Windows NT Workstation may be the perfect fit. It provides essentially all the services available under Windows NT Server, but limits you to 10 connections. This chapter tells you how to set up Windows NT Workstation 4.0 to be your network server.

Part IV: Using E-Mail, and Remote Access

In Part IV, we move on to an assortment of specialized communications services available with Windows NT Workstation 4.0, including e-mail and remote access.

Chapter 10, "Configuring Windows NT Messaging," covers installing, configuring, and using Windows NT Messaging and connecting to a Microsoft Exchange Server running on a Windows NT Server computer on your LAN.

Chapter 11, "Using E-Mail in Windows NT 4.0," covers installing, configuring, and using the Microsoft Mail client software, as well as third-party SMTP mail clients.

Chapter 12, "Using Remote Access Service and Dial-Up Networking," covers installing, configuring, and using Windows NT Workstation 4.0 remote access features. Dial-Up Networking allows your computer running Windows NT Workstation 4.0 to establish outbound dialup TCP/IP or IPX/SPX network connections to remote hosts, including Windows Network hosts, NetWare servers, and the Internet. Remote Access Service (RAS) lets your computer running Windows NT Workstation 4.0 function as a RAS server, allowing other computers to dial in and establish a network connection to your computer.

Part V: Using the Internet

In Part V, we explain how to connect Windows NT Workstation 4.0 to the Internet, from the perspectives both of using Internet services provided by others and of providing services to others via the Internet. We cover using client-side Internet tools like Web browsers and client software for ftp, news, and Telnet. We go on to show you how to bring up your own Web site and how to use Internet tools to build an internal "intranet" for your company.

Chapter 13, "Understanding the Internet and TCP/IP," provides an overview of the Internet and takes a detailed look at the Internet Protocol (IP) suite that provides its foundation. We provide a short history of the Internet, and make some educated guesses about where it might be headed. We also examine in detail the most important protocols and services used on the Internet. If you're not quite sure what people mean when they talk about Network Layer protocols, or what exactly a Domain Name Server does, this chapter is for you.

Chapter 14, "Connecting to the Internet," tells you what you need to know to connect to the Internet, whether you are looking for a simple single-user dialup connection or a high-speed leased line multiuser connection. You will learn how to choose the type of telephone service appropriate for your needs and how to select an Internet Service Provider.

Chapter 15, "Using Web Browsers," covers choosing, installing, and using Web browser software, with an emphasis on Microsoft Internet Explorer and Netscape Navigator. It also explains how to use search engines like Yahoo! and AltaVista to locate information on the Web.

Chapter 16, "Using ping, ftp, news, and Telnet," covers selecting, installing, and using Internet utilities other than Web browsers, in particular clients for ftp, USENET News, and Telnet. We examine the best individual stand-alone clients available for each of these purposes, and go on to examine some of the best Internet suites, which bundle all or many of these clients in a single product.

Chapter 17, "Building Your Own Web Site," covers the essentials of bringing up your own Web site, including selecting and installing a Web server and understanding the basics of how to create Web pages using HTML.

Chapter 18, "Building an Intranet," introduces the concept of an intranet. You can employ the same technologies, notably Web servers and browsers, used on the Internet to build a private TCP/IP-based intranet. With this intranet, you can share internal company information with your employees, using standard Internet tools while maintaining security.

Special Features in the Book

Que has more than a decade of experience writing and developing the most successful computer books available. With that experience, we've learned what special features help readers the most. Look for these special features throughout the book to enhance your learning experience.

Chapter Road Maps

Each chapter begins with a road map, or brief list of topics to be covered in that chapter, so you can tell at a glance what information is included. It also provides a useful outline of the key topics you will be reading about.

Notes

Notes present useful or interesting information that may not be essential to understanding the topic at hand. Although you can safely skip over Notes without fear of missing key information, they often provide a more in-depth explanation of subjects covered in the general body text. Notes look like this:

> **Note**
>
> You can use the <u>A</u>dvanced button in the Session Profile dialog box to set advanced options for a profile, including Network Timeout, port selections, passive transfer options, and firewall parameters. You will almost never need to alter any of these parameters from their default values. If you have trouble connecting to a site, contact the site administrator (usually **ftpadmin@sitename.domain**) or your local ftp administrator and explain the difficulty. You may be told to alter one or more of the parameters in the Advanced dialog box. Otherwise, don't touch them.

Internet References

Throughout this book, you will find Internet references that point you to World Wide Web addresses or online addresses where you can go for additional information about the topics discussed, or download software. Internet references look like this:

On the Web

Que's WWW site can be found at:

http://www.mcp.com/que

Tips

Tips present brief advice about using little-known or often-overlooked techniques or resources that can save you time or make things easier. Tips look like this:

> **Tip**
>
> Keeping up with all the Internet utilities available is no easy job. Many are updated frequently, and worthwhile new applications appear frequently. One easy way to keep current with what's out there is to point your Web browser to **http:// www.cwapps.com** and check out Stroud's Consummate Winsock Applications List. CWSApps is updated frequently, and includes both ratings and more detailed reviews of individual products. You can locate software by name or by product category. Bookmark this site on your Web browser and visit it every month or so.

Cautions

Cautions inform you of potential traps, pitfalls, and problems that may be caused by a particular procedure. Cautions also tell you what to avoid doing entirely, and what procedures may have unexpected results. Cautions look like this:

> **Caution**
>
> Junk e-mail is becoming an increasing problem. Using only a few lines of Java, it is possible for any server you access to download and store the information you enter in this section.
>
> If you want to use Java but do not use Navigator for e-mail or news, help keep yourself off junk e-mail mailing lists by leaving this section blank. If you want to use Navigator's e-mail or news clients, but don't care about Java, you can disable Java and JavaScript processing by choosing Options, Security, and finally the General tab. You can then safely enter the information in this section.
>
> If you want to use both Java and Netscape's e-mail and news, resign yourself to knowing that whatever information you enter here will probably be made available on numerous junk e-mail lists.

Cross References

Throughout the book, you see references to other sections and pages in the book, like the one next to this paragraph. These cross references point you to related topics and discussions in other parts of the book.

▶ See "Fundamentals of Data Storage and Representation" p.16

Troubleshooting

Troubleshooting sections attempt to anticipate problems that you may run into while following certain instructions or working with specific features. Troubleshooting sections are set up in a Problem/Solution format:

> ### Troubleshooting
>
> *I can access the Web now, but I have no URLs to try and don't know where to start.*
>
> Choose Search Internet Directory of Services to search for sites of interest through Yahoo, one of the big net search services (it's free except for your usual CIS connect time).

Sidebars

Sidebars present detailed information about a topic that belongs in that section, but doesn't necessarily fit into the body text, perhaps because it is of interest only to some readers, or perhaps because it covers a topic in more depth than most readers will need. Sidebars look like this:

> ### Are Web Transactions Secure?
>
> There has been a great deal of discussion as of late in both trade journals and the general media about security on the Web. On a monthly basis, it seems, we hear stories about Internet security being cracked. People who think nothing of giving a credit card number to an anonymous voice on an 800 line, or of seeing their waiter disappear for 20 minutes with their credit card, seem convinced that using the Web to purchase something via credit card will hopelessly compromise security. So how safe is the Web anyway?
>
> Unless you have good reason to suspect that someone in the National Security Agency desperately wants your credit card number, you can feel safe using even export-level encryption. Incidentally, because they are available worldwide via the Internet, downloadable versions of products that provide encryption—including both Navigator and Internet Explorer—are the export version. Contact Microsoft or Netscape on their Web pages to find out how to upgrade your encryption to the domestic-only level

Underlined Hot Keys, or Mnemonics

Hot keys in this book appear underlined, just as they do on screen. For example, the F in File is a hot key, or shortcut, for opening the File menu. Hot keys are used liberally throughout Windows NT itself and all Windows application programs to provide shortcuts to commonly used menus, commands, buttons, and other features. To use a hot key, simply hold down the Alt key and press the letter associated with the item. For example, hold down Alt and press the E key to open the Edit menu.

Shortcut Key Combinations

Like hot keys, shortcut key combinations allow you to substitute keyboard shortcuts for using your mouse to delve down through menus to achieve a particular purpose. For example, if you want to paste information contained in the Clipboard into the current document, you can do so in one of two ways. You can either click the Edit menu to open it and then click Paste, or you can simply hold down the Ctrl key and press V, represented in the text as Ctrl+V. Most available shortcut key combinations are displayed within the menu to the right of the menu selection itself.

Using a shortcut key combination almost always takes less time and effort than doing the same thing by navigating through menus with your mouse.

Menu Commands

Instructions for selecting menu commands take this form:

Choose File, Properties.

This means click the File menu to open it and then click the Properties item contained within the File menu.

The Start button that debuted in Windows 95 is now a part of Windows NT Workstation 4.0, along with the rest of the Windows 95 Graphical User Interface (GUI). When you need to select an item from the Start menu, the command takes the form:

Open the Start Menu and select Programs, Accessories, Dial-up Networking.

Note that, in this case, only the first selection (Programs) offers a hot key selection. Simply dragging the mouse to highlight the Programs menu item displays the contents of the Programs menu. Menus may contain other menu folders and executable programs. Subsidiary menus are displayed when you highlight them—you needn't click them.

Typeface Enhancements

This book uses the following typeface enhancements to indicate special types of text, as shown in the following table:

Typeface	Description
Italic	Italics are used to indicate new terms and variables in commands or addresses.
Boldface	Bold is used to indicate text you type, Internet addresses, and other locators in the online world.
`Computer type`	This command is used for on-screen messages and commands (such as DOS Copy or UNIX commands).
MYFILE.DOC	File names are set in all caps to distinguish them from regular text.

Part I

Getting Started

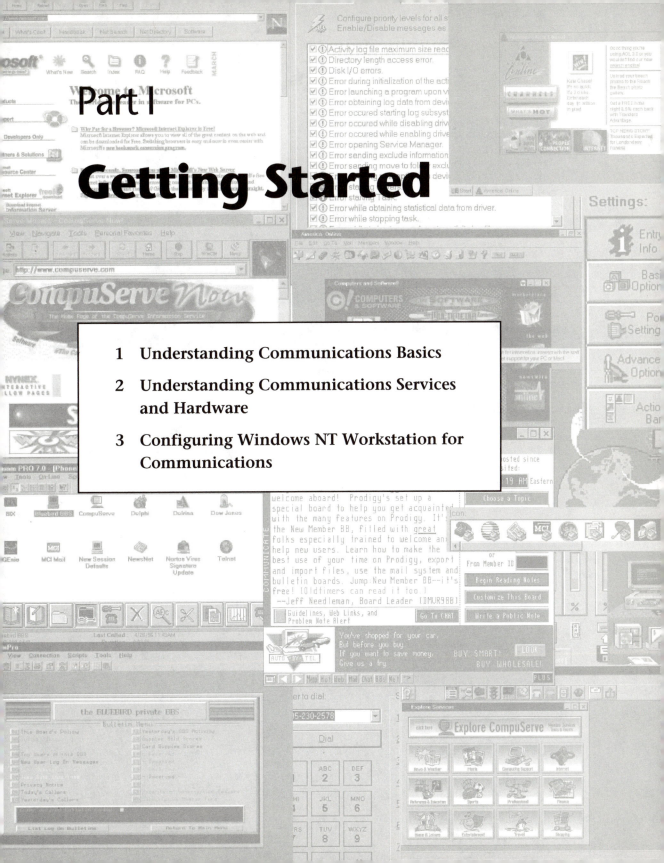

CHAPTER 1

Understanding Communications Basics

by Robert Bruce Thompson

Microsoft Windows NT Workstation 4.0 is an operating system that was designed to communicate with other computers. Like its close relatives, Windows NT Server 4.0 and Windows 95, Windows NT Workstation 4.0 provides a full complement of communications services and utilities to support local area networking, dial-up asynchronous communications, Internet access, and more.

To get the maximum advantage from the built-in communications capabilities of Windows NT Workstation 4.0, you first need to understand some fundamental concepts about computers in general and data communications in particular. If you can explain the implications of analog versus digital data transmission and already understand the finer points of packet switching, then you may not need to read this chapter. If, on the other hand, you are not completely clear about the difference between ASCII and EBCDIC, then reading this chapter will give you a solid grounding in the fundamentals of data communications.

In this chapter, you learn

- How computers store and represent data internally
- How data is communicated between computers
- What kinds of data communications you can use to link computer systems and networks
- What services you can access using data communications
- What communications services and facilities are bundled with Windows NT Workstation 4.0

Fundamentals of Data Storage and Representation

To understand computer communications, you need to have at least a working understanding of the way computers represent, code, store, and transfer information. Unfortunately, many people never take the few minutes necessary to gain this working knowledge. As a result, most users never really understand how computers communicate. So take a few minutes to review some basic math so you have a firm foundation for enjoying the rest of the book.

Decimal and Binary Numbering Systems

Because people have ten fingers, most human societies use *Base 10* for counting and arithmetic. We use nine symbols, 1 through 9, to represent the possible digits with Base 10, and we use a special symbol, 0, as a placeholder to represent no value being present. Base 10 is also called the *decimal numbering system*.

Multiplying a number by itself is called raising that number to a power. For example, 10 times 10 equals 100, which can also be referred to as 10 to the second power, or 10^2. Similarly, 10 times 10 times 10 equals 1,000, which can also be referred to as 10 to the third power, or 10^3. By convention, any number raised to the zero power equals 1.

Using Base 10, the number 1 represents one unit, or 10 raised to the zero power (10^0). The number 10 represents 10 raised to the first power (10^1). The number 100 represents 10 raised to the second power (10^2), and so on. In any Base 10 number, the far right number is called the units place, the next place to the left is called the tens place, the next the hundreds place, and so on. The number 4,321 has 1 in the units place, 2 in the tens place, 3 in the hundreds place, and 4 in the thousands place.

We can represent any Base 10 unit value by combining different quantities of powers of 10. For example, the number 1,059 can be represented as:

$$
\begin{array}{rl}
 & 1 \times 10^3 = 1{,}000 \\
+ & 0 \times 10^2 = 0 \\
+ & 5 \times 10^1 = 50 \\
+ & 9 \times 10^0 = 9 \\
\end{array}
$$

Base 10 seems natural to us because we grew up using it. Some societies have used other bases, however. Many ancient societies used Base 12, and the Mayans used Base 60. That our clocks have 12 hours and our circles have 360 degrees is an artifact of these differing bases.

Computers are most comfortable dealing with simple *either/or* situations. A switch is *either* on *or* it is off. A voltage is *either* present *or* it is not. Accordingly, computers use *Base 2* numbering, also called *Binary*. In Base 2, the only two symbols used to represent digits are 0 and 1. Counting in binary takes a little getting used to.

Say we're sitting next to each other and we're both going to count to 10, but you're going to do it in decimal and I'm going to do it in binary. You start by saying 0, which I echo. You then say 1, which I also echo. You then say 2. Oops. I'm out of symbols because I only have 0 and 1 to work with. How do I get around this? The same way you will when you reach 9. You have to move one place to the left and start over with 1 in the tens place and 0 in the units place, or 10. I have to do the same thing, but I have to do it much sooner and much more frequently. Here's how the count goes:

Table 1.1 Counting with Binary Numbers Versus Counting with Decimal Numbers			
Decimal	**Expanded Decimal**	**Binary**	**Expanded Binary**
0	0×10^0	0	0×2^0
1	1×10^0	1	1×2^0
2	2×10^0	10	$(1 \times 2^1) + (0 \times 2^0)$
3	3×10^0	11	$(1 \times 2^1) + (1 \times 2^0)$
4	4×10^0	100	$(1 \times 2^2) + (0 \times 2^1) + (0 \times 2^0)$
5	5×10^0	101	$(1 \times 2^2) + (0 \times 2^1) + (1 \times 2^0)$
6	6×10^0	110	$(1 \times 2^2) + (1 \times 2^1) + (0 \times 2^0)$
7	7×10^0	111	$(1 \times 2^2) + (1 \times 2^1) + (1 \times 2^0)$
8	8×10^0	1000	$(1 \times 2^3) + (0 \times 2^2) + (0 \times 2^1) + (0 \times 2^0)$
9	9×10^0	1001	$(1 \times 2^3) + (0 \times 2^2) + (0 \times 2^1) + (1 \times 2^0)$
10	$(1 \times 10^1) + (0 \times 10^0)$	1010	$(1 \times 2^3) + (0 \times 2^2) + (1 \times 2^1) + (0 \times 2^0)$

Using decimal numbering, each digit can represent any one of 10 possible states. With binary numbering, each digit can represent only two states. A *binary digit* is called a *bit*. A bit is the smallest piece of information possible to have. A bit can represent exactly two states of a given entity: true or false, yes or no, on or off.

Grouping Bits and Encoding Information

Because a bit is such a small unit of information, it makes sense to group bits together. Doing so achieves two things. First, a group of bits allows an entity to be represented in more than two states. While a single bit can represent only two states, a two-bit group can represent 2^2 or four states. A three-bit group can represent 2^3 or eight states, a four-bit group can represent 2^4 or 16 states, and so on. Second, grouping bits together allows information to be handled in larger chunks, which reduces overhead.

To decide how many bits to group together to form a standard information handling unit, you must first examine the type of information you want to represent and store. Most of the time, that information will be letters and numbers. Take a look at how many bits you need to represent the alphabetic and numeric symbols.

One of the first methods used for coding alphabetic and numeric data (also called alphanumeric or alphameric data) for communication was Samuel F. B. Morse's Morse code. It was developed in the early 1800's for telegraphy. Morse code uses variable length combinations of short dots and longer dashes to represent alphabetic and numeric symbols. This ad hoc system worked well by assigning short combinations to frequently used letters. For example, the most frequently used letter in the English language is "e", which is represented in Morse Code by a single dot. The next most frequently used letter is "t", which is represented by a single dash. Less frequently used symbols are represented using several dots and dashes. Whatever its benefits in practice, Morse code does not use a binary method for representing symbols.

Five-Bit Encoding Systems

Attempts to automate the telegraphy process made it desirable to use a binary method to code alphanumeric data using fixed symbol lengths. Emile Baudot (pronounced Baw-doe) developed such a system by using 5-bit groupings to represent each symbol. Using a five-bit grouping yields a possible 2^5 or 32 states for a symbol unit. Because the Roman alphabet has 26 characters in most countries, this does not leave enough symbols remaining to represent numbers, punctuation characters, and so on. Baudot encoding uses two special characters, LTRS and FIGS, to shift the meanings of other characters. Having sent a LTRS symbol, all following symbols are recognized by the recipient as alphabetic until a FIGS symbol is sent. At that point, all following symbols are recognized as numeric symbols until a LTRS symbol is again received. Obviously, this is a rather clumsy method. Five bits is not quite enough to serve our needs.

Six-Bit Encoding Systems

The next step was to use 6-bit grouping, which yields a possible 2^6 or 64 states for a symbol unit. At first glance, 6-bit encoding appears to offer more than enough options to represent the alphabetic, numeric, and punctuation symbols we need. We can represent the 26 alphabetic characters, the 10 numeric symbols, and still have lots of room left over for punctuation marks and such. Upon closer examination, however, a problem becomes apparent. We don't really need 26 alphabetic characters. We need 52 of them. An uppercase "A" needs to be distinct from a lowercase "a". If we choose to allocate 52 of 64 states for alphabetic characters and 10 for numeric symbols, we have only two left over to represent everything else.

As a matter of historic interest, the Digital Equipment Corporation (DEC) line of PDP-8 minicomputers used 6-bit encoding, and was sold well into the 1970's. DEC got around the uppercase/lowercase problem by using only 26 symbols to represent the alphabet and then using two of the remaining symbols as "shift-in" and "shift-out" characters to indicate whether a given alphabetic character should be recognized as uppercase or lowercase. Although DEC made it work with the PDP-8, using a 6-bit symbol set is clearly a bit too tight for comfort.

Seven-Bit Encoding Systems

The next step is to use 7-bit grouping to yield 2^7 or 128 states for a symbol unit. With 7 bits, we finally arrive at a workable grouping. We can allocate 52 symbols to the upper- and lowercase alphabet, 10 symbols to numbers, others for punctuation, and still have quite a few left over for other uses, such as control characters (tabs, carriage returns, page breaks, and so on).

The 7-bit grouping has been standardized as ASCII, an acronym that stands for American Standard Code for Information Interchange. ASCII is now a world-wide standard for representing symbols on systems ranging from personal computers to supercomputers. Nearly any computer you work with today uses ASCII encoding to store information.

Eight-Bit Encoding Systems

From the computer's point of view, seven is an ugly number. It's not "even"—computers use powers of two. The next step up, 8-bit encoding, uses 2^3 or 8 bits to represent 2^8 or 256 possible symbol combinations, which doubles the 128 symbols available with seven-bit encoding. The following sections describe what you can use all these extra symbols for.

Extended ASCII. Extended ASCII uses the eighth bit to represent an additional 128 symbols. Everyone needs the 128 symbols, 0 through 127, represented using the first seven bits of standard ASCII. The upper 128 symbols, 128 through 255, are also called high-order ASCII, and they are not standardized. Each computer manufacturer can use these upper 128 characters to represent any symbols it chooses, and in the early days of computers they did just that.

When IBM shipped the first PC in the early 1980s, they chose to define their version of high-order ASCII to include a useful set of foreign alphabetic characters, some box-drawing and shading symbols useful for character graphics, and several general purpose symbols that are not included in seven-bit ASCII. IBM's early dominance in the PC industry made this upper ASCII definition, referred to as the IBM Character Set, a standard in the PC-compatible world.

It is important to understand, however, that the IBM Character Set is only one way of defining high-order ASCII. Other manufacturers chose to define the upper symbols differently. For example, a particular high-order ASCII value may represent a completely different symbol on an Apple Macintosh than the same ASCII value represents on an IBM. Extended ASCII also varies from country to country by taking into account the need for special symbols particular to different languages and cultures.

EBCDIC. The Extended Binary Coded Decimal Interexchange (or Interchange) Code, or EBCDIC (pronounced eb-suh-dik) is a proprietary 8-bit encoding system used by large- and mid-range IBM computer systems. EBCDIC stores one alphabetic character or two decimal characters per byte. Unless you are connecting to large IBM systems, you will seldom encounter EBCDIC.

Large Bit-Count Encoding Systems

It's easy to forget that the whole world doesn't use a character-oriented alphabet. In particular, rather than building words from component characters, oriental languages use ideograms or pictograms, each of which represents a specific word with a single symbol. So, while western languages that use the Roman alphabet can assemble vocabularies comprising hundreds of thousands of words using just a few alphabetic symbols, an eastern language may require thousands of discrete symbols, each representing a specific word.

Recent versions of Microsoft Windows include support for *Unicode*, which uses 16 bits to represent 2^{16} or 65,536 symbols. The advantage of Unicode encoding is that the huge number of discrete symbols it allows permits languages based on ideograms and pictograms to have all or most of their vocabulary represented by single symbols. The disadvantage is that Unicode requires more storage space. Representing a simple letter "a" requires 16 bits in Unicode versus the 7 or 8 bits required to represent the same character using ASCII.

Defining Standard Terms

Until now, I've been referring generically to groupings of bits into larger units. There are, however, standard terms used to refer to such groupings of various sizes.

The Byte

A group of eight bits is called a *byte*. A byte is the standard unit grouping used by computer systems to record and manage data. As mentioned, the byte is an organized grouping of 8 bits, and can represent 2^8 or 256 different values, which range from 0 through 255. Each of these values can be assigned a specific symbol using one of the encoding methods previously described.

For example, the decimal ASCII value 065, which can also be represented in binary notation as 01000001, corresponds to the uppercase letter "A". Similarly, the decimal ASCII value 097, which can also be represented as the binary value 01100001, corresponds to the lowercase "a". Note that each of these values has a zero as its first or most significant bit, indicating that these are true 7-bit ASCII values. Toggling the most significant bit for the latter of these values from 0 to 1 yields 11100001, or the decimal ASCII value 225, which corresponds in the IBM character set to the symbol "β". Figure 1.1 illustrates how these three characters are represented in ASCII.

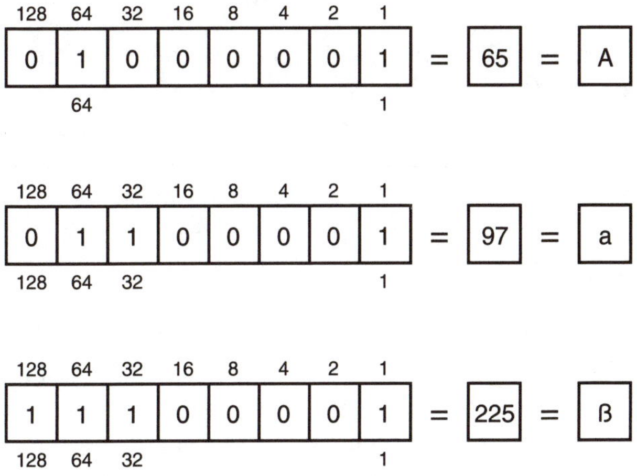

Fig. 1.1
The bytes representing the symbols A, a, and β.

With one exception, the whole world calls a byte a byte. That exception is France, which in its effort to keep the French language from being polluted by foreign words and phrases, insists on referring to a byte as an octet. Strangely, the word octet is increasingly being used in the data communications industry to refer to a byte.

The Nibble and Hexadecimal Notation

There are times when a byte is too large a grouping. For example, if you are storing purely numeric data, it is wasteful to use an entire 8-bit byte, which is capable of storing 256 discrete values, to store only one of 10 numeric symbols. You can instead divide the byte in half and store one full numeric character in each half of the byte. You thereby double your storage density and halve the storage space required for a given amount of data.

This part of a byte is called, appropriately enough, a *nibble*. A nibble comprises four bits, and can therefore represent 2^4 or 16 discrete symbols. Storing only the 10 decimal values in these 16 positions would waste space, so some bright computer person came up with the idea of fitting the storage chunk to the available space by using Base 16 to represent the numeric data. Base 16 is also called *hexadecimal notation*. Using hexadecimal notation, the first 10 numbers, 0 through 9, are the same as decimal and mean the same thing.

It's when you get to decimal 10 that decimal and hexadecimal part ways. Instead of having only 10 symbols to represent units (as in decimal notation), hexadecimal uses 16 discrete symbols, with the six additional single symbols representing the decimal values 10 through 15. This begs the question of what to use to represent these additional symbols.

By convention, hexadecimal notation assigns the letter "A" to the decimal value 10. Decimal 11 is represented as "B" and so on, with hexadecimal F representing the decimal value 15. This means that decimal values between 10 and 15 can be stored using only one symbol rather than the two symbols required by decimal notation. Again, when you arrive at "F," you've run out of symbols. Counting in hexadecimal, the number that follows F is 10, which corresponds to decimal 16.

The Word

On occasion, you will hear the term *word* used to describe a unit of computer storage. A word consists of two or more bytes. Unlike the other units previously discussed, the word is not standardized. Instead, it depends on the particular hardware implementation. For example, the Intel 80286 processor—a 16-bit processor—uses a 16-bit or 2-byte word length. The Intel 80386, 486, and Pentium processors use a 32-bit or 4-byte word. Large computers systems may use words comprising 48 bits, 64 bits, or more. The term *word* refers to the way a particular processor manipulates data internally. A processor that communicates 32 bits at a time with memory and other storage is said to use a 32-bit or 4-byte word size.

How Bytes are Counted

One of the most enduring causes of confusion in the computer industry is the way in which large numbers of bytes are counted and referred to. This results from the otherwise very convenient fact that every third power of 10 corresponds to every tenth power of two. For example, compare the following:

2^{10} or 1,024	$\cong$	10^3 or 1,000
2^{20} or 1,048,576	$\cong$	10^6 or 1,000,000
2^{30} or 1,073,741,824	$\cong$	10^9 or 1,000,000,000

In decimal notation, 10^3 represents thousands, 10^6 represents millions, and (in the United States) 10^9 represents billions. The close binary equivalents are respectively referred to as kilo (K), mega (M), and giga (G). The problem arises when these close equivalents are used interchangeably, as they often are— even by experienced computer people. People may refer to the round number 1,000 as 1K, which is really 1,024. Conversely, they may refer to 1M (which is really 1,048,576 bytes) as one million bytes. It's been going on for years, it usually doesn't make a significant difference, and no one seems to care.

> **Note**
>
> Incidentally, when you refer to a giga-something, pronounce each letter "g" hard, as in "guy" instead of soft as in "German."

Fundamentals of Data Communications

Now that you've established a solid grounding in the mathematics of data communications, examine some fundamental concepts regarding how data is communicated.

Requirements for Communications

Establishing communication requires four elements: a sender, a recipient, a message, and a transmission path. These four elements are illustrated in figure 1.2. All enhancements beyond these four required elements are used to increase the reliability of communication, to increase its speed, to make it more secure, to reduce its cost, or some combination of these factors.

Fig. 1.2
Sender, recipient, message, and transmission path.

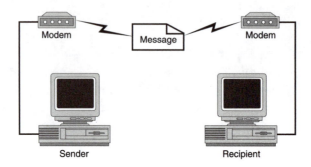

Analog versus Digital

The difference between analog data and digital data is simple, but understanding this difference is critical to understanding computer communications. *Analog data* can have any value between two extremes on a continuum. *Digital data* can occupy only defined discontinuous locations on that continuum.

To understand the difference between analog and digital, assume you want to upgrade the lighting in your den to allow you to have anything from complete darkness to bright light.

Using analog methods, you might install a 1,024 watt light bulb and connect it to a continuously variable dimmer switch, as shown in figure 1.3. By adjusting that dimmer switch, you can light the room using anything from 0 watts and complete darkness to the full 1,024 watts and brilliant light. Depending on how finely the dimmer switch can be adjusted, you might find that 12.3 watts gives an appropriately dim ambiance while you're watching a movie on your home theater system, while 267.8 watts is about right for playing ball with your dog. You probably don't know exactly what wattage you're using—and you probably don't care. You just adjust the dimmer until the lighting level looks about right. You can select any of an unlimited number of values ranging from 0 watts on the low end to 1,024 watts on the high end.

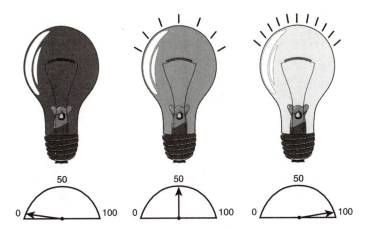

Fig. 1.3
An analog control lighting system allows you to vary the lighting level continuously between defined extremes.

If you decide to install a digital system instead, you no longer have the luxury of using a continuously variable dimmer. Digital values are 0 or 1, off or on. To accommodate your variable lighting needs, you might install 16 individual, 64-watt light bulbs that are controlled by individual switches. Together, the 16 light bulbs total the same 1,024 watts as the analog system. The digital lighting system, shown in figure 1.4, allows you to choose from 16 lighting levels, depending on how many of the switches you turn on. As compared with the analog system, the difference is that you can choose only among the available discrete steps. You might really want 12.3 watts, but what you can have is either 0 watts or 64 watts—nothing in between.

If you decide that the available digital steps are not fine enough, you might choose to replace the 16 64-watt light bulbs and switches with 1,024 individual one-watt light bulbs, each controlled by its own switch. By doing so, you reduce—but do not eliminate—the distance between steps. What you want may still be 12.3 watts. What you can have with your new upgraded digital system is either 12 watts or 13 watts.

Fig. 1.4
A digital control lighting system allows you to vary the lighting level by selecting discrete steps between defined extremes.

This stepping function is a characteristic of digital systems. Analog systems are continuously variable along the continuum. Digital systems can occupy only defined values within that continuum.

You might wonder why anyone in his right mind would install the digital system, with its plethora of bulbs and switches, instead of the analog system with its single bulb and single switch. After all, the analog system is simpler and it lets you choose exactly what you want instead of settling for a close approximation.

In reality, of course, no one is going to install the digital system described—or even the analog one for that matter. Nevertheless, this example illustrates the one key advantage that digital systems have when compared with analog systems that makes digital the technology of choice for communicating data. Digital values are precise. You either have 12 switches turned on or you don't. In contrast, analog values are only approximations. You may try to turn the dimmer to the same location as you used the last time, but you can never reproduce the same value exactly. The last time, your 12.3 watt lighting scheme may have really been 12.29 watts. Next time it may be 12.31 watts, or even 12.9 watts.

To see why this difference is crucial, consider two real-world applications, one digital and one analog.

For the analog example, shown in figure 1.5, print an original document on a laser printer. Then using a photocopier, which is an analog technology, make a photocopy of the original you just printed. Then, make a photocopy of the photocopy. Continue photocopying photocopies until you have made a total of 24 photocopies, each of the preceding copy. The result is called a 25th generation copy. Because of the imprecise nature of analog data, each succeeding generation is further and further removed from the value of the original. You'll be lucky if you can even read the finer print in the last copy you make. This degradation is inherent to the analog representation of data. If you ever copied a copy of an audio- or videotape, you've seen this phenomenon in operation. Depending on how critical your eye (or ear) is, you might or might not notice a difference from one generation to the next. You will certainly notice the difference between copies that are several generations apart.

Original   5th Generation   10th Generation

Fig. 1.5
Analog replication introduces additional inaccuracy with each succeeding generation.

For the digital example, shown in figure 1.6, save your document to a floppy disk. Then make a copy of the floppy disk. Then make a copy of that copy. Continue copying copies until you have made a total of 24 copies, each of the preceding copy. Compare the data on the original floppy disk with the data on the 25th generation copy and you will find that there is no difference between the original and the 25th generation copy—assuming that your floppy drive is working correctly and all of the disks were perfect. Because digital data is discrete, it can be reproduced exactly, with the reproduction completely indistinguishable from the original.

Original   5th Generation   10th Generation

Fig. 1.6
Digital replication allows each succeeding generation to exactly match the original source.

To borrow a concept from the target shooting world, consider the terms *accuracy* and *precision*. If you fire 10 shots at a 3" bullseye and put all 10 into the bullseye, but the shots cover the full 3" circle, you are shooting accurately but not precisely. If you put all 10 shots into a 1/2" group, but that group is located 10" from the bullseye, you are shooting precisely but not accurately. The contrast between accuracy and precision is shown in figure 1.7. Analog data is accurate at the expense of precision. Digital data is precise at the expense of accuracy.

Fig. 1.7
Analog accuracy
versus digital
precision.

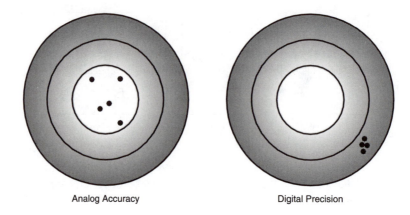

Analog Accuracy   Digital Precision

All of this is important to data communication because the degradation inherent to analog transmission of data makes it a less reliable means of communicating data precisely than is digital transmission. Analog transmission works well if only an approximation of the original data is needed by the recipient.

For example, if you are listening to an FM radio station while driving to work, it doesn't much matter that what your radio receives isn't exactly what left the transmitter. Any minor differences are subsumed by the losses and distortions inherent in receiving, decoding, and amplifying the signal before it reaches your speakers, which are themselves an imperfect means of reproducing the original signal content. Similarly, millions of people happily watch videotapes at a resolution of about 230 lines versus the 400 lines or so that are visible when watching the program directly as it is broadcast. In short, people are good at filling in the blanks when some data is missing or distorted.

Computers, however, are literal entities. If you transfer a one million-byte computer file from one system to another, the original file must be replicated exactly at the receiving end for that file to be usable. If even a single bit differs between the original and the copy, the data represented by the file will be corrupted or the file itself may be unusable. A single bit error could, for example, change a "9" in a spreadsheet to a "0". If the error occurs in the cents place, it may not matter much to anyone but the accountants; if it's in the millions place, it matters even to Bill Gates. For data communication between computers, no loss or distortion whatsoever is acceptable.

If data needs to be transferred at high speeds or over long distances, or both, some means of amplifying, cleaning up, and re-transmitting the data will probably be needed at one or more points along the transmission path.

Because an analog copy is never exactly like the original, each such step results in additional generational degradation as previously described. Although digital data is also subject to some degradation as distance and speeds increase, the fact that it is possible to exactly replicate digital data means that the data arriving at the destination can be exactly the same as the data that left the origination point, which is not possible with analog transmission technologies.

Standards and Protocols

If I speak only English, I can communicate readily with millions of people in the United States and elsewhere in the world. If you speak only Spanish, you can communicate with millions of people in Spain and in Latin America. However, if the two of us try to communicate, we're going to have trouble getting the message across. There may be a lot of noise and arm waving, but ultimately little real information will be transferred between us.

Even if we speak nominally the same language, communication difficulties can easily arise. An American conversing with a Briton, or for that matter someone from New England trying to talk to someone from the deep South, can have problems getting his meaning understood. What I regard as plain unaccented English, you may hear as a nearly impenetrable dialect. Vocabularies vary. Different words may be used to refer to the same thing, or the same word may be used to mean different things. Even regional and cultural differences in body language can make communicating harder than it should be.

In the same way, successful communication between computers requires not only that the two communicating computer systems speak and understand a common language, but that they use the same conventions and protocols to do so. For computers, the requirements are more rigorous than they are for people. People are good at filling in the blanks, making reasonable assumptions, and otherwise doing what it takes to communicate information. Computers have no such creativity or flexibility. They are literal-minded, and require that communication be done in a predictable and repeatable fashion.

If two computers are to communicate with each other, hundreds of issues must first be decided. What form will the data take? How fast will they communicate? Will each computer acknowledge receipt of each block of data, and, if so, how? How will errors and the need for re-transmissions be handled? How will one computer tell the other that it is temporarily too busy to accept further data? What physical connectors will we use on the cable connecting the two machines? For that matter, what kind of cable will we use? What voltage will we use to signal with? These and hundreds of other issues must be decided in minute detail by all parties concerned before communication can take place.

Standards Types

There is an old joke among computer people that says standards must be a good thing because we have so many competing ones. Standards develop in one of two ways:

- *De facto standards* are those that develop by common usage, usually because one company decided how to do something and was dominant enough and had a good enough solution that everyone else adopted it. In Latin, *de facto* means "by fact."

- *De jure standards* are those that are developed, promulgated, and maintained by a formal standards process, backed by a government or industry organization. The Latin term *de jure* translates to "by law."

Hundreds of standards of both types are used in day-to-day life and in data communications. All of us obey numerous *de jure* standards—embodied as traffic laws—just driving to work. Without such properly enforced standards, driving becomes a nightmare, as anyone who has driven in Italy can attest. *De facto* standards, although they don't have the force of law, can be just as important as *de jure* standards. For example, the QWERTY keyboard is a *de facto* standard. Just imagine the confusion and lost productivity that would result if every computer manufacturer used a different keyboard layout. Dominant *de facto* standards are sometimes incorporated as *de jure* standards.

Standards Bodies

The need for standards has resulted in the growth of organizations that are responsible for developing and promulgating standards. Some of these organizations are created by national or international government bodies, while others are industry trade groups. The following are some of the more important standards bodies that address data communications issues:

- *American National Standards Institute (ANSI).* ANSI sets numerous standards relating to telecommunication and networking. ANSI is a non-governmental membership body formed in 1918, and is the U.S. representative to the ISO, described in one of the bullets that follow.

- *International Telecommunication Union (ITU).* The ITU Telecommunications Standards Sector (ITU-T) is the group formerly known as the CCITT (Comite Consultatif Internationale de Telegraphique et Telephonique), which in English translation means the Consultative Committee for International Telegraphy and Telephony. The ITU-T sets numerous standards that apply to data communication using the public telephone network. The V-series of standards (such as the V.34 modem standard), and the X-series of standards (such as the X.25 packet switching standard, and the X.400 and X.500 mail standards) are products of the ITU-T.

■ *Institute of Electrical and Electronic Engineers (IEEE).* IEEE is best known for the 802 series of networking standards. For example, Ethernet networks are defined by the 802.3 standard, and Token Ring networks by 802.5. The IEEE also works closely with other organizations, including the National Institute of Standards and Technology, the Networking Centre in the UK, and many other national standards organizations.

■ *International Organization for Standardization (ISO).* ISO sets standards for national and international data communications. ANSI is the United States representative to ISO.

■ *Electronic Industries Association/Telephone Industries Association (EIA/TIA).* EIA/TIA is best known in the networking arena for the EIA/TIA-568 Commercial Building Telecommunications Wiring Standard, which is used to specify requirements for structured telephony and network cabling systems. EIA/TIA also sets standards relating to pathways and spaces and to other aspects of building cabling.

Synchronous and Asynchronous Communication

Communication between computer systems can be done synchronously or asynchronously. When two systems are communicating *synchronously*, they share a common time reference. When two systems communicate *asynchronously*, no such common time reference exists between the systems.

Because systems communicating asynchronously have no common time reference, each byte sent is treated as a separate entity and must be surrounded by framing bits. The sending system first sends a start bit to tell the receiving system that data is about to come in. It then sends the eight bits of the data byte itself, followed by one or more stop bits to tell the receiving system that it is finished sending that particular byte.

Basically, this means that each byte sent asynchronously requires at least 10 bits: the eight data bits of the byte plus at least one start bit and one stop bit for framing. Thus, an asynchronous connection can never yield more than 8/10 or 80 percent efficiency in using the nominal bandwidth.

Systems communicating synchronously, on the other hand, have a common time reference to work with. This means that the receiving system is always "in sync" with the transmitting system and knows when each byte is due to start and stop, thus reducing the need for framing. Rather than the byte-level framing used by asynchronous systems, synchronous systems use framing at the block level. Blocks may range in size from a few bytes to eight kilobytes or more, which reduces framing overhead from the 20 percent range typical of asynchronous systems to a small fraction of one percent.

The advantage to synchronous communications is that bandwidth is used more efficiently because there is less overhead involved in coordinating the transfer of information. The disadvantage is that more complicated and expensive equipment is required on both ends to establish and maintain the clocking reference. Conversely, asynchronous communication is simple to establish and to maintain using less expensive equipment, at the expense of using bandwidth less efficiently.

As data communication methods have improved, this distinction between synchronous and asynchronous has become much less evident. Early low-end modems communicated only asynchronously. If you needed synchronous communications, you bought a more specialized and expensive modem. Modern modems begin each call asynchronously, but during the negotiation process they establish a synchronous connection. The connection between your computer and the modem remains asynchronous, but this is a fast link and bandwidth is of little concern. The connection between the modems themselves runs synchronously, making the most of the little available bandwidth.

Reliable and Unreliable Communications

The terms *reliable* and *unreliable* as applied to data communication are used differently than in everyday life. You might expect that reliable communications might be typified by your telephone, which almost always works. Unreliable communications might be represented by your cable television, which probably fails much more frequently.

In data communication, the terms *reliable* and *unreliable* have nothing to do with what percentage of the time the communication system is working properly. Instead, they refer to whether transmitted data is acknowledged by the recipient as having been received. In a reliable communications system, the sender always knows whether the data has been received properly because the recipient acknowledges each block of data as it is received and requests re-transmission of blocks that are lost or garbled. In an unreliable communication system, the sender simply transmits data on the assumption that it will be received properly.

Implementing a reliable communication system increases the probability that data will be received at the expense of increasing the overhead required to maintain the communication channel. Reliable communication is therefore inherently slower and more expensive than unreliable communication.

Bandwidth and Transmission Speeds

The term *bandwidth* refers to how much data can be transmitted per unit time. Data communication transmission speeds are measured and discussed in bits per second, which is abbreviated bps and pronounced "bips."

Data transmission speeds vary widely, depending on the application and the type of link used. Dialing in to a remote computer using regular telephone lines gives you a bandwidth measured in the low thousands of bits per second. Connecting to another machine on a local area network may allow transmission speeds of one hundred million bits per second or more.

Low bandwidth communication is measured in kilobits per second, which is abbreviated Kbps and pronounced either "killo-bips" or "kay-bips." One Kbps is an even 1,000 bps—not 1,024 bps as you might expect. Data communication terminology uses prefixes based on decimal rather than binary numbering.

High bandwidth communication is measured in megabits per second, which is abbreviated Mbps, and nearly always pronounced "megga-bips" although occasionally as "em-bips." One Mbps is one million bits per second.

Very high bandwidth communication is measured in gigabits per second, which is abbreviated Gbps, and nearly always pronounced "gigga-bips" although occasionally as "gee-bips." One Gbps is one billion bits per second. Transmission speeds in the Gbps range are becoming more common with the widespread deployment of fiber optic cables.

When you see a number representing communication speed, look carefully at the case of the "b". A speed of 1 MBps, or one megabyte per second, is considerably faster than the similar appearing 1Mbps, or one megabit per second. Although data communication speeds are conventionally stated using bits rather than bytes, you will sometimes find exceptions.

Communication Modes

When a communication channel has been established, the question arises of who has the right to transmit, who must listen, and when. The three communication modes commonly used are called simplex, full-duplex and half-duplex.

- *Simplex communication mode* means that one station transmits at all times and all other stations only receive. Television and radio broadcasting are examples of simplex communication. Simplex communication is inherently unreliable because it makes no provision for recipients to communicate with the transmitting station.

- *Half-duplex communication mode* means that, although any station may both send and receive data, only one station may be transmitting at any given time. A two-way radio or walkie-talkie operates in half-duplex mode.

- *Full-duplex communication mode* means that any station can simultaneously both send and receive messages without corrupting the data. Face-to-face discussions and telephone conversations are good examples of full-duplex communication.

Simplex mode, shown in figure 1.8, is used only in specialized circumstances, notably broadcasting. Simplex mode has little application in data communications between computers, simply because it is a unidirectional mode and computers usually need bidirectional communication.

Fig. 1.8
Simplex mode allows communication only in one direction.

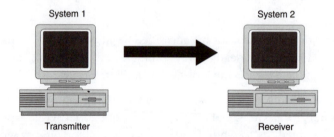

System 1   System 2

Transmitter   Receiver

Half-duplex mode, shown in figure 1.9, is very commonly used in data communication. Although it limits communication to one direction at any time, because each station is given an opportunity to transmit, bidirectional communication can occur. If a second station attempts to transmit at the same time as the first, both transmissions are garbled. While a station is transmitting, it cannot hear others that are also transmitting. Some provision must be made to ensure that no two stations can transmit simultaneously or, if simultaneous transmissions do occur, that the resulting garbled messages can be recognized as lost and can be retransmitted.

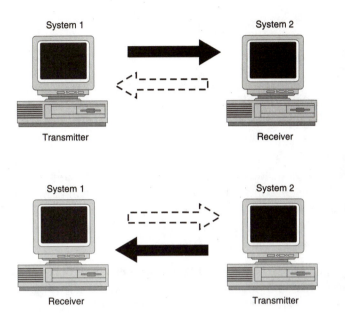

Fig. 1.9
Half-duplex mode
allows communi-
cation in both
directions, but not
simultaneously.

The chief advantage to half-duplex mode is that it uses bandwidth efficiently. Because only one station can transmit at one time, that station can use the full available bandwidth, rather than being required to share it with other transmitting stations. Another advantage to half-duplex is that it simplifies management; because only one station is transmitting at any given time, no overhead is incurred to manage multiple simultaneous transmissions to keep their content separated.

One disadvantage to half-duplex mode is that any half-duplex system introduces turnaround delay. If two stations are communicating on a half-duplex link, when one station finishes its transmission, a finite amount of time must pass before the link can automatically reconfigure itself to allow the second station to begin transmitting. In some applications, this turnaround delay is unacceptable, so full-duplex mode must be used instead.

Full-duplex mode, shown in figure 1.10, is used less commonly in data communication. With full-duplex, all stations may transmit and receive simultaneously. Although full-duplex has the advantage of not requiring arbitration of bandwidth demands by individual stations, it has two main drawbacks.

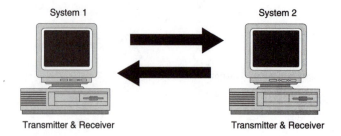

First, because bandwidth must be shared between a transmit channel and a receive channel, maximum throughput is reduced. If half of the available bandwidth is allocated to each purpose and your application is heavily weighted towards one or the other function, then your throughput will be lower than on a half-duplex link.

For example, a network file server typically spends most of its time transmitting data in response to user requests. Files on a server are read much more often than they are written. A user opens a file stored on the server and the file server must transmit the contents of that file to the user. The request may be very small, typically only a few bytes. The file, on the other hand, may be very large—a megabyte or more. Using full-duplex mode in this situation would mean that the transmit channel of the server would be in constant use sending files to users, while the receive channel would see only occasional traffic as users sporadically requested files. If the transmit and receive channels had each been allocated 50 percent of the bandwidth, one channel would be almost unused while the other would be running flat out most of the time. For this reason, full-duplex is inappropriate in most data communication environments.

The second drawback to full-duplex mode is that it is complicated and expensive to implement. Managing multiple simultaneous transmissions adds a level of design complexity and thereby increases costs.

One data communication environment where full-duplex is common is in dial-up asynchronous modem communications, where the turnaround delay inherent in half-duplex communications is often unacceptable.

Error Checking and Correction

Any time data is communicated there is the danger that portions of it will be lost or distorted. Human communication is more forgiving of such errors than computer communication. A momentary buzz on the telephone line, a cellular hand-off, or a flicker in your TV picture may be annoying, but little or nothing is lost when these errors occur. A similarly small data loss or drop-out could be catastrophic in data communications.

Parity

The first and simplest means of improving the reliability of data communication, and one familiar to modem users, is called *parity*. Asynchronous communication uses single byte framing. This single byte contains eight bits, but because the ASCII character set requires only seven bits to represent all available symbols, the eighth bit is unused. Rather than let it go to waste, the eighth bit can be used as a primitive means of error detection. Under this scheme, the otherwise unused eighth bit is called the *parity bit*.

When the transmitting station frames a character, or byte, it counts the number of 1's and 0's in the 7-bit data portion of the byte. Using *even parity*, if the number of 1's in the 7-bit data stream is even, the parity bit is set to 0. If the number of 1's is odd, the parity bit is set to 1. Using *odd parity*, the situation is reversed. The parity bit is set to 0 when the number of 1's in the data portion of the byte is odd and sets the parity bit to 1 if the number of 1's in the data stream is even.

When the receiving station receives the byte, it counts the number of 0's and 1's in the data portion of the byte and compares the result of this tabulation with the state of the parity bit. If the two do not correspond, it knows that an error has occurred and can request that the transmitting station retransmit the byte. The process of calculating parity values is illustrated in figure 1.11.

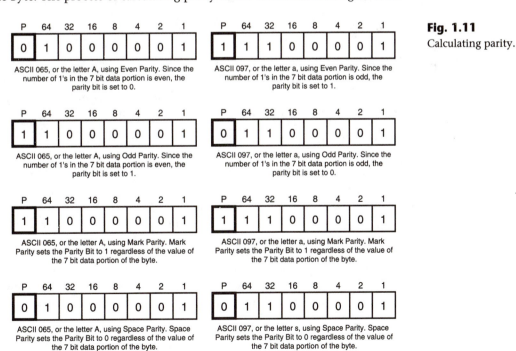

Fig. 1.11
Calculating parity.

ASCII 065, or the letter A, using Even Parity. Since the number of 1's in the 7 bit data portion is even, the parity bit is set to 0.

ASCII 097, or the letter a, using Even Parity. Since the number of 1's in the 7 bit data portion is odd, the parity bit is set to 1.

ASCII 065, or the letter A, using Odd Parity. Since the number of 1's in the 7 bit data portion is even, the parity bit is set to 1.

ASCII 097, or the letter a, using Odd Parity. Since the number of 1's in the 7 bit data portion is odd, the parity bit is set to 0.

ASCII 065, or the letter A, using Mark Parity. Mark Parity sets the Parity Bit to 1 regardless of the value of the 7 bit data portion of the byte.

ASCII 097, or the letter a, using Mark Parity. Mark Parity sets the Parity Bit to 1 regardless of the value of the 7 bit data portion of the byte.

ASCII 065, or the letter A, using Space Parity. Space Parity sets the Parity Bit to 0 regardless of the value of the 7 bit data portion of the byte.

ASCII 097, or the letter s, using Space Parity. Space Parity sets the Parity Bit to 0 regardless of the value of the 7 bit data portion of the byte.

Two other forms of parity are also available. Strangely enough, each of them does very little to improve the reliability of data communication. In each of these other schemes, the content of the data portion of the byte is totally ignored. The first of these is called *mark parity*, which requires that the parity bit always be set to 1. The second is called *space parity*, which requires that the parity bit always be set to 0. The only protection offered by mark parity and space parity occurs if the parity bit itself is changed during transmission, which only occurs once in every eight single-bit errors.

A final form of parity is *no parity*. This simply means that all 8 bits are used for data transmission and therefore no spare bit is available to use for parity.

Parity in any form is a poor means of ensuring reliable data transmission for several reasons. First, it can reliably detect only single bit errors. If two bits are altered, say a 0 to a 1 and a 1 to a 0, the parity calculation yields the same result as it would if the byte had been received correctly. Second, if a single-bit error does occur, one time in eight it will be the parity bit itself that was altered, and the 7-bit data portion of the byte came through fine, resulting in needless retransmissions. Third, parity only detects errors, albeit inefficiently. It does nothing to correct them. More sophisticated schemes can detect an error (and can do so more reliably than parity methods), and they can actually correct the error without requiring that the data be retransmitted.

Checksums and Cyclic Redundancy Checks

The deficiencies of parity as an error checking method led to the adoption of other error checking schemes based on the use of checksum and cyclic redundancy check (CRC) methods. Both of these methods are used to ensure the integrity of a block of data, as opposed to the single byte for which parity is used. A block can range in size from 128 bytes to 4K or more.

Using a checksum or a cyclic redundancy check, the value of a bit (0 or 1) and its position within the byte contribute to the check value. For example, because the bytes 00000001 and 10000000 both contain exactly one "1," their parity values are identical. For a checksum or CRC, however, these are very different values. The first byte has a decimal value of 1 and the second a decimal value of 128. Accordingly, a checksum or CRC calculated against these bytes yields different results for each.

A *checksum* is a value that the sending station calculates by summing the binary values of each byte contained in the block and then truncating the most significant bits to the size of the checksum portion of the block. The sending station then appends the checksum value to the data block and sends the result to the receiving station. When the receiving station receives the block, it then separates the data block from the checksum value, recalculates the checksum against the data block, and compares the resulting checksum value with the checksum value received. If these values differ, the recipient knows that the data was damaged in transit and can request that the sender resend it. The process of creating a checksum is illustrated in figure 1.12.

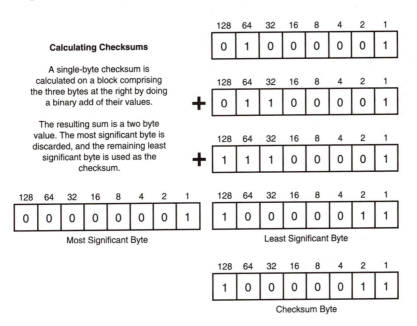

Fig. 1.12
Calculating a checksum.

Checksums can detect single-bit errors and some multiple-bit errors, and are a much better method of ensuring data integrity than simple parity. Checksums are seldom used today, having been superseded for most purposes by the much superior cyclic redundancy check.

A *cyclic redundancy check* is another method used to ensure the integrity of transmitted data. Unlike the checksum, which simply does a binary sum and appends the result, the CRC uses a sophisticated mathematical algorithm to calculate an error checking value. CRC divides the binary data values against a fixed binary number and appends the modulo to the data block as a check value. The modulo is the remainder which results from an integer division. The process of creating a CRC value is illustrated in figure 1.13.

Fig. 1.13
Calculating a
cyclic redundancy
check.

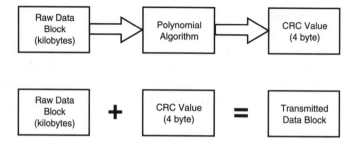

A CRC value can occupy one byte or several bytes. Allocating a larger number of bytes to the CRC value increases the chance that a data transmission error will be detected. A 1-byte CRC provides 2^8 or 256 possible values, a 2- byte CRC offers 2^{16} or 65,536 values, and so on. Each additional checksum byte multiplies the possible values by a factor of 256.

The number of bytes used depends on the size of the data block itself. Four-byte CRC values are commonly used with 1K data blocks, yielding 2^{32} or more than four billion possible values for the check data. When applied to a data block in the small kilobyte range, this number of possible states for the check value almost guarantees that any transmission error will be detected.

Transmission Media

For communication between a transmitting station and a receiving station to occur, a transmission path must exist between them. This path can take the form of a wireless link using radio or light waves, such as a cellular phone or the remote control for your television. It can also take the form of a cable that physically connects the two stations together, such as a computer connected to a local area network. Finally, it can take the form of a switched connection, which temporarily connects the two systems either physically or virtually, such as a telephone. Take a look at each of these in more detail.

Wireless Connection Paths

Wireless connection methods are referred to by communication experts, somewhat pedantically, as unbounded transmission media. Until recently, wireless methods were uncommon in the workaday data communications that you and I might deal with, although they were commonly used as major components in the national data communications infrastructure in the form of satellite data communications. The only direct contact most of us had with wireless data communications might have been setting up a wireless bridge to link the networks in two buildings that were difficult to connect using cable, or perhaps in using a VSAT disk to link back to main headquarters.

Wireless is, however, beginning to come down to the workstation level, with network adapter cards using laser infrared signaling or spread-spectrum UHF signaling becoming more commonly seen. These devices address two increasingly common problems. First, the proliferation of notebook computers and the increasing importance of local area networks to the core business of organizations has made it desirable to break the hard-wired link formerly required for network workstations. This need to "plug in anywhere" is easily accommodated by a properly designed wireless LAN system. Second, it is becoming increasingly difficult to wire existing buildings for communication. Conduits are full and getting more so. If your building is listed on the National Register, it may be undesirable to drill holes in walls to run cable, and it may be illegal. Again, wireless technology addresses the problem.

Two major concerns exist with any wireless transmission media. First, because wireless methods require you to broadcast your data, it may be easily accessible to outsiders. This is less of a concern with infrared methods, because the signal seldom escapes the room in which it is used. Using radio frequency methods poses more of a problem. Although the signals are typically of very low power and spread-spectrum methods are used to distribute the data across several frequencies, the possibility that your data will be compromised by an eavesdropper cannot be overlooked. Manufacturers of wireless devices are addressing this problem with built-in dynamic encryption, and wireless security will probably soon cease to be an issue for any but the most sensitive data.

The second problem with wireless, in particular radio frequency methods, is simple congestion. A limited band of frequencies is available for use by these devices. Their low transmitting power makes it unlikely that you might interfere with a user across town or even in the next building. However, as these devices become more commonly used, the chance that you might mutually interfere with a user on the next floor of your building increases dramatically. If this problem is not addressed by government allocating more frequencies for this type of use and by manufacturers incorporating better methods to isolate users, the resulting confusion could make us all look back fondly on the boom days of CB radio.

Hard-Wired Connection Paths

When most people think of two computers communicating, they think about a cable linking the two machines. Cable is a mature and well-understood technology. Thousands of types of data communication cable exist, each optimized for a particular use. Most cable uses a copper conductor to transmit electrical signals. Fiber optic cable, which uses light waves to transmit data, is becoming much more common as its price drops. If your computers are connected in a local area network, almost certainly some type of cable is used to connect them.

Using cable to connect computers has several advantages. It's inexpensive, it offers high data transmission rates, and it's relatively secure against eavesdropping. If cable has one primary disadvantage, it is that cable requires a physical connection between the machines. If you need to connect to a system across the country, or even one across town, running cable isn't a practical choice.

Until you begin to explore the subject, you won't believe how much there is to know about cable and the devices used to connect it. If you're responsible for building a local area network, take the time to learn at least the fundamentals. The "wire is wire" attitude has probably caused more LAN problems than any other mistake. Cabling is discussed fully in Chapter 7, "Building a Network Infrastructure."

Switched Connection Paths

Having a dedicated connection to each computer system with which you need to communicate is practical on a local area network. However, it rapidly becomes impractical as the distance between the computer systems increases. Two facts make a solution to this problem possible.

First, although you may need to communicate with one or many remote computers on a regular basis, you probably don't need a full-time dedicated connection to each of these computers, and you can probably live with slower data throughput than you have on your locally connected systems. Second, many other people have a similar need to communicate with remote computers. The solution is called *switching*, and it works by sharing resources. The same connection resources that allow your computer in Winston-Salem to communicate with another computer in San Francisco can be used by someone else while you're not using them.

There are three methods of creating switched connections between stations, called circuit switching, message switching, and packet switching.

Circuit Switching. *Circuit switching*, shown in figure 1.14, creates a temporary dedicated channel between the stations. The circuit is created, called *buildup*, when the connection is initiated. The circuit is then destroyed, called *teardown*, when the connection is terminated. Every time you dial your telephone you use circuit switching to complete the connection.

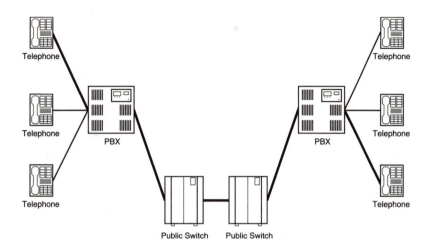

Fig. 1.14
Circuit switching
dedicates connec-
tion resources for
the duration of the
connection.

Conceptually, circuit switching works by connecting each station via a dedicated cable to a central switching station, which itself connects to hundreds
or thousands of individual stations. When Station A wants to connect to
Station B, the connection is made temporarily at the switch by joining the
dedicated line from Station A directly to the dedicated line of Station B.
When the connection terminates, the junction is removed. Because multiple
central stations can themselves be connected via trunk lines, you can establish a connection to any station that's connected to any part of this network
by running through more than one switch.

For the duration of the connection, circuit switching dedicates the resources
necessary to sustain the connection. When the connection terminates, these
resources again become available to use in building other connections. During the course of the connection, circuit switching provides dedicated bandwidth. The advantage to this is that the bandwidth is always available when
needed, which eliminates delay and makes circuit switching appropriate for
voice, video, and other real-time applications. The drawback is that unused
bandwidth cannot be reallocated to other communications. For example, if
there is a pause during your telephone conversation, that unused bandwidth
goes to waste rather than being used to carry another conversation.

Circuit switching limits the number of connections that can exist simultaneously to some finite number based on the resources available. When all of
these resources are in use for existing connections, attempting to make another connection fails until one of the original connections terminates and
its resources are returned to the pool for re-use. For example, if you attempt
to place a telephone call on Christmas Day or during a weather emergency,

you may hear the fast-busy reorder tone that indicates all circuits are busy. Until one of the ongoing conversations concludes, no resources are available to establish your connection. When you can establish a connection, you have absolute claim on the resources needed to support it until you terminate the connection.

Circuit switching is used in computer data communications in two ways. First, it is used to allow a workstation equipped with a modem to establish a connection to a central host using ordinary telephone lines. Second, it is sometimes used to connect two central hosts on a more or less permanent basis.

Message Switching. *Message switching,* shown in figure 1.15, is also referred to as store-and-forward messaging. In a message switching system, the entire message is moved from one connection point to the next until it reaches its ultimate destination.

Fig. 1.15
Message switching uses minimal connection resources, but does not offer real-time performance.

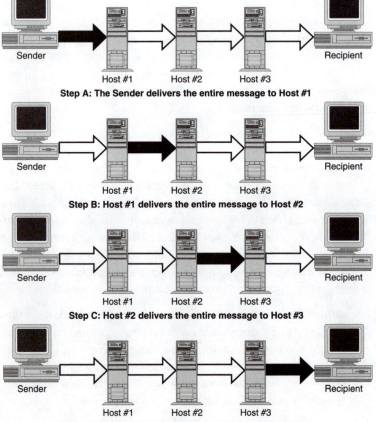

Step A: The Sender delivers the entire message to Host #1

Step B: Host #1 delivers the entire message to Host #2

Step C: Host #2 delivers the entire message to Host #3

Step D: Host #3 delivers the entire message to Recipient

Sending a letter from coast to coast via the U.S. Mail provides a good example of how a message switching system operates. You place an envelope—the message—in your mailbox, which is the first connection point. The letter carrier picks up this message—and perhaps several others stored in your mailbox—and carries it to the branch post office, the second connection point. At the branch post office, the message is stored and then forwarded to the main post office or to a central sorting facility, the third connection point. It then makes its way to a sectional center facility and is then put on a truck or a train for forwarding to the destination SCF. At this point, the process is reversed, and your envelope makes its way down the chain until the letter carrier places it in the destination mailbox.

Message switching creates a dedicated connection to the next switch, transmits the entire message and then terminates the connection. The recipient switch stores or buffers that message in its entirety until it can create a temporary connection to the next switch, forward the message in its entirety to that switch, and then terminate the connection. This process continues until the message reaches its ultimate destination.

The advantage of message switching is that it uses very few resources in relation to the amount of data conveyed. Because a connection exists only for the time required to transmit the message, little bandwidth is wasted. The one major drawback to message switching is that it does not provide a real-time connection, and is therefore inappropriate for voice, video, and interactive data connections.

The most common application of message switching in computer data communications is for storing and forwarding e-mail messages and UseNet news articles. Otherwise, it is little used.

Packet Switching. *Packet switching*, shown in figure 1.16, creates a virtual connection between two stations, as opposed to the physical connection used in circuit switching and message switching. The connection resources used to build this virtual connection can be used simultaneously to provide other virtual connections.

Fig. 1.16
With packet switching, each packet may take a different route through the network and arrive in a different order than it was sent.

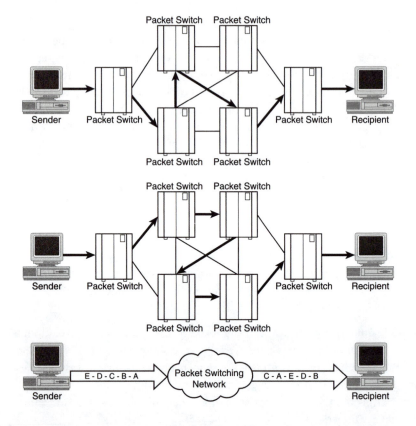

Using packet switching, a message to be transmitted is first broken into smaller blocks, called *packets* or *frames*. To each of these packets is added a header section, which includes address information for the originating and destination stations. Each packet is an individual entity and is transmitted and handled as such. Once assembled, these packets are then sent to a central packet switching device, which examines each incoming packet and uses the address information contained in that packet to route that packet either to its ultimate destination or to an intermediate switch. At intermediate switches, this process is repeated until the packet reaches the recipient.

Packet switches do not dedicate resources to any particular connection. Any packet switch may connect to other packet switches using several routes. Inherent to packet switching is the concept that route is immaterial. It doesn't matter how they get there, as long as they do get there. Successive packets from the same message may arrive at the destination via completely different routes. The first packet might travel from Winston-Salem to San Francisco with only a single intermediate hop to a switch in Chicago. The very next packet may travel first to New York, hop a satellite up-link to Houston, bounce back to Atlanta and then travel straight to San Francisco. The following packet may see London and Tokyo before it arrives. Because routing resources are allocated dynamically, each packet is routed by the fastest or least congested means available at the millisecond when that packet arrives.

Packet switching has two major advantages. First, the fact that redundant routes between packet switches are available means that if one route goes down, packets can be routed via alternative routes, though perhaps with slower performance. Second, unlike circuit switching, packet switching has no absolute limitation on the number of connections that can be handled by a switch. Because all bandwidth is shared, other connections can continue to be added subject only to the cumulative throughput available. As each additional connection is added, the other connections experience proportional degradation in throughput, but each station always has a chance to transfer data.

Balanced against these advantages are several disadvantages. First, using packet switching results in unpredictable arrival of information. One packet may arrive at the destination in 250 milliseconds, while the next packet takes 400 milliseconds to make the trip. Also, packets do not necessarily arrive in the order in which they were sent. This unpredictability makes packet switching inappropriate for real-time applications like voice and video imaging, although it is an ideal technology for bursty computer data communications. Second, the overhead involved in building the packets originally, routing them through various switches, and reassembling them at their destination is considerable. Essentially, with packet switching you spend a lot of money to provide high performance switches so you can use lower performance, less expensive, non-dedicated links. Contrast this with circuit switching, which can use relatively low-performance and inexpensive switches, but requires expensive dedicated links between the switches.

Packet switching is a widely used technology in computer data communication. Packet switching uses virtual circuits, of which three types are available—the standard virtual circuit, the switched virtual circuit, and the permanent virtual circuit.

Virtual Circuit. A standard *virtual circuit,* shown in figure 1.17, uses a connectionless service to communicate packets between stations. Connectionless means that no connection exists between the originating station and the receiving station. The originating station creates packets and sends them to the packet switch, which then forwards them to intermediate switches and ultimately to the receiving station. Each packet is treated independently of all other packets, and each may follow a different path to the destination.

Fig. 1.17
A virtual circuit allows any connected station to communicate with any other. Each packet may take a different route through the network and arrive in a different order than it was sent.

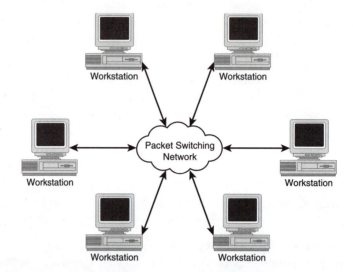

Standard virtual circuits provide connections in a parallel one-to-many environment. Any station connected to the packet switching network using a virtual circuit can at any time transmit data to and receive data from another station similarly connected. A transmitting station indicates the desired destination station by including the destination network and station addresses in each outgoing packet. Any station connected to the packet switching network can "see" all packets, but it acts only on those addressed to it. The most visible implementation of virtual circuit packet switching is the Internet, which handles billions of such packets every day, routing them to and from stations all over the world.

You might use virtual circuit packet switching if you had several branch offices located in different cities that needed to be connected. By connecting each branch office to its local point of presence (POP) for the same packet switching service, each office can communicate at any time with the other branch offices over the network. This easily beats the first alternative, providing each branch office with a dedicated line to each other office, on the basis of price alone—not even considering the additional complexity and management needed to support so many dedicated connections. It also beats the second alternative, having each branch office dial in to another branch office or to the main office as needed, on the bases of simplicity, functionality, and cost.

Switched Virtual Circuit. A *switched virtual circuit*, shown in figure 1.18, uses a connection-oriented service to communicate packets between stations. *Connection-oriented* means that a specific route through the network is temporarily built between the communicating stations when the connection originates. This route continues to be used for the duration of the connection, and is torn down when the connection terminates. If one element of the route fails during the connection, the switch automatically substitutes another route. Otherwise, the route remains fixed for the duration of the connection. Network resources are allocated to the connection when it is made, and are usable only by that connection so long as it exists. This means that only a finite number of switched virtual circuits can be in use at any one time on a particular switch.

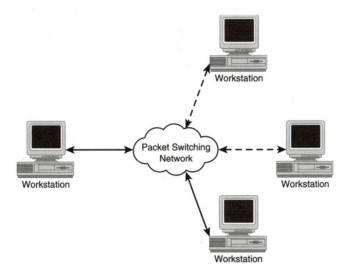

Fig. 1.18
A switched virtual circuit allows any connected station to communicate with any other, but only by making an explicit request to connect to that station. A station may be linked to only one station at any given time.

Switched virtual circuits provide connections in a serial one-to-many environment. This means that any station using a switched virtual circuit packet switched connection can communicate with any other station so connected, but only one at a time. Station A can establish a connection to Station B. If Station A then needs to communicate with Station C, the original connection must be torn down and a new connection must be established between Stations A and C.

In this respect, using a switched virtual circuit to communicate data is similar to using a circuit switch for voice telephone communications. In fact, switched virtual circuits ordinarily require a dialing process similar to that of voice telephony. The difference is that, unlike the circuit-switched telephone call, the switched virtual circuit data call does not monopolize the available bandwidth of a circuit. It instead shares the circuit with other switched virtual circuits and uses bandwidth only when needed to transfer data.

Switched virtual circuits are used commonly in data communications, with the most familiar examples being X.25 packet switching and Switched 56K service.

Permanent Virtual Circuit. A *permanent virtual circuit*, shown in figure 1.19, uses a connection-oriented service to communicate packets between two defined end stations. Conceptually, a permanent virtual circuit is similar to the traditional data leased line, and is used for the same purpose. The connection is established by the telephone company or other service provider at the time the circuit is installed, and never varies. For this reason, permanent virtual circuits are inherently point-to-point connections.

Fig. 1.19
A permanent virtual circuit establishes a fixed connection between two designated stations similar to a traditional leased line, but using the packet switching network.

You might use a permanent virtual circuit to establish a permanent connection between two file servers located remotely from each other. The advantage to a permanent virtual circuit is that you pay only for the data you actually communicate. With the leased line, you pay 24 hours a day, 365 days a year whether you use the connection heavily or not at all.

Types of Communications

Now that you have a good understanding of the fundamentals of how data communication works, take a look at some of the ways communications are actually used in the real world. But first, a little more background. To understand the differences between types of communications, it is important to understand the crucial difference between a multiuser system and a local area network.

A traditional *multiuser system* like a minicomputer, mainframe, or UNIX system uses a powerful central computer system called a host. A multiuser system is shown in figure 1.20. Programs and data are stored on the host, and all processing is done by the host processor. Connected to this host are dumb terminals, which are basically just a video display and keyboard, and have little or no processing power of their own. A PC can run terminal emulation software, which simply makes it appear as a dumb terminal to the host. The connection between terminals and the host typically runs at low kilobit per second speeds. UNIX and VAX/VMS are examples of traditional multiuser operating systems.

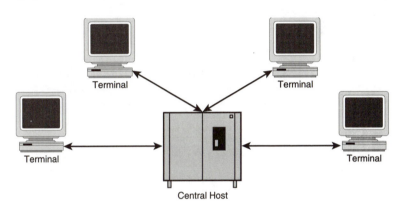

Terminal

Terminal

Terminal

Terminal

Central Host

Fig. 1.20
With a multiuser system, all processing is done at the host.

A traditional *local area network* (LAN), shown in figure 1.21 and described in more detail in the following section, connects a group of computer systems together. One or more of these computer systems runs the network operating system (NOS), and acts as a server to provide shared access to disk drives, printers, and other shared resources located on the server. With minor exceptions, other than the network operating system itself, no programs run on the server. Other computer systems function as client workstations and run the actual application programs locally. The connection between workstations and servers typically runs at multi-megabit per second speeds. Novell NetWare and Banyan VINES are examples of traditional network operating systems.

Fig. 1.21
With a local area network, some or all programs run on the workstations.

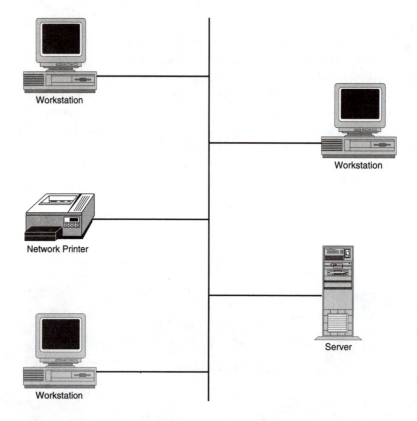

The key difference between a multiuser system and a local area network is where the actual application programs run. On a multiuser system, all application programs run on the central host. On a local area network, all application programs run on the individual client workstations. If you need to speed up program execution on a multiuser system, you buy a more powerful host. If you need to speed up program execution on a network, you buy faster workstations.

Microsoft Windows NT blurs the distinction between multiuser systems and networks. It is a hybrid, with aspects of both methodologies. In addition to the file and printer sharing services typically provided by a network operating system, Windows NT Server also allows you to run user programs on the server itself. A server doing so is called an Application Server, and it provides the same functionality as a traditional multiuser system.

Local Area Networks

A *local area network* is a group of computer systems located in close physical proximity, typically within one building. Each of these computers is provided with a network adapter card, which allows it to connect to the network cabling system. Once connected—by using standard common data communications protocols—these systems can exchange data and share resources like files and printers. In broad terms, there are two types of computers connected to a local area network.

A computer that provides services to the network users is called a *server*. Some servers are general purpose, and may simultaneously provide shared disk storage, access to network printers, shared access to e-mail, and so forth. Some servers are specialized, and provide only one or a few functions. Your network may, for example, have a server dedicated to providing network fax services or shared access to a mainframe computer system. Servers run specialized software to allow them to provide these services. For example, a general purpose server may run Novell NetWare or Microsoft Windows NT Server to provide shared file and print services. Another server may run Netscape Commerce Server software to provide World Wide Web (WWW or Web) services to Internet users.

A computer that uses some or all of these network services is called a *client* or a *workstation*. A client computer system runs special software to allow it to access the services provided by various servers. Windows NT Workstation 4.0 has client software built-in to allow it to access many common services, including Microsoft Networking, Novell NetWare, and the Internet.

Historically, local area networks were divided into two categories. *Client/server* or *server-based* networks dedicated one or more computer systems solely to providing network services. *Peer-to-peer* networks did not dedicate a computer system as a server, but allowed each client to share its resources with other clients on the network. Client/server networks were considered expensive and complicated to manage, but they provided high performance. Peer-to-peer networks were considered inexpensive and easy to manage, but at the expense of providing lower performance.

The advent of Windows has blurred this distinction. Windows 3.11 for Workgroups, Windows 95, and Windows NT provide built-in high-performance peer networking services. Each can, as a client, access resources shared by any of the others functioning as servers. If your situation demands the power and speed of a dedicated server running a traditional client/server network operating system, Windows NT Server provides the horsepower needed while integrating gracefully with its close relatives. For smaller networks, Windows NT Workstation 4.0 can perform as a very respectable server, providing shared resources to Windows 3.11 for Workgroups and Windows 95 clients.

Dial-up Asynchronous

For many people, their first experience with data communications comes when they connect a modem to their computer and use their telephone line to call a bulletin board system or a commercial online service like CompuServe or America Online. These people are using a dial-up asynchronous connection.

You establish a dial-up asynchronous connection by running general purpose communications software like HyperTerminal or ProComm Plus on your workstation. This turns your expensive computer into an inexpensive dumb terminal. This software controls your modem, dials the number of the destination computer's modem and establishes a link with it, and then uses asynchronous protocols to provide a terminal window on the remote host. When you're connected, you can use services on the remote host as though you were using a locally connected terminal.

What you don't have with an asynchronous dial-up connection is a network link. The protocols used to establish and maintain the dial-up link provide only terminal functionality. You have no network access to disk drives, printers, or other network resources located on the remote system.

For example, if you need to retrieve and edit a Microsoft Word document file that's stored on the hard drive of the remote system, you must first request that the remote system send the file to you. You then manually initiate a "receive file" function from within your communications program, and wait while the remote system transfers the file to you and your system saves it to your local hard drive. Only then can you open and edit the Word document file. When you have made your changes and saved the Word document file on the local hard drive, you must then reverse the process and transfer the file manually back to the remote system if you want the version stored on the remote system to be current.

Contrast this process with what would have occurred if you had a network connection. With the network connection, you could load Word on your local computer, browse a list of disk drives located on the remote system, point to the document, and double-click to retrieve it. When you finish making changes, you simply save the document to the drive located on the remote machine.

Dial-Up Networking

Dial-Up networking (DUN) uses the same equipment and techniques as dial-up asynchronous does, but with a different end result. In dial-up asynchronous, you connect to a host in terminal mode. This means that all programs run remotely on the host, and your computer is used only to offer you a terminal window. With DUN, the link is instead used to establish a network connection between the local server, called the *DUN server*, and your remote workstation, called the *DUN client*. Your remote workstation can access network services just as though it were locally connected to the network, albeit usually at a much slower rate.

DUN uses special remote networking protocols like Point-to-Point Protocol (PPP) and Serial Line Internet Protocol (SLIP) to establish and maintain the network link. When this link has been established, you can run normal local area network transport-level protocols like TCP/IP, IPX/SPX, and NetBEUI to access network services on the remote server.

Using DUN to access network services on a remote server is just like using those same services on a locally-connected server—with one exception. Speed. Your local area network connection probably runs at 10 million bps or faster. Your dial-up networking connection probably runs at considerably less than one percent of that speed.

A small data file that loads instantaneously when accessed locally takes several seconds or longer to load across the remote connection. A directory list that pops up instantly on your locally connected computer may take a second or two to come up on the DUN client. Because loading huge program files like Microsoft Word across the remote link would take several minutes, you will find that in practical terms you must run these files from the local hard drive of the DUN client. Otherwise, DUN offers essentially the same functionality as a local connection.

You can use DUN to connect to different types of DUN servers. For example, if you set up the workstation on your desk as a DUN server, you can use your notebook computer as a DUN client to connect to your desktop machine back at the office when you travel. You can then check your mail, update your calendar, and otherwise behave as though you were seated in front of your office desktop. Another application of DUN might be to use your notebook system as a DUN client to connect to an Internet service provider. For the duration of the connection, your notebook computer has an actual network connection to the Internet. You can run your World Wide Web browser, use ftp to transfer files, and enjoy live Internet access.

I

Getting Started

Internetworks, Wide-Area Networks, and the Internet

A local area network comprises two or more computers located in close physical proximity and connected using cables. Local area networks serve the needs of businesses well, but there may come a time when business needs dictate that you connect your local area network to one or more other networks.

When two or more self-sufficient local area networks are connected together, either directly by using cables or indirectly by using facilities provided by the telephone company or other data communications providers, the result is called an *Internetwork*. The networks comprising an internetwork can be close together, perhaps simply on different floors of the same building. They can also be widely separated, perhaps in different countries. Connected networks that are widely separated geographically are called *wide-area networks* (WANs), shown in figure 1.22.

Fig. 1.22
Wide-area networks connect local area networks together using routers.

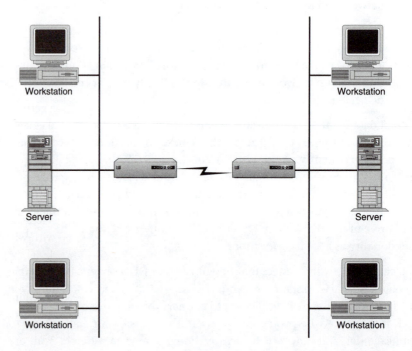

Perhaps the best example of a wide-area network, and one that comes immediately to mind for anyone who reads the newspaper, is the Internet. The Internet is an international wide-area network with millions of connected computers, tens of millions of users, and thousands of gigabytes of data. Over the past couple of years, the Internet has become a major force—some would say *the* major force—in computing. In the final section of this book, you learn in detail how to get on the Internet, both as a user of services provided by others and, if you want, as a provider of services yourself.

Types of Services

There isn't much point in connecting computers together to allow them to communicate unless you get some benefit from doing so. To be useful, data communications must enable you to do something you couldn't do before, or at least to do something faster or less expensively than you could without its presence.

Fortunately, there are numerous useful data communications applications available today. With the Internet leading the cause, more are becoming available all the time. Take a look at some of the things you can do with a "wired" computer.

E-Mail

People love to communicate, and the explosion of the usage of e-mail proves it. E-mail allows you to send messages to and receive them from anyone from a coworker down the hall to a business associate on the other side of the world. E-mail is getting better all the time, because more people are getting connected and because the software is improving in functionality and in the capability to communicate with other mail systems.

If you work for a medium or large company, you almost certainly have access to an e-mail network. Even if you work for a small company, chances are better every day that you will find yourself with e-mail access to your coworkers and to the world. At home, the explosion of commercial online services and the Internet means that there's an excellent chance that someone with whom you want to exchange e-mail already has private access or soon will.

E-mail software has improved dramatically in the past two or three years. Originally, e-mail was limited to plain ASCII text messages, and exchanging mail with someone using a different mail software package was problematic at best.

Using modern e-mail software, you can format messages just like word processing documents. You can use fonts and colors to enhance them, you can include graphics, and you can attach files. Some e-mail software even allows you to include audio and video clips with your mail message. The days of plain text-mode e-mail are gone forever.

The explosion of the Internet and the broad acceptance of Internet standards like Simple Mail Transfer Protocol (SMTP) and Multipurpose Internet Mail Extensions (MIME) means that the type of e-mail software you choose to use is increasingly less important. If you use Windows Messaging mail, I use Pegasus Mail, and our friend uses Eudora mail, the three of us can still exchange messages and attachments because all three of these products can understand and use SMTP and MIME. No longer are users limited to exchanging mail only with others who use the same e-mail software. E-mail has become so common that many people are starting to refer to it simply as "mail," and qualifying traditional mail as the U.S. Mail or "snail mail." Nowadays, if someone tells you that he'll mail you a document, chances are he means that he'll e-mail it to you.

Windows NT Workstation has excellent built-in support for e-mail. In Chapter 10, "Configuring Windows NT Messaging" and in Chapter 11, "Using E-mail in Windows NT 4.0" you'll learn in detail how to set up and use Windows Messaging to provide e-mail.

Bulletin Board Systems

At its simplest, a *bulletin board system* (BBS) is simply a computer system equipped with a modem and telephone line. BBSes run specialized software that allows other computers to call in, connect to it, and make use of the services it offers. For example, callers can exchange e-mail, transfer public domain and shareware program files to and from the bulletin board, and perhaps play games.

BBSes originated in the late 1970's as a means for technically-oriented computer hobbyists to exchange programs and information. Their users were often pigeon-holed as young, male computer "nerds." For the first few years of their existence, this was perhaps a fair characterization. It is no longer. BBS callers today are male and female, young and old, rich and poor, black and white, computer gurus and computer tyros. Anyone can find something worthwhile on BBSes today.

BBSes have now matured. Depending on whose count you believe, there are at least 30,000 BBSes, and perhaps more than 50,000, throughout the United States. Even small towns are likely to have a BBS or two, and in major cities you can often choose from dozens or even hundreds of BBSes. Some of these systems are general purpose, while others cater to particular interests, which may be narrowly defined. For example, you can find BBSes with emphases ranging from NASCAR auto racing to Libertarian politics to AIDS awareness.

BBSes have also outgrown their isolated nature. In the past, a BBS was connected only with its own callers. Today, a BBS is likely to be connected to national and international networks for exchanging e-mail. BBSes have grown in other ways as well. Years ago, the typical BBS had only one modem and one telephone line, which limited it to serving one caller at a time. The largest BBSes today may have 1,000 or more telephone lines and modems installed, tens of gigabytes of files available for download, and packet switched access for long distance callers. All large BBSes, and many smaller ones, offer at least some level of Internet access. Many offer complete Internet services to their callers. In fact, it can be difficult to put your finger on what exactly separates these large BBSes from the commercial online services like CompuServe.

BBSes are now used heavily by corporate America. Companies have recognized that a BBS offers a fast, inexpensive, and effective method of communicating with their customers. Price lists, product specifications, program updates—all of these and more can be made available to any customer with a modem, 24 hours a day, 365 days a year. A BBS can also be a very useful platform for internal company communications. It can provide e-mail services throughout the company, allow staff members to exchange work, serve as a central announcement area, and allow sales people on the road to access company information.

Many people predicted the death of BBSes, at first due to competition from commercial online services, and later due to competition from the Internet. The opposite seems to be the case, however. Certainly, single-line hobbyist boards can be started with only a small investment in time and money, and therefore tend to be ephemeral, springing up and collapsing on almost a weekly basis. Overall, however, the use of BBSes, both public and private, is growing by leaps and bounds.

Commercial Online Services

Commercial online services like CompuServe, America Online, Prodigy, and The Microsoft Network have exploded. Just a few years ago, online services were the province of corporate researchers, writers, and technical staff. With today's commercial online services, you're as likely to find an eight year old researching a school paper, a working mom working on her master's degree, or a grandfather exchanging e-mail with his grandchildren.

The commercial online services provide a structured, content-rich environment with something for everyone. Each service provides special interest groups and forums that focus on a variety of topics, from Archeology to Zoology. Online encyclopedias and other reference resources are abundant. News, weather, and current events are there for the browsing, as are thousands of well-organized and maintained public domain and shareware files. You can shop in an online virtual mall for coffee, wine, clothing, furniture, and more. Value-added services feature special content from real-time stock quotations to credit reports to premium data bases. If it makes any sense at all to have something available online, you can probably find it somewhere on a commercial online service.

Right now, commercial online services are in the odd position of both growing faster than they ever have and yet having a clouded future. As of July 1996, America Online had more than six million paying subscribers, and CompuServe nearly five million. Each of these services is adding new subscribers at the rate of hundreds of thousands per month. Why, then, in the face of these impressive numbers, do many people predict coming bad times for these online services? The one-word answer is the Internet.

Just consider the news concerning three of the major commercial online services in one two-week span at the end of February 1996. First, H&R Block, the owner of CompuServe, announced that it planned to spin off the online service, maintaining only a 20 percent stake. Next, Sears announced that it was abandoning its stake in Prodigy. Next, Microsoft, which had recently announced a corporate restructuring and a change in emphasis of the Microsoft Network from a commercial online service to an Internet service, found that the development team for the Microsoft Network had departed *en bloc* to form another company that would focus on providing Internet tools.

The reason for all of this is, quite simply, that commercial online services charge primarily by the hour while Internet access is available for a flat monthly rate. People are voting with their dollars, and what they're telling the commercial online services is that they don't like to have a meter running while they're working online. AT&T drove yet another nail into the coffin of the commercial online services when, in March of 1996, they announced that any AT&T long distance subscriber was eligible for five free hours per month of Internet service for an entire year, and that heavier users could have unlimited Internet access for $20 per month. That's a pretty tough act to follow.

The main reason for the explosive growth in subscriptions to commercial online services is that they provide Internet access in a form that ordinary people can use. What the commercial online services do not seem to understand is that all of these new subscribers have only a secondary interest in the proprietary content available on the service; what they really want is to get on the Internet. As less expensive alternatives (like the AT&T plan) become widely available, these new subscribers will depart in droves. The commercial online services will be left with an overbuilt infrastructure, high costs, and few subscribers willing to pay the rates necessary to support that cost structure. Can it be coincidence that America Online, which is generally considered to provide the best Internet access of the major online services, is currently growing faster than the other online services combined?

Commercial online services make the argument—and it is a good one—that their content is structured and therefore expensive to maintain. They say the Internet, however, is a completely unstructured anarchy where it is difficult to locate the information you're looking for. They're right, but potential customers aren't buying it. Although commercial online services pay lip service to consumers' desire for flat-rate pricing, their flat rate plans offer such limited access to so few services that nearly all of their users spend a significant amount of time in the so-called premium areas, with the meter ticking away by the minute.

Standing apart from this crowd of general purpose commercial online services are the specialized commercial online services typified by Dialog and Dow-Jones News Retrieval. Rather than focusing on a general audience, these services specialize in providing information that is of interest to only a relatively small, well-defined market niche. They are the province of corporate, law, and medical librarians and other skilled researchers. Rates commonly begin at $100 per hour, and very specialized services, such as a patent law database, may charge $1,000 per hour or more. Still, if the information you need is available on one of these specialized services, they can provide the easiest and least expensive means of tracking it down.

The World Wide Web and Other Internet Services

If you read the newspaper, watch the television news, or even just listen to office conversations around the water cooler, you've heard about the Internet. Until recently the province of computer professionals and university computer science departments, the Internet has exploded into the mass consciousness of the American public.

Everyone from school children to grandmothers wants to be on the Net. Small businesses that until recently may have done their accounting manually now offer their products and services online via the World Wide Web. Proving the concept of the "killer app," all of this excitement and growth can be traced to two related events.

The 1993 introduction of the Mosaic Web browser, designed by Marc Andreessen of the National Center for Supercomputing Applications (NCSA) at the University of Illinois, brought a graphical user interface (GUI, pronounced goo-ey) to the Internet. Until then, the Internet was essentially a character-mode service. It was ugly, hard to use, and most people found it just about impossible to find what they were looking for.

The introduction of Mosaic changed all of that. Suddenly, you could browse Internet services and sites from within a graphic shell. The Web browser was an idea whose time had come, and today you can choose among scores of browsers. Andreessen left NCSA, formed Netscape Communications to market his Netscape Navigator program, and made it the overwhelming *de facto* standard Web browser (see fig. 1.23). Microsoft got into the act by releasing its Internet Explorer browser. Most of these browsers are inexpensive or free, simply because the companies that produce them want their browser to be the standard. This will enable the companies to sell related software.

Fig. 1.23

You can use the Netscape Web Browser to access the Microsoft home page.

The second event that allowed the Internet to explode was the development of *search engines*. Before search engines, you pretty much had to know not only exactly what you were looking for, but exactly where to find it. Locating something somewhere among the thousands of Internet sites was impractical, because no index existed. Search engines like Lycos, Yahoo, and AltaVista do the work for you (see fig. 1.24). They scan thousands of sites per day, update their databases accordingly, and offer all of this information to you in a searchable format.

The Internet is more than just the World Wide Web, although you wouldn't know it from the amount of press attention the Web gets. Thousands of publicly accessible file transfer protocol (ftp) sites hold freely downloadable files by the gigabyte. The USENET has thousands of discussion groups, with topics ranging literally from aardvarks to zebras. By reading the newspaper, you might reasonably believe that the Internet and USENET are cesspools of child pornography and kinky pictures. Yes, these things are there, but they make up a *tiny* fraction of what's available.

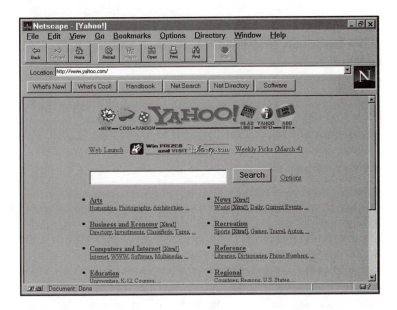

Fig. 1.24
The opening screen of the Yahoo! search engine.

Windows NT Workstation 4.0 gives you the tools you need to access and use the services on the Internet. You learn in Chapter 16 "Using Web Browsers" and Chapter 17 "Using ping, ftp, news, and Telnet" just what else you need to do to get connected.

Windows NT Workstation Communications Services Overview

Microsoft Windows NT Workstation 4.0 includes numerous standard communications features. It provides all of the tools you need to connect to a local area network, to access the World Wide Web and the other services available on the Internet, to connect to a variety of services using your modem and phone line, and more. Here are some of the communications tools and services provided by Windows NT Workstation 4.0:

■ *Full local area network support* provides everything you need to connect to your local area network, including support for a wide range of network protocols, client software for Microsoft and Novell networks, file and printer sharing, and network management and analysis tools. In addition to being a capable and well-behaved network client, Windows NT Workstation 4.0 can perform credibly as a server for a small network.

■ *Microsoft Exchange* includes Microsoft Mail and Microsoft Fax. Microsoft Mail provides high-quality e-mail services for your local area network and the Internet. Microsoft Fax, used with your fax modem and telephone line, allows you to send and receive fax transmissions right from your desk.

> **Note**
>
> Although fax functionality will not ship with the initial release of Windows NT Workstation 4.0, Microsoft has announced that they will ship a service pack before the end of 1996 that will update Windows NT Workstation 4.0 to include fax functions.

■ *Dial-Up Networking* allows a computer running Windows NT Workstation 4.0 to connect to a remote network server using a modem and a standard telephone line. That computer can then access network services and otherwise participate in the network as though it was locally connected. The converse is also true. You can set up your Windows NT Workstation 4.0 as a Remote Access Service (RAS), and it can then provide network services to remote Dial-Up Networking clients.

■ *Internet access tools* allow you to surf the Internet for free programs, cruise the World Wide Web to find information, and more.

■ *HyperTerminal* is an entry-level communications program that may be all you need to connect to local bulletin board systems and commercial online services.

Network Support

Microsoft Windows NT Workstation 4.0 provides built-in networking support unparalleled by any other workstation operating system—with the possible exception of its close relatives, Microsoft Windows NT Server 4.0 and Microsoft Windows 95.

Transport Protocols

Microsoft Windows NT Workstation 4.0 provides built-in support for the network protocols you are most likely to need to link seamlessly to existing server-based and peer-based local area networks and to the Internet.

- *NWLink* IPX/SPX compatible transport protocol allows you to connect with Novell NetWare 3.x and 4.x file servers. During installation, Microsoft Windows NT Workstation 4.0 recognizes available Novell NetWare servers on the network and configures itself accordingly.

- *NetBEUI* transport protocol allows you to connect to workstations and networks running older versions of Microsoft Networking, including Windows 3.11 for Workgroups.

- *TCP/IP* transport protocol, in addition to being an excellent choice if you are building a network of your own, allows you to connect to the Internet.

Client Support

Microsoft Windows NT Workstation 4.0 provides built-in support for Microsoft Networking, as well as standard client software for Novell NetWare 3.x and 4.x networks. The client for Novell NetWare provides full support for NetWare Directory Services (NDS).

Services

Microsoft NT Workstation 4.0 provides numerous network services, which you will learn about in detail later in the book. You can install file and printer sharing for Microsoft networks to allow other Microsoft Networking clients on your network to share your files and printers, and vice versa. Installing file and printer sharing for NetWare networks allows the same for Novell clients.

Windows Messaging System

Windows Messaging provides a single point for managing all types of messages. This Universal Inbox allows you to receive, respond to, and manage incoming e-mail, faxes, and more. Windows NT Workstation 4.0 also includes the supporting software and services you need to create and manage a mail system for a small business.

Windows Messaging allows you to send messages to and receive them from other Messaging users connected to a Windows NT or Windows 95 network. You can attach files and other binary objects created in other applications, and invoke the originating application by clicking the object. You can use fonts, colors, and other text attributes to make your message standout. You can use folders to store, organize, and sort your messages and attachments in various ways.

Microsoft Mail

The *Microsoft Mail Client* software that comes standard with Windows NT Workstation 4.0 probably provides all of the features you need in an e-mail package, including the capability to send mail to and receive it from local users and the Internet.

The *Postoffice* software supplied with Windows NT Workstation 4.0 allows you to create and manage a single postoffice that can serve all of the e-mail users on a small local area network. If your needs grow, you can expand to an enterprise mail system by purchasing Microsoft Mail server software or Microsoft Exchange Server software to allow you to create additional post-offices on other servers or networks while continuing to use the mail client software originally installed.

Windows Messaging does not limit you to using the Microsoft Mail Client. You can substitute any MAPI 1.0–compliant e-mail software and use it from within Windows Messaging. If your existing mail system is not MAPI compliant, you can continue to use it from outside Messaging.

Microsoft Fax

Microsoft Fax is an intrinsic part of Windows Messaging. Using Microsoft Fax with your fax modem and telephone line allows you to send faxes directly from your desktop and from within your applications as easily as printing a document. Incoming faxes come directly to your Windows Messaging Universal Inbox, and can be printed, stored, and otherwise managed as easily as e-mail or any other message.

> **Note**
>
> Although fax functionality will not ship with the initial release of Windows NT Workstation 4.0, Microsoft has announced that they will ship a service pack before the end of 1996 that will update Windows NT Workstation 4.0 to include fax functions.

Microsoft Fax allows you to create, edit, and store cover pages using the included cover page designer. You can edit the rather pedestrian cover pages supplied with the software, or create new ones from scratch. You can incorporate fonts and graphics to dress up your cover pages.

Microsoft Fax offers enhanced functionality when compared with an ordinary fax machine. Using Microsoft Fax, you can exchange confidential documents with other users protecting the documents with digital signatures and public key encryption. You can also attach binary objects to a fax, which can then be received by another Microsoft Fax user.

Microsoft Fax is intelligent enough to recognize the capabilities of the fax device on the receiving end and adjust its behavior accordingly. If it is connected to a standard fax machine, Microsoft Fax recognizes its limitations and sends the data, including attached binary objects, as an ordinary fax transmission. If the receiving device is a Microsoft Fax, all extended capabilities and features are used.

Microsoft Fax also lets you share a fax modem and, more importantly, a fax telephone line. A single fax modem and telephone line installed on any workstation in a Microsoft Networking workgroup can be used by any workstation connected to that network to send and receive faxes. Microsoft Fax is fully compatible with nearly any fax modem you might choose, including support for high-speed fax standards like ITU-T v.17, v.29, and v.27.

Dial-Up Networking

Dial-Up Networking allows a remote computer running Windows NT Workstation 4.0 to use a modem and an ordinary telephone line to establish a link to a Microsoft network. When the link is established, the workstation can access network resources as though it were connected locally to the network. Volumes, directories, and files located on the network are accessible to the workstation simply by clicking from within Explorer. Documents can be printed to a shared printer on the network. The remote user has full access to e-mail and other Messaging services.

The Windows NT Workstation 4.0 Dial-Up Networking client software can access the following: a Dial-Up Networking server running Windows NT 3.1, 3.5, or 4.0 Remote Access Server; a server running Windows 95 Dial-Up Networking services. As long as the protocols are set up correctly on both client and server, the remote client can access all of the network resources available to the locally connected workstation running the server software.

Internet Access Tools

Microsoft Windows NT Workstation 4.0 provides all of the protocols and ser-
vices you need at the operating system level to get connected to the Internet.
That's the good news, because getting this low-level stuff correct is the hard
part. The bad news is that the application-level tools that come bundled with
Windows NT Workstation 4.0 are, not to put too fine a point on it, pathetic.
Fortunately, making this problem go away is easy.

If there is one thing you can find in abundance on the Internet, it's software
designed to use on the Internet itself. Although there is some garbage out
there, many of the programs available for free download are not only best-of-
breed in terms of features and functionality, but most of them are free or very
inexpensive.

For example, Microsoft makes available Internet Explorer, a first-rate Web
browser, for free. Almost any Internet-related program or utility you can
imagine is out there somewhere. About the only downside to using these free
and inexpensive programs is that you have to find them and evaluate them
yourself. Even here, Que has done most of the work for you. The enclosed
CD-ROM disk includes most of the utilities you will need, and each of them
is top-notch.

HyperTerminal

The HyperTerminal communications applet is a simplified version of
Hilgraeve HyperAccess communications software. If your requirements for
dial-up asynchronous communications are casual, you may find that this
application is all you need. For those whose needs are more demanding,
Chapter 4, "Using Communications Programs," covers the best of the
industrial-strength, general purpose, communications software packages. ❖

CHAPTER 2

Understanding Communications Services and Hardware

by Robert Bruce Thompson

A standalone PC is connected to nothing but the power outlet. A Local Area Network, or LAN, is just that—local. It may connect workstations within a single building, or perhaps within a group of buildings in a campus environment. At some point, you will probably want to extend the reach of your PC or your LAN beyond these boundaries. You may need to connect your PC or LAN to the Internet, or you may need to connect branch offices to your headquarters. You may simply need to use your PC to access services provided by a commercial online service or remote host.

For most companies, linking a standalone PC to the world or extending a Local Area Network outside its natural boundaries means using connection services provided by telephone companies and other carriers. Today, even very large corporations, which in the past maintained their own private data networks, are increasingly turning to the public data network to serve their data communications needs. Improvements in the security and reliability of the public data network have made the costs of maintaining such private networks difficult to justify. In a classic business school "make or buy" decision, the emphasis has shifted to buy.

This chapter introduces the variety of data communications services and technologies available. Each of these technologies requires different connecting hardware to service the link. In the case of newer and higher speed technologies, the connecting hardware needed is not a consumer item. You are well advised to simply use what the carrier provides or purchase whatever he recommends, down to the manufacturer, model, and perhaps even to the ROM revision level.

For asynchronous dial-up connections, and increasingly for ISDN, the connecting hardware is standardized. You can choose the best component to meet your needs and your budget and purchase it separately. Because most readers will be primarily interested in dial-up and ISDN connections, we will take a close look at the connecting hardware used with each of these services.

In this chapter, you learn to

- Recognize the various data communications services available from telephone companies and other carriers
- Choose the most appropriate and cost effective service for your data communications needs
- Select the communications hardware used with the various services

Choosing Communications Services

Life was simpler before we had so many choices. You simply called the telephone company and asked them what services were available and how much each of them cost. You then picked the service that best fit your requirements and your budget. There was no need to negotiate price, because the prices for each service were fixed by Public Utilities Commission tariffs. Once the service was installed, if something broke, you called the telephone company and they fixed it. Of course, there weren't all that many services available, and those that were cost an arm and a leg.

Things have changed a lot. Nowadays, you can choose among hundreds of services provided by scores of carriers. Similarly named services may vary dramatically in both performance and cost, while different carriers may refer to identical services using dissimilar names. Prices vary all over the map, and if you aren't careful you can end up spending a lot more than you need to for a lot less than you expected. Many of these services are not under tariff, so the carrier can charge you as much or as little as the competition and your knowledge of the market will allow.

The good news is that with this diversity and competition comes better services at more affordable prices. Chances are that you can find the service you need at a price you are willing to pay. In this section, we examine the various services that may be available to you. Note that all of these services may not be available in all areas, although most of them should be available in most places.

If you are located in a major metropolitan area you will probably be able to choose among more services from more carriers than you will if you are in a rural area. This is not universally true, however. Many small rural telephone companies have converted completely to the modern digital switching equipment that makes many of these services possible, while many telephone companies located in major cities are still using older switches that cannot support high speed digital data communications. Even if your site is served by a modern digital switch, your telephone company may be unable to sell you services the switch is capable of providing, simply because the phone company has not filed a tariff with the Public Utilities Commission to provide these services.

Finding out what services are available to you from which providers and what each of them will cost is half the battle. The worst thing about using telephone company services is that you have to deal with the telephone company. Telephone companies deliver voice service. That's what they're good at, and they do it very well. When it comes to data, the story is different. To find out the answer to an apparently simple data question, you will often find yourself buried 12 levels deep in automated attendants, placing multiple calls to 800 numbers, and spending long periods on hold. At the end of all this you will usually end up leaving a message for the one person in the whole phone company who knows the answer to your data question, because he has eight other callers already on hold.

Tip

When you are ordering services from the telephone company, ask lots of questions and never assume anything. A service identical or closely similar to the one you are initially offered may be available under a different name and a different tariff at a very different price.

For example, I have two residential voice telephone lines, and wanted the second line to ring when the first was in use. I was first offered a service called Residential Hunting, at a cost of $16 per line per month, or $32 per month over the cost of the phone lines themselves. Upon further questioning, the service representative located a similar service called Call Forward on Busy, which accomplished the identical function, but with more flexibility, and at a total cost of only $1 per month. It pays to ask a lot of questions.

Competing carriers often do a better job of answering your questions, but they may or may not provide the service you need at a price competitive with the telephone company. It is almost always worth it to spend the time needed to check all the alternatives. You will likely be paying a substantial monthly bill for data communications services for some time to come, so take the time early on to make sure you make the best decision from the beginning. It's easy to assume that the telephone company will offer only the stodgy, high-priced services, but this isn't necessarily the case. Check out the carriers who specialize in data communications, certainly, but don't overlook Ma Bell.

In order to compare these services intelligently and to judge which is optimum for a particular situation, you must first have at least a basic understanding of each. Let's take a look at some of the available services.

Understanding Facilities versus Services

Throughout this section, we will be discussing various data communications alternatives available from the telephone company and from competing carriers. It's important as you consider your alternatives for you to understand the difference between a facility and a service.

- *Facilities* are the physical infrastructure and low-level protocols used to deliver data to your site. The copper twisted pair which connects your site to the telephone company central office is an example of a facility.

- *Services* are higher level collections of protocols delivered to your site using a facility, and intended to provide a turn-key communications solution. Frame Relay is an example of a service.

This situation is made all the more confusing because one facility may be used to deliver many different types of services. For example, the copper twisted pair cable facility that links your site to the telephone company central office may be used to provide analog voice service, analog leased line service, and other services. The fiber optic Synchronous Optical Network (SONET) facility may be used to deliver Frame Relay, ATM, voice, and other services.

Similarly, a particular service may be delivered using more than one type of facility. For example, Basic Rate Interface (BRI) ISDN service is typically delivered using the existing copper twisted pair facility which already links you to the telephone company central office. The Primary Rate Interface (PRI) ISDN service, which operates at a much higher data rate than does BRI ISDN, will be delivered to your site via T carrier facilities using twisted pair copper, coaxial cable, or perhaps fiber optic cable.

Adding to the confusion is the fact that a facility in one environment is instead a service in another. For example, when a T1 line is used to deliver PRI ISDN, the T1 is the facility upon which the ISDN service is delivered. You may instead choose to install a T1 line to link two of your offices and use that T1, for example, simply to carry TCP/IP data between the sites. In this case, you are essentially using a telephone company facility—the T1 line—to carry a service that you provide yourself. In this case, the telephone company re-gards the T1 line as a service.

As a general rule, facilities are exclusively provided by your local telephone company. Services may also be provided by the local telephone company, or you may contract with third parties to provide services that are then deliv-ered by using telephone company facilities. Even this is changing, however, with the entry of long-distance carriers into the local services market.

Analog Telephone Lines

Analog telephone lines are familiar to anyone who has ever used an ordinary telephone. Also called Plain Old Telephone Service, or POTS, analog tele-phone lines were the earliest method used to communicate information on telephone lines, and are still the most common means used to provide residential and business voice telephone service. When you pick up your tele-phone at home to call a friend or to order a pizza, you are almost certainly us-ing an analog telephone line on this *Public Switched Telephone Network*, or PSTN.

The present analog telephone network dates, at least conceptually, to the first public telephone networks that were installed in the late 19th century. Mate-rials, methods, and equipment have been updated frequently since then, but the concept remains the same. The telephone line enters your home on a single pair of copper conductors. From your home, this pair leads first to a satellite connection point, where it is cross-connected to a large multi-pair line that ultimately terminates in the *Central Office (CO)* for your *exchange*.

All other subscribers on your exchange similarly have pairs of copper wire that physically connect them to the Central Office. These connections from homes and businesses to the Central Office are collectively called the *local loop,* shown in figure 2.1. Because, as we learned in Chapter 1, analog signals are attenuated and distorted with increasing transmission distance, local loops are limited in length. Although amplifiers and other equipment can be used to condition the signal and thereby extend the length of the local loop, the practical limit to the local loop is generally set at perhaps 12 or 15 miles of actual copper, or something less than this in terms of map distances. This means that the Central Office you are served by is almost certainly within a 10 mile radius of your home or business.

An exchange is the first three digits of your seven digit local number. For ex-ample, for the telephone number 555-1212, the exchange is 555. Because in an ordinary telephone number four decimal digits follow the exchange seg-ment, each exchange can theoretically support up to 10,000 telephone lines,

Fig. 2.1

The telephone
company local
loop connects all
users of a single
exchange to the
central office
telephone switch.

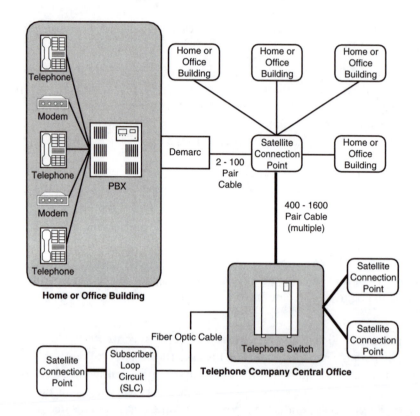

from 555-0000 to 555-9999. In reality, the number is somewhat less than
this. Some numbers are reserved for internal telephone company use. Others
were disconnected recently and will not be reassigned until they have
"rested" for a while to prevent new subscribers from receiving calls intended
for the person who was previously assigned that telephone number. A typical
exchange may have between 6,000 and 9,000 active subscriber numbers, although an exchange in a small rural area may have only a few hundred subscribers.

A small Central Office may have only a single exchange, and may provide
telephone service for only a few hundred or a few thousand subscribers. A
large Central Office may have as many as ten or more separate exchanges,
and may provide telephone service for upwards of 100,000 subscribers.

The Central Office contains switching equipment that can connect your pair
to any other pair that terminates in the Central Office. If you place a telephone call to another subscriber of your own Central Office, also called an *intra-CO* call, the connection is made completely within that Central

Office. An intra-CO call is shown in figure 2.2. In essence, the switch simply connects your pair to the pair of the person you are calling and the conversation can proceed.

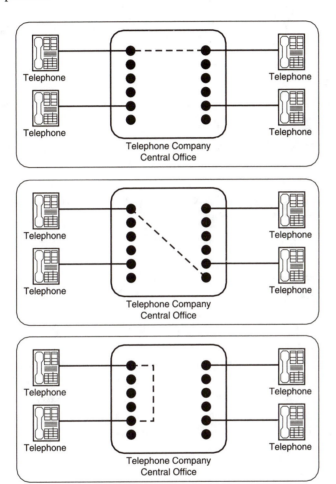

Fig. 2.2
The originating and receiving stations for an intra-CO local call are both within the same central office.

If instead you place a call to someone who is connected to a different Central Office, also called an *inter-CO* call, the switch at your Central Office routes your call via a *trunk line* to the destination Central Office, where that switch connects your inbound call to the pair of the party you are calling. Trunk lines are high speed communications paths that are used to link switches at different Central Offices. An inter-CO call is shown in figure 2.3.

Fig. 2.3
An Inter-CO local call connects two stations that are members of different central offices.

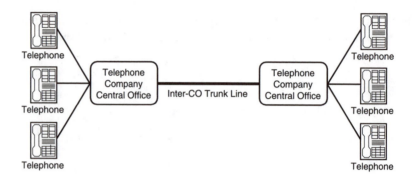

In the last 10 years, the demand for telephone lines has grown incredibly. Part of this is due to population growth, certainly, but the lion's share is due to the proliferation of additional services that use telephone lines. Fax machines, modems, and security systems all require phone lines, and all are becoming more common in homes.

In the past, the telephone company could safely assume that the average home would have only one telephone line. When planning to provide phone service to a new subdivision of 500 homes, for example, the phone company twenty years ago would have probably run a 600 pair or 800 pair cable to the satellite connection point for that subdivision. They knew that an occasional doctor, lawyer, minister or businessman would want a second home telephone line, and they installed some spare pairs to allow for new homes being added and so forth, but the average number of telephone lines per residence was still very close to 1.00. If it was a very wealthy subdivision, the telephone company might plan for as many as 1.25 lines per residence to account for home business needs, lines for teenagers, and so on, but the fact is that 20 years ago, or even 10, the average home had only a single line.

That has certainly changed. Many middle- and upper-middle class homes now have separate lines for their computers. They may also have a separate line for a fax machine or a security system, and separate lines for teenagers have become very common, thanks in part to promotion of this by the telephone companies themselves. Many people now telecommute or run full time home-based businesses, both of which increase the demand for phone lines.

In a recent conversation with BellSouth, I learned that, although the majority of homes served by BellSouth still have only a single line, those to which BellSouth provides more than one telephone line average more than 4.5 lines each. With seven telephone lines installed at my home, I expected to hold some kind of all-time record for number of telephone lines installed at a residence. Not so, according to BellSouth. Not even close.

Supporting this increased demand using the older copper technology would require running large numbers of large multi-pair cables substantial distances, which is neither cheap, nor in some cases, with conduits becoming full, even practical. The alternative is to use a device called a *Subscriber Loop Circuit*, or SLC, which is pronounced "slick." Telephone companies think SLCs are the best thing since sliced bread. You may not be so happy about being connected to one. Here's why:

The telephone company installs a SLC at the satellite location to which your home or business telephone line is connected. The part of the link from your location to the SLC still runs on copper pairs, so you have no way of knowing that your connection is via SLC. The connection from the SLC to the Central Office is made using a single fiber optic link, which is much easier and less expensive than running a copper pair all the way back to the Central Office for every subscriber pair. The SLC multiplexes, or muxes, the telephone conversations onto the fiber link between the SLC and the Central Office, and then demultiplexes, or demuxes, them so that they can be routed to the local destination through the copper loop.

> ### Tip
>
> If when using a communications program you see a random series of characters appear sporadically on your screen—usually √ and °—it is a safe assumption that a poorly tuned SLC is at fault. This problem, caused by phase jitter on the SLC, is not apparent with voice communications, but can wreak havoc with data and fax transmissions.
>
> If you experience problems with data communications on your phone line that you suspect may be due to phase jitter on a SLC, don't tell the telephone company that you are having problems with your modem. Don't mention phase jitter or SLCs. They'll just tell you that they don't guarantee voice lines for use with data, and offer to try to sell you a specially conditioned data line.
>
> Instead, play dumb and tell them that your fax machine isn't working properly and that some faxes you receive are scrambled. They understand fax machines, and will probably fix the problem quickly.

They say that familiarity breeds contempt. Because analog telephone service is so familiar to all of us, it's easy to go to extremes with it. Some people won't even consider using a dial-up telephone line for serious data communications, no matter how good a choice it might be for a particular application. Others look first to a dial-up solution even when another choice might offer better throughput and lower costs.

Most people think of dialup as being suitable only for use by a standalone workstation in establishing a temporary link to a remote host, bulletin board system, or commercial online service. Although this is certainly the most common application for dial-up, don't rule it out for providing a semi-permanent link between two networks. For example, you might have a main office and a manufacturing plant located in the same town, each with its own network. If the only data that needs to be communicated between these networks is e-mail and an occasional file transfer, your cheapest, easiest, and best method may be simply to install an ordinary telephone line and a modem at each site and use dial-up routers to link the networks. You'll drive the telephone company nuts by placing what they consider ordinary telephone calls that last a week or a month, but there's not a lot they can do about it.

> **Tip**
>
> One way to extend the reach of flat-rate dial-up asynchronous links is to order a Foreign Exchange or FX line. Paying for an FX line simply substitutes a flat rate, albeit higher than that charged for a standard local flat rate telephone line, for the per minute toll charges that you would otherwise incur.

I live in Winston-Salem, North Carolina. Greensboro, North Carolina is about 30 miles away. Telephone calls to Greensboro from Winston-Salem and *vice versa* incur a per-minute toll charge. By ordering an FX line installed at my office in Winston-Salem, I am assigned a telephone number that belongs to a local Greensboro exchange. When a Greensboro caller dials this number, it rings in Winston-Salem, and neither the caller nor I pay a per-minute toll for the call.

If you plan to use dialup to link two locations that are in close proximity but outside each other's local calling area, and if these connections will be either frequent or of long duration, or both, then investigate using FX lines.

Note that FX lines may be unidirectional insofar as the toll free aspect goes. In other words, the FX line described above allows a Greensboro caller to call the author in Winston-Salem without incurring a toll. The converse is not necessarily true. If you have two sites as described, and each needs to call the other, determine whether a single FX line can be used or whether you must install a separate FX line at each location.

Consider dial-up asynchronous as just one building block in your data communications tool kit. Dialup is appropriate when you need a simple, low-speed link using familiar equipment. Dialup is often most appropriate when it is used to link two locations within a local calling area with a flat-rate calling plan, although it may also be the best choice when a toll call is involved, particularly for applications that require polling or other sporadic access.

Leased Analog Lines

Leased Analog Lines, shown in figure 2.4, are an anachronism in today's data communication environment, although they are still in widespread use and indeed still being actively marketed by the telephone companies. They originated in the days when state-of-the-art data communication meant mainframes linked to remote character-mode terminals. Most of them are still used for that purpose, or something very similar.

Getting Started

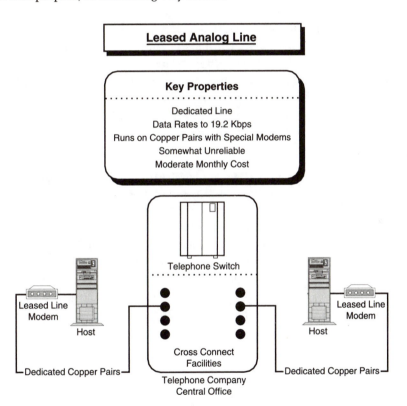

Fig. 2.4
Leased analog lines.

A Leased Analog Line provides a dedicated connection from point-to-point without running through a switch, eliminating the variations in connection quality that occur with dial-up analog lines. A Leased Analog Line may connect only two locations, or it may be spanned to additional locations, which is called multi-point or multi-drop. If more than two locations use the connection, the bandwidth is shared among them. At each location, a special modem designed for Leased Analog Lines provides the connection.

Leased Analog Lines are available with data rates ranging from 2.4 Kbps to 19.2 Kbps in several steps. The vast majority of Leased Analog Lines run at either 9,600 bps or 19.2 Kbps. Hardly anyone is willing to pay a monthly service charge to maintain a 2,400 bps or 4,800 bps leased line. Fewer and fewer people are willing to do so for the "high speed" 9,600 bps and 19,200 bps versions.

Leased Analog Lines are available in several types. For example, a Type 1 line is intended for Basic Voice service and a Type 9 line is intended for Telephotographic applications. About the only Type of any interest to anyone anymore is Type 5, which is intended for basic data.

Because the link is dedicated rather than being switched, the telephone company can provide *conditioning* for the line to improve its data transmission characteristics. Several types of conditioning are available, of which the most common are C-conditioning, which is further subdivided into C1 through C8, and D-conditioning. You don't have to understand conditioning to use it. Your terminating equipment will be labeled with the *line type* and *conditioning* required. All of this used to matter a great deal to the mainframe data communications types, but is now simply a matter of historic interest, if that.

Leased Analog Lines can be used to connect two or more locations that are served by the same Central Office. In this situation, the cost can be relatively low as leased line costs go, perhaps in the range of $150 to $200 per month for connecting two locations. In this situation, it usually makes more sense to instead install a flat-rate dial-up voice grade analog telephone line at each end and use v.34 modems to provide a 28.8 Kbps link. The reality is that, for almost any application, v.34 modems on standard dial-up lines provide both better performance and lower cost than any Leased Analog Line. You end up spending about half as much or less on monthly service and getting twice or more the throughput.

Leased Analog Lines can also be used to connect two or more locations that are served by different Central Offices. In this situation, the monthly cost skyrockets, often to within striking distance of $1,000 per month, even when the two Central Offices involved are local to each other. The reason for this high cost is that a dedicated pair of conditioned copper wires is needed between the Central Offices, which doesn't come cheaply. When you consider that this same pair of copper wires that is dedicated to the slow analog link could instead be used to provide a much higher speed link, it is obvious that we are consuming a very expensive resource to provide a very low performance link.

Because a Leased Analog Line is dedicated, you pay the fixed monthly charge regardless of how much or how little data you communicate. About the only time it makes any sense to consider installing a Leased Analog Line is when you need a low-speed connection between two sites—such as, to link two e-mail servers—and your only realistic alternative to the Analog Leased Line is to use a long distance dial-up connection. In this situation, you must determine how many hours per day the connection will be in use and compare the flat monthly cost of the Analog Leased Line versus the cumulative hourly cost of using a long distance dial-up connection.

The break-even point usually occurs at about four hours of usage per business day, meaning that if you truly need the connection to exist eight or nine hours a day, five days a week, the Analog Leased Line may be the less expensive choice. Before you make this determination, however, first decide if the connection really must be up continuously. If for example, the link will be used to exchange e-mail or for occasional database queries, perhaps a dial-on-demand solution using standard long distance lines will end up being considerably cheaper, because the connection is made only when needed and then drops once you have finished using it. Many long distance calls may be placed each day, but each will be of short duration, and the total cost may well be lower than the fixed monthly cost of the Analog Leased Line.

Another alternative to consider in this situation is using a Foreign Exchange or FX line, described in the earlier section "Analog Telephone Lines." Because an FX line offers what amounts to flat rate long distance calling, you can install an FX line at one of the sites and have the other site dial in to it without incurring an hourly charge. The two sites can connect at 28.8 Kbps using v.34 modems, and all it costs is the fixed monthly charge for the FX line, which is usually a small fraction of the cost of an Analog Leased Line.

One drawback to the FX method is that flat rate calling may be unidirectional. That is, if you install an FX line at Site A, then Site B can dial-up Site A with no per-minute long distance charges. If Site A instead calls Site B, then normal per-minute long distance charges will apply. This is not normally a problem, since you can usually configure your equipment to determine which site will call the other each morning or if the connection is lost during the day. If for some reason you need each site to be able to call the other and not incur toll charges either way, simply install an FX line at each site. The FX line costs will double, but will still probably be substantially less than the cost of the Analog Leased Line.

One final drawback to Analog Leased Lines needs to be addressed. Over the course of many years working with a variety of analog and digital data communications lines of various types from several providers and at many locations, my experience with Analog Leased Line reliability has not been good.

Relative to Digital Leased Lines, Analog Leased Lines seem to go down much more frequently and take longer to repair. Consider all of your alternatives carefully before deciding to use Analog Leased Lies.

Digital Data Service (DDS) and Switched 56

Digital Data Service (DDS) lines, shown in figure 2.5, can be considered simply as a digital version of the traditional Leased Analog Line. DDS provides a full duplex synchronous connection at data rates ranging from 2,400 bps to 56 Kbps.

Fig. 2.5
Digital Data
Service (DDS).

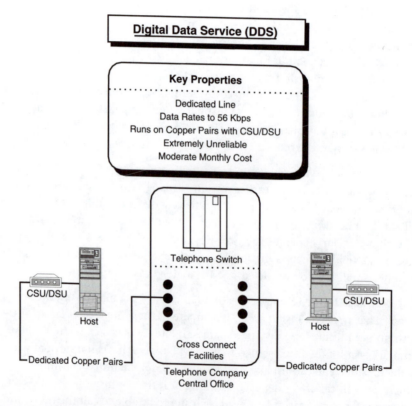

DDS uses T Carrier physical facilities, and is limited to providing point-to-point connections. Unlike Leased Analog Lines, which require a special leased line modem at each end of the connection to perform digital-to-analog and analog-to-digital conversions, DDS lines are digital end-to-end. The terminating equipment used on each end of a DDS line is called a *Channel Service Unit/ Data Service Unit*, or CSU/DSU. Your router or other equipment connects to the CSU/DSU using a standard EIA-232D serial connection at lower DDS data rates, or using a v.35 connection at higher data rates.

Like a Leased Analog Line, Digital Data Service uses a dedicated line, meaning that you pay a fixed monthly charge regardless of the amount of traffic passed by the link. DDS ranges in price from inexpensive for low-speed, short haul connections to moderately expensive for longer distances and higher speeds.

Another service designated Switched 56 or something similar is available from many providers. Switched 56, shown in figure 2.6, uses the same facilities as BRI ISDN, and provides similar functionality to a single ISDN B channel. Rather than using a dedicated, non-switched link as does DDS, Switched 56 is routed through the provider's data switching equipment, allowing you to establish sequential one-to-many connections.

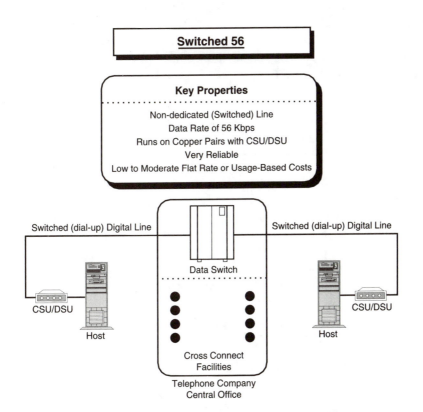

Fig. 2.6
Switched 56.

Switched 56 is both named and tariffed in various ways. It may be flat rate within a Central Office service area. It may instead be time-sensitive, distance-sensitive, or both, even within the service area of a single Central Office. Flat-rate Switched 56 often compares favorably in cost with dial-up asynchronous. BellSouth Centrex users, for example, pay a flat rate of about

$30 per month for this service. If you need to connect two locations within a single CO, and if 56 Kbps is fast enough for your application, and if flat-rate Switched 56 is available, it will often be your best choice.

DDS and Switched 56 links are much more reliable than Leased Analog Lines. While outages occur relatively frequently with Leased Analog Lines, a DDS link will often go from one year to the next without failing. Switched 56 links are not quite as reliable as DDS, but nearly so. With either digital service, problems are normally resolved much more quickly than they are with a Leased Analog Line.

Integrated Services Digital Network (ISDN)

Integrated Services Digital Network (ISDN), shown in figure 2.7, is a service devised by telephone companies in the 1970s to provide an end-to-end switched digital service. An ISDN line is divided into channels. A Data or "D" Channel is used for call setup and control. One or more Bearer or "B" Channels carry data or voice traffic.

Fig. 2.7
Integrated Services
Digital Network
(ISDN).

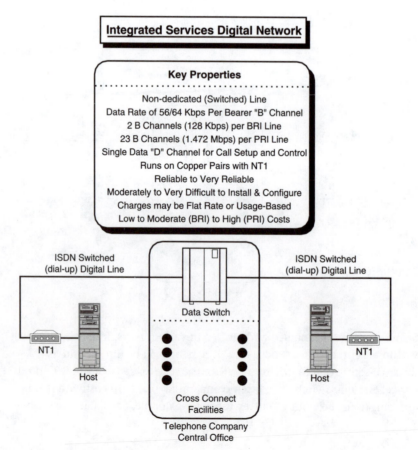

Integrated Services Digital Network

Key Properties

Non-dedicated (Switched) Line
Data Rate of 56/64 Kbps Per Bearer "B" Channel
2 B Channels (128 Kbps) per BRI Line
23 B Channels (1.472 Mbps) per PRI Line
Single Data "D" Channel for Call Setup and Control
Runs on Copper Pairs with NT1
Reliable to Very Reliable
Moderately to Very Difficult to Install & Configure
Charges may be Flat Rate or Usage-Based
Low to Moderate (BRI) to High (PRI) Costs

ISDN Switched
(dial-up) Digital Line

ISDN Switched
(dial-up) Digital Line

Data Switch

NT1

Host

NT1

Host

Cross Connect
Facilities

Telephone Company
Central Office

ISDN is commonly offered in two configurations. The *Basic Rate Interface* or
BRI, shown in figure 2.8, may have one or two 64 Kbps B Channels and a
single 16 Kbps D Channel. The *Primary Rate Interface* or PRI, shown in figure
2.9, may have as many as 23 64 Kbps B channels and one 64 Kbps D channel.

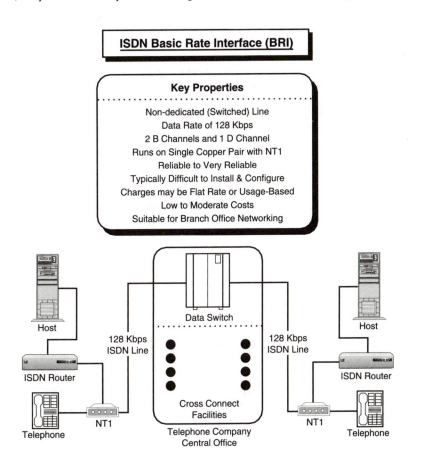

Fig. 2.8
ISDN Basic Rate
Interface (BRI).

A PRI is intended for use with central site routers and digital PBXs. A PRI is
conceptually similar to, and priced at the same level as, a channelized T1
used to deliver analog voice channels to a PBX or via a Channel Bank to a
modem rack. For PRI service, the telephone company charges first for a T1
circuit, then for channelization of the T1, and then finally for one Network
Access Register, or NAR, for each B Channel. Installation charges for the PRI
will amount to several thousand dollars, but the monthly service charges will
usually be less than that for 12 BRIs. Installing a PRI will usually be cheaper
overall, and will certainly be cleaner than installing wiring for and then
maintaining a dozen BRI interfaces on a router.

Fig. 2.9
ISDN Primary Rate
Interface (PRI).

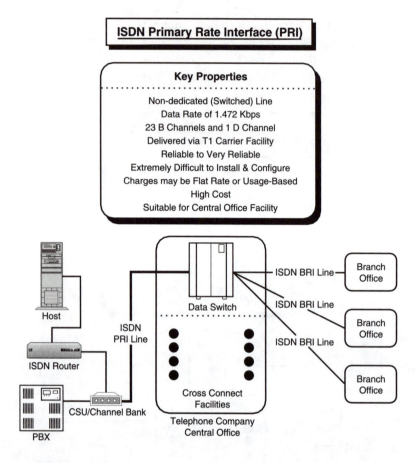

A BRI is by far the most common ISDN interface. It is commonly configured with two B channels and one D Channel. Although the D channel is sometimes used in specialized circumstances for transferring data, such as credit card verification, the primary purpose of the D channel is for call setup and management.

The ISDN network, and it really is a network, uses the CCITT Q.931 and Q.921 specifications to define the network and data link protocols. An important feature of any ISDN device, especially for data applications, is its ability to report the Q.931 transactions to the user for trouble shooting purposes. If you have a problem with your ISDN line, and can capture the Q.931 transactions, and if you can find someone at the phone company who knows what Q.931 is, you can resolve the problem in a matter of days, rather than weeks.

A 64 Kbps B channel can carry either voice or data traffic if it is properly provisioned. Voice traffic is defined as a connection from an ISDN line to an analog voice line. The digital to analog translation occurs on the Central Office switch to which the ISDN line is connected. Data traffic is defined as a call from one ISDN line to another ISDN line, whether the connection is used to carry voice or actual computer data. This distinction is important because most telephone companies charge, in addition to the monthly service for the line itself, for measured service on "data" calls. They may also charge for measured service on "voice" calls, but usually at lower rates than those charged for data.

In some areas, due to switch limitations, the telephone company may be unable to provide a clear channel, especially for inter-CO and long distance calls. In these situations, the B channel data rate will be reduced from 64 Kbps to 56 Kbps. This is handled automatically on most ISDN equipment when receiving a call, but you may have to specify the 56 Kbps speed when dialing out from your equipment. ISDN can also interoperate with Switched 56 devices. The only special thing you may have to do to call a switched 56 device is to specify the 56k speed when dialing.

A BRI is equivalent to two phone lines. Each B Channel will be assigned one or more Service Profile Identifiers (SPIDs) by the telephone company. A SPID is usually the telephone number for that channel with as many as four additional digits added. The telephone company installer will usually label the demarcation with the SPID numbers. Also, the telephone company switch may or may not require that the SPID be programmed into your ISDN device. In any event, keep this number in a safe place for future reference.

You can connect more than one ISDN device to a single BRI. Each device may have its own phone SPID, or devices may share SPIDs and use sub-addressing. With sub-addressing, multiple devices connected to a single BRI are each assigned a sub-address. Each device can then be accessed by dialing an additional digit. For example, if your BRI is assigned the phone number 555-5555, you could access the first device by dialing 555-55551, the second device by dialing 555-55552, and so on.

In many respects, ISDN is both too little and too late. It is a 1970s technology struggling for acceptance in the 1990s. When ISDN was designed, computer networks were in their infancy and personal computers did not exist. The world has changed, but ISDN is stuck in the 1970s.

ISDN is also hampered by incompetent marketing on the part of many telephone companies and by inadequate technical backing on the part of nearly all of them. At many telephone companies, even finding someone who can take your order for ISDN is sometimes almost impossible. Once the order has been placed, you may wait weeks or even months for the line to be installed. Once the line is installed, there is a good chance it won't work. Most telephone companies have trained very few installers and technicians on the vagaries of ISDN, and the explosion in demand for ISDN has made this trained staff in very short supply.

The availability of ISDN is spotty. If you live outside a major city, chances are that ISDN isn't available at all. Even if ISDN is offered in your service area, it may not be available at your site. If you need to link two offices in the same city, you may well find that ISDN service is available for one but not for the other, even if both offices are served by the same Central Office.

Another damper on the widespread acceptance is the wide differences in the prices charged by different carriers. In one place you might be charged $90 per month for a BRI and have to pay per-minute usage charges as well. Drive 10 miles across the state line and you may find that a BRI costs $30 per month flat rate, with no usage charge. In states served by multiple telephone companies, you may find that two sites that are literally two miles apart have a similar differential in cost because they are each served by a different operating company with different tariffs. This situation may well change as AT&T, MCI, and other long distance carriers enter the local telephone service market over the next few years, introducing competition to the heretofore monopoly market for local telephone services.

Perhaps the biggest problem with ISDN is its complexity. Anyone can order a standard analog telephone line and plug a telephone into it with a high level of certainty that it will work. ISDN has hundreds of parameters that must be set correctly before anything will work. Various organizations, notably Intel, have attempted to standardize settings in such a way that anyone who wants ISDN can simply order a standard group of settings by name, such as "Intel Blue." These and other efforts are beginning to pay off, although it may be years before ordering and installing an ISDN line is as straightforward as doing the same for an ordinary phone line.

Still, ISDN is worth exploring, if only because it offers relatively high throughput at a (usually) relatively low price. A BRI running at 128 Kbps nearly quintuples the throughput of the best dial-up connection using v.34 modems running at 28.8 Kbps. ISDN makes the most sense in four situations.

First, if you want to link a standalone PC to an Internet Service Provider for dial-up Internet access, the speed of ISDN gives you a much more usable link than does a 28.8 Kbps dial-up connection. Web pages snap when you access them, and file transfers take one fifth the time. Many ISPs provide dial-up

ISDN access for the same price as analog dial-up access, and even those that do charge a premium for ISDN access normally don't charge too much of one. Thus, for the incremental cost of installing an ISDN line at your location you can more than quadruple your access speed to the Internet.

Second, for most small LANs an ISDN network link to the Internet will be more than sufficient, and costs a small fraction of what a T1 connection would cost. For example, in many cities, PSI offers an ISDN network link for about $300 per month, plus the cost of your ISDN line. Thus, for perhaps $350 or $400 per month, you can provide every workstation on your LAN with full Internet access running at 128 Kbps. Using a T1 instead would increase throughput to 1.544 Mbps, but at a cost of perhaps $2,500 to $3,500 per month. For many small companies, ISDN means the difference between being able to afford to connect their LANs to the Internet and having to make do with standalone dial-up access by individual users.

Third, ISDN is the best thing to happen to branch office networking in years. Many companies have one or more local branch offices, manufacturing plants or other facilities, each with its own Local Area Network. Naturally, these companies would like to link these remote locations to the LAN at the main office. Until the advent of ISDN, doing so was often impractical, for two main reasons. First was the sheer cost involved—thousands of dollars for the equipment needed at each branch office and thousands more for the leased line service to connect the offices. Second was the complexity of the connecting equipment, which required a highly skilled data communications specialist to install and maintain. The availability of simple ISDN branch office routers under $1,000 and of relatively inexpensive 128 Kbps BRI ISDN service eliminates both of these problems, making branch office networking practical for thousands of small companies that previously could afford neither the equipment and service nor the technical expertise needed.

Fourth, ISDN makes telecommuting practical by allowing people who work at home to have full access to the company network. As telecommuting becomes more common, many companies are installing one or more PRIs at the headquarters office and using them to support a BRI installed at each telecommuter's home. With an ISDN link to the network, a remote user can access files and printers on the company LAN with what appears to the remote user as nearly local performance. At first glance, the 128 Kbps throughput of ISDN appears closer to 28.8 Kbps dial-up throughput than it is to the 10 Mbps throughput typical of a LAN. Although this may be true in theory, in practice an ISDN link "feels" almost like a local connection.

If you attempt to run a network connection through a 28.8 Kbps dial-up link, you are always aware that you are on the other end of a slow telephone line. For example, when you retrieve a file from the server into Microsoft Word that would be loaded instantly on a local connection, it instead takes several seconds to be displayed on your remote workstation. When you access a database, screen draws that would be instant on the local connection again take several seconds to complete. With ISDN, this lag is almost eliminated. Most users, most of the time, can tell little difference between the ISDN link and the local one.

If one or more of these situations applies to you, consider using ISDN if it is available. Even with all of its problems and aggravations, ISDN can still be a useful addition to your data communications tool kit.

Asymmetric Digital Subscriber Line (ADSL)

In many ways, ISDN is both too little and too late. Although the 128 Kbps data rate provided by the Basic Rate Interface is nearly five times the speed available with 28.8 Kbps v.34 modems, the graphics-rich environment of the Internet and the World Wide Web could really use higher throughput than even that provided by ISDN.

From the telephone companies' point of view, the problem with delivering high data rates to homes and businesses has always been the local loop, the so-called "last mile." Connections between Central Offices and satellite distribution points are now largely made using fiber optic technology, which supports data rates in the gigabit per second class. The choke point is the local loop, the final link between your home or business and the telephone company facilities. Millions of miles of local loop connect millions of homes and businesses to Central Offices, and much of this local loop was installed long before personal computers and the Internet existed.

The impending entry of cable television companies into the competition for delivering high speed data to homes and businesses has caused telephone companies to reconsider their alternatives for providing such service. Much time, effort, and money has been expended by the telephone companies in attempting to overcome the limitations of the local loop so that they can provide high data rate connections without replacing these millions of miles of local loop.

The results of all this research is a technology called *Asymmetric Digital Subscriber Line* or ADSL. ADSL, shown in figure 2.10, is the Great White Hope of the telephone companies in their impending war with cable television companies to be your digital data provider. ADSL provides very high data rates using the existing local loop, eliminating the costly and time-consuming process of running fiber to each home or business to be served. Not coincidentally, the wide spread deployment of ADSL will sound the death knell for ISDN, since ADSL will do everything that ISDN does, but better, faster, and cheaper.

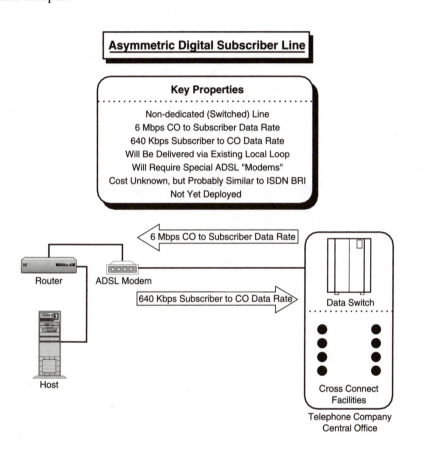

Fig. 2.10
Asymmetric Digital Subscriber Loop (ADSL).

Although ADSL is a full duplex technology, the Asymmetric portion of its name means that data is transmitted and received at different rates. Under the current standard for ADSL, your home or office will receive data from the Central Office at 6 Mbps, which is nearly 50 times the data rate provided by an ISDN BRI, and within striking distance of local Ethernet speeds. Data sent from your location will be transmitted to the Central Office at only about one tenth that rate, or 640 Kbps, which is still five times ISDN BRI throughput.

When you think about it, this imbalance in channel speed suits many applications perfectly. For example, for most people and companies, using the Internet and other network services means receiving huge amounts of data—downloading graphics-heavy Web pages, using ftp to download a program update, listening to audio clips, and perhaps watching a video clip or two. All of this material is transmitted to you at 6 Mbps. On the other side, the amount of data outbound from your site is usually relatively small.

About the only situation for which ADSL may be inappropriate is when this common usage pattern is reversed. If, for example, your site hosts a heavily used Web server, most of the traffic on the link may originate at your site and be carried by the slower 640 Kbps back channel portion of the link. Even this, however, may not be a problem. Even the "slow" portion of the link still transfers data at nearly half T1 speed, which is certainly not to be sneezed at.

A variant of ADSL called *Symmetric Digital Subscriber Line*, or SDSL, should be available in many locations by the end of 1996. SDSL is similar in concept to ADSL, but uses full duplex symmetric channels to provide T1 level throughput of 1.544 Mbps on both the transmit and receive channel, again using the local loop.

The only downside to ADSL is that it may not be widely implemented for some time to come, although telephone companies are burning the midnight oil to make ADSL access a reality. Contact your telephone company and ask them their plans for deploying ADSL. The trouble is, finding out about ISDN, difficult though it is, is child's play compared to finding anyone who can tell you anything about ADSL. Be prepared to call a lot of toll-free numbers, speak to a lot of telephone company employees who have no earthly idea what you are talking about, be referred from place to place and spend a long time on hold. When your search for the Holy Grail is over and you finally do find someone at the phone company who is knowledgeable about ADSL, get his full name and direct extension and record it indelibly somewhere where you won't lose it. You have just captured a pearl beyond price.

T Carrier Transmission and Services

T Carrier transmission technology is used to carry the bulk of the data transmitted by leased digital lines (see fig. 2.11). T Carrier will be familiar to many readers in its most common form, called *T1*. T1 uses two copper pairs to provide full duplex digital signaling at 1.544 Mbps. T1 and other T-carrier services are shown in table 2.1.

Table 2.1 T Carrier Data Rates—DS0 through DS4

Digital Signal (DS) Level Rate	T Carrier Designation Transmission Media	DS0 Channels	T1 Equivalents	Approx-imate Data
DS0 UTP Copper		1	1/24	64 Kbps
DS1 UTP Copper	T1	24	1	1.5 Mbps
DS1C UTP Copper	T1C	48	2	3 Mbps
DS2 UTP Copper; Coax	T2	96	4	6 Mbps
DS3 Coax; Microwave; Fiber Optic	T3	672	28	45 Mbps
DS4 Fiber Optic	T4	4032	168	275 Mbps

Channelized T1 uses Time Domain Multiplexing (TDM) to divide this 1.544 Mbps cumulative throughput into 24 equal channels, each of which has 64 Kbps throughput. This 64 Kbps channel is the building block from which T1, as well as all faster T carrier connections, is formed. It is called *Digital Signaling Level 0*, or DS0.

The DS0 signaling speed of 64 Kbps was chosen because it provides just enough digital bandwidth to allow digital voice transmission with voice quality equal to the 3 KHz bandwidth provided by a standard analog telephone line. A T1 line may be used to carry 24 voice channels simultaneously. Alternatively, it may be used purely for data transmission at 1.544 Mbps, or for some combination of voice and data which total 24 channels and 1.544 Mbps throughput.

Each DS0 channel is sampled 8,000 times per second. Each sample is 1 byte (8 bits) wide, yielding the 64Kbps data rate of the DS0 channel. 24 DS0 channels combined into a single T1 provide 24 X 64 Kbps, or 1.536 Mbps. An additional 8 Kbps channel is used to control framing, with 1 bit used per frame at 8,000 frames per second. Summing the 1.536 Mbps provided for data channels and 8 Kbps used for framing yields the 1.544 Mbps throughput nominally provided by a T1 line.

Fig. 2.11
T Carrier services.

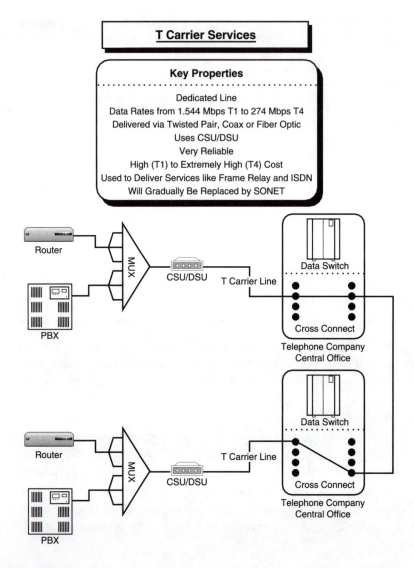

T Carrier Services

Key Properties

Dedicated Line
Data Rates from 1.544 Mbps T1 to 274 Mbps T4
Delivered via Twisted Pair, Coax or Fiber Optic
Uses CSU/DSU
Very Reliable
High (T1) to Extremely High (T4) Cost
Used to Deliver Services like Frame Relay and ISDN
Will Gradually Be Replaced by SONET

Fractional T Carrier

There is a large gap between the maximum 56 Kbps throughput available
with DDS and the 1.544 Mbps throughput provided by T1. For many applications, 56 Kbps is inadequate, but full T1 throughput is overkill, both in terms
of throughput and in terms of cost. Many carriers have addressed this problem by offering *Fractional T1* services. Fractional T1 allows you to buy just as
many DS0 channels as you need to meet your requirements, and to pay for
only this number of channels.

> ### Tip
>
> If you are considering using Fractional T1, make sure to determine where the break even point lies between the charges for Fractional T1 service and for full T1 service. This break even point is normally somewhere between four and eight DS0 channels, or 256 Kbps and 512 Kbps. If you need higher throughput, the full T1 will both be less expensive and provide higher throughput than Fractional T1.

Fractional T Carrier is also offered in the T3 market. The T1C and T2 facilities shown in the previous table above as intermediate between 1.544 Mbps T1 and 45 Mbps T3 are not commonly used. If your requirements fall between those provided by T1 and T3, you can instead purchase Fractional T3. With Fractional T3, you purchase just as many T1 equivalents as you need, which are then delivered to you via T3 transmission facilities. Once again, a break even point exists, typically between five and eight T1 equivalents, at which it is less expensive simply to purchase the full T3.

Provisional T1

Ordinary T1 lines provide dedicated point-to-point service. That is, when you order a T1, you indicate which two locations you want to connect. Provisional T1 service allows you instead to install a full T1 or Fractional T1 at one location and to use it to connect to multiple other locations, each of which has a DS0 or Fractional T1 link installed.

Figure 2.12 shows a typical use of Provisional T1 to link a main headquarters office to several branch offices. The main office may have one or more full T1 connections. Each branch office may have a DS0 or a Fractional T1 connection. The links from the main office to the branch office may be intra-CO, inter-CO, or a combination.

T Carrier Service Costs

The prices of T Carrier services are based upon bandwidth and distance. For example, a T1 linking two locations near each other might cost $600 to $1,000 per month, while a T1 linking two more remote locations might cost twice that. Linking the nearby locations with a T3 might cost $10,000 or $12,000 per month, with the more distant pair again perhaps double that amount. Monthly service charges for a T Carrier line of a given speed vary depending both upon your geographic location and upon the carrier you select. The general trend in T Carrier pricing has been significantly downward for the last several years.

Fig. 2.12
Provisional T1.

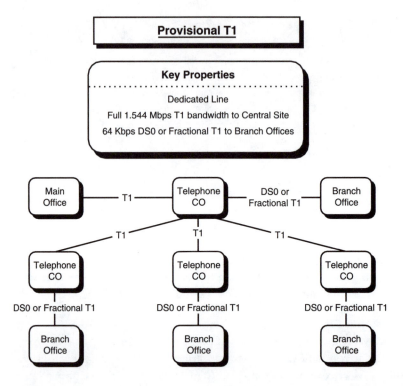

If your T Carrier line is supplied by your Local Exchange Carrier (LEC) to link two points within its service area, you will pay a single monthly charge to that LEC. If instead your T Carrier line is provided by an Interexchange Carrier (IXC) like AT&T or MCI, you will incur an additional monthly charge from the LEC to provide the local loop segment of the line, which connects the IXC Point of Presence (POP) to your sites.

In addition to the monthly service charge, there are some up-front costs you need to plan for:

■ Installation of the line can be quite expensive, typically ranging from several hundred dollars to several thousand dollars, depending on the carrier you select and the speed of the line. You may be able to reduce or eliminate this installation charge if you are willing to commit to keeping the line in service for a specified number of years. The monthly service charge itself may also be reduced if you can commit to an extended term.

■ You will need to purchase at least one DSU/CSU for each end of the links, although these components may be supplied as a part of the installation charge. If the link is critical, you might consider purchasing one or even two spares rather than depending on having a failed CSU/ DSU repaired quickly. Even with a service contract or warranty that guarantees swap out by overnight courier, your link may well otherwise be down for a day or more. A DSU/CSU for a T1 line is typically priced at about $1,000 each, and a T3 DSU/CSU will be $5,000 or more.

X.25

X.25, shown in figure 2.13, provides connection-oriented, reliable services via packet switching at the Network Layer of the OSI Model. Originally designed by CCITT to operate using a network infrastructure which was then largely analog, X.25 devotes a great deal of overhead to ensure reliable delivery, and is therefore very inefficient. X.25 runs at a maximum data rate of 56 Kbps.

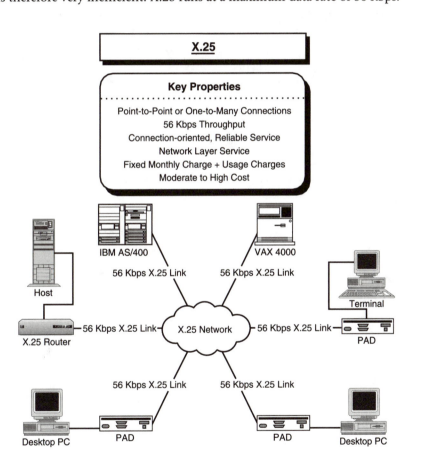

Fig. 2.13
X.25.

Because it operates at the Network Layer, X.25 may be used either with a Permanent Virtual Circuit to establish a permanent point-to-point link or with a Switched Virtual Circuit to establish a switched one-to-many communications environment.

In terms of connecting hardware, X.25 requires a Packet Assembler/Disassembler, or PAD, at each connected site. At the source, the PAD takes a stream of serial data and assembles it into X.25 packets for transmission to the network. At the destination, the PAD disassembles the incoming stream of packets and reconstitutes the serial data stream. PAD functionality is built into X.25 ready routers. You can also purchase standalone PADs to allow single remote standalone terminals or PCs to access the X.25 network.

Although X.25 is technologically obsolescent, it remains a CCITT/ISO standard and is the oldest commercially available packet switching service. Accordingly, X.25 is universally available worldwide, and may be your only available choice for connecting diverse sites, particularly those located in third-world countries. If, for example, you need to link main offices located in Chicago, Canberra, and Capetown to branch offices located in Rawalpindi and Rangoon, you will probably find that X.25 is the only common alternative.

X.25 is moderately expensive to very expensive, depending upon the locations of the sites you need to link and how much traffic will travel that link. Charges normally include a fixed monthly portion to cover the cost of the local loop connection and a usage charge per thousand packets (kilo-packets) transmitted. Consider using X.25 only if you must. Other networking transport methods offer both much higher throughput and much lower cost.

Frame Relay

Frame Relay, shown in figure 2.14, provides connectionless, unreliable services using variable length frames. Frame Relay is so named because it operates at the MAC sub-layer of the Data Link Layer of the OSI Model, and therefore communicates at the frame level. Although Frame Relay does not reach to the Network or Packet level, it is still thought of and referred to as a packet switching technology. Frame Relay is available at speeds ranging from 56/64 Kbps (DS0) to 1.544 Mbps DS1/T1.

In many respects, Frame Relay is the replacement technology for X.25. One of the design considerations for X.25 was to provide guaranteed delivery and error correction as a part of the protocol. This was necessary because, in the early years of X.25 at least, it was running on a primarily copper-based analog public network.

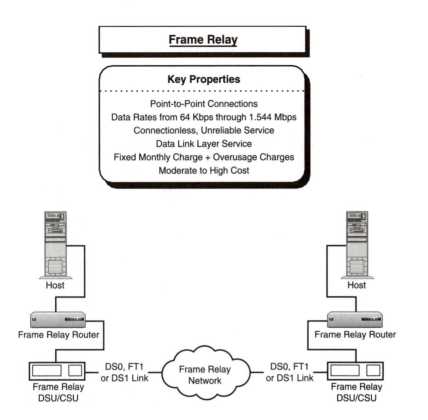

Fig. 2.14
Frame Relay.

Getting Started

As the public network has migrated to digital technology and fiber optic media, it has become more reliable by an order of magnitude or more. Transmission errors caused by the network itself have been greatly reduced, and the need for the protocol to provide its own error handling has been reduced. Thus, the high overhead and corresponding performance penalty incurred by X.25 to perform these now redundant error checking functions has become an increasingly undesirable and unnecessary burden. Frame Relay eliminates this burden and, by doing so, provides higher throughput than X.25.

Because Frame Relay operates only up to the ISO Data Link Layer, it deals only with Data Link Layer frames rather than Network Layer packets. This means that only the hardware addressing native to the Data Link Layer is present, and the software addresses native to the Network Layer are not. Frame Relay is therefore limited, at least for now, to using a Permanent Virtual Circuit to establish point-to-point connections.

Frame Relay can, however, still be used as a one-to-many connection method simply by installing a single Frame Relay connection at each remote site and establishing a PVC to the central site for each remote. The central site still has only a single physical connection to the Frame Relay network, but serves as the terminus for the several remote site PVCs.

Like X.25, Frame Relay is priced based on a combination of first, a fixed monthly charge for the local loop connection and second, on usage. Unlike X.25, however, the usage charge is a fixed monthly charge based on how much throughput you specify. When you purchase Frame Relay services, you specify a Committed Information Rate, or CIR, as shown in figure 2.15.

For example, you might determine that a branch office requires a guarantee that 128 Kbps throughput be available at all times. You purchase a CIR of 128 Kbps for this branch office, and the Frame Relay vendor installs the link, using a 1.544 Mbps T1 line to connect your branch office to its POP. You then pay for that CIR level every month, whether you are using it or not.

Your throughput is not limited to that specified by the CIR, however. All the CIR does is guarantee the Frame Relay service provider that you will pay for that much throughput each month. You may transparently use as much additional throughput as you wish when you wish to use it, but you will pay extra for doing do. These penalties for over-usage of bandwidth can add up quickly, so it pays both to choose a CIR initially that corresponds closely to your estimated actual needs and to review actual usage frequently. If you find that you are frequently paying for utilization above your CIR, it is time to bump up the CIR. It's cheaper to do so in the long run.

Although in our example the branch office has a CIR of 128 Kbps, it can use throughput up to the 1.544 Mbps limit of its physical link. It might do so, for example, in the mornings, when many people are simultaneously logging on to a remote server, or in the afternoons when everyone is saving his work and preparing to go home at the same time. It may also peak at various times during the day or week when you are particularly busy. For example, you may find that your branch office receives many calls the first thing Monday morning, requiring heavy database access to a remote server, which, in turn, drives up the bandwidth demand on the Frame Relay link.

Negotiating Frame Relay Services

When you negotiate for Frame Relay services, pay careful attention to the vendor's policy on exceeding the CIR. Determine what period is used to calculate the average throughput. You will want it to be calculated on a daily or weekly basis, while the vendor would prefer to calculate it on an hourly or per minute basis. Which period you use makes a big difference on how often you will exceed a given CIR, and accordingly on how high you must set the CIR to avoid exceeding it.

Also find out what the vendor's policy is on charging for these peaks. Some vendors allow you to exceed the CIR occasionally without penalty, while others charge for each peak. Find out how often and by how much you can exceed the CIR without being assessed additional charges.

All of this is negotiable, no matter what the salesman tells you. Your goal is to negotiate the lowest possible CIR and to get the vendor to be as forgiving as possible of peak utilization that exceeds that CIR. His goal is to get you to set your CIR as high as possible. He would like to see it set high enough that you will never exceed it. The two of you can compromise somewhere in the middle. That way, he gets reasonable monthly revenue from you and you get the data communications path you need at an almost guaranteed flat monthly charge.

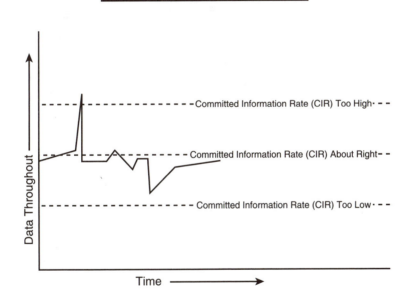

Fig. 2.15
Frame Relay Committed Information Rate (CIR).

Asynchronous Transfer Mode (ATM)

Asynchronous Transfer Mode (ATM), shown in figure 2.16, is also referred to by some as Cell Relay, and is thought by many to be the future of internetworking. ATM operates at the MAC sub-layer and LLC sub-layer of the OSI Data Link Layer. ATM provides connection-oriented, unreliable data transmission using fixed length 53-byte cells. Again, although ATM does not reach to the Network or Packet level, it is still thought of and referred to as a packet switching technology. ATM is currently available at speeds ranging from 44.736 Mbps DS3/T3 to 2.488 Gbps OC-48.

Fig. 2.16
Asynchronous
Transfer Mode
(ATM).

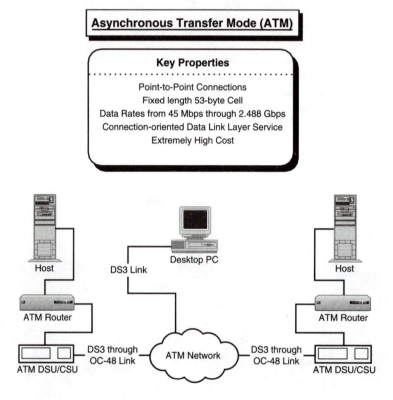

Like Frame Relay, ATM operates only as high as the OSI Data Link Layer, and is therefore limited to providing point-to-point connections using Permanent Virtual Circuits. Unlike Frame Relay, ATM is a connection-oriented service and uses fixed-length 53-byte cells. Because it is connection-oriented, ATM is appropriate for applications that require real-time network response, such as video and multimedia.

The fact that Frame Relay uses variable length frames means that Frame Relay switching equipment must use powerful processors and a large amount of memory to process and buffer these variable length frames. Because it instead uses fixed length cells, and therefore knows exactly what to expect incoming traffic to look like, ATM switching equipment can be designed specifically to handle only this one cell size. ATM switches are therefore much more efficient and much faster for any given hardware level than are Frame Relay switches.

ATM is unique in that it is not only a WAN technology, but can extend to the desktop as well. Heretofore, there has been a sharp dividing line between Data Link Layer LAN technologies like Ethernet and Data Link Layer WAN technologies like X.25 and Frame Relay. Routers are used to link the LAN portions of the internetwork to the WAN portions. For example, your current router may have an Ethernet interface to connect to your LAN and a Frame Relay interface to connect it to the public data network.

With ATM, this gap disappears. You can run ATM network interface cards in your workstations and servers at all locations and use the ATM network to provide Data Link Layer connections end-to-end for the entire internetwork, eliminating your routers. Or so goes the theory, anyway.

In practice, ATM is just beginning to be deployed, and widespread commercial availability is still some time off. The real reason that ATM has not yet been widely adopted is simply its high cost. A typical ATM network interface card is still priced in the four figure range, and ATM service itself will be very expensive at the very high data rates that will initially be offered.

Although ATM network services are currently being deployed using T Carrier technology at data rates up to 45 Mbps T3 and using SONET or SMDS technology at data rates up to 2.488 Gbps OC-48, there is no reason that ATM cannot be used at T1 and even Fractional T1 data rates. Similarly, as production volumes ramp up, the cost of ATM network interface cards will drop dramatically.

In short, ATM is a technology for the future. In one or two years, chances are you won't be running ATM. In five years, chances are you will.

Switched Multimegabit Digital Service (SMDS)

Switched Multimegabit Digital Service (SMDS), shown in figure 2.17, provides connectionless, unreliable services at the OSI Network Layer. In many ways, SMDS can be thought of as a higher speed alternative to Frame Relay and as a lower speed alternative to ATM.

As specified by the IEEE 802.6 WAN committee, SMDS is intended to use Distributed Queue over Dual Bus (DQDB) at the ISO Physical Layer. However, SMDS implementations currently being deployed use T Carrier technology at the ISO Physical Layer to provide data rates ranging from 1.544 Mbps T1/DS1 through 45 Mbps T3/DS3. SONET implementations at higher data rates may be deployed in the future (see the following section), depending on how widely and how quickly ATM is adopted. SMDS uses the same 53 byte cells at the OSI Data Link Layer as does ATM, with the intent of making eventual migration from SMDS to ATM easier.

Fig. 2.17
Switched
Multimegabit
Digital Service
(SMDS).

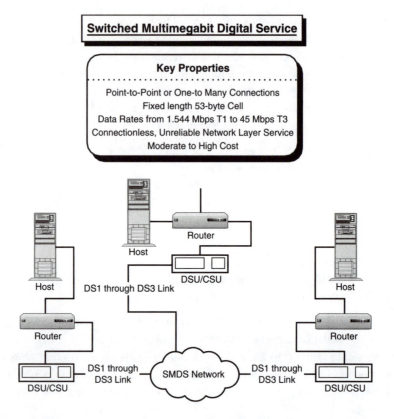

SMDS is really a stopgap technology. Although it is relatively new and not yet widely deployed, its replacement—in the form of ATM—is already gaining ground. SMDS ranges in price from moderate at lower speeds to quite expensive at higher ones.

Synchronous Optical Network (SONET)

The *Synchronous Optical Network*, or *SONET*, shown in figure 2.18, is now being deployed by AT&T, MCI, and other carriers. SONET operates on fiber optic media, and provides ultra-high speed Time Domain Multiplexing (TDM) transmission facilities. SONET will ultimately replace T Carrier technology. Even as this is written, the Internet backbone is being shifted from T3 facilities to SONET, with the migration expected to be completed by 1997 or 1998.

Full SONET offers data rates ranging from 51.84 Mbps Optical Carrier 1 (OC-1) through 2.488 Gbps OC-48. As with T carrier services, Fractional SONET services will be marketed to those who need something less than a full OC-1 SONET connection. Because SONET uses the same 64 Kbps DS0 data rate increments as do other digital services, Fractional SONET implementations will be available from 64 Kbps DS0 through full OC-1. Again like T carrier, a break even point will probably exist at some small fraction of full OC-1 SONET data rates where it becomes more economical simply to go with the full OC-1. Table 2.2 compares SONET data rates with T-carrier data rates.

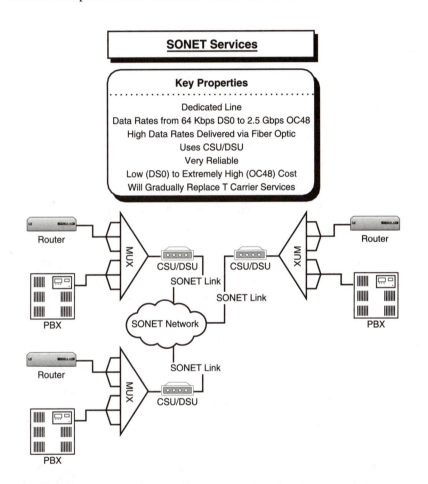

Fig. 2.18
Synchronous Optical Network (SONET) Services.

Getting Started

Table 2.2 SONET OC Data Rates versus T-Carrier Data Rates			
SONET Carrier (OC) Level	**Approximate OC Data Rate**	**Digital Signal (DS) Level**	**Approximate DS Data Rate**
		DS0	64 Kbps
		DS1	1.5 Mbps
		DS2	6 Mbps
		DS3	45 Mbps

(continues)

Table 2.2   Continued

SONET Carrier (OC) Level	Approximate OC Data Rate	Digital Signal (DS) Level	Approximate DS Data Rate
1	52 Mbps		
3	156 Mbps		
		DS4	274 Mbps
9	467 Mbps		
12	622 Mbps		
18	933 Mbps		
24	1244 Mbps		
36	1866 Mbps		
48	2488 Mbps		

Unlike T Carrier technology, which simply provides a connection path at the ISO Physical Layer and MAC portion of the Data Link Layer upon which other services can be carried, SONET makes provisions for value added network services. This means that providers can—instead of simply reselling commoditized T carrier transmission facilities—concentrate on providing turnkey network services, including Virtual Networks and Broadband ISDN.

The ultimate direction of the public data network will be ATM running on SONET.

Point-to-Point Protocol (PPP)

The *Point-to-Point Protocol*, or *PPP*, has become the universal Data Link protocol for TCP/IP connections over serial interfaces. Defined as an Internet standard in RFC 1661 and many others, PPP is the protocol of choice for serial connections between routers and from end nodes to routers.

Unlike its predecessor, *Serial Line Internet Protocol*, or *SLIP*, PPP allows several OSI Network Layer protocols, most commonly IP and IPX, to share the same connection. Recent enhancements to the PPP protocol such as Multilink PPP, or MPPP, solve such problems as standardizing the channel bonding on ISDN connections, and have been rapidly embraced by the user community.

High Level Data Link Control Protocol (HDLC)

High Level Data Link Control, or *HDLC*, is a bit-oriented, sliding window ISO standard protocol based on the IBM Synchronous Data Link Control, or

SDLC, protocol. HDLC has been adopted by the ITU/CCITT as Link Access Procedure B, or LAP-B, and by ANSI as Advanced Data Communications Control Procedure, or ADCCP.

You must be careful when using HDLC between two different manufacturer's equipment. Many vendors—for example, Cisco—use proprietary versions of HDLC and do not go out of their way to advertise that fact.

Bypassing the Telephone Company

Until recently, the telephone company has essentially held a monopoly on providing data communications by virtue of their in-place facilities. If you needed data communications facilities, you had little choice but to use those offered by the telephone company, and at whatever price they happened to charge.

This is changing, however. Service providers that previously delivered their services over facilities leased from the telephone companies are beginning to install their own physical facilities, often based on fiber optic loops within a metropolitan or downtown area.

Depending on your needs, you may be able to provide your own facilities. One of the most aggravating situations you run into with data communications is when you need to link two sites separated by perhaps a few blocks, or even a couple of miles. In many cases you can see one site clearly from the other, and yet when you call the telephone company you find that they'll charge you $600 or $1,000 a month for a T1 to link the two sites. You can either pay this outrageous charge every month from now until eternity, or you can do something else.

For many companies, the something else means installing a private link between the two sites using microwave or low-powered laser technology. Until a few years ago, using microwave technology meant going through an involved FCC licensing process, which was both time consuming and expensive, to get the FCC license necessary to run the relatively high power microwave installations then available.

Today, devices based on low-power, spread spectrum microwave or low-power lasers have eliminated the need for licensing. These devices provide a communications link over line-of-sight distances ranging from several blocks to several miles. The spread spectrum technology helps to ensure a reliable path by compensating for interference. They also offer better throughput than a T1 from the phone company does. Typical low-power devices range from 2.5 Mbps to 10 Mbps, and sometimes higher. If a 56 Kbps link is adequate for your needs, you will find very inexpensive devices designed to provide this level of throughput over a short haul.

Some of these devices are designed as bridges that just happen to use radio waves or infrared to connect to their counterpart on the far end. Others appear to existing routers as just another leased line link. In either event, for a one-time charge of $2,500 to $5,000 per end, you can eliminate the monthly charge from the phone company and have better performance in the bargain.

Satellite Services

Innovative methods of delivering data to consumers via nontraditional methods are popping up everywhere. Although these services are nonstandardized and their availability varies from place to place, they can sometimes be the best and most cost-effective alternatives available.

For example, Hughes Networking sells the DirecPC service to those who want high speed Internet access at an affordable price. You purchase a satellite dish and receiver for about $1,000, and still dial in to the Internet through a participating ISP. The downlink provides available bandwidth of 1.2 Mbps in theory, and about 400 Kbps in practice. DirecPC is priced by usage starting at $16 per month with 30M, with an additional $0.60 per M during off-peak hours.

On the Web

DirecPC can be reached at: **www.direcpc.com**.

In what may become one of the most significant attacks on the telephone company data communications monopoly, Cable TV companies are starting to get into the ISP business. One of the more promising initiatives is @Home, a consortium lead by cable industry giant TCI. @Home plans to build its own high speed backbone, and to provide local cable TV operators with the standards and expertise to provide high-speed 10 Mbps Internet connections to existing cable TV customers. @Home is currently in the development phase, and will take several years to implement fully.

Choosing Communications Hardware

Each of the data communications facilities we have examined requires connecting hardware designed specifically for that facility. For example, a Leased Analog Line requires a special Leased Line modem. DDS and T Carrier digital facilities are terminated by a Channel Service Unit/Data Service Unit (CSU/ DSU) appropriate for the speed in question. Dial-up Analog Lines are terminated by a standard modem.

Serial Ports

Serial Ports come in several varieties. Familiar to most of us are the standard EIA-232D asynchronous serial ports, one or two of which are supplied standard with most newly purchased PCs. Because they provide only low-speed asynchronous serial services, these ports are limited to use with analog dial-up links. Other types of serial communications are used for low speed synchronous applications like Leased Analog Lines. Still other protocols and standards are used for digital and high speed applications, such as, EIA-422, EIA-423 and v.35.

Fortunately, ports, connectors, and cables for these specialized applications are standardized, making it unnecessary for most users to be concerned about them. If you plan to install one of these services, give both your hardware vendor and the service provider full particulars of your existing router or terminal equipment, the service you propose to install, and the terminating hardware you plan to use. Between the three of you, you should be able to come up with the information necessary to choose the appropriate cables and ports.

Enhanced Serial Port Standards

Since the 1981 introduction of the IBM PC, personal computers have used one of three methods to communicate with peripheral equipment. Over the years, these methods have become completely standard, allowing a device that uses any of them to be connected to any PC.

The first method, called RS-232C or, more properly, EIA-232D, is the common garden-variety *serial port* or comm port. It communicates at speeds ranging from 300 bps to perhaps 38.4 Kbps over distances from several feet to perhaps 150 feet. Serial ports are used to connect peripheral devices like modems, terminals, printers, plotters and mice.

The second method, the *Centronics parallel port*, communicates at speeds an order of magnitude higher than a serial port, but is limited to working over a distance of perhaps 10 feet. Parallel ports are almost exclusively used to connect printers, although some plotters and a very few modems use parallel connections.

The third method, the *Small Computer System Interface*, or SCSI, communicates at speeds of up to 20 Mbps over distances of at most five or 10 feet. SCSI is used primarily to connect disk drives, tape drives, and similar peripherals, although SCSI printers, scanners, and other peripherals are available.

All three of these technologies are mature, inexpensive, widely implemented, well understood, and well suited to the purpose for which they were designed. All three may also soon be as obsolete as the 8-track tape. In 1996 and 1997, two challengers to the 15-year dominance of these standards will take center stage. Both of these new technologies offer high data rates using thin cables and simple connectors. One, and perhaps both, of these new technologies is likely to become as ubiquitous in a few years as are serial, parallel, and SCSI today.

Like the gradual replacement of 5.25" floppy disks and drives with 3.5" ones, these new standards will coexist with existing standards for the next few years. Your next PC may well come equipped with all three of the existing technologies and both of the newer ones. By the turn of the century, however, serial, parallel and SCSI are likely to be about as common as vinyl record albums.

These two new standards are superficially similar, and appear to have a fair degree of overlap in terms of the purpose they serve. On this basis, some industry observers expect a horse race between the technologies, with a clear winner once the dust settles. Most, however, see the two technologies as being fundamentally complementary rather than competitive. Each has its own strengths and neither can fully substitute for the other.

Universal Serial Bus. The first of these new would-be standards is called the Universal Serial Bus, or USB. As the brainchild of Intel and Microsoft, USB is almost guaranteed to succeed in the market. Making its success even more likely, USB is a very inexpensive technology. The logic will be built into motherboards as a standard feature at essentially zero incremental cost, and the USB connector itself sells for less than a dollar in production quantities. By the time you read this, Intel will have begun shipping all motherboards with standard USB support. Other manufacturers are almost certain to follow.

More than 100 companies have announced plans to provide USB-compliant peripherals, including mice, modems, printers, and other components. As is usually the case with a new technology, these USB peripherals will initially be priced somewhat higher than ones using the older technology. As production ramps up and as computer manufacturers begin bundling USB peripherals with their systems, this price premium will rapidly disappear. By mid to late 1997, USB peripheral prices will likely be the same or lower than those using the older technologies.

USB provides 12 Mbps bandwidth using a thin cable and a simple four pin connector. It allows as many as 126 peripheral devices to be connected to the bus, with cable segments as long as five meters connecting the components. USB allows components to be connected and disconnected on-the-fly.

FireWire (IEEE P1394). The second new standard was developed jointly by Apple and Texas Instruments, and has been adopted as IEEE standard P1394. Everyone calls it *FireWire*. Like USB, FireWire uses a thin cable of up to four and one-half meters and a simple connector, this time with six pins rather than four. Also like USB, FirxeWire allows as many as 63 peripherals to be daisy chained.

FireWire will be an order of magnitude faster than USB, running initially at 50 Mbps, with 100 Mbps, 200 Mbps, and 400 Mbps not far behind. This places it squarely in the sweet spot for replacing SCSI to support hard disk drives and other high-speed peripherals. Eventually, FireWire may also be used in high-performance video subsystems, making full-screen, full-motion video not only possible, but commonplace. With increased speed comes increased cost, and FireWire is likely to be an expensive technology, at least initially.

FireWire has the backing of the consumer electronics giant Sony, which sees it as a natural for providing the link needed to support the long-discussed convergence of computers and home electronics. Also backing FireWire is Adaptec—which sees it as a replacement for the SCSI technology currently used in high-end disk drives—and major PC industry players including Apple, IBM, and Compaq.

FireWire is likely to debut in 1997 as a niche product in applications that require its high performance. It will probably never be as commonly used as USB nor as inexpensive, but it is likely to survive.

Transition to Enhanced Serial Port Standards. The transition from traditional I/O standards to USB is likely to occur quickly and without many problems. The typical PC today ships with two serial ports and one parallel port. As USB is phased in, one or two USB ports will likely replace one of the two standard serial ports on newly produced PCs, allowing them to support both new and old peripherals.

The very first USB capable systems will probably include an unused USB port or two intended simply for future compatibility. As a major backer of USB, Microsoft is likely to release patches to Windows 95 and Windows NT that will integrate support for USB into the operating system. Soon thereafter, newly shipping systems will begin to use USB for minor peripherals like keyboards and mice.

Backwards compatibility will be ensured in two ways. First, those with existing systems will be able to purchase inexpensive expansion cards that will provide one or two USB ports, allowing these older systems to use most new USB peripherals. From the opposite tack, inexpensive USB-to-serial and USB-to-parallel converters will also be available to allow using older peripherals with USB systems.

Because millions of serial and parallel devices will remain in use for years after USB ships, and indeed will continue to be produced, it is likely that computer systems produced well beyond the turn of the century will continue to include standard serial and parallel ports, particularly because these ports cost almost nothing to include. These older technology ports will gradually be phased out as old technology peripherals reach the end of their useful lives and the demand for backward compatibility disappears.

Understanding Modems

Computers use digital signaling, while the telephone system today still largely uses analog. In order for two computers to communicate across a telephone line, some means must be used to convert the sending computer's digital signal into an analog signal that can be transferred across the telephone line. At the far end, the incoming analog signal must again be translated into a digital signal understandable by the receiving computer. The device used to perform this translation is called a *modem*. The term modem is derived from *mo*dulation/*dem*odulation, the process used to perform the translation from digital to analog and vice versa.

A Brief History of Modems

AT&T invented the modem in 1956. The first modems were available only from the telephone company and operated at 300 bits per second, or 300 baud. Early modems used acoustic coupling technology. You dialed the phone manually, listened for another modem on the far end, and then placed the telephone handset into two rubber cups on your modem. Communications then proceeded, albeit slowly in modern terms. All early modems used the Bell 103 standard to transfer data at 300 bits per second. ITU-T v.21 is the international standard equivalent to Bell 103.

The next step in modems was direct connect. Rather than using rubber cups to cradle the handset, direct connect modems have an RJ-11 jack on the modem itself that allows the telephone line to connect directly into the modem. Direct connection allowed speeds to be increased somewhat. Although the first direct connect modems still offered only 300 bps connection rates, 1200 bps modems using the Bell 212A standard soon appeared.

Note

The term RJ-11 comes from *the Universal Service Ordering Code* (*USOC*) term *Registered Jack* (*RJ*) formerly used by Ma Bell to designate both the physical properties of jacks and plugs and the connection pin-outs used to wire them. Although the USOC RJ terminology is no longer officially used, it became so dominant after being used for so many years that nearly everyone (including the phone company) continues to use it.

An RJ designation originally specified two items:

- The physical properties of the jack, including its dimensions and the number of conductors it provides. For example, an RJ-11 jack uses a physical connector that provides six positions to connect wires. It is therefore properly referred to as a 6-position (or 6P) jack.

- The pinouts used to connect the wires to the jack. For example, an RJ-11 jack connects only two wires to the centermost two conductors of the six positions available on the jack. An RJ-14 jack uses the same physical connectors, but connects four wires to provide two telephone lines on a single jack. Almost everyone refers to an RJ-14 jack—or any other 6P jack—as an RJ-11.

RJ-11 is used casually to any 6P jack, regardless of how many conductors are used and how they are pinned out. Similarly, RJ-45 is commonly used to refer to any 8P jack—including jacks properly referred to as RJ-45S, RJ-48, and so on—regardless of the number of conductors installed or their pinouts. Although these usages are technically incorrect, everyone uses them.

Bell 212A modems were for years the standard for businesses, and later for home use. Bell 212A modems provide full duplex asynchronous or synchronous communications at 1200 bps using the public telephone network. By quadrupling the throughput of the earlier 300 bps modems they made character mode dial-up activities bearable. 1200 bps modems actually run at 600 baud, but encode 2 bits per baud to double throughput. ITU-T v.22 is the international standard equivalent to Bell 212A.

Up until this point, AT&T had a monopoly on modems. It was actually illegal to connect a modem not supplied by AT&T to your telephone line. When the government withdrew this monopoly, other manufacturers were free to provide modems based on existing standards and to develop enhanced standards of their own. The good news for users was that this new found competition caused the price of modems to drop rapidly at the same time that their performance was increasing. The bad news was that, with the departure of the Bell standards, each manufacturer was on its own in developing standards. The first non-Bell standard modems were just that—nonstandard. For several years, it was common to find proprietary "high-speed" modems from various manufacturers running at 2,400 bps, 4,800 bps, or more. The problem was that these modems would talk only to another identical modem.

Modern Modems and the CCITT

This incompatibility problem was finally solved when manufacturers decided, in their own interests as well as that of users, to make modems that were compliant with CCITT standards. The first such modems used the CCITT v.22*bis* standard to allow full duplex asynchronous and synchronous communications at 2,400 bps. V.22bis modems still communicated at 600 baud, but encoded 4 bits per baud.

The next step up was CCITT v.32 modems, which communicate at 9,600 bps using 2,400 baud signaling with 4 bits encoded per baud. Very soon thereafter, the CCITT v.32*bis* standard increased data rates to 14,400 bps, again using 2,400 baud signaling but with 6 bits encoded per baud.

The need for speed is always uppermost in the minds of modem manufacturers. After the introduction of v.32*bis* 14,400 bps modems, there was a quiet period during which modem manufacturers seemed to be gathering their strength for the jump to the next speed level.

Everyone knew that this next step would again double communications rates to 28,800 bps, but the CCITT had not yet finalized this next standard, although details of the proposed standard were readily available. Modem manufacturers elected not to wait, and began building modems based on the partial proposed standard as it then existed. These so-called v.fast and v.fast class modems were compliant with the proposed standard, at least to the extent that anyone could hit a moving target, but again minor incompatibilities often made it difficult or impossible to communicate between modems made by different manufacturers. Fortunately, v.fast modems were only a short-term aberration, the CCITT finally finished the follow-on v.34 standard, and standards-based modems began shipping soon thereafter.

The current ITU-T v.34 standard provides data rates of 28,800 bps, using 2,400, 3,000 and 3,200 baud signaling. The v.34 standard is widely believed to be the last modem standard that will ever be proposed, because current modem speeds are pushing the limits of how fast it is physically possible to transfer data on a standard telephone line. If v.34 isn't fast enough for you, you need to be looking at a technology other than dial-up communications on standard analog telephone lines.

Nearly any modem offered for sale today will be either 14,400 bps v.32bis model or a 28,800 bps v.34. V.32*bis* modems, the cutting edge of technology only a couple of years ago, are now commodity items, selling for as little as $50. Even name brand v.34 modems, which sold in the $300 to $800 range in mid-1995, are now available for as little as $100. Don't consider buying anything other than a v.34 modem. It's probably the last modem you'll ever buy.

Enhanced Modem Functions

The first modems were used only to transfer data. Each modem model was designed and engineered from the ground up, using discrete logic and custom Very Large Scale Integration (VLSI) chips. Sales volumes were still relatively small. Although standards-compliant, individual modem models were unique in their designs.

With the introduction of v.32 and v.32*bis,* modems became a mass-market item. Chip set manufacturers like Rockwell began producing what amounted to modems on a chip. A would-be modem manufacturer no longer had to actually design and engineer a modem, but could simply purchase purpose-built chip sets, incorporate some supporting circuitry, add a couple of jacks for phone and line connections, and wrap it all in a case. With this development, the number of modem manufacturers and models exploded.

The chip set manufacturers quickly noticed that they could at little cost enhance the functionality of their offerings by incorporating support for related telephony functions like fax and voice mail. Although these extended features may be useful in a modem intended for personal dial-up access, they often simply get in the way on a modem intended to provide a dedicated link between networks, such as for dial-up networking.

Baud versus Bits per Second

Another issue that seems to confuse a lot of people is that of *bps* versus *baud*. Both are used to measure how fast data can be transferred across a telephone line, but they measure very different things. To understand why, we have to understand a little bit about the process of transferring data between two computers (which use digital signaling) connected by an ordinary telephone line (which uses analog signaling).

Before transmission, the digital bit stream from a computer, which is measured in bits per second, must first be translated to an analog signal usable by the telephone line. An ordinary telephone line offers 3 kilohertz (KHz) of analog bandwidth, which translates, according to Bell Labs, to a maximum analog signaling rate of 6,000 baud.

Baud is a measure of how many times per second the analog line state changes, and is related only indirectly to data throughput. A single analog state change, or baud, can carry information about either a single bit or multiple bits, depending on the encoding method used to translate the digital signal to an analog signal. Using multiple bit encoding techniques, the bit per second rate can therefore exceed the baud rate. The progress in modem standards illustrates how encoding ever more bits per baud has increased overall throughput:

- Bell 103-compatible modems communicate at 300 baud using Frequency Shift Keying (FSK) modulation to code 1 bit per baud, yielding throughput of 300 bits per second.

- Bell 212-compatible modems communicate at 600 baud using Differential Phase Shift Keying (DPSK) modulation to code 2 bits per baud, yielding throughput of 1,200 bits per second.

- CCITT v.22bis modems communicate at 600 baud, but using Quadrature Amplitude Modulation (QAM) to encode 4 bits per baud, yielding throughput of 2,400 bits per second.

- CCITT v.32 modems communicate at 2,400 baud, using Trellis Coded Modulation with Viterbi Decoding (TCM) to encode 4 bits per baud, yielding throughput of 9,600 bits per second.

- CCITT v.32bis modems communicate at 2,400 baud, again using TCM, but this time to encode 6 bits per baud, yielding total throughput of 14,400 bits per second.

- ITU-T v.34 modems communicate at baud rates ranging from 2,400 to 3,200 and use a variety of encoding methods to yield total throughput as high as 28,800 bits per second.

Understanding ISDN Hardware

When the telephone company installs an ISDN BRI on your premises, they will provide a two-wire U interface, usually on an eight pin RJ45 or RJ48C jack. The BRI must then be powered, conditioned and converted to a four wire S interface. This is done using a Network Termination device called an NT-1.

A basic NT-1 with a single U and S interface connectors costs about $150. Many ISDN devices are equipped with an integrated NT-1. This may or may not be a good feature. If the integrated device does not provide an additional S interface you won't be able to plug other ISDN devices into your BRI. Also if the integrated NT-1 is damaged by a power surge or by lightning, you'll have to replace the entire device.

There are many types of ISDN equipment you can buy for your Windows NT Workstation, but they generally fall into one of two categories:

- *Terminal Adapters* are available in internal and external versions. They provide one or two serial ports, and may also provide an analog port to connect a standard analog telephone device like a fax machine, answering machine, or modem. Terminal Adapters act like modems, and generally cannot deliver the full 512 Kbps compressed bandwidth to your workstation.

- *ISDN Network Interface Cards* are available only as internal devices. They are similar conceptually to a standard network interface card, and provide higher throughputs than do Terminal Adapters. Because of the instantaneous call setup times provided by these cards, and because many telephone companies measure service, most of these devices may be configured to drop the connection after a specified period of idle time. Some telephone companies also disconnect calls after long periods of inactivity.

Most ISDN devices make provisions for combining the two 64 Kbps B Channels to provide a single 128 Kbps pipe. There are several different methods to achieve this. The two most common methods are called BONDing and MPPP. BONDing, or Bandwidth ON Demand, is an inverse multiplexing technique. MPPP, or Multilink Point-to-Point Protocol, is an extension to PPP that allows PPP packets to be divided among several interfaces and recombined at the destination.

MPPP has two advantages. First, it is an IETF standard, and well supported by various manufacturers. Second, MPPP is not limited to combining the two B channels on a single BRI. It can also combine two or more BRIs to yield cumulative throughput greater than 128 Kbps. To increase throughput, many ISDN devices also allow PPP packet compression using either the LZ or Stac Electronics algorithm. Such compression can yield a 4:1 improvement in throughput when used with compressible data, such as Web pages.

Understanding Leased Line Connecting Hardware

Leased line connecting hardware is specific to the type of leased line you install. Leased Analog Lines use special leased line modems. Because Leased Digital Lines do not require analog-to-digital and digital-to-analog conversion, they do not require a modem. They do, however, use an equivalent device called a Channel Service Unit/Data Service Unit, or CSU/DSU, which interfaces the digital line to your equipment.

Channel Service Unit (CSU)

A *Channel Service Unit* is used to terminate a DDS or T Carrier line at the customer's premises. The CSU conditions this line. It enforces the selected framing method, e.g., Extended Super Framing (ESF), Super Framing (SF), and so forth. The CSU also ensures that the proper 1's density is transmitted and received, such as B8ZS, NRZI, and so on.

Data Service Unit (DSU)

A DSU is used to interface a serial device, most commonly a router or multiplexer, to a CSU. The DSU converts the router serial interface, e.g., v.35 or EIA-232D, to match the protocol used by the CSU, e.g., DDS or T1.

Integrated Service Unit

Almost no one uses the proper term, *Integrated Service Unit*, or *ISU*, to refer to the combination of a CSU and a DSU. Instead, everyone simply calls it a *CSU/ DSU*. The vast majority of DDS hardware is sold as an integrated CSU/DSU. It is seldom necessary to purchase the CSU separately from the DSU. Stand-alone CSUs are commonly used in channelized T1 applications such as an ISDN PRI. ❖

CHAPTER 3

Configuring Windows NT Workstation for Communications

by Dan Balter

The decade of the 1990's has seen an absolute explosion in the growth of computer telecommunications. PC data communications cover the gamut from online services like America Online, CompuServe, Prodigy, and others to electronic mail and faxing to Home Pages on the Internet's World Wide Web. The PC world is now discovering many of the benefits of data communications, but, at the same time, we are coming up against the problem of limited bandwidth which controls the speed of our data communications.

Higher speed data access options that were virtually unheard of by many people just a year or two ago are now becoming part of popular PC lingo. Data communications technologies like ISDN, T-1, and ATM are starting to play much more prevalent roles as our needs for faster data communications speeds increase, especially for accessing real time, higher fidelity video and audio sources. Version 4.0, the latest release of Windows NT Workstation, is ready to take advantage of the new data communications revolution.

In this chapter, you'll learn how to set up and configure your Windows NT Workstation PC using modems with 28.8 kilobits per second access speeds over ordinary phone lines. You'll see how to install and configure both internal and external ISDN terminal adapters for up to 128 kilobits per second access speeds over digital phone lines. You will also learn how to connect two Windows NT Workstation computers together using a Direct Connection so that you can copy files between them.

Installing and Configuring Serial Ports

Most personal computer peripherals (*except most printers*) that work with sending and receiving data utilize serial communications to accomplish their tasks. A serial connection converts and transfers data literally "bit-by-bit" with one bit following the other. A data bit is the fundamental level of information that a computer stores. The term "bit" actually takes its name from the term *binary digits*: numeric values that must be either *zero* or *one*. These values correspond to electrical voltages of either *On (1) or Off (0)*. A serial connection is quite different from a parallel connection, which is used by most printers today. Parallel connections send information 8 bits at one time, and 8 bits are equivalent to one byte. So, *parallel* communications work at the *byte* level and *serial* communications work at the *bit* level.

Communications Hardware

Whenever discussing computer data communications, it is always good to understand certain basic terms. You must have two types of equipment to connect, transfer, and receive data: *Data Terminal Equipment* and *Data Communications Equipment*. Data Terminal Equipment (DTE) includes the computer itself along with its monitor, keyboard, mouse, and disk drives. The serial ports located in the rear of the computer are also considered to be part of the DTE. Data Communications Equipment (DCE) is what you connect to a computer (DTE). Modems and ISDN terminal adapters are examples of DCE.

DCE is responsible for transmitting and receiving data communications to and from DTE. Data Communications Equipment gets physically connected to a computer either as an *internal* device, which is installed into an available expansion slot inside of the computer, or as an *external* device by attaching a serial cable from the modem or terminal adapter (DCE) to one of the computer's (DTE's) COM ports. COM ports provide the necessary serial communications interface so that a data communications connection can be established. IBM-compatible personal computers follow specific guidelines for their COM ports.

What's a UART and Why Does the RS-232 Standard Matter?

The true "heart" of serial communications input and output (I/O) lies in the integrated circuitry that a computer's COM ports are attached to. Serial port circuitry is sometimes built directly into a computer's motherboard or else it is a small circuit board that gets plugged into an available expansion slot inside of the computer. The actual device that controls serial I/O is called a UART. UART stands for *Universal Asynchronous Receiver/Transmitter*. A UART is built into all serial port cards as well as into *internal* communications circuit board cards like internal modems. The original IBM PC used serial ports with a UART model number of 8250 that had a specific design and capability. As technology has improved, most newer serial ports today sport the 16550 UART. The 16550 UART is a 16-bit device which can pass data to the motherboard's RAM much faster than older UARTs.

RS-232 is a standard for communication between serial ports (UARTS) established by the Electronics Industries Association (EIA). It is officially titled the *EIA Interface Standard RS232c*. The RS-232 standard specifies all of the important parameters of interfacing between Data Terminal Equipment and Data Communications Equipment. The technical details of communications transmission speed, impedance, control handshaking, and other requirements are all spelled out by the RS-232 standard.

PC Communications Ports

Usually, a personal computer will have at least one serial COM (communications) port at the rear of the computer. Serial ports come in two types: 9-pin ports and 25-pin ports. For most serial communications, either type should suffice. The important thing to remember is that you need to use the appropriate cable connector for each type of port. If you find that you have a serial cable with a 25-pin connector on the end of it, but the computer's serial COM port is only 9-pin, you can easily find an inexpensive adapter at most computer stores to bridge this gap. It's easy to differentiate between serial ports and parallel ports: COM ports are always *male* connectors and parallel ports are always 25-pin *female* connectors.

Installing a Serial Port. If your computer does not have a serial port, or, if you want to add an additional serial port, you will need to install one in order to connect your PC to a serial communications device like a modem. To install a serial port, follow these steps:

1. Make sure that an expansion slot is available inside of your computer by looking at the back of it to see whether all of the openings have been used up.

2. Power down the PC and unplug it from the electrical wall outlet.

3. Open up the computer.

4. Unscrew one of the metal slides (used to keep dust out of the computer) of an open expansion slot and remove it so that you will be able to install the serial port card into that slot.

Caution

Before inserting the serial port card, READ the documentation that comes with it! The card will be set to a *default* base memory address and a *default* IRQ (Interrupt Request line number) by the factory. These settings determine the COM port number that the serial card will use. Serial ports can be set to COM1:, COM2:, COM3:, or COM4:. You may have to select a different COM port number depending on the devices that you already have installed on the computer, the base memory addresses, and IRQ's that are already being used by those devices. See table 3.1 for a list of COM ports and their associated base memory addresses and IRQ settings.

5. Set the jumper(s) located on the serial card to the appropriate setting(s) that the computer requires for the COM port (see table 3.1).

Tip

To find out which IRQs and base memory addresses are being used by the computer's devices, click the Start button, select Programs, Administrative Tools, and click Windows NT Diagnostics. The Windows NT Diagnostics dialog boxes appear. Click the Resources tab to obtain resources information and then click the IRQ button at the bottom of the dialog box to view all of the IRQs that are presently being used by various devices (see fig. 3.1). The I/O Port button will show you information on the various memory addresses that are being used by different devices. The Devices button will display information for each type of device attached to the computer. Select the device that you want to view information on and then click the Properties button to see specific information on each device (see fig. 3.2).

Table 3.1 IBM-Compatible PC Serial COM Port Memory Addresses and IRQ Settings

Serial Port	Base Memory Address	Interrupt Request #
COM 1	03F8	4
COM 2	02F8	3
COM 3	03E8	4
COM 4	02E8	3

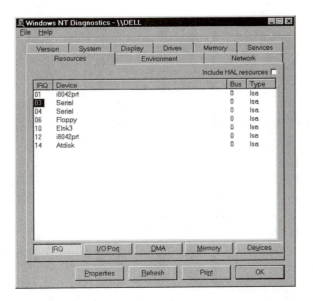

Getting Started

Fig. 3.1
The Resources page of the Windows NT Diagnostics dialog box.

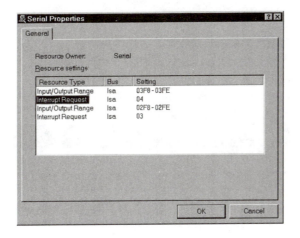

Fig. 3.2
The Serial Properties sheet of the Windows NT Diagnostics Utility.

6. Insert the serial card into the available expansion slot.

7. Once the card is seated properly, fasten it with the screw from the protective metal slide that you removed earlier.

8. Close up the computer and re-attach all of the proper cables.

9. Power on the PC. Use the Windows NT Diagnostics tool (or some other utility) to see whether the computer properly recognizes the new serial COM port.

Once a serial port has been installed and is available, you are ready to connect data communications devices directly to it. In the next section of this chapter, we will look at how to install and configure both internal as well as external modems under Windows NT Workstation.

Installing and Configuring Modems

Believe it or not, computers and ordinary telephone service are far from being a perfect match for each other. Computers work exclusively with *digital* information. At the bit level, this information is represented by zeros and ones. Telephones, on the other hand, work only with *analog* information. Telephones convert sound waves into electrical impulses that are analogous to the sounds that are fed into them. Modems derive their namesake from their capacity to translate (or **Mo**dulate) a computer's digital data signals into an analog signal that telephone lines can carry. Modems must also re-translate (or **Dem**odulate) the analog telephone signals back into digital signals for the computer on the other end of the communications loop. Hence the name modem (**mo**dulator/**dem**odulator).

Understanding Common Telecommunications Terminology

Before you voyage off into the online world, table 3.2 lists some basic data communications terms that you should know.

Table 3.2 Basic Telecommunications Terms and Settings	
Term	**Explanation**
Access Speed or Line Speed	This term is sometimes referred to incorrectly as baud rate. This term refers to the speed of a data telecommunications session. It can be expressed in either *bits per second (bps)* or *kilobits per second (kbps)*. In 1996, one of the more common modem speeds is 28,800 bits per second, which can also be expressed as 28.8 kilobits per second. This is where the moniker "28.8 modem" comes from.

Term	Explanation
COM Port Number	This is the number of the serial port where the modem (or other terminal adapter) is physically connected. Traditionally, *each* communications software package would need to know information about the modem (including to which COM port it is attached) in order for the software to utilize it. With operating systems like Windows 95 and Windows NT 4.0, all of the configuration information can be entered only once and retained by the operating system. By using the new built-in Telephony API (API stands for Application Programming Interface), all Telephony-enabled software can access the modem's settings automatically *without* having to re-configure all of those settings for each software program.
Parity	This is essentially a method for the communications software to *verify* that the data that it is receiving is really the correct data that was meant to be sent. Usually this setting can be left at "none" unless you are trying to access data from a location that specifies some other setting.
Data Bits	This setting involves configuring the modem to recognize how many binary digits should be used to symbolize one character of information. The normal default is 8.
Stop Bits	This setting is used to notify the modem as to how many binary characters will be used between each stream of serial data bits to indicate that a full character has been transmitted. Stop Bits act as a break between character transmissions. Generally, this setting should be set to 1.
Duplex	When data flows simultaneously to the modem as well as from the modem, this is known as Full Duplex. Whenever the modem is required to take turns sending and receiving data, this is known as Half Duplex. Full Duplex should suffice in most situations.
Protocol	Computer networking and telecommunications are chock full of different types of protocols. Protocols function as rules that computers must follow to properly transfer data files. Protocols are sort of like languages– when transferring files between two PCs, both computers *must* "speak" the same protocol. Your choice of protocol can usually be made right before you start attempting to send or receive a file.

(continues)

Table 3.2 continued	
Term	**Explanation**
Download	To receive a file from another computer.
Upload	To send a file to another computer.
Terminal and Terminal Emulation	These terms apply whenever you are accessing a mainframe (host) computer, a bulletin board service (BBS), or some of the online services (CompuServe, etc.) that support non-proprietary software. Each different type of online service or connection will stipulate the type of *Terminal Emulation* that it requires for you to access it. It's called emulation because the communications software is just emulating (or simulating) the type of terminal that you would have to be using if you were actually working on that system locally. Two of the more generic terminal emulations are VT100 and ANSI.
The AT Command Set	All communications software dictates the actions of a modem via a set of standard commands that have come to be known as the AT Command Set (pronounced "A" "T"). Most communications software manuals list several of the AT commands. Hayes Microcomputer Products Company originally developed these commands and they quickly became a de facto standard. Two of the most common AT commands are *ATDT,* which generates a dial tone and then instructs the modem to dial the a phone number the follows the command. (such as, "ATDT 1-800-555-1212") and *ATH,* which tells the modem to hang up.

Installing Internal Modems

Installing an internal modem card is very similar to installing a serial port card. First, you need to turn off the computer. Second, you need to unplug all of the cables that are attached to the computer, including the power cord. Third, you need to configure the modem card jumper settings for the proper COM port, base memory address, and IRQ line so that it will not conflict with any other devices that are already connected to the computer. Many newer communications cards are software-configurable. These cards allow you to set the proper IRQs and memory addresses through the manufacturer's proprietary software utility program that ships with the card. Fourth, after you have properly configured the modem card, you can open up the computer and insert the modem card into an available expansion card slot. Finally, fasten down the modem card with the proper screw, close up the computer, and re-connect all of the cables. When you turn the PC back on again, your modem should be ready for the software portion of the installation. Don't forget to connect a phone line cord from a telephone wall jack to the phone line connection port located on the modem itself.

> **Tip**
>
> On some modems, both internal and external, it actually matters to which phone line port you connect your telephone cord. Some modems will *only hear a dial tone* when you plug the phone cord into the port labeled "Line", not the port labeled "Phone". On these particular modems, the "Phone" port can only be used as a *pass-through* convenience to which you can add a telephone. In order for these modems to access a dial tone, you must plug the phone cord from the telephone jack into the "Line" port.

Installing External Modems

External modems are easier to install than internal ones, provided that your computer has an available serial port to connect to. With an external modem, you simply take it out of its box, connect one end of a serial cable to the modem and the other end to the computer's available COM port. Next, Attach one end of the power cord that comes with all external modems to the modem and plug the other end into a nearby electrical outlet. Finally, remember to connect a phone cord from a telephone jack to the external modem's "Line" connection port. After that, you should be ready to begin the software phase of the modem installation and configuration routine.

> **Note**
>
> External data communications devices are almost always more expensive than their internal counterparts. Functionally, there is no difference between internal and external communications equipment. However, when you are connecting an external device to an existing serial port, you do *not* need to be concerned with IRQ or memory address settings. In addition, there may be times when you need to reset (turn off and back on) the communications device. With an external device, resetting it is easy; just press its power switch. To reset an internal device, you must at least reboot the computer. Many times, though, a simple reboot is *not* sufficient to reset the device. In a lot of cases, resetting an internal device means having to *turn off your computer and then turn it back on.* For this one reason alone, I know many consultants who shy away from internal communications devices. If you have ever had to reboot a file server because its internal modem was not functioning properly, you can really appreciate this rationale.

Installing and Configuring a Modem Using the Install New Modem Wizard

Windows NT Workstation 4.0 borrows much of its new gadgetry from Windows 95. Installing a new modem under Windows NT 4.0 is no exception. After you have properly installed the modem hardware (internal or external), you can then proceed to make the operating system aware of its existence. To use the Install New Modem Wizard, do the following:

1. Click the Start button, select Settings, and click Control Panel.

2. Double-click the Modems icon located inside of the Control Panel window. The Install New Modem dialog box appears (see fig. 3.3).

Fig. 3.3
The first of the
Install New
Modem Wizard
dialog boxes.

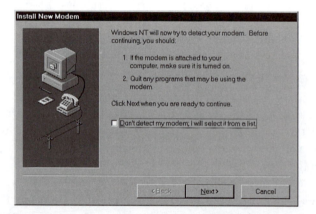

3. If you do *not* want the Install New Modem Wizard to automatically try to detect your modem, click the Don't Detect My Modem checkbox. You will then have the opportunity to choose the proper make and model of your modem from a list supplied by Windows NT. You will also have the option of using a configuration disk that may have been supplied by your modem's manufacturer.

4. Click Next to continue. If you permit the Wizard to try and detect your modem, you will see a status window displayed showing you the different COM ports that Windows NT is checking to try and find your modem (see fig. 3.4).

5. Click Next to accept the modem brand and model that Windows NT automatically detected. If the information is incorrect, click the Change button (see fig. 3.5).

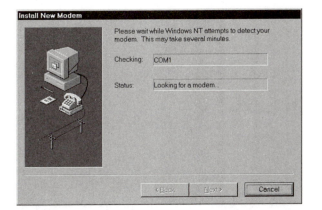

Fig. 3.4
The Install New Modem Autodetection Status windows lets you know exactly what is happening.

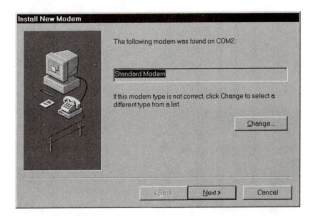

Fig. 3.5
Either accept or change the modem type in this dialog box.

6. From the Install New Modem manufacturer and model selection window, click the name of your modem's manufacturer in the Manufacturers list box and then click the model of your particular modem from the Models list box (see fig. 3.6).

7. If you have a disk provided by the modem manufacturer, click the Have Disk button. Type in the proper drive letter and path and then click OK to have Windows NT install the modem drivers supplied by the manufacturer. You may still need to select the correct model of modem. Click the correct model to select it.

8. After you have selected the proper manufacturer and model, click the OK button.

Getting Started

Fig. 3.6
Click the manu-
facturer and model
of your modem in
this dialog box.

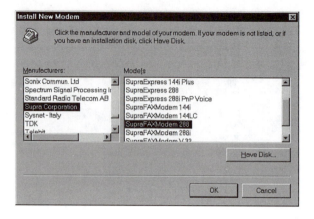

9. Click Next to continue with the installation.

10. Click Finish for the final Install New Modem dialog box to complete
the modem installation process (see fig. 3.7).

Fig. 3.7
Click Finish and
the setup is
complete.

Working with Your Telecommunications Configuration

After you have successfully completed the Install New Modem Wizard and
you have set up the modem, the Modems Properties sheet appears (see fig.
3.8). From this sheet, you can change any modem settings that you would
like, plus, you can further configure telephone dialing attributes as well as
many other telecommunications parameters for your Windows NT Workstation computer.

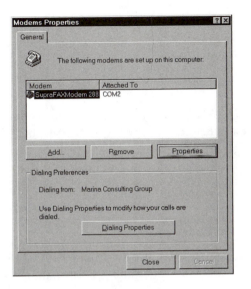

Fig. 3.8
The Modems
Properties sheet
lists the modems
setup on your
computer.

Dialing Properties

To configure your modem's dialing properties, click the Dialing Properties
button from the General tab of the Modems Properties sheet. The Dialing
Properties sheet appears (see fig. 3.9). You can configure several dialing characteristics for your modem here.

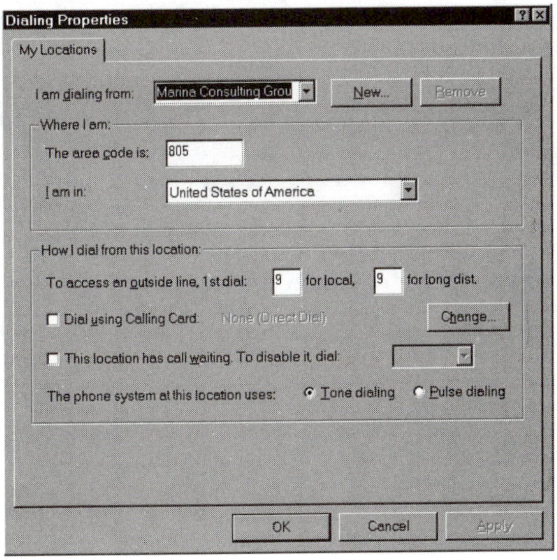

Fig. 3.9
The Dialing
Properties sheet
allows you to
configure dialing
characteristics for
your modem

■ You can set up one or more dialing locations by typing in a name for the location in the I Am Dialing From drop-down list box and then clicking the New button.

■ Enter the area code and select the country for the location in the Where I Am section.

■ In the How I Dial From This Location section, enter any outline line access numbers that may be required by the telephone system currently used. Many offices require that you dial a 9 before you can make either a local or long distance call. If this is true for your location, type a **9** in the For Local, box and another **9** in the For Long Dist. box.

■ If you want the modem to dial using a telephone calling card, mark the checkbox labeled Dial Using Calling Card and then click the Change button. From the Change Calling Card dialog box, select the appropriate calling card service by using the Calling Card To Use drop-down list box (see fig. 3.10). Enter your number in the Calling Card Number box. If your calling card service is not listed, you can click the New button to create a customized entry for your particular calling card company. After you have entered all of the necessary calling card information, click OK.

Fig. 3.10
Select the correct calling card service for the Calling Card to use drop-down list.

■ If your location has call waiting, you can mark this checkbox if you would like to disable it while the modem is online. Select from the drop- down list or type in the appropriate numeric sequence for disabling call waiting in your specific area. You may need to check with your local telephone company for this information.

■ Click the Tone dialing option button if you have the common push-button type phone service; otherwise, click the Pulse dialing option if you have the old rotary-style phones.

Click the OK button when you have completed filling in all of the necessary items for the Dialing Properties dialog box. Repeat this process for each dialing location that has different dialing parameters.

Working with Other Modem Properties

From the Modems Properties sheet, you can add additional modems by clicking the Add button if you happen to have more than one modem connected to the computer. You can also remove any of the modems that are listed in the Modems Properties sheet by clicking the name of a modem to select it and then clicking the Remove button. Removing a modem in this manner does not physically remove it, of course, it only removes all references and configuration settings for it from the Windows NT operating system. To view and change properties of an installed modem, click the name of the modem whose properties you wish to work with and then click the Properties button.

You will see the Properties sheet displayed for the modem that you selected (see fig. 3.11). On the General tab, you can change the COM port setting that the modem is connected to by selecting a different COM port from the Port drop-down list box. You can vary the modem's Speaker volume by dragging the speaker volume control lever with your mouse. You can also select the maximum transmission speed for the modem from the Maximum speed drop down. You can mark the Only Connect At This Speed checkbox to restrict the modem's connections to a particular number of bits per second.

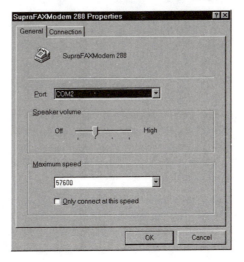

Fig. 3.11
The Modem Properties sheet for the modem you've selected.

When you click the Connection tab of the modem's Properties dialog box, you can view the Connection preferences for Data bits, Parity, and Stop bits (see fig. 3.12). You can change any or all of these items by selecting a different setting from their respective drop-down list boxes; however, Windows NT's default settings usually should be adequate. Change these settings at *your own risk.* You can also modify Call Preferences by clearing the Wait for Dial Tone Before Dialing checkbox. You can elect to *not* Cancel the call if not connected within 60 seconds by clearing this checkbox, or you can type in a different number of seconds for canceling a call.

Fig. 3.12
The Connection page shows the preferences for data bits, parity, and stop bits.

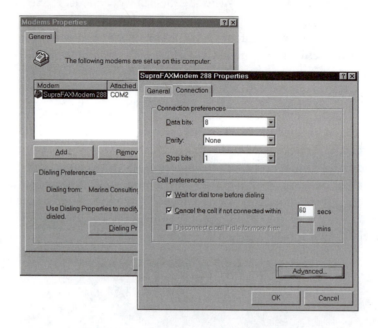

Click the Advanced button to view or change Advanced Connection Settings (see fig. 3.13). From here, you have the option of changing any of the default advanced settings. Again, I must stress that you should exercise a good deal of caution whenever you attempt to change modem settings. *Any changes can render your data communications configuration inoperative.*

Fig. 3.13
The Advanced Connection Settings dialog box allows you to make choices about error control and flow control.

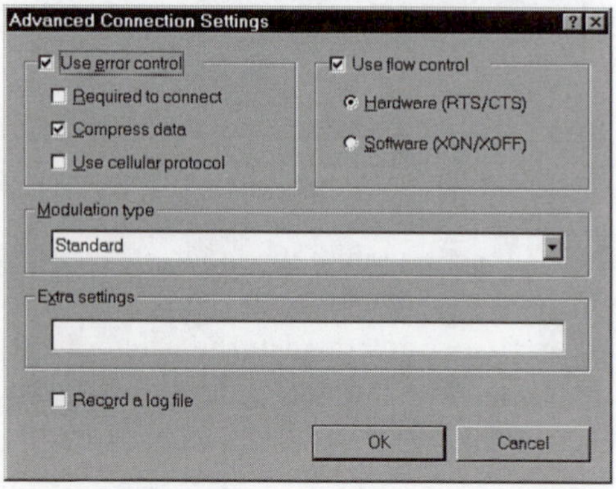

The one advanced modem connection setting that may prove useful *without* possibly damaging your configuration is the Record a Log File checkbox located at the bottom of the Advanced Connection Settings dialog box. By marking this checkbox, Windows NT will create a log file in the *WINNT* (system root) directory that will be named "ModemLog_*nameofmodem*.txt". As an example, we can see that the name of the modem that I have installed on my Windows NT Workstation computer (Supra FaxModem 288) becomes part of the log filename as shown in figure 3.14. If you double-click this text file in My Computer or in the Windows NT Explorer, you can view this log file in the Notepad editor (see figure 3.15).

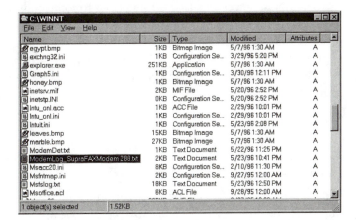

Fig. 3.14

The modem log filename is displayed in the My Computer Window.

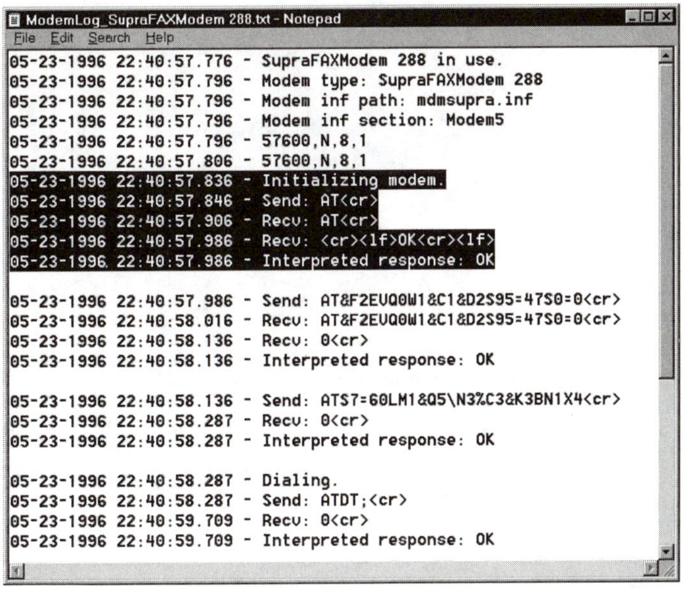

Fig. 3.15

The modem log file opened up in Notepad.

Click OK to close the Advanced Connection Settings dialog box and again click OK to close your modem's Properties sheet with the General and Connection tabs. Finally, click the Close button for the main Modems Properties sheet to close it down.

Testing Your Modem's Setup: Making Sure That It Works!

After you have physically connected the hardware, run the Install New Modem Wizard, and properly configured any additional settings, you are then ready to put your handy work to the ultimate test: will your modem connect? Well, there's only one sure way to tell—try connecting to some online service, a bulletin board service (BBS), or connect to your favorite Internet service provider. The way that I'm choosing to test my new modem setup, the one that appears in all of the figures for this chapter so far, is by attempting to connect to one of the popular online services, CompuServe, where I already have a user account.

The first and easiest test that you can try, is to see if your modem will simply hear a dial tone and then dial a phone number. You can use the Phone Dialer program that ships with Windows NT Workstation 4.0. To run the Phone Dialer program, follow these steps:

1. Click the Start button, select Programs, Accessories, and then click Phone Dialer. The Phone Dialer dialog box appears (see fig. 3.16).

Fig. 3.16
The Phone Dialer Program dialog box.

2. Type in a valid telephone number. (You may want to use a phone number that will ring a nearby telephone so that you can actually hear your modem causing the phone to ring.)

3. Click the Dial button. The Phone Dialer program should cause your modem to dial the phone number that you entered.

4. Click the Hang Up button on the Call Status dialog box after you hear the modem dialing the phone number.

> **Tip**
>
> If you are unable to get any Windows communications software to dial the modem, try going to a command prompt and entering AT modem commands directly from there. This can help determine whether you are encountering a hardware problem or a software-related Windows NT problem. At a command prompt, type **"echo ATDT > COM#:"** and press Enter (replace the # sign with the number of the COM port your modem is attached to). If you hear a dial tone from the modem, you can rest assured that you do *not* have a hardware problem. Type **"ATH"** at the command prompt and press Enter to have the modem hang up the phone line.

If you want to be *real sure* that your modem is setup and working properly, there is no better test than actually connecting and accessing some type of service or data online. Windows NT Workstation ships with another handy tool for connecting to BBSes and various online services: the HyperTerminal program. To run HyperTerminal, do the following:

1. Click the Start button, select Programs, Accessories, and then click HyperTerminal.

2. When this program starts, it will ask you for the name of the connection that you wish to make—for example, CompuServe (see fig. 3.17).

3. Choose an icon for this new connection from the row of available icons displayed by clicking one of them.

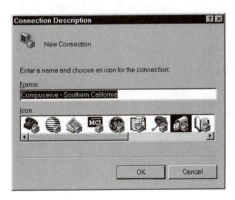

Fig. 3.17
HyperTerminal's Connection Description dialog box asks for the name of the connection you want to make.

4. Click OK to proceed to the Phone Number dialog box. Type in the telephone number for the connection that you want to make (see fig. 3.18).

Fig. 3.18
HyperTerminal's
Phone Number
dialog box allows
you to enter
details for the
number you want
to dial.

5. Click OK to bring up the Connect dialog box.

6. From the Connect dialog box, click the Dial button to have HyperTerminal instruct the modem to dial the telephone number and make the connection.

7. If all goes well, the connection should be established and you will be online similar to the illustration for connecting to CompuServe in figure 3.19.

Fig. 3.19
Through
HyperTerminal,
you are now
connected online
to the CompuServe
information
service.

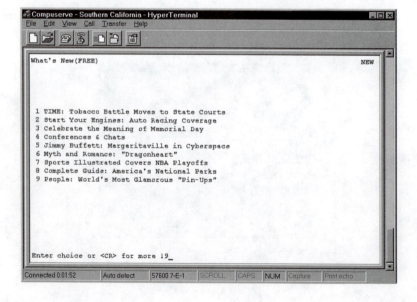

8. When you are done working online, click the Disconnect icon on the toolbar or choose Call, Disconnect to hang up the phone line and go offline.

9. To exit HyperTerminal, click the X icon in the window's upper-right corner or select File, Exit.

10. HyperTerminal will ask you if you want to save your settings for the new connection that you have just configured. Click Yes to save the connection information, click No to exit and *not* save the connection settings, or click Cancel to *not* exit the program and return to the HyperTerminal window.

Installing and Configuring ISDN Adapters

Many people believe that the next wave of telecommunications technology to support the mounting bandwidth cravings of the masses will be ISDN: Integrated Services Digital Network. ISDN provides telephone service with all digital signaling. What this means to you and me is the sorely needed increased data transfer speed for all kinds of data communications such as real time video and audio.

ISDN's Basic Rate Interface (BRI) service actually provides the consumer with three separate *channels* for communications which use the very same copper wires that regular analog telephones use. These three channels are referred to as two "B" channels and one "D" channel, or, 2B+D. But not only do you get three channels with BRI, the two B channels can theoretically deliver up to 64 kilobits per second (kbps) line speed each. That's a total speed of up to 128 kbps! The third channel is a called the D channel or the common channel. It travels at just 16 kbps and is used only for housekeeping chores like setting up calls, monitoring the communications network, and the like.

ISDN has many, many facets to consider. Ultimately, ISDN can be a godsend but getting it installed and configured correctly can become a major nightmare! Fortunately, there are now some excellent references at our disposal for learning about all of the nuances of ISDN. Required reading for anyone who is interested in ISDN is *Special Edition Using ISDN* by James Y. Bryce and published by Que Corporation. This book is an outstanding guide to ISDN.

On the Web

There are also Web Pages of note on the Internet:

Dan Kegel's ISDN Page at:

http://www.alumni.caltech.edu/~dank/isdn

James Bryce's home page at:

http://www.bryce.com/~bryce

Microsoft has an ISDN page on its web site at:

http://www.microsoft.com/windows/getisdn

Besides containing general information on ISDN, you can actually request ISDN telephone service through the Microsoft page! You can find out whether your local telephone company offers ISDN service in your area and, if it is offered, you can discover approximately how much it would cost for installation and monthly service charges. ISDN orders placed through this Web page are confirmed later by phone through your local phone company representative.

Using an ISDN Adapter

You can find a few different ISDN adapters out in the marketplace these days, more than you could find just one or two years ago. Although the Motorola BitSURFER has become a rather popular choice among some ISDN users, I was intrigued by an external adapter that was recently announced by U.S. Robotics. The Courier I-Modem with ISDN/V.34 supports *both* analog *and* digital telecommunications *without* any reconfiguration. This feature comes in real handy since there are not yet that many online services, BBSes, or businesses and individuals who support ISDN access. I have found it necessary to constantly switch back and forth between utilizing ISDN for my Internet connection while still using 28.8 kbps analog phone connections for things like my CompuServe e-mail and for downloading updated software and networking drivers off of corporate bulletin boards that do not support ISDN access. For more information on U.S. Robotics and their products, you can call 708-982-5001.

On the Web

U.S. Robotics web site at:

http://www.usr.com

Good Terms to Know

Before diving head first into the world of ISDN, check out Table 3.3 for a few key terms you may come to know and love.

Table 3.3   Important ISDN Terminology

ISDN Term	Definition/Description
Service Profile Identifier or SPID Number	This number is assigned by the telephone service provider. This number can be *one* of your assigned ISDN phone numbers with a prefix added. You need to configure your ISDN terminal adapter with this number. Since BRI contains two B channels, you get two different ISDN telephone numbers when you install an ISDN line.
Directory Number	This number is also assigned by your local phone company. This is also required configuration information for your terminal adapter.
Switch Protocol Type	The type of telephone switch varies from telephone company to telephone company. Check with your local provider for the correct type. This is necessary information for your terminal adapter.
NT-1 Device	An NT-1 device is required to connect ISDN terminal adapters to your telephone company's wall jack (this is known as the U interface). One (and only one) NT-1 device can be connected on any one given ISDN BRI line at any one given time! All ISDN adapters that will use the same BRI line *must* connect through the *same* NT-1. Some terminal adapters have an NT-1 device *built-in*. This feature can be beneficial if you have only one or two ISDN users on that BRI line. However, if you have multiple ISDN users on one BRI line, each with their own adapters, you will be better off with a separate external NT-1 device.

(continues)

Table 3.3 Continued

ISDN Term	Definition/Description
RJ-45	This is the type of phone wire connector that ISDN terminal adapters and ISDN wall jacks use. It is very similar to a standard RJ-11 phone cord connector except that it is *wider*. RJ-45 is the same connector specification that is used for 10BaseT Ethernet (also referred to as unshielded twisted pair) networking cables.
Point-to-Point Protocol (PPP)	This protocol is widely used by Internet Service Providers (ISPs) to give their customers access to the Internet.
PPP Multilink Protocol	A standard being proposed for ISDN *channel aggregation*. For example, combining two B channels of 64 kbps each to gain one communications circuit of 128 kbps.
BONDING	A trademark of the BONDING Consortium which stands for **B**andwidth **ON D**emand **In**teroperability **G**roup. This is another method of channel aggregation for combining two B channels for up to 128 kbps access speed. This method works through *inverse multiplexing* of ISDN signals. You can peruse some text documents on this subject by pointing your Web browser to: **http://www.hep.net.ftp/networks/bonding**.

Physically Connecting an External Terminal Adapter

An external ISDN adapter looks very much like a modem. It attaches to a computer in much the same fashion, too. Simply connect a serial cable between the adapter's 25-pin female connector and one of your PC's available serial COM ports. Next, connect ordinary twisted pair telephone cable with RJ-45 connectors on each end from an ISDN wall jack to your NT-1 device. Remember, all ISDN terminal adapters *must* be connected through an NT-1 device or they will not function. Some adapters have built-in NT-1 devices.

For these adapters, just plug one end of the phone cable directly into the connector plug marked "U". "U" is an ISDN designation pointing to the telephone company's side of the circuit. The customer's side begins where the cabling goes from the NT-1 device over to the terminal adapter(s). The last step is to plug in the power cord for the adapter.

The Software Side of Installation and Configuration

Now you need to inform Windows NT Workstation that you have attached an ISDN terminal adapter to the computer. To install the necessary software components, perform the following steps:

1. Click the Start button, point to Settings, and click Control Panel.

2. From the Control Panel window, double-click the Modems icon.

3. The Modems Properties sheet appears. Click the Add button to install a new terminal adapter.

4. When the Install New Modem dialog box appears, you can opt to try and have Windows NT detect the ISDN adapter or you can mark Don't Detect My Modem; select the I Will Select It from a List checkbox instead. For ISDN adapters, I suggest that you mark the checkbox and manually choose the appropriate adapter listing.

5. Click the Next button to proceed to the following dialog box which displays a list of Manufacturers and Models of modems and terminal adapters. If you can find your specific manufacturer and model, click the appropriate entries. Otherwise, click the Have Disk button if you have a disk supplied by the manufacturer.

6. If you click Have Disk, you will see the Install From Disk dialog box displayed. Type the proper path for the terminal adapter's installation files in the drop-down list box or click Browse to locate them. Click OK after you have entered the installation path information and/or inserted the manufacturer-supplied disk.

7. Next you should see a second Install New Modem dialog box listing different models of modems and terminal adapters. Click the proper one to select it and then click Next (see fig. 3.20).

8. The subsequent Install New Modem dialog box asks you about the COM ports that you want to install the terminal adapter on. Click either All Ports or Selected Ports. If you select Selected Ports, be sure to click which COM port(s) that you want it installed on (see fig. 3.21).

Fig. 3.20
The Install New
Modem dialog box
with the U.S.
Robotics Courier
I-Modem selected.

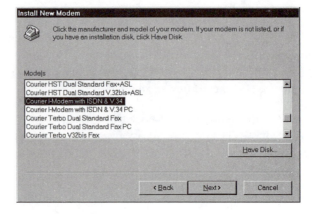

Fig. 3.21
The Install New
Modem COM
ports selection
dialog box.

9. Click Next to continue. Windows NT will then install the necessary software components for your ISDN terminal adapter (you may be prompted for the location of your Windows NT setup files).

10. Click Finish to complete the process. The adapter should now be installed (see fig. 3.22).

11. Click Close to exit from the Modems Properties dialog box.

After you have gone through the Install New Modem procedure, you should see the name of your ISDN terminal adapter along with the number of the COM that it is connected to listed in the Modem Properties dialog box (see fig. 3.22). From this dialog box, you can make any necessary adjustments to Windows NT's properties for the adapter by clicking the Properties button (just like an analog modem). You can also set up dialing properties for the ISDN line by clicking the Dialing Properties button.

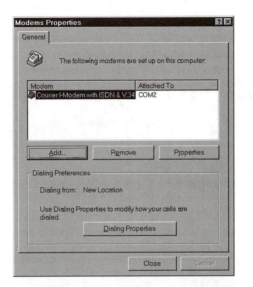

Fig. 3.22
The Modem
Properties dialog
box After Success-
ful Installation of
an ISDN Terminal
Adapter.

Tip

ISDN lines do *not* require that you dial a "9" for an outside line, even if your regular business telephone service requires it. Do not enter any special prefix for local or long distance ISDN service for your adapter's dialing properties unless instructed to do so by your ISDN service provider. Adding a "9" to an ISDN phone number will not permit a connection.

Proprietary Terminal Adapter Configuration Software. ISDN terminal adapters must be configured properly in order to function. ISDN adapters require more setup information than analog modems. Your terminal adapter should ship with at least one disk that contains some sort of configuration management software for the adapter. The U.S. Robotics Courier I-Modem comes with a disk labeled I-Modem Configuration Manager.

On my initial attempt to set up the U.S. Robotics Courier I-Modem terminal adapter, I was unable to get it to function properly. After conferring with my Internet service provider, I called U.S. Robotics for technical support. The support engineer had me extract some vital statistics from the I-Modem by using a terminal window in a communications software program like Procomm Plus for Windows. We entered in two AT commands for the I-Modem: ATi5 and ATi7 (see figs. 3.23 and 3.24). We discovered that the adapter's firmware version (ROM) was not the most recent. This was probably causing the problem. Fortunately, the Courier I-Modem uses updatable flash

ROM. So, I used one of my analog modems to dial up and connect to U.S. Robotics 24-hour tech support BBS (1-847-982-5092) and I had to download a file named IE010104.ZIP to upgrade the adapter's flash ROM.

Fig. 3.23
The Procomm Plus Terminal window shows ISDN Terminal Adapter information by issuing the ATi5 command.

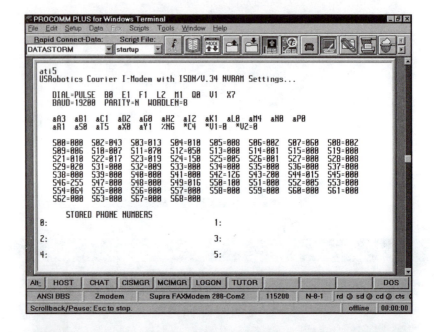

Fig. 3.24
The Procomm Plus Terminal window shows ISDN Terminal Adapter information by issuing the ATi7 command.

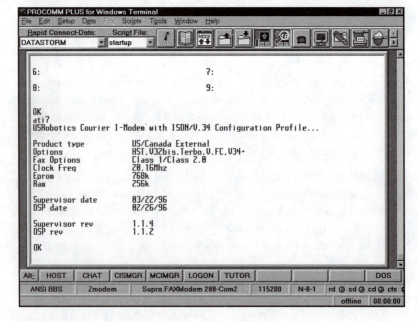

After downloading the file, I unzipped it into an empty subdirectory on my hard drive. For my specific model of the I-Modem (model 1), I was told by the tech support engineer to run the GO.BAT file which comes as part of the downloaded zip file. The flash ROM upgrade process should be run at an actual DOS prompt, not within a Virtual DOS Machine window, if at all possible. So, I first had to boot DOS and then run the upgrade program. The exact syntax that I ran was "GO.BAT 2". The process took about ten minutes to complete, but it solved the connection problems that I was having.

The next step after performing the Windows NT Install New Modem procedure is to run your terminal adapter's configuration software program. For the I-Modem, you should insert the I-Modem Configuration Manager disk into the A:\ or B:\ drive, click the Start button, click Run, type **A:\Setup.exe**, and click OK to install the Configuration Manager program (see fig. 3.25). After installing the software, double-click Courier I-Modem Manager icon from the U.S. Robotics program group folder to start to program (see fig. 3.26). Click Continue to arrive at the main configuration dialog box.

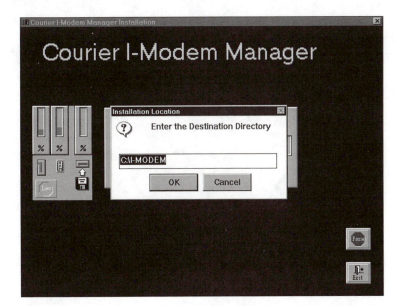

Fig. 3.25
The U.S. Robotics Courier I-Modem Configuration Manager software installation routine.

Click the COM port where your adapter is connected to the computer and then click Open COM to enter and view the adapter's configuration settings (see fig. 3.27). This is where you must enter all of the required information for the adapter to function properly. The I-Modem is somewhat unique in that it supports both ISDN and analog calling. The Courier I-Modem Configuration Manager has both a Data Channel section and an Analog Device Channel section for this very reason.

Fig. 3.26

The opening dialog box of the U.S. Robotics Courier I-Modem Configuration Manager.

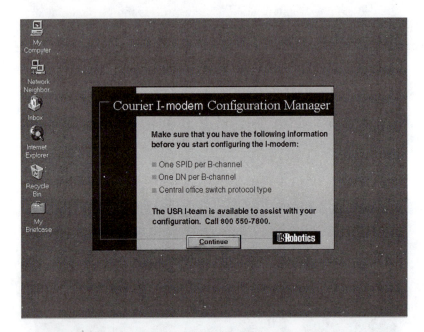

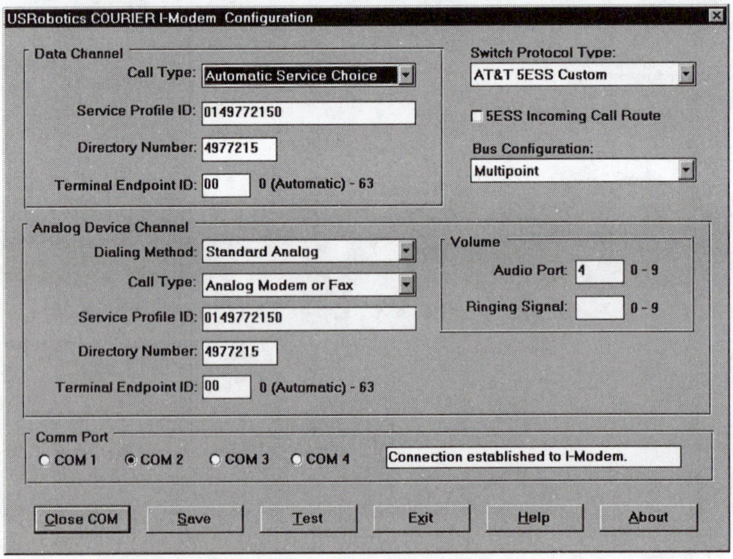

Fig. 3.27

U.S. Robotics Courier I-Modem Configuration Manager Settings dialog box is used to enter the adapter's configuration information.

Fill in these settings for the Data Channel section:

- *Call Type.* It is best to set this to Automatic Service Choice.

- *Service Profile ID (SPID).* Type in the number assigned to you by your ISDN service provider (local phone company).

- *Directory Number (DN).* Type in the number assigned to you by your ISDN service provider (local phone company).

- *Terminal Endpoint ID.* Set this to 0 (Automatic) unless instructed otherwise by the telephone company.

- *Switch Protocol Type.* This setting depends on your particular area and local phone company. You will probably need to ask the phone company about this one. For my area, I am required to set this to AT&T 5ESS Custom.

- *5ESS Incoming Call Route.* Mark this checkbox if you will be using this feature.

- *Bus Configuration.* Select either Multipoint or Point To Point.

For the Analog Device Channel section, you can simply accept the default selections for the Dialing Method and the Call Type. The SPID and Directory Number should be entered exactly the same as in the Data Channel section. The Terminal Endpoint ID should also be set to 0 (Automatic) unless you entered a different setting in the Data Channel section as advised by your local ISDN service provider.

When you have finished entering in all of the settings, you can click the Test button to try out the configuration. If all has gone well, you will get a Switch Test Completed message box telling you that the Switch Connection Test has completed successfully. Click OK to leave the message box. To save your configuration settings down to the ISDN adapter, click the Save button at the bottom of the dialog box. You should see a message box displayed to let you know that the configuration values were saved to the adapter. Click OK to remove the message box. Click the Close COM button to close down the COM port connection to the adapter and then click Exit to leave the I-Modem Configuration Manager program.

Testing Your ISDN Adapter

Now let's put our ISDN configuration to the test! One of the best ways to test out your ISDN adapter is to dial up an Internet service provider (ISP) who offers ISDN access. In my area, Franklin interNet is one of the few ISPs who have *local* ISDN phone numbers (long distance ISDN calls are more expensive, just like regular phone service). You can use the Dial-Up Networking Tool that ships with Windows NT Workstation 4.0 to connect to the Internet. Dial-Up Networking is covered in great detail in Chapter 13, "Using Dial-Up Networking."

To use Dial-Up Networking, click the Start button, point to Programs, Accessories, and click Dial-Up Networking. After setting a Dial-Up Network entry for your ISP, click Dial to connect. You can configure your Dial-Up Networking session entry to either pop up a terminal window after connecting, or it can run a script to log you on to the ISP's network (see fig. 3.28). Once you have successfully connected and logged on, you're home free to explore the World Wide Web using Microsoft's Internet Explorer, which installs as part of Windows NT 4.0 at 64 kilobits per second! If your ISDN terminal adapter supports Bonding which combines two B channels together for effective throughput of up to 128 kilobits per second, you can really surf the Net in style! Unfortunately, U.S. Robotics is still working on the Bonding implementation for the Courier I-Modem as of May, 1996. So, I-Modem users will just have to be patient and wait a little while for the firmware and software upgrades that will support ISDN Bonding.

Fig. 3.28
Dial-Up
Networking's
Terminal window.

Internal ISDN Adapters

Setting up an internal ISDN terminal adapter is much the same as an external one. Of course, the physical connection is different; you need to have an open expansion slot inside of your computer to install an internal ISDN adapter card. Just like an internal modem or serial card, you must make sure that the adapter's base memory address and interrupt request line (IRQ) do not conflict with another device inside of the PC. On many models, you can configure the base memory address and IRQ settings through a software utility program that comes with the adapter. Be sure that the jumper switches on the internal adapter card are set to allow software configuration. Refer to the manufacturer's manual for specific information.

After you have opened up the computer, physically installed the adapter card, and then closed the PC back up, it's time to configure the adapter using the proprietary software disk(s) that come with it. For example, to configure the U.S. Robotics Sportster ISDN 128K internal adapter, you can click the Start button, click Run, type **A:\setup** (or **B:\setup**), and click OK to launch the program (see fig. 3.29). From the Board Configuration dialog box, enter all of the pertinent information for your ISDN channels (see fig. 3.30). The Sportster ISDN adapter supports the new WinISDN interface for Windows 95. For Windows NT, you need to separately purchase the Windows NT Driver for the Sportster ISDN 128K Internal adapter. The Windows NT driver has a list price of $150 if purchased directly from U.S. Robotics.

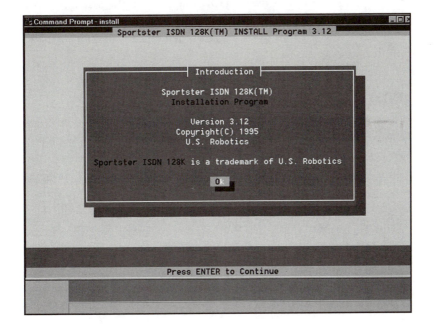

Fig. 3.29
U.S. Robotics Sportster ISDN 128K Internal Adapter Configuration Program.

Fig. 3.30

U.S. Robotics
Sportster ISDN
128K Internal
Adapter Board
Configuration
dialog box.

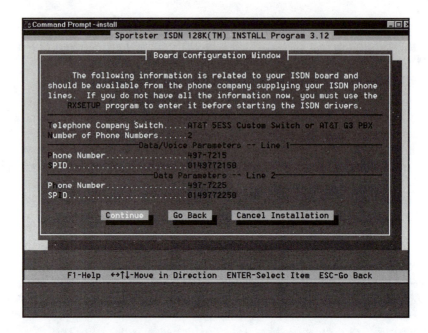

When you have completed the configuration settings for the adapter card, you can go to the Control Panel. Double-click the Modems icon and then click the Add button. The Install New Modem dialog box appears. Go through each of the same steps that are outlined previously in this chapter in the section on installing an external ISDN adapter with the Install New Modem dialog box. After you successfully setting up the adapter under the Windows NT Modems Properties sheet, you can then proceed to connect using your ISDN phone line.

Summing It All Up

From high speed ISDN connections for Internet access to support for Direct Cable Connections between computers, Windows NT Workstation 4.0 is ready for the next revolution in data communications. In this chapter, we examined how to install and configure both analog modems as well as digital ISDN adapters. We went over some of the basics of ISDN to get you started on it while taking advantage of the latest rev of Windows NT. The future demands higher bandwidth and Windows NT 4.0 can certainly help to get you there. ❖

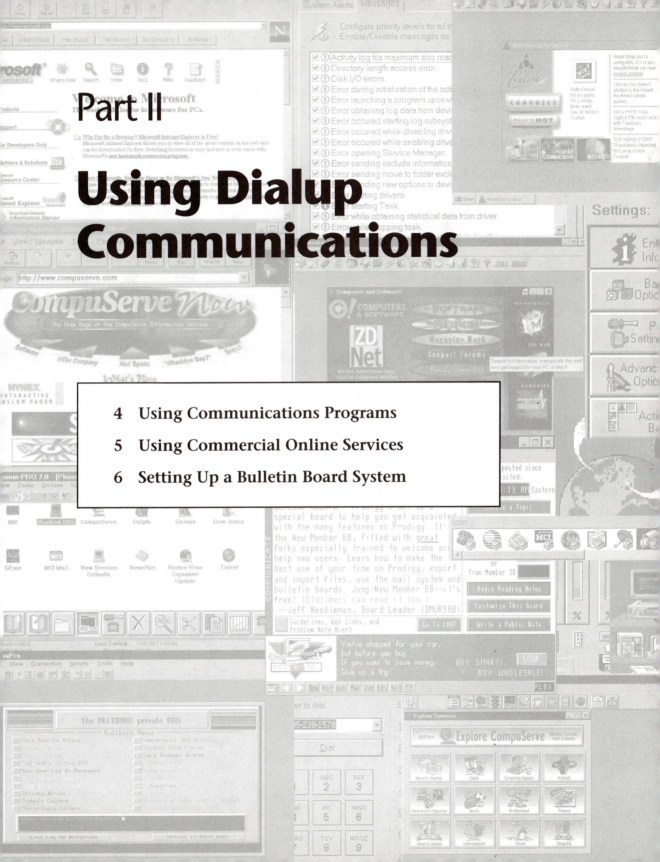

Part II

Using Dialup Communications

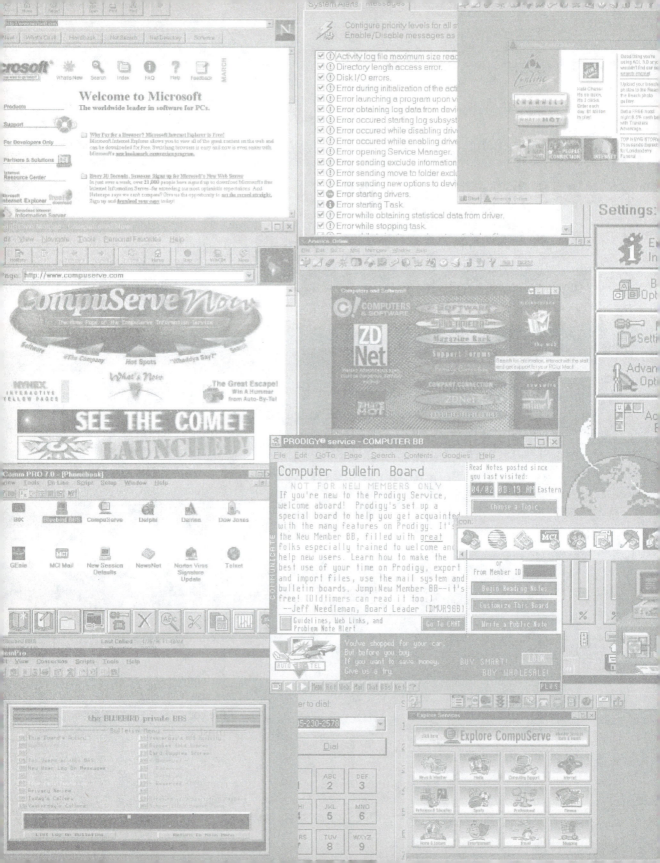

CHAPTER 4

Using Communications Programs

by Robert Bruce Thompson

Just a few years ago, writing a chapter on communications programs would have been very straightforward. General purpose communications programs, like ProComm Plus and Crosstalk, occupied a tightly defined market niche. They used your phone line and modem to establish a dial-up asynchronous connection between your PC and a BBS or a commercial online service, such as CompuServe or GEnie. Once connected, the program shifted to terminal emulation mode and essentially converted your PC to a dumb terminal, allowing you to access character-mode information on the service. The competing products had similar feature sets. One might have a little bit better scripting language support and another might emulate more types of terminals, but there were few really significant differences between the products.

Three things changed all that. First, fax protocols for modems were standardized and became widely supported by industry-standard chip sets, allowing modem manufacturers to build fax capabilities into their modems at little or no incremental cost. Second, the commercial online services began providing proprietary Windows-based graphical client software, and the use of general purpose communications software to access these services accordingly declined precipitously. Third, the advent of the Internet shifted the online focus of many users from BBSes and commercial online services to the Internet in general and the World Wide Web in particular.

In order to sell in volume today, a communications program must attempt to be most things to most people. First, it must still provide the dial up asynchronous terminal emulation functions that traditionally formed the core feature set of a communications software product. Beyond this, it must also offer either full-featured native fax functionality or, alternatively, tight integration with either the fax support built into Windows or with an add-on faxing product of its own. In addition, the importance of the Internet in today's online environment means that a good communications program must, at a minimum, support the Internet File Transfer Protocol (ftp) and Telnet terminal emulation protocols. Many communications software packages go further, bundling clients for the World Wide Web and perhaps for less frequently used Internet services, such as Gopher and Archie. A few continue to focus only on the functions traditionally provided by a general purpose communications program.

This chapter takes a close look at the traditional functions of a general purpose communications program—primarily terminal emulation and file transfer support. The faxing and Internet aspects common to many of today's communications programs are important enough that each has been allocated a chapter of its own. However, the traditional functions of terminal emulation and file transfer are still key factors for many users.

In this chapter, you learn to

- Evaluate the most fundamental feature of a general purpose communications program—how many terminals it emulates and how well

- Evaluate the second most important feature of any communications program—how many file transfer protocols it supports and how efficient they are

- Recognize other important features of communications programs

- Realize when Windows NT HyperTerminal may be all the communications program you need

- Compare three of the major communications programs—Mustang QModemPro, Symantec WinComm Pro, and Quarterdeck ProComm Plus—, and choose which is better for your particular requirements

- Install and configure McAfee VirusScan NT to detect viruses

Communications Program Features

Like other modern applications programs, communications programs have become the victims of "feature bloat." Many of these features serve no useful purpose in routine work. These features are present simply to satisfy the marketing folks' demands for "checklist" features—ones that a purchasing agent may insist on before allowing the product to be purchased. Some features, however, are important. This section looks at the features that make a difference in product usability and convenience.

Terminal Emulation

A sea change in computing occurred in the early 1970s when Digital Equipment Corporation (DEC) introduced a Video Terminal, called the VT-52, with the PDP-8 minicomputer. Video Display Terminals were available before then, but they were essentially "glass teletypes" that simply displayed output on a CRT in much the same way that it would have appeared if sent to a printer.

The VT-52 changed that by placing the display under programmatic control. Where and how characters and other screen elements were displayed could be determined by the program, using non-displayed control codes called *escape sequences*. The VT-52 was the first mainstream terminal to have these capabilities. As often occurs in technology when you're the first to come up with a workable solution, the VT-52 and its descendants became a *de facto* standard. Since then, many competing terminals have evolved, each with its own proprietary set of escape sequences.

The essence of a general purpose communications software program is to emulate a terminal, thus allowing the user to connect to a remote host and perform functions as though he were using a locally connected terminal. It is vital that the communications software provide a high quality emulation of at least one of the terminal types supported by the remote host.

General purpose communications software programs vary in terms of how many and which terminal emulations they support, and in terms of the quality of those emulations, such as how fully the emulated terminal is really imitated. Because terminals are hardware devices with capabilities of their own, not all features of all terminals can be fully emulated on the PC platform.

As a simple example, if a particular terminal has 20 function keys, some accommodation must be made on a PC that has only 12 function keys. This is typically done by using function keys 1 through 10 in conjunction with the Shift key to emulate function keys 11 through 20. How fully and how well such anomalies are accommodated is the mark of a good terminal emulator.

The advent of the graphical Windows environment has made it much easier to provide full terminal emulation. In the past, special hardware capabilities of terminals, such as double-high double-wide characters, were difficult or impossible to replicate exactly on a character-mode PC. Windows and TrueType fonts have made it that much easier to accommodate such differences. Although such things as missing keys can be imitated only imperfectly, a terminal emulator today is much superior to those available a few years ago under DOS.

> **Tip**
>
> Make sure the communications program you choose offers complete flexibility in remapping your keyboard for each supported terminal emulation. Even more useful is the capability to remap the same emulation in different ways for different hosts, that is, remapping by session rather than simply by terminal type.
>
> This means, for example, that if you want to use DEC VT-102 emulation to contact two VAX hosts running different applications, one of which uses PF10 as the "save" key and the other of which uses PF4, you don't have to choose. You can map the VT-102 emulation for the first host to use a specific key as the "save" key, and then remap the VT-102 emulation for the second host to use the same physical key as the "save" key, even though it's sending a different escape sequence.

There are still problems in the way some programs provide terminal emulation, not so much because of technical or hardware limitations as because of poor programming. You might think that one DEC VT-220 emulation would be much like another, and you would be right as long as only the basic terminal functions were being used. When less commonly used features are needed, the comparison breaks down. A good terminal emulator will support these uncommon features and offer you the flexibility to reconfigure the program to fit your exact needs. A poor terminal emulator will do neither.

Take a look at some of the terminal emulations that should be provided by the communications program you choose.

ANSI-BBS

ANSI-BBS, also called BBS-ANSI, or simply ANSI, originated as DEC VT-100 ANSI, but has since evolved to support various enhancements desirable in a BBS environment, including music and color. ANSI-BBS is almost-but-not-quite DEC VT emulation. If you access a BBS with your terminal emulation set to VT-100 or higher emulation, everything will work—almost. You'll see an occasional escape sequence displayed on screen as something like [la][2J, but otherwise the text will be readable. Minor though the differences are, you really want a good ANSI-BBS emulation if you'll be calling BBSes. ANSI-BBS is the standard character-mode emulation used by all BBSes. It is so standardized that nearly any communications package will offer a usable version of it.

Remote Imaging Protocol (RIP)

RIP is the BBS world's answer to graphical user environments like Windows. The slow speed of dial up asynchronous connections realistically limits BBSes to using character mode displays. Transferring Windows graphics would result in unacceptably slow performance. RIP gets around this problem rather cleverly, allowing the use of attractive displays, push buttons, and the mouse. It does so by caching standard large graphics on the local workstation hard drive. When you first contact a new BBS running RIP, any custom graphics files specific to that BBS are transferred to you and stored on your local hard drive. When a graphic is needed for display, instead of being transferred across the slow dial-up link, it is simply loaded from your local disk cache. A RIP screen is shown in figure 4.1.

Fig. 4.1
Remote Imaging Protocol (RIP) graphics provide attractive graphics displays using slow dial up connections.

If contacting BBSes is important to you, make sure your communications program supports RIP graphics. Otherwise, ignore it.

Digital Equipment Corporation VT Series

Since the introduction of the VT-52 in the early 1970's, DEC has continued to update, enhance, and expand the capabilities of the VT series through the VT-1xx, the VT-2xx, the VT-3xx, and finally the VT-4xx. The DEC VT series has become a *de facto* standard, supported on systems ranging from small UNIX hosts to mainframes and supercomputers.

Various terminal types have been offered in the different families, from basic character-mode dumb terminals to intelligent graphics terminals. If you're operating in a DEC environment, the finer distinctions among these various close relatives may be important to you. Otherwise, make sure your communications software supports, at a minimum, DEC VT-52, VT-100, or VT-102 and VT-220 emulations.

Although most communications programs provide several DEC VT emulations, the quality of these emulations varies greatly. Some relatively unknown and free products provide better emulations than the big-name products. For example, early versions of ProComm Plus had deficient DEC VT emulations out of the box, while the free Kermit program offered superior emulation. If DEC VT emulation is important to you, test programs for the completeness of their emulations before you standardize on them. Don't make any assumptions.

Other Emulations

Most communications programs offer numerous other terminal emulations, including models from IBM, Televideo, ADM, and Wyse. Again, unless you have a specific application that requires one of these emulations, their presence or absence is immaterial to selecting a communications program. If you do require a particular emulation, verify that the emulation is nominally provided by the communications software you are considering, and that the implementation provided by that software includes the features you need.

File Transfer Protocols

File transfer protocols are sets of rules that are used to allow two computer systems to transfer files between them, regardless of what type of computer system is doing the sending and what type is receiving. File transfer protocols are used to detect and correct transmission errors when uploading and downloading files, and to format the data correctly for the receiving system. The concept of file transfer protocols originated back when modems had no error detection and correction built-in, and it was up to the communications program to make sure the file arrived without being corrupted. Both the transmitting and receiving computer systems must be running the same file transfer protocol in order to transfer files successfully.

File transfer protocols perform their function by first breaking the file to be sent into equal-size blocks. The transmitting program performs a *checksum* or *cyclic redundancy check (CRC)* calculation on each block and appends the result to that block. When a block arrives at the destination, the recipient does the same calculation against the received data block and compares the result against the received checksum or CRC. If the results differ, the program assumes that the data block has been corrupted in transmission and requests that it be re-sent.

The high speed of modems today pushes the envelope insofar as how fast it is possible to transfer data across an asynchronous dial-up link. As a result, if it is to be usable at all, any modem that operates at v.32bis (14,400 kbps) or higher must include native error correction, usually in conjunction with data compression.

A few years ago, a battle for dominance in modem hardware error correction and data compression occurred. On one side was the CCITT, with the v.42 error correction protocol and the v.42bis data compression protocol; on the other side was Microcom, with its Microcom Networking Protocol (MNP) series of protocols. This battle is over, and the CCITT standards won. Any mainstream modem you buy today will include CCITT (now called ITU-T), v.42 error detection, and v.42bis data compression. The MNP series of standards has been pretty much relegated to specialty applications like cellular data transmission.

Because all modems now have error detection and correction built-in, it might seem at first glance that using a file transfer protocol would be superfluous. After all, why use software to accomplish something that your hardware is already doing? In fact, file transfer protocols are just as necessary as they always were, although their emphasis has shifted somewhat. They're still needed to break the file into blocks and to take care of the administrative functions needed to actually get the file from the transmitting computer to the recipient. Take a look at some of the basic concepts of file transfer protocols.

Understanding File Transfer Protocol Concepts

Although file transfer protocols vary greatly in features and performance, many of them have several general concepts in common. Some perform similar functions in different ways. The following are some of their similarities and differences:

- *Block Size.* Before a file can be transferred, it must first be broken down into equal size chunks. This is done for administrative and error-correction reasons. After all, you wouldn't want to send a 5M file as a single chunk only to have the recipient turn around and tell you there had been an error in one byte and that the whole file therefore needed to be resent.

  In general, the larger the block size, the more efficient the transfer, because calculating the checksum or CRC and performing other administrative tasks is done less frequently with larger blocks. However, on a noisy line larger block sizes can actually be less efficient; if an error occurs, the entire block must be resent. Different protocols use different block sizes. The Zmodem protocol can use block sizes of 8K or greater. Older protocols like Xmodem and Kermit use block sizes of 128 bytes or less.

Older and less sophisticated file transfer protocols, like Xmodem, use a fixed block size. Newer and more sophisticated file transfer protocols, like Zmodem, can vary block size dynamically, increasing it when line conditions are good and decreasing it as they detect noise on the line.

■ *Windowing and Streaming.* Early file transfer protocols, like Xmodem, worked sequentially. The sender assembled the first block, calculated and appended the checksum or CRC, and sent the block to the recipient. The recipient verified that this first block had been received correctly, and then sent an acknowledgment (ACK) to the sender. Only when it received this acknowledgment did the sender transmit the following block. Although this process worked, it was extremely inefficient. Streaming and Windowing are two methods used to greatly reduce the latency involved in the sequential transfer and verification method.

   • *Windowing (or Sliding Windows).* Allows the sender to transmit multiple blocks before receiving an acknowledgment from the recipient. The number of blocks that can be sent without receiving an ACK is called the *window size*. Because each block is numbered and therefore identifiable by both sender and recipient, the recipient can verify blocks as it has time to do so, and can request that any numbered block be retransmitted if necessary. This means that under a windowing scheme, blocks may be transmitted out of order. If the sender has sent as many blocks as are allowed by the Window Size without receiving an ACK from the recipient, it pauses until an ACK is received.

   • *Streaming.* Like windowing, this allows the sender to transmit multiple blocks without receiving an ACK. The difference is that with streaming, the sender assumes that everything is working correctly, and continues to send blocks until the recipient tells it otherwise. The recipient notifies the sender only if a problem occurs. As with windowing, blocks are numbered to allow the recipient to request that a specific block be resent if needed.

■ *Duplex.* Older file transfer protocols are half-duplex, meaning that data transmission occurs in only one direction at a time. This means that each time the sender finishes sending a block, it then switches into receive mode to allow the recipient to acknowledge that block. This process is very inefficient, and greatly slows data transfers. Newer protocols are full duplex, meaning that either station can transmit data at any time.

- *Batch Mode.* Most file transfer protocols allow you to send only a single file at a time. If you need to send 10 files, you must do so as 10 separate transfers. Some protocols support *batch mode*, which allows you to send two or more files in a single step.

Understanding File Transfer Protocol Types

There are a bewildering array of file transfer protocols available in most general purpose communications programs.

The Xmodem Family. In the late 1970's, the first BBS was brought up to allow computer hobbyists to connect their home-built systems to share information. Even in those days, when a 300 bps modem was a rare and expensive piece of equipment, the need to transfer files made it obvious that some form of file transfer protocol was needed. Ward Cristensen started it all by writing the Xmodem protocol. Since then, Xmodem has been extended, enhanced, and renamed, with the newly-developed variants of it being called Ymodem and Zmodem.

XModem. The original Xmodem protocol is a single-file, half-duplex protocol that uses 128 byte blocks and a 1-byte checksum. Despite its age and inefficiency, Xmodem remains useful today as a least common denominator. Almost any system you're likely to contact supports it, meaning that it can be used as a last resort if your system and the remote host have no other file transfer protocols in common. It's slow and inefficient, but it will get the job done.

The first major enhancement made to Xmodem, called Xmodem-CRC, substituted the use of a cyclic redundancy check (CRC) for the checksum error detection method used by the original implementation. CRC is a much more robust method of detecting errors, and should be used in preference to checksum when available. Most Xmodem implementations can successfully determine when CRC is available at the far end, and negotiate its use between them. However, some Xmodem implementations that don't support CRC choke on the request to use CRC and require that you manually specify Xmodem on your end rather than allowing negotiation to occur.

As the quality of telephone lines and modems improved, it became obvious that the 128-byte block used by the original Xmodem implementation was a serious impediment to throughput. The next enhancement to Xmodem was to increase its block size to 1,024 bytes. This version, called *Xmodem-1K* or *1K-Xmodem*, is often incorrectly referred to by some communications programs and BBS software as Ymodem. Like standard Xmodem, Xmodem-1K is a single file, half-duplex protocol.

> **Tip**
>
> If you have problems transferring a file from a BBS after specifying Ymodem on the BBS side and on your communications software, try choosing Ymodem on the BBS and Xmodem-1K on your end.

As modems further improved and began to incorporate hardware error detection and correction, Xmodem was again enhanced. Because adding software error detection and correction to a transfer that's already running on a link that uses hardware error detection and correction can actually slow throughput, 1K-Xmodem-G eliminates software error detection and correction entirely. 1K-Xmodem-G is a streaming single-file protocol.

> **Caution**
>
> Like other file transfer protocols that don't provide error detection and correction, 1K-Xmodem-G is intended for use only with modems that provide hardware error detection and correction. Attempting to use 1K-Xmodem-G and similar protocols on a link without such hardware error detection and correction will result in transferred files being corrupted. Although any modem that runs at v.32 9,600 bps or above is capable of providing hardware error detection and correction, your link may not have negotiated such protection. Do not use these protocols unless you are certain that hardware error detection and correction is in use.

Ymodem. The next step in the evolution of Xmodem was the development of Ymodem. Ymodem is similar to 1K-Xmodem, using 1,024 byte blocks. It differs in that it is a batch mode protocol, meaning that multiple files can be sent in a single step. Like 1K-Xmodem-G, Ymodem-G is simply a non-error corrected version of the main protocol that's intended for use with error correcting modems.

> **Tip**
>
> If your system and the remote system have only the Xmodem and Ymodem protocols in common, choose any variant of Ymodem in preference to any variant of Xmodem. Although the advantage may not be great, particularly if you're transferring only a single file, true Ymodem implementations are typically somewhat more efficient at transferring data.

Zmodem. The final enhancement to the Xmodem family of protocols came when Chuck Forsberg of Omen Technologies created Zmodem under contract with the Telenet packing switching service. Telenet was concerned because the delays inherent in packet switching caused timing problems for the existing Xmodem and Ymodem protocols. They commissioned Forsberg to write an improved Xmodem family protocol, and then placed the resulting Zmodem protocol in the public domain.

Zmodem is certainly the last protocol in the Xmodem family alphabetically, and is probably the last in terms of features and function. Forsberg did a superb job with Zmodem, incorporating numerous new features and enhancements to existing ones. Zmodem is a very efficient, full-duplex batch-mode protocol. It supports windowing and streaming. Unlike many earlier protocols, it sends information about file attributes to the receiving station, including file name, file size, and date/time stamp information. One of the nicest features of Zmodem is called *crash recovery*. With older protocols, when a transfer failed, you had to restart the transfer from the beginning of the file. With Zmodem running in crash recovery mode, a failed transfer can be restarted from the point where it failed, thus eliminating the need to resend all of the data that had already been received successfully.

Tip

Due to the foresight of Telenet in releasing the Zmodem protocol specification into the public domain, implementations of Zmodem are available on nearly every platform, including UNIX and DEC VAX/VMS. Zmodem is also the standard protocol on nearly all BBSes. If your system and the remote host support Zmodem, choose it in preference to any other protocol. It's the fastest and most robust protocol available.

Kermit. Kermit was developed by Frank da Cruz at Columbia University and released into the public domain. The original version has been enhanced with the addition of sliding windows and long block lengths, but Kermit remains one of the slowest protocols available. That said, it's also essential to have on your system.

Like Xmodem, one real advantage of Kermit is its ubiquity. Implementations of Kermit are available on any system, from a long obsolete CP/M micro to the largest supercomputers. The second unique strength of Kermit is its flexibility. Because it was designed with the intention of allowing file transfers between unlike systems, Kermit is the protocol most likely to work. It may work slowly, but it does work. The same can't be said for the alternatives. The third advantage of Kermit is that it's designed to allow 8-bit binary files to be sent across 7-bit connections. Kermit uses a technique called *eighth bit quoting* to convert bytes with a significant high-order bit into a 7-bit form for transmission.

> **Tip**
>
> Use Kermit only as a protocol of last resort. If you need to transfer a file from a mainframe or a minicomputer, Kermit may be the only common protocol. Similarly, if you have to transfer a binary file across a 7-bit connection, Kermit will do it for you when others can't.

By the way, in case you were wondering, Kermit was named after Jim Henson's famous frog. It isn't easy being green.

CompuServe Quick-B (CIS-B) and Quick-B+ (CIS-B+) Protocols. In the early days of CompuServe, it became obvious that the Xmodem and Ymodem protocols then dominant on BBSes had some severe drawbacks when used on the CIS packet switching network. Both Xmodem variants were designed for use on standard asynchronous dial up connections, and neither accommodated the delays inherent in a packet switched network particularly well. Zmodem was still in the future, so CompuServe came up with their own proprietary protocol, designed for the exigencies of packet switched data transfers.

CIS-B+ is the native file transfer protocol for CompuServe; it's used there and nowhere else. Most general purpose communications software packages support CIS-B and/or CIS-B+ simply because, in the days before CompuServe introduced its own graphical front end software, the service was typically accessed with a general purpose communications software program. That they continue to provide CIS-B support in newer versions is probably due as much to inertia as anything else, although a few users do continue to access CompuServe in character mode with standard communications programs.

Specialized File Transfer Protocols. The protocols discussed previously are general purpose protocols that are intended to transfer files between systems of varying types. Various special-purpose file transfer protocols exist, which are tightly focused on providing file transfers to and from one particular type of system, typically a mainframe or another system that offers no flexibility.

For example, the IND$FILE is used exclusively to transfer files to and from IBM mainframes and minicomputers. It's a rather primitive protocol, offering throughput and functionality similar to that of Xmodem. IND$FILE is indispensable however, because it provides specialized functions to allow you to control the functioning of supporting hardware, like protocol converters.

If you need to transfer files to and from a mainframe or you need to accommodate the needs of a remote host, make sure the communications software you select supports the protocol you need. Otherwise, you can ignore these specialized file transfer protocols.

Propriety and Standalone File Transfer Protocols. Many general purpose communications programs that have been around for a long time offer their own proprietary file transfer protocols. These protocols were originally written simply as a means of getting around the limitations of Xmodem and other early protocols. The arrival of Zmodem, Kermit, and other widely supported enhanced protocols made these proprietary protocols functionally obsolete. However, they continue to be provided with later versions of communications software simply for backward compatibility.

Another fad that flourished for a while, particularly in the BBS environment, was the proliferation of stand-alone file transfer protocols. Because BBS software and general purpose communications software typically used to access these BBSes made it easy to add external file transfer protocols, it seemed as though there was a new and improved external file transfer protocol popping up about once a month. Some of these protocols made true improvements to the state of the art, but none of them offered enough of an advantage over Zmodem or was widely supported enough to become a standard.

Choosing File Transfer Protocols

Most general purpose communications software programs offer a choice of many file transfer protocols. You can safely ignore most of these, but make sure the program you choose provides at least the following:

- *Zmodem* for everyday general usage. Set Zmodem as the default protocol in your communications program, and always use it when available in preference to any other protocol.

- *Xmodem* as a least common denominator to ensure that you can always transfer files to and from any PC-based remote host, however old and obsolete the communications software running on it. Ymodem is also worth having, but having Xmodem available is essential, although you may never have to use it.

- *Kermit* as another least common denominator, and for transferring files to and from mainframes and other systems with unusual requirements.

- *Specialized protocols* as required by your particular situation.

II

Dialup Communications

Scripting

A scripting language is included with any full-featured communications program. Originating as simple macro processors, these scripting languages have evolved into full-fledged programming languages that offer most of the power and flexibility of a standard general-purpose programming language, such as BASIC or C. Although some communications programs depend on runtime interpreters to execute their scripts, many include compilers that allow the script source code to be compiled into p-code for subsequent running. This offers faster execution of the scripts, and an added measure of security by concealing passwords and other account information from casual prying eyes.

A comprehensive scripting language is primarily useful in a corporate environment, where the MIS department may want to develop custom communications applications using the scripting language provided by their standard communications software package. Few ordinary users will write a script for their communications program, and most will never edit a previously written script.

One aspect of scripting can be of use to ordinary users, however, and that is the capability of a good communications program to generate its own script files based on keystrokes entered by the user. This feature, generically referred to as *learning mode*, allows the user to activate it and then log on to a host while the communications program captures the information typed by the user and the responses received from the remote host.

The resulting automatically generated script can then be stored and invoked the next time the user wants to log on to that host, thus eliminating the need to re-enter the account information each time. Here is an example of a script file automatically generated by ProComm Plus.

```
proc main
    waitfor "color graphics? [y/n]"
    transmit "y^M"
    waitfor "available?"
    transmit "y^M"
    waitfor "FIRST name:"
    transmit "john^M"
    waitfor "LAST name:"
    transmit "doe^M"
    waitfor "John Doe?"
    transmit "y^M"
    waitfor "Password:"
    transmit "doejohn^M"
    waitfor "bypass the logon bulletins?"
    transmit "n^M"
    waitfor "More? [Y/n/ns] "
    transmit "n^M"
endproc
```

Other Program Features

Communications programs provide a host of other features, some of which are useful to most users on a day-to-day basis, and others that have specialized purposes that will be of interest to only some users. The following sections take a short look at some of these features and how they might be important to you.

Dialing Directory

The *dialing directory* concept, pioneered by Datastorm's ProComm and subsequently adopted by nearly every communication program on the market, provides a consolidated screen that displays each of your destination hosts or sessions as an individual phonebook entry (see fig. 4.2). Although in today's Windows environment, individual icons for each session may take the place of a tabular display, the concept remains the same. You can view numerous sessions at a glance and select a specific session to learn more about its properties. Dialing a particular destination is as simple as double-clicking the corresponding icon or table entry.

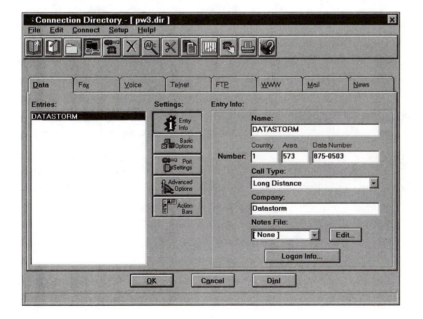

Fig. 4.2
ProComm Plus Connection Directory.

Each entry includes specific information about a particular session, including the phone number, communications parameters, terminal emulation, default file transfer protocol, and so on. It may also include data about when you last connected to this site, the total time you have spent online with it, and so on.

A good communications program makes it easy to create a new entry in the dialing directory, depending on stored default parameters for much of its information. For example, if you create a new entry for a BBS, chances are you want to use ANSI-BBS terminal emulation and Zmodem file transfer.

Telephony Application Programming Interface (TAPI)

Anyone who has worked much with Windows 3.1*x* communications knows about the problems that resulted from trying to share a single communications resource, such as a modem or a phone line, between two or more applications. The architecture of Windows 3.1*x* made such sharing difficult or impossible. If, for example, you had WinFax Pro running minimized to receive faxes but wanted to make a quick call with ProComm Plus to check your e-mail, you first had to exit WinFax before ProComm Plus could use the comm port.

With Windows 95 and Windows NT 4.0, Microsoft has addressed these problems by introducing TAPI. *TAPI* allows multiple applications to gracefully share a single comm port, modem, and telephone line. All of the communications applets included in Windows NT are TAPI-enabled, as are many third-party communications applications. Applications that are not TAPI-compliant continue to behave as they did under Windows 3.1*x*, seizing the comm port and refusing while they're running to release it for use by other applications.

Vendors have taken two approaches to the issue of sharing communications resources. Some products, such as Mustang's QModemPro and Symantec's WinComm Pro, are TAPI-enabled. These products co-exist well with each other and with the applets bundled with Windows NT. Other products, like Quarterdeck's ProComm Plus, instead of providing TAPI compliance to allow other products to co-exist peacefully, simply provide all the communications functions they think you need in a single program, rendering port contention a non-issue.

In the long run, TAPI compliance may become an important issue, as voice functions as well as fax and data are integrated. In the short run, if you find an all-in-one product that does everything you need to do, TAPI shouldn't be a concern for you.

Session Log

Most communications programs keep a session log, which you can examine to find which hosts you connected to, when, and for how long. Some programs can provide a very detailed log, including information about the names and sizes of files you uploaded or downloaded, the time required, and the efficiency to do so. The original purpose of these logs was to allow users of BBSes to rectify their long distance bills and for users of commercial online services, like CompuServe, to verify that they were not being charged for time they had not incurred. Session logs aren't that important to most users any more, but there are times when having one available is useful.

Scroll Back Buffer

A good terminal emulation program differs from a real terminal in at least one respect. With the real terminal, when data scrolls off the screen it is gone forever. With the terminal emulation program, the data is stored temporarily in a buffer. You can return to it as needed for viewing. When the amount of received data exceeds the size of the buffer, the data is replaced on a first-in-first-out basis. Any competent communications program will provide such a buffer. A good one will allow you to specify the size of the buffer to fit your needs.

Capture to File or Printer

Most communications programs allow you to capture an entire session to either a disk file or to the printer. This can be particularly useful the first time you access a BBS or online service, by allowing you to capture new user tips, policy statements, and other information for subsequent perusal offline. It can also be very useful if you find yourself using an expensive online search service, such as Dialog, for research. Instead of trying to read and remember information while paying a dollar a minute or more, you can simply dump it to a disk file or to the printer and read it later.

Host Mode

Some communications programs, particularly those that originated in a BBS environment, offer a *host mode*, which is a kind of mini-BBS. Host mode allows your computer to serve as a BBS, answering the phone and allowing users to log in, read mail, transfer files, and so on. Although you probably wouldn't want to use host mode to run a real BBS, it can be a lifesaver in special circumstances. For example, if you need to transfer a file to a coworker in another office, you might simply bring up host mode. He then calls your temporary mini-BBS, transfers the file, and logs off.

Network Support

Other than at large corporations who have the staff and technical resources to support modem sharing on a network, the rule of thumb is still pretty much that each user who needs asynchronous dial up communications gets a modem and a phone line. Still, a good communications program will at least be network aware. If modem sharing on the network is or may become an issue for you, look for support for Int14, NCSI/NASI, and NetBIOS.

Multiple Site Support

Notebook computers have become ubiquitous, and no computer is more likely to have communications software installed than a notebook. A desktop system is unlikely to be moved. A call placed to a given host will always originate from the same location on a desktop system. Notebooks, on the other hand, move around a lot. You may call a given host from your office one day, from your home that evening, and from a hotel room next week.

The best communications software packages realize that a static originating location is a thing of the past for many users. They make provision for differing originating locations, allowing you to use the same dialing directory entry to contact a given host wherever you may be calling from. If you designate your present site as being your office, for example, the program knows to prepend a 9, to get an outside line. At home you don't have to dial 9 to get an outside line—well, most of us don't—so when you designate your present site as being at home, the program doesn't prepend the 9,.

If you do a lot of dial up calling, and do so from differing locations, make sure the program you choose has strong support for multiple sites.

Choosing a Communications Program

Choosing a communications program, like choosing any other software, is highly personal. There are a variety of products available for Windows NT Workstation, ranging from simple programs with few advanced features to powerhouses with every feature imaginable. With power comes added complexity, however. If you're a casual or infrequent user of communications software, you may well be better off with a simpler product.

The following sections examine four excellent communications programs, each of which occupies its own niche on the continuum from simplicity to power. These programs are:

- *HyperTerminal* is bundled with Windows NT 4.0 Workstation, and provides a competent, if minimalist, communications program. It offers a useful assortment of terminal emulations, including VT100 and ANSI. Supported file transfer protocols include Xmodem, Ymodem, Zmodem, and Kermit. You won't find any support for fancy scripting and other bells and whistles, but if you're a casual user of asynchronous dial up communications, HyperTerminal may be all you need.

- *QmodemPro*, by Mustang Software, is a communications program in the traditional mold. Qmodem originated in the BBS environment, and it shows. You won't find things like built-in faxing, and support for the Internet is limited. What you will find is competent scripting, support for a variety of terminal emulations and file transfer protocols, and numerous features designed to ease the time you spend online with BBSes and online services. If HyperTerminal is a bit short in features for your needs, consider QmodemPro as the next step up.

■ *WinComm Pro*, by Symantec, is mid-way between QModemPro and ProComm Plus in terms of features and functions. It's available as a standalone product or as a tightly integrated part of the Symantec/ Delrina CommSuite, which includes the popular WinFax Pro software and Cyberjack Internet Suite. As a standalone communications package, WinComm Pro offers you more choices, more power, and more flexibility than QmodemPro, but fewer than ProComm Plus. It manages to conceal enough power to satisfy almost any user behind a friendly, uncluttered interface that won't intimidate beginners.

■ *ProComm Plus*, by Quarterdeck, wants to be the only communications package you'll ever need. In addition to providing a full—some would say overwhelming—complement of traditional communications package features, ProComm Plus incorporates an excellent fax package and a full set of Internet tools, including Internet mail, a news reader, clients for ftp, Telnet and Gopher, a Winsock compliant TCP/IP stack of its own, and even a Web browser. ProComm Plus is the industrial strength package. It does an amazingly good job of fitting all of these functions into a usable interface, but the result is still more likely to intimidate beginners and casual users than the other packages.

Windows NT HyperTerminal

Windows NT HyperTerminal, shown in figure 4.3, takes the refreshing approach of trying to be most things to most users, without falling into the trap of throwing in everything but the kitchen sink in an attempt to satisfy everyone. You won't find a huge assortment of terminal emulations or file transfer protocols in HyperTerminal, but those you do find are the half dozen most likely to be used by most people. You'll also find a few features that might surprise you, such as support for multiple sites.

The upside of this limited functionality is ease of use. Because there are few choices to be made, almost anyone can get comfortable using HyperTerminal in a very short time. You can't beat the cost, either. It comes bundled with Windows NT. Windows NT HyperTerminal is a trimmed down version of Hilgraeve's HyperAccess. Although the 32-bit version of HyperAccess was not available for review in time for this book, it may well be available by the time you read this.

Fig. 4.3
Windows NT
HyperTerminal.

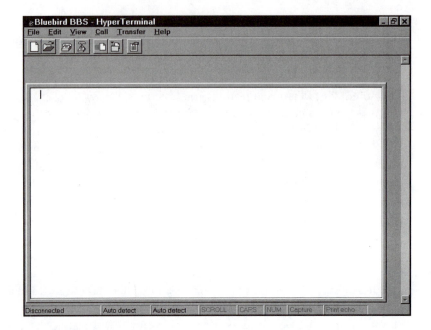

Mustang QModemPro

QmodemPro, shown in figure 4.4, is a communications package from the old school dressed up with a modern face and support for Windows services and standards like OLE, MAPI, and TAPI. QmodemPro comes from the BBS world, and it shows. Everything about this product focuses purely on asynchronous dial up communications.

The QModemPro dialing directory, shown in figure 4.5, is called the *Phonebook* and uses Windows 95/NT conventions. Each entry is represented with an icon. You can store five telephone numbers for each entry, along with account information (such as username and password). Data, Telnet, and voice entries can share the same phonebook.

QmodemPro provides decent script language support, although it doesn't have the power or the flexibility of the ProComm Plus ASPECT script language. For those who want to write complex applications in QmodemPro script, the SLIQ (Script Language Interface for Qmodem) language offers most of the tools needed, including a compiler and debugger. The language itself is similar to BASIC in vocabulary, syntax, and power.

The Quicklearn script recorder can be used easily, even by a beginner, to automate logons. Using it is a simple matter of defining a name for the script and then logging on normally. QModemPro automatically switches to Quicklearn mode, records your keystrokes as you log on, and then creates a script to automate future logons.

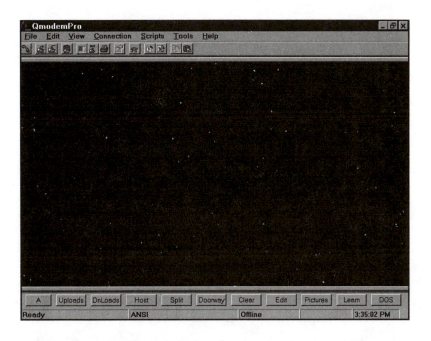

Fig. 4.4
QModemPro
terminal screen.

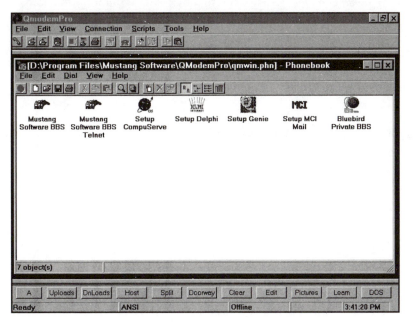

Fig. 4.5
QmodemPro
dialing directory
(Phonebook).

QmodemPro supports three important Windows standards:

■ *MAPI (Mail Application Programming Interface).* Allows you to transfer text, images, and files from QmodemPro to other MAPI-enabled applications, like Windows Messaging or IBM/Lotus Notes.

- *TAPI (Telephony Application Programming Interface).* Allows QmodemPro to share a modem with other TAPI-compliant applications. This means, for example, that you can run QmodemPro simultaneously with Exchange FAX or the Remote Access Service without conflict.

- *OLE (Object Linking and Embedding) 2.0.* You can use drag and drop within your communications sessions. You can create shortcuts to frequently called phonebook entries simply by dragging them to the desktop and dropping them. Similarly, while a QmodemPro session is active, you can transfer files simply by highlighting them in NT Explorer, dragging them to QmodemPro, and dropping them into the file transfer window.

Internet support in QmodemPro is limited to a Telnet client, but that client allows you to use most of the features of QmodemPro, including terminal emulation, file transfer protocols, macros, and scripting when you Telnet in to a remote host or BBS. In essence, you can continue to use QmodemPro, but on a Telnet connection rather than a dial up one. QmodemPro supports the RSA MD5 Message Digest Algorithm for security.

- *Terminal Emulations.* QmodemPro provides 35 terminal emulations, including:

  ADDS VP60

  ADM3A

  ANSI

  Avatar

  DEC VT52, VT 100, VT 102, VT 220, and VT 320

  Debug ASCII

  DebugHEX

  Data General DG 100, 200, and 210

  Hazeltine 1500

  Heath 19

  IBM 3101 and 3270

  RIPscrip

  TTY

  Televideo TVI 910, 912, 922, 925, 950, and 955

  Vidtex

  Wyse 30, 50, 60, 75, 85, 100, and 185

■ *File Transfer Protocols.* QmodemPro provides 10 file transfer protocols, including:

ASCII

CompuServe B+

Kermit

Xmodem (checksum and CRC)

Xmodem-1K

Xmodem-G

Ymodem

Ymodem-G

Zmodem

Installing QmodemPro

QmodemPro uses a standard Windows setup routine, including a Setup Wizard to guide you through the installation procedure. After entering your name, company, and serial number, you are given the opportunity to select the main installation directory, which defaults to C:\Program Files\Mustang Software\QModemPro\.

You then select the Setup Type you prefer, choosing Typical Installation, Compact Installation, or Custom Installation. Because a full installation of QmodemPro requires only about 6M of disk space, it is usually better to simply install the whole program. You are then prompted to select a program group, with setup defaulting to creating a new group named QmodemPro for Windows 95. You may also add QmodemPro to an existing program group. As you continue through setup, you next select the default modem to be used by QmodemPro, enter your telephone area code, and select your country code. When you have entered this information, the program files are copied to the destination directory and QmodemPro setup completes the installation.

QmodemPro may be uninstalled by using Add/Remove Programs in the Control Panel.

Creating a New Phonebook Entry with QmodemPro

Creating a new dialing directory entry in QmodemPro is a simple matter of right-clicking in the dialing directory, and choosing New. The Add Phonebook Entry dialog box appears, as shown in figure 4.6, with three tabbed pages allowing you to supply the information required to create the new entry. The Connection tab allows you to enter general information about the connection—name, primary telephone number, alternate telephone numbers, connection type, and so on.

II

Dialup Communications

Fig. 4.6
The Add
Phonebook Entry
dialog box allows
you to supply
information to
create the new
entry.

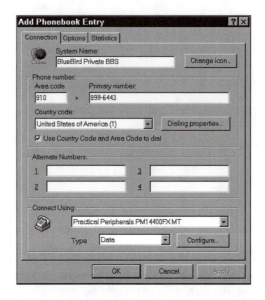

The Options tab, shown in figure 4.7, allows you to enter information about the terminal emulation and file transfer protocols to be used for this connection, your account information, the script to be used, and so on.

Fig. 4.7
Enter information
about the terminal
emulation here.

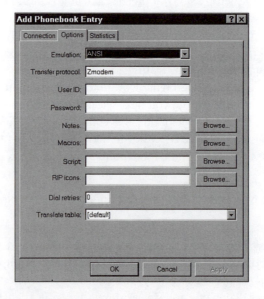

The Statistics tab, shown in figure 4.8, displays information about the date, time, and duration of your last connection to this host; the total number of files you have uploaded and downloaded; and the total number of times you have connected.

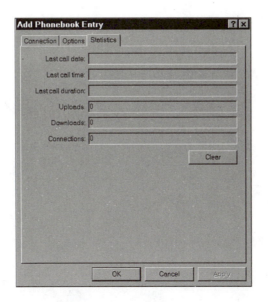

Fig. 4.8
The Statistics page displays date, time, and duration.

Using QmodemPro to Make a Connection

Using QmodemPro to connect to a remote host is as easy as double-clicking an icon in the dialing directory. The dialing directory is replaced by the terminal screen. The Dialer dialog box, shown in figure 4.9, displays call progress, history, and dialing status while the connection is being made.

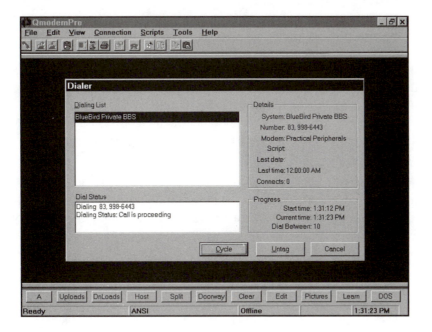

Fig. 4.9
QmodemPro Dialer.

II

Dialup Communications

After the connection is made, the Dialer dialog box closes and you are left with a very clean terminal mode screen, shown in figure 4.10.

Fig. 4.10
QmodemPro is online with Bluebird BBS.

Symantec WinComm Pro

WinComm Pro, shown in figure 4.11, is one of the three or four best general purpose communications programs on the market. WinComm Pro is available either as a standalone product or as part of the Delrina CommSuite 95, which also includes the WinFax Pro fax software and the CyberJack Internet Suite. Delrina was recently acquired by Symantec Corporation, so by the time you read this the product will probably be relabeled as a Symantec product. If WinComm Pro looks familiar the first time you fire it up, it's because it and Windows NT HyperTerminal both derive from the Hilgraeve HyperAccess communications software.

WinComm Pro offers a clean, uncluttered interface that makes it easy for beginners and casual users to get the job done without worrying about the underlying details. At the same time, a lot of power lurks behind the pretty face. Advanced users will find that WinComm Pro offers most or all of the configuration options they need, albeit perhaps buried several layers down.

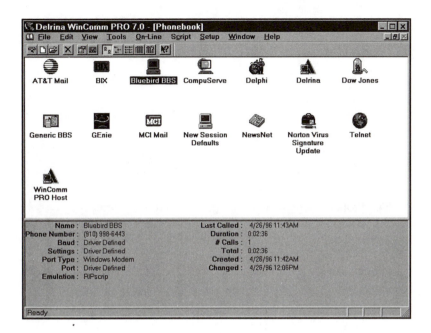

Fig. 4.11
WinComm Pro
main screen.

WinComm Pro provides all of the amenities you expect from a high-end general purpose communications program. It includes a comprehensive scripting language. Scripts may be compiled for faster execution. It provides a reasonably wide selection of terminal emulations, including RIPScript. You'll also find all the file transfer protocols you're likely to need, including good implementations of Zmodem and Kermit. WinComm Pro is TAPI-compliant, so you can use it simultaneously with other TAPI-compliant applications, including all of the communications applets included with Windows NT Workstation.

■ *Terminal Emulations.* WinComm Pro provides a reasonably large selection of terminal emulations, although not as extensive a list as QModemPro or ProComm Plus. The most notable omission is the lack of any support for the popular Wyse series of terminals that are commonly used on UNIX systems. Available emulations include:

ADM3A

ANSI

CompuServe

DEC VT52, VT 100, VT 102, VT 220, and VT 320

IBM 3101 and 3278

RENX 3278

RIPscrip

TTY

Televideo TVI 925 and 950

Wang

- *File Transfer Protocols.* WinComm Pro provides a reasonable selection of file transfer protocols, although again not as extensive a list as either QmodemPro or ProComm Plus. The most surprising holes are the absence of either ASCII or CompuServe B+ protocols. Available file transfer protocols include:

HyperProtocol (a proprietary Hilgraeve file transfer protocol)

Kermit

Xmodem

Xmodem-1K

Ymodem

Ymodem-G

Zmodem

Installing WinComm Pro

WinComm Pro uses a standard Windows setup routine, including a Setup Wizard to guide you through the process. After accepting the license agreement and entering your name, company, and serial number, you are given the opportunity to choose one of the following installation types:

- *Typical Installation.* Installs WinComm Pro 7.0, the Delrina Image Manager, the Delrina Zip Manager, and the default phone book entries, requiring about 15M of disk space.
- *Compact Installation.* Installs only WinComm Pro 7.0, and requires about 11M of disk space.
- *Custom Installation.* Installs only the components you select.

After you choose an installation type, the setup program first checks to make sure there's enough available disk space to install the files you select. It then prompts for the main and subsidiary installation directories, defaulting to C:\Program Files\Delrina\WinComm\.

If you chose to install Delrina Image Manager, you are then asked whether you want to use it as the default program to handle JPG and GIF image files. Similarly, if you install Delrina Zip Manager you may choose whether or not you would like it to be used to handle all ZIP files.

> **Caution**
>
> Selecting yes during installation of Delrina Image Manager sets these programs as the default for handling their respective file types by creating a file extension association in the Registry. This means that all files with the extension JPG or GIF will be handled by the Delrina Image Manager by default and that all ZIP files will be handled by Delrina Zip Manager.
>
> Although both of these programs are reasonably competent at what they do, you might not want to do this. WinZIP, for example, is a much better choice for handling ZIP files and LView Pro is superior for handling JPG and GIF files.

You are then asked to complete the Dialing Preferences dialog box, shown in figure 4.12. Enter information about your telephone number, prefixes and suffixes needed to access an outside line, long distance service, international calling, and so on.

Fig. 4.12
WinComm Pro dialing preferences.

After you complete this step, you then select a modem from a list of installed modems or you install a new modem. Specify the program group to which the WinComm programs will be added, with the default being WinComm Pro 7.0. As a final step, you are given the option to complete an online registration process. The WinComm Pro files are then installed and the setup program configures your system.

You can uninstall WinComm Pro using Add/Remove Programs in the Control Panel.

Creating a New Phonebook Entry with WinComm Pro

WinComm Pro is centered on its dialing directory, called the *Phonebook*, shown in figure 4.13. Phonebook entries, called *Sessions*, are represented by individual icons.

Fig. 4.13
WinComm Pro Phonebook.

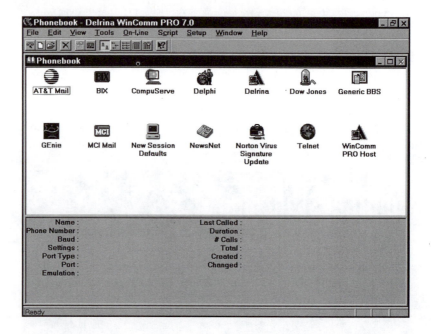

To create a new entry, choose File, New to open the New Session Wizard. You are prompted to enter the Session Name and Telephone Number, as shown in figure 4.14.

Fig. 4.14
Enter session name and telephone number.

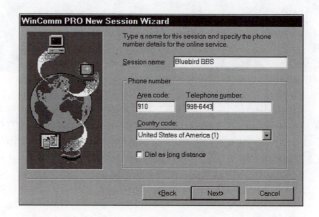

You are then prompted for the <u>C</u>onnection type and <u>T</u>erminal emulation to be used, shown in figure 4.15.

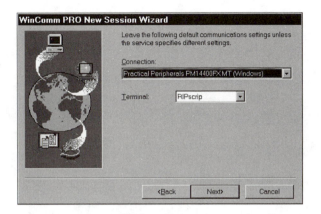

Fig. 4.15
Specify connection type and terminal emulation.

After you do so, the new Session appears as an icon in the Phonebook.

Modifying Session Properties

Right-click a session icon and choose <u>P</u>roperties to modify any of the parameters associated with that session. The Session Properties dialog box includes seven tabs, which between them control all aspects of the selected session.

The General tab, shown in figure 4.16, allows you to modify destination and user information.

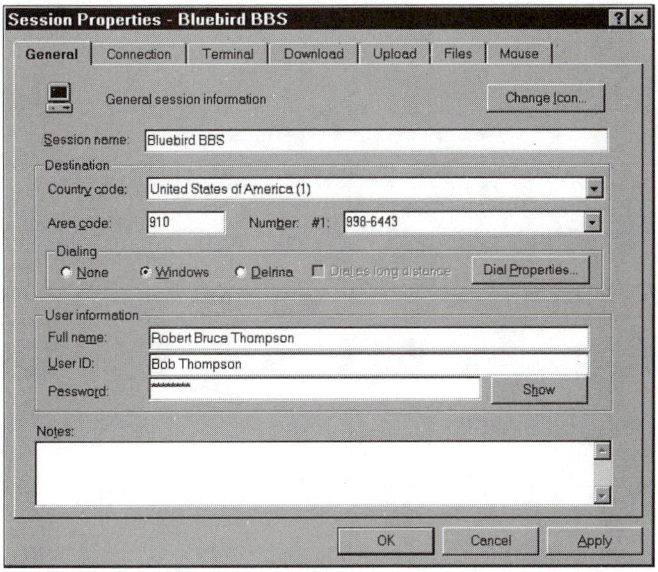

Fig. 4.16
You can modify destination and user information.

The Connection tab, shown in figure 4.17, allows you to specify the connection type, which modem is to be used, how often and how many times the call should be retried, and so on.

Fig. 4.17
Specify connection type and modem information here.

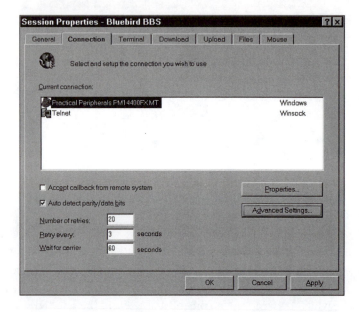

The Terminal tab, shown in figure 4.18, allows you to specify the type of terminal emulation to be used, colors and fonts, terminal window sizing, and terminal window control.

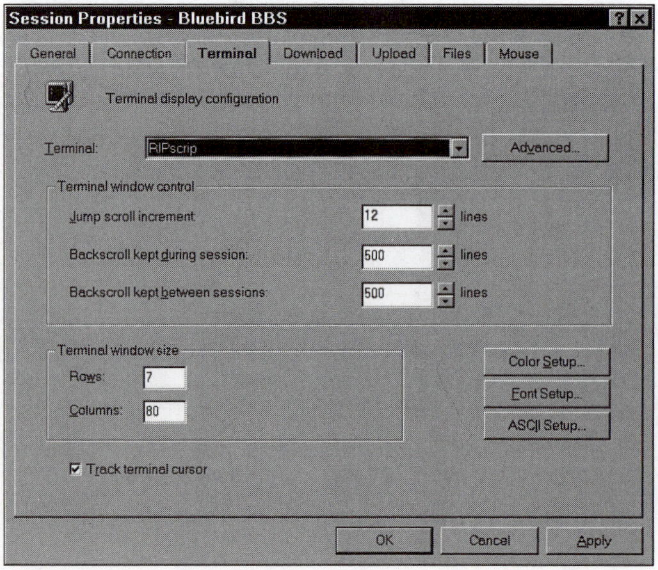

Fig. 4.18
Specify terminal emulation, window sizing, and window control.

The Download tab, shown in figure 4.19, allows you to specify the file transfer protocol to be used, the destination folder for downloaded files, destination file naming options, the action to take if the destination file name already exists, whether to view image files as they are downloading, and whether to scan for viruses as the file is downloading.

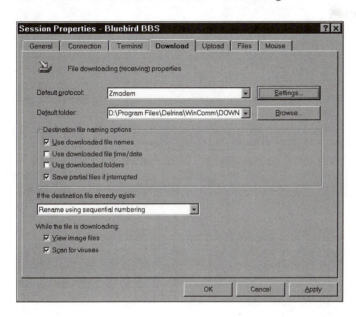

II

Dialup Communications

Fig. 4.19
You can specify your file transfer protocol.

The Upload tab, shown in figure 4.20, allows you to specify the default file transfer protocol to be used when uploading files and the default file folder in which files to be uploaded can be found.

The Files tab, shown in figure 4.21, allows you to specify a script or program to be run before the connection is made, another to be run when the connection is made, and a third to be run if a file transfer is aborted. It also allows you to specify locations for the scroll back file, the log file, and the screen capture file for that session.

The Mouse tab, shown in figure 4.22, allows you to specify mouse behavior in the terminal window for this session.

You can modify the parameters for any session individually, affecting only that session. You can also modify the properties of the New Session Defaults icon to change the default settings that will be used when you create a new session. Any changes made to the New Session Defaults only affect new sessions created after the changes are made.

Fig. 4.20
You can also specify the default file transfer protocol to use when uploading.

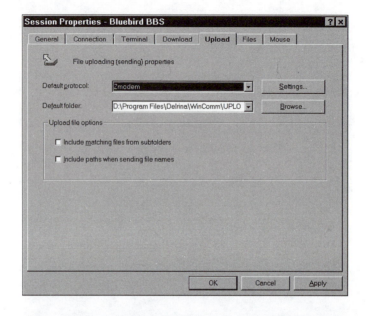

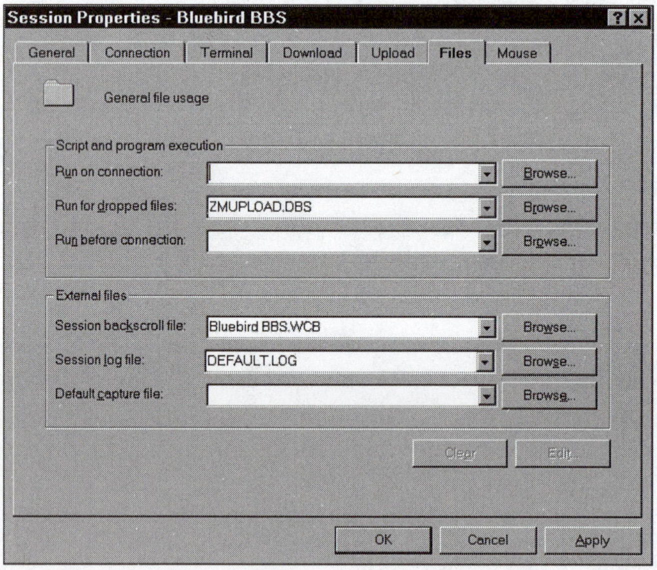

Fig. 4.21
Specify locations for the scroll back file and log file.

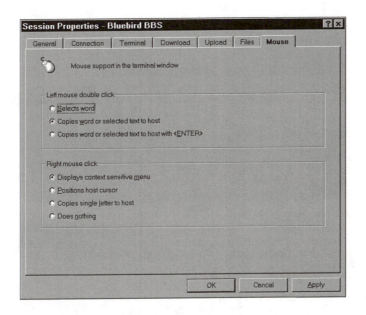

Fig. 4.22
Make your mouse
behave properly
from this page.

Using WinComm Pro to Make a Connection

To use WinComm Pro to establish a session with a remote host, simply
double-click the session icon in the Phonebook. The terminal screen and the
Connect dialog box appear. The Connect dialog box, shown in figure 4.23,
displays call progress while the connection is being made.

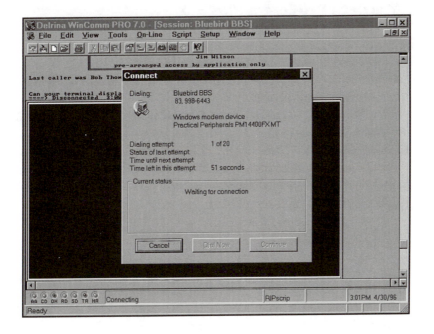

Fig. 4.23
WinComm Pro
Connect dialog
box.

When the connection has been established, the Connect dialog box closes, leaving you connected to the remote host in terminal mode, as shown in figure 4.24.

Fig. 4.24
WinComm Pro online with Bluebird BBS.

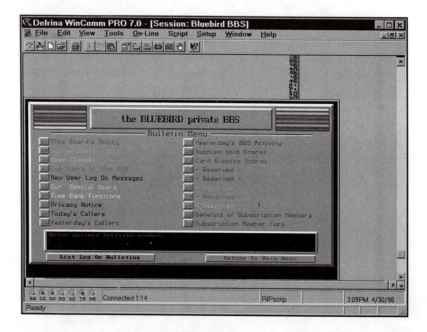

Quarterdeck ProComm Plus 3.0

The ProComm Plus splash screen prominently displays the phrase "Everything You Need to Communicate On-Line," and they mean it. The bad news about ProComm Plus 3.0 is that it isn't TAPI-compliant, so it doesn't cooperate gracefully with other communications programs. The good news is that you probably won't care, because ProComm Plus integrates just about every communications feature imaginable into a single program. In addition to all of the features you would expect in a general purpose communications program, ProComm Plus 3.0, shown in figure 4.25, adds fax support as good as anything else on the market and a full complement of competent Internet tools, including clients for Mail, News, ftp, Telnet, and the World Wide Web.

If you're looking for a single program to serve all of your communications needs, ProComm Plus is a strong candidate. If you can't find a particular communications feature in ProComm Plus 3.0, chances are you don't really need it anyway.

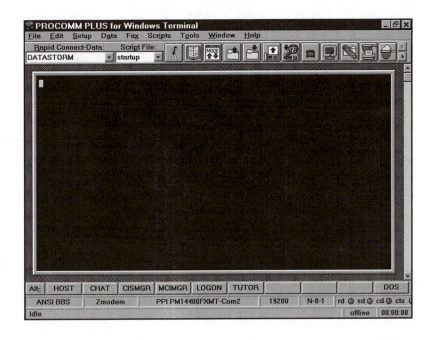

Fig. 4.25
The ProComm Plus
main screen.

■ *Terminal Emulations.* ProComm Plus provides 36 terminal emulations, including:

ADDS 60, ADDS 90

ADM 31, ADM 3A, ADM 5

ANSI-BBS

AT&T 4410, AT&T 605

DEC VT52, DEC VT 100, DEC VT 102, DEC VT 220, and DEC VT 320

Data General DG 100, DG 200, and DG 210

Esprit 3

Heath 19

IBM 3101, IBM 3161, IBM 3270, and IBM PC

RIPscrip 1.54

TTY

Televideo TVI 910, TVI 912, TVI 920, TVI 922, TVI 925, TVI 950, and TVI 955

Vidtex

Wyse WY-50, WY-60, WY-75, and WY-100

■ *File Transfer Protocols.* ProComm Plus provides 11 file transfer protocols, including:

ASCII

CompuServe B+

Kermit

IND$FILE

Raw ASCII

Xmodem (checksum and CRC)

1K-Xmodem

1K-Xmodem-G

Ymodem

Ymodem-G

Zmodem

Installing ProComm Plus

ProComm Plus 3.0 uses a standard Windows setup routine. After entering your name, company, and serial number, you are given the opportunity to choose one of the following installation types:

■ *Express Installation.* Installs the entire ProComm Plus suite of programs, with all options. A complete installation requires about 40M of disk space.

■ *Custom Installation.* Installs only the components you select.

If you choose Custom Installation, you first specify the drive and directory to which ProComm Plus will be installed. The program files occupy about 8M of disk space. You may also select which supporting files are to be installed, as follows:

■ *Utility and other Options.* Occupies up to 13M of disk space, and allows you to install the BBS QWKMail offline mail reader, support for RIPscrip, the Action Bar Editor, help for the ProComm Plus program and its ASPECT scripting language, the Dialog and ASPECT editors, the Scheduler, the User Window Editor, the GIF graphics viewer, and the ProComm Plus Readme file.

■ *Connection Directories.* Occupies up to 304K of disk space, and allows you to install import utilities for Web HTML pages, HyperAccess versions 1.0 and 2.0x, ProComm Plus DOS 2.01, ProComm Plus Windows 1.x/2.x, QmodemPro 1.0, Telix 3.1x, the USBBS List, WinComm Pro

1.0/1.1, and WinFax Pro 3.0/4.0. You can also install lists of Cool Internet Sites, Modem Vendor BBSes, and 50 Popular U.S. BBSes.

- *Scripts*. Occupies up to 6M, and allows you to install scripting support for BBS Chat, CompuServe Manager, ProComm Plus Hints, a Host Mode Script, PC-to-PC File Transfer, Logon Scripting, MCI Manager, and Remote Script Commander.

- *Network Connections*. Occupies up to 128K, and allows you to install support for NetBIOS, Int14, Extended Int14, NASI Windows Support for NetWare Connect, and NCSI/NASI Support for DOS Drivers.

- *Tutorial Script*. Allows you to install a 720K interactive tutorial.

- *Fax Utilities and Other Options*. Occupies up to 5.5M of disk space, and allows you to install support for scanners, fax forwarding, fax merging, sample cover sheets, fax cleaning, DOS, and the Cover Sheet Editor.

- *Internet*. Occupies up to 3M of disk space, and allows you to install support for Ping, ftp, Telnet, and the ProComm Plus Web browser, called Web Zeppelin. Installing the Web browser also installs support for Internet Mail and USENET News.

After you make your selections, the files are copied from the distribution media to your hard drive. ProComm Plus installs a Windows 95 fax driver and prompts you to restart your computer.

When the system restarts, ProComm Plus runs a configuration script. You are first prompted to verify your name and company information and to enter your voice and fax telephone numbers and your fax Calling Station ID (CSID).

ProComm Plus then begins the modem configuration procedure, shown in figure 4.26. You are given the opportunity to specify your modem manually or to allow the setup routine to automatically detect and configure it. The ProComm Plus modem database contains information about more than 1,000 discrete modem models, and will almost certainly detect and configure properly any modem you are likely to have installed.

After the modem has been detected and configured, you provide information about your area code and dialing prefixes required to get an outside line, to place long distance calls, and so forth. ProComm Plus then creates program groups and offers you the option of viewing the README file and completing online registration.

Fig. 4.26
ProComm Plus
modem installa-
tion.

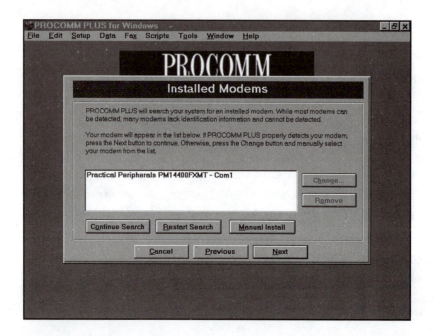

The final step is Internet setup. You are first asked whether you will access the Internet using a dial-up connection or via a direct LAN connection. You may configure your existing dial-up or LAN connection or create a new one. After the connection is configured, you are given the opportunity to enter account information for your mail server and news server. After you do so, you may run the Tutorial. ProComm Plus is fully configured and ready to use.

You can uninstall ProComm Plus using Add/Remove Programs in the Control Panel.

Creating a New Connection Directory Entry with ProComm Plus

ProComm Plus originated the Dialing Directory concept, and this latest version centers on the Connection Directory, an expansion of the original concept to include access by other than traditional dial up means. An entry in the Connection Directory includes information about every means you can use to contact that entity. You can enter information about each entry in eight classes, including Data, Fax, Voice, Telnet, FTP, WWW, Mail, and News.

You aren't likely to have entries in all eight of these classes for any given connection. For example, for a BBS, you will probably have entries only for the Data class, and perhaps in the Voice class for the system operator's voice telephone number. For an Internet site, you may have entries for one or more of the classes, such as Telnet, ftp, WWW, Mail, and News. For an individual, you may maintain contact information for Data, Fax, and Voice.

Take a closer look at configuring each of these classes. The information used here is only for example purposes, so substitute your own information. To create a new entry in your connection directory, choose Edit, New Entry or simply click the New Entry icon.

ProComm Plus Data Class Properties. The Data tab, shown in figure 4.27, allows you to enter information about a dial up connection, typically a BBS or online service. You may enter the name, company name, telephone number, and communications parameters, including parity, data bits, stop bits, terminal emulation, and default file transfer protocol. The Call Type field specifies whether the call is internal, local, long distance, or international, thus allowing ProComm Plus to automatically append the correct prefixes and suffixes to the telephone number to be dialed. The Data Connection field specifies the modem or other service to be used to make the connection. You may also assign this connection to a group, such as BBSes, which allows you to arrange your connections into a hierarchical folder structure.

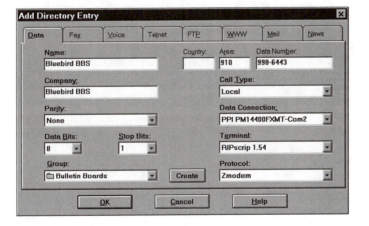

Fig. 4.27
ProComm Plus
Data Class
properties.

ProComm Plus Fax Class Properties. The Fax tab, shown in figure 4.28, allows you to enter information about a fax connection, including the fax telephone number, the type of call—internal, local, long distance, or international—and the modem or other service to be used for the connection. Like Data Class entries, Fax Class entries may be assigned to a group.

II

Dialup Communications

Fig. 4.28
ProComm Plus Fax
Class properties.

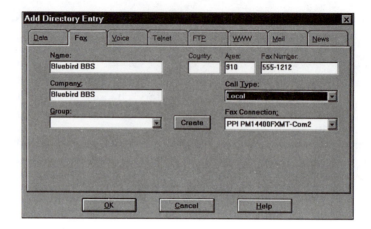

ProComm Plus Voice Class Properties. The Voice tab, shown in figure 4.29, allows you to enter information about a voice connection, including the voice telephone number, the type of call, and the modem or service to be used to make the connection. Again, you may use the Group field to assign the entry to a folder. For example, if you have several individuals who you call at a particular company, you can create a group for that company and assign the individual Voice Class entries to that group.

Fig. 4.29
ProComm Plus
Voice Class
properties.

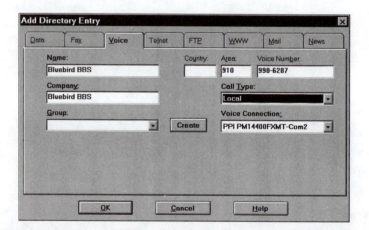

ProComm Plus Telnet Class Properties. The Telnet tab, shown in figure 4.30, allows you to enter information about a Telnet connection, including the host name or Internet IP address for the Telnet host, the terminal emulation to be used, and the default file transfer protocol. Although it may seem strange to use terminal emulations (such as ANSI-BBS) and file transfer protocols (such as Zmodem) that are usually associated with dial-up asynchronous connections on the Internet, an increasing number of BBSes are accessible via

Telnet. This means that rather than placing a long-distance call to a BBS, you can access it via your existing Internet connection without losing any of the terminal emulation or file transfer features available via dial up connections.

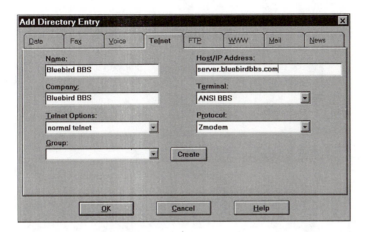

Fig. 4.30
ProComm Plus
Telnet Class
properties.

ProComm Plus ftp Class Properties. The FTP tab, shown in figure 4.31, allows you to enter information about an ftp connection, including the host name or IP address and the default host directory. You may use anonymous ftp by checking the Anonymous Logon checkbox. Leaving it unchecked allows you to enter a Logon ID and password for non-anonymous ftp access. If you created a custom ftp options set in Setup, you can select it under FTP Options; otherwise the default is Normal FTP. The Passive Mode field is useful only if you are behind an IP firewall. Enabling Passive Mode essentially reverses the roles of the ftp client and ftp server, allowing the client to take control of the connection.

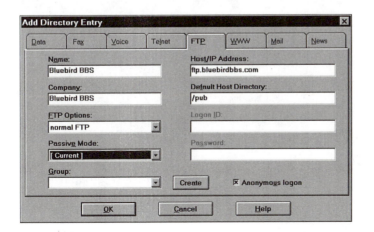

Fig. 4.31
ProComm Plus FTP
Class properties.

II

Dialup Communications

ProComm Plus WWW Class Properties. The WWW tab, shown in figure 4.32, allows you to enter information about a WWW connection, including the address of the Web server and the font size to be used by the ProComm Plus browser.

Fig. 4.32
ProComm Plus
WWW Class
properties.

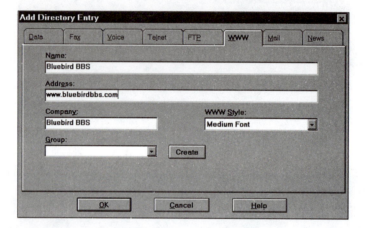

ProComm Plus Mail Class Properties. The Mail tab, shown in figure 4.33, allows you to enter information about an Internet Mail connection, including the name, company, group, and e-mail address.

Fig. 4.33
ProComm Plus
Mail Class
properties.

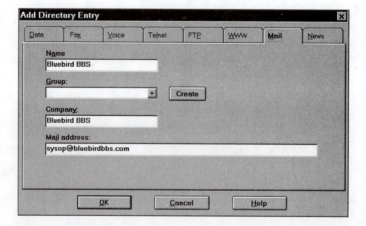

ProComm Plus News Class Properties. The News tab, shown in figure 4.34, allows you to enter information about a USENET News connection, including the name, Connection Directory Group, and the Newsgroup name.

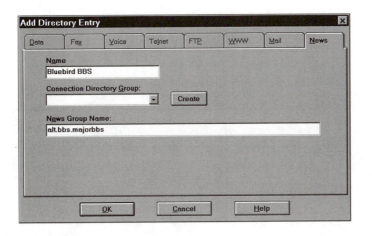

Fig. 4.34
ProComm Plus
News Class
properties.

Using ProComm Plus to Make a Connection

To use ProComm Plus to establish a session with a remote host, simply
choose Rapid Connect, Data, and choose a connection from the list. Groups
you have defined appear as folders in this list, allowing you to drill down to
the connection you want to initiate. The Dialing status screen, shown in
figure 4.35, appears and displays call progress while the connection is being
made.

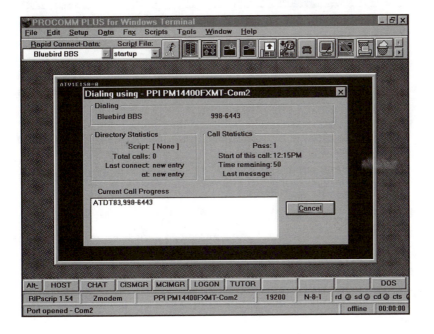

Fig. 4.35
ProComm Plus
Dialing status
screen.

When the connection has been established, the Dialing status screen disappears, leaving you connected to the remote host in terminal mode, as shown in figure 4.36.

Fig. 4.36
ProComm Plus
online with
Bluebird BBS.

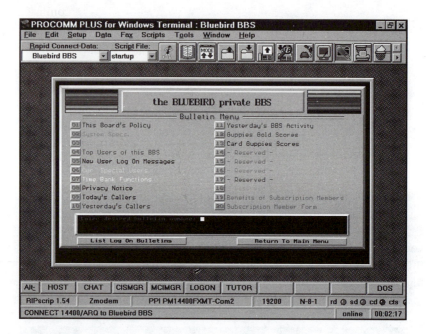

Protecting Against Viruses

When talking about communications software, the subject of viruses inevitably arises. Without minimizing the very real danger that a virus can present, the fact is that damage caused by computer viruses is nowhere near as common nor usually as catastrophic as many people believe. In the course of more than 10 years working with thousands of PC's in scores of offices and making more than 20,000 connections to BBSes, I have seen a virus infection fewer than 10 times. Most problems attributed to a virus infection are simply a result of improperly configured hardware, buggy software, and thumb-fingered users.

Although a variety of shareware and commercial virus scanning products are available, some of which claim to scan for thousands of viruses, the majority of these viruses do not exist in the wild. The policy of some virus scanner vendors of paying a bounty for each newly discovered virus has lead to many viruses being created for no reason other than for claiming the bounty. Only a couple hundred or so viruses are in general circulation, and fewer than a dozen are really common. Of this number, some are relatively benign, and many, although malignant, are relatively easy to deal with.

Online services in general and BBSes in general have gotten a very bad and largely unjustified rap concerning viruses. It is not likely that your computer will be infected by a virus contained in a file downloaded from commercial online services or a well-run BBS oriented toward adult users. All commercial online services and all responsible BBS system operators take great care to scan files for viruses before posting them publicly for download.

> **Caution**
>
> The situation on teen-oriented and pirate BBSes is very different. Download files from these systems at your own risk. As a general rule, if the BBS allows the use of "handles" rather than real names, you should treat any file downloaded from that BBS with suspicion. Also, if you find commercial software posted for download, avoid the temptation to do so. You will often find that such commercial software is infected with a virus, sometimes intentionally.

The Internet has brought a new dimension to the virus problem. Most people regularly connect to one or two commercial online services and perhaps a half dozen BBSes. If you find an infected file among those you have down-loaded, it's usually easy to remember where you got that file. BBS users form a closely knit community, and a BBS that posts infected files soon finds itself without users. Similarly, commercial online services go to great lengths to prevent this from occurring—and those few times that it has, the situation has been quickly corrected.

The Internet changes this completely. Because you can jump from one side of the planet to the other with the click of your mouse, you may well download a file from a site and later be unable to recall from where the file originated. The thousands of Web servers and ftp sites on the Internet make it much easier, whether intentionally or unintentionally, for infected files to remain available for download.

All of this said, you are considerably more likely to lose data as a result of a disk crash, a power failure, or because of thoughtless actions than because of a virus infection. When I lose data, it's almost always a case of familiarity breeding contempt. At the "Are you sure? Y/N" prompt, I always confirm without thinking about it. Don't you? This has lost me quite a few files over the years.

As a first priority, then, configure the Recycle Bin to save your deletions. Then buy and use both a tape backup drive and an uninterruptable power supply. After you have done all of these, you can think about installing a virus scanner.

My favorite is from McAfee, but equivalent products are available from Symantec and many other vendors. Use whichever you feel most comfortable with. Any of them will catch any of the viruses you're likely to see in the real world. Don't be too impressed by how many viruses each claims to detect, and don't pay too much attention to the comparative claims. All of the virus scanners are good—but, none are perfect.

On the Web

Visit McAfee's home page at

ftp.mcafe.com   The files are located in the /pub/antivirus directory.

McAfee VirusScan NT 2.5 Overview

McAfee VirusScan NT 2.5, shown in figure 4.37, is representative of the better virus scanning products available. It runs as a native NT Service, installing the McAfee Alert Manager and the McAfee Task Manager. The Antivirus Console allows you to manage your local workstation and remote workstations that also run McAfee Antivirus. McAfee makes it easy to keep your virus signature files current so a new virus doesn't take you by surprise. It has an AutoUpdate feature that will automatically log in to the McAfee server, download the latest virus signature file, and update your system accordingly.

Fig. 4.37
McAfee VirusScan
NT.

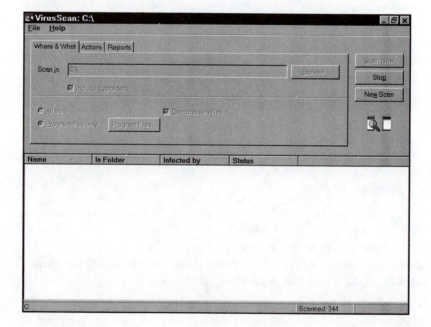

Installing McAfee VirusScan NT

McAfee VirusScan NT uses a standard Windows setup procedure, using an installation wizard to automate the entire process. For the installed product to work correctly, you must install it while logged on as a user with administrative privileges. You can install it to the default C:\WIN32APP\VirusScanNT directory, or specify an alternate directory. After you specify a program group (or accept the default McAfee VirusScan NT group), the files are copied to the destination folder.

If you want to scan network drives, you have to supply a username and password for an account that has access to the network drives in question. Make sure you have this information available before beginning the installation. As the final step, the setup procedure asks if you would like to install Network Alert definitions to allow you to be notified of events via network messages.

Using McAfee VirusScan NT

McAfee Antivirus has two major components. The virus scanning program does the actual scanning for viruses. The McAfee Antivirus Console, shown in figure 4.38, allows you to configure and manage the use of the scanning program.

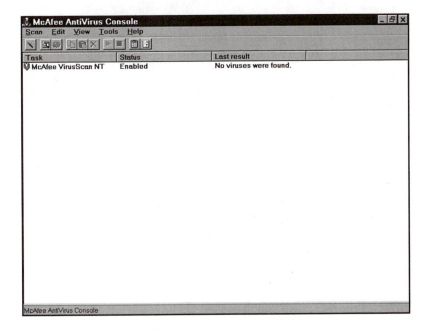

Fig. 4.38
McAfee Antivirus Console.

The Antivirus Console AutoUpdate feature allows you to automatically download and install current virus signature files. If you have an updated signature file on disk, you may use the Update Location tab of the AutoUpdate Properties sheet, shown in figure 4.39, to specify the location of these files. Alternately, you can tell the program to get the updated signature file itself via ftp, using a shell script specified on this tab. After the updated file has been downloaded, it's stored in the location specified on this tab.

Fig. 4.39
You can specify current virus signature files on the Update Location page.

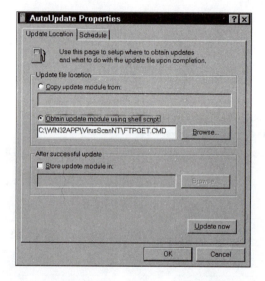

The Schedule tab of the AutoUpdate Properties sheet, shown in figure 4.40, allows you to specify how often and when the program should update your virus signature file. The default is to disable the AutoUpdate Scheduler. If you check the Enable scheduler checkbox, the program defaults to updating on a monthly basis.

The McAfee Antivirus Console Alert Properties sheet allows you to specify when and how the program notifies you of anomalous events, such as a virus being detected. Configured using the Alert Properties System Alerts tab, shown in figure 4.41, the program defaults to recording alerts in the system Event Log. You may also set it to the Event Log on another computer system, allowing you to establish a central point where virus alerts are received. You may also, if you want, configure the program to run an external program when an alert is received, doing so either only the first time an alert is received, or each time an alert is received.

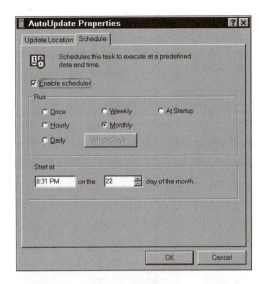

Fig. 4.40
Use the Schedule
page to specify
how often the
program should
update your virus
signature file.

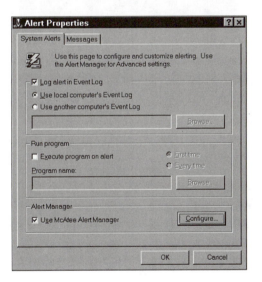

Fig. 4.41
This page allows
you to configure
and customize
alerting.

II

Dialup Communications

The Alert Properties Messages tab, shown in figure 4.42, allows you to enable
and disable alert messages and to configure priority levels.

McAfee Antivirus products, as well as the rest of their line of network management software, are available on a shareware basis. Fully functional evaluation copies can be downloaded directly from **ftp.mcafee.com**. You may
also visit their Web site at **www.mcafee.com**.

Fig. 4.42

You can configure
priority levels for
all system
messages here.

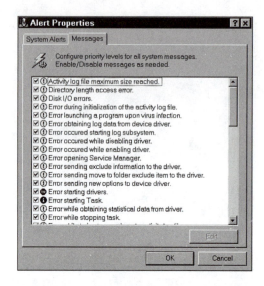

CHAPTER 5

Using Commercial Online Services

by Kate Chase

The simple truth is that major commercial online services—those members-only, subscription-based systems like CompuServe and America Online—have never been cheaper, faster, easier to use, or more competitive than right now.

A few years ago, as the race for Internet access began to take on nuclear proportions, such services turned their attention to offering fast-and-easy on-ramps to the Information Superhighway for those who chose not to concern themselves over the differences between WinSocks or choosing a Web browser. As a result, second-string players like America Online, known more as a friendly cyberspace community than a heavy-duty technical resource, shot quickly into top place from a few hundred thousand members to more than five million. Meanwhile, the more staid CompuServe introduced WOW!, service just for Windows 95 users and apparently targeting brand-new computer owners.

However, times—and focus—change rapidly in the online world. The introduction of lower-cost Internet access alternatives like those opened by AT&T WorldNet in early 1996, coupled with the faster speed of direct net connections over entering the Internet via one of the big commercial services, have made these services shift their emphasis back to providing original content for their members. What this translates to for you is that you may find more areas of interest on specific services such as expanded home and business tax areas, real estate offerings, job listings, professional networks and small business owner forums, along with the technical support you expect to find online.

In this chapter, you learn about

- How to join and use the Big Three commercial online services
- Other general interest online services

- Other specialty online services
- The future of online services in today's Net-hungry world

The Big Three

While commercial online services have sprung up everywhere in the last few years, only three services (CompuServe, America Online, and Prodigy) have managed to come out on top in the online membership wars. Their recent booming success is at least due in part to their quickness in introducing popular Internet features—world-wide e-mail, USENET newsgroups, and the World Wide Web—just as the rush to the Net began.

How you choose which, if any, of these large commercial services depends on what your needs are. What the major services all share is a successful Windows interface (with enough basics built in to help even the newest members navigate their online systems quickly and easily), at least some Internet access, and a broad range of interests represented. Because they're so competitive, you can pretty much expect that as one drops prices, the others will follow; however, prices have stabilized over the last year.

CompuServe (CIS)

Let's first look at the "Granddaddy" of today's current major online services, CompuServe (CIS). Not only is CIS the oldest, it may become the first to fully jump to the Web, as it has announced plans to move it's entire base of operation and membership onto the World Wide Web over the next few years.

Established in 1979 and owned by H & R Block, CompuServe became the premiere service for serious online computer users long before the rest of America discovered modems. Today, it continues its emphasis on hard-hitting technical support and shareware, but CompuServe has also expanded to offer something for everyone—parents and kids, computer novices as well as veteran users, buyers and sellers, and small and large business owners.

If you've tried CompuServe in the distant past, you should appreciate both the added functionality as well as the graphical ease of the Windows version of their software, offering you point-and-click access to over 3,000 online areas. You no longer have to memorize those UNIX-style arcane commands or suffer through setting up terminal software to access. A Favorites Place option available right on the software's top toolbar, for example, allows you to mark select sites from CompuServe's many layers of online areas so you can readily find your way back on return trips. This would have saved me a fortune several years ago, and the prices were much higher then.

Getting CompuServe Software

You can access CompuServe without its Windows CompuServe Information Manager (WinCIM) using a PC terminal communications package, but it's not advised for the faint of heart.

Often, copies of WinCIM are packed into copies of popular computer magazines like *PC World, NetGuide,* and *Windows Magazine,* so you might want to check out back issues for a CompuServe disk or CD.

If you can't locate one, and you have access to the World Wide Web through another service or Internet provider, you can download the software directly from their Web site or you can call 1-800-848-8990 and ask for their introductory software. You want CompuServe V2.0.1 or later since this version improves on a number of features, including Internet tools.

You can download WinCIM from CompuServe's WWW site at:

On the Web

http://www.compuserve.com/down.html

Even if you have access to CompuServe software from another source, you'll still need a temporary User ID and password to create an account. If you don't have these packed with your software, call the 800 number above.

Connecting through TCP/IP

If you're already a CIS member, and you're connected to the Internet by means of a local area network connection, you can use this to connect to CIS. To do this, from WinCIM, choose Special from the CIS menu bar, then choose Session Settings, Connector, then select INT14 from the list. When the LAN button displays, choose Configure and double-check to make certain the Host Name listed is **gateway.compuserve.com** and the Host IP Address is blank. Then choose OK, and then OK again. Make your connection to the Internet via your LAN, launch WinCIM, and you're there!

Setting up a CompuServe account. Once you have the CompuServe WinCIM software, just follow instructions for installing the software, which is usually Run (from Windows NT Start) A:\SETUP.EXE for disk-based software and D:\DEMO.EXE for the WinCIM V2.0.1 Exploring CompuServe CD. Then choose CompuServe under Available Programs (also from the Windows Start menu) to launch WinCIM, and sign on to create your account.

CompuServe Pricing. Over the past year, a big drop in CompuServe pricing has made it affordable for many and on a par with its rivals. For a standard plan of $9.95 a month, you receive membership and five hours of online access. Each additional hour will cost you $4.80. New members can take advantage of their trial offer—a free month's membership and 10 free hours—to get acquainted with the service.

CompuServe also has many premium areas, like magazine searches as well as credit inquiry and specialty service areas which are priced on a per-transaction basis. Check out the fees as you enter any of the areas marked with a "$." They vary from $1.50 for a magazine search "match" on up.

You can use either a major credit card or electronic transfer of funds from your checking account to pay your monthly bill.

Getting Technical Assistance. If you have problems installing the WinCIM software or just can't get on the service after you've established an account, call 1-800-848-8990. These lines can be ferociously busy, though, so members who can access the service are advised to try to get online for technical assistance.

To do this, select Services from the WinCIM menu bar, then select Go, and when the little dialog box pops up in the middle of your screen, type, **SUPPORT**.

Table 5.1 Places to Go	
Go word	**Service**
BILLING	CompuServe Account Information
FILEFINDERS	CompuServe's Online File Search Utilities
INTERNET	Internet Services (Web, ftp, Telnet, USENET)
MAIL	CompuServe e-mail (lets you send Internet e-mail)
MICROSOFT	The Microsoft Connection
SUPPORT	Member Support
USENET	USENET Newsgroups
WCIMSUPPORT	Support for WinCIM software
WINSHARE	Windows Shareware Forum
WINSUPPORT	Windows Support Forum
WINUTIL	Windows Utilities Forum

Tip

<u>G</u>o is your command to shuttle you to specific sites around the service. You can access <u>G</u>o by typing Ctrl+G, or by selecting Services from the WinCIM menu bar, then choosing <u>G</u>o. A dialog box will appear; this is where you type the name of the area you want to visit, like MICROSOFT or WINSHARE.

Basic Features

Before you sign on, the main areas of interest found on the service are represented on the graphical Explore CompuServe screen, which loads when you launch WinCIM, as shown in figure 5.1.

Fig. 5.1

If you're a business person looking for professional "people" networking or financial information, check the Professional or Finance icons on Explore Compu-Serve. Click one to start connecting and it will deposit you right at the entry of these categories.

If you think CompuServe is for still just for nerds, think again. Though CompuServe forged its reputation on its technical resources, the service has really expanded to offer enough variety to appeal to everyone, offering star appearances by hotshots from a wide range of industries, extensive support forums and file libraries, popular live chat, net access, and even lots of shopping opportunities.

Logging in one day, the What's New screen gave an indication of that diversity. The offerings included a position paper by former GOP presidential candidate Steve Forbes on the Chinese threat to Taiwan, a guide to America's national parks, online help for migraine sufferers, and that day's new issue of *Time Magazine,* as well as a look at what notables would be visiting CompuServe soon.

Tip

Online and feeling very confused? Click the large yellow question mark at the far left hand of your CIS toolbar to load CompuServe's extensive online help file.

E-mail

WinCIM lets you know that you have e-mail waiting if there's a number printed below the envelope or Mail icon on the WinCIM toolbar. For example, 3 would indicate you have three pieces of unread or undeleted mail waiting in your mailbox for disposition.

To retrieve your mail:

1. Access your mail menu by selecting Mail, then Get New Mail options from the WinCIM menu bar, or

   Click the envelope or Mail icon on your WinCIM toolbar.

2. Highlight an e-mail from the list and double-click it to read it.

To compose new mail:

1. Pull down Mail from the WinCIM menu bar, and then click Create/ Send Mail.

2. From the Recipient List screen, provide the recipient's name, CompuServe ID or Internet mailing address, and which Address Type (i.e., CompuServe).

3. Once that's done, you can add the recipient's information to your address book by selecting first Add, then Copy.

   Click OK.

4. The next screen, as shown in figure 5.2, is where you actually compose the message.

5. Enter a Subject for the e-mail (required).

6. Type in the body of the message.

7. To send:

   Now: choose Send Now, or

   Later: choose Out-Basket.

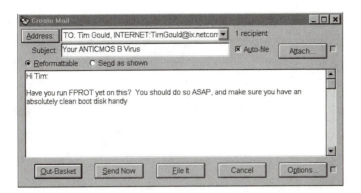

Fig. 5.2
Use the Attach option when composing e-mail to bundle a file or file archive along with your message. You can also request a receipt for mail delivery.

> **Note**
>
> You can also use Windows Messaging to send and receive mail on CompuServe. For more information on using Windows Messaging System, see "Configuring Windows NT Messaging" in Chapter 10.

Just as this book went to press, CompuServe announced plans to offer e-mail access via touch-tone telephones. Using a special Smart Card paid calling card, members choosing this option can use their touch-tone phones to call a special number to get their e-mail read to them by a Max Headroom-style voice system. The cost is 25 cents a minute, and the custom option also enables you to place long distance phone calls using your account. Call CompuServe for availability, because you have to have the Smart Card in order to participate.

Internet Access

Once you're a CompuServe member, Internet access is very easy, but a tad confusing. For example, if you click the Internet (globe) icon from Explore CompuServe you'll be signed on and delivered to the entry to CompuServe's World Wide Web Gateway. This is fine since the Web is probably the part of the Internet with the heaviest traffic, but it's not the only component of the Internet to be found online.

Let's try to draw you a more exact map.

To reach CompuServe's NCSA Mosaic Web browser and access to the World Wide Web:

1. From offline, launch WinCIM and click the Internet (globe). This will sign you on to CompuServe and direct you to the Web gateway.

   From online, click the Globe icon on the WinCIM toolbar.

2. Once there, click any icon to jump onto the Web.

Troubleshooting

I can access the Web now, but I have no URLs to try and don't know where to start.

Choose Search Internet Directory of Services to search for sites of interest through Yahoo, one of the big net search services (it's free except for your usual CIS connect time).

---

3. By default, CompuServe will begin to load its own home page into your Web browser, as shown in figure 5.3.

You can stop this by clicking Stop.

Fig. 5.3
CompuServe offers its own direct dial-up Web access as part of its WinCIM installation. Time spent connecting to the Web this way is billed at the usual connect rates to your CIS account, but may be a little faster than connecting through the regular WinCIM front-end.

4. Use the Web Page dialog box just below the Mosaic browser toolbar to type in a URL you want to visit.

If you want to keep a record of Web sites you want to revisit often, you can do this using Hotlists. To include a Web site in your Hotlists, choose Navigate, Add Web Page to Hotlist.

To reach CompuServe's entire Internet lineup, **Go INTERNET** (see fig. 5.4) and choose from USENET newsgroups, ftp, Inbound Telnet, and again, the Web.

Fig. 5.4
Choose USENET
newsgroups to
subscribe to and
access/read
USENET
newsgroups you
select. You'll find a
tool for searching
the newsgroups by
keyword at Go
USENET.

Dialup Communications

Computing Support

Now this is where CompuServe stashes its true gold mine of resources, whether it's discussing Windows NT new version release dates with Microsoft honchos on the bulletin boards, getting the latest printer driver, or registering your shareware directly online.

Not only will you have access to the strongest selection of computing vendor support available on any online service, you can also touch base with a number of different sources on any given problem. Let's say your office is having a miserable time printing from the Hewlett-Packard Deskjet since upgrading your Windows NT server. Don't limit yourself to simply visiting the Personal Operating Systems Forum in The Microsoft Connection, not when you can ask in the Hardware and Windows Support Forums available at **Go SIGS.**

Because the offerings are so plentiful, you need to find a sane launch pad for finding the computer support resources available on CompuServe. One good place to start is the Computing Support Directory.

To reach it:

1. Launch WinCIM.

2. Click the Computing Support icon from Explore CompuServe screen.

3. You'll be automatically signed on and transported to the main Computing Support entry screen, where you can select from a number of options, including What's Hot, Reference, Shareware Services (where you can register your shareware online), Featured Shopping, News, and Find a File.

Click Computing Support Directory to bring you to a screen where you may search for support or vendor by keyword, company name, or product (see fig. 5.5).

You can also browse through the list of categories, and click one you want to explore.

Fig. 5.5

Categories listed in the Computing Support Directory include Accounting/Finance/Tax, Computer Systems and Components, Desktop Publishing, and Operating Systems (including all releases of Windows).

Finding NT Support Online. Because you're already aware that you can obtain assistance from a number of different venues on CompuServe, let's choose one area to locate as an example. The Microsoft Connection seems as good as any for finding some Windows NT help, so follow these steps for finding it:

1. From online, **Go Microsoft**.

2. From The Microsoft Connection screen, you'll be met with choices: use Microsoft FileFinder, download a Microsoft-customized version of WinCIM, get sales information, or visit areas like the Microsoft KnowledgeBase (an excellent resource also available on the Web) or the

Microsoft Software Library.

Choose MS Product Support Forums.

3. Double-click Microsoft Personal Operating Systems.

4. Select Windows NT Forum (or Windows NT Service Pack Download Area).

5. At the Join screen, click Join and you're connected to the forum.

Microsoft KnowledgeBase:

http://www.microsoft.com/kb/

On the Web

Select NT Files available. You can perform a quick search of select Windows NT files available on CompuServe with **GO: PCFF** and searching on criteria like Windows and NT and Utility or Windows and 32 and Application.

Here are just a few of CompuServe's Windows NT files:

■ *CUTIL.ZIP* by clySmic software, a collection of 32-bit desktop utilities usable on both Windows 95 and Windows NT. It features a drag-and-drop wallpaper selector as well as a random wallpaper generator EXE file and system information utilities.

■ *FAXNET.ZIP* by Jon Krahmer is also known as FaxMail Network for Windows. It adds a Faxbar to all your Windows programs for truly easy fax access, and supports OCR as well as Fax to PCX Breakup.

America Online (AOL)

If there's a "Little Engine that Could" of online services, America Online is probably it. Just a few years ago, not many recognized the name of the formerly Apple/Macintosh-only service, fighting its way up from a paltry 100,000 or so members.

Today, with nearly six million members and rising rapidly, AOL has become the "everyman's" online service, mingling friendly technical support with an easy-to-use Windows interface, and a wide selection of general interest content. Its appeal has made it a favorite with big business looking to establish storefronts in cyberspace, too, like Century 21's plan to open up real estate services there, Ticketmaster selling show seats, and Gateway Computers' long-established support base online.

Its rapid growth has also garnered America Online more than its share of criticism as well. For example, Internet denizens were horrified when AOL opened the gate to USENET newsgroup access to its then more than one

II

Dialup Communications

million members, many of whom had no prior experience with net etiquette or finding what they needed. The fast rise also led to wide reports of performance problems as the service struggled to keep up with its burgeoning membership roster. The reports appear intermittent these days.

Getting America Online Software

Since you can only use America Online's proprietary software to connect with the service, you will need to have it before you can create an AOL account.

If you've bought a PC magazine in the last year, you'll likely have a small pile of AOL disks. Make certain you have at least V2.5, which incorporates a full World Wide Web browser, or even better V3.0 (which became fully available in June of 1996).

Failing that, you can:

- Call 1-800-827-6364 and progress through the voice menu system to order.
- Ask a friend with an AOL account to order you a copy by going to keyword: **FRIEND** (they get free hours in return).
- With your modem and communications software (not AOL software), phone the America Online Technical Support BBS at 1-800-827-5808. If your modem supports speeds at or above 9600 bps, you can download the software there on a free call.

Setting Up an America Online Account. Once you have the Windows version of America Online software, just follow instructions for installing the software, which would usually be Run (from Windows NT Start) A:\SETUP.EXE for disk-based software. Then choose America Online under available Programs (also from the Windows Start menu) to launch AOL and sign on to create your account.

America Online Pricing. Pricing here is fairly simple, because unlike CompuServe and Prodigy with their mix of free and premium areas, America Online has very few additional-fee services. This means that just about everything you will do online is covered under the same connection fee—chatting, downloading, using electronic mail, or reading message boards.

First-time members are entitled to 10 free trial hours with the first month's membership fee waived. After that, you'll pay the $9.95 basic subscription each month, billed to your credit card or electronically transferred from your checking account. The monthly fee gives you five free hours online, with additional time billed at $2.95 per hour.

Getting Technical Assistance. Can't get AOL's software to install properly, or forget your password? Customer Service offers several different options for you to reach them.

- Call 1-800-826-6364.

- If you can get online, and have a technical problem, type Ctrl+K, a dialog box will pop up, in which you need to type **TECHLIVE** which transports you to a free (you won't be charged for connect time while you're in there), live technical help area.

- If you can get online and have a Customer Service or billing related problem, type Ctrl+K, and in the dialog box which appears, type **SERVICE** (also a free area).

- If you have a fax or fax/modem, try America Online's free FAX Link service by calling 1-800-827-5551 from a touch-tone telephone. A voice menu will lead you through a selection of available help topics, then prompt you for your fax number. FAX Link will then send you a list by fax in anywhere ranging from a few moments to a few hours. Phone FAX Link's 800 number again to request up to five of the topics from the list sent to you, and these will in turn be faxed to you. Yes, you can repeat the process to get additional topics sent to you.

Tip

Navigating America Online is fast with the use of keywords linking you from one place to another (see Table. 5.2). To use them, type Ctrl+K or pull down the Go menu from the AOL menu bar then select Keyword. In the dialog box that appears, type the name of the site you wish to visit, like **WINFORUM** to reach the Windows Forum, or **TAXES** to reach the Computing Tax Forum. You can also type World Wide Web URLs in the dialog box to load the browser and take you directly to the desired home page.

Table 5.2 Frequently Used Keywords

Keyword	Gets You to:
@TIMES	*The New York Times* online edition, complete with classified ads
APPS	PC Applications Forum (supports all manner of applications, such as Microsoft Office and offers a lot of business software)

(continues)

Table 5.2 Continued	
Keyword	**Gets You to:**
BILLING	America Online Account Information
BUSINESS WEEK	*Business Week Magazine*
COMPUTING	Computing Forums (listing of all categories)
FILESEARCH	Online file search tool
INTERNET	Internet Forum (Web, ftp, Gopher/WAIS, USENET, Inbound Telnet)
MOTLEY FOOL	Popular Investment/Stocks forum
SERVICE	Customer Service Department
TECHLIVE	Free, live Technical Support for AOL software
WINFORUM	Windows Forum (supporting all versions of Windows)
WINMAG	CMP Publications' *Windows Magazine*

Basic Features

America Online's major departments are on display for you as soon as you first log on through the Main Menu. Such departments include Today's News, Personal Finance, Clubs and Interests, Computing, Marketplace, and Internet Connection, to name a few.

Yet the software won't linger at Main Menu (which remains open behind the next screen), moving instead to the In the Spotlight page, as shown in figure 5.6. You can locate more features from AOL's toolbar (see Table 5.3).

Table 5.3 Options on AOL's Toolbar	
Toolbar Icon	**Description**
(mailbox)	Your e-mail box; flag up means you have unread mail
(letter)	Compose Mail. Also use Ctrl+M
(Remote control)	Channels—AOL's many departments
(Hot)	What's Hot—previews special events or places
(profile faces)	People Connection—live, general interest chat
(magnifying glass and disk)	Filesearch—search file database
(graph)	Stock quotes and portfolios

Toolbar Icon	Description
(news)	Today's News
(globe)	Internet Connection
(shopping cart)	Online shopping in Marketplace
(My AOL)	Customize AOL to fit your preferences
(clock)	Online Clock, reports current time and your time online
(printer)	Print
(file cabinet)	Save important data to filing cabinet
(heart folder)	Favorite Places, remember and revisit select sites
(?)	Help and Support Services
(Find)	Locate areas on the service
(Keyword)	Shortcut to areas you want to visit

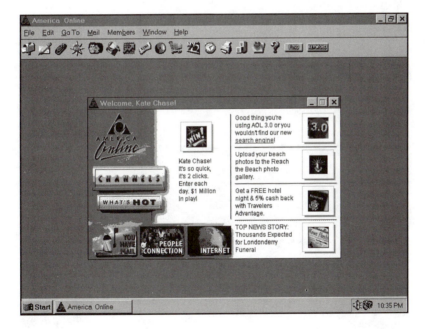

Fig. 5.6
The Spotlight lets you access your new mail, check out the hour's leading news story, and select spotlighted online sites to visit.

Dialup Communications

E-mail

Of all the online services, America Online has perhaps the simplest e-mail format.

- ■ Ctrl+M lets you compose e-mail
- ■ Ctrl+R lets you read your new e-mail

■ Use the <u>M</u>ail option from AOL's menu bar to set flashsessions (can download your e-mail for reading and offline response), check mail you've sent, as well as check mail you've read.

One nice extra with the new AOL 3.0 software is that you can use stylized text in e-mail and other communications, allowing you to select from font size, color/background color, and appearance (bold, underline, italic). You can even send hyperlinks in e-mail to help someone get to a specific location directly from that e-mail.

Internet Access

America Online's Internet offerings are fairly robust—even if surfing the net from AOL can sometimes get pretty slow. Besides inbound Telnet, a built-in Web browser, and access to net mail, newsgroups, and mailing lists, America Online also offers Gopher/WAIS and FTP service, plus the ability to create your own Web home page.

To reach the Internet's

■ *e-mail and mailing lists.* See previous "E-mail" section.

■ *ftp.* Type keyword **FTP**.

■ *Gopher/WAIS.* Type keyword **GOPHER**.

■ *Internet services.* Type keyword **INTERNET** or click the globe icon from the AOL toolbar (see fig. 5.7).

Fig. 5.7
AOL's Internet Connection offers direct access to most features except the net's IRC live chat and outbound Telnet.

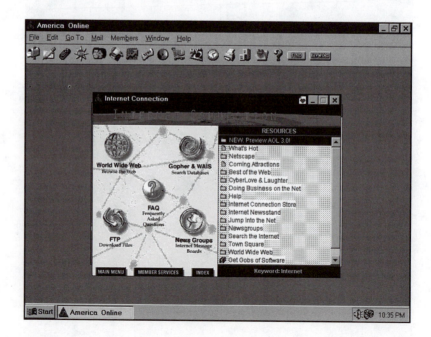

- *Newsgroups.* Type keyword **NEWSGROUPS**, from which you can search, add/remove, read and reply.

- *Telnet.* Type keyword **TELNET**.

- *Web.* Type keyword **WEB** or press Ctrl+K for keyword then type the URL of the Website you wish to visit in the dialog box.

Computing Support

One more way America Online makes it a little easier can be witnessed here, because America Online packs almost all of its computing support content—from files to vendors to live discussions—all under one umbrella at keyword **COMPUTING** (see fig. 5.8).

Fig. 5.8
From keyword COMPUTING you can locate forum-based support for PC applications, hardware, DOS, networking, and game-playing, read computing magazines, and visit vendors like Symantec and Hewlett-Packard.

Dialup Communications

Finding NT Support Online. Again, you have an advantage in that Windows NT support is centralized in one area: the Windows Forum at keyword **WIN FORUM**, which offers support, files, and live help sessions for all versions of Microsoft Windows, including NT.

Unfortunately, with all the attention required to provide help with the fairly new Windows 95, Windows NT support on America Online tends to be sketchy. Forum news, however, reports the forum is undergoing a reorganization to beef up its content, including direct links to Win-related net sites and further development of online NT resources. Monday nights, the Windows Forum hosts a live Windows NT discussion, 8:30 p.m. Eastern Time, at keyword **WIN FORUM** (choose Conference Room, then select Windows NT Conference Room) while the message boards and small collection of NT utilities and references are always open.

You can locate the Windows NT Resource Center right from the Windows Forum's main menu, as shown in figure 5.9.

Fig. 5.9
Support for Windows 3.1, Windows 95, and Windows NT are all housed at keyword: **WIN FORUM**.

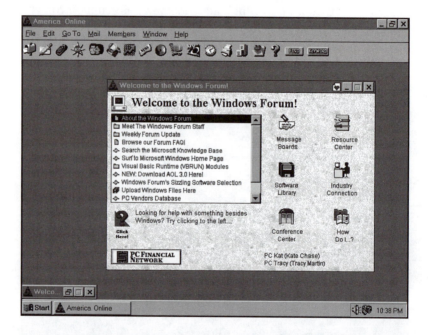

Select NT Files Available. To find Windows NT files on America Online, type keyword **WIN FORUM,** select NT Resource Center, and check out the Software Libraries emphasizing Windows NT and full 32-bit shareware and public domain files. You can also check out Ziff-Davis' network's ZD NET online at keyword **ZD NET.**

Here's one available by using keyword **FILESEARCH**:

- *TBNTPREV.EXE* (Turbo Browser) by Pacific Gold Coast Software is a premier Windows NT visual file manager which can take the place of Windows Explorer and some add-ons. It permits automatic viewing of many types of files (databases, graphics, icons, cursors, documents, clip art, and multimedia files), as well as supports file compression and encryption/decryption and text search (including offline HTML search or fuzzy search).

Prodigy (P*)

If your demands are more serious and technical, this online oldtimer, Prodigy, may not be robust enough for your regular use. But let's examine some of its features.

Even though Prodigy was the first of the online services to release the very popular Windows-based Web access and browser in 1995, the online gold rush hasn't been as fortunate for Prodigy as it has for America Online and CompuServe. As those services hired new people and expanded resources, Prodigy cut jobs and hasn't grown nearly as fast as its two major competitors. Sears, which jointly owns the service with IBM, tried to sever its ties for years before Prodigy was bought out by investors in 1996.

The role Prodigy has played in the online community has been an important one as the easiest, if not the most feature-packed, of the major online services. Over the past few years, in addition to plugging in Internet access, Prodigy has broadened its regular offerings to include live chat, and downloads (mostly through ZD Net, discussed earlier under America Online). While even this expansion hasn't fully turned the financial tide for Prodigy, which is fighting to hold onto its third place status among the Big Three, Prodigy has survived many past rumors of its demise. It may rally through these interesting times as well.

Getting Prodigy Software

You can look for free Prodigy disks in any recent computing magazine (you want V1.2 or later) since the only way to use Prodigy is by using their software. However, you need a user ID and temporary password to access the service to establish an account, so even if you have the software, you'll need to call the number below to get a user ID if you don't have one.

If you can't find any free disks, you can order a copy by calling 1-800-PRODIGY.

Setting up a Prodigy Account

Once you have the Windows-version Prodigy software, just follow instructions for installing the software, which would usually be Run (from Windows NT Start) A:\SETUP.EXE for disk-based software. Then choose Prodigy under available Programs (also from the Windows Start menu) to launch Prodigy and sign on to create your account.

Prodigy Pricing. One plus with Prodigy is that it offers you the choice of a standard monthly membership plan or a special bargain plan for frequent users.

Under the Value Plan, you pay a monthly fee of $9.95, which includes five hours of CORE access. You then pay $2.95 for each additional hour you're online, with extra fees accessed for some Plus areas online. The Mutual Fund Analyst on Prodigy is one example of a plus area, charging a daily fee of $5.95 for investment guidance.

With the 30/30 plan, a $30 monthly fee nets you 30 online hours.

New members receive the first month's membership free, along with 10 free hours to preview the service.

Tip

Several of your Prodigy account information needs can be accessed by pressing Ctrl+T to get the Tools menu, from which you can alter your password, modify your personal information, check your account, get print options, and configure Prodigy for AUTOLOGON capability.

Getting Technical Assistance. If you can't sign on to Prodigy, you can call 1-800-PRODIGY for help. Like the other online service customer lines, Prodigy's tend to be jammed so expect to wait anywhere from a few minutes to the better part of an hour to talk with a representative.

If you can't get online between the hours of 10 a.m. and 2 a.m., you can seek live assistance at JUMP: HELP. You can also reach the Member Assistance area by clicking the blue underlined (hypertext linked) Member Help option anywhere you see it online.

Tip

JUMP is the fastest way to move about Prodigy. To JUMP, press Ctrl+J or select Go To from Prodigy's menu bar then choose JUMP (or NAVIGATE). A Goto dialog box will appear. Type in the name of a Prodigy site you want to visit or make your best guess. If Prodigy doesn't recognize the JUMPword, it will provide a list of known sites to browse through (see Table 5.4).

Basic Features

Prodigy dishes up a little bit of everything, without much exhaustive detail in any one area. You can shop through vendors like Office Max, check your horoscope, get information about Business and Finance, surf the Web, or search through Prodigy's topic-oriented bulletin boards.

Table 5.4 Prodigy JUMPword list	
JUMPword	**Prodigy Site**
BOARDSA-Z	Prodigy's Main Bulletin Boards menu
BUSINESS	Business and Finance online spotlight
COMPUTER BB	Computer Bulletin Board
COMPUTERS	Computers Main Menu
COMPUTING	Computing Main Menu
HELP	Customer Service support area (free)
INTERNET	Prodigy's Internet Services
MAIL	Prodigy Mailbox
ZDNET	Ziff-Davis Net (Plus area)

E-mail

Prodigy Mailbox is actually a separate utility called when you request it, like selecting Mail from the Prodigy toolbar. The result can be frustratingly slow on older PCs and/or slower modems.

As Mailbox loads, your list of new, as well as received but undeleted, mail appears along with information about status (new or read), date received, who sent it, and the subject of the communication. Highlight a piece of mail you wish to read, and click it. That e-mail will open in a small text window below the e-mail listing, which you can resize as necessary.

To reply to this e-mail, select the e-mail again from the Mailbox listing and click Reply or select Reply from the open e-mail screen. An empty e-mail screen will appear about the received e-mail screen, and will automatically be addressed to the sender of the original mail with the subject line left intact. Type your reply, then click Spellcheck and Send, or just Send to post the e-mail.

To compose new mail, select Write from the Prodigy Mailbox screen, and a new mail message screen will open (see fig. 5.10). Provide the intended recipient's e-mail address (you can send mail across the Internet from Prodigy, as well as receive it), tab down to the Subject and provide a title, then tab to the main body of the e-mail and write your message. When you're satisfied, click Send to post it.

II

Dialup Communications

Fig. 5.10
Did you notice
that Prodigy
Mailbox has a
Spellcheck feature
built in?

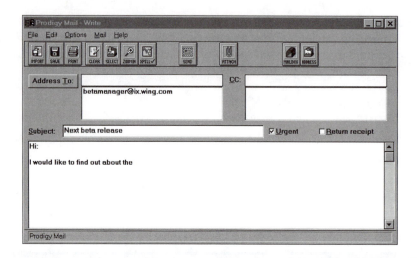

Troubleshooting

Wait, I'm confused. What does the blue marker in the bottom right of my Prodigy screen do?

This is Prodigy's blue billing indicator, which reports FREE, CORE, and PLUS access depending on where you are and what you're doing on the service. FREE means you're not paying for connect time. CORE means you're located in a regular online area which does count against your connect time, but accesses no additional fees for access. PLUS means you've entered a premium service, like ZD Net or Homework Helper.

Internet Access

JUMP INTERNET transports you right to Prodigy's net gateway, from which you can browse the Web. You can also launch the Web software directly by clicking on the Web button from the Prodigy toolbar available at the bottom of your Prodigy screen. Internet e-mail capability is built into Prodigy Mailbox. USENET newsgroups are also accessible.

What many find is that Prodigy's Web access seems faster than web surfing through rivals America Online and CompuServe, perhaps partly due to lower traffic and partly to something Prodigy connected right. Loading a Web search engine like Lycos at **http://www.lycos.com** can take me more than four or five minutes connecting to America Online at a modem speed of 14.4K, while it typically takes me less than 90 seconds to do so via Prodigy.

II

Dialup Communications

> **Tip**
>
> Need a shortcut for visiting a particular Web site? Just **JUMP**, click the WWW option on the GoTo screen which pops up, then type the exact URL of the Web site you wish to load in the dialog box. Prodigy auto-loads the Web browser and tries to connect you with the site.

Computing Support

A few jumpwords take you to the core of Prodigy's computer support offerings. For example, **JUMP COMPUTING** spotlights special features and events online as well as available through direct links to the Internet, particularly locations on the Web as well as related Usenet newsgroup discussions.

JUMP COMPUTERS takes you to the virtual lobby of hardware and software manufacturers with support bases on Prodigy. You'll also see links to related special support groups such as the IBM Club.

Because Bulletin Boards on Prodigy seem to offer the largest base of communication, let's look at how to navigate one on Prodigy, using as the example the Computer Bulletin Board, as shown in figure 5.11.

Fig. 5.11
You can select to read Bulletin Board posts going back only so far or look for posts from a specific Prodigy member.

1. From online, type **JUMP COMPUTER BB.**
2. Click Choose a Topic.
3. In the dialog box that appears, type **Windows** or select Windows/Windows 95 from the list.

4. Click Begin Reading Notes.

5. From the Read Post menu choose from options available to navigate through the postings.

To compose a new post for publication on Prodigy's Computer BB, select Options from the Read Post menu, from which you can then select a new subject or topic.

Prodigy still does not offer a great deal in the form of downloadable files, and you can find the majority of what's available in two locations:

- In the Bits and Bytes collection. **JUMP COMPUTING**, select blue underlined File Libraries option, from the next screen choose File Libraries again, and you'll see a library listing.

- ZD Net, a premium extra on Prodigy, available at **JUMP ZD NET**. Check the file descriptions carefully here, since they indicate the price you'll be charged for downloading a particular file, with most fees ranging from $2-5.

The Microsoft Network (MSN)

Microsoft is no novice to offering online support, having guested on other online services for several years. And it took just seven months from the time it launched the Microsoft Network service in August 1995 to reach the one million member mark.

But with MSN's software accessibility limited to being packed into one or two versions of their Windows operating system platforms, coupled with its less than full Internet features, and relative scarcity of vendors, the Microsoft Network's future seems cloudy. There are already rumors that MSN will ultimately change from a regular online service to a gigantic, possibly subscription-based (you pay a fee) Web site.

Getting MSN software

You will need Microsoft's proprietary MSN software to access the Microsoft Network, and luckily (since it's not currently available separately) you will find it built right into your Windows NT desktop after installation.

If you experience any difficulties in signing on to MSN for the first time, you can reach their technical support team as outlined later in this section under, "Getting Technical Assistance."

Setting Up an MSN Account

To establish a new account with the Microsoft Network, just click the MSN icon on your Windows NT desktop, which brings up an MSN information screen about types of services offered.

1. Select OK to continue establishing a new MSN account.

   If you happen to already be a member needing to set up MSN on a new computer, you can click the bottom left corner box marked, "Click Here if you are already a member..." then click OK.

2. The next screen will prompt you for your local area code, then the first three digits of the phone number you are calling from.

3. Select OK to continue.

4. A screen will announce it needs to help you locate a primary access number for you to use each time you call MSN, and hopefully within your local calling area. Select Connect to allow the software to dial the information number.

5. MSN will dial the information number, download any information needed to find the primary access number along with any quick updates needed for you to use the network, then it will hang up, and open a window in which you can start filling in your account information.

   Select Tell us Your Name and Address.

6. Supply the needed information about yourself and locale, then select OK.

7. Choose Next, then select a way to pay.

   MSN is one of the services which absolutely requires a major credit card like MasterCard or Visa for payment. While Microsoft says it's investigating other possible arrangements like electronic transfer from checking accounts or prepaid debit cards, you're currently out of luck if you don't do plastic.

8. Provide the required credit card information, then select OK.

9. Select Then, Please Read The Rules.

   Basically, these are your rules of the road for being a member on the Microsoft Network, giving you some guidelines about what is, and what isn't acceptable on the service.

10. Select I Agree; if you don't agree, you can't join.

11. Select Join Now.

12. Select Connect to let your system dial MSN using your newly found primary access number to finish your account application.

13. You now need to choose your own Member ID and Password, then click OK.

    One benefit of MSN is that it lets you easily choose your own member name, instead of recommending alphanumeric combinations like on many other services. Many members just use their first name, or first name and first initial of their last name. For example, someone listing in MSN's member directory as Bill Gates of Redmond, Washington can be reached at Member ID "BillG."

14. Next, you will be asked to choose if you want full Internet access.

    Select Yes if you want access to expanded features like the World Wide Web (which, sadly, is not available through all local access numbers, including mine). If MSN detects Internet access capability from another online service, you will be asked if you want to let MSN remove your other net configuration. What this means is that if you want to continue to access the Internet from the other service provider, you should choose No.

    Select No if you only want access to Usenet newsgroups and net e-mail through MSN.

15. Select Finish.

You're now the newest member of the Microsoft Network!

To sign on for your first session:

1. From your Windows NT desktop, double-click the MSN icon, which brings up the Sign In screen as shown in figure 5.12.

Fig. 5.12
The MSN Sign In screen allows you to check the bottom left corner box to "remember" your password. This is convenient, but be careful using this option if others have access to your PC.

2. Type your Member ID and Password.

3. Select Connect.

> **Note**
>
> The Sign In screen includes an option entitled Settings. Use this to change your access number(s), dialing information, or modem, as well as specifying whether you want to connect using another dial-up Internet access provider or connect through your local area network.

4. It may take a few minutes to complete your first Sign In as your registration information gets transmitted to Microsoft. But, once you make it to the MSN Central screen (see fig. 5.13), you're there! Well, you will still need to get through the welcome messages from Microsoft Founder Bill Gates and MSN chief, Laura Jennings.

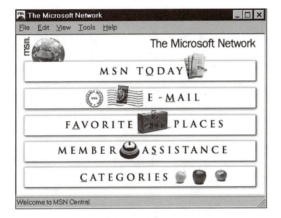

Fig. 5.13
MSN Central offers you fast and easy routing to the key offerings on MSN. Select E-Mail, Member Assistance, or Categories, Favorite Places, or view MSN Today to get a round-up of online highlights like Taxtime'96.

Dialup Communications

MSN Pricing

Microsoft offers two pricing schemes—a standard option and a frequent user plan. Under the first, you pay a monthly fee of $4.95 per month which includes three free hours of online access, with each additional hour costing $2.50. With the frequent user option, you pay $19.95 per month which covers 20 free hours plus a 20% discount (or $2/hour) on each additional hour you're online past that. Your first month online is free of charge.

Like many of the other services, Microsoft Network requires a major credit card to establish an account, but Customer Service indicates that they are exploring other payment options which they may implement in the future.

Getting Technical Assistance

Microsoft offers two ways for you to get help with malfunctioning MSN software.

- Online: Select Member Assistance, then select Member Support.

  You will receive a short form in which you can type in your problem and submit it to support staff for a reply, which generally comes in the form of e-mail about 24 hours later.

- Offline: Call 1-800-386-5550 and follow the voice menu to the best match for the kind of technical problem you are experiencing.

> **Tip**
>
> The wait for help via the phone can be very long. For instance, I called early one Thursday morning and waited just under 37 minutes for help. If you can make it online, try using Member Assistance instead. You'll get an e-mail reply within 24 hours.

Basic Features

Because the Microsoft Network is the newest of the commercial services, it hasn't quite had the time yet to become quite as packed with members and online offerings as its more established competitors. But less traffic and fewer than a million different options can be advantages to many new to online communications.

> **Tip**
>
> Go words aren't mentioned much online, but they act like fast links to desired spots on MSN without having to wade through unnecessary screens. To use them, go to MSN Central, pull down the Edit menu from MSN's menu bar, point to Goto, then click Other Location. Type the Go word of the area you want to visit in the dialog box which appears.

There are two main screens for accessing the greater components of the service, like electronic mail, business and finance, and computers and software. The first we discussed in the previous section, MSN Central, and the second is MSN Today (see fig. 5.14).

Let's take a look at some of the basic features you're apt to utilize or visit on MSN.

E-mail

As you first sign in to MSN, it will alert you with a text note at the bottom of your screen if you have e-mail waiting. If you blink, you may miss it, particularly if you're accustomed to the highlighted mail notification on America

Online or Prodigy. One plus about MSN's mail system is that it is integrated into Windows Messaging, available as part of your Windows package, and offers integrated communications services like e-mail, fax options, and even MSN itself as part of your desktop.

Fig. 5.14
The MSN Today screen acts as a sort of spotlight for special events and new online offerings, changing daily, and providing quick access to standard sites like the online Directory, Calendar of Events, and departments like Business and Finance.

To read new mail:

1. Select E-Mail from the MSN Central screen, or

If you're offline, click the Inbox icon on your Windows NT desktop.

2. A screen entitled, Inbox—Microsoft Exchange will appear as shown in figure 5.15.

The MSN toolbar above the e-mail listing provides some basic mail tools.

To read a listed piece of e-mail, place your cursor on the e-mail you want and double-click.

3. The e-mail message will open for you to read.

Additionally, you can choose from the open message screen to save the message as a text file to your disk, send it to your printer, forward it to someone else, copy it elsewhere, or simply delete it to eliminate it from your Inbox.

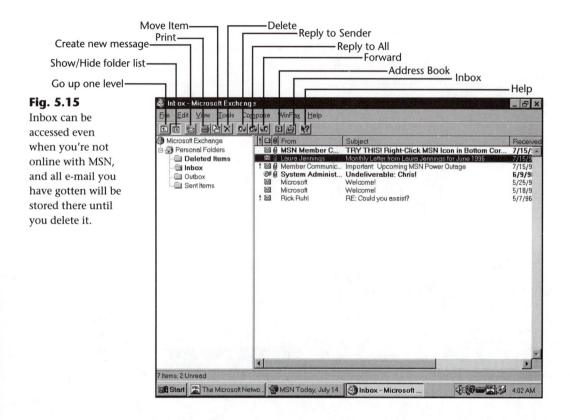

Fig. 5.15
Inbox can be
accessed even
when you're not
online with MSN,
and all e-mail you
have gotten will be
stored there until
you delete it.

To create e-mail:

1. Select the Create New Message icon from the toolbar, or

Select Compose from the top menu bar, then select New Message.

2. Write your e-mail.

Tip

Need to send mail to someone on another online service or elsewhere on the Net?
MSN mail lets you do that; just remember to add the @address.xxx to the person's
e-mail ID when you send mail, like this—**72340.167@compuserve.com** or
KateChase@aol.com.

---

3. Click the yellow envelope icon at the far left side of the toolbar to Send.

Internet Access

As you'll find, MSN doesn't offer a full range of Internet services at this time.
What you will have access to is Internet e-mail, Usenet newsgroups, and the

World Wide Web. For the Web, you'll need to download additional software to use, and you may encounter a problem if your local access or primary dialing number won't support Web surfing. In the latter event, you will need to decide if accessing the Web from MSN is important enough for you to incur toll charges by calling a Web-capable node outside your local calling area.

To reach MSN's Internet Center:

1. Go to the MSN Central Screen, then select Categories.

2. From the Categories listing, scan down the list until you locate Internet Center.

3. Double-click the Internet Center folder to open it.

To participate in Internet Newsgroups:

1. Double-click the Internet Newsgroups folder in Internet Center.

2. Double-click NetNews, which provides you with a listing of Newsgroup categories.

3. Double-click a category of interest to you, and folders representing each of the discussion groups within each category pop up.

4. Click folders until a listing of messages in that Newsgroup is presented on your screen.

5. Choose a message listing you wish to read, and click it.

Setting up Web access through MSN:

1. Follow the previous instructions 1-2 for reaching The Internet Center.

2. Select the Getting on the Internet icon which produces a screen offering Setup Instructions. In reality, this means you need to download additional software to make MSN Web-capable.

3. Select Setup Instructions.

4. Select Troubleshooting: How to Reinstall MSN, then click the star available on your screen.

    You'll get a screen advising you of how long the download will take (often 20-25 minutes at average 14.4K access), as well as stating that once the download is complete, MSN will disconnect you.

5. Click Yes.

6. You will be instructed to close all applications before continuing. Do so.

7. Click OK. Windows will then restart your computer.

8. When Windows reappears, you should now have an Internet icon on your desktop.
    Double-click the Internet icon.

II

Dialup Communications

9. Select Next.

10. Select Connect Using my <u>P</u>hone Line, or select Connect Using my LAN.

11. Select Next.

12. Select <u>U</u>se The Microsoft Network

13. Select Next.

14. Select Yes.

15. Select Next.

16. Click OK.

To get on the Web via MSN, just double-click the Internet icon. If you're not already connected, you will also need to Select Connect to Sign In. By default, the Microsoft Network will load its own Web home page as a jumping-off place.

Naturally, you want to explore other Web sites, so have your list of "want-to-visit" sites handy, complete with their URLs (Uniform Resource Locator, a special Net-specific address).

To specify a new Web site to visit:

1. Select <u>F</u>ile from the top menu bar, then <u>O</u>pen.

2. When the Open Internet Address dialog box pops up, carefully type the URL for your desired site. For example, if I want to reach the U.S. Government's FedWorld site, I would type: **http://www.fedworld.gov/** or **http://www.doc.gov** to access the Department of Commerce's Web site.

General and Business Interests

When you're not sure where to start finding what you want on MSN, it's positively time to explore the Categories option available from the MSN Central screen. This is where you locate major departments such as Business and Finance, Computers and Software, News and Weather, Home and Family, and the Internet Center which then guide you down into the meat of the service.

Troubleshooting

Help! I'm getting lost with all these open MSN screens. How do I find out if my PC vendor has a support area on MSN?

To find a specific vendor or service online, go to the MSN Central screen and select MSN Today. From the left-hand listings of categories, select Directory to let you view

> specific online listings sorted by Category. You have the option of resorting them alphabetically, which I found much easier to wade through.

Try double-clicking Business and Finance to bring up that category's features, leading to online areas for Federal Express, Fidelity Online Investment Center, Hoover's Business Resources, and Dun & Bradstreet Information Services.

Computing Support

You might expect that of all the companies running these commercial services, Microsoft's certainly got the relationships and resources to have perhaps the preeminent Computing Support area online. But it doesn't, at least not yet.

What it does have, besides a few online computing vendors like Symantec, is Microsoft and that's important. One advantage to that, for instance, is sometimes it's just faster to download Windows drivers from MSN than it is to pull them off Microsoft's ultra-busy web site.

You can download the latest Windows drivers at:

http://www.microsoft.com/windows/

On the Web

To reach the Microsoft Network's Computers and Software center, go to your MSN Central screen and select Categories, then choose Computers and Software. You will find hardware and software support, gaming publishers like Yoyodyne Entertainment, and bulletin boards for posting messages to ask questions and provide suggestions for others.

Finding NT Support Online

You can locate some discussions of Windows NT as a workstation and server on some of the resources already cited earlier in the section, "Computing Support."

Through a little exploration, we were able to locate two primary areas on MSN to find select Windows NT files. Unfortunately, as we were working on this book, Windows NT 4.0 was still in beta, so the offerings were pretty much for NT 3.51 Workstation or Server or earlier. Hopefully, this will change dramatically by the time you Sign In.

The first is the Shareware Forum. To reach it, go to the MSN Central screen, and select MSN Today. From MSN Today's left-hand listing, choose Computers and Software. You'll be presented with a Computers version of MSN Central advising you of select chats, special events, and permanent forums you might be interested in. On the right-hand side of the screen, under the listing Featured, scroll down to locate Shareware Forum, then double-click. Of the icons displayed, double-click Shareware Files, then double-click Windows 32-bit files.

The second area is part of Microsoft's own support forum. You can reach it by returning to the Computers and Software screen as outlined above. From the right-hand Featured list, select Microsoft to bring you to the Microsoft Forum. From the next screen, choose either Windows NT Workstation or Windows NT Server. Select Support Desktop, then choose the Windows NT Workstation and Server Software Library.

If you discover a must-have utility, just follow the prompts for downloading to your system.

Other Online Services

Not all of today's online services are huge, and not all appeal to a mass audience, focusing in on specialized niches, like financial information, gaming and entertainment, or library-based search needs. Let's take a look at a few of them, briefly.

General Interest

As was mentioned before, several online services are awaiting roll-out even as I type this, but two general interest services are known by name to many—Delphi and GEnie. At one time, both of these commercial services were part of the "Top Five" systems, but times haven't been as kind to them.

Delphi

While Delphi had the full complement of Internet services well ahead of any of the other big commercial companies, and was backed by wealthy publisher Rupert Murdoch's vast resources, it did so without the graphically pleasing Windows-based Internet tools packed into the proprietary software offered up by successes like CompuServe and America Online. This may be part of the reason that Delphi has virtually faded from the cyberspace map over the last few years. Gossip passes along the grapevine that Delphi may disappear as a full online service altogether, as Apple Computer's eWorld did early this year.

One advantage to Delphi, if you can still find them open, is that you can establish an account using your modem and a terminal communications package (since they have no proprietary software).

To do so:

- Set your terminal software to dial 1-800-895-4002.
- When the modem connects, press RETURN till you get a prompt.
- At the prompt, type username **JOINDELPHI**.
- At the prompt, type password **FREE** (you need a major credit card for immediate access).

You can also reach Delphi at 1-800-695-4005 or 1-617-491-3342.

GEnie

A division of General Electric, GEnie seemed to lose steam in the online membership wars even before the race for the Internet gathered momentum a few years back. Then GEnie simply failed to get its much-promised net access in place long after people began to demand to be "wired."

Though GEnie's members were loyal, using GEnie could be a problem since it, too, lacks any proprietary software. Thus, you have to contend with the clunkiness of a terminal communications package to connect to GEnie.

Late in 1995, General Electric said it was putting this long-running online service up for sale, and then G.E. itself formed a separate Internet division to focus on "business productivity solutions."

You can contact GEnie at 1-800-638-9636 or 301-251-6415.

Specialty Services

Specialty services appeal to a particular audience, rather than offering broad-based areas and content aimed at the masses. One example of this would be The Sierra Network, produced by Sierra Games, devoted to game-playing for kids of all ages.

But there are far more heavy-hitting specialty services out there for business persons and those needing key research abilities. Two of the best known of these are discussed in more detail below.

Dialog

Established in 1972 and owned by Knight-Ridder Information, Dialog continues to be the premier serious research service available by modem worldwide.

Why Dialog is a favorite among research librarians, scientists, students, and busy business folks is no mystery. Its resources include abstracts from millions of documents, access to over 100 top newspapers around the world, as well as to thousands of magazines and other periodicals. If something has been in print, there's a good chance you can locate a reference to it here.

Probably more than a few of us owe our Master's degrees to Dialog's very existence.

You can use any terminal software package and your modem to connect to Dialog. But navigating the system is made easier with the company's DialogLink software available in Macintosh, DOS, and Windows versions, at an additional charge.

Pricing is different here, too, because you pay by the kilobyte of retrieved information, but you can save time by having search results saved to your Dialog mailbox. You can't simply call up and join Dialog either, since they require you to fill out an application in advance. To get an application, call Dialog at 1-800-334-2564.

To see Dialog in action first, try visiting a large library close to you—a university library might be perfect since many have Dialog accounts for research. For a fee, many of these libraries will perform a search for you and sometimes let you sit in on the process.

Dow Jones

If you guessed that an online service with the name Dow Jones might be financial in focus, you're right.

Dow Jones News/Retrieval is a division of the same company which publishes the *Wall Street Journal*, the content of which is largely featured on the service. You'll also find services like stock and mutual fund information garnered from heavyweights such as Dun & Bradstreet and Standard and Poor's.

Aimed at the business person or investor, Dow Jones was one of the first to boast personalized news content based on the specific interests of a particular subscriber. You select the categories you're interested in, and then choose to ignore or explore the rest.

Dow Jones TextLink software makes navigating the service fairly straightforward, too.

To contact Dow Jones about an account, call 1-800-522-3567.

Future of Online Services

What's that old Chinese curse?

"May you live in interesting times!"

This could very well be the cross that movers and shakers among the online services must bear right now, because these are decidedly interesting times stealing forward to an uncertain future.

Just in the past year, Apple's eWorld folded rather suddenly after a long, tough ride. The Interchange online service which never made it out of beta was scrapped by AT&T after they spent a fortune acquiring it from the Ziff-Davis computer publishing empire. Talk is afoot that Microsoft isn't pleased with the response to MSN and may turn it into a gigantic Web page, and the same has been rumored for the ailing Prodigy. America Online has seen tremendous growth, but how far away is its ceiling, with other providers offering cheaper and usually faster Internet access?

Even AOL CEO Steve Case, who reportedly became a millionaire overnight in 1993 when the company's stock went public, has to be worried about Time Warner's planned debut of LodeRunner. This new online service boasts one very pivotal difference: Cable modem connections will allow access at speeds up to 100 times faster than current AOL and CompuServe service.

As the next few years unfold, look for online services to seem perhaps less like glorified computer bulletin board systems, and more like television networks. America Online, for example, has started tossing about the word "channels," meaning new or expanded areas of content. AOL also seems to be pushing the concept of online "stars" like the Motley Fool crew and NetGirl, perhaps hoping you'll become as loyal to certain "programs" online as more of us once were to favorite TV shows.

But this also means the "mainstreaming" of online services will continue. This is good on the one hand, because it means that more people from all walks of life and regions of the world can become a part of the information and social gold mines of cyberspace. It's very likely by the year 2000, a good many more of us will be shopping there, taking classes there, communicating with friends and business associates there, and even ordering our lunch pizzas there. On the other hand, it may mean online services will become even more like television networks in that you'll have to wade through a quantity of channels to find the quality of programming you want. ❖

II

Dialup Communications

CHAPTER 6

Setting Up a Bulletin Board System

by Kate Chase

Long before CompuServe and America Online became household names, people both in this country and the world communicated via the computer bulletin board system (BBS). Born in wintry Chicago in 1978 when software designed by Ward Christensen first answered the phone on a CP/M-based Northstar computer operated by Randy Seuss, BBSes became the prototype for today's big commercial online services.

Though they're the oldest medium for popular personal computer/modem communications, bulletin boards are still very viable today and remain a daily part of telecommunicating life. True, BBSes tend not to be as glitzy and broadly feature-packed as their mega-sized commercial siblings. However, BBSs and their system operators, known as sysops, have tried to keep pace by offering increasingly sophisticated technology in a friendly format, like advanced Internet access, online shopping/ordering, and new avenues to provide customer support.

Bulletin boards were once primarily for modem hobbyists, but a BBS can function in many roles. It can serve as a community information server, a technical support tool to offer software updates and help material, a shopping mall, or an office communications network. They can be open to the world, or access can be limited to specific persons you designate.

We will look at considerations in planning and setting up a business-based BBS under Windows NT. In the process, we'll touch on everything from design to specific software to maintenance issues that will keep your BBS running smoothly and looking well-kept, something your BBS customers will demand whether you let them access freely or charge a fee.

In this chapter, you'll learn to

- Recognize typical BBS features
- Design, select, and establish your BBS
- Consider security, maintenance, and Internet connection
- Find resources for BBS system operators

The BBS as a Business Tool

Naturally, you need to know a bit more about bulletin board systems and what features may benefit you before you decide to establish one.

Simply put, a BBS is an online service in which customers, or users, connect using their PCs, modems, and terminal communications software to a special host program, which can run on anything from old 8-bit Commodore 64s to today's ultra-fast P-200s and beyond to the mini and mainframe computer realm. You may be surprised at how nice a BBS you can design and implement on a fast 486 with a sizable amount of hard disk storage and a few hundred dollars for software, a standard Hayes-compatible modem, and a spare phone line. This can provide a low-end trial to see if this medium can work for you.

First, you need to know what kind of features are commonly available to you when creating your own BBS:

- *Live chat/teleconferencing*. With multiple phone lines you can give your customers the option of communicating real-time with your support personnel or other customers. With special add-ons, you can include global chatting to other BBSes or Internet Relay Chat (IRC), a large talk network component of the Internet.
- *E-mail*. Have e-mail limited to your BBS system and those with access to it, or establish gateways to other networks like Fidonet (the largest international hobbyist BBS with thousands of nodes across the globe). With the proper connections like an SMTP gateway, you can give your users the ability to send and receive Internet e-mail quickly and easily. Note that most serious BBS software gives you the ability to read and respond to e-mail offline, so customers have the option of communicating with you without tying up the BBS lines.
- *Message Bases*. Like e-mail, this can be a local "conversation" where customers can communicate by posting notes or messages that can be set to be read only by those with staff-access to the BBS or by the general populace. But you can also gateway these to other BBSes. For

example, Fidonet calls this Echomail offering topical message bases to any Fido BBS that subscribes, or allow your customers to explore USENET newsgroups via an Internet connection.

- *Software Libraries*. Give your customers access to software updates, technical information, tips, and downloadable graphic images of products.

- *Doors*. Even older than Windows, BBS doors are add-on programs that allow users to select specialty features like completing a market survey, playing a game, or product ordering.

- *Specialty additions*. Discussed more later, you can get add-ons to process check and credit card payments, create an online mall, provide very specialized order-taking, and more.

Knowing some of what a BBS can offer, let's examine some of the factors that you should consider when making your decision. For example, if you're looking for an on-ramp to the Information Superhighway you can construct at your own pace, there may not be a cheaper way to test the waters than by setting up a bulletin board.

What Do You Want To Accomplish?

It's important to know how you can use this BBS in your business before you even begin looking at software. Consider some of the ways BBSs are currently utilized for commercial purposes (yet, many operate freely, with no membership costs or advertisement) to see if any of the applications fit your goals.

Ways a Business Can Use a Bulletin Board

Since we've already discussed standard BBS features, you know what you can have, but how you implement these features—and customize them for your business—to help you meet the goals for your BBS will be your signature.

What are some standard applications for the BBS in the business world?

- *Technical Support Center*. Provide your customers with a BBS to provide software updates, get latest information on product releases, post questions and get responses from support staff, and place orders for new versions.

  The U.S. government operates a BBS called FedWorld just for locating federal information, like congressional votes, IRS tax forms in PC readable format, and consumer tips (see fig. 6.1).

Fig. 6.1
Uncle Sam's very own FedWorld BBS lets you go online with the government to check on congressional bills coming up for vote or check out housing information.

- *Online Shopping Mall.* With the advent of cybersales, you could develop a network of wholesaler contacts, set up a BBS oriented to sales of a product listing of your own selection as a distributor, then process orders and payments electronically. Today's BBSes allow you to add snazzy graphics advertising your wares, and sound options to promote events or demo available music for purchase.

- *As an Employee Resource.* Set up a dialup BBS for your outside sales force to call in orders and check on product availability. Establish one oriented to personnel for work schedules, upcoming events, accumulated sick and vacation time, or online educational resources.

- *As a Community-Oriented Service.* Many newspapers, local Chambers of Commerce, professional organizations, medical services, and other public and private sector groups provide public BBSes as a means of giving local service information with the added bonus of some "good neighbor" advertising.

  For example, many accounting and tax preparation firms pool resources to offer a BBS or Web site with tax and financial planning tips.

Would a Web Site Be Better?

The World Wide Web is definitely the hottest component of online communications right now, whether personal or business-related. The current level of consumer excitement over it can mean big revenue to those who get noticed.

Yet that same excitement leads to a lot of traffic problems on the Web, and a tendency for good sites to go neglected as thousands of new Web entries come online each week. While there are tens of thousands of BBSes globally as well, the competition isn't anywhere near as fierce as on the Web. Thus, you can be a small fish in the large Web pond, or a bigger fish in the smaller BBS pond.

Cost-effectiveness can be a factor. To provide the kind of materials on your Web site that you could on a bulletin board would probably require leasing Web services from an outside contractor, or investing perhaps a minimum of $2,000 in software and other equipment, along with the labor to establish it (unless you have an HTML guru in your workplace already) and a Pentium dedicated as a Web server and Internet connection. The fancier you want to make your home page, like adding Web chat capability, the more behind-the-scenes resources are required. The same amount of money and equipment would buy you a comparatively higher degree of capability with a BBS.

Having a BBS hardly precludes you from having a Web presence. Once you decide to connect your BBS to the Internet, either on debut or at some future time, you can find software and hardware modules to make it possible for customers to reach your BBS through the World Wide Web, as shown in figure 6.2, featuring your own home page. This will be discussed later in this chapter in the section, "Connecting Your BBS to the Internet."

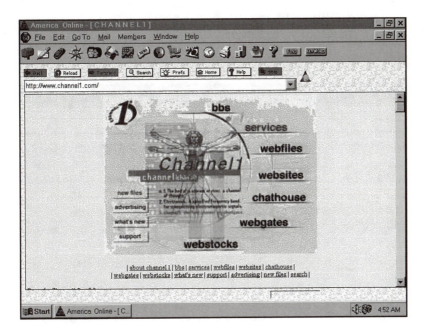

Fig. 6.2
Channel1, a Cambridge, MA-based commercial BBS and Internet Service Provider, offers inbound Telnet access to their system to reduce long distance access charges.

II

Dialup Communications

Research and Review the Results

The very best way to determine what is currently available with today's bulletin boards and how you might use these features and implementations to your advantage is to do some field work—study your computer, terminal communications software, and modem.

Locate some BBSes that relate to your field to see what other businesses are doing, and you may want to check out other types of bulletin boards as well, just for ideas. If you have an account on any of the major online services (see Chapter 5, "Using Online Services"), you can find BBS lists pretty easily. On CompuServe, you can download a national BBS listing updated monthly from Ziff-Davis' Computer Shopper Forum at **GO: CSHOPPER**. On America Online, as another example, type Ctrl+K or **keyword: FILESEARCH** then search on BBS LISTS.

On the Web

You can locate these on the Web, too, by using one of the big Web search engines like the one at:

http://www.lycos.com

or visiting a site like Boardwatch Magazine's at:

http://www.boardwatch.com

or Computer Shopper's Web site at:

http://www.cshopper.com.

To get you started, we have provided a short listing of business-based BBSs available for public access, shown in Table 6.1.

Table 6.1 Some Business Bulletin Boards		
Company/Service	**Phone No.**	**Focus**
Channel One	1-617-354-8873	Boston area information, ISP
FedWorld	1-703-321-3339	Gateway to Uncle Sam online
FedWorld/Tax Forms	1-703-321-8020	Just tax forms
Hamptons Online	1-516-283-1114	Community service and info, ISP
Microsoft	1-206-637-9009	Technical support
Whole Earth 'Lectronic Link	1-415-332-6106	Premiere subscription BBS, ISP

Quick Approach to BBS Hopping

Now that you have some BBS access numbers to try, let's cover the fastest way to get online to check one out.

1. From Windows NT, click Start, Programs, then Accessories.

2. Double-click Hypertrm, the included Windows 95/NT Windows terminal software.

3. A screen marked Connection Description appears. Type a name or title for the connection session, then choose an icon from the provided selection (see fig. 6.3). Click OK.

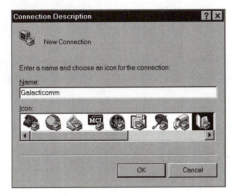

Fig. 6.3
Since we're calling Galacticomm's BBS to check out their setup, Galacticomm is what we named this session.

4. When the window pops up, type in the Area Code and phone number of the BBS you want to call and then click OK.

5. When a Connect dialing screen pops up, click Dial.

HYPERTRM dials the number and offers you a status screen letting you know how things are going. When you're connected, as shown in figure 6.4, the status screen disappears and you're presented with the opening screen of the BBS you just connected with, prompting you for your name.

Note

Most bulletin boards require your terminal communications software's parameters be set to 8-N-1. This refers to 8 bits, no parity, and one stop bit.

Fig. 6.4
BBSes like FedWorld and Galacticomm are free access, meaning you only pay any long distance connect charges. Some are subscription-based so you must pay a fee to access the full BBS.

As you visit established BBSes, feel free to take notes on what type of BBS software is being used (this is standardly provided), how easy it allows you to navigate the service, and anything special the business itself offers via the BBS which may spark an idea of your own. Most systems allow you to post a message to the system operator or sysop, as well. Don't be afraid to ask questions, since other sysops can be one of your best resources for technical assistance and brainstorming fresh approaches.

Deciding How Big a Commitment to Make

As touched upon earlier, you can start a BBS offering of just a single-line, or launch with a much larger multi-line system which gives dozens of customers access simultaneously.

Young teenagers, for example, set up their own BBSes everyday using their existing PCs and modems and downloaded shareware or public domain BBS software (like Maximus, a Fidonet-compatible shareware BBS package) for the cost of one extra phone line into their room.

The Cost Factor

For a business system where you have the basic equipment (dedicated BBS computer, phone line, and Hayes-compatible modem), as little as $100 for a package like Mustang Software's Wildcat! for Windows95/NT can get you up and running with a one- or two-line BBS within a few hours.

However, the closer you approach a fully-serviced Internet-linked BBS, the steeper the expenses become until you're in the range of several hundred dollars per month just for an ultra-fast Integrated Services Data Network (ISDN) 24-hour Net link. You also need to factor in the telephone and electricity expenses.

While many BBSes operate freely—this is standardly the case with company support systems—many thousands of BBSes operate on a subscription basis, usually paid by check or credit card for three months to a year in advance. Such fees often average from $10-30 per month, with the higher end usually the norm with fuller featured BBSs—offering full Internet service in addition to other specialty services, like extensive software collections or global chatting.

Labor—Your BBS Operator

The broader your goals, the more likely you will need to designate a part- or full-time operator to run the BBS. This is especially true if you create a very interactive BBS that allows customers to post questions with a promise of a speedy reply, or lets customers place or check on the status of orders. Clients notice when questions go unanswered or out-dated material is left online, not to mention if the BBS becomes unavailable for long periods of time due to technical difficulties. This can lead them to stop using your BBS as a resource, something you don't want if you've made a substantial time and cost commitment in establishing it. Remember the labor factor as a continuing role in your BBS's success when making your plans.

What qualifications should a sysop have? This depends on the software and equipment you choose, and the size of operation you plan. Some of the software is amazingly easy to install and get operational but you need someone with talent and perseverance to tweak it to perfection, then keep it running smoothly. You may be able to do the job yourself or see if someone else in your business already has BBS or ISP experience to draw upon.

For example, with almost no modem communications experience whatsoever, I was quickly able to get a Fidonet node BBS up and running echomail back and forth within Connecticut in the late 1980s. But to finally override a very pesky hidden security feature with a specialty modem I was using required the help of an experienced sysop, who worked with me by phone while I typed furiously at the keyboard.

If you're planning a larger scale operation, you could easily get by with someone already on your staff who is knowledgeable about PCs, Windows NT, and communications service, and able to devote some of his or her time to BBS maintenance. Ideally, the person should have solid experience in system troubleshooting, since this can be a big part of what a sysop does.

In a typical week, a BBS sysop can expect to read and write a good deal of e-mail, run routine maintenance like the purging of old messages and files, monitor system activity, provide access to new customers, replace or upgrade malfunctioning hardware and software, do regular backups, and reset the BBS many, many times.

Equipment

Besides the modem, software, phone line, and computer we have talked about for a very basic BBS set up, you may find yourself clamoring to add nice additions like a multi CD-changer (for CD-ROM based file collections on BBSs offering a large software base) or ISDN capability.

While ISDN capability and connecting are discussed later in "Connecting Your BBS to the Internet," making hardware configuration decisions for your BBS is not a lightweight issue. If you're running a small system, then you probably can start out comfortably with the items mentioned above (your PC, modem, BBS software, and phone line).

The larger the system you anticipate opening, the greater your hardware needs are likely to be. File-intensive systems—those offering thousands of software titles—demand a large amount of storage space, and perhaps the aforementioned multi CD-changer to handle download requests for software kept offline (off your local hard disk). Systems focusing on live chat capabilities are more apt to need additional modems and phone lines to accommodate the hours many users choose to spend on chat-based BBSes, and may feel a stronger push to be connected via some type of network so that BBS users can chat with users on other BBSes either locally or globally.

BBS Software

Strangely enough, you would think BBS software developers would have leaped to the 32-bit possibilities under Windows NT. In truth, however, just having BBS software available in a Windows version at all is a fairly recent phenomenon, and NT-specific software is still rarer.

Troubleshooting

Why doesn't the BBS software I bought for Windows 95 work properly under Windows NT 4.0? They look so similar!

An editorial in Windows NT Magazine (June 1996) suggests that less than 50 percent of Windows 95 logo applications will run under Windows NT 4.0. So, you can't assume that BBS software written for Windows 95, an earlier version of Windows NT, and certainly many written for Windows 3.x, will run properly on your Windows NT 4.0 setup. Check with the technical support department of your BBS software publisher to see if the BBS software you wish to use is fully Windows NT 4.0-compatible.

We're going to take a quick look at some of the more popular BBS packages you may have heard about already. There are more available, and ones like PowerBBS provide a downloadable shareware version you can get on many of the commercial online services. A few public domain BBS software packages like Opus are also available.

Some Popular Titles

Easy to install and configure, Excalibur is used by more than 12,000 BBSes globally, and runs under Windows, Windows 95, and Windows NT. It supports Internet connection, LANs too, and includes built-in security options and graphics support, plus developers' tools to create new programs for your Excalibur BBS.

The Bread Board System (TBBS)

One of the older BBS software packages, eSoft's The Bread Board System (TBBS) bills itself as an "industrial-strength" BBS provider. Internet- and LAN-capable, with all the classic BBS features, eSoft also offers option modules to add onto TBBS or other software.

Of particular note is eSoft's IPAD (Internet Protocol Adapter) package, an add-on that provides a turnkey-style approach to Internet access for those without any experience in connectivity. According to eSoft, it can work with almost any BBS software, but those using TBBS or Durand Communications' MindWire Web server can potentially just remove the unit from its box and establish a single cable link connection to create an Internet link, providing you have a physical line out to the net already established (see "Connecting Your BBS to the Internet," later in this chapter).

On the Web

A demo of IPAD is available at their Web site at:

http://www.esoft.com

The Major BBS

Galacticomm was offering commercial-style, multiple line-capable BBS software long before most people heard of cyberspace. You will also notice a lot of business-based BBSes running it. One advantage here is that Major BBS software runs well under Galacticomm's WorldGroup Web server package, which offers a sizable modular expansion inventory. If you think you may evolve into offering Web-based service, you may want to investigate this. For a good indication of Major BBS's qualifications, definitely visit Galacticomm's own bulletin board at (954) 583-7808.

On the Web

You may want to surf to Galacticomm's Web site too, but it's only WorldGroup-related, available at:

http://www.gcomm.com

PowerBBS

This package differs from many in that it is a 32-bit graphical user interface (GUI), with easy installation, fully customizable menus, and inbound Telnet capable. It starts at $189 for a 4-node pack. You can find a Windows version on CompuServe using **GO PBBS** or call their BBS at (516) 938-0506.

PowerBoard BBS 2.0

Produced by NuIQ Software, a standard 4-node package retails for $99 and the 99-node professional pack for $249. PowerBoard bills itself as the first BBS package to support the Windows Internet Protocol (WIP) standard, and the only BBS platform that runs equally well under both Windows and DOS. There is no Windows NT-specific version currently available. Log onto their BBS at (914) 833-1479.

On the Web

You can test drive the BBS format on PowerBoard Web site at:

http://www.nuiq.com

Wildcat! BBS

See the later section "Walking Through a Sample BBS Setup" for expanded details on Wildcat's features. Two strong benefits with Mustang's Wildcat!: it's very quick to configure and Mustang offers support for it on several online services. Check their BBS at (805)873-2400.

Specialty Add-ons

While a few major names produce the rather small roster of general application BBS software available, you will find more selection to be had (depending on your software type) in add-ons for your BBS.

Add-ons can run the gamut from political polling software to intricate game modules to advanced financial/transaction service applications. If you know in advance of a particular add-on product you might want—for example, credit-card processing—check to make certain the BBS software is compatible with the add-on. Sometimes add-ons are written to run under all major BBS software, and sometimes just for a select one or two. Many packages provide a developer's kit to help BBS sysops and interested programming pros and amateurs create add-ons of their own.

To get an idea of what's available, here's just a sampling of the add-ons you can get your hands on:

- American Banking System sells BBS-specific software to facilitate accepting check payments online (they also offer credit card payment/processing, online shopping, and Web server options). You can reach them at **http://www.absbank.com**.

- Logicom offers a service to allow your BBS customers to pay for BBS access or products by charging a fixed fee directly to their telephone bills, invoked by dialing a 1-900 number from their standard touch-tone telephones.

Walking Through a Sample BBS Setup

Sure, we can tell you that BBS software itself is fairly easy to set up—remember, we said the tweaking could be the time-killer—but walking through a sample BBS software installation should give you an even clearer picture.

Choosing from the few available with an NT-specific version, let's try setting up Mustang Software's Wildcat! V5 BBS for Windows 95/NT.

Wildcat's System Requirements

First, we need to check the software's operating requirements to make certain we have what is necessary. As a general rule, if you have what it takes to run Windows NT, you probably have what you need just to test-drive the BBS software on a single-line setup, if you have a modem and spare phone line.

Wildcat! says it needs:

- A minimum 486/33 PC compatible, with a Pentium preferred for greater than two phone lines

- 16M or more recommended for Windows NT-based sysops with 32M preferred by many
- More than 30M of hard disk space available
- CD-ROM drive
- Hayes compatible modem, preferably 14.4K bps or faster
- Voice grade telephone line (the kind you use daily) for dial-in BBS customers
- Available standard communications ports, though it is possible to use other devices (optional) such as ISDN adapters and multi-port cards which are Windows NT 4.0 compatible

How to Install

Mustang made the installation pretty easy. On my P-133, for example, it took well under 10 minutes from start to finish, placing me on the threshold of designing my service.

If you have Wildcat! 5 for Windows 95/NT, you can follow along as we install the software.

1. With NT already running, simply quit all other applications you may have open.

2. Place the Wildcat! 5 CD into your CD-ROM drive.

   NT should auto sense the CD's presence and the Wildcat! 5 menu appears, as shown in figure 6.5.

Fig. 6.5
More than 50,000 BBSes around the world use Wildcat! 5 BBS software.

3. Click the Wildcat! Install icon.

   The "Welcome to the Wildcat! for Windows 95/NT Setup program" appears. Click Next.

4. Next, you're prompted for a destination for the Wildcat! software on your hard disk. Choose a different location by selecting the Browse option, or use the default location provided: **C:\WC5**. Click Next.

5. Select the Group to install Wildcat! into.

   By default, it will be placed in its own Wildcat! 5 folder but you can also choose to add it to an existing folder. Click Next.

6. Files are then copied from the CD to your designated destination on your hard disk. Then a window pops up announcing that Setup is Complete!

   Click OK to continue.

7. You need to provide your Wildcat! Registration information (see fig. 6.6) including registration number, line count, and product key. You will locate these codes on the back label of your Wildcat! installation CD.

   Click OK once and you are notified that your registration data is being saved. Click OK again to continue.

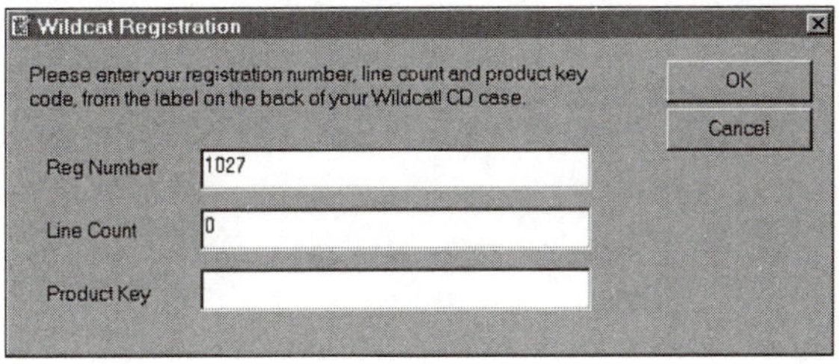

Fig. 6.6
Don't toss away your Wildcat! 5 installation CD jacket. You'll need the codes on the back label of the jacket if you reinstall the BBS.

8. The Welcome to Wildcat! screen appears, then informs you that the wizard will help you install an upgrade to an existing version of Wildcat! or load one for the very first time. Choose Create a New Configuration and click Next.

9. You are then informed the installation is complete, and offered the option to install the HoTMetaL free HTML authoring tool. Click OK to install it, or click Cancel to abort the HTML tool installation.

Finally, a Group populated by Wildcat! configuration tools appears. Believe it or not, your BBS software is now installed, and ready to configure to your custom specifications.

A Quick Look at Wildcat! 5 Controller Files

Controller programs are located within the Wildcat! 5 program group created during installation (see fig. 6.7). These controller programs help you create, enhance, or make corrections to your BBS setup.

Fig. 6.7

Repair or enhance your BBS setup using your Wildcat! 5 tools.

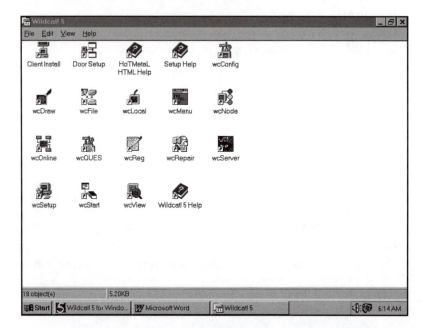

- *wcConfig*. Your Wildcat! BBS configuration tool (see "How to Customize", later in this chapter).
- *wcDraw*. Loads an ANSI draw program for creating ANSI graphics for your menus or simple graphical screens.
- *wcFile*. Lets you add files from CDs to your file database.
- *wcLocal*. Use this to log into the BBS locally (from your BBS keyboard).
- *wcMenu*. Create and edit BBS menus.
- *wcNode/wcNodeW*. Edit your node information.
- *wcOnline*. Brings the BBS active to a Waiting for Calls state and monitors activity.
- *wcQues*. Create and edit BBS questionnaires.
- *wcQWK*. Permits you to import and export mail in QEK/REP packet format for offline reading.
- *wcRepair*. Fixes the corrupted index on BBS database.
- *wcRun*. Runs wcCode programs from batch file.

- *wcServer*. Loads the server to control access to all BBS databases and configuration files.

- *wcSetup*. Your Wildcat! setup file; use to create a new BBS or upgrade an existing setup.

- *wcStart*. Lets you create a Wildcat startup sequence.

> **Tip**
>
> You can run wcStart each time you load Windows NT. To do so:
>
> **1.** Click <u>S</u>tart, Settings, Taskbar.
>
> **2.** Click the Start Menu Programs tab.
>
> **3.** Click Add.
>
> **4.** Use Browse to locate the WCSTART.EXE icon in your Wildcat! group folder and double-click it.
>
> **5.** Add the command line **/run,** so this line reads:
>
>   [drive letter]:\dirname\wcStart.exe /run
>
> **6.** Click <u>N</u>ext, then double-click the Start Menu folder.
>
> **7.** Provide the name you want for the Start Up menu, then click <u>F</u>inish.

- wcSyspw. Lets you assign a system password.
- *wcView*. View node activity (see who is on).

Preparing for Your First Test Call

Mustang makes it particularly easy by giving you a 10-step "quick access" route to allow you to get a skeleton BBS up and ready to accept a test call in a matter of minutes. This skeleton won't be what you want to ultimately make available to your employees or customers, but it's great not only for those who demand immediate gratification but for those who need to get something up quickly for test purposes.

To create the skeleton service:

1. With WildCat! running, double-click the wcServer icon in the Wildcat5! Group.

This launches the Server component of your BBS Software which runs minimized on the desktop. You'll know it is loaded when you see its red-and-white icon appear next to the clock on the Windows NT taskbar.

2. Double-click wcConfig.

A screen pops up entitled General Information, as shown in figure 6.8.

Fig. 6.8
Likely, if you're setting up a BBS for your business, it will bear your business name. But if you choose something more creative, try to research first to avoid duplicating the name of an already established BBS.

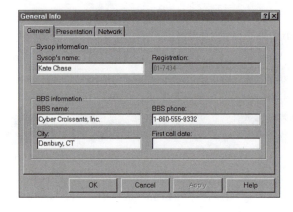

3. Provide your name—or your sysop's name—and give your BBS its name. Click OK.

4. Select Node 1 from the wcConfig group and then click Edit.

5. From the Node Settings screen, select the COM Port your BBS modem resides on, as well as the Modem type (see fig. 6.9).

   Leave the Computer Name option blank at this time. When you're satisfied, click OK.

6. Once again at the Node Settings screen, repeat step 5 except choose Node 2 and click Edit. This time, you need to configure your BBS for Local (from your keyboard) log-ons.

Fig. 6.9
Most BBS software requires a Hayes compatible modem. You may find best results with your BBS when using a very standard modem type, such as U.S. Robotics or Hayes.

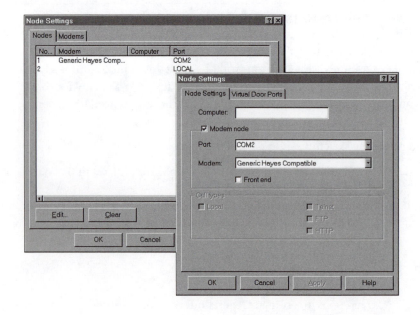

Click the box marked Local.

Click OK to shut this window, then click OK again to close the Node Settings window.

7. Return to the Wildcat! 5 Group and double-click wcLocal.

This option is always most exciting the first time you run it, because local mode allows you to log onto your BBS to see it the same way your customers will when they first enter.

You will be prompted for your name and password, as shown in figure 6.10. Remember to use the same name the very first time you log in that you used as Sysop Name in the previous steps.

Fig. 6.10
Don't lose your system password and don't write yourself a note reminding you of the password then post it where others can see.

8. Click the Security option on the toolbar under wcConfig.

You can now provide yourself with sysop-level access to your BBS, giving you additional options for performing behind-the-scenes work via your BBS that your customers cannot see.

Explore your skeleton BBS, then type **G** to log off your BBS. Now it's time to get ready for the first real incoming BBS call.

9. From the Wildcat! 5 Group, double-click wcOnline.

The Wildcat Online Controller screen appears. Immediately, Wildcat! reports that it is initializing the modem on Node 1, but will soon be ready to accept its first call as the Status message changes to Waiting for Calls.

10. Finally, test your BBS by placing the first remote call into the system. You can do this using one of the following methods:

■ Use an available second phone line and modem on this PC or another in your home or office to directly dial into the BBS.

- Ask a knowledgeable colleague or another sysop to test the line for you while you watch at your local console (the BBS keyboard).
- Log in through TCP/IP networking, if available.

If you are done testing your connection, close *wcOnline* to commence the creative part of BBS sysoping: the planning and design on your BBS.

> ## Troubleshooting
>
> *When I select wcLocal, it reports "no nodes are available" and nothing happens.*
>
> Return to Node Settings and make sure you selected Local for Node 2. Then retry wcLocal.

What Your Customers Don't See

As a sysop, you will have capabilities, known in BBS parlance as privileges, that those accessing your BBS from the outside will not have. This means you will find options available on your BBS' menu that you can see, but your customers or users will not.

Typically, those with standard access can reach a BBS' general areas with the ability to post and read in main message areas, download or upload files, chat, and have a set amount of time which they can spend on your BBS, all designated by you.

If you wonder what the average user sees, log onto your BBS locally and create a new account for yourself using a different screen name or handle, and look around. This is good for catching potential security problems, because you may spot an option available to general customers that you didn't want.

How to Customize

The wcConfig menu is like a control panel guiding your entry to performing the customization necessary to turn Mustang's software into your online service, with 18 major configuration options or tools available to you.

Looking at the menu, as shown in figure 6.11, let's take a quick look at what each does.

- *General Info.* Gives your name, sysop's name, and so on.
- *System Security.* The heart of Wildcat's system protection.
- *Colors.* Define custom colors for menus, backgrounds, and more.
- *Configuration.* Set paths for your BBS and any added Doors.

Fig. 6.11
Making your BBS uniquely a customer or employee service of your business requires customization based on what information or options you want to offer provided in an easy, clear fashion for the reader.

- *Node Settings*. Select the appropriate node.

- *Security Profiles*. Assign acceptable parameters for daily and per call customer BBS time limits; how often to let them try again after a logon failure.

- *Access Profiles*. For every security profile, there's a matching access profile covering download limits and options for running nodes off your BBS; including where a customer can go on your BBS.

- *File Areas*. Create, populate, and maintain file libraries.

- *Conference Areas*. Create and edit conference areas for your BBS.

- *Doors*. Add specialty Door applications like lottery results, game, or news service.

- *Offline Mail.* Configure your system to handle offline mail readers to cut down on customer or employee time spent online reading message and mail bases.

- *Languages*. Translate menus and other system information into other popular languages.

- *CD-ROM*. Add CD-ROM-based files to your BBS software collection.

- *QWK Networking*. Configures for Wildcat!'s built-in Echomail support; useful if you want to connect two or more BBSes together to "mirror" conferences on one to another.

- *ANSI Draw*. Configure for and create ANSI graphics for your BBS.

- *Menus*. Develop menus to drive different areas of your BBS.

- *Questionnaires*. Take the pulse of your public through polls, surveys, and other customer input tools.

- *File Management*. Determine the organization and maintenance for your system.

Issues in Designing Your BBS

Software like Mustang's does indeed allow you to create the basic shell of a bulletin board in less than an hour. This gives you a feel for the features you have to work with, and a good preview of problems you may want to address before you make the BBS available to your intended audience.

But a good online service—from the smallest free community BBS to the largest of the large commercial subscriber networks—requires a good design with clear goals so it's easy for your audience to use. This means that while you can create a basic service very quickly, plan to spend at least a few weeks or even months, depending on your intended enterprise, deciding what you want to make available and how. Then try to deliver it in a simple but attractive way.

Before we discuss just some of the decisions and considerations you will need to make before launching your BBS, let's revisit an earlier recommendation: do your research on other BBSs, particularly ones related to your business-type, to see what is currently available. Don't hesitate to consult other sysops because they can provide an invaluable technical and professional support, letting you know what has worked for them, and what hasn't.

If you don't know any as you start this project, do try the earlier suggestion of leaving questions for the sysop as you visit other BBSs doing research. Contact your local computer users' group since many not only run a BBS in cooperation with their group activities, they often have an active sub-group of BBS sysops within their membership roster. Visit any of the major online services on which you may have an account. Prodigy, America Online, and CompuServe, for example, all feature BBS areas if not specific BBS support areas (you can find Mustang Software on AOL, for example, by using keyword: **MUSTANG**).

Deciding Who Has Access

As you define the focus of the bulletin board you're designing, one of the decisions to make is who your audience is. If you want it accessible to employees or specific contractors only, it is important to release the BBS access number only on an as-needed basis, with your sysop perhaps preassigning account names and passwords only to those on a designated access list.

If your interest is in providing customer-only support, then simply limit BBS information to the clients you want to use it. For example, a customer could not get access to your BBS unless they could correctly offer their account number and prearranged password at log-in.

Most commonly, however, general access to a BBS is open to anyone who chooses to call. On subscription BBSs, how much access a customer or user gets may be dependent on whether they have signed a subscription agreement with the sysop and paid the fee. Typically, a small selection of message boards and file libraries may be available to non-subscribers logging in, but the meat of the BBS is only available with paid access.

Who gets access to the service is different from the issue of who gets what type of access. Briefly put, BBS software allows you to configure for different forms of access, with only the sysop and specified helpers getting access to tools to make changes to the BBS itself or to read private e-mail.

How Customers Access

Knowing how you want your customers to connect with your Bulletin Board is important because some avenues will cost you more than others. These are the options usually available:

- *Standard phone line*. You get a standard line from your local phone company, and customers directly dial into your number. If the call is long distance to your BBS, the call is charged against the customer's phone bill, as would any toll call.

- *BBS Direct*. A service from Concentric that offers call-in points in major cities. Customers connect to BBS Direct through a local phone call, and then BBS Direct links them with the long distance BBS, at a cost below premium toll charges. Both customers and sysops pay a fee for the connection, however. For more information, you can reach them at Concentric 1-800-745-2747.

- *Inbound Telnet*. Discussed earlier (see "Would a Web Site Be Better"), this option is available to you only if you have connected your BBS to the Internet (as covered in "Connecting Your BBS to the Internet" later in this chapter) and have a Web server up and running. What this means is that customers with Web access through their ISP can surf to your BBS by entering through your Web page. If their ISP is a local call for them, there will be no long distance connection charges.

- *800 number*. Now relatively rare, an 800 number allows your customers to connect with your BBS while you pick up the charges as a WATS line. This can be very attractive for customers and a great public service, but it's so cost prohibitive that many companies formally offering an 800 number-accessible BBS have switched to another method.

■ *900 number*. Not in common use, this alternative lets your customers connect to you minus a long distance connection fee. But they pay the premium 900 number per-minute charges, often ranging from $.99 to $5. This option doesn't tend to be popular with customers, and they will generally only justify it if you offer a very specialized, desired service they could obtain no other way.

Making Policies Regarding Your BBS

The BBS of today not only exists in a competitive market, it exists in a time when policies and laws regarding conduct, freedom and means of speech, and accountability in cyberspace are just beginning to be written by our lawmakers.

The Telecommunications Reform Act of 1996, for example, includes a potent section called the Communications Decency bill, which promises stiff penalties for anyone transmitting obscene materials over the Internet, but does little to define what materials could be definitively categorized as obscene. This part of the Telecom Act was set aside for the time being as unconstitutional, since it impinges on the First Amendment of the Constitution, which guarantees free speech, but the implications for sysops could be troublesome if this clause of the Act is implemented.

Another court case found Prodigy at least partially responsible for objectionable content on its service, for which someone took them to court. The court said that since Prodigy exercised some editorial control over the content available on its service, this held them at least partly accountable for what is published on Prodigy.

Thus, given the instability of the political climate concerning how we'll conduct our business over the Internet in the future, it's wise for those operating a BBS, particularly one attached to your livelihood, to develop guidelines for exactly what content is and is not acceptable, as well as general policies for how to handle emergencies *before* they crop up.

For example, computer viruses are becoming more and more prevalent as increasingly more people are online to help pass them around. If your BBS accepts uploads from customers or users, you should scan for viruses in these uploads before making them available to the general BBS population to download. This is true, too, of files you may want to put online for download that may have been stored off the network or stored where no virus checking is routinely performed. Many sysops will tell you the fastest way to smear your reputation in cyberspace is to make an infected file available to unsuspecting users.

Connecting Your BBS to the Internet

Why the appeal for establishing Internet service on your BBS? Obviously, one very good reason is its current popularity. People not yet "wired" may not quite comprehend what the Internet is, but they know it's supposed to be very cool and a place they should visit very soon. This may bring you customers.

It also can be an information tool for your staff. They can read industry-related USENET newsgroups, do research on the Web, participate in professional net mailing lists, and exchange e-mail with colleagues around the world.

But there are drawbacks to Internet connectivity as well. As one example, a gateway out onto the Internet can be an open door to your private business computer network unless you implement a firewall—think of it as a big security net—over that part of your network and computerized records you want sealed off from prying visitors.

Since there are people who do nothing but research new ways to defeat security measures, a firewall isn't something to take lightly, and isn't something to leave in place just assuming its presence makes it secure. So if you open your system up onto Internet, be prepared to take system security very seriously and expect to constantly monitor it for weaknesses if you don't care to have a hacker find them for you.

There are other considerations, too. For one, establishing a connection to the Internet can be costly for a small business, and can be troublesome. Even the best connections go up and down, and can require more maintenance time when they do.

For the last few years, many very small operations have sought to cash in on the influx of consumers jumping on the Information Superhighway by becoming Internet Service Providers (ISPs). For some, this meant going from a tiny operation one day to a massively popular, financially sky-rocketing business seemingly the next.

But the tide is turning as big players like AT&T are offering both business and residential customers inexpensive Internet access as part of their regular phone service. This leads some industry analysts to predict that the small ISPs may soon fade away, leaving only a handful of giants to provide the bulk of the nation's Internet service, much as traditional phone service is currently handled.

If you're still eager to establish your own net connection, understand that you won't "hook" directly into the Internet itself. Many BBSes offering Internet connectivity do so through a single high speed (56 kbps) connection to a larger ISP (like your phone company), who provides a Net feed for a charge. The more competitive systems, or those with greater Internet demands, opt for at least a T1 line (which can pass data at up to 1.544 Mbps) on up to full ISDN connection.

ISDN, or Integrated Data Services Network, is highly desirable because it can move incredible amounts of data very quickly, far faster than standard digital-analog phone lines. It's also easier for your phone company to deliver because they don't have to convert digital material back to analog for the last leg of the "data jump" from the phone company to the phone line coming in on your PC, as they do with other transmissions.

But your phone company isn't eager to have to upgrade all its connections to fully accommodate the kind of throughput possible under ISDN, so it charges a premium rate for the connection, about $500 per month for a 24-hour dedicated connection in my area. This pricing excludes many small BBSes and businesses from jumping on ISDN's growing bandwagon, so cost is a consideration.

Speed is a factor, and you want the highest speed connection you can afford to the Internet. In the past, BBS software itself limited the speed at which your BBS could connect to 19.2 kps or 28.8, but newer versions, including Mustang's Wildcat!, now support speeds of up to 115.2 kps.

Some of the BBS software companies make connectivity to the Internet particularly easy by offering turnkey hardware add-ons, usually starting at around $400, to make it fairly easy for someone without serious network experience to make the connection in less than a half hour, providing they already have an account through a larger ISP. IPAD, available from eSoft and mentioned already in the section on "BBS Software" is one, while NuIQ, makers of PowerBoard BBS, sell something similar which they developed in cooperation with MurkWorks.

Note

If you're using Microsoft Windows NT Server 4.0, as opposed to Workstation, at your business, you have access to the Internet Information Server. This is a built-in package offering a comprehensive Web, ftp, and gopher server so you won't need to purchase these separately as add-ons unless you opt to go with another server package.

Additional Resources for the BBS Sysop

Here are just some of the Net-based resources available for sysops and sysops-to-be:

- Material covering issues related to BBS sysoping, including legal decisions, government regulations, and case analysis is available via Anonymous ftp from **oak.oakland.edu** by looking in **/pub/misc/bbs**.

- Formerly ONE BBSCON, ISPCON (for Internet Service Providers Convention) is the largest annual meeting of BBS system operators and Net providers held annually in late summer. Get information at **http:// www.ispcon.com**.

- The American BBS Association, 850 N Main Street, Dayton, OH 45405; is a national association for BBS sysops with its own BBS available at (513)228-1020.

- Sysop News is a Web site specifically for BBS sysops, featuring news on the BBS industry. Visit **http://www.sysNews.com**.

- USENET newsgroups covering the topic:

  alt.bbs

  alt.bbs.ads

  alt.bbs.allsysop

  alt.bbs.doors

  alt.bbs.internet

  alt.bbs.lists

  alt.bbs.majorbbs

  alt.bbs.powerboard

  alt.bbs.wildcat

  alt.bbs.wildcat.wccode

- Internet mailing list forum focusing on the sysop looking for a profit (or just to lose less money) and to market their BBSes more effectively. It is more business-focused than technical. Send questions via e-mail to **Ted.Kraus@property.com**. To subscribe, send e-mail addressed to **LISTSERV@property.com**. In the body of the message, type: **SUBSCRIBE SYSOPS-GROUP Your_Real_Name**.

II

Dialup Communications

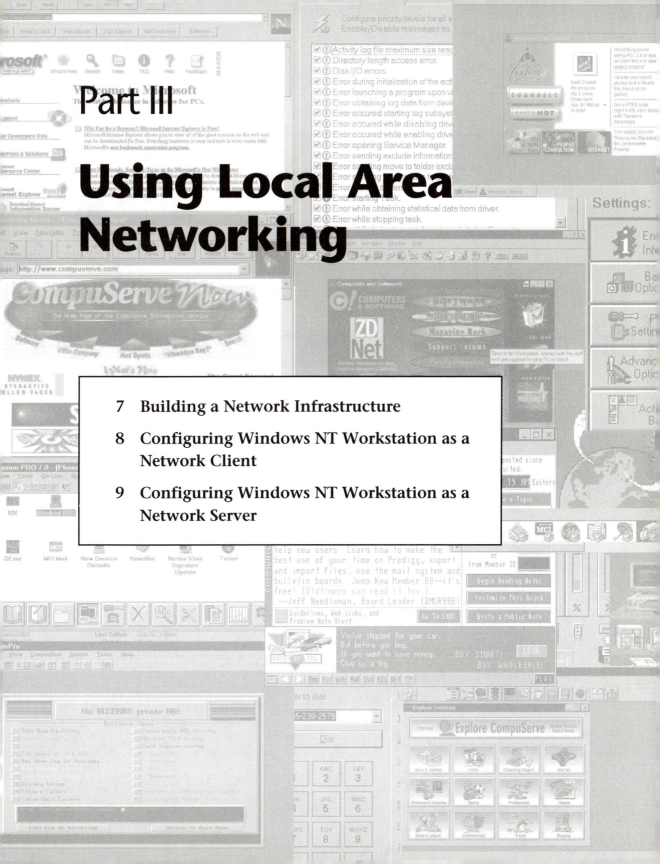

Part III

Using Local Area Networking

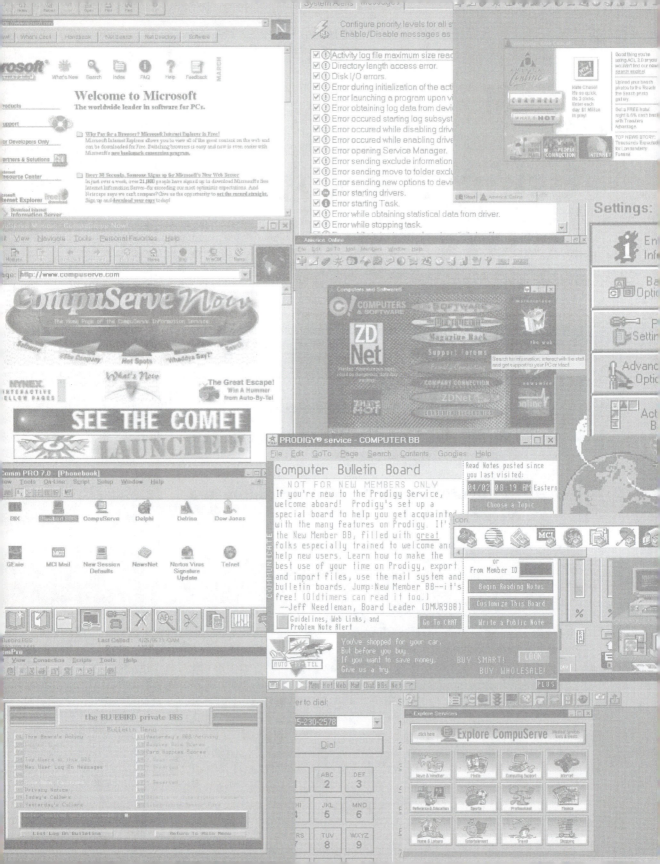

CHAPTER 7

Building a Network Infrastructure

by Robert Bruce Thompson

Microsoft Windows NT Workstation 4.0 is not only an excellent workstation operating system for many small businesses, it can provide the nucleus of a capable Local Area Network. The built-in networking features of Windows NT Workstation allow it to perform as a simple, low-cost and high-performance server operating system in a small network environment.

The differences between Windows NT Workstation 4.0 and Windows NT Server 4.0 are largely a matter of degree. Windows NT Server, for example, allows an unlimited number of workstations to be connected as clients, while Windows NT Workstation limits client connections to 10. Windows NT Workstation does not include the built-in RAID disk redundancy features of Windows NT Server, and supports only two processors rather than the four processors supported by the server version. The Windows NT Server Remote Access Server (RAS) supports 256 simultaneous dial-in clients, while Windows NT Workstation RAS supports only one. Windows NT Server provides several services and utilities to make managing a larger network easier, which are not included with Windows NT Workstation.

For many small businesses the simplicity and low cost of Windows NT Workstation make it an ideal choice as the network operating system for a small server-based network. Using Windows NT Workstation as a server operating system gives you the best of both worlds—the simplicity and low cost of a traditional peer-based LAN and the high performance and flexibility of a traditional server-based network.

Using Windows NT Workstation as the foundation of a small network is not limited to small businesses. Larger companies can use the advanced networking features of Windows NT Workstation to build small workgroup or branch office networks without incurring the expense and added complexity of installing a Windows NT Server solution at each site.

If you decide to use Windows NT Workstation as the core of your network, selecting and installing the proper network infrastructure—cabling, network interface cards and other network components—will ensure that your network works reliably and is easy to maintain and expand. Spending some time planning your installation will pay off down the road in fewer problems and easier growth.

This chapter tells you what you need to know to build such an infrastructure for your Windows NT Workstation based network, whether it supports five users in a small business or is simply a small part of an enterprise network in a large corporation.

In this chapter, you learn to

- Use the OSI Reference Model as a framework for understanding networking concepts
- Choose the best media access method and cabling topology for your environment
- Select appropriate network adapters and other active network components to optimize network performance and allow for future growth

Understanding the OSI Reference Model and the DARPA Model

Networking is a complicated business if you try to understand everything at once. Breaking a problem down into smaller chunks makes it easier to understand than attempting to assimilate everything at once. The *OSI Reference Model* and the *DARPA Model* are conceptual frameworks that do just that. The OSI Reference Model is the newer, and now *de jure* standard network model. The older and closely similar DARPA Model, also called the Department of Defense or DoD Model, is still important as a *de facto* standard because it is used to describe the largest of all networks, the Internet.

By breaking down the complex subject of computer networking into seven layers, the OSI Reference Model allows you to first understand each layer in isolation, then to understand the relationship between adjoining layers, and finally to understand the subject as a whole. The DARPA Model takes a similar approach, but uses only four levels to encompass the same subjects. To many people, this theoretical approach at first seems a bit too academic to be of much use in the real world. One soon learns, however, that it is essential to have a firm grounding in theory in order to truly understand how a network operates.

It is important to understand that any network model, including the OSI Reference Model, is simply a framework that allows you to think about networking in an organized way. From this model are developed *protocols* that operate at one or more levels of the model and specify in detail how particular tasks are to be accomplished. For example, IEEE 802.3 Ethernet is a protocol that operates at the lower two levels of the OSI Reference Model. From protocols are developed *implementations*, which are physical manifestations of one or more protocols. For example, a 3Com 3C509 Ethernet card is an implementation of the 802.3 10BaseT protocol standard.

Interestingly, although the OSI Reference Model is the declared standard, few protocols based on the OSI Model are actually used. On the other hand, the DoD Model, which is now only a *de facto* standard, forms the basis for the *Internet Protocol Suite*, commonly called TCP/IP, which carries the majority of the public and private internetworking traffic throughout the world.

The seven layers of the OSI Reference Model begin at the lowest level with the networking hardware itself—the cabling and interface cards used to physically connect the computers with each other. The intermediate layers deal with the low-level functions of packaging data, ensuring its integrity and moving it to its destination. The upper layers deal with the interface between the network and the applications software running on the workstation and, ultimately, the interface with the user. Let's take a closer look at each of the levels of the OSI Reference Model and how they relate to the DoD Model, as shown in figure 7.1.

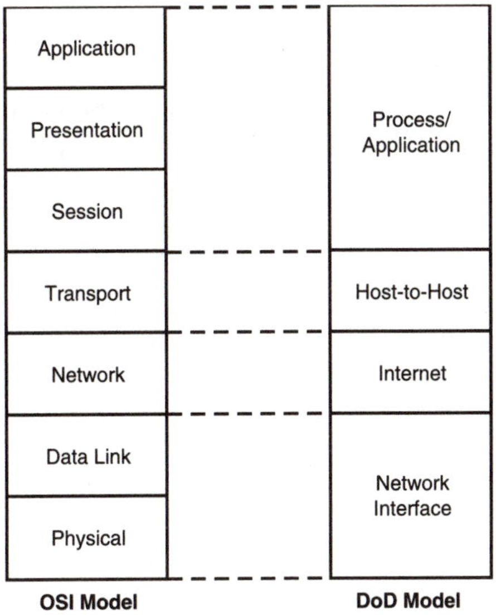

Fig. 7.1
The OSI Reference Model and the DoD Internet Model provide a framework for understanding networking concepts.

III

Local Area Networking

The Physical Layer

The Physical Layer of the OSI Reference Model is concerned with the physical, mechanical, and electrical characteristics of your network hardware. Things like what type of cable and connectors are to be used and what voltages will be used to signal are specified at the physical layer.

The Physical Layer specifies how data is to be placed on and retrieved from the network, which is referred to as the Media Access Method. For example, the IEEE 802.3 Ethernet specification and the IEEE 802.5 Token Ring specification are Physical Layer standards.

At the Physical Layer, data has not yet been organized; instead, it is treated simply as a raw stream of bits or electrical voltages. The OSI Physical Layer corresponds to the lower half of the DoD Network Interface Layer, which may also be called the Network Access Layer or the Local Network Layer.

The Data Link Layer

The Data Link Layer is concerned with the error-free delivery of data. It organizes the raw bit stream received from the Physical Layer into organized groupings of bits, called *frames*, and transfers the frames between devices on a single network. The Data Link Layer is the transition between network hardware and upper-layer protocols.

Frames vary in size depending on the media access method in use, but are of fixed size for a particular media access method. For example, an 802.3 Ethernet network may use a fixed frame size of 1514 bytes, while an 802.5 Token Ring network may use a fixed frame size of 4202 bytes.

In addition to the raw data provided by the Physical Layer, the Data Link Layer appends control information contained in a header to each frame. This header contains information like the hardware address of the station that originated the frame, the hardware address of the specified destination, the length of the data block included within the frame, information concerning the higher-level protocols for which the frame is intended, and a CRC or Checksum section to allow detection of errors. Hardware addresses contain no information about the actual geographical location of a device. An Ethernet II frame is shown in figure 7.2.

The Data Link Layer is usually treated as two sub-layers. The *Media Access Control* (MAC) sub-layer defines the relationship at the hardware level between Physical Layer devices, like Network Adapter Cards, and the Data Link Layer. The *Logical Link Control* (LLC) sub-layer defines the relationship between the MAC sub-layer and Data Link Layer devices and drivers.

The OSI Data Link Layer corresponds to the upper half of the DoD Network Interface Layer.

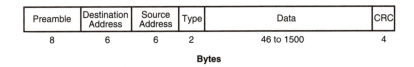

Preamble	Destination Address	Source Address	Type	Data	CRC
8	6	6	2	46 to 1500	4

Bytes

Fig. 7.2
An Ethernet II frame contains user data and the addresses for the source and destination devices.

The Network Layer

The *Network Layer* handles routing between networks and the timely delivery of data. It organizes frames received from the Data Link Layer into *Packets*. Packets encapsulate the frame and append a Network Layer header, which includes *Network Addresses* for the source and destination stations. Network Layer addresses are software or logical addresses rather than the hardware addresses used at the Data Link Layer. Network addresses can contain information about the geographical location of an address, allowing packets to be routed to distant networks.

The *Internet Protocol* (IP) portion of the TCP/IP protocol suite and the *Internet Packet Exchange* (IPX) portion of the Novell IPX/SPX protocol suite are Network Layer protocols. The OSI Network Layer corresponds closely to the DoD Internet Layer.

The Transport Layer

The *Transport Layer* is responsible for delivering data reliably. Building up and tearing down connections, packet sequencing, acknowledgments, and flow control are done at the Transport Layer.

The *Transmission Control Protocol* (TCP) and *User Datagram Protocol* (UDP) portions of the TCP/IP protocol suite and the *Sequenced Packet Exchange* (SPX) portion of the Novell IPX/SPX protocol suite are examples of Transport Layer protocols. The OSI Transport Layer corresponds closely to the DoD Host-to-Host Layer.

The Session Layer

The *Session Layer* provides mechanisms to establish and maintain communications between applications, including access authentication and session management. For example, when you log in to a server and are validated by the server you are using Session Layer services. The Session Layer also performs such services as verifying that adequate disk space is available to fulfill a workstation's storage request, notifying the user that a printer is offline, and so forth.

The *Remote Procedure Call* (RPC) protocols used by many network operating systems function at the Session Layer. The OSI Session Layer corresponds to the lower third of the DoD Process/Application Layer.

The Presentation Layer

The *Presentation Layer* is responsible for formatting, representing, and translating data. Functions like ASCII to EBCDIC translation, compression/decompression of data, and encryption/decryption of data occur at the Presentation Layer. The OSI Presentation Layer corresponds to the middle third of the DoD Process/Application Layer.

The Application Layer

The *Application Layer* provides the interface between the network and the application software being run by the user. The OSI Application Layer corresponds to the upper third of the DoD Process/Application Layer.

Relationships Between the Layers and Inter-Device Communication

In either network model, a given layer is a provider of services to the layer immediately above it and a consumer of services provided by the layer immediately below it. For example, the OSI Transport Layer provides services to the Session Layer above it, and in turn receives services from the Network Layer below it.

When two connected devices are communicating, the connection exists between the corresponding layers on the two devices, as shown in figure 7.3. Data passes down the Model on the source device and is operated upon by the services provided at each lower layer. When the data reaches the Physical Layer of the source device, it is communicated as a bit stream to the Physical Layer of the destination device, where the process is reversed. The data is passed up through each layer of the Model on the destination device, undergoing the processing particular to that layer, until it reaches the layer corresponding to where the data originated on the source device.

The OSI Reference Model and the IEEE

The OSI Reference Model does not explicitly specify all functions particular to each of the seven layers. The *Institute of Electrical and Electronic Engineers* (IEEE) 802 Committees remedy this for the Physical Layer and the Data Link Layer by providing detailed specifications referred to as the 802.x series of standards. These committees range widely in purpose. They specify standards for numerous data communications disciplines including, for example, Metropolitan Area Networks (802.6) and Local Area Network Security (802.10).

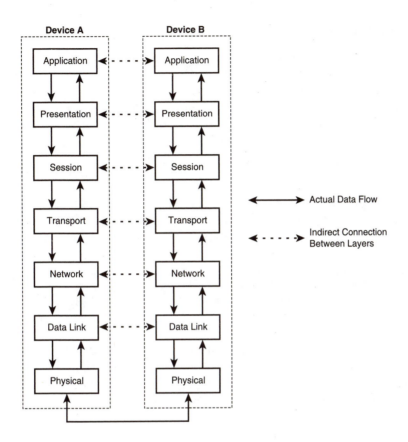

Fig. 7.3

OSI Model Inter-Device Communications occur between corresponding layers on the two devices.

For our purposes, the most important of these IEEE 802.x committees are:

- *IEEE 802.1*. Serves as an umbrella over the functions of the other 802.x committees. The 802.1 committee is also responsible for the Spanning Tree protocol used by bridges, which is covered later in this chapter.

- *IEEE 802.2*. Responsible for the Logical Link Control (LLC) sub-layer of the OSI Data Link Layer. The IEEE has "sub-divided" the OSI Data Link Layer into the Media Access Control (MAC) sub-layer and the LLC sub-layer. The MAC sub-layer is the lower of the two, and interfaces with services provided by the Physical Layer. The LLC sub-layer interfaces to the Network Layer above it.

- *IEEE 802.3*. Defines Ethernet and its variants, including 10Base5, 10Base2, 10BaseT and 100BaseT.

- *IEEE 802.5*. Defines Token Ring.

III

Local Area Networking

Selecting a Media Access Method

If you are building a small network from scratch for a small business or for a branch office of a larger business, the first important decision you must make is which media access method to use. This decision is comparable in importance to a railroad's choice of which gauge to use—how far apart do we put the tracks? Everything devolves from this decision, including your choice of active network components, the type of cabling that you will install, and ultimately the performance, reliability, and cost of your network.

If you are instead building a workgroup network that will interconnect locally with a larger existing local area network, this decision will, in essence, already have been made for you. Still, understanding media access method issues will be helpful to you in integrating your new small network with the large existing one. In this section we will examine the available alternatives and make several recommendations.

In the previous section we learned about the ISO Reference Model and the purpose of its various layers. Media access methods are addressed in the first, or Physical Layer and the second, or Data Link Layer. These layers are the realm of the Institute for Electrical and Electronic Engineers, or IEEE. The IEEE is a standards body that codifies and publishes official standards documents. Among these are the IEEE 802 series of standards, which cover media access methods for local area networks among other related issues. The IEEE develops these standards in cooperation with various industry bodies. Once a standard has been adopted and promulgated, all manufacturers of equipment addressed by that standard ensure that their products are in full compliance with the standard in question. This is why, for example, you can freely mix Ethernet cards made by any manufacturer with the assurance that they will all talk to each other properly.

Media Access Methods

Several *media access methods* are commonly used on local area networks running Windows NT, including ARCnet, Ethernet, and Token Ring. Newer high-speed technologies like 100VG-AnyLAN and 100BaseT are becoming more common. You will learn about each of these technologies in the following sections.

ARCnet

One of the oldest media access methods still in use is ARCnet, shown in figure 7.4. Developed in 1977 by DataPoint Corporation, ARCnet (Attached Resource Computer Network) was deservedly popular in the early- and mid-1980s. Its combination of simplicity, low cost, and reasonable performance made it a good choice at a time when Ethernet was extremely expensive and Token Ring did not yet exist. Thousands of Novell NetWare 2.x networks were installed using ARCnet, many of which are still running today.

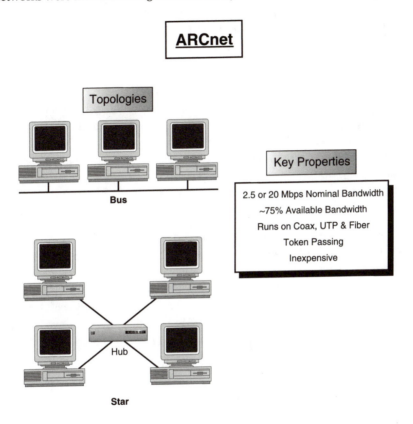

Fig. 7.4
ARCnet uses a
Token-Passing
access method.

ARCnet uses a token-passing access method. A *token* is a small binary object generated by the ARCnet hardware that is passed from station to station in an orderly, predetermined manner. Only one token can exist at a time, and a station must possess the token in order to transmit data on the network. When the station has completed its transmission it passes the token on to the next station. In this fashion, every station is guaranteed an opportunity to transmit, and no station can interfere with another station's transmission.

In ARCnet, a station with data to transmit waits to receive the token, referred to as the Invitation to Transmit. When the station receives the token, it issues a Free Buffer Inquiry. Upon receiving an ACKnowledgment it transmits a data packet and again waits for an ACK, upon receipt of which it passes the token

III

Local Area Networking

on to the next station. ARCnet passes the token in turn from each station to the station with the next-higher logical address, regardless of the physical layout of the network. ARCnet cards are typically configured by means of an 8-position DIP switch, allowing assignment of station address values from 0-255. Address 0 is reserved for broadcasts, so an ARCnet network can never have more than 255 attached workstations. Intrinsic to ARCnet is the ability of the network to automatically reconfigure itself as stations are added and removed.

ARCnet originally operated on 93-ohm RG-62 coaxial cable in a bus topology with a data throughput of 2.5 million bits per second (Mbps). Newer ARCnet equipment can be run on unshielded twisted pair cable and fiber optic cable as well as the original RG-62 coax. The topology has also been extended from the original bus to include star topologies using a combination of active and passive hubs. Thomas-Conrad now markets ARCnet cards that operate at 20 Mbps, as well as Thomas-Conrad Networking System (TCNS) 100 Mbps cards which derive from the ARCnet standard.

Because ARCnet was never adopted as an official IEEE standard, it never achieved wide industry acceptance. It has since gone into a steep decline, despite the efforts of Thomas-Conrad and others to enhance and extend its functionality and performance. The ARCnet market is currently replacement-only, because essentially no one is installing new ARCnet networks. A glance at the Microsoft Windows NT Hardware Compatibility List (HCL) reveals that the only ARCnet support provided is a generic Thomas-Conrad driver. If you happen to have an ARCnet network in place, you may choose to run a Windows NT Workstation as a server on it. Otherwise you should not consider ARCnet.

Token Ring

Introduced by IBM in 1986, Token Ring has a lot going for it, balanced by a few negatives. Token Ring, shown in figure 7.5, is fast, reliable, and well supported by IBM in both the PC and heavy iron environments. Balanced against this are two factors: First, Token Ring is extremely expensive when compared with Ethernet alternatives. The price of one name-brand Token Ring card will buy between two and five name-brand Ethernet cards. This cost disparity holds true across the range of networking hardware you will need—hubs, routers and so forth. Second, Token Ring has not achieved wide industry acceptance, due initially to IBM's restrictive licensing policies and subsequently to the market dominance of Ethernet. As a result, your choice of network interface cards and other active network components is restricted to only a handful of vendors with Token Ring, whereas with Ethernet you can choose among scores of vendors.

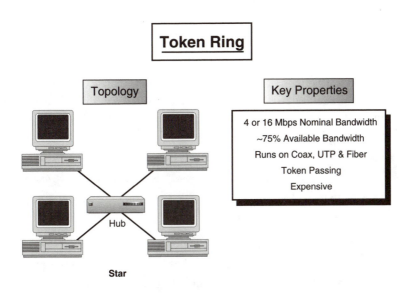

Fig. 7.5
Token Ring uses a binary token to control media access.

Like ARCnet, Token Ring uses a token-passing access method, but with a somewhat different mechanism. In Token Ring, a station with data to be transmitted first waits for an idle token. It changes the status of the token to busy, appends a destination address, attaches data to the token, and passes the burdened busy token to the next station. Because in Token Ring each station functions as a unidirectional repeater, receiving data from the downstream station, regenerating it, and passing it to the upstream station, this next station regenerates the burdened busy token and again passes it along to the next station in sequence. This process continues until the burdened busy token reaches its destination. At the destination, the recipient extracts the data from the token and sends an ACKnowledgment to the originating station. Upon receiving this ACK, the originating station generates an idle token and passes it to the next station.

Because it is critical to Token Ring that exactly one token exist on the ring at any given time, one station is designated an *active monitor*. It is the responsibility of this station to monitor the ring for unusual conditions, including the absence of a token, a damaged token, or multiple tokens coexisting. When such a condition is found, the active monitor corrects the problem and returns the ring to normal operating conditions.

Token Ring uses a star-wired ring topology in which each station is connected by an individual cable run to a concentrator called a Multi-Station Access Unit, or MAU. In the early days of Token Ring, I disassembled an IBM MAU and was surprised to find that it literally contained a tiny ring to which the eight individual station ports were connected.

Token Ring originally operated on 150-ohm shielded twisted pair cable arranged in a star-wired ring with data throughput of 4 Mbps. Newer Token Ring equipment can operate on unshielded twisted pair cable and fiber optic cable as well as the original shielded twisted pair cable. The throughput has also been upgraded to 16 Mbps. Many newer Token Ring components can operate at either 4 Mbps or 16 Mbps to ease transition from the older technology to the newer.

> **Note**
>
> A Token Ring network segment must be exclusively 4 Mbps or 16 Mbps. The two speeds cannot coexist on the same ring.

Token Ring, including its enhancements, has been adopted as standard 802.5 by the IEEE. Its market share is second only to Ethernet, although the growth of new Token Ring networks has slowed as Ethernet has increased its dominance. Although there are large numbers of Token Ring networks installed, Token Ring remains in essence a niche product. It is primarily limited to exclusive IBM shops and to those locations with a need to interconnect their networks to IBM minicomputers and mainframes. Although IBM's commitment to Token Ring remains strong, even IBM has been forced to bow to market realities and begin offering Ethernet as an option.

One other market niche in which Token Ring remains strong is one that requires real time response, primarily manufacturing locations with networked numeric control and process control requirements. Ethernet is *stochastic*, which means that response time is unpredictable and influenced heavily by the volume of network traffic on the wire at any given time. Token Ring, on the other hand, is *deterministic*, which means that it has a predictable response time under load. This single factor can mandate Token Ring for real time environments.

Ethernet

Invented by Bob Metcalfe in 1973 and developed as a commercial product by Digital Equipment Corporation, Intel, and Xerox (DIX), *Ethernet* is the media access method of choice for most new networks being installed today, and for good reason. Ethernet, shown in figure 7.6, is inexpensive, performs well, is easily extensible, and is supported by every manufacturer of network equipment. Ethernet has become the networking standard by which all others are judged.

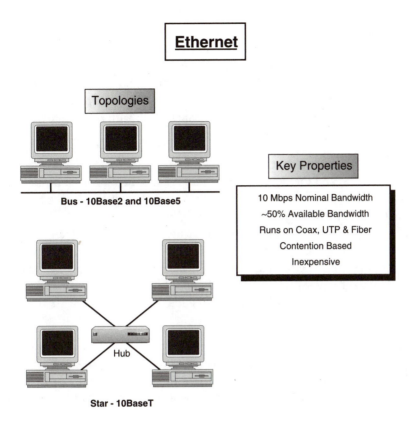

Fig. 7.6
Ethernet uses contention to control media access.

Ethernet is based on a contention scheme for media access known as *CSMA/CD*, or *Carrier Sense Multiple Access with Collision Detection. Carrier Sense* means that each Ethernet device on the network constantly monitors the *carrier* present on the cable and is able to determine when that carrier is idle and when it is in use. *Multiple Access* means that all Ethernet devices on the cable have an equal right to access the carrier signal without obtaining prior permission. Because Ethernet is a *baseband* system, only one transmission can be present on the wire at any one time. *Collision Detection* means that if two or more Ethernet devices transmit simultaneously and thereby corrupt all of the data, this data *collision* will be detected and can subsequently be corrected.

Unlike token-based schemes, any Ethernet station is permitted to transmit at any time it has data to be sent. When a station needs to transmit, it first listens to make sure the carrier is free. If so, it begins transmitting the data.

The original Ethernet specification, referred to as *10Base5*, operated on 50-ohm thick coaxial cable in a *bus topology* with a data throughput of 10 Mbps and a maximum segment length of 500 meters. Concerns about the

III

Local Area Networking

cost and difficulty of working with thick coax cable brought about the *10Base2* specification, which runs the same data rate over thinner and cheaper RG-58 coaxial cable, but limits segment length to only 185 meters. With the introduction of the *10BaseT* specification, Ethernet was extended from the original physical bus topology to a physical star topology running on inexpensive unshielded twisted pair cable, again with a data rate of 10 Mbps.

High Speed Ethernet Variants

As the load on an Ethernet cable increases, the number of collisions inevitably also increases and the cumulative throughput begins to fall. The traditional solution to this problem has been to divide a heavily loaded network into multiple segments by using bridges, which are covered fully in the following section on active network components. The use of bridges to create additional segments essentially breaks the network into multiple neighborhoods. Local traffic within a neighborhood is kept local and only traffic which needs to cross segment boundaries does so.

To address these perceived Ethernet performance problems, three contending high-speed challengers have arisen. The first, *Full Duplex Ethernet*, doubles bandwidth to 20 Mbps. The remaining two, *100BaseT* and *100VG-AnyLAN*, compete at the 100 Mbps level. All of these competitors propose to achieve their bandwidth increases using existing cable in at least one of their variants.

A major attraction of both 100 Mbps proposed standards is this ability to run on existing *voice grade cable*, the assumption being that a network can be easily upgraded to 100 Mbps without requiring significant changes to the in-place cable plant. The truth is somewhat uglier. Although standard networks require only two pairs, four pair cable has traditionally been installed to provide spare pairs. Although you cannot run two 10BaseT devices on a single four pair, cable, the extra two pairs are often used to run analog dial tone or other signaling applications. Also, since bad pairs do occur, some four pair cable runs will be found to have two pairs in use for the network, one bad pair, and only one spare pair. Such a cable is not usable for either of the 100 Mbps competitors. One final factor that will make many installed cabling plants unusable for 100 Mbps is that these spare pairs often exist only from the workstation jack to the first equipment room, where you will usually find them carefully twisted around the sheath of the cable but not cross connected to anything. As a result, most cabling systems, even though they use four pair cable throughout, in reality provide only two usable pairs. So much for an easy and cheap upgrade without having to touch your cable plant.

An alternative exists to these proposals to increase overall network throughput by increasing the data transfer rate of each device attached to it. The use of switching hubs, covered fully in the "Selecting Active Network Components" section later in this chapter, grants each workstation what amounts to a dedicated 10 Mbps Ethernet link to the switch. The switch is connected to the rest of the network using very high-speed links and handles contention for this high-speed bandwidth, providing bandwidth on demand to each workstation. The result is that each workstation behaves as though it has a full-speed Ethernet link directly to the server. It is impossible to predict at this point which, if either, method will dominate.

Full Duplex Ethernet. *Full Duplex Ethernet* is one recent scheme for increasing bandwidth beyond the 10 Mbps available with standard Ethernet. An Ethernet device may be transmitting or receiving, but it cannot do both simultaneously. Full Duplex Ethernet devices, on the other hand, transmit and receive data simultaneously, thereby doubling effective bandwidth to 20 Mbps.

Full Duplex Ethernet devices are designed to work on 10BaseT networks using unshielded twisted pair cabling, and achieve their higher data rates simply by placing data on the transmit pair and receive pair simultaneously. Although Full Duplex Ethernet can coexist with standard 10BaseT Ethernet on the same cabling system, implementing Full Duplex Ethernet requires that network interface cards, hubs, bridges, routers, and other active network components be upgraded or replaced to support it.

Another problem is that the additional bandwidth provided by Full Duplex Ethernet is available only when linking two devices, both of which have data to be transmitted simultaneously. A typical Full Duplex Ethernet workstation-to-server link often shows little or no performance improvement over standard Ethernet because the majority of the traffic between them is inherently of a half-duplex nature.

Full Duplex Ethernet is superficially attractive for linking devices that communicate large amounts of data between them, such as server-to-server links. In this situation, the increased bandwidth of Full Duplex Ethernet can indeed be realized. However, better alternatives are available for this type of link which provide higher data rates and have less impact on the required network infrastructure.

Full Duplex Ethernet is likely to disappear as superior high-speed alternatives become available to replace it. Do not consider it for your network.

100BaseT. Of the two competing 100 Mbps proposed standards, *100BaseT* was first out of the starting gate. 100BaseT remains conceptually close to Ethernet roots, using CSMA/CD media access combined with one of two signaling methods. *100BaseX* signaling combines CSMA/CD and FDDI Physical Layer specifications and runs on two pairs of a Category 5 cable. 100BaseX can also run on shielded twisted pair or fiber. The *4T+ signaling* method runs CSMA/CD on four pairs of Category 3 cable.

At the Data Link Layer the major change involves timing. CSMA/CD based systems function on the assumption that all collisions will be detected. The maximum cabling length in an Ethernet network is limited by *Round Trip Delay* time or *RTD*. The RTD of the entire network must be small enough that the two devices located farthest from each other can detect a collision in progress. The much higher signaling speed used by 100BaseT means that such collisions are present on the cable and detectable for a much shorter span. As a result, the maximum end-to-end cabling length for a 100BaseT network is 250 meters, or one-tenth that of a 10BaseT network.

100VG-AnyLAN. The second of the 100 Mbps proposed standards is *100VG-AnyLAN*. Although it is often considered to be an extended version of Ethernet, 100VG-AnyLAN is really not Ethernet at all. It replaces Ethernet's CSMA/CD media access method with a *demand priority* method more similar conceptually to that used by Token Ring, although access to the cable is arbitrated by a centralized controller rather than by possession of a token. In fact, the 100VG-AnyLAN specification permits using Token Ring frames as well as Ethernet frames.

100VG-AnyLAN is named for a composite of its 100 Mbps transmission rate, its ability to run on four pairs of Category 3 Voice Grade or VG cable, and its support for both Ethernet and Token Ring frame types. 100VG-AnyLAN can also be run on two pairs of Category 5 cable, on shielded twisted pair, and on fiber.

In contrast to the relatively minor changes made at the Data Link Layer by 100BaseT, 100VG-AnyLAN does a wholesale replacement. This is reflected in the fact that 100VG-AnyLAN is under the umbrella of the new IEEE 802.12 committee rather than the 802.3 committee that covers Ethernet and 100BaseT.

With 100VG-AnyLAN, all stations constantly transmit an IDLE signal to the hub. When a station has data to transmit, it sends a request to transmit to the hub. When a request arrives at the hub, the hub transmits an *incoming* (*INC*) signal to the other stations. These stations then cease transmitting the IDLE signal, which frees the line for traffic. After the hub has received the frame from the source station and forwarded it to the destination, it sends an IDLE signal to all stations that did not receive the frame and the cycle begins again.

A request can be either a *Normal Priority Request* (*NPR*) or a *High Priority Request* (*HPR*). An NPR arriving at the hub is serviced immediately if no HPRs are outstanding. HPRs are always given initial priority in processing over NPRs. However, if HPRs exist when an NPR arrives at the hub, a timer is started on the NPR. After a certain time has passed, the NPR is promoted to an HPR and processed. This priority demand system allows high priority traffic such as real-time video and audio frames to be processed *isochronously*.

The major drawback to 100VG-AnyLAN is that the complexity and processing power required at the hub is similar to that required for a switching hub but does not provide the benefits of switching. For the cost of the required 100VG-AnyLAN network cards and hubs, you can instead install switched Ethernet with much less effort and superior results.

Other High-Speed Media Access Methods

Several other high-speed alternatives exist. Each of these has at one time or another been proposed as a desktop standard, and each has failed to become such a standard because of the very high cost of network interface cards and hub ports. As a result, each has been largely relegated to use in network backbones.

Fiber Distributed Data Interface (FDDI). Developed by the ANSI X3T9.5 Committee, the *FDDI* specification describes a high-speed, token-passing network operating on fiber optic cable. In its original incarnation, FDDI was intended to operate on dual counter-rotating fiber rings with a maximum of 1,000 workstations and a transmission rate of 100 Mbps. FDDI, shown in figure 7.7, can support a large physical network. Stations can be located as much as 2 kilometers apart, and the total network can span 200 kilometers. Like Token Ring, FDDI is deterministic and offers predictable network response, making it suitable for isochronous applications like real-time video or multimedia.

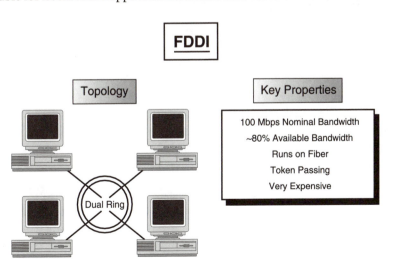

Dual Counter-Rotating Ring

Fig. 7.7
Fiber Distributed Data Interface (FDDI), like Token Ring, uses a binary token to control media access.

III

Local Area Networking

Two classes of FDDI station exist. *Class A stations*, also called *dual-attached stations*, attach to both rings using four fiber strands. This offers full redundancy, since failure of one ring simply causes traffic to shift to the other, allowing communication to continue uninterrupted. Class B stations, also called *singly attached stations*, connect only to the primary ring, and do so via a star wired hub. During a ring failure, only Class A stations participate in the automatic ring reconfiguration process.

FDDI is commonly seen in network equipment rooms, providing the network backbone used to link hubs and other active network components. FDDI to the workstation is rarely seen, appearing primarily in U.S. government and large corporate locations where the resistance of fiber optic cable to electronic eavesdropping outweighs the large additional cost of installing FDDI.

Copper Distributed Data Interface (CDDI). The FDDI specification actually makes provision for two Physical Layer *Physical Media Dependencies* (*PMDs*). Traditional FDDI operates on a fiber PMD. *CDDI*, more properly referred to as *Twisted Pair Physical Media Dependent* (*TP-PMD*) is exactly analogous to FDDI, but runs on Category 5 unshielded twisted pair cable rather than fiber. The high cost of purchasing and installing fiber optic cable was the original motivation for the development of TP-PMD. As fiber installation costs have decreased dramatically, the justification for TP-PMD has become more difficult due to other advantages of fiber optic cable. By its nature, fiber optic cable does not generate electrical interference, nor is it subject to being interfered with. Also, because FDDI is often used to link separate buildings on a campus, the fact that fiber is an electrical insulator allows you to use it without considering issues like lightning protection and building grounds. Do not consider using TP-PMD in your network.

Asynchronous Transfer Mode (ATM). *ATM* competes with FDDI for the network backbone. Although it is usually thought of as running at 155 Mbps on fiber media, ATM hardware is in fact available running at data rates ranging from 1.544 Mbps T1, through IBM's 25 Mbps implementation, up through the telephone company's OC-48 multi gigabit per second rates, and on various media including fiber optic cable and unshielded twisted pair. Although ATM to the desktop has from time to time been proposed as a standard, the extremely high cost of ATM adapters and hub ports has limited it to use as a network backbone technology.

ATM is defined at the Physical Layer and Data Link Layer of the OSI Reference Model. It is a high bandwidth, low latency transmission and switching methodology similar in concept to traditional packet switching networks. It combines the high efficiency and bandwidth utilization of packet switching networks with the guaranteed bandwidth availability of circuit switching networks. ATM uses fixed-length 53-byte cells, each of which contains 48 bytes of data and 5 bytes of header information. Fixed cell length reduces processing overhead and simplifies the design and construction of the very high speed switches required for ATM speeds. The speed and switching capabilities of ATM were major factors in its selection by the ITU (formerly CCITT) as the methodology of choice for broadband Metropolitan Area Networking. ATM is a demand-priority isochronous technology, and therefore suitable for real-time applications such as voice, video, and multimedia.

Recommendations

If you have an existing ARCnet, Token Ring, or Ethernet network in place that is adequate for your needs, there is no question. Use what you have. All of these are supported by Windows NT, and all will provide at least adequate performance.

If you will be installing a new network or substantially upgrading and expanding an existing one, give strong consideration to using Ethernet. The performance and expandability constraints of ARCnet make it a strong candidate for replacement when your network needs to grow. Most firms replacing ARCnet networks choose not the newer, high-performance ARCnet variants, but instead use Ethernet. Similarly, many firms considering large-scale expansions of an existing Token Ring network, particularly one running at 4 Mbps, find that the limited selection and high cost of 16 Mbps Token Ring network interface cards and active network components make it financially feasible to replace the entire Token Ring network with Ethernet and still come out money ahead.

Consider installing a new Token Ring network only if you find yourself in one of the three following special situations:

First, if you are building a workgroup network that needs to connect to a large-scale existing Token Ring network, you realistically have little choice but to use Token Ring. Although it is possible to build a new Ethernet network and bridge it to the existing Token Ring network, doing so will both cost more than it would to simply install Token Ring for your new network and introduce additional complexity.

Second, if your business depends heavily on IBM mainframes and minicomputers, you may find that a Token Ring environment makes sense for you. Even then, you should balance carefully the costs of upgrading your mainframe or minicomputer to Ethernet versus the cost of installing a full Token Ring network for all of your PCs.

Third, if your new network will connect to real-time process control or numeric control systems that require a deterministic network to offer predictable response times, you may have no choice but to use Token Ring. Again, although it is possible to use Ethernet for your general networking and use Token Ring only for those portions of the network that require deterministic access, doing so in a small network environment will be both more costly and more complex than simply using Token Ring throughout.

Do not consider using Full Duplex Ethernet. Its marginal performance improvement comes at a high cost in adapters and active network components, and it is an obsolescent technology. Both of the competing 100 Mbps standards require careful thought before committing. Do not consider 100VG-AnyLAN for now. Although it holds twice the market share of 100BaseT, it is expensive and provides little incremental benefit. 100BaseT, on the other hand, may make sense now. Dual 100/10 Mbps network interface cards are standardized and are available now for little more than 10BaseT 10 Mbps cards. Although 100BaseT hub ports are still quite expensive, you might want to consider installing 100/10 Mbps capable cards with the intent of upgrading your hubs and other active network components later as needed.

If your situation requires high bandwidth to the workstation, consider carefully exactly which needs high bandwidth and just how much bandwidth each really needs. Examine the possibility of using switched Ethernet to provide a dedicated 10 Mbps link to each of these workstations. For tasks like high resolution medical imaging that need more bandwidth than that provided even by switched Ethernet, consider installing fiber to the affected workstations and running FDDI or ATM to those workstations only. Keep in mind that doing so demands $1,000 workstation NICs rather than $100 ones and $2,000 hub ports instead of $200 ones.

In most networks, the only place for fiber running ATM or FDDI is in the backbone. Use these technologies to establish a high-speed backbone to link your hubs and leave the workstations to copper.

In the end, you will probably decide that either Ethernet or 100BaseT is the way to go. A properly designed Ethernet network offers high performance and reliability, and does so at a price much lower than that of the alternatives. In conjunction with a properly designed cabling system, Ethernet networks are easily upgradable by replacing hubs and other central components as needed while leaving the majority of the network, including workstation NICs, in place. In addition, Ethernet's market dominance ensures that you will always have many competing products to choose from. In a competitive market like Ethernet, manufacturers are constantly improving performance and reliability and reducing prices. What else could anyone ask for?

Designing a Network Cabling System

The importance of cabling to the performance and reliability of your network cannot be overstated. The cabling system is to your network what your circulatory system is to your body. Experienced network managers will tell you that the majority of problems in most networks are due to cabling and connector problems. A properly designed, installed, documented, and maintained cabling system allows you to avoid these problems and concentrate on running your network.

Another issue addressed by a well designed and properly documented cabling system is that of maintainability. If your cabling system is a rat's nest, a simple station add may turn into an all-day affair, as you attempt to locate spare pairs, determine in which equipment closet they terminate, and so on. By contrast, adding a station on a properly structured cabling system takes only a few minutes. If your company is like most, you probably don't have enough skilled network staff to do all that needs to be done. In terms of time saved, the presence of a good cabling system can be just like having one more full-time staff member.

Craftsmanship is the single most important factor in the reliability of a cabling system. Give the same raw materials to a good cook and a bad one. The good cook turns them into a delightful meal, while the bad one turns out an inedible mess. Give the same cable and connectors to a good installer and a bad one. The good installer gives you a properly installed and reliable cabling system, while the bad one turns out a cabling system that will cause you no end of problems.

The question of installing the cabling system yourself versus contracting it out often doesn't receive the attention it deserves. Many companies make the mistake of pricing out the cable and connecting hardware needed to do the job and forgetting that cable installation is a very labor-intensive process. When quotes arrive from the cabling contractors, the company is shocked at the price difference between the raw materials cost and the quoted prices, and decide on that basis to do it themselves. For most companies, this is a major mistake. Unless your company is large enough to have staff members dedicated to installing LAN cabling, you should probably contract it out. Don't expect the voice guys in telecommunications to install LAN cabling. They don't have the equipment or the experience to do the job properly.

As this is written, professionally installed LAN cabling starts at about $50 per run. The price can be much greater, depending on the type of cable required, the number of runs to be made, the difficulty of installation, and so forth. Obviously you can expect to pay more if you live in New York City than if you live in Winston-Salem.

III

Local Area Networking

Having made the decision to contract your LAN cabling out, don't make the mistake of deciding on the installer purely on the basis of price. If you put your cabling contract out to bid, as you should, you will probably find that most of the low responses come from companies that specialize in business telephone systems. These guys walk the walk and talk the talk. They really believe that they are competent to install LAN cabling. They are not. They will provide references of companies that they have installed LAN cabling for. Don't even bother to call the references. They wouldn't know a good cabling system if it bit them.

Like singles versus doubles tennis and duplicate versus contract bridge, voice cabling and LAN cabling appear superficially to be very similar, but are in fact quite different. The best quality cabling and connectors installed according to best voice grade industry practices result in a cabling system that is at best marginal for data.

In my consulting practice, I frequently see LAN cabling systems installed by voice grade specialists. On the one hand, the obvious care taken to do a neat installation is admirable. Cables are bunched and tied off, routed neatly to the punchdown blocks, and so forth. Too bad that this neat installation is pretty much useless for data. Category 5 cable, which when properly installed allows the sheath to be stripped back less than 1/2 inch from the point of connection, has been stripped back 18 inches to make for a neater installation. Of course, it is no longer really Category 5 cable, thanks to the installer's neatness. The cable is connected to 66 punchdown blocks rated for voice only instead of to data grade 110 blocks. The sad part is that the installer walked away convinced that he'd done a good installation. The really sad part is that the customer thinks so too.

If you want your cabling installed right, throw out the bid responses from the telephone specialists and make sure that you pick a company that installs LAN cabling for a living. Let's look at what you need to know to talk to your cabling company intelligently.

Don't make the mistake of thinking that designing and installing a proper cabling system is less important for a small network than it is for a larger one. Again, if you are installing a workgroup network that will connect to an existing large network, many of the decisions concerning cabling may already have been made. You may even find that the in place cabling structure will support your new network without any additions or changes. At worst, you may have to extend the existing cabling system to serve your new network.

If, however, you are building a new network for your small business or installing a new network at a remote branch office, it may well be up to you to select and install the proper cabling to support your network. Doing the cabling right is even more important to the success of your network in this environment than it is in a larger scale environment. If the cabling malfunctions, or if you simply need to connect another workstation where someone forgot to install a data jack, you probably won't have an on-call staff of experts from the MIS department to come and fix the problem.

Network Topologies

There are many ways to arrange your cabling. These are referred to as topologies. Physical topology describes the way in which the physical components of your cabling are arranged. Electrical topology describes the way in which it functions as an electrical circuit. Logical topology describes the way in which the system functions as a whole. Physical and logical topologies do not necessarily go hand in hand. It is possible to have a physical topology of one type supporting a logical topology of another. It is also possible to have a hybrid physical topology.

Only three of the many possible physical and logical topologies are commonly used in LAN cabling. These are the Bus, the Star, and the Ring.

Bus topology, shown in figure 7.8, uses a straight piece of cable to which workstations are connected along its length, either directly or by means of drop cables. A bus has two ends, each of which is physically terminated with a resistor of the appropriate value to prevent signal reflection and standing waves.

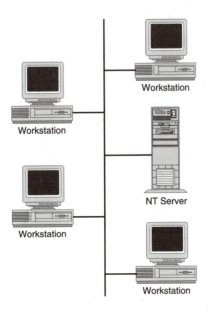

Fig. 7.8
Bus topology is simple and inexpensive, but unreliable and difficult to troubleshoot.

The main advantage of a physical bus topology is that it is simple to run and typically uses less cable than any other physical topology. The main disadvantage of a physical bus is that a break anywhere on the cable results in all workstations being unable to communicate.

Ethernet runs on a bus topology. The older 10Base5 and 10Base2 Ethernet implementations use a logical bus running on a physical coaxial cable bus. The newer 10BaseT Ethernet implementation uses a logical bus running on a physical unshielded twisted pair cable (UTP) star. ARCnet also runs on a logical bus. Early ARCnet implementations ran a physical bus on RG-62 coaxial cable. Later ones use a logical bus running on a physical UTP star.

Star topology, shown in figure 7.9, uses a central concentrator or hub. Each workstation is connected directly to the hub with a cable to which nothing else is connected. Each end of each cable run in a star is terminated, but this termination is internal at the hub and the workstation NIC.

Fig. 7.9

Star topology is reliable, inexpensive, and easy to troubleshoot.

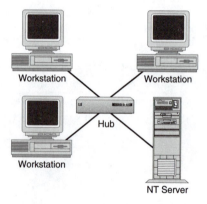

The main advantage of a physical star topology is ease of maintainability and troubleshooting. A cable problem affects only the single device to which that cable is connected, making problem isolation much easier. The only real disadvantage of a physical star is that it typically requires somewhat more cable and labor to install, which is a minor issue in the overall scheme of things. The physical star has become the topology of choice for most new network cabling installations.

10BaseT Ethernet and newer implementations of ARCnet run a logical bus on a physical star. Token Ring runs a logical ring on a physical star. No common networking method uses a logical star topology.

Ring topology, shown in figure 7.10, is simply a bus topology in which the terminators have been eliminated and the ends of the cable connected to form a closed ring. In a ring, each device connects to exactly two other devices forming a closed circle.

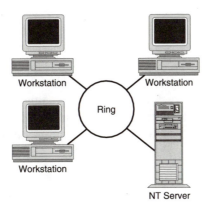

Fig. 7.10
Ring topology is unreliable and difficult to troubleshoot.

A physical ring topology shares the advantages and disadvantages of a bus. It requires less cable than the star, but like the bus is difficult to troubleshoot and subject to complete failure if a break occurs in the ring.

FDDI runs a logical ring on a physical ring. Token Ring runs a logical ring on a physical star.

Cable Types

Thousands of types of cable are available, and only a few of them are appropriate for connecting your LAN. One of them is probably exactly right for your needs. In the following sections you learn how to select the right cable for your own requirements.

Coaxial Cable

Coaxial cable, called coax for short, is the oldest type of cable used in network installations. It is still in use and still being installed today. Coax comprises a single central conductor, surrounded by a dielectric insulator, surrounded by a braided conducting shield. This assemblage is then covered by an insulating sheath. Coaxial cable is familiar to anyone with cable television.

Coax has a lot going for it. It is a mature technology. It is inexpensive, offers high data throughput, and is resistant to electrical interference. These advantages are balanced by a few disadvantages. Coax is difficult to terminate properly and reproducibly. Because coax is typically used in a physical bus topology, many connections are required, increasing the chances of a bad connection taking down the entire network.

Three types of coax cable are commonly seen in network installations:

The original Ethernet 10Base5 specification uses Ethernet coax. Ethernet coax is a 50 ohm cable also called Thick Net. It is about as big around as your thumb, is inflexible and therefore difficult to run, and is by far the most expensive type of coax treated in this section, typically costing $1 or more per foot. Connections are made to Thick Net using piercing tap transceivers, whereby an actual hole is drilled through the sheath, shield, and dielectric to reach the center conductor. Thick Net is most common now as a network backbone in older installations. The sole advantage of Thick Net is that it allows a maximum cabling run of 500 meters. Almost no Thick Net is being installed today.

The difficulty and expense of working with Thick Net resulted in the Ethernet 10Base2 specification, which uses RG-58 coax. RG-58 is a 50 ohm cable also called Thin Net or Cheapernet. Thin Net is less than a quarter inch in diameter, is flexible and therefore easy to install, and typically costs 15 cents per foot. Thin Net cables terminate in a *barrel nut connector* (*BNC*). A Thin Net network is run as a daisy chain, with each workstation using a T-connector to allow connection of one cable coming in to the workstation and another going out. The end stations have only a single cable with the other connection terminated. An Ethernet network running on Thin Net has all of the advantages of Thick Net except that maximum cable length is limited to 185 meters. Thin Net cabling is still commonly found connecting Ethernet workstations, and is still being installed new today, although there are better alternatives. Thin Net is also used at many sites as a backbone media to connect hubs and other active network components together.

ARCnet networks were originally installed using RG-62 coax. RG-62 is a 93-ohm cable also used to connect some types of IBM mainframe devices. Except for the differing impedance and types of devices it is used to connect, RG-62 is otherwise similar to Thick Net and Thin Net cable. Like them, it must be terminated at each end.

If your network will be very small—fewer than 10 workstations all located in close physical proximity—you may be tempted to use Thin Net coax to avoid the cost of buying a hub. If you insist on doing so, at least purchase pre-made cables in the appropriate lengths to connect each device rather than trying to terminate the coax yourself. For any larger network, do not even consider using coax.

Shielded Twisted Pair Cable

Shielded twisted pair (*STP*) cable comprises insulated wires that are twisted together to form pairs. These pairs are then twisted with each other and enclosed in a sheath. A foil shield protects the cable against interference. Depending on the type of cable, this shield may lie immediately beneath the sheath, protecting the cable as a whole, or individual pairs may be shielded from other pairs. The sole advantage of STP cable relative to unshielded twisted pair (UTP) cable is the greater resistance of STP cable to electromagnetic interference. STP cable is very expensive, typically costing from two to five times as much as equivalent UTP cable. IBM Token Ring was originally designed to run on STP cable, and that is still about the only place where you are likely to see it installed. Most new Token Ring installations are done using UTP cable. Don't consider using STP cable for your network.

Unshielded Twisted Pair Cable

Unshielded twisted pair (*UTP*) cable is the dominant type of cable used in network cabling installations today. Like STP cable, UTP cable is constructed from twisted pairs of wire, which are then in turn twisted with each other and enclosed in a sheath. The UTP cable normally used for workstation cabling includes four such twisted pairs, although UTP cable is available in pair counts ranging from two to more than 1,000. The twist reduces both spurious emissions from the cable and the effects of outside electromagnetic interference on the signal carried by the cable. UTP cable is available in thousands of varieties, differing in pair count, sheath type, signal carrying ability, and other respects. UTP cable used for network wiring has a nominal impedance of 100 ohms.

UTP cable is now both the *de facto* and *de jure* standard for new network cabling installations. It is inexpensive, easy to install, supports high data rates and is reasonably resistant to electrical interference, although less so than the other types of cable discussed here. Typical four pair UTP cable ranges in price from 3 cents to 50 cents per foot, depending on the signal carrying ability of the cable and the type of sheath. Don't consider using anything but UTP cable for your network. Even very small networks will benefit from the advantages of UTP cable.

A piece of UTP cable appears upon casual examination to be a simple item. Nothing could be further from the truth. A quick glance at just one manufacturer's catalog reveals hundreds of different types of UTP cable. Only a few of these are appropriate for any given task, and one is probably exactly right. Let's take a look at some of the variables to consider when specifying UTP cable.

- *Conductor Type*. UTP cable is commonly available in 22, 24, and 26 American Wire Gauge (AWG) using either solid or stranded conductors. Although 22 AWG cable has some advantage in terms of the distance a

III

Local Area Networking

signal can travel without degradation, this is primarily of concern in analog phone systems and is outweighed by the additional cost and other factors for data wiring. Data station cabling should be done using 24 AWG solid conductor cable. Use stranded cable only for patch cords and similar jumpers where the flexibility of stranded conductors is needed.

- *Pair Count.* UTP cable is available in pair counts ranging from two to more than 1000. UTP cable runs made to the workstation are almost universally four-pair cables. High pair-count cables—25-pair, 50-pair, 100-pair, and greater—are used primarily in voice wiring as riser cables to concentrate station runs and link floors within a building. Pair count is inextricably linked to the signal carrying capability of the cable, with higher signaling rates being limited to smaller cables. Until 1994 not even 25-pair cable was available that met the minimal Category 3 data standards. Although such 25-pair cable is now available from AT&T, you should still as a matter of good practice avoid using riser cables to carry data. When you find yourself wishing you had a riser cable, it probably means that you should instead install a hub at that location and use fiber or another backbone media to link that hub to the rest of the network.

- *Sheath Material.* UTP cable designed for inside wiring can be purchased with either general purpose sheathing or Plenum rated sheathing. The sheath of general purpose cable is usually constructed of polyvinyl chloride (PVC). PVC sheathing is acceptable for wiring that will be run inside conduit or in spaces not used to route HVAC (Heating, Ventilation, and Air Conditioning) source and return. Plenum cable uses sheathing constructed of Teflon or a similar compound. Its use is mandated by law and by the National Electrical Code (NEC) if the cable will be exposed within an HVAC plenum. When exposed to flame, PVC sheath produces toxic gases while plenum sheath does not.

- Unfortunately, plenum sheathing is extremely expensive. The same box of Category 5 cable that costs $130 with PVC sheathing may cost nearly $400 with plenum sheathing. Don't even think about using PVC cable where you are required by the NEC to use plenum. First, doing so breaks the law. Second, if an inspector finds PVC cable where you should have used plenum, you'll be required to rip it out and replace it. Third, if a fatal fire ever does occur at your site you would hate to wonder for the rest of your life whether your decision to save a few bucks on cable cost someone their life.

- *Quality Grades.* UTP cable varies widely in terms of how fast a signaling rate it will support and over what distance. The terms Type, Level, and Category are used and often misused interchangeably. The IBM Cabling System defines a variety of cables, each of which is designated a "Type." Underwriters' Laboratories (UL) runs a LAN cabling certification plan which assigns "Level" ratings to various qualities of UTP cabling. The Electronic Industry Association/Telephone Industry Association (EIA/TIA) has a similar program that rates UTP cables by "Category."

To offer just one example, IBM Type 3 is a UTP cable used in the IBM Cabling System, and is in fact the only UTP cable defined within that system. Type 3 cable is intended to carry analog telephone signals and low speed data traffic—1 Mbps and 2 Mbps terminal traffic and 4 Mbps Token Ring. In terms of electrical characteristics and signal carrying ability, Type 3 cable corresponds roughly to Underwriters' Laboratories (UL) Level 2 cable. The lowest Category assigned by the EIA/TIA system is Category 3, which is substantially superior to Type 3. UL rates cable at Levels 1 through 5, with Levels 3, 4, and 5 corresponding to the EIA/TIA Categories 3, 4, and 5. So although you may hear someone refer to Category 2 cable, no such thing exists.

You can spend a long time learning everything there is to know about UTP cable. Fortunately, you don't need to. The EIA/TIA has developed minimum specifications, called Categories, for grades of cable appropriate for various uses. All you have to do is pick a cable Category that meets your requirements and your budget.

Category 3 Cable, or Cat 3 for short, is the minimum level you should consider for any new cable installation. Using the standard two pairs of the available four pairs, Cat 3 cable supports data rates as high as 10 Mbps Ethernet, and may be used over short runs for 16 Mbps Token Ring. Cat 3 can support the newer 100 Mbps technologies like 100BaseT and 100VG-AnyLAN, but only by using all four pairs. Cat 3 typically costs about $60 per 1000 foot spool in PVC sheathing, and about $125 per spool in plenum sheathing. Cat 3 is used almost exclusively now for voice cabling, with only about 10 percent of new data cabling being done using Cat 3.

Consider very carefully before deciding to install Category 3 cable. Although you can certainly save a few dollars now by installing Cat 3 instead of a higher grade cable, that wire is going to be in your walls for a long time. In five or ten years, you may rue the decision to install Cat 3. Do so only if your budget is such that using Cat 3 is your only option.

Category 4, or Cat 4 Cable is an obsolescent product. Its reason for existing was simply that it was marginally better than Cat 3, allowing 16 Mbps Token

Ring networks to operate over greater distances than are supported on Cat 3. It is now stuck in the middle—not much better than Cat 3 and not much cheaper than Cat 5. Cat 4 typically costs about $110 per 1000 foot spool in PVC sheathing, and about $250 per spool in plenum sheathing. Only 5-10 percent of the data cabling being installed new is with Cat 4, and most of that is probably being done by organizations that simply have always specified Cat 4 and are continuing to do so. Do not consider Category 4 Cable for your network. Unless you will be running 16 Mbps Token Ring, in which case you should be installing Cat 5 cable anyway, Cat 4 offers no performance advantage but costs substantially more than Cat 3.

Category 5, or Cat 5 Cable is the cable of choice for most new network installations. Cat 5 cable supports 100 Mbps data rates using only two pairs, and offers the potential for carrying data at gigabit rates. Cat 5 typically costs about $130 per 1000 foot spool in PVC sheathing, and about $350 per spool in plenum sheathing. About 80-85 percent of all new data cabling installed is done using Category 5 cable. The huge demand for Cat 5 cable has resulted in the manufacturer of the sheathing material being unable to meet demand, particularly for the plenum variety, so Cat 5 cable can be hard to come by. For flexibility some organizations have gone to the extent of specifying Cat 5 cable for all of their cabling, including voice. You should specify Cat 5 cable for your network. Since the majority of the cost to run cable is in labor, you will likely pay only a 10-20 percent overall premium to use Cat 5 rather than Cat 3. This additional cost can easily be justified for most organizations by the additional flexibility that Cat 5 offers over the 15 to 25 year life of a typical cabling plant.

Fiber Optic Cable

Fiber optic cable has become increasingly common in network installations. Just a few years ago, fiber was an esoteric and extremely expensive technology. Although fiber optic cable was initially positioned for use as a network backbone, most networks continued to use coax to carry backbone traffic. Fiber itself was expensive, the active components were costly and in short supply, and even something as simple as putting a connector on a fiber optic cable was a difficult and expensive process. In recent years, large reductions in the cost of the fiber media itself, improvements in the means used to terminate it, and the widespread availability of inexpensive fiber-based active network components have made fiber optic cable a realistic alternative for use as a network backbone.

Fiber optic cable consists of glass fiber conductors, or strands, contained within a central core. Each strand is surrounded by cladding material and covered by a tough high-density polymer coating. One or more pairs of these individual fiber strands are then assembled into a core assembly that is then covered by a sheath. The strands themselves are composed of very pure germanium doped silica optical glass, and are analogous to the individual conductors in a traditional copper cable. The cladding material that surrounds each individual fiber is also composed of optical glass, although of different optical characteristics, and is used to reflect back the signal carried by the fiber core to keep it contained within the strand. The polymer coating is used to protect the fiber strands against abrasion and breakage during handling, and also adds physical strength to the conductors themselves.

Fiber optic cable offers the highest bandwidth available of any type of cable. It has very low signal attenuation, allowing it to carry signals over long distances. The complete absence of crosstalk allows multiple high-bandwidth links to exist within a single sheath. Fiber optic cable is completely immune to electromagnetic interference, and conversely, because it does not radiate, is secure against eavesdropping. Fiber optic cable is much smaller in diameter and lighter than copper cables capable of carrying the same bandwidth, and is therefore easier to install. Lastly, because many fiber optic cables have no metallic components, they are electrical insulators and can therefore be used to link buildings without concerns about lightning protection and grounding issues. Set against all of these advantages are a few disadvantages. The installed cost of fiber optic cable is still somewhat higher than that of copper, and the active network components designed to work with it also cost more. Lastly, fiber optic cable is typically more fragile than copper cable, requiring careful attention to bend radii and handling requirements when installing it.

In broad terms, fiber optic cable is available in two varieties: Multimode and Single mode. *Multimode (MM) fiber* is the type used in LANs. It uses inexpensive low-power LED light sources for signaling, and can connect two devices separated by as much as two or three kilometers. MM fiber is available in two core diameters. 50 micron cores conform to ITU-T (formerly CCITT) specifications and are used primarily in military applications. 62.5 micron cores are the type used in LANs.

Single mode (SM) fiber is used primarily in Metropolitan Area Networks (MANs) and other long-haul high volume applications where its ability to carry data for long distances is important. The signaling equipment used with single mode fiber is very expensive, however, because it uses higher powered laser light sources to communicate.

Unless you have a true need for either the high data rates or the security provided by fiber optic cable, do not consider installing it to your workstations.

III

Local Area Networking

The cost of the fiber itself, and in particular the costs of connectorizing it, are still much too high for such casual use in most LANs. Do, however, consider installing fiber optic cable to link equipment rooms. If you are in a campus environment, fiber optic will usually be the best choice for linking the individual buildings. Fiber, like copper, requires two conductors to make a circuit. When you install fiber, be sure to install plenty of spare strands. The price differential between 6-fiber cable and 12-fiber cable is not great, and you will probably be glad to have those spare strands in the future. Many companies install fiber optic cables with at least twice as many fibers as they actually need initially, leaving the spare fibers unterminated for future use.

Structured Cabling Systems

The need for standardization of cabling was recognized long ago by companies like IBM and Digital Equipment Corporation. In the days when most organizations were single vendor shops, these companies developed standardized cabling schemes like the IBM Building Wiring System and OpenDECConnect, which were designed primarily to support their own equipment, with consideration to other vendor's equipment added only as an afterthought, if at all. Cable and connector companies like AMP and Leviton developed competing systems. The result was that the cabling of a building wired to one company's specification was often unsuitable for use with another vendor's equipment. The advent of open systems and the proliferation of multi-vendor environments made such a situation intolerable.

The Electronic Industries Association and Telephone Industries Association (EIA/TIA) recognizing this need for a truly standards-based wiring specification, developed, in cooperation with IBM, AT&T, DEC and other vendors, the EIA/TIA 568 *Commercial Building Telecommunications Wiring Standard*. This specification incorporated the best features of each competing standard to develop a composite standard that supported any vendor's equipment and at the same time ensured backward compatibility with existing cabling systems installed using the propriety cabling standards of each participating vendor. The vendors in turn updated their own specifications to full compliance with EIA/TIA 568. As a result, you can purchase a cabling system from many vendors with the assurance that, so long as it is EIA/TIA 568 compliant, it will support any industry-standard networking scheme.

If you purchase an installed cabling system, you should specify full compliance with both the EIA/TIA 568 Wiring Standard and the EIA/TIA 569 *Pathways and Spaces Standard*. If you design and install the cabling system yourself, you should pay close attention to the provisions of both the EIA/TIA 568 and 569 specifications, even if you do not intend your cabling system to achieve full compliance. Both of these specifications may be purchased from Global Engineering Documents at 1-800-854-7179. Order these documents if you plan to design and install the cabling system yourself. If you intend to contract the installation you probably don't need to buy the documents.

EIA/TIA 568 incorporates elements specifying horizontal or station cabling, backbone cabling, wiring closets, entrance facilities, and cabling administration.

Horizontal cabling, also called station cabling, is used to connect the office data jack to the wiring closet, where other station runs from offices in the same vicinity also terminate. EIA/TIA 568 specifies a physical star topology, and requires at least two horizontal runs to each office, terminating at two separate jacks. At least one of these runs must be 100-ohm UTP cable of at least Category 3. The second run may be UTP cable, 50-ohm coax, 150-ohm STP or multimode fiber optic. The coax and STP cables are allowed for compatibility with earlier vendor-proprietary standards, and are seldom installed in new cabling systems today. Fiber optic cable is seldom run because of cost. Nearly everyone simply installs multiple UTP cables. A typical installation would be one Category 5 cable for data and a second Category 3 cable for voice, although many companies use Category 5 exclusively for future flexibility. Because the cable itself is inexpensive and it does not require much more labor to pull several cables, many companies as a matter of policy pull four, six, or even eight cables to each work area, giving themselves a great deal of flexibility in the future as to furniture arrangements, office sharing, and so forth.

EIA/TIA 568 also addresses the matter of how the cable will be terminated at the office jack. Like cables, jacks are rated. In the past it was common to use expensive Cat 5 jacks only to terminate runs intended for data use and to use inexpensive Cat 3 jacks on voice terminations. The decreasing cost of Cat 5 jacks has made this practice less common. Two methods of connecting the cables to the jacks are allowed within the 568 standard, differing only in which cable conductors are connected to which pins of the jack. Consult with your vendor to determine whether the 568A or 568B method is more appropriate for you.

Wiring Closets are central locations to which horizontal cables run. Although EIA/TIA 568 differentiates between wiring or telecommunications closets and equipment rooms, for all intents and purposes most LAN managers use these terms interchangeably. By definition, an equipment room contains both equipment and wiring, while a wiring closet contains only wiring. It is at the wiring closet that each horizontal cable terminates and is connected to a device called a punchdown block. *Punchdown blocks* have many pins to which the individual cable conductors are connected using a physical impact punchdown tool. These blocks allow large numbers of conductors to be connected reliably and in an organized fashion.

Voice cables are connected to a group of blocks called the *voice field* and data cables to a group of blocks called the *data field*. From these blocks, voice cables are cross connected to the voice riser cable, typically a large multi-pair Level 2 UTP cable that runs to the main telephone equipment room. Data cables may be cross connected using either cross connect wire or jumper cords and a patch panel. They may connect to small pair count Category 3 data riser cables and thence to an equipment room where a hub is located, or they may connect to a hub located in that room.

EIA/TIA 568 specifies a maximum horizontal cable run of 90 meters from the office jack to the first punchdown block. The drop cable from the office jack to the equipment may be up to three meters long. Six meters are allowed for interconnection within the wiring closet, giving a total of 99 meters from the equipment to the hub. If your floor plan would require longer runs than these, EIA/TIA 568 requires additional equipment rooms and hubs, with the hubs linked by a backbone cable. In practice, this 99 meter limit is usually rounded up to 100 meters and then ignored. Depending on the quality of the cable and what you are running on it, you can get away with exceeding these distance limits. It is common to run 10BaseT on Category 5 cable for 150 meters and even 200 meters. However, what you can get away with using today's technology you won't necessarily be able to get away with using tomorrow's higher speed technologies, so pay close attention to the EIA/TIA 568 distance limitations and try very hard to live within them.

Riser Cables are more commonly used in voice cabling than in data cabling. The lower requirements of voice cabling mean that it is possible to use large multi-pair voice grade cables, often comprising 100 or more pairs, to connect station runs from local wiring closets to the central telephone equipment room. The largest Category 3 cable now available is 25 pairs, and Category 5 cable is not available in pair counts beyond those used for station runs. Accordingly, it is normal practice to place a hub in each wiring closet at which data cables terminate and cross connect to that hub using patch cords and patch panels. About the only place where you see data cables cross connected to risers is in a wiring closet that serves so few workstations that it is not worthwhile to install a hub. These workstations are served instead by merely running additional data grade wiring from the wiring closet to the nearest location with a hub. These are not in fact riser cables at all, but simple extensions of the station wiring, and the horizontal cabling for these worksta-tions can be thought of as terminating at the hub location and as merely passing through a wiring closet where they happen to have been joined to another length of cable. This practice is frowned upon, but the realities of life sometimes make it necessary.

Backbone Cables are those used to link active network components located in various equipment rooms and wiring closets. Backbone cables may be STP, UTP, coax, or fiber. The decreasing cost of fiber has made its use increasingly common as a data backbone. It is often accompanied by one or more Cat-egory 5 UTP cables installed "just in case" to back up the fiber.

Backbone cabling is commonly found in star, ring, and mesh configurations. In a star, backbone cabling is run from the main equipment room to each subsidiary equipment room and to any wiring closets that contain active net-work components. In a ring configuration, backbone cable runs from the main equipment room to the first subsidiary equipment room, from there to the next equipment room, and so on. From the final equipment room, it is then run back to the main equipment room, closing the ring. In installations using both star and ring backbones, it is common to see redundant cabling routed differently to minimize the chances of a cable cut causing loss of the backbone. The final backbone topology is the *mesh*, which runs cable from each equipment room and wiring closet to every other equipment room and wiring closet. This topology can be thought of as a multiple star configura-tion in which each equipment room is the central point of one star. Running a full mesh can be difficult unless you have conduit linking each equipment room to all other equipment rooms, but it does have the advantage of guar-anteeing that you will always be able to create a high speed link from any equipment room to any other.

Recommendations

Whether your cabling system will support five workstations in a small office or 500 workstations in a multi-building campus, there are several guidelines that you should adhere to ensure that your cabling system provides the ser-vice that you expect.

- Design and install your cabling system in full compliance with the EIA/TIA 568 *Commercial Building Telecommunications Wiring Standard*, using a star topology running on unshielded twisted pair cable. To the extent that your floor plan allows, adhere closely to the EIA/TIA 569 *Pathways and Spaces Standard*.

- Pay careful attention to the quality of even the smallest components used. Just as a chain is no stronger than its weakest link, your cabling system will be no better than the quality of the worst component that is a part of it. Good installations are often spoiled by using substandard small components. Don't scrimp on patch cords and drop cables.

■ Have your cabling installed by LAN cabling specialists. Using the highest quality components means nothing if the craftsmanship of the installer isn't up to par. Use the expertise of your cabling vendor. Listen to their advice, and ignore it at your peril.

■ Install new voice cabling at the same time you are cabling for data. It is a great temptation to make do with existing voice cabling, but you will find that the advantages of having a single integrated cabling system more than make up for the small additional cost.

■ Install Category 5 cable exclusively for data and install lots of it. Install at least Category 3 cables for voice, and consider carefully using Category 5 for voice as well as data. Make sure that you specify different color cable sheaths for voice and data runs. Consider the EIA/TIA 568 requirement for two runs to each office to be an absolute minimum. Run a voice cable, a data cable, and a spare cable to each wall box, and leave the spare cable unterminated, with sufficient slack on each end to allow you to terminate later as needed. Consider putting three such cable runs into wall boxes on at least two walls of each office. You will bless your foresight in the coming years.

■ Make absolutely certain that your cable installer fully documents every single conductor of every single cable he installs. Horizontal cables, riser cables, and punchdown blocks should be numbered and pin assignments provided. You should be able to trace any conductor from the wall jack, through punchdown blocks and patch panels to the final termination. If your cabling plant will be a large one, consider purchasing a cable management software package to record this information initially and then keep up-to-date with changes and adds to the cabling. Assign one person responsibility for making changes to the cabling plant and then make it known that making physical changes to the cabling system without recording them is a serious offense.

Scaling the Cabling System to Your Needs

Although in general terms the characteristics of a good cabling system are similar no matter what the size of the installation, there are some special considerations based on the scale of the installation.

Small Cabling Systems often make compromises that would be unacceptable in a larger installation. This is done to some extent for cost reasons, but largely because small cabling systems are inherently simpler to work with than large ones. During his first visit to a major wiring closet, a friend of mine summed it up by saying that there appeared to be eight million wires there, all of them white, blue, or orange. Cabling is fundamentally simple, but even simple things can be overwhelming in large numbers.

The easiest definition of a small cabling system is one in which all wire runs terminate to one location, often the same location that hosts the hub, the server, and possibly coffee maker and copy machine. If your cabling plant will be small by this definition, you can compromise on equipment room layouts, number of cable runs, and even on the extent to which you require the vendor to document the system. Do not, however, compromise on the basic topology or on the quality of the components and craftsmanship. Many small networks are cabled using daisy-chained coaxial cable looped from desk to desk to avoid the cost of installing UTP and a hub. Don't make this mistake or you will pay for it in decreased reliability and increased maintenance.

Medium Cabling Systems are those in which at least one wiring closet exists in addition to the main equipment room. It is in medium cabling systems that a backbone first appears, because active network components in a medium network are distributed throughout the facility. A formal structured cabling system becomes, if not an absolute requirement, at least a highly desirable item in a medium cabling system. If you will have a medium cabling system, give strong consideration to installing a formal structured cabling system. If you will be maintaining the cabling system yourself, consider using Category 5 UTP or coax as a backbone to avoid the expense and difficulty of working with small numbers of fiber runs. If you will contract installation and maintenance of your cabling system, go ahead and use a fiber backbone for its greater bandwidth and future flexibility.

Large Cabling Systems are those in which the cabling system connects a large building or multiple buildings within a campus. Installation of a full formal structured cabling system is essential to the ongoing maintenance of a large network. Install a full fiber backbone for your large network, and in particular use fiber to link multiple buildings. Consider installing a fiber ring or a fiber mesh between the buildings to prevent a single cable cut from severing communications. Pay particular attention to the requirements for wiring closets and equipment rooms specified in *Pathways and Spaces*, and make every effort to ensure that you have at least the minimum floor space specified for each. Conduit space becomes critical in a large cabling system, both in terms of size and routing. Make sure that you have conduit installed to link each wiring closet and equipment room to every other such space. Determine adequate

III

Local Area Networking

numbers and sizes for each of these conduit runs, and then double both. Regard a cable management software package as mandatory to successfully maintaining your large network.

Designing for Expandability and Ease of Maintenance

The first principle here is to over-wire your station runs. It costs very little more to run two cables than it does to run only one. If you have a location that you are absolutely positive will never need more than one cable run, go ahead and run a spare anyway, leaving the spare unterminated with enough slack on both ends for future use. Yes, you will probably end up with a lot of $10 pieces of cable left unused in the wall for eternity, but the first time you desperately need one of those cable runs will more than pay for every extra run you made. Don't scrimp on cable runs. They're cheap and easy to make when the cabling system is being installed. They're expensive and difficult or impossible to make later on.

The second principle is to over-wire your backbone and riser runs. If a 25-pair riser will do the job now, go ahead and put in a 50-pair or even a 100-pair riser. If a 6-fiber cable will carry your present traffic, go ahead and install a 12-fiber cable instead. The cable itself is cheap. What costs money is labor, and most of the labor is spent terminating the cable. By installing more pairs than you need and leaving them unterminated you have the best of both worlds. Having the extra pairs in place costs next to nothing, but they are there and can be terminated if and when you need them.

The third principle is to pay close attention to the physical environment of your wiring closets and equipment rooms. Nothing is more miserable than trying to maintain a cabling system in an overheated or freezing closet while holding a flashlight in your teeth. Make sure your wiring closets and equipment rooms are well-lighted, properly ventilated, and provided with more electrical receptacles than you think you'll ever need. Your equipment will be much happier, and so will you when you need to make changes to the cabling.

Getting Professional Help and Using Vendors' Expertise

Make it a point to choose your cabling installer as early in the process as possible. Check references and visit sites where your prospective installers have installed cabling systems on a scale similar to your own. Having chosen a cabling installer, if only in your own mind, then use that cabling installer's experience to help you design your cabling system. Get them involved very early in the process, ideally at the floor plan stage. You will find that a good cabling system installer can help you avoid pitfalls that you might not have noticed on your own. Do not expect them to work for free. If you will eventually bid out the installation of your cabling, then offer to pay a good cabling system installer up front to help with design, making it clear to them that they will be bidding competitively for the installation itself. Alternatively, choose a good network consultant and buy a day or two of his time to help with the design phase. Whatever means you choose, make sure that you have it right before actual cable pulling begins. You will be living with this cabling system for many years, and the time to get it right is sooner rather than later.

Keeping It Structured

A properly designed and installed structured cabling system is a thing of beauty. It will support almost any networking technology you want to install now and down the road. It will make routine day-to-day changes and adds quick and easy. About the only thing it won't do is protect itself from someone with a punchdown tool and an emergency request for a wiring change. Once you have a structured cabling system in place, make sure it stays structured. All it takes is a few emergency changes that aren't recorded to turn your nice new structured cabling system into an unstructured mess. Make it very clear from the beginning that only designated persons are allowed to make wiring changes, and that these changes must be recorded in an acceptable format. Install a cable management software package and use it religiously. Install good locks on all wiring closets and equipment rooms and keep close control over who has access to the keys. Protect the structure of your cabling system and make sure that 15-minute jobs don't turn into 8-hour jobs.

Selecting Active Network Components

If the cabling system is the arteries and veins of your network, then the *active network components* are its heart. By itself, the cabling system is just dead wire. Active network components bring that wire to life, putting data on it and allowing the various parts of your network to communicate with each other.

In our consulting practice, we frequently find organizations that have chosen active network components from a variety of vendors. A company might have Cisco routers, Cabletron hubs, DEC bridges, and Hewlett-Packard servers. All are fine suppliers, and each makes top notch equipment. Some have very broad product lines while others specialize to a greater or lesser extent in particular market segments. The fact remains, however, that the purchasers of this equipment in retrospect would have done better to select their components from only one or two of these suppliers rather than attempting to pick best of breed from the market as a whole.

If you remember only one thing from this section, make it this: *The single most important factor in choosing active network components is to maintain consistency.* Having chosen one manufacturer as your supplier, it is easy to be seduced by another manufacturer's component that is a bit cheaper or has a nice feature or has better specifications. Don't fall into this trap. You will pay the price later in dollars, time, and aggravation when you find that you can't solve a problem related to the interaction of the two manufacturer's components because neither will take responsibility or that you have to purchase a second $5,000 network management software package because neither manufacturer's management software will work with the other's product. Real estate brokers tell us that the three most important factors are location, location, and location. In choosing active network components, the three most important factors are consistency, consistency, and consistency. All else is secondary.

Network Interface Cards

A Network Interface Card, commonly referred to as a NIC, is used to connect each device on the network to the network cabling system. Network Interface Cards operate at the Physical Layer and the Data Link Layer of the ISO Reference Model. A Network Interface Card provides at the Physical Layer the physical and electrical connection required to access the network cabling and to use it to convey data as a bit stream. At the Data Link Layer, the NIC provides the processing that assembles and disassembles the bit stream on the cable into frames suitable for the Media Access Method in use. Every device connected to the network must be equipped with a network interface, either by means of a peripheral Network Interface Card or by means of similar circuitry built in to the component directly.

A Network Interface Card is media dependent, media-access-method dependent, and protocol independent. Media dependent means that the NIC must have a physical connector appropriate for the cabling system to which it is to be connected. Media-access-method dependent means that even a card that can be physically connected to the cabling system must also be of a type that supports the media access method in use. For example, an Ethernet card designed for UTP cable can be connected to but will not function on a Token Ring network wired using UTP cable. Protocol independent means that a particular NIC, assuming that appropriate drivers are available for it, may communicate using a variety of higher level protocols, either individually or simultaneously. For example, an Ethernet NIC may be used to connect a workstation simultaneously to a LAN server running IPX/SPX and to a UNIX host running TCP/IP.

It's common in the industry to differentiate between NICs intended for use in workstations and those intended for use in servers. Conventional wisdom says that inexpensive NICs are fine for use in a workstation where performance is less of an issue, but that for your server you should buy the highest-performance NIC you can afford. In fact, although you can use any NIC in any computer system it will fit, be it workstation or server, you should pay close attention to selecting NICs for both your workstations and your servers. Installing very high performance NICs in your server and using low-performance NICs in your workstations is actually counter-productive. Because in this situation the server NIC can deliver data so much faster than the workstation NIC can accept it, the network is flooded with retransmissions requested by the workstation NIC. These constant retransmissions greatly degrade network performance. The solution is simple. Balance the performance of the NICs you use in your workstations with the performance provided the server NIC.

Choosing Workstation NICs

To choose the best NICs for your workstations, you must consider several factors, including compatibility, performance, and cost. In the following sections, you learn how to balance each of these factors in your decision.

Bus Types. The first consideration in choosing a workstation NIC is the workstation's bus type. There are two schools of thought on this issue. The first holds that you should install a NIC that uses the highest performance bus provided by that workstation. For example, if the workstation has both Industry Standard Architecture (ISA) and VESA Local Bus (VLB) slots, choosing a VLB NIC rather than an ISA NIC results in better performance. The second school believes that the advantages of standardization outweigh the incremental performance benefits of matching the card to the workstation. Members of this group, faced with a mixed workstation environment of ISA, Peripheral Component Interconnect (PCI), and VLB systems would choose ISA NICs for all workstations. There is something to be said for each of these positions, but on balance I favor the second, for reasons described in the following sections.

Throughput. The theoretical maximum throughput of an Ethernet network is 1.25 megabytes per second (MBps), determined by dividing 10 megabits per second (Mbps) by an eight-bit byte. The true throughput on a working network will be much lower due to protocol overhead, network traffic, collisions, retransmissions, and so on.

Out of curiosity, we experimented to determine the real-world throughput of Ethernet cards. We set up a network consisting of a single server and a single workstation. We first equipped both systems with 3Com 3C509 Ethernet cards, which are generally considered to be at or near the top in performance for ISA cards. We measured a sustained throughput of 0.80 MBps using these cards. We then replaced the $100 3Com cards with $25 Addtron AE-200JL-N Ethernet cards and repeated the measurements. We found that the inexpensive Addtron cards provided a sustained throughput of 0.78 Mbps, performance essentially indistinguishable from that of the 3Com cards. Although these *ad hoc* benchmark tests were not particularly scientific or rigidly controlled, they do suggest that throughput should not be a major consideration when choosing network interface cards. Note that this is not intended to advocate the use of Addtron cards or to criticize 3Com cards. There are many good and valid reasons why you might choose higher priced cards rather than inexpensive clone cards, but promised throughput should not be one of them.

Software Configurable versus Jumper Configurable NICs. Network Interface Cards have various settings that may need to be adjusted before the card can be used. Nearly all cards are configurable for Interrupt Request (IRQ). Many require setting Direct Memory Access (DMA), base address, and media type. All ARCnet cards and some Token Ring cards allow the network address to be set by the user. One important factor that contributes to the usability of a NIC is whether these settings are made using physical jumpers or by using a software utility. A card that requires setting physical jumpers is inconvenient. Making a change involves disassembling the computer, removing the card, setting the jumpers, and then putting everything back together. It's often necessary to go through this process just to examine how the card is currently set. A software configurable card, on the other hand, can be both examined and set simply by running a program. Fortunately, most cards which ship today are configurable with software. Don't consider buying one that is not.

Remote Boot. Some Network Interface Cards support remote boot. *Remote boot capability* simply means that the NIC itself contains all the files needed to boot the workstation and connect it to the network. These files are generated by the network administrator and stored on a ROM chip installed on the NIC.

Several years ago diskless workstations had a brief vogue based on a two-fold justification. The first was the lower cost of workstations not equipped with hard disks and floppy drives. This issue has faded in importance with the plummeting cost of drives as well as the emergence of Microsoft Windows as a corporate standard and the desirability of using a local hard disk to host Windows swap files. The second issue is one of security. A workstation that has no drives protects against theft of company data by making it impossible for a dishonest employee to copy information to a floppy disk. It also makes protecting the network against viruses much easier. Because workstation users cannot boot their computers or run programs from a floppy disk, this potential source of infection is removed and only the server must be protected.

This protection does, however, have its price. Many organizations have found that the reduced costs of diskless workstations are illusory. The net result of using diskless workstations is to trade a small savings in hardware acquisition costs for a large additional expense in the skilled labor required to install and maintain them. Still, some organizations find that the security provided by diskless workstations is worth the additional cost and aggravation. If yours is such an organization, the availability of remote boot must be a mandatory check list item on your network interface card specifications. Otherwise, give this feature no weight in your selection.

Name Brand NICs versus Clones. As mentioned above, the relative performance of name brand versus clone NICs should normally not be a deciding factor in your purchase decision. However, name brand NICs justify their considerable price premium in several ways.

The best reason to pay the premium for a name brand NIC is that part of that premium goes to pay for better quality control and reliability. In working with thousands of name brand and clone NICs over the years, I've very seldom seen a name brand NIC that was dead on arrival, and almost never experienced a failure of a name brand NIC that was not due to some easily explained problem like a lightning strike. With clone NICs the story is not so happy. On one occasion I received a shipment of 10 clone NICs of which six were DOA. All four of the remaining NICs and several of the replacement ones failed for no apparent reason shortly after being installed. The choice is yours, but most LAN administrators recognize that the relatively small amount of money saved by buying clone NICs can be rapidly swamped by the costs of just one network failure attributable to using cheap cards.

Another good reason to pay the extra cost of name brand NICs is the availability of support. If you have problems with a name brand NIC you can usually get them resolved with a telephone call to the manufacturer's tech support line. With a clone NIC it may not even be immediately obvious who manufactured the card, and getting any support at all may prove impossible.

III

Local Area Networking

Similarly, name brand NICs are well supplied with frequently updated drivers by the makers of both the NIC and the network operating system. Getting the latest driver for a name brand NIC is as simple as contacting the manufacturer's ftp site or bulletin board system. On the other hand, network operating system (NOS) makers write very few drivers for clone NICs, so it is up to the NIC manufacturer to write the drivers for each NOS. As a result, the newest available drivers for a clone NIC are often a version or two behind the current software release. Whether they'll be updated as new versions of the software are released is anyone's guess.

Yet another reason to buy name brand NICs is manageability. Developing network management standards like SNMP (Simple Network Management Protocol) and RMON (Remote Monitoring) are supported first by the manufacturers of name brand NICs and only much later, if ever, by the cloners. If network management down to the workstation level is something you would like to implement—or even to leave open as an option—make sure that the NICs you buy will support it when you want it.

A final reason to prefer name brand NICs to clones is consistency. Subtle and very difficult to resolve network problems can occur because of something as simple and apparently minor as a ROM revision. The difference between an Ethernet card with a 1.21e ROM and a 1.21f ROM may not seem large, but similar small differences have been known to cripple a workstation or even to down a network. Even the name brand makers are not faultless in this respect. I once received a shipment of 100 Ethernet cards in a box sealed by the manufacturer and was surprised to find a mixture of three ROM rev levels within that single box. However, at least with name brand NICs it is usually possible to find out the reason for ROM revisions and whether the changes need be of concern to you. With clone cards you're usually on your own, and purchasing additional cards with the same ROM rev levels is almost always a hit or miss situation.

For all of these reasons it's a good idea to buy name brand network interface cards in bulk. Specify on your purchase order not just the quantity and model number but also the ROM revision number you require. Make it clear to the vendor that you will reject cards with different ROM revision numbers and then stick to your guns. When your order comes in, you will probably find that the vendor has ignored your instructions and just shipped you a box of the card that you ordered, but at least you will then be in a good position to demand that the incorrect ones be exchanged for ones with the proper ROM rev level.

Choosing Server NICs

All the same factors that apply to choosing workstation NICs also apply to choosing server NICs, with a few more thrown in for good measure. While a workstation NIC is responsible for handling only the traffic of its own workstation, a server NIC must process traffic from many workstations in rapid sequence. Doing so demands a high speed link to the I/O system of the server. Accordingly, NICs intended for use in servers are universally designed to use a high speed bus connection.

Until recently this need for speed meant that server NICs were either EISA or MCA cards. The advent of PCI, which transfers four bytes at a time on a 33 MHz mezzanine bus for a total throughput of 132 MBps, has made both EISA and MCA obsolescent. The pending extension of PCI to 64 bits will allow it to transfer eight bytes at a time, doubling throughput to 264 MBps. All newly designed servers are PCI-based. If they offer EISA or MCA slots, it is only for compatibility with legacy expansion cards. Even IBM, the originator and long the sole champion of MCA, has begun offering PCI-based servers.

Another factor that is of little concern in workstation NICs but more important in server NICs is that of processor utilization. All NICs require some assistance from the system processor, but a properly designed server NIC should minimize this dependence. This issue is of particular concern with 100BaseT server NICs. I've seen one server equipped with four such NICs in which the overhead associated with handling the NICs themselves occupied more than 50 percent of the processor. Find out what level of processor utilization your proposed server NICs require, and favor those with low utilization.

Deciding which network interface card to install in your server is straightforward. If you have a PCI server, as you should, install name brand PCI NICs. In choosing the brand of NIC, simplify global network management issues by giving first preference to a card made by the manufacturer of your other active network components. Alternatively, choose a card made by the server manufacturer to simplify server management. Obviously, if your server and your active network components are made by the same supplier you have the best of all worlds and a seamless network solution.

One of the most valuable pieces of real estate in your network is a server expansion slot. Even though a typical server has many more slots than a workstation, the competition for these slots is intense. When your boss reads an article on disk redundancy and decides that your server needs to be duplexed, there goes another slot. The marketing and sales guys demand that you bring up Remote Access Services, so you add a multiport serial card and lose yet another slot. The Chief Financial Officer (CFO) says the mainframe guys won't link to your network and insists that you have to link to theirs—there goes another slot. After a while you start to look at those four Ethernet cards taking up four slots and think there must be a better way. There is, and it takes the form of a multi-port NIC. These devices combine the function of more than one NIC onto a single card. They are available in dual- and quad-NIC versions from a variety of suppliers. If your LAN will be Ethernet, as it probably should be, and if you will segment it, as you should, consider carefully how many server slots you will have available and whether you should purchase a dual-port or quad-port NIC.

Repeaters

Repeaters, shown in figure 7.11, are used to amplify and rebroadcast a signal, extending the distance that the signal may be run reliably on a particular type of cable. They function exclusively at the Physical Layer of the OSI Reference Model. Repeaters are media dependent and protocol independent. As purely electrical devices, repeaters are unaware of the content of the signals that they process. They simply regenerate the signal and pass it on.

Local Repeaters are used to extend signaling distance within the confines of a LAN. Remote repeaters are used to extend a LAN segment, often by means of fiber optic cable, to a remote location without requiring installation of a bridge or router. The workstations at the remote site appear logically to be on the same local segment as that to which the remote repeater is attached.

Hubs, bridges, routers, gateways, and all other active network components include basic repeater functionality. You should use standalone local repeaters as needed to manage cable length limitations within your network. You should use standalone remote repeaters to extend your LAN to remote locations that do not justify installation of a bridge or router.

Simple Hubs (Multi-Port Repeaters)

Hubs are used as concentrators to join multiple workstations with a single link to the rest of the LAN. A hub has several ports to which workstations are connected directly and one or more ports that may be used in turn to connect the hub to the backbone or to other active network components. A hub functions as a multi-port repeater. Signals received on any port are immediately retransmitted to all other ports on the hub. Hubs function at the Physical Layer of the ISO Reference Model. They are media dependent and protocol independent. Hubs come in a wide variety of sizes, types, and price ranges.

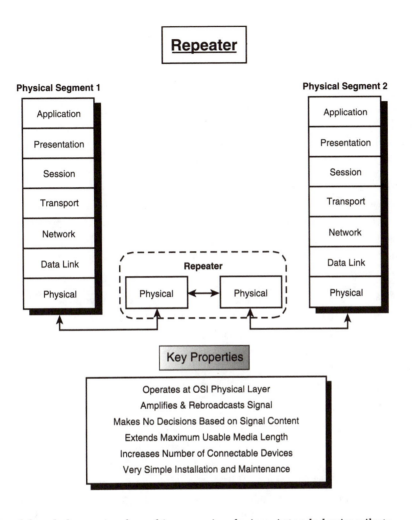

Fig. 7.11
Repeaters amplify
signals to allow
longer segments.

Standalone hubs are simple and inexpensive devices, intended primarily to serve a self contained workgroup in which the server is connected to one port, the workstations to other ports, and no interconnection to a larger network exists. They range in size from 4-24 ports. Depending on port count, standalone hubs vary in size from about that of a modem to about that of a pizza box. They normally operate on low voltage supplied by a power brick similar to that used to power external modems. They normally consume about as much power as a night light.

Standalone hubs offer little or no expandability. This is not usually a problem because these hubs are inexpensive and can simply be purchased in a size appropriate for your needs. Standalone hubs usually offer no provision for management, although high-end standalone hubs may have management

III

Local Area Networking

features standard or as an option. Manageability is not normally a major issue in the small workgroup environment for which these hubs are intended.

A typical name brand 8-port standalone unmanaged hub has a street price of under $200, or less than $25 per port. Hubs with higher port counts may cost somewhat more on a per-port basis. Hubs that include management features may approach $100 per port. If your network comprises only a few workstations that are all located in close proximity, a standalone hub is an excellent and inexpensive way to connect these systems.

Make sure that any standalone hub you buy has *jabber protection*. This feature monitors each port for constant uncontrolled transmission that will flood the network. If this condition is detected, jabber protection temporarily shuts down the offending port while allowing the remainder of the ports to continue functioning. This function is commonly referred to as partitioning by hub manufactures.

Stackable hubs are a fairly recent development. In the past, you had to choose between a standalone hub, which provided little functionality but a low price, and a chassis hub, which provided enterprise-level functionality but at a very high cost. Stackable hubs do a good job of blending the best characteristics of both other types of hub. They offer much of the expandability and management capabilities of chassis hubs at a cost not all that much greater than standalone hubs.

What distinguishes a true stackable hub is that it possesses a backplane which can be used to link it directly to a similar hub or hubs, melding the assembled stack into a single hub running a single Ethernet bus. Although standalone hubs may be physically stacked and joined simply by connecting a port on one to a port on the next, the result is not a true stack. To understand why, it's necessary to understand that Ethernet places a limit on the maximum number of repeaters that are allowed to separate any two stations. A device connected to any port of any hub in a stack of stackable hubs is connected directly to the single bus represented by that stack. As a result, any two devices connected to that stack can communicate while going through only the one repeater represented by that stack. The "stack" of standalone hubs, on the other hand, results in two stations connected to different hubs within that "stack" going through at least two repeaters to communicate.

Stackable hubs are commonly available in 12-port and 24-port versions. Some manufacturers also offer 48-port versions. The street price of stackable hubs ranges from about $50 to $250 per port, depending on port density and what, if any, management options are installed. For most organizations, these hubs offer the best combination of price, features, and expandability available.

Manageability is another consideration in choosing standalone or stackable hubs. This is simply the ability of a hub to be configured and monitored from a remote workstation running specialized software. Although protocols like Simple Network Management Protocol (SNMP) and Remote Monitoring (RMON) are standardized, their implementations are not. This means that it's unlikely that you will be able to manage one manufacturer's hub with remote software intended for use with another manufacturer's hub. This is yet another reason to stick with one manufacturer for your active network components.

Although hub manufacturers attempt to represent "dumb" or unmanaged hubs as a separate category from "smart" or manageable hubs, the reality is that manageability is just one more feature that may be standard, optional, or unavailable on a particular hub. Most low-end standalone hubs are not manageable and cannot be upgraded. High-end standalone hubs and most stackable hubs either come with management standard or at least offer it as an option. Unless yours is a very small network, you should buy manageable hubs, or at least ones that can be upgraded to manageability.

Bridges

Bridges, shown in figure 7.12, are used to divide a network into mutually isolated segments while maintaining the whole as a single network. Bridges operate at the Data Link Layer of the ISO Reference Model. They work with frames, which are organized assemblages of data rather than the raw bit stream upon which hubs, repeaters, and other Physical Layer devices operate.

Most bridges are media access layer dependent. A bridge designed to connect to an Ethernet network cannot connect to a Token Ring network. There are some highly specialized *translational bridges* that will convert Ethernet to Token Ring, but this function is better served by a router due to the differences in the frame sizes. Bridges are protocol independent above the Data Link Layer. It doesn't matter to an Ethernet frame or to the bridge that directs it whether that frame encapsulates an IP packet, an IPX packet, or some other type of packet at the logical level. A bridge simply sees that the frame originated from a particular hardware address and needs to be sent to another hardware address.

Frames include, in addition to the raw data itself, a header that identifies the address of the source station and the address of the destination station. Frames use physical rather than logical addresses. When a workstation transmits an Ethernet frame to the server, the source address is the MAC (Media Access Control) or hardware address of the workstation's Ethernet card, and the destination address is the MAC address of the Ethernet card in the server.

III

Local Area Networking

Fig. 7.12
Bridges link
multiple segments
on a single LAN.

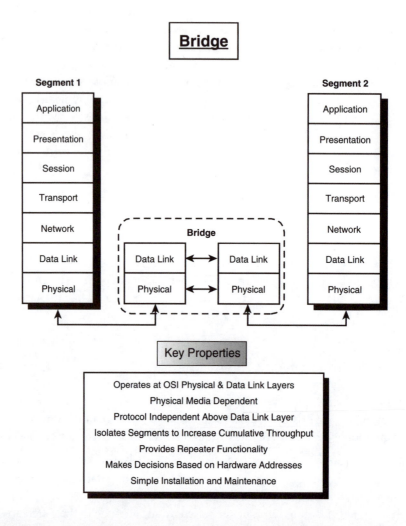

A bridge divides a single network cable into two or more physical and logical segments. The bridge listens to all traffic on all segments and examines the destination hardware address of each frame. If the source and destination hardware addresses are located on the same segment, the bridge simply discards that frame since the destination can hear the source directly. If the source and destination addresses are located on different segments, the bridge repeats the frame onto the segment where the destination address is located. Traffic with both source and destination addresses on the same segment is kept local to that segment and not heard by the rest of the network. Only traffic whose source and destination addresses are on different segments or a broadcast is forwarded to the network as a whole.

When used properly, bridges can significantly reduce the total volume of traffic on the network. This is particularly important on Ethernet networks, because as the network grows and the traffic volume increases, collisions become more frequent and the overall performance of the network degrades.

Another important characteristic of bridges is that they negate the impact of repeaters. Ethernet allows a maximum of four repeaters to intervene between the source and destination stations. Using a bridge, a frame on the source segment may pass through as many as the legal limit of four repeaters before reaching the bridge. When the bridge places that frame on the destination segment, it may again pass through as many as four repeaters on its way to the destination station. This can be an important design consideration in Ethernet networks, particularly those that are large and physically widespread.

Defined in the IEEE 802.1 specification, the *Spanning Tree Algorithm (STA)* detects loops within a bridged network. The STA allows a bridge to determine which of available alternate paths is most efficient and forwards frames via that path. Should that path become unavailable, a bridge using STA can detect that failure and select an alternate path to prevent communications from being severed.

Routers

Routers, shown in figure 7.13, are used to connect one network to another network. Routers operate at the Network Layer of the ISO Reference Model. They work with packets, which are composed of a frame encapsulated and with logical addressing information added.

Routers are media independent. A router designed to process IP packets can do so whether it is physically connected to UTP cabling or to a coax cable. Routers are protocol dependent above the Data Link Layer. A router designed to process IP packets cannot process IPX packets and vice versa, although multiprotocol routers do exist that are designed to process more than one type of Network Layer packet.

Packets are encapsulated within a Data Link Layer frame. Packets include a header that identifies the address of the source station and the address of the destination station. Packets use logical rather than physical addresses. Unlike bridges, which require the source and destination address to be on the same network, router addressing allows the destination address to be on a different network than the source address.

III

Local Area Networking

Fig. 7.13
Routers are used to link separate networks.

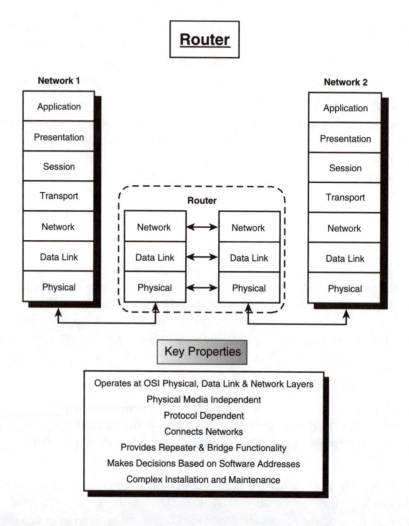

Routers are much more complex than bridges, and are accordingly more expensive and require more configuration. A bridge makes a simple decision. If the destination address is on the same segment as the source address, it discards the frame. If the two addresses are on different segments, it repeats the frame. A router, on the other hand, must make a complex decision about how to deliver a particular packet to a distant network. A router might have to choose the best available route from a variety of alternatives.

It is important to understand that routers work with the logical addressing information contained in Network Layer packets, and not all upper layer protocols provide this information. Windows NT Server includes native support for TCP/IP, IPX/SPX, and NetBEUI. TCP/IP and IPX/SPX packets include the Network Layer logical addresses needed by routers, and are referred to as *routed* or *routable* protocols. NetBEUI packets do not include this Network Layer information, and accordingly are referred to as *non-routed* or *non-routable*. This means that if you are using TCP/IP or IPX/SPX transport, you have the choice of designing your network around bridges, routers, or both. If instead you are using NetBEUI, bridging is your only alternative, because routers cannot handle NetBEUI packets.

Easily confused with routed versus non-routed protocols, but completely different in concept, are *routing protocols* themselves. These refer not to the ability of user packets to be handled by a router, but instead to the protocols used by routers to communicate between themselves. Routing protocols fall into two categories. The older *Distance Vector protocols*, typified by Internet *Routing Information Protocol* (*RIP*) and Novell RIP, are simpler and less robust than the more recent *Link State protocols* typified by *Open Shortest Path First* (*OSPF*) and *Novell Link State Protocol* (*NLSP*).

Distance Vector protocols generate relatively large amounts of administrative traffic and are limited in the size of network they can support. The complexity and size of the routing tables used by Distance Vector protocols increases geometrically with the addition of each subnetwork. Link State protocols generate relatively smaller amounts of administrative traffic and can support much larger internetworks, but require correspondingly more powerful router hardware to handle them. Consider the potential size of your internetwork before deciding on a brand and model of router, and question the vendor carefully concerning the routing protocols that the router will support and the size of internetwork it is capable of handling.

Routing versus Bridging

There is a great deal of confusion about the differences between bridges and routers and about when the use of each is appropriate. This confusion is increased by the availability of *Brouters*, which are simply devices that combine the function of both bridges and routers.

The differences between the two are really the difference between a single network and an internetwork. A group of connected devices that share a single common network layer address are defined as a single network. Bridges are used to join segments within a single network. Routers are used to join separate networks.

Bridges function at the Data Link Layer and work with hardware addresses, which provide no information about the geographical location of the device. Routers function at the Network Layer and work with logical addresses, which can be mapped to a geographical location.

Routers have the following advantages over bridges:

- *Bridges do not communicate with other bridges and routers on the network.* Routers continuously communicate with each other, updating information on availability and loading present on various paths. Accordingly, a router can make intelligent decisions about how to route traffic while a bridge cannot.

- *Routed networks are much more robust than bridged networks.* Failure of a particular link in a routed network results in immediate communication between the routers concerning the failure. Traffic is immediately shunted to the best remaining path, and communication continues uninterrupted. A similar failure on a bridged network results in an extended break in communications while the bridges relearn the locations of all accessible devices.

- *Bridges can forward only the frame size for which they are configured.* A bridge designed to forward 1514 byte Ethernet frames when presented with a 4202 byte Token Ring frame simply discards it. Routers can break down larger frames, encapsulate the fragments in smaller packets, and reassemble them at the destination. This allows routers to handle a variety of frame sizes and types and offers greater flexibility.

Bridges have the following advantages over routers.

- *Bridges are inexpensive compared to routers.* Routers must do a great deal of processing to decode Network Layer information and act upon it, while bridges make a simple decision based on the hardware address.

- *Installing and configuring a bridge is trivial, while installing and configuring a router requires a great deal of expertise.* Bridges simply plug into the network and begin learning about their environment. Routers must be programmed initially, and as the network changes, this programming must be updated. Anyone can install a bridge and then simply walk away from it. Putting in a router demands someone who knows what he is doing.

- *Bridges are protocol independent above the Data Link Layer, while routers are not.* If you are using a non-routed protocol like NetBEUI you have no alternative to using a bridge. Non-routed protocols have no Network Layer information within their packets, leaving a router nothing to work with.

Gateways

A *Gateway*, shown in figure 7.14, is used to translate between incompatible protocols, and can function at any one layer of the ISO Reference Model, or at several layers simultaneously. Gateways are most commonly used at the upper-three layers of the ISO Model. For example, if you have some users using the *Simple Mail Transfer Protocol* (*SMTP*) for e-mail and others using the *Message Handling System* (*MHS*) protocol, a Gateway could be used to translate between these two protocols so that all users could exchange e-mail.

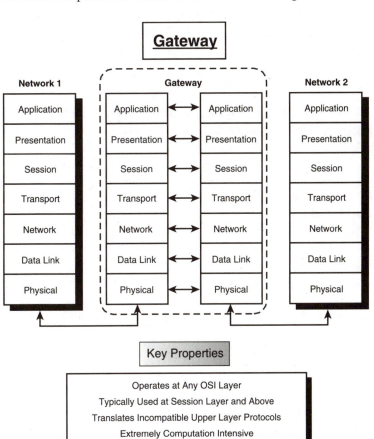

Fig. 7.14

Gateways are used to translate dissimilar upper-level protocols.

Because of the work they must do to translate between fundamentally incompatible protocols, gateways are usually very processor intensive and therefore run relatively slowly. In particular, using a gateway to translate transport protocols—such as TCP/IP to and from IPX/SPX—usually creates a bottleneck. Use a Gateway only if it is the only solution available, and then only on an interim basis while you migrate to common shared protocols. Gateways are typically very difficult to install and maintain, and the translations they provide are often imperfect at best, particularly at the upper ISO layers.

Note

The Internet community uses the term gateway to refer to a router.

Enterprise Hubs, Collapsed Backbones, Ethernet Switches, and Virtual LANs

Traditional routed and bridged networks are gradually giving way, particularly in larger networks, to newer methods that depend on high speed switching to direct traffic.

Enterprise Hubs

Enterprise hubs or *chassis hubs* are in fact much more than hubs. These devices are based on a wall-mounted or rack-mounted chassis that provides two or more passive backplanes into which feature cards are inserted to provide the exact functionality needed. Cards are available to provide hubs for Ethernet, Token Ring, FDDI, and ATM networks. Other cards may be installed to provide routing, bridging, gateway, management, and other functions.

An enterprise hub is something you buy only if you have to. The unpopulated chassis alone may cost more than $10,000. The cards used to populate it are likewise expensive, both in absolute terms and on a per-port basis. Why, then, would anyone buy an enterprise hub instead of a pile of stackables? Three reasons: to establish a collapsed backbone, to implement Ethernet switching, and to build a virtual LAN.

Collapsed Backbones

Collapsing the backbone simply means to move all active network components into a single physical cabinet and then to link them using a very high-speed bus. Rather than locating hubs and other active network components in equipment rooms near the workstations, these components are reduced to cards contained in a single chassis sited centrally. This scheme has certain perceived advantages both in terms of management and in terms of implementing technologies like switching and virtual LANs.

Ethernet Switches

To understand Ethernet Switches, it is first necessary to appreciate the progression in hub design and functionality from simple standalone hubs and stackables to the modern full featured chassis hub.

- Standalone hubs are simple repeaters. All devices connected to any port on a standalone hub are connected to the single segment represented by that hub.

- At the entry level, chassis hubs and a few stackables provide a backplane that supports multiple segments. Each hub card is, in effect, a standalone hub operating on its own segment. A station's segment is determined by which physical hub card it is connected to. Using multiple hub cards segments traffic, but does nothing to interconnect the separate segments. Moving traffic between two or more of these segments requires a bridge or router.

- At the next step up, a chassis hub replaces physical assignment of ports to segments with a switched matrix, which allows logical assignment of any port to any segment. This is a static rather than dynamic assignment. A port is assigned to a particular segment until the network manager intervenes to change the assignment. At this level, the chassis hub still provides no interconnectivity between ports located on different segments. The only real difference between this arrangement and the one described above is that port assignments can be changed programmatically rather than by going out and physically moving a jumper cord. The ability to make these changes programmatically is typically provided by adding a management card to the chassis. This is the level at which many installed chassis hubs are working.

- The next logical step is to provide self-contained bridging and routing functions within the chassis hub. This is accomplished by adding a card or cards to the chassis to provide these connectivity functions, in effect combining your hubs, bridges, and routers into a single box. Many installed chassis hubs and nearly all newly purchased ones function at this level.

- The final step in the evolution of the hub is to provide a switching backplane that can connect any port to any other port dynamically and under control of the hub itself. Rather than linking a port to a segment, the hub links a port directly to another port via building up and tearing down dedicated logical channels on its high speed backplane as needed, in effect assigning each port to its own segment. It is at this level that your chassis hub essentially becomes a switch.

III

Local Area Networking

The single characteristic that distinguishes a hub from a switch is that on the hub all traffic generated by any port is repeated and heard by all other ports on the hub while a switch instead establishes virtual circuits that connect the two ports directly. Traffic on this virtual circuit cannot be heard by ports not a part of the virtual circuit. In essence, the hub resembles a CB radio conversation while the switch resembles a telephone conversation. To look at it another way, each device attached to a switch port is for all intents and purposes connected to its own dedicated bridge or router port.

Switches use one or both of two methods to process traffic. *Store-and-Forward* processing receives and buffers the entire in-bound frame before processing it, while *Cut-Through* begins processing the inbound frame as soon as enough of it has arrived to provide the destination address. A Cut-Through switch therefore never has possession of the entire frame at any one time. The advantage of Cut-Through is raw speed and increased throughput. The advantage of Store-and-Forward is that because the entire frame is available at once, the switch can perform error checking, enhanced filtering, and other processing on the frame. Both methods are used successfully, and in fact many switches incorporate elements of both types of processing.

The first and most common type of switch is the *segment switch*, which is conceptually similar to a bridge or a router. Functioning as a switched learning bridge, the segment switch provides basic filtering and forwarding between multiple segments.

The next step up in switches is the *Private LAN Switch*, in which each port can connect to any other port via a dedicated virtual segment built up and torn down as needed by the switch itself. So long as the software is properly written and the backplane has sufficient cumulative bandwidth, every pair of ports can, in theory, communicate with each other at full network bandwidth without contention or collision. In practice, of course, some ports (such as servers) will be much more popular than others, so the theoretical cumulative throughput of any switch can never be reached. A private LAN switch simply extends the concept of bridging multiple segments to reduce traffic to its ultimate conclusion of providing each device with its own segment.

It's also possible to add routing functionality to a switch. The switches discussed above filter and forward frames and otherwise function as bridges at the Data Link Layer of the OSI Reference Model. *Routing Switches* extend this functionality to working with the Network Layer of the OSI Model. The level of routing functionality varies by manufacturer and model, from those on the low end, which provide *barrier routing*, to those on the high end, which essentially provide each device with a dedicated router port. Routing Switches are expensive components, and as the level of routing functionality increases, so does the price.

Virtual LANs

Like modern PBX telephone switches, network switches are dumb in the sense that the switch hardware itself simply provides a high performance foundation but does not provide the functionality of the switch. This functionality is controlled by firmware. Implementing a *virtual LAN* in firmware is the logical conclusion of switching technology.

Switching is itself the logical conclusion of the use of segmenting to reduce traffic. However, reducing traffic to the extent that a particular frame or packet is received only by the designated port raises a fundamental problem. We have until now been considering only user traffic, those frames and packets that contain user data. There is, however, another type of traffic on a LAN. Overhead or administrative traffic comprises frames and packets used by the network to maintain itself. Novell servers generate *Service Advertising Protocol* (*SAP*) traffic to inform all devices on the LAN of the services available from that server. Routers use *Routing Information Protocol* (*RIP*) and other protocols to communicate routing information to each other. All of this administrative traffic is no less essential for not carrying user data. Without it, the LAN does not run. For switching to reach its ultimate utility, we must somehow ensure that this overhead traffic is heard by all devices that need to hear it.

The solution to this problem is the *virtual LAN* or *VLAN*. A VLAN allows any arbitrary group of ports to be clustered under programmatic control. Just as all the users attached to a traditional Ethernet segment hear all the traffic present on that segment, all the users on a VLAN hear all the traffic on the VLAN. The difference is that VLAN users can be located on different physical networks and scattered broadly geographically.

With a traditional hub, the physical port into which a workstation is connected determines which network that workstation belongs to. With a switch the physical port no longer determines which network the workstation belongs to, but the workstation must still belong to a network physically located on that switch. With a VLAN, any workstation plugged into any port located on any switch may be logically configured to be a member of any network. This feature of VLANs breaks the dependency of physical location to network membership, allowing users to be relocated anywhere within the internetwork and still remain a member of the same network.

Some of the building blocks of VLAN technology have been around for several years, but the technology as a whole has not yet been fully implemented. The high costs of fast data links has also contributed to the slow adoption of VLANs. As the technology continues to mature and the cost of high-speed data links continues to drop, VLANs will become an increasingly common part of the network landscape.

Recommendations

Throughout this chapter you've learned what you need to know to design a proper network infrastructure. As you begin to design your own network, keep these points in mind:

- *Scale the infrastructure to your needs, keeping in mind that most networks grow.* In a typical network, installed components should have at least 25 percent of their capacity unused, and should be easily expandable to at least 100 percent additional capacity. If your initial configuration puts you at or near capacity on a particular component, install the next level up. Plan for growth.

- *Choose one manufacturer for your active network components and then buy all of them from that one manufacturer.* Standardize as much as possible, even to the extent of using the same model within the manufacturer's line when possible.

- *Consider purchasing only manageable components, or those that can be upgraded to manageability.* If your entire network can run from only one hub and is likely to remain small then you can safely avoid the extra expense of manageability. Otherwise, look to the future.

- *Get outside help to design and implement your network.* Use your vendor's expertise to help you avoid bad design decisions. Consider hiring an independent network consultant at least to sign off on the final design, and ideally to help in the initial design phase. Get advice from your peers in other companies as to what works and doesn't work for them.

- *Understand fully the differences between bridges and routers and use them as appropriate to control network traffic.*

- *Provide standby UPS power in each equipment room and make sure that each active network component is connected to it.*

- *Provide full lightning protection to supplement that provided by the UPS.* Protect all wires connected to the network in any fashion, including AC power, telephone lines, and leased lines. Ideally, you should provide such protection for each workstation as well. At the very least, protect key active network components like bridges, routers, and servers by installing data line protectors.

■ *Purchase standby spares for critical network components.* Even if your system is under maintenance contract, having a spare hub available can make the difference between being down for 15 minutes and being down for a day.

CHAPTER 8

Configuring Windows NT Workstation as a Network Client

by Robert Bruce Thompson

An ideal network client operating system would install and configure the network client software automatically, support a wide variety of transport and core protocols, provide a single unified logon to servers running different network operating systems, provide robust security, and do so while using minimal system resources. Microsoft Windows NT Workstation 4.0 does all of this and more. While it is not yet perfect, it is far and away the best network client operating system yet delivered.

As multi-site, multi-platform internetworks become common and user demands for Internet access increase, network administrators increasingly find themselves supporting multiple transport protocols. The Internet and most private internetworks use TCP/IP; NetWare servers understand only IPX/SPX; and many peer networks use NetBEUI. Your NetWare servers run NetWare Core Protocol (NCP) and your Windows NT Servers run Server Message Block (SMB). Mobile users need PPP Dial-Up Networking. Tying all of these diverse systems and protocols together requires a workstation operating system that allows you to support all of these protocols simultaneously and still have enough memory left to run applications. Windows NT Workstation 4.0 provides all the tools you need to get these jobs done.

In this chapter you learn to

- Install and configure network adapter drivers
- Install and configure client support for Novell NetWare servers
- Install and configure network transport protocols, including NetBEUI, NWLink and TCP/IP

Windows NT Workstation 4.0 Networking Features

The release of Windows NT Workstation 4.0 was a red letter day for many network managers. In one fell swoop, Windows NT Workstation 4.0 eliminates most of the client-side problems that have plagued LAN administrators for years. Its built-in support for Novell NetWare and its extensible architecture allow Windows NT Workstation 4.0 to be, if not all things to all people, at least most things to most people. Some of the more important networking features of Windows NT Workstation 4.0 are:

■ *Multiple Client Support.* With earlier generation workstation operating systems, installing client software for more than one type of network operating system was problematic at best. The client software was provided by the NOS vendors, and conflicts often occurred when installing the second client. Even if you did install and configure support for a second NOS successfully, the additional memory required often made it difficult to run applications on the workstation. Sane LAN managers didn't even think about trying to install support for a third NOS. All of this changes with Windows NT Workstation 4.0 and its built-in support for multiple clients. Out of the box, Windows NT Workstation 4.0 provides full native support for Novell NetWare, including NetWare Directory Services (NDS) on Novell 4.x servers. It also, of course, fully supports Microsoft Networking, including LAN Manager, Windows 3.11 for Workgroups, Windows 95, and Windows NT Server.

■ *Multiple Protocol Support.* Windows NT Workstation 4.0 has built in support for TCP/IP, IPX/SPX, and NetBEUI, which among them are the transport protocols used on the vast majority of networks. It supports the two major network core protocols, with full support for Microsoft SMB (Server Message Block) and support for Novell NCP (NetWare Core Protocol). It supports both Microsoft Network Driver Interface Specification (NDIS) and Novell Open Datalink Interface (ODI). It supports a wide variety of standard communications protocols like named pipes and remote procedure calls. In short, Windows NT Workstation 4.0 out-of-the-box provides every protocol you are likely to need. In the unlikely event that a building block you need is missing, its extensible architecture means that a third party product may be written to fill the void.

■ *Simultaneous Connection to Multiple Networks.* While Windows 3.1 allows you to connect to only one network, and Windows 3.11 for Workgroups to only two, Windows NT Workstation 4.0 places no such limitation on you. In Windows NT Workstation 4.0 you can connect to as many different networks as you would like.

■ *Single Network Logon.* If you have servers running more than one NOS, Windows NT Workstation 4.0 allows you to connect to all of them simultaneously at login, as long as you keep user names and passwords identical on the various servers. Windows NT Workstation 4.0 automatically processes login scripts on Windows NT Servers and NetWare servers.

■ *Automatic Reconnection.* When a downed server comes back up, Windows NT Workstation 4.0 reconnects to that server automatically, and re-maps drive letter assignments and printer connections as they were before the failure.

■ *Automatic Client Setup.* Windows NT Workstation 4.0 makes it easier than ever before to install and configure network clients. During setup, it nearly always detects the network interface card in the workstation and automatically installs the appropriate 32-bit protected mode drivers. Although Windows NT Workstation 4.0 does not offer full Plug-'N-Play support, it does automatically detect and configure most network adapter cards and other devices. Setup and configuration is done from the Network option in Control Panel, with setup information stored in the registry, eliminating the need to maintain configuration files manually. System policies and user profiles may be established to automate installation and control user access to resources.

■ *Peer-to-Peer Networking.* When Microsoft shipped Windows 3.11 for Workgroups with built-in peer networking, many wondered whether third-party peer networks like LANtastic and PowerLAN could survive. With Windows NT Workstation 4.0, Microsoft has upped the ante. Any Windows NT Workstation 4.0 client can share its disk and printer resources with other workstations on the network.

■ *Dial-Up Networking.* Windows NT Workstation 4.0 comes equipped for remote access. The dial up networking client supports connection to TCP/IP, IPX/SPX, and NetBEUI networks, via Point to Point Protocol (PPP), Serial Line Internet Protocol (SLIP) and NetWare Connect. For complete information on Dial-Up Networking, see Chapter 12, *"Using Remote Access Service and Dial-Up Networking."*

■ *Long Filename Support.* With Windows NT Workstation 4.0, Microsoft eliminates the old DOS 8.3 file naming convention barrier. Windows NT Workstation 4.0 allows a file name to be as long as 255 characters, or 260 characters including the path.

III

Local Area Networking

- *Higher Network Performance.* Windows NT Workstation 4.0 uses 32-bit protected mode client software, drivers, and protocols, offering significantly better performance than that provided by older 16-bit real mode drivers. Network performance is further enhanced by the caching of network data, allowing frequently accessed network data to be read from the local cache rather than repeatedly transferred across the network. In addition to offering faster data access, this also reduces network congestion by cutting down traffic.

- *Minimal Conventional Memory Usage.* Saving the best for last, Windows NT Workstation 4.0 does all of these things while consuming minimal system resources. Installing multiple clients and protocol stacks used to be a juggling act, always keeping one eye on free conventional memory. Windows NT Workstation 4.0 eliminates this problem, by using Windows memory to run network client software, drivers, and protocols.

Installing and Configuring Network Adapters

Windows NT Workstation 4.0 includes a large database with information about hundreds of common network adapters and their default settings. If there is an adapter installed in the workstation, chances are that Windows NT Workstation 4.0 will automatically detect it and load the proper drivers for it during the installation process. However, if your adapter is an uncommon model, or if your adapter is set to other than default settings, you may have to intervene to provide the proper drivers and settings.

Tip

If your network adapter is software configurable, either verify that the manufacturer supplied adapter configuration utility will run under Windows NT Workstation 4.0, or keep a copy of the adapter configuration utility available on a DOS bootable floppy disk. Most adapter configuration utility programs are DOS based, and many will not load or function properly under Windows NT Workstation 4.0. Having a DOS bootable floppy disk allows you to reboot the system under DOS, make the necessary changes to the adapter, and store these changes in non-volatile RAM. When you reboot your system into Windows NT Workstation 4.0, the changed settings remain in effect.

Note

The most common situation in which Windows NT Workstation 4.0 misidentifies an installed adapter is when you are using an adapter that offers both a native mode and a mode that emulates another model of adapter. For example, a clone Ethernet card may offer both its own proprietary native mode and an emulation of a Novell NE2000 card. If you have previously configured the adapter as an NE2000, Windows NT Workstation 4.0 may instead identify it as the actual underlying model, requiring you to manually configure Windows NT Workstation 4.0 to see the adapter as an NE2000.

If this occurs, you can either change the adapter settings to the defaults expected by Windows NT Workstation 4.0, or you can alter Windows NT Workstation 4.0 settings to correspond to those to which the adapter is actually set. If your adapters are software-configurable, keep a copy of the configuration software provided with the adapter handy because you may need it to alter the settings on the adapter. If, instead, the adapter settings must be changed by using jumpers, you may be able to avoid opening each workstation by using the adapter as is and instead altering the Windows NT Workstation 4.0 driver settings to correspond with these jumpers.

When you install Windows NT Workstation 4.0, the setup procedure attempts to detect installed network adapters automatically. If automatic identification fails, if you need to change settings for an installed adapter, or if you need to install a new adapter, you can do so from the Network icon of Control Panel. Unlike earlier Windows versions, which required that some network settings be changed by manually editing text files in various locations, Windows NT Workstation 4.0 centralizes core network installation and configuration functions within the Network icon of Control Panel.

Tip

If Windows NT Workstation 4.0 apparently identifies your adapter successfully, but you still can't communicate with the network, the most likely cause is that the IRQ, DMA or Base Address of the adapter doesn't match the settings used by Windows NT Workstation. Windows NT Workstation 4.0 may install the adapter using the manufacturer's default settings, which may not correspond with the actual settings of the adapter. You can correct this mismatch by altering the settings from within Windows NT Workstation 4.0 for IRQ, DMA or Base Address as needed to correspond to the actual settings of the adapter.

III

Local Area Networking

To install a Network Adapter, take the following steps:

1. From Control Panel, double-click the Network icon to display the Network property sheet, shown in figure 8.1.

Fig. 8.1.
The Network property sheet allows you to install and configure network components.

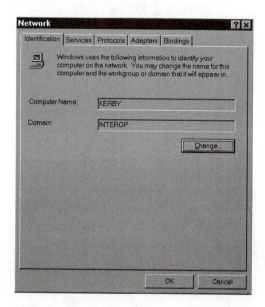

2. Click the Adapters tab to display the Adapters page, shown in figure 8.2. Installed adapters are shown in the Network Adapters dialog box. In this case, an adapter has not yet been installed, so the box has no entries.

Fig. 8.2
The Adapters page allows you to install and configure network adapters.

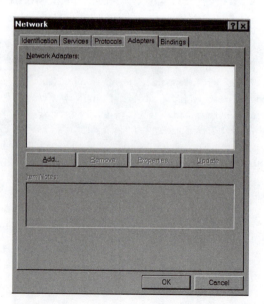

3. Click <u>A</u>dd to display the Select Network Adapter dialog box. Windows
NT Workstation 4.0 first builds a list of available adapters, as shown in
figure 8.3. After a few seconds, the Select Network Adapter dialog box
presents an alphabetized list of adapters available to be installed, shown
in figure 8.4.

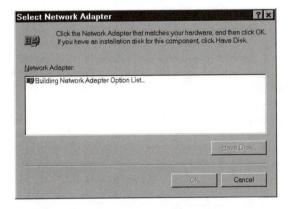

Fig. 8.3
Windows NT
Workstation 4.0
builds a list of
available adapters.

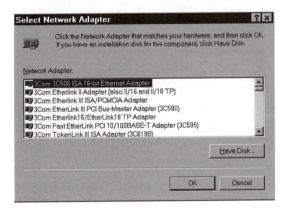

Fig. 8.4
The Select Network
Adapter dialog box
displays a list of
the adapters
available to be
installed.

4. Scroll down through the list and click the adapter you want to install to
highlight it. In this case, we are installing a Novell NE2000 Compatible
Adapter, as shown in figure 8.5.

III

Local Area Networking

> **Note**
>
> If your adapter does not appear on the list, you may still be able to use it. You have two possible alternatives. First, refer to your adapter documentation to determine if it can emulate an adapter that does appear on the list. For example, many Ethernet adapters emulate the Novell NE2000. If your adapter can emulate a supported adapter, configure your adapter to emulate the supported adapter and attempt to install it as such. Second, you can install a driver provided by the adapter manufacturer using the Have Disk option. Use this method only if the manufacturer has written a driver specifically for Windows NT Workstation 4.0. Using a Windows NT Workstation 4.0 driver provided by the manufacturer of the network adapter may provide more features and better performance than using the equivalent driver provided with Windows NT Workstation 4.0 itself.

Fig. 8.5

The Novell NE2000 Compatible Adapter is highlighted for installation.

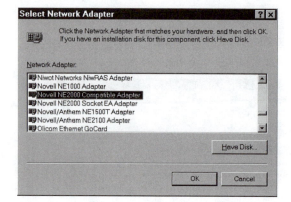

5. Click OK to display the <adapter-name> Network Card Setup dialog box, shown in figure 8.6. The appearance of this dialog box varies, depending on the particular card you are installing. It allows you to set parameters for the card you are installing, including Interrupt Request Level (IRQ Level), I/O Port Address, Direct Memory Access (DMA) and so forth. This particular card requires that only IRQ Level and I/O Port Address be configured, so no other items appear.

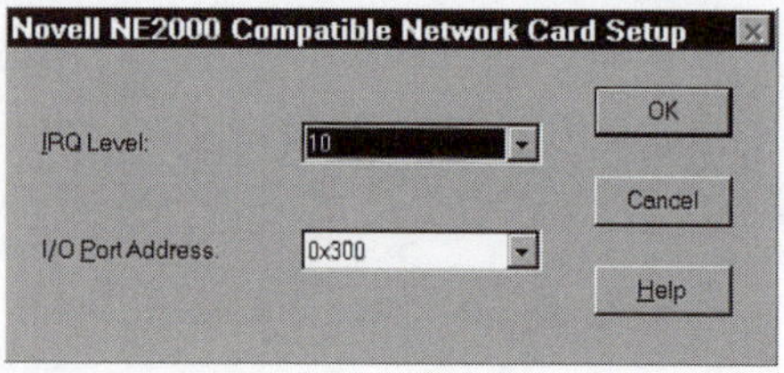

Fig. 8.6

The <adapter-name> Network Card Setup dialog box allows you to configure adapter parameters.

Caution

The automatic detection process used by Windows NT Workstation 4.0 to locate network adapter cards determines only the manufacturer and model of the card installed. Windows NT Workstation 4.0 cannot detect the IRQ Level, I/O Port Address, and other configuration parameters for the card, so it uses default values for these parameters. If you have changed the physical settings of your network adapter from the default values, be sure to change the default values used by Windows NT to correspond with the actual settings.

6. When you have finished setting parameters in the <adapter-name> Network Card Setup dialog box, click OK. If your computer has an enhanced bus, in this case a PCI bus, Windows NT 4.0 displays the <adapter-name> Adapter Bus Location dialog box shown in figure 8.7. Select the appropriate bus Type and Number from the drop-down lists. Note that this dialog box does not appear if your computer uses an Industry Standard Architecture (ISA) bus.

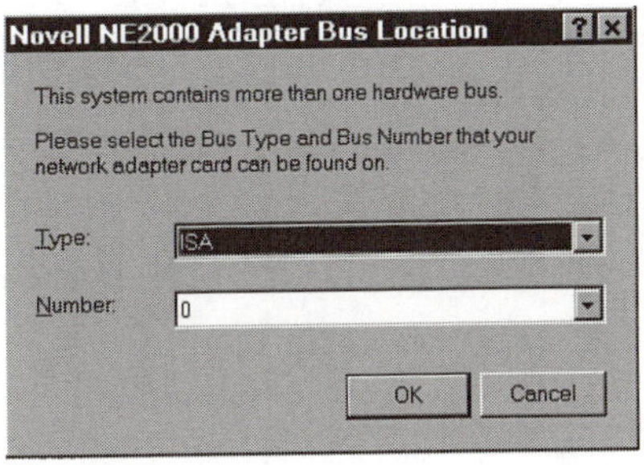

Fig. 8.7
The <adapter-name> Adapter Bus Location dialog box allows you to specify to which system bus your adapter is connected.

7. When you have selected the appropriate bus Type and Number from the <adapter-name> Adapter Bus Location Dialog box, click OK to display the Windows NT Setup dialog box, shown in figure 8.8. Enter the drive and directory where the Windows NT Workstation 4.0 distribution files are located, and click Continue to begin copying files. If you are installing from a CD-ROM to a computer running an Intel processor, the distribution files are located in the \i386 directory of your CD.

8. After all files have been copied, the Network property sheet reappears, showing the Adapters page with the newly installed adapter visible, as shown in figure 8.9. Click Close to complete the installation. Windows NT Workstation 4.0 configures, stores, and reviews bindings, as shown in figure 8.10.

III

Local Area Networking

Fig. 8.8
The Windows NT Setup dialog box prompts you to specify the location of the files to be installed.

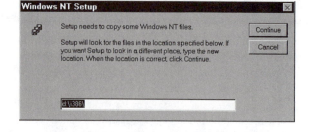

Fig. 8.9
The Network property sheet shows the newly installed adapter.

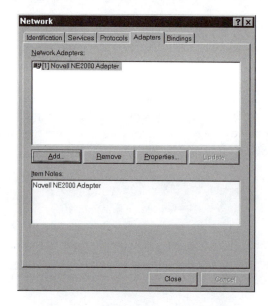

Fig. 8.10
Windows NT Workstation 4.0 configures, stores, and reviews the bindings for the newly installed adapter.

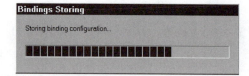

9. After the bindings have been configured, stored and reviewed, Windows NT Workstation 4.0 displays the Network Settings Change dialog box, shown in figure 8.11, to notify you that you must restart the computer before the changes will take effect. Click Yes to restart the computer immediately or click No to return to the Windows NT Workstation 4.0 desktop. If you choose the latter, your newly installed network adapter will not be available for use until you restart the system later.

Fig. 8.11
The Network
Settings Change
dialog box prompts
you to restart your
computer so that
the changes can
take effect.

Installing and Configuring Network Services

Windows NT Workstation 4.0 makes several default choices for a network adapter, whether it is automatically installed during Windows NT Workstation 4.0 installation or it is installed manually later. IPX/SPX (NWLink) and NetBEUI transport protocols are both installed, allowing the client workstation to operate with Windows Microsoft NT Server, Novell NetWare, and Microsoft Workgroup networks. Client support for Microsoft Networks is installed automatically. These default settings are designed to work for the most common network environments.

There are three common reasons to change these default selections. First, you may need to install client support for Novell NetWare servers on your network. Second, you may need to install client support for various services provided by Windows NT servers on your network. Third, you may want your workstation to provide services to other computers on the network. These and other functions are provided by Windows NT Workstation 4.0 by using *network services*.

Installing Novell NetWare client support

Unlike Windows 95, which provides a named client for Novell NetWare support, Windows NT Workstation 4.0 installs client support for NetWare as a network service. The NetWare client support provided by Windows NT Workstation 4.0 goes a step beyond that provided by Windows 95 by offering standard support for Novell NetWare Directory Services (NDS). NDS support allows Windows NT Workstation 4.0 to provide full featured client support in a NetWare 4.x server environment. To install Novell NetWare client support, take the following steps:

1. From Control Panel, double-click the Network icon to display the Network property sheet (refer to figure 8.1).

2. Click the Services tab to display the Services page, shown in figure 8.12. Installed services are shown in the Network Services. Verify that Client Service for NetWare does not appear in this list before proceeding.

Fig. 8.12
The Services page
displays installed
network services.

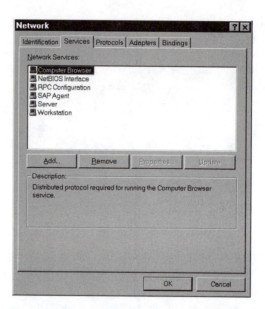

3. Click <u>A</u>dd to display the Select Network Service dialog box shown in
figure 8.13.

Fig. 8.13
The Select
Network Service
dialog box allows
you to specify the
network service to
be added.

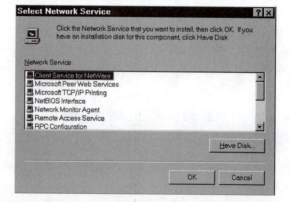

4. Highlight Client Service for NetWare and click OK to display the Windows NT Setup dialog box, shown in figure 8.14.

5. Enter the drive and directory where the Windows NT Workstation 4.0
distribution files are located, and click Continue to begin copying files.
If you are installing from a CD-ROM to a computer running an Intel
processor, the distribution files are located in the \i386 directory of
your CD. The Windows NT Setup dialog box shown in figure 8.15 displays progress as the files are copied.

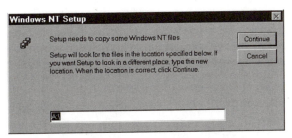

Fig. 8.14
The Windows NT Setup dialog box allows you to specify the location of the files to be copied.

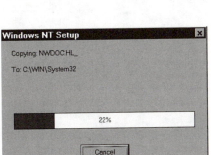

Fig. 8.15
Windows NT Setup displays progress as the files are copied.

6. After all files have been copied, the Network property sheet reappears, showing the Services page with the newly installed service visible, as shown in figure 8.16. Click Close to complete the installation. Windows NT Workstation 4.0 configures, stores, and reviews bindings, as shown in figure 8.17.

7. After the bindings have been configured, stored, and reviewed, Windows NT Workstation 4.0 displays the Network Settings Change dialog box, shown in figure 8.18, to notify you that you must restart the computer before the changes will take effect. Click Yes to restart the computer immediately or click No to return to the Windows NT Workstation 4.0 desktop. If you choose the latter, your newly installed network service will not be available for use until you restart the system later.

III

Local Area Networking

Fig. 8.16
The Network property sheet shows Client Service for NetWare as an installed service.

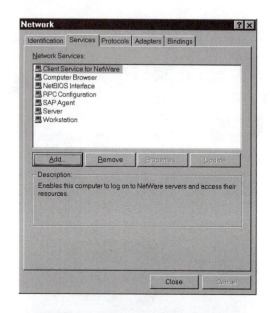

Fig. 8.17
Windows NT Workstation 4.0 configures, stores, and reviews the bindings for the newly installed service.

Fig. 8.18
The Network Settings Change dialog box prompts you to restart your computer so that the changes can take effect.

Installing and Configuring Network Protocols

Windows NT Workstation 4.0 provides optional support for seven protocols. These protocols include:

- *AppleTalk Protocol.* Used to provide connectivity in an Apple Macintosh network environment. It is useful only when installed on NT server, or with a third party product, so it is only described here briefly.

- *DLC Protocol.* Used primarily in the Windows NT environment to provide connectivity to network printers using the Hewlett-Packard JetDirect network connection. The DLC Protocol is also used to connect to IBM mainframe computers.

- *NetBEUI Protocol.* Used to provide connectivity with network clients running Windows 3.11 for Workgroups and other NetBEUI-based peer networking software.

- *NWLink IPX/SPX Compatible Transport.* Used primarily in the Windows NT environment to provide connectivity to Novell NetWare networks, although some system administrators choose to run a purely Windows NT Server based network using NWLink as the primary transport.

- *Point To Point Tunneling Protocol.* Provides packet level encryption on PPP connections, allowing insecure public networks (like the Internet) to be used to transfer private data.

- *Streams Environment.* STREAMS originated in the UNIX System V environment. STREAMS establishes a standard method for passing messages bidirectionally between layers of a protocol stack. STREAMS is useful in the Windows NT environment primarily for developers and programmers who are writing interfaces to UNIX systems.

- *TCP/IP Protocol.* Used to provide connectivity to the Internet and to UNIX systems. Many network administrators choose TCP/IP as their primary transport even when Internet or UNIX connectivity is not an issue, since TCP/IP is well suited for large and complex networks.

Installing the DLC Protocol

The DLC (Data Link Control) Protocol is primarily used in the Windows NT environment to support DLC network printers, e.g. Hewlett-Packard LaserJet printers that connect to the network directly using the HP JetDirect network connector. Using the DLC protocol in conjunction with a DLC printer allows you to place that printer at any convenient network connection point without requiring space and other resources for a PC to drive that printer.

Only one computer on the network needs to run the DLC protocol to make the DLC printer available to all clients on the network. If your network includes a Windows NT server, you normally configure that server to provide the DLC connection, if one is needed to support a JetDirect printer. The only

III

Local Area Networking

common reason to run DLC on your Windows NT Workstation computer is if it is functioning as the "server" for a small network that requires DLC printer support.

If you are running TCP/IP transport on your network, there is little reason to enable DLC for network printing. The JetDirect can be configured to provide a direct network printer connection using IP and lpd. Using IP instead of DLC has one big advantage if your network is a part of an internetwork. DLC is not a routable protocol, that means that using it limits access to the shared printer to clients that are on the same local network as the DLC printer. Using IP instead allows any client on a routed internetwork to access the shared printer.

> **Note**
>
> Installing the DLC protocol automatically enables the DLC JetDirect driver, which is supplied by Hewlett-Packard and bundled with Windows NT.

To install DLC Protocol support, take the following steps:

1. Follow steps one through three from the preceding list to display the Select Network Protocol dialog, shown in figure 8.19.

Fig. 8.19
The Select Network Protocol dialog box allows you to specify the network protocol to be added.

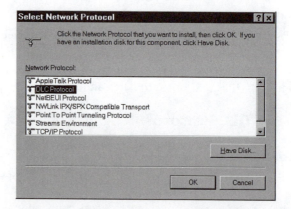

2. Highlight DLC Protocol and click OK to display the Windows NT Setup dialog box, shown in figure 8.20.

3. Enter the drive and directory where the Windows NT Workstation 4.0 distribution files are located, and click Continue to begin copying files. If you are installing from a CD-ROM to a computer running an Intel processor, the distribution files are located in the \i386 directory of your CD.

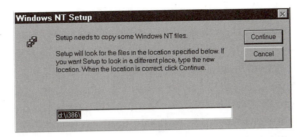

Fig. 8.20
The Windows NT
Setup dialog box
allows you to
specify the
location of the
files to be copied.

4. After all files have been copied, the Network property sheet reappears, showing the Protocols page with the newly installed protocol visible, as shown in figure 8.21. Click Close to complete the installation. Windows NT Workstation 4.0 configures, stores, and reviews bindings.

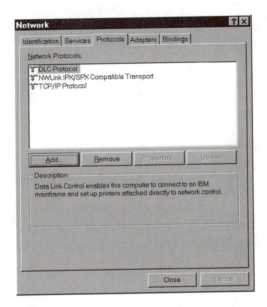

Fig. 8.21
The Network
property sheet
shows DLC
Protocol as an
installed protocol.

5. After the bindings have been configured, reviewed, and stored, Windows NT displays the Network Settings Change dialog box to notify you that you must restart your computer before the changes will take effect. Click Yes to restart the computer immediately or click No to return to the Windows NT Workstation 4.0 desktop. If you choose the latter, your newly installed network protocol will not be available for use until you restart the system.

The DLC Protocol has no user configurable parameters, as indicated by the grayed out Properties button in figure 8.21.

Installing the NetBEUI Protocol

NetBIOS Extended User Interface (NetBEUI) is a fast and simple transport protocol used by Windows 3.11 for Workgroups and other peer LANs. It requires very little management, but because NetBEUI packets do not contain network header information, NetBEUI is not routable, making it inappropriate for larger networks. If Windows NT Workstation 4.0 detects the presence of NetBEUI on the network during installation, it automatically installs NetBEUI support. You will normally need to make few changes to the NetBEUI configuration.

To install and configure NetBEUI Protocol support, take the following steps:

1. Follow step one from the preceding list to display the Select Network Protocol dialog box, shown in figure 8.22.

Fig. 8.22

The Select Network Protocol dialog box allows you to specify the network protocol to be added.

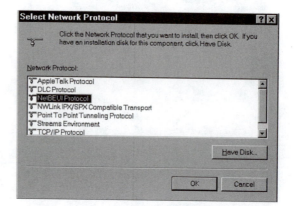

2. Highlight NetBEUI Protocol and click OK to display the Windows NT Setup dialog box, shown in figure 8.23.

Fig. 8.23

The Windows NT Setup dialog box allows you to specify the location of the files to be copied.

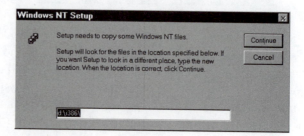

3. Enter the drive and directory where the Windows NT Workstation 4.0 distribution files are located, and click Continue to begin copying files. If you are installing from a CD-ROM to a computer running an Intel processor, the distribution files are located in the \i386 directory of your CD.

4. After all files have been copied, the Network property sheet reappears, showing the Protocols page with the newly installed protocol visible, as shown in figure 8.24. Click Close to complete the installation. Windows NT Workstation 4.0 configures, stores, and reviews bindings.

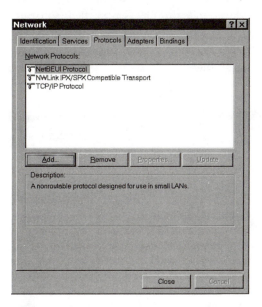

Fig. 8.24
The Network property sheet shows NetBEUI Protocol as an installed protocol.

5. After the bindings have been configured, reviewed, and stored, Windows NT displays the Network Settings Change dialog box to notify you that you must restart your computer before the changes will take effect. Click Yes to restart the computer immediately or click No to return to the Windows NT Workstation 4.0 desktop. If you choose the latter, your newly installed network protocol will not be available for use until you restart the system.

The NetBEUI Protocol has no user configurable parameters, as indicated by the grayed out Properties button in figure 8.24.

III

Local Area Networking

Configuring NWLink IPX/SPX Compatible Transport

NWLink is the Microsoft implementation of the IPX/SPX transport protocol originally developed by Novell for NetWare. NWLink is the default transport protocol used by Windows NT Server and is fully interoperable with IPX/SPX running on NetWare servers and clients. Windows NT Workstation 4.0 installs the NWLink protocol automatically when the Client Service for NetWare is installed. The Client Service for NetWare uses the NWLink protocol exclusively.

Most workstations will require little or no change to the default settings for NWLink. If the workstation is running Novell client software when Windows NT Workstation 4.0 is installed, the setup program configures Windows NT Workstation 4.0 NWLink settings to correspond to those in the Novell NET.CFG configuration file.

To configure NWLink, take the following steps:

1. From the Control Panel, double-click the Network icon to display the Network property sheet. Click the Protocols tab to display the Protocols page, shown in figure 8.25.

Fig. 8.25
The Protocols page allows you to select the protocol for which the properties are to be modified.

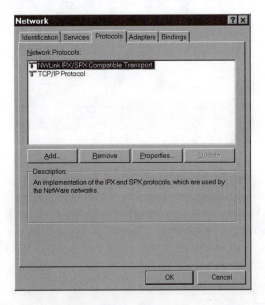

2. Highlight NWLink IPX/SPX Compatible Transport and click Properties to display the NWLink IPX/SPX Properties property sheet, shown in figure 8.26.

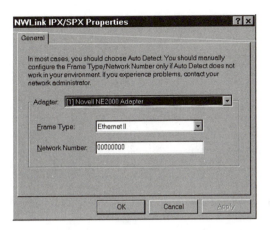

Fig. 8.26
The NWLink
IPX/SPX
Properties
property sheet
allows you to
modify NWLink
properties for the
selected adapter.

3. If you have only one network adapter installed in your computer, that adapter is displayed in the Adapter list box. If you have more than one adapter installed, use the drop-down list to select the adapter for which you want to set properties.

4. Select a frame type from the Frame Type drop-down list. The available choices vary depending on the type of adapter. For a Token Ring adapter, the choices are Token Ring and Token Ring SNAP. For an Ethernet adapter, the choices are: Auto Detect, Ethernet_ 802.2, Ethernet_ 802.3, Ethernet_ II, and Ethernet SNAP.

Choosing the Correct Ethernet Frame Type

If an otherwise functional Windows NT Workstation 4.0 client is unable to see a NetWare server on an Ethernet network, the problem is almost certainly a frame type mismatch. NetWare can use any of four Ethernet frame types: Ethernet_802.2, Ethernet_802.3, Ethernet_II and Ethernet_SNAP. The frame types being used by the server and the workstation must be identical for communication to take place.

The Windows NT Workstation 4.0 IPX/SPX protocol defaults to frame type Auto Detect, which usually succeeds in detecting the frame type being used by the NetWare server. If auto detection fails, you may need to explicitly set the frame type.

NetWare 3.11 and earlier servers default to the Ethernet_802.3 frame when using Ethernet. The corresponding Windows NT Workstation 4.0 frame type is Ethernet_ 802.3. NetWare 3.12 and higher servers default to Ethernet_802.2 frames, for which the corresponding Windows NT Workstation 4.0 frame type is Ethernet_ 802.2.

(continues)

III

Local Area Networking

(continued)

For an Ethernet network, Novell recommends using the Ethernet_802.2 frame type and Microsoft recommends that Windows NT Workstation 4.0 be set to frame type Auto Detect. They are both wrong.

Ethernet_802.2 uses the OSI 802.2 LLC specification, and is the most recent standards-based Ethernet frame. Ethernet_ II is an older specification that was originally developed by Digital Equipment Corporation, Intel, and Xerox (DIX). Newer isn't always better, however. The majority of Ethernet traffic worldwide still uses Ethernet_ II frames. All active components understand how to handle Ethernet_ II frames. On the Internet, Ethernet_ II always works. The same cannot be said for Ethernet_ 802.2.

If your workstations need Internet access, if your network includes a UNIX host, or if you plan to use SNMP management on your NetWare servers, do yourself a big favor and run Ethernet_ II. Even if you have no current need for these services, using Ethernet_ II now will make the transition easier in the future if you do need to add them. There are no performance or other drawbacks to using Ethernet_ II versus Ethernet_ 802.2. Set your Windows NT frame type to Ethernet_ II on both workstations and servers and add Ethernet_II frame support to each of your NetWare servers.

5. Enter a valid eight byte hexadecimal Network Number. Leave this value set to all zeroes if you want Windows NT to automatically determine and use the appropriate network number.

6. After you complete the preceding information, click OK to accept your changes and return to the Network property sheet. Click Close to complete the configuration. Windows NT configures, stores, and reviews the bindings.

7. After the bindings have been configured, reviewed, and stored, Windows NT displays the Network Settings Change dialog box to notify you that you must restart your computer before the changes will take effect. Click Yes to restart the computer immediately or click No to return to the Windows NT Workstation 4.0 desktop. If you choose the latter, the changes you have made to you NWLink configuration will not take effect until you restart the system.

Installing and Configuring the Point-to-Point Tunneling Protocol

The Point-to-Point Tunneling Protocol (PPTP) allows you to use the Internet to securely communicate confidential corporate data between sites. PPTP creates one or more virtual private networks (VPNs) which use public means to transfer private data. Because the data is encrypted while in transit, it cannot be compromised, although it can be intercepted.

Note

Point-to-Point Tunneling Protocol is used only with dial-up connections. To use it, not only must both the originating and destination networks support PPTP, but so must the Internet Service Provider who provides the Internet connection to both networks. For more information about using PPTP, see Chapter 12, "Using Remote Access Service and Dial-Up Networking."

To install Point-to-Point Tunneling Protocol support, take the following steps:

1. From Control Panel, double-click the Network icon to display the Network property sheet. Click the Protocols tab to display the Protocols page. Click Add to display the Select Network Protocol dialog box, shown in figure 8.32 with Point-To-Point Tunneling Protocol highlighted.

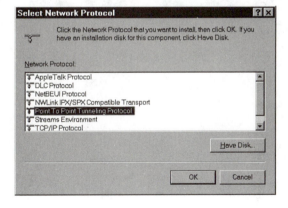

Fig. 8.27
The Select Network Protocol dialog box allows you to specify the network protocol to be added.

2. Highlight the Point To Point Tunneling Protocol and click OK to display the Windows NT Setup dialog box, shown in figure 8.28.

3. Enter the drive and directory where the Windows NT Workstation 4.0 distribution files are located, and click Continue. If you are installing from a CD-ROM to a computer running an Intel processor, the distribution files are located in the \i386 directory of your CD.

Fig. 8.28
The Windows NT
Setup dialog box
allows you to
specify the
location of the
files to be copied.

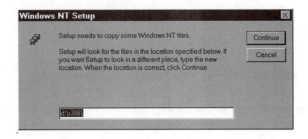

4. Windows NT displays the PPTP Configuration dialog box, shown in figure 8.29. Select a value for Number of Virtual Private Networks from the drop-down list and then click OK to continue. Each VPN represents a remote LAN that can be accessed via the Internet using the PPTP protocol.

> ### Note
>
> If Remote Access Service (RAS) is not already installed, Windows NT Setup installs RAS and allows you to configure it before proceeding.

Fig. 8.29
The PPTP
Configuration
dialog box allows
you to specify the
number of private
virtual networks to
be configured.

5. After all files have been copied, the Network property sheet reappears, showing the Protocols page with the PPTP protocol visible, as shown in figure 8.30. Click Close to complete the installation. Windows NT Workstation 4.0 configures, stores, and reviews bindings.

6. After the bindings have been configured, reviewed, and stored, Windows NT displays the Network Settings Change dialog box to notify you that you must restart your computer before the changes will take effect. Click Yes to restart the computer immediately or click No to return to the Windows NT Workstation 4.0 desktop. If you choose the latter, your newly installed network protocol will not be available for use until you restart the system.

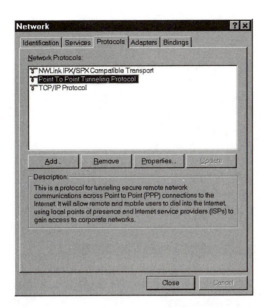

Fig. 8.30
The Protocols page of the Network property sheet, showing Point-to-Point Tunneling Protocol installed.

The PPTP Protocol has only one user configurable parameter, Number of Virtual Private Networks. You can reset this value at any time from the Protocols page of the Network property sheet. To do so, highlight the Point-To-Point Tunneling Protocol entry and click Properties.

Installing the Streams Environment

The Windows NT Workstation 4.0 Streams Environment allows transport layer drivers developed in the UNIX Streams environment to be easily ported to Windows NT. If you don't know what Streams is, you probably don't need to install it. If you do need Streams, install it with the following steps:

1. From Control Panel, double-click the Network icon to display the Network property sheet. Click the Protocols tab to display the Protocols page. Click Add to display the Select Network Protocol property sheet, shown in figure 8.31 with the Streams Environment highlighted.

2. Click OK to install the Streams Environment. The Windows NT Setup dialog box prompts you for the location of the files. Enter the drive and directory where the Windows NT distribution files are located and click Continue to begin copying the files.

3. After all files have been copied, the Network property sheet reappears, with the Protocols page with the PPTP protocol visible, as shown in figure 8.32. Click Close to complete the installation. Windows NT Workstation 4.0 configures, stores, and reviews bindings.

III

Local Area Networking

Fig. 8.31
Install the Streams
Environment from
the Select Network
Protocol property
sheet.

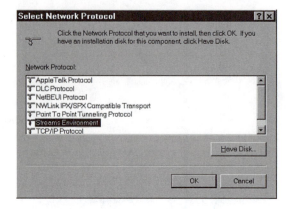

Fig. 8.32
The Protocols page
of the Network
property sheet,
showing the
Streams Environ-
ment installed.

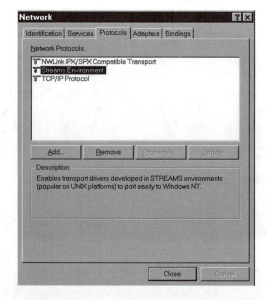

4. After the bindings have been configured, reviewed, and stored, Windows NT displays the Network Settings Change dialog box to notify you that you must restart your computer before the changes will take effect. Click Yes to restart the computer immediately or click No to return to the Windows NT Workstation 4.0 desktop. If you choose the latter, the Streams Environment will not be available for use until you restart the system.

The Streams Environment has no user configurable parameters, as indicated by the grayed out Properties button in figure 8.32.

Installing and Configuring the TCP/IP Protocol

Windows NT Workstation 4.0 does not install support for the TCP/IP transport protocol by default. If your network includes UNIX hosts, or if your workstations will access the Internet, you need to install and configure TCP/IP support. NetBEUI and IPX/SPX were both designed for use on Local Area Networks, and require very little configuration and management. TCP/IP was instead designed for use in internetworks, and requires that the administrator have both a deeper understanding of the protocol and the willingness to configure and manage it.

Installing the TCP/IP Protocol

To install and configure the TCP/IP Protocol, take the following steps:

1. From Control Panel, double-click the Network icon to display the Network property sheet. Click the Protocols tab to display the Protocols page, shown in figure 8.33.

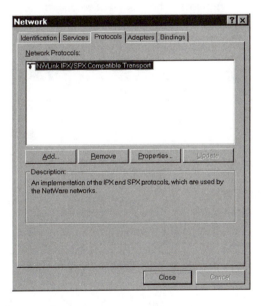

Fig. 8.33

Add the TCP/IP Protocol from the Protocols page of the Network property sheet.

2. Click <u>A</u>dd to display the Select Network Protocol dialog box and click TCP/IP Protocol to highlight it, as shown in figure 8.34.

III

Local Area Networking

Fig. 8.34
The Select Network Protocol dialog box allows you to specify the network protocol to be added.

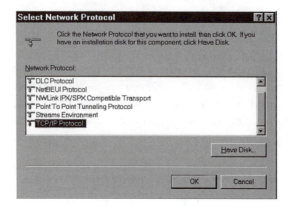

3. Click OK to display the TCP/IP Setup dialog box, shown in figure 8.35. Click Yes if there is a DHCP server on your network and you want it to provide an IP address for this computer. Click No if there is no DHCP server on your network, or if you want to assign the IP address for this computer manually. In this example, we elect to provide the IP address manually by clicking No.

Fig. 8.35
The TCP/IP Setup dialog allows you to use DHCP to provide an IP address for this computer.

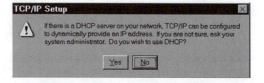

4. Windows NT displays the Windows NT Setup dialog box, shown in figure 8.36, to prompt you for the location of the distribution files. Enter the drive and directory where the Windows NT Workstation 4.0 distribution files are located, and click Continue. If you are installing from a CD-ROM to a computer running an Intel processor, the distribution files are located in the \i386 directory of your CD.

Fig. 8.36
The Windows NT Setup dialog box allows you to specify the location of the files to be copied.

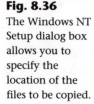

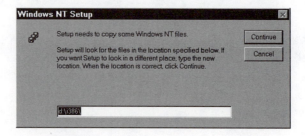

5. After the files are copied, Windows NT displays the Network property sheet with the TCP/IP Protocol visible, as shown in figure 8.37. Click Close to complete the installation.

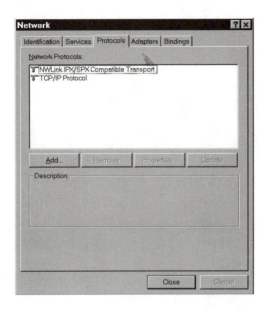

Fig. 8.37
The Network property sheet Protocols page shows the TCP/IP Protocol as installed.

6. After the bindings have been configured, reviewed, and stored, Windows NT displays the Network Settings Change dialog box to notify you that you must restart your computer before the changes will take effect. Click Yes to restart the computer immediately or click No to return to the Windows NT Workstation 4.0 desktop. If you choose the latter, the TCP/IP Protocol will not be available for use until you restart the system.

Configuring the TCP/IP Protocol

After you have installed the TCP/IP Protocol, as described in the preceding section, you must configure it before it can be used. To configure the TCP/IP Protocol, take the following steps:

1. From Control Panel, double-click the Network icon to display the Network property sheet. Click the Protocols tab to display the Protocols page, shown in figure 8.38.

2. Click TCP/IP Protocol to highlight it and then click Properties to display the IP Address page of the Microsoft TCP/IP Properties property sheet, shown in figure 8.39. The IP Address page allows you to specify how your computer is allocated an Internet Protocol (IP) address.

III

Local Area Networking

Fig. 8.38
Configure the
TCP/IP Protocol
from the Network
property sheet
Protocols page.

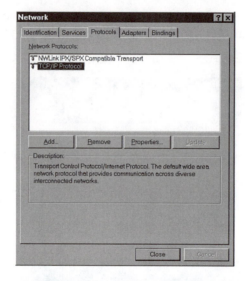

Fig. 8.39
The Microsoft
TCP/IP Properties
property sheet
allows you to
configure the
TCP/IP Protocol.

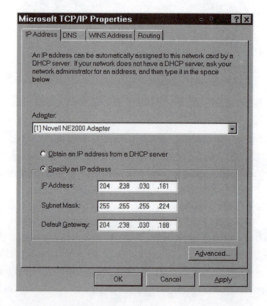

3. If you have only one network adapter installed in your computer, Windows NT fills in the Adapter list box with that adapter. If you have more than one adapter installed, use the drop-down list to select the adapter for which you want to configure TCP/IP properties.

4. Choose either Obtain an IP address from a DHCP server or Specify an IP address.

If your network includes a Windows NT Server running the Dynamic Host Configuration Protocol (DHCP) service, select Obtain an IP address from a DHCP server. The DHCP server allocates an IP address to the workstation automatically at startup.

If your network does not include a DHCP server, or if you simply want to specify the IP address for this workstation manually, select this option. Enter the appropriate IP Address, Subnet Mask and Default Gateway in the fields provided.

> **Caution**
>
> Use extreme care when you enter these numbers. If any are entered incorrectly, problems ranging from subtle conflicts to a network crash can result.

5. Click Advanced to display the Advanced IP Addressing dialog box, shown in figure 8.40.

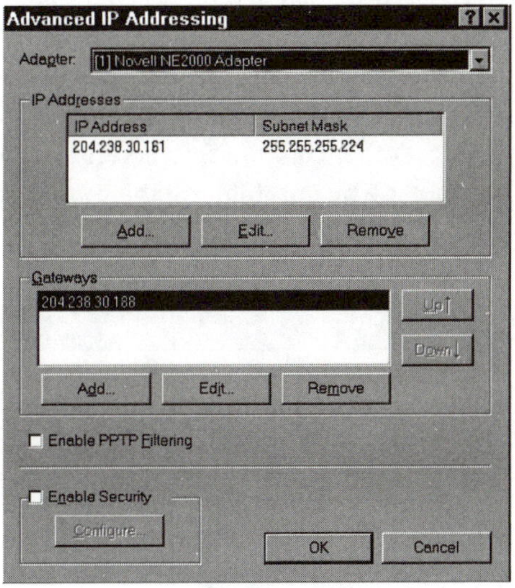

Fig. 8.40
The Advanced IP Addressing dialog box allows you to configure multiple IP addresses and Gateways, and to configure security options.

6. If you have only one network adapter installed in your computer, Windows NT fills in the Adapter list box with that adapter. If you have more than one adapter installed, use the drop-down list to select the adapter for which you want to configure Advanced IP Addressing properties. The Advanced IP Addressing dialog allows you to specify the following items:

III

Local Area Networking

- *IP Addresses*. Use A<u>d</u>d, <u>E</u>dit, and Remo<u>v</u>e to modify the IP addresses assigned to the selected network adapter. You can specify as many as 16 IP addresses per adapter. You can use multiple IP addresses on a single adapter to make a single physical computer appear to the network as multiple virtual computers. This might be useful, for example, if you want to run multiple independent Web servers on a single computer, with each Web server being discretely addressable.

- *Gateway*. Use A<u>d</u>d, Ed<u>i</u>t and Re<u>m</u>ove to modify the Gateway's configuration. Gateways are searched in the order they are shown in the <u>G</u>ateways list box. If more than one Gateway is listed, you can use <u>U</u>p and D<u>o</u>wn to modify the search order.

- *Enable PPTP <u>F</u>iltering*. if selected, this check box enables packet filtering for the Point-to-Point Tunneling Protocol.

- *E<u>n</u>able Security*. if selected, this check box allows you to specify TCP/IP security parameters by clicking the Configure to display the TCP/IP Security dialog box shown in figure 8.41. You can specify which TCP Ports, UDP Ports, and IP Protocols on your computer are available to the network. By default, all ports and protocols are available. You might, for example, set these parameters to allow other computers to access a Web server running on your computer while prohibiting them from accessing other TCP/IP services.

Fig. 8.41
The TCP/IP Security dialog box allows you to specify which ports and protocols are available on the network.

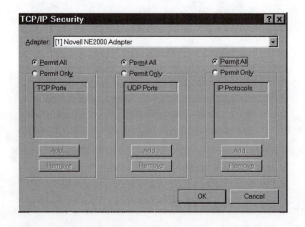

7. After you complete Advanced IP Addressing, click OK to return to the Microsoft TCP/IP Properties property sheet. Click the DNS tab to display the DNS page, shown in figure 8.42.

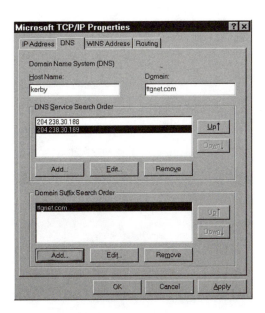

Fig. 8.42
The DNS Page allows you to configure Internet Domain Name System properties.

8. Enter values for each of the following items:

   - *Host Name.* Enter the IP name of this computer.

   - *Domain.* Enter the Internet domain of which this computer is a member. Don't confuse this value with the Windows NT domain.

   - *DNS Service Search Order.* Use Add, Edit, and Remove to provide the IP addresses for one or more DNS servers. The IP address that appears first in this list is the Primary DNS, and is used whenever it is available. The IP address that appears second in the list is the Secondary DNS, and is used only if the primary DNS is unavailable. Use Up and Down to modify the search order.

   - *Domain Suffix Search Order.* Use Add, Edit, and Remove to provide the names of Internet domains to be searched. This feature allows partially-qualified names to be resolved. For example, if your primary Internet domain is WIDGET.COM but you frequently access a host named NTS that belongs to the domain GADGET.COM, specifying GADGET.COM as a secondary search domain allows that host to be resolved when specified simply as NTS rather than as NTS.GADGET.COM.

9. After you complete the DNS page, click the WINS Address tab to display the WINS Address page, shown in figure 8.43.

III

Local Area Networking

Fig. 8.43
The WINS Address page allows you to configure the Windows Internet Naming Service.

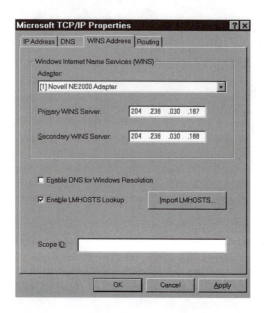

10. If you have only one network adapter installed in your computer, Windows NT fills in the Adapter list box with that adapter. If you have more than one adapter installed, use the drop-down list to select the adapter for which you want to configure WINS Address parameters. The WINS Address page allows you to specify the following items:

    • *Primary WINS Server.* Specify the IP address of the primary server that provides WINS address resolution for this computer. If you do not have a WINS server on your network, leave this blank. Windows NT then uses the local LMHOSTS file in conjunction with name query broadcasts to resolve IP addresses from the NetBIOS computer name, which limits you to resolving addresses on the local network.

    • *Secondary WINS Server.* Specify the IP address of the secondary server that provides WINS address resolution for this computer.

    • *Enable PPTP Filtering.* if selected, this check box enables packet filtering for the Point To Point Tunneling Protocol.

    • *Enable DNS for Windows Resolution.* if selected, this check box allows WINS and DNS to function together to resolve Windows names and IP addresses. Mark this checkbox if you have both WINS and DNS servers on your network and you want to use DNS for name resolution and to have DNS support in UNC names.

- *Enable LMHOSTS Lookup*. if selected, this check box causes Windows to use the LMHOSTS file for address resolution. You can click Import LMHOSTS to use the contents of an existing LMHOSTS file. An LMHOSTS file maps NetBIOS computer names to IP addresses, and must be maintained manually on each client. A NetBIOS name server like the WINS server bundled with Windows NT Server centralizes the mapping of NetBIOS computer names to IP addresses, and greatly reduces the effort needed to maintain these maps.

- *Scope ID*. You should normally leave this field blank. However, if your internetwork is running NetBIOS over TCP/IP and has been assigned its own scope identifier, you may enter that value here. Doing so limits communication between computers on the NetBIOS over TCP/IP internetwork to those that have identical values for scope id.

11. After you complete the WINS Address page, click the Routing tab to display the Routing page, shown in figure 8.44.

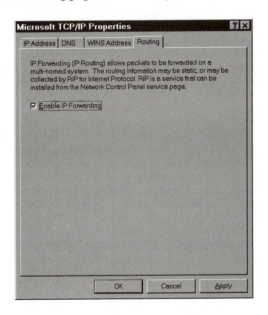

Fig. 8.44
The Routing page allows you to specify whether Windows NT will forward IP packets.

12. If you want this computer to function as an IP router, mark the check box Enable IP Forwarding.

13. Click OK to accept the changes you have made to Microsoft TCP/IP Properties and display the Network Settings Change dialog box, shown

III

Local Area Networking

in figure 8.45. Click <u>Y</u>es to restart the computer immediately or click <u>N</u>o to return to the Windows NT Workstation 4.0 desktop. If you choose the latter, the changes you have made to the TCP/IP Protocol will not take effect until you restart the system.

Fig. 8.45
The Network Settings Change dialog box prompts you to restart your computer to allow the Microsoft TCP/IP Properties settings you have made, take effect.

CHAPTER 9

Configuring Windows NT Workstation as a Network Server

by Dan Balter

The Workstation edition of Windows NT can provide a stable and secure network environment for smaller offices and organizations. It costs virtually the same as Windows 95, but it offers enhanced features that are not available in Windows 95. These significant features account for improved multitasking for 32-bit programs, more control over file access with the NTFS file system, and much better network administration tools with its Performance Monitor, User Manager, Task Manager, and Event Viewer.

In this chapter, you learn to

- Consider hardware and security issues
- Work with memory, disk space, and processor requirements
- Configure the server computer for optimal performance
- Share resources

Why Windows NT Workstation as the Dedicated File Server?

For smaller-sized environments, Windows NT Workstation 4.0 can serve as a much more robust host than either Windows for Workgroups or Windows 95. Although Windows NT Workstation is not as fault tolerant or feature-rich as its big brother, Windows NT Server 4.0, it offers a much more secure and reliable network operating system than Windows 95 while providing the same updated interface.

Windows NT Server is the preferred network operating system for medium to large scale organizations where central administration, security, system fault tolerance, advanced TCP/IP services, or Apple Macintosh client support are required. Additionally, Windows NT Server provides its users single domain log on capability for accessing all available network resources. It is also the *only* platform that supports Microsoft's BackOffice suite of server applications.

What is a Workgroup?

Workgroup is the term used to describe one of the two Microsoft networking models. A workgroup is a collection of networked personal computers having *peer-to-peer* connectivity with each other so that each PC in the workgroup can have access to, and can share resources with, each of the other PCs. Each computer user that is part of a workgroup is individually responsible for making his/her files and printers available to other users in the workgroup. If Joe Smith wants to access computers named X, Y, and Z, a user account with his user name (such as JSmith) *plus* a password for his user account must be added to each computer that he wants to access. In this example, the user account name of JSmith would have to exist on all three of the computers that Joe wants to use. If a workgroup becomes very large (50 to 100 PCs or more) managing all the redundant user accounts on multiple computers can be quite overwhelming.

How Does a Workgroup Differ from a Windows NT Server Domain?

The Microsoft networking domain model provides for a *central point* of administration for resource sharing and access permissions. A domain administrator is fully responsible for managing domain resources and user accounts which can even span multiple servers. Workgroups do *not* provide for centralized management. Access to remote disk drives and remote printers must be granted and updated for every user at each separate computer on the network. Furthermore, workgroups do not accommodate *roving* users well unless they log on to different machines as *guest* users, or already have an account on each specific computer that they want to work on. Domains allow users to move from workstation to workstation and log on to the network *without* requiring that they have a user account on each workstation nor that they log on as guest users. With Window NT Server, users log on to a specific domain, not necessarily onto a particular computer.

When Should You Use A Workgroup for Networking?

You should employ the workgroup networking model generally only in smaller settings where you have two to ten or maybe even as high as 20 workstations on a local area network. But there are other important considerations before you choose a workgroup. If you have substantial security concerns or if your organizational setting has many roving users, you may well be better served by implementing the domain model. In addition, if you are concerned about your network server's fault tolerance capabilities like disk duplexing or disk striping with parity you will need to run Windows NT Server since it supports domains. If security, roving users, and higher levels of fault tolerance are not very important issues and if you are dealing with a relatively small number of workstations with users who are somewhat savvy about computers in general, then a workgroup setup is tailor-made for you.

Hardware Considerations, Security Issues, and Multitasking Settings

According to Microsoft, the *minimum* requirements for a computer to run Windows NT Workstation 4.0 are listed in Table 9.1:

Table 9.1 Windows NT Workstation 4.0 Requirements		
Hardware Category	**Minimum Requirements**	**Recommendations**
CPU Platform	Intel 80486—33 Mhz or higher; MIPS, Alpha, or PowerPC RISC-based systems.	Faster is always better. Up to 2 microprocessors are supported.
Memory	Intel Platform = 12M	The more RAM the better. RISC computers = 16M. 32M of RAM offers very good *standalone* performance.
Video Display Card	VGA or higher	SVGA works well.
CD-ROM Drive	At least one CD-ROM Drive is required unless installing NT over a network connection.	4X speed drives are acceptable. 6X and 8X or faster drives and provide better performance. SCSI interface recommended.
Floppy Disk Drive	One 3.5" floppy drive Required for Intel-based computers.	
Pointing Device	Not strictly required.	A mouse or other type of pointing device is strongly recommended.

(continues)

Table 9.1   Continued

Hardware Category	Minimum Requirements	Recommendations
Available Disk Space	RISC-based computers require 136M of free space. SCSI disk drives are preferred by Windows NT and provide better throughput than EIDE drives.	One or more hard drives containing at least 108M of space. Of course, the more the better.
Network Adapter Cards	One or more network adapters cards are needed to connect Windows NT Workstation to the network.	Check the Windows NT Hardware Compatibility List (HCL) to ensure functionality.
Different Manufacturers and Models of Computer Hardware Products	Components that have been tested with Windows NT 4.0 HCL to ensure functionality.	Check the Windows NT HCL to ensure functionality for all components.

Just because a hardware component is *not* listed on the Hardware Compatibility List (HCL) does not necessarily mean that it won't work with Windows NT. However, when you verify that a component is listed on the HCL, you may very well save yourself a lot of headaches. If you are not careful, you can find yourself having major problems with an installation or configuration of a system that turns out to be unsolvable due to an incompatible hardware component.

Remember that the requirements listed in Table 9.1 for running Windows NT Workstation are only the *minimum* requirements. When you use a Windows NT Workstation computer as one or more servers in a network, those requirements will usually need to be bumped up quite a bit. Disk space and RAM are always at a premium, especially under the demands of a network server.

If you plan on using your Windows NT Workstation computer as both a server and a workstation, you may want to convert some or all of your hard drive partitions from the DOS-compatible FAT (File Allocation Table) file system to the much more secure Windows NT NTFS file system. NTFS can prohibit even local users from viewing, accessing, or deleting any files or folders that you designate. You should consider using the NTFS file system for any semi-sensitive or confidential data such as financial or payroll information.

When you use Windows NT Workstation as a server computer, you should configure its multitasking capabilities so that it adequately splits its CPU time slices between all the network users that will be connected to it. To change the system's multitasking priorities, follow these steps:

1. Right-click the My Computer desktop icon.

2. Select Properties from the pop-up menu. Skip to step number 5.

-OR-

3. Open the Start Menu and select Settings, Control Panel.

4. Double-click the System icon.

5. Click the Performance tab (see fig. 9.1).

6. In the Application Performance section, click and drag the slider bar all the way to the left so that the foreground application performance boost reads None. This setting tells Windows NT to make both foreground and background applications equally responsive.

7. Click OK to accept the new setting and close the dialog box.

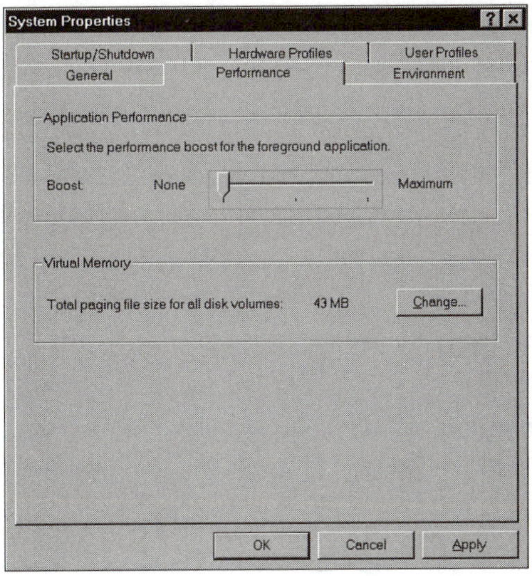

Fig. 9.1
The Windows NT Workstation Tasking dialog box.

III

Local Area Networking

Memory, Disk Space, and Processor Requirements

Available random access memory (RAM), the type of hard disk controller(s), the throughput of the hard drive(s), the amount of available hard disk space, and the type, speed, and number of microprocessors all help determine a computer's performance capabilities. For a network server computer, these elements can often make the difference between a *slow* network and a *faster* network.

Memory should be considered the most important component. A generous amount of RAM can usually make up for slower processor speeds, single processor machines, or even for hard drives that are not as fast as the current state-of-the-art. Windows NT loves memory. The more RAM, the better, and Windows NT will utilize as much memory as you can throw at it. Added memory allows Windows NT to *cache* more data and application code from the hard drive(s). The more information that the system can keep in memory, the less often that it will need to access any of the hard drives and the faster information can be served to all the networked users. Disk access is often the first bottleneck on a network server computer. Adding more RAM can usually solve this problem.

Hard disk space is probably the second most important element. In this day and age of "more, faster, and bigger", the size of both application files and data files are growing at a tremendous rate. It is very easy to underestimate future disk space needs, especially for multiple users in a networked environment. No simple formula exists to determine proper disk space requirements. One general rule of thumb is to add up the number of megabytes for all the application programs that you will install on the server computer plus the 108M minimum available space that Windows NT Workstation needs for installation. Take that number and multiply it by three. If the result is over 2G, install disk space that approximates that amount. If the result is equal to or less than 2G, install 2G worth of storage for the time being. With the price of hard drives becoming more and more affordable, this is an area where you can usually afford to splurge.

> **Note**
>
> Only Windows NT Server provides for disk mirroring, disk duplexing, and disk striping with parity (RAID level 5). However, Windows NT Workstation does support disk stripe sets *without* parity (RAID level 0). Although disk striping without parity does *not* offer any fault tolerance (if one disk drive fails, the entire stripe set will fail), it does offer improved throughput. A regular, frequent backup policy might provide sufficient fault tolerance in exchange for the enhanced throughput that disk striping can give.

There are some disk drive configuration options that you should think about. Disk striping is available in Windows NT Workstation. Disk striping permits you to combine the free space on multiple disk drives (you can use any number of drives from 2 up to 32 total) and create one volume that spans all the disk drives in the stripe set. This can result in increased throughput in disk I/O. Even if you choose not to use disk striping, you can improve some of the performance of your Windows NT system by installing at least two physical hard drives with a separate hard disk controller card for each drive. By having each drive with its own controller, more disk reads and writes can be performed simultaneously. Furthermore, you can place a Windows NT paging file on each disk drive partition that can also improve the system's performance.

The microprocessor that your system will use is probably the least important of the three components we're discussing. This is not to say that the CPU is not important or that having a multiprocessor Windows NT computer as a server isn't advantageous. It can be very beneficial! But, in the scheme of things, with everything else being relatively equal, you should put your money first on memory, then on disk space, and then on processor power. The reason for this is simple: network file and print services are not very processor intensive. Generally, you will see more performance gain from a 90 Mhz Pentium server with 64M of RAM than a 166 Mhz Pentium with 32M of RAM.

How Secure Does the Network Server Need To Be?

Regardless of the type of file system that the Windows NT Workstation computer is using (either NTFS or FAT), the network administrator can set the permission level for each shared folder that each user (or group of users) can have. Access permissions for users that connect to shared folders consist of:

- *No Access*
- *Read*
- *Change*
- *Full Control*

However, if you would like more detailed control over shared folders, if you need to exercise permissions on a file by file basis, or if you need to control the access to folders and files for users who log on directly to the server computer to use it as a workstation, you need to install the NTFS file system.

FAT Disk Partitions. The File Allocation Table (FAT) file system hails from the days of the original IBM PC and DOS. It provides a basic hierarchical directory and subdirectory organizational structure for computer files. The FAT file system offers little in terms of security. You can set four attributes for files and subdirectories: Hidden, System, Read Only, and Archive. But that's about all you can do. These attributes must apply to all users. You cannot selectively apply them depending on the user. Furthermore, it only takes a small bit of knowledge to know how to change the attributes. Almost anyone who has worked with PCs for a little while is capable of mass destruction on a FAT-based computer system.

NTFS Disk Partitions. The newer NTFS file system was designed with a high level of computer security in mind. In fact, both Windows NT Workstation and Server have U.S. government certifiable C-2 level security built in. An NTFS partition is invisible to other file systems like FAT. Even if someone boots a computer from a floppy disk, NTFS partitions cannot be seen or accessed. The NTFS file system gives you a lot of flexibility in the type of access permissions you can assign to users of the system as shown in Table 9.2. In addition to the No Access, Read, Change, and Full Control options you can specify for remote users, NTFS permits you to grant various combinations of permissions to both *remote* and *local* users. You can apply NTFS access permissions to both individual users and groups of users. NTFS also gives you the ability to monitor your users' file access activities through its file auditing feature. The file auditing feature is accessible with the Event Viewer utility.

When you install Windows NT Workstation, the setup program asks you if you want to convert any or all of the computer's hard disk partitions from existing FAT file systems over to NTFS. You can also elect to convert FAT partitions over to NTFS at a later time by using the Convert command line utility. To use Convert to change a partition's file system to NTFS, go to a command prompt window and use the following syntax:

```
Convert drive letter: /FS:FAT [/v]
```

You can't convert the drive that you are currently accessing. The /v parameter is for verbose mode and this is optional. Verbose mode provides additional message output to the screen to keep you updated on the NTFS conversion process. Another thing to keep in mind before converting to NTFS is that NTFS volumes are faster for *random* reads and writes whereas FAT volumes are faster for *sequential* reads and writes.

Caution

Converting a FAT partition to an NTFS partition is a *one-time, irreversible* procedure. You can never convert an NTFS partition to a FAT partition and if you convert a boot partition to NTFS, you will no longer be able to boot MS-DOS, OS/2, Windows 3.x or Windows 95 from that partition. Even booting DOS from a floppy disk will not allow you to access any NTFS drives (although now someone has come up with an MS-DOS utility that will allow you to read an NTFS partition). The only way to revert back to FAT once you have converted to NTFS is to backup, reformat the partition(s), and reinstall the operating system.

Table 9.2   NTFS File System Standard Permissions

Access Permission Options	Applies To Folders (Directories)	Applies To Files
No Access	Yes	Yes
List	Yes	No
Read	Yes	Yes
Add	Yes	No
Add & Read	Yes	No
Change	Yes	Yes
Access Not Specified	Yes	No
Special Access (Custom)	Yes	Yes
Full Control	Yes	Yes

To view access permissions for a *folder* located on an NTFS partition, right-click the folder and select Properties when viewing the folder from My Computer or Windows NT Explorer. Click the Security tab of the folder's Properties sheet. Click the Permissions button. The Directory Permissions dialog box appears (see fig. 9.2). You can add, change, or remove permissions for users or groups from this dialog box. To remove permissions, click a user or group name from the Name list and then click Remove. To change permissions, click the user or group name that you want to modify and then select a different permission from the Type of Access drop-down list.

Fig. 9.2

The Windows NT Workstation Directory Permissions dialog box.

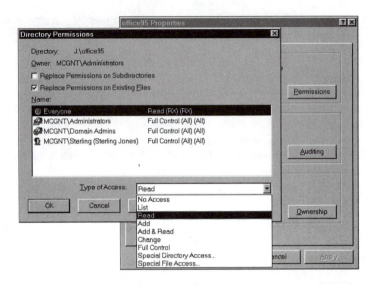

To add permissions for a user or group, follow these steps:

1. Click Add.

2. From the Add Users and Groups dialog box, click a user name or group name and then click Add for each group or user that you want to grant permissions to.

   You can click the Show Users button to show the names of the user accounts for the system.

   You can click the Members button to view the members of any group that you select.

3. Select the permission(s) that you wish to grant from the Type of Access drop-down list (see fig. 9.3).

4. Click OK when finished.

Before you are done working with the Directory Permissions dialog box, mark the Replace Permissions on Subdirectories checkbox if you want the changes that you have made to the access permissions to cascade down to all the subdirectories beneath the current directory. Mark the Replace Permissions on Existing Files checkbox if you want the changes that you have made to the access permissions to affect the files within the current directory as well as the directory itself. Click OK when you are finished with the Directory Permissions dialog box and click the OK button one more time to exit from the folder's Properties sheet.

Setting file access permissions works exactly the same way as setting folder-level (or directory-level) permissions. Select a file that is stored on an NTFS volume, right-click the file, select Properties, click the Security tab, and then click the Permissions button. From here, you can add, change, or remove permissions for users and groups who access the file. NTFS folder and file permissions override share level permissions and provide for more granularity of control over network resources.

Fig. 9.3
The Windows NT Workstation Directory Permissions Add Users and Groups dialog box.

Tip

Windows NT Workstation 4.0 offers a directory-level permission called Access Not Specified. This permission prevents files from inheriting permissions from the current directory. The files retain the permissions that they had before becoming a part of the directory.

Standard predefined NTFS permissions are simply made up of individual NTFS permissions. These basic individual permissions are the building blocks for NTFS folder and file security. These individual security options can be combined in many ways to obtain customized Special Access permissions. NTFS individual permissions are as follows with their abbreviations in parentheses:

- *Read (R)*
- *Write (W)*
- *Execute (X)*
- *Delete (D)*
- *Change Permissions (P)*
- *Take Ownership (O)*

III

Local Area Networking

> **Tip**
>
> It's much easier to assign permissions to groups of users rather than to individual users. In the same vein, it is also easier to grant access permissions to entire folders (directories) instead of dealing with innumerable individual files within several different folders. Finally, you will find that if you stick to issuing just the standard NTFS set of permissions rather than creating Special Access permissions, your life as a network administrator will be that much easier.

Configuring the Server Computer for Optimal Performance

Earlier in this chapter we discussed the importance of setting Windows NT Workstation's Tasking priorities so that foreground and background applications are given equal status in terms of CPU time slicing. Another way of improving the system's performance is to set up one or more additional paging files. This is especially useful if your system has two or more separate physical hard drives with individual controllers. Windows NT paging files provide necessary virtual memory for the system. Even with tons of RAM installed, Windows NT really requires at least one paging file which it creates at the time of installation. Two or more paging files on separate physical disks allow for additional virtual memory for the system and for simultaneous reads and writes. This allows the system to access its virtual memory faster.

To set up additional paging files

1. Right-click the My Computer icon (or open the Start menu and select Settings, click Control Panel, and double-click the System icon).
2. Click the Performance tab.
3. In the Virtual Memory section, click the Change button.
4. In the Drive box, click a drive letter that does not already have a paging file.
5. Enter an Initial Size and a Maximum Size based on the available disk space for that drive and the size of the first paging file (see fig. 9.4).
6. Click the Set button.
7. Click OK to close the Virtual Memory dialog box.
8. Click OK again to close the System Properties sheet and have your new paging file settings take affect.

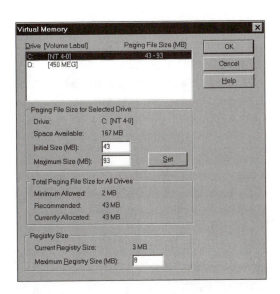

Fig. 9.4
Windows NT Workstation's Virtual Memory dialog box.

Implementing a Network Workgroup

You can start a network workgroup on your Windows NT Workstation computer when you install Windows NT or at a later time. The process is essentially the same whether you choose to do it at the time of installation or not. For this example, let's assume that you already have a Windows NT Workstation up and running and now you want to add network connectivity.

1. Open the Start menu, select Settings, click Control Panel, and then double-click the Network icon. The Network dialog box appears (see fig. 9.5).

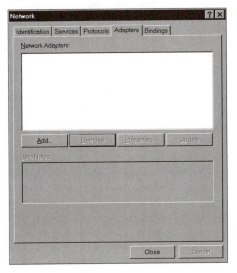

Fig. 9.5
Windows NT Workstation's Network dialog box.

III

Local Area Networking

2. From the Adapters tab, click the <u>A</u>dd button to tell the system the type of network adapter card that is installed.

3. Click the name and model of the adapter that you have installed in the computer so that Windows NT can load the proper driver for it (see fig. 9.6). Click the <u>H</u>ave Disk button if your network adapter is not listed or if you have a disk that was provided by the network adapter card manufacturer. Click OK after selecting the proper network adapter card for your system.

Fig. 9.6
Windows NT
Workstation's
Select Network
Adapter dialog
box.

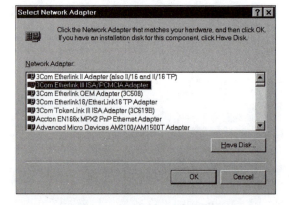

4. Select the correct I/O <u>P</u>ort Address, <u>I</u>nterrupt Number, and <u>T</u>ransceiver Type for the network adapter card (see fig. 9.7). Click OK when you have finalized the settings.

5. Windows NT Setup will ask you for the location of the installation files. Type in the proper drive letter and path and then click Continue (see fig. 9.8). You may need to insert the Windows NT Workstation CD-ROM to complete this procedure.

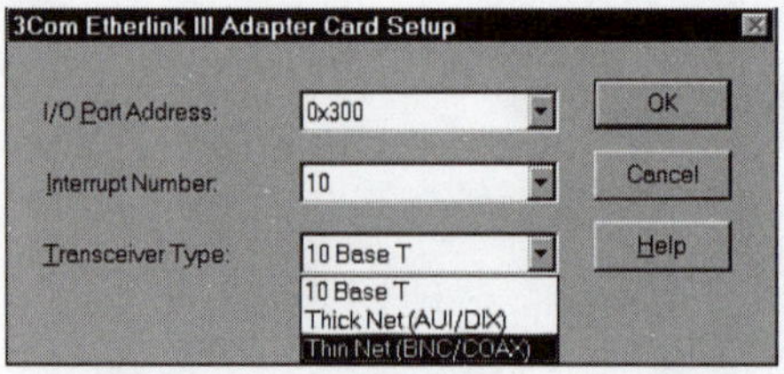

Fig. 9.7
The Windows NT
Workstation
Adapter Card
Setup dialog box.

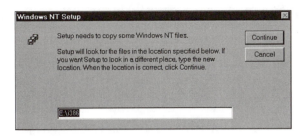

Fig. 9.8
The Windows NT
Workstation Setup
dialog box.

6. If the network card driver is successfully installed, the name of the card
   will be listed under Network Adapters on the Adapters tab of the Network dialog box. Click the Protocols tab to add one or more network
   protocols, which are the type of transport mechanisms (networking
   dialects) that your network requires.

7. Click the Add button to add a protocol. The Select Network Protocol
   dialog box appears (see fig. 9.9). Select a network protocol from the list
   or click Have Disk to choose a different protocol than those listed. Click
   OK to continue.

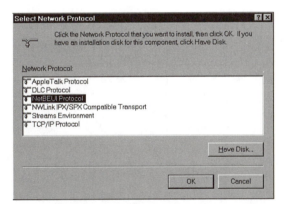

Fig. 9.9
The Windows NT
Workstation Select
Network Protocol
dialog box.

III

Local Area Networking

Tip

For a small network, Microsoft's NetBEUI protocol is quite sufficient. However, for
medium to larger networks you should probably opt for a protocol like TCP/IP or
NWLink (IPX/SPX). If you are integrating Windows NT into an existing network
environment that already has protocols running such as TCP/IP (on Ethernet networks) or IPX/SPX (Novell NetWare networks), you will probably want to choose one
or more of those existing protocols.

> **Caution**
>
> The NetBEUI protocol is *not* routable. In a network environment where routing is required, you should choose a protocol like TCP/IP, NWLink (IPX/SPX), or another routing-capable protocol.

8. Windows NT Setup will again ask you for the location of the setup files. Type in the drive letter and path and then click Continue. Once the protocol has been successfully installed, you will see it listed in the Network Protocols box (see fig. 9.10).

Fig. 9.10
The Network dialog box's list of installed network protocols.

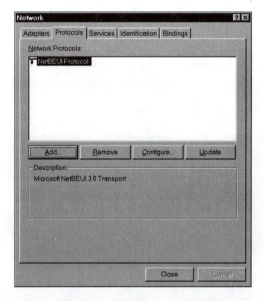

9. Click the Identification tab and then click the Change button. The Identification Changes dialog box appears (see fig. 9.11).

10. The computer should already have its own unique name that is different from any of the other computers on the network (if it does not, you will need to change it now). In the Member Of box, click the Workgroup option button and type in the name of your workgroup. For this example, we will be creating a new workgroup for the **Sales** office of our organization.

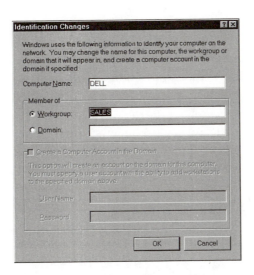

Fig. 9.11
The Network
Identification
Changes dialog
box.

11. Click OK after you have verified that the Computer Name is unique to
your network and after you have typed in a name for your Workgroup.
A Network Configuration message box should appear welcoming you as
a member of the workgroup (see fig. 9.12).

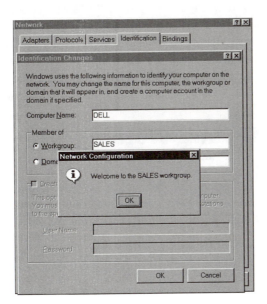

Fig. 9.12
The Network
Configuration
Welcoming
message box.

12. Click OK on the welcoming message box. At this point, you have successfully installed the correct network adapter card driver, installed at least one compatible network protocol, and you have properly identified your network server so that other workstations will be able to connect to it.

13. Click the Close button for the Network dialog box to implement the changes that you have made. Windows NT then displays a message box alerting that you need to restart the computer for your new networking changes to take affect (see fig. 9.13).

Fig. 9.13
The Network
Settings Change
message box.

14. Click Yes to restart the system.

One surefire way to see whether you have succeeded in establishing network connectivity is to double-click the Network Neighborhood icon. If you have previously set up other computers as part of the same workgroup, you should be able to see those *network nodes* as soon as the system boots back up again (see fig. 9.14). You should also be able to browse computers located in other workgroups and domains within the same physical network, if they are using one of the same network protocols as your computer. You can double-click the Entire Network icon to view other workgroups and domains.

Setting Up and Working with Users and Groups

Unless you want some or all the users on the network to access your server's resources using a Guest password, you need to establish a user name account and password for each user that will be connecting to your Windows NT Workstation server computer. You will also need to set up access permissions for the users. Access permissions vary depending upon each user's position in the organization and his/her specific needs for various types of information (such as, financial, marketing, or personnel data).

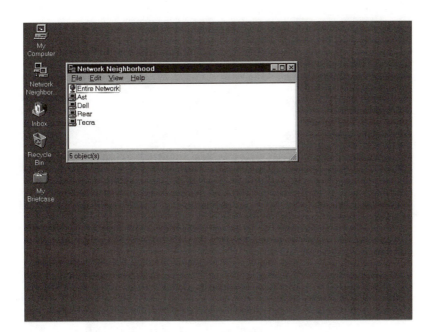

Fig. 9.14
The Network Neighborhood window after properly configuring Windows NT Workstation for networking.

Adding and Managing Users and Groups

You add, delete, and change users and groups through Windows NT Workstation's User Manager tool. You'll find this applet located under Start, Programs, Administrative Tools. Click User Manager to start the program. To add a new user, choose User, New User (see fig. 9.15). The New User dialog box appears (see fig. 9.16). Type in a User Name which is the user's network identification that the person will use to log on to this server computer. The User Name is limited to 20 characters and is *not* case sensitive. It cannot contain spaces nor any of the following characters:

" / \ [ ] : ; [vb] = , + * ? < >

The Full Name and Description fields are optional. Passwords can be no more than 14 characters long and passwords *are* case sensitive (however case sensitivity does *not* matter when logging on from DOS, Windows for Workgroups, or Windows 95 computers). If you do not want the user to have a password, clear the Password text box and leave it blank. Verify the password that you typed by typing it again in the Confirm Password text box.

The User Must Change Password at Next Logon checkbox is marked by default. Clear this checkbox if you do not want to require the user to change his/her password the first time that he/she logs on.

Fig. 9.15
User Manager
dialog box and the
User menu.

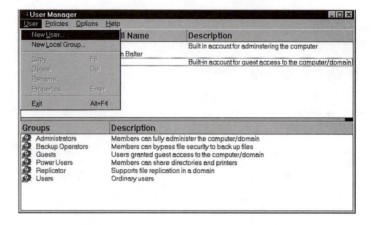

Fig. 9.16
User Manger's
New User dialog
box.

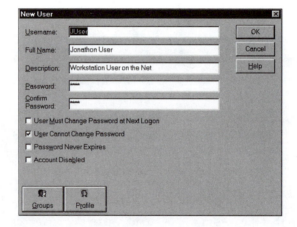

Mark the User Cannot Change Password checkbox if you want to retain complete control of the user's password.

Mark the third checkbox if you want to allow that the user's Password Never Expires.

The last checkbox permits you to have the user's Account Disabled. This option is good for extended periods of absence (like vacations) where you do not want to chance that anyone unauthorized might try to access that user's account. You can also use this option instead of immediately deleting the user's account in the case of the person leaving the organization.

Click the Groups button on the bottom of the dialog box to view which group(s) the new user automatically becomes a member of (see fig. 9.17). New users automatically attain membership in the Users group. To make the user a member of other groups, click one of the groups listed under Not Member Of and then click the Add button. To remove the user from one of the groups, click the group name listed under Member Of and then click the Remove button. Click OK to close the Group Memberships dialog box when you are finished.

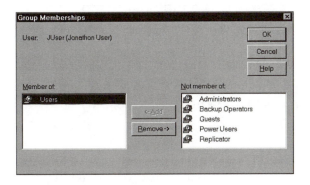

Fig. 9.17
User Manger's New User Group Membership dialog box.

Click the Profile button on the New User dialog box to configure User Profile settings. If you want a script file (a .BAT or .CMD file) to run every time the user logs on to the server computer, you can type in the name of that Script file. The Script file must be located in the \\"Winnt Root"\System32\Repl\ Import\Scripts folder. The User Environment Profile dialog box also provides the ability to set a custom path for storing specific information about the user's desktop settings if he/she is connecting to this computer from another Windows NT Workstation computer. You can specify a Home Directory for the user. This Home Directory can be either a folder located on the *user's* local workstation (Local Path), or, it can be located on the server's computer (Connect). To have it located on the server's hard drive, click Connect and then type in the full path name. You can use the %USERNAME% environment variable to have Windows NT create a folder with the user's name as the name of the Home Directory (see fig. 9.18). Click OK when you are done to return to the New User dialog box.

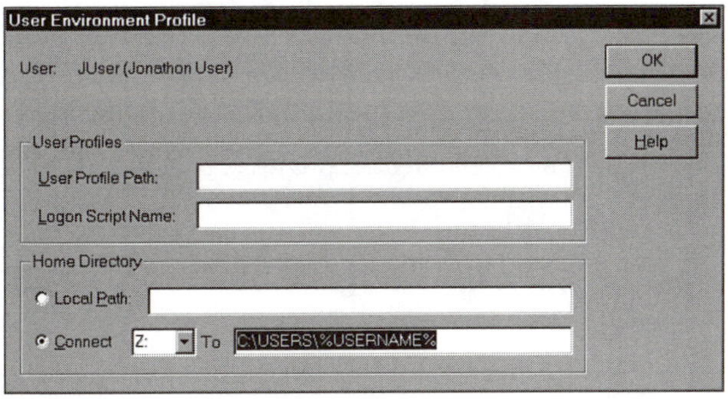

Fig. 9.18
User Manger's User Environment Profile dialog box.

III

Local Area Networking

> **Note**
>
> At times, User Manager may display a message box indicating that it cannot create a Home Directory for the user. In these instances, you need to manually create the directory.

Click OK to add the new user. You will see the new user displayed in the User Manager window. To make any changes to an existing user, double-click the user name. To delete a user or users, select the user by clicking it, or select multiple users by holding down the Ctrl or Shift keys and clicking each user that you wish to delete. Press the Delete key or choose User, Delete. You can make changes to multiple users by selecting them and then choosing User, Properties. You are able to change common properties that the users all share.

You can create your own groups with User Manager. Any groups that you add will co-exist with Windows NT Workstation's default groups. To create a new group

1. Choose User, New Local Group. The New Local Group dialog box appears (see fig. 9.19).

Fig. 9.19

The New Local Group dialog box.

2. Type in a name for the new group along with a description.

3. Click the Add button to add members to the new group (see fig. 9.20). You will see the Add Users and Groups dialog box.

4. Click the user(s) that you wish to add to the group and click Add.

5. Click OK when you have added all the users that you want to add to this group.

6. Click OK for the New Local Group dialog box.

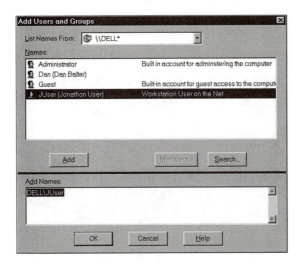

Fig. 9.20
The New Local Group's Add Users and Groups dialog box.

You can delete groups the same way that you can delete users: click the group(s) that you want to delete and either press the Delete key or choose User, Delete.

Sharing Resources and Establishing Access Control Permissions

Once you have set up the necessary connectivity for your network and then added the appropriate user accounts, you are ready to make key resources (folders, files, and printers) available to the remote users. This process is called *sharing*. Windows NT has two levels of access control permissions: Share-level and User-level. Share-level access control is used for both types of Windows NT file systems, FAT and NTFS. User-level access control can only be implemented under NTFS. Both types of access control permit you to limit which users view, change, or delete shared information. User-level access control provides greater pinpoint control as well as control over users who have access to logging on the local server computer.

Share Level Access Control

You can make any folder on your Windows NT Workstation system available to remote users by simply sharing it. Before you attempt to share a folder, you must be logged on as a member of either the Administrators group or the Power Users group. To share a folder

1. From the My Computer window or Windows NT Explorer, right-click the folder that you wish to share.

2. Select Sharing from the pop-up menu. The folder's Properties sheet appears with its Sharing tab displayed (see fig. 9.21).

Fig. 9.21
The Properties sheet displaying its Sharing tab.

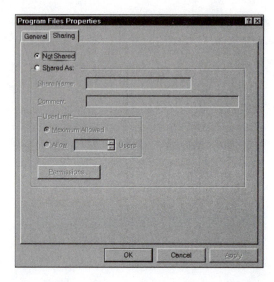

3. Click the Shared As option button to activate sharing for the folder.

4. Type in a Share Name if you want a different share name than the name of the folder which becomes the share name by default.

5. Type in a Comment, if desired.

6. You can set a User Limit on the share to restrict concurrent usage to a certain number of users. Windows NT Workstation enforces its own maximum concurrent user limit of 10 users—this limit *cannot* be exceeded. You must select a number between 1 and 10.

7. Click Permissions to view the default permissions that Windows NT Workstation automatically assigns to every new share (see fig. 9.22). Notice that it defaults to granting Full Control to Everyone (all users).

8. Click OK to close the Access Through Share Permissions dialog box.

9. Click OK for the Properties sheet to establish the share (see fig. 9.23).

If the share name you are assigning is longer than a standard MS-DOS eight-character directory name, Windows NT alerts you that DOS-based workstations, Windows 3.x, and Windows for Workgroups 3.x client computers will *not* be able to access the share. Once the share has been created, the shared folder will display a hand underneath its icon (see fig. 9.24).

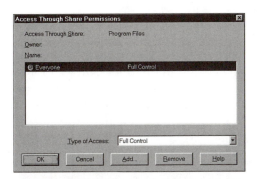

Fig. 9.22
The Access Through Share Permissions dialog box.

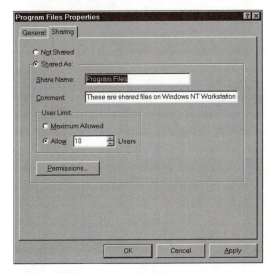

Fig. 9.23
The Sharing page is complete.

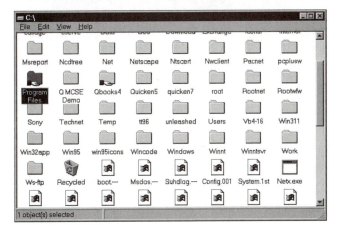

Fig. 9.24
A Shared Folder icon.

Restricting Network Access

You can limit the access users have to each individual share. For this example, let's assume that you have a folder on the C:\ drive of your Windows NT Workstation computer called DATA that contains a subfolder named DOCS. Drive C:\ is using the FAT file system, so you can only limit its sharing by using the standard set of folder sharing permissions: No Access, Read, Change, and Full Control. Because it is much easier to work with groups when assigning permissions, you should implement permissions on a group basis whenever possible.

The DOCS folder contains company documents. You want all users to be able to read the documents, but you only want members of the Sales Managers group to have the ability to make any changes or to be able to delete the documents. To set these access permissions

1. From either My Computer or Windows NT Explorer, right-click the C:\DATA\DOCS folder and select Sharing.

2. Leave the Share Name as "Docs" and click the Permissions button. You will see the Access Through Share Permissions dialog box (see fig. 9.25). Notice that by default Everyone (all users) has Full Control permission—this means that any user will be able to access this folder and he/she can perform *any* action on its files, including changing or deleting them!

Caution

It's a good idea, in general, to immediately remove the default Full Control permission for the global Everyone group. Not only does this permission allow *anyone* complete access to every share that you create, it also *overrides* any more restrictive permissions (*except No Access*), since all users are a part of the Everyone group. If you want to limit access to a particular folder to only Power Users by granting the Power Users group Full Control and the Users group No Access, members of the Users group will *not* be able to access the share. However, if you grant the Users group Read permission and the global Everyone group still has Full Control, members of the Users group will *retain* Full Control permissions! Be very careful about the way you establish access permissions!

---

3. Click the Remove button to remove the default Full Control permissions for the Everyone group.

4. Click the Add button to add permissions. The Add Users and Groups dialog box appears (see fig. 9.25).

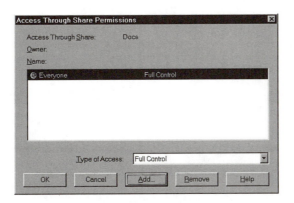

Fig. 9.25
The Access
Through Share
Permissions dialog
box.

5. Click Show Users to view the users names on the system.

6. Click the Sales Mangers group and then click the Add button
(see fig. 9.26).

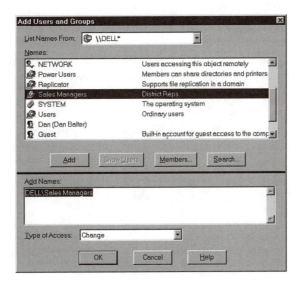

Fig. 9.26
The Add Users and
Groups dialog box.

7. From the Type of Access drop-down list, select the Change permission.

8. Click OK to return to the Access Through Share dialog box.

9. Click Add again.

10. Click the Users group and then click the Add button.

11. Select Read from the Type of Access drop-down list.

12. Click OK to return to the Access Through Share dialog box
(see fig. 9.27).

Fig. 9.27
The Access
Through Share
Permissions dialog
box after setting
new permissions.

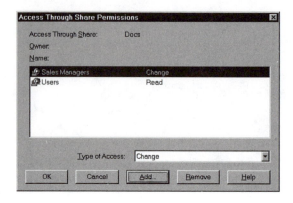

13. Click OK to return to the Sharing tab of the Properties sheet for the Docs folder.

14. Click OK for the Properties sheet to complete the configuration of this new share.

Sharing Resources with "Guest" Permissions

There may be times when you have new users on the network that you have not been able to add to the Windows NT Workstation server computer, or, you may have users that usually don't need access to the files or printers on the Windows NT Workstation machine, so they don't have user accounts on the server. For these types of users, you can still allow them access to the computer, if you want to. Windows NT automatically installs a Guest user account. The Guest account has a blank password by default. You should assign a password to the account if you are not going to disable it. Depending on the folder, you will probably want to strongly limit Guest access permissions. You should use the built-in Guest group to do this.

When a network user tries to connect to a Windows NT Workstation computer that he or she does not have an account on, the user is prompted for a password in order to access each particular resource. Using a Windows 95 client PC as an example, if a user without a network account on the server PC tries to access the Windows NT Workstation computer, the user is prompted by a message box to type in the proper password for Guest access. If the user enters an incorrect password, the client PC issues a message box warning that the password is incorrect. Once the user enters a valid password, he or she is granted access to the resource.

Administrative Shares

Windows NT Workstation automatically creates its own shared folders every time it boots. These shares are called *administrative shares*. Administrative shares are distinctive due to the conspicuous dollar sign ($) that is added to each share name. The root folder of every hard drive becomes an administrative share by the Windows NT system. Figure 9.28 shows administrative shares generated by Windows NT using the Server utility found in the Control Panel and clicking the Shares button. The dollar sign prevents these shares from being browsed over the network, so they are hidden. No one can see that administrative shares are available, you have to already know that they exist to use them. Even if users know about these shares, they *cannot* connect to them unless they are members of the Administrators group. You can create your own administrative shares, just add a dollar sign ($) to the end of any share name. To connect to an administrative share, click the Connect To Network Drive icon from the File Manager window in Windows for Workgroups, or from Windows 95, choose Tools, Map Network Drive from the Explorer window (see fig. 9.29). You must *manually* type in the computer name and path.

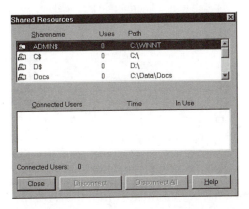

Fig. 9.28
The Server Utility's Shared Resources dialog box showing default administrative shares.

Fig. 9.29
The Windows 95 Explorer's Map Network Drive dialog box.

III

Local Area Networking

Access Control Using NTFS Security

You can more finely control access permissions on hard drives that have been formatted with the NTFS file system instead of the FAT file system. You share folders the same way on an NTFS volume as on a FAT volume. The difference is that you are given more alternatives for the types of access that you can allow under NTFS. In the earlier section, "NTFS Disk Partitions," we covered the various types of NTFS permissions. NTFS permissions apply to both remote users accessing the share over the network *as well as* to any user who happens to work interactively on the local Windows NT Workstation computer.

> **Note**
>
> Whenever NTFS and share-level access permissions conflict, the *most restrictive* access permissions prevail. If a shared folder has Full Control permission for a user or group, but the NTFS permission is only Read, that user will only retain Read access to the files in that folder. On the other hand, if a shared folder is granted Change permission for a user or group, but its NTFS permission is Special Access with only Read (R), Write (W), and Execute (E), the user or group will *not* be able to delete any of the files. The more restrictive Read, Write, and Execute permissions will override the less restrictive Read, Write, Execute, and Delete capabilities that comprise the Change access permission.

If you find that the standard NTFS permissions do not suffice for certain circumstances, you can customize the permissions to better suit a given situation. To set Special Access NTFS permissions for a folder (directory)

1. From My Computer or Explorer, right-click a folder that is located on a hard drive that has been formatted with the NTFS file system.

2. Select Properties from the pop-up menu. When the Properties sheet appears, click the Security tab.

3. Click the Permissions button to display the Directory Permissions dialog box.

4. It's a good idea to delete the permissions for the global Everyone group. Click the Everyone group, if it is displayed, and click Remove.

5. Click the Add button. The Add Users and Groups dialog box appears.

6. Click the Users group to select it and next click the Add button to add permissions to this group. Don't worry about the type of access for the moment.

7. Click OK to return to the Directory Permissions dialog box.

8. Click the Type of Access drop-down list and select Special Directory Access. The Special Directory Access dialog box appears (see fig. 9.30). These permissions affect the directory itself.

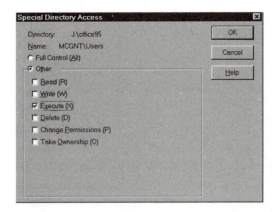

Fig. 9.30
The Special Directory Access dialog box.

9. Mark the Read (R), Execute (X), and Write (W) checkboxes to grant permission only to read, write, and run executable files from this directory for members of the Users group. These NTFS permissions will override any lesser-restrictive share-level permissions that have been granted to remote users.

10. Click OK to return to the Directory Permissions dialog box.

11. Click the Type of Access drop-down list again and this time select Special File Access. The Special File Access dialog box appears. These permissions affect the files within the current directory.

12. Mark the Read (R), Execute (X), and Write (W) checkboxes and clear any other checkboxes.

13. Click OK to return to the Directory Permissions dialog box.

14. Mark the Replace Permissions on Subdirectories checkbox if you want these Special Access permissions to trickle down to any and all of the subdirectories that are beneath the current one. Leave the Replace Permissions on Existing Files checkbox marked unless you do not want these Special Access permissions to affect the files contained within the directory.

III

Local Area Networking

15. Click OK to go back to the Security tab of the Properties sheet.

16. Click OK to close the Properties sheet.

Even if Full Control is granted as a share-level permission, the NTFS permissions shown in this example will only allow the user or group to Read, Write, or Execute the files contained in the folder.

Sharing Printers

Sharing printers on a Windows NT Workstation computer is a very easy and straightforward process. Once you have installed one or more printers, you can share printers in the same way that you set up shares for folders. To share a local printer with remote network users

1. Open the Start menu and select Settings, Printers, or double-click the Printers icon inside of the My Computer window or the Explorer window. The Printers window opens.

2. Right-click the printer icon that you wish to share and select Properties. The Printer Properties sheet appears.

3. Click the Sharing tab to access the printer's sharing properties.

4. Click the Shared option button and type in a descriptive name for the Share Name such as HP4-SalesOffice (see fig. 9.31).

Fig. 9.31
The Printers
Properties sheet's
Sharing tab.

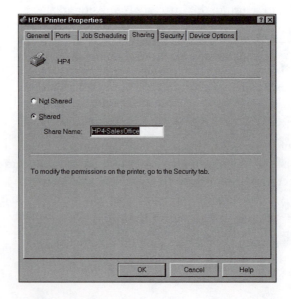

After you have shared a printer, you will want to set up some access permissions for it, just like you set up access permissions for files and folders. To work with a printer's access permissions

1. While you are still in the Printer Properties sheet, click the Security tab.

2. Click the Permissions button to view the Printer Permissions dialog box (see fig. 9.32).

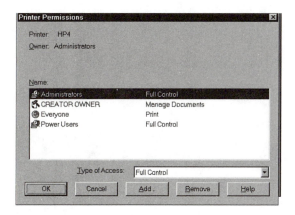

Fig. 9.32
The Printers Permissions dialog box.

3. To remove a user or group from the permissions list, just click the name of the user or group and then click Remove.

4. You can add users or groups to the permissions list by first clicking the Add button. The familiar Add Users and Groups dialog box appears.

5. Click the user name or group name that you wish to add permissions for and then click the Add button.

6. From the Type of Access drop-down list, select the type of access permission that you want to assign to the user or group.

7. Click OK to accept your new access permissions and return to the Printer Permissions dialog box.

8. Click OK to close the Printer Permissions dialog box and click OK again to close the Printer Properties sheet.

III

Local Area Networking

Printer permissions cover a full range of printing activities. Table 9.3 outlines the major printing activities and their associated access privileges.

Table 9.3 Windows NT Workstation Printer Permissions

Activity	Full Control	Manage Documents	Print Documents	No Access
Printing	X	X	X	
Control Job Settings for a User's own Documents	X	X	X	
Pause, Restart, and Delete a User's own Document	X	X	X	
Control Job Settings for All Documents	X	X		
Pause, Restart, and Delete All Documents	X	X		
Share Printers	X			
Change Printer Properties	X			
Delete Installed Printers	X			
Change Printer Permissions	X			

Monitoring Network Connections

It's always a good idea to keep track of who's accessing your Windows NT Workstation computer at any given time and what resources they are using. The Server utility can help you keep tabs on network usage. To work with the Server applet follow these steps

1. Open the Start menu and select Settings, and Control Panel.

2. From the Control Panel, double-click the Server icon. The Server utility will start (see fig. 9.33).

You can view connection information and perform the following actions through the Server utility:

Fig. 9.33
The Server Utility.

- The Server utility shows you the current number of Sessions, Open Files, File Locks, and Open Named Pipes under its Usage Summary. To view the users that are currently connected to your computer, click the Users button.

- The Users button displays the User Sessions dialog box which shows all the current Connected Users and their computer names (see fig. 9.34). You can click a Connected User and then click the Disconnect button to disconnect that session, if you find that necessary. You can also disconnect all the current users. Click the Close button to close this dialog box.

- Click the Shares button to view Shared Resources together with Connected Users (see fig. 9.35). Click Close to close this dialog box.

- Click the In Use button to see all the Open Resources that are currently being accessed (see fig. 9.36). You can opt to click one of the resources and then click the Close Resource button to shut down the user's access to that resource. You also have the option of clicking the Close All Resources button. These types of measures should be rarely used—data loss is almost guaranteed by shutting down resources in this way. In addition, you will not win over many friends if you exhibit this type of behavior very often. Click Close to return to the Server.

- The Replication button concerns the importing of files from Windows NT Server computers.

- The Alerts button allows you to have your Windows NT Workstation computer send any administrative alerts to other computers on the network.

III

Local Area Networking

Fig. 9.34
The User Sessions
dialog box.

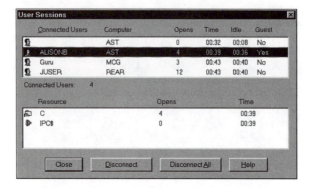

Fig. 9.35
The Server Utility's
Shared Resources
dialog box.

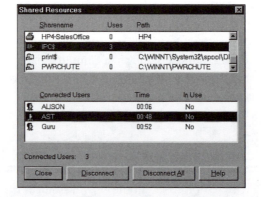

Fig. 9.36
The Server Utility's
Open Resources
dialog box.

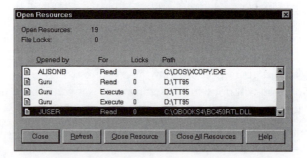

Windows NT Workstation Can Act as a Big Server for a Smaller Environment

As you can see, Windows NT Workstation can more than adequately serve the connectivity needs for smaller networks. The workgroup networking model works well for organizational groups where central administration is not paramount and where the users can be trusted to maintain their own shared resources.

Windows NT Workstation can provide a robust networking platform along with strong security to protect important files from being accessed by unauthorized users. You can integrate Windows NT Workstation into a mixed network environment by implementing protocols that ship with the product to connect with Novell NetWare networks as well as many others. If you are a seasoned NetWare technician, you will be comfortable with the organization of a Windows NT-based LAN, especially in the area of security. Now, with version 4.0, Microsoft brings its high-end network operating system up-to-date by incorporating Windows 95's enhanced look and feel. ❖

III

Local Area Networking

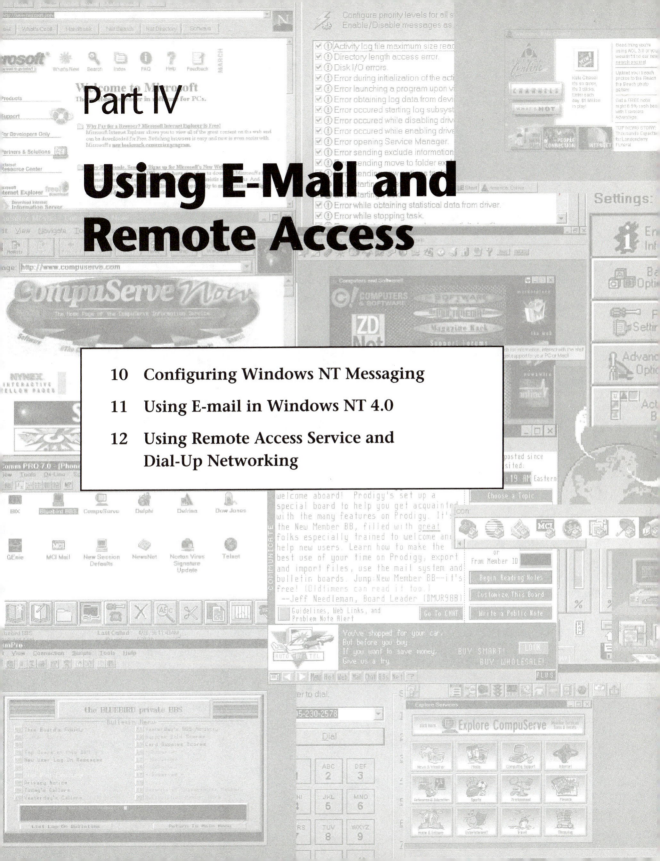

Part IV

Using E-Mail and Remote Access

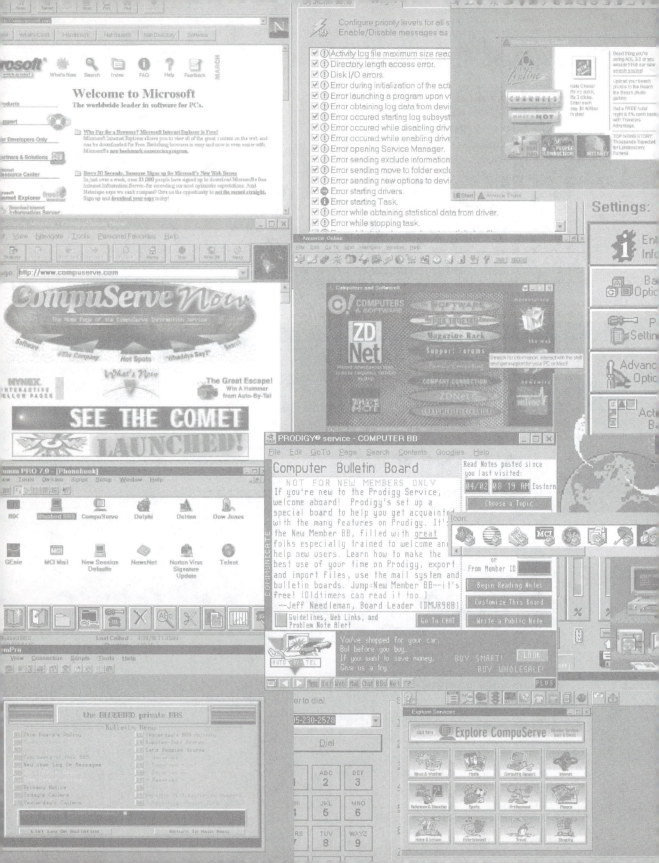

CHAPTER 10

Configuring Windows NT Messaging

by Jim Boyce

Windows NT includes an e-mail feature named Windows NT Messaging (referred to in the remainder of the chapter as simply Messaging) that enables you to combine much, if not all, of your e-mail into a single inbox. With Messaging, you can send and receive e-mail to a Microsoft Mail post office, the Internet, and CompuServe. Messaging's support for Internet and CompuServe e-mail gives you a gateway to send and receive messages to almost anyone in the world who has an e-mail account on the Internet or on an online service such as CompuServe, America Online, Prodigy, or others.

> **Note**
>
> The Windows NT Messaging feature that is included with Windows NT is almost identical to the Microsoft Exchange client included with Windows 95. The Messaging client and the Microsoft Exchange client in Windows 95 are not the same as the Microsoft Exchange client designed by Microsoft for the Microsoft Exchange Server product. The Microsoft Exchange client for the Microsoft Exchange Server provides additional features not supported by the versions included with Windows NT and Windows 95. In fact, Microsoft changed the name of the client to Windows NT Messaging (from Exchange) to differentiate between the "light" client and the full-featured client supported by the Microsoft Exchange Server product.

This chapter helps you install and configure Messaging to enable you to send and receive e-mail and faxes, both locally on your network and through your modem to remote sites and services.

In this chapter, you learn to

- Install Messaging

- Configure Messaging and service providers

- Create and edit a Messaging profile

- Set up your personal message store and address books

- Add other e-mail and fax services to Messaging

- Set up Messaging for remote mail access

- Customize Messaging

Installing the Messaging Client

Microsoft Messaging is a typical Windows NT application (see fig. 10.1) that works in conjunction with various *service providers* to enable you to send and receive e-mail and faxes. You can think of a service provider as an add-on module that enables the Messaging client to work with specific types of mail and online services. For example, Windows NT includes service providers that enable it to work with Microsoft Mail and the Internet.

Fig. 10.1

Messaging provides a unified inbox for all of your e-mail.

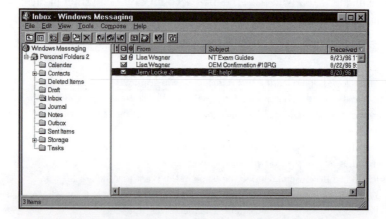

Installing and configuring Messaging consists of four phases, which are described in the following list:

- *Install Messaging.* You can install Messaging when you install Windows NT, or you can easily add Messaging to your PC at any time after you install Windows NT.

- *Create at least one profile.* Your Messaging settings and service providers are stored in a Messaging *profile.* Each profile can contain one or more service providers to support different e-mail and fax systems. A profile is a collection of settings you can use to specify which service providers and settings you want to use with Messaging.

- *Add a personal information store and address book.* You need somewhere to store your messages, so the third phase in configuring Messaging is to add a personal information store to your profile, along with an address book to store e-mail and fax addresses. With Windows NT Messaging, the personal information store is referred to as your personal folder.

- *Add service providers.* The final phase of installing Messaging is to add the service providers you want to use to your profile. These could include Microsoft Mail, CompuServe Mail, and Internet Mail.

Note

The CompuServe Mail provider for Windows NT Messaging (called CompuServe Mail for Microsoft Exchange) was designed to work with the Windows 95 version of Messaging. It is included on the Windows 95 CD, but is not included with Windows NT. You can retrieve an updated version of the CompuServe Mail provider from CompuServe (**GO CSMAIL**). This updated version adds features not included with the original release (such as connection to CompuServe through the Internet) and works with Windows NT Messaging.

You can even get a cc:mail service for Messaging from Transend Corporation at:

On the Web

http://www.transendcorp.com/n

Setup doesn't automatically install Messaging when you install Windows NT. Instead, you must specifically select Messaging as an option to install when you run Setup. Or you can add Messaging after installing Windows NT. The following sections explain how to install the Microsoft Messaging client software. Later sections explain how to create and modify Messaging profiles, add service providers, and set other Messaging options.

Installing Messaging During Windows NT Installation

If you have not yet installed Windows NT, you can install Messaging at the same time you install Windows NT. To install Messaging, use the following steps:

1. Start the Windows NT Setup program as explained in Chapter 4, "Installing Windows NT."

2. Proceed through the installation until the Setup Options dialog box appears (see fig. 10.2) and prompts you to select the type of installation you want. Choose Custom; then choose Next. (The Typical, Portable, and Compact selections will not install Messaging.)

Fig. 10.2
Select the Custom option to install Messaging with the rest of the Windows NT components.

3. When the Select Components dialog box appears, mark the Microsoft Messaging checkbox, then click the Details button.

4. When the Microsoft Messaging property page appears, select the service provider(s) you want to use with Messaging (see fig. 10.3). When you've made your selections, choose Next.

Fig. 10.3
Choose one or more service providers from the Get Connected dialog box.

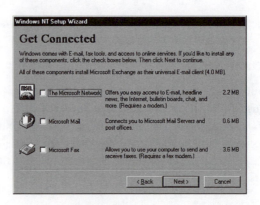

> **Note**
>
> If you forget to add a service provider when you install Windows NT or add Messaging to your system, you can add the service provider later.

   5. Follow Setup's remaining prompts to complete the installation process.

After Setup completes the installation process and you start Windows NT, you see an Inbox icon on the desktop. This is the object you will later use to start Messaging. Before using Messaging, however, you need to complete the configuration process. Skip to the section "Creating and Editing User Profiles" later in this chapter to learn how to complete the configuration process for Messaging.

> **Troubleshooting**
>
> *When Messaging starts, I receive error messages that my Internet Mail server is not available. I don't have an Internet Mail server and don't use Internet Mail. What's wrong?*
>
> You probably have installed the Internet Mail service provider by mistake. Open Control Panel and choose the Mail and Fax icon. From the list of installed services, choose Internet Mail; then choose Remove. Windows NT prompts you to verify that you want to remove the Internet Mail service provider from your profile. Choose Yes to remove the service from your profile.

Adding Messaging After Installing Windows NT

If you didn't install Messaging when you installed Windows NT, don't worry—it's easy to add. Use the following steps to add Messaging after installing Windows NT:

   1. Choose Start, Settings, Control Panel to open the Control Panel.

   2. Double-click the Add/Remove Programs icon to open the Add/Remove Programs Properties sheet.

   3. Click the Windows NT Setup tab, and the Windows NT Setup page appears.

4. Scroll through the Components list to locate and select Microsoft Messaging; then choose Details.

5. In the Microsoft Messaging dialog box, place a checkmark beside Microsoft Messaging, then place a checkmark beside each of the service providers you want to use, and choose OK.

6. Choose OK again. Windows NT adds the necessary software to your system.

> **Note**
>
> If you will be using Messaging for local e-mail (on the LAN, for example) with the Microsoft Mail provider, you must first create a postoffice on a computer that will act as your mail server. For steps and tips on setting up a postoffice, see the section, "Setting Up a Workgroup Postoffice," later in this chapter. You should have the postoffice in place before you begin configuring your profile(s). If you are using only the Internet Mail or CompuServe Mail providers, you don't need a workgroup postoffice.

Creating and Editing User Profiles

Besides installing Messaging, you need to configure at least one user profile. The following section explains user profiles to help you understand how to create and edit them.

Understanding Profiles

A collection of information stores, address books, and service providers is called a *user profile*. For example, you might use a profile that contains your personal information store, one address book, a Microsoft Mail service provider, and a CompuServe service provider. In addition to giving you a means of grouping the service providers and information store you use most often into a named group, Messaging profiles also store the settings for each item in the profile. Figure 10.4 shows items in a typical Messaging profile.

If you're like most people, you will use a single profile. But you can use multiple profiles. For example, if you use CompuServe Mail very seldom, but use Microsoft Mail all the time, you might want to place the CompuServe Mail provider in a separate profile. When you have to use CompuServe Mail, you can make the CompuServe Mail profile active (explained in the next section); then start Messaging to use it.

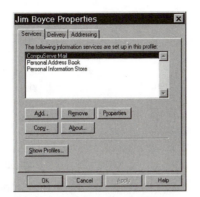

Fig. 10.4
A Messaging profile stores your Messaging settings by name.

Tip

Information stores and address books are service providers, just like Microsoft Mail, CompuServe, and other service providers. All these service providers are often referred to as just *services*. A personal information store is really just a set of special Messaging folders in which you store your messages, and is something you must add to your default profile—Messaging doesn't create an information store for you automatically.

Configuring Profiles

As with most configuration tasks in Windows NT, you create and edit user profiles from the Control Panel. When you install Messaging, Windows NT does not create a default profile for you. So, you must create your own profile after installing Messaging. To create a default profile, open the Control Panel; then double-click the Mail icon to display the Mail properties sheet similar to the one shown in figure 10.5.

Fig. 10.5
Use the Mail property sheet to create and modify Messaging profiles.

From the Mail property sheet, you can add services to a profile, delete services, set properties for services, and create and view other profiles. You also can set the properties of services in a profile. If you are using the CompuServe Mail provider, for example, you can specify your CompuServe user ID, password, and other properties that control how and when the CompuServe provider logs on to CompuServe to send and receive your CompuServe mail.

Each service is different, so the properties that you can set for each service varies. Later sections, "Setting Up Personal Folders," "Setting Up Address Books," and "Adding Other Information Stores," explain how to add services and set their properties. The following section explains how to create and delete profiles.

Creating and Deleting Messaging Profiles

As explained earlier, you must create a default profile, or you might want to use more than one Messaging profile to store different sets of properties and services. You can create a profile in one of two ways—create a completely new profile or copy an existing profile. Regardless of which method you use, you can edit the profile to add, remove, or edit services after you create the profile.

You can easily create a Messaging profile from scratch or copy an existing profile. Windows NT provides a wizard to step you through the process of creating a profile. Use the following steps to create a new Messaging profile:

1. Open the Control Panel and double-click the Mail icon to display the Mail property sheet.

2. If one or more profiles already exist, click the Show Profiles button to display the Microsoft Messaging Profiles property sheet.

3. Click the Add button, and the Inbox Setup Wizard appears.

4. Click the Use the Following Information Services option button.

5. Place a checkmark beside each of the services you want to include in your profile. Deselect any services you don't want included in the profile; then choose Next. If other profiles have already been created, the wizard displays a new dialog box prompting you for a name for your new profile.

6. Enter a unique name for your profile; then choose Next.

7. Depending on which services you selected, the wizard prompts you for information to configure the services. Refer to the sections later in this chapter that describe setup options for services to help you configure the services.

8. When you have finished configuring the services, the wizard displays a final dialog box showing the name for your new profile. If this is the first profile you've created, the wizard provides a name automatically. Choose Finish to complete the profile creation process.

To copy an existing profile, follow these steps:

1. Open the Control Panel and double-click the Mail icon to display the default profile property sheet.

2. Click the Show Profiles button to display the Mail property sheet shown in figure 10.6.

Fig. 10.6
With the Mail property page, you can create a new profile or copy an existing profile.

3. Select the profile you want to copy; then click Copy. A dialog box prompting you to enter a name for your new profile appears (see fig. 10.7).

4. In the New Profile Name text box, enter a unique name for your new Messaging profile; then choose OK. Windows NT then copies all the services and settings in the selected profile to your new profile.

IV

Communications

Fig. 10.7
Enter a unique
name for your new
profile.

5. Use the steps explained in the following sections of this chapter to configure the services in your new profile.

> **Tip**
>
> After you create a profile, you need to specify it as your default profile before you can use it with Messaging. See the section "Setting Your Default Profile" later in the chapter to learn how to begin using your new profile.

Setting Your Default Profile

Although you can create as many Messaging profiles as you want, you can only use one profile at a time. You have two options for specifying which profile Messaging uses. Each time you want to use a different profile, you must exit Messaging, use the Control Panel to specify which profile to use, and then restart Messaging. Or you can configure Messaging to prompt you to specify which profile to use each time Messaging starts.

To specify a default profile, follow these steps:

1. Open the Control Panel and double-click the Mail icon.
2. Click the Show Profiles button.
3. From the drop-down list labeled When Starting Microsoft Messaging, Use This Profile, choose the profile you want Messaging to use as a default.
4. Choose Close; then start Messaging to verify that it is using the correct profile.

To have Messaging prompt you to select a profile each time Messaging starts, follow these steps:

1. Start Messaging (double-click the Inbox icon on the desktop).
2. Choose Tools, Options to display the Options property sheet.

3. From the control group named When Starting Microsoft Messaging, choose the option labeled <u>P</u>rompt for a Profile to be Used. Then choose OK. The next time you start Messaging, you'll be prompted to select which profile you want to use.

To learn about other general Messaging options you can specify, see the section "Setting General Messaging Options" later in this chapter.

Setting Up Personal Folders

Without a place to store all your messages, Messaging wouldn't be much use to you. So each profile should include at least one *information store*. An information store is a special type of file that Messaging uses to store your messages, and Windows NT refers to a message store as Personal Folders. Whether the message is a fax, an e-mail message from your network mail post office, or other service, incoming messages are placed in the Inbox folder of your default information store. A typical information store contains the following folders:

- *Deleted Items*. This folder contains all the messages you have deleted from other folders. By default, Messaging does not delete items from your information store unless you select them in the Deleted Items folder and delete them. As explained later in the section "Setting General Messaging Options," you can configure Messaging to immediately delete a message instead of moving it to the Deleted Items folder.

- *Inbox*. Messaging places all your incoming messages—including error and status messages generated by the various service providers, e-mail, and faxes—in the Inbox.

- *Outbox*. Items that you compose are placed in the Outbox until the appropriate service delivers the message automatically or you manually direct Messaging to deliver the message(s).

- *Sent Items*. By default, Messaging places in the Sent Items folder a copy of all messages you send. You can configure Messaging not to keep a copy of sent messages (see the section "Setting General Messaging Options" later in this chapter).

In addition to the folders listed previously, you can add your own folders to an information store. And you're not limited to a single information store—you can add as many information stores to a profile as you like. The folders in each information store show up under a separate tree in the Messaging window. Figure 10.8 shows Messaging with two information stores being used.

Fig. 10.8

You can use as many information stores in a profile as you like.

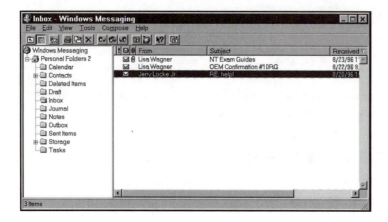

Adding multiple message stores to a profile is useful mainly for copying messages between message files. If you are using the latest version of the Microsoft Mail service provider that supports shared folders, however, you can add a shared folder message store to your profile. The shared folder enables you to share messages with other users.

There is one other reason to add a set of personal folders to your profile: you can't change the encryption method on an existing Personal Folders Store, but you can specify the type of encryption to use on a secondary set of personal folders when you add the folders to a profile. The two stores are identical in function, so if you want to use a different level of encryption for your message file for extra security, add a Personal Folders item to your profile, copy your messages from the original Personal Folders to the new one, and then remove the original Personal Folders from your profile. Make sure that you configure Messaging to use the new personal folders to store incoming messages, as explained in the next section.

Configuring Your Personal Folders

You can change a handful of settings for Personal Folders. To change properties for a Personal Information Store, use the following steps:

1. Open the Control Panel and double-click the Mail icon.

2. If you want to set properties for Personal Folders in a profile other than the default profile, choose the Show Profiles button, select the profile you want to change; then choose Properties.

IV

Communications

3. Select Personal Folders from the list of services in the profile; then choose Properties. The Personal Folders property sheet shown in figure 10.9 appears.

Fig. 10.9

Use the Personal Folders Property sheet to set properties for the information store.

4. Set the properties for the Personal Folders according to the following descriptions and your needs:

- *Name.* If you like, enter a new name for the Personal Information Store. This name will appear in the profile instead of "Personal Folders."

- *Change Password.* Click this button to change the password for your Personal Information Store. The four properties you can set in the password dialog box are described in table 10.1.

Table 10.1 Password Properties for an Information Store

Property	Purpose
Old Password	Enter in this text box the current password, if any, for the Personal Information Store.
New Password	Enter in this text box the new password you want to assign to the Personal Information Store.
Verify Password	Enter in this text box the new password you want to assign to the Personal Information Store to enable Windows NT to verify that you have entered the password correctly.
Save this Password In Your Password List	If you want the password stored in your password cache so you don't have to enter the password each time you open Messaging, place a checkmark in this checkbox.

- *Compact Now.* Choose this button to compress (compact) your Personal Information Store. Windows NT compresses the file, reducing its size. Compressing a message store has no effect on your ability to use the file to store messages.

- *Comment.* If you want to add a short comment about the Personal Folders, enter it in this text box.

After you have specified all the necessary properties, choose OK; then choose OK again to save the changes.

Adding Other Information Stores

As explained earlier, you can add as many information stores to a profile as you like. These additional stores are also called Personal Folders, and they have the same structure and function as your default Personal Folders. You can add a new Personal Folders file to a profile or add an existing file. Adding an existing file enables you to easily import messages from other information stores that you or others have created separately.

To add an information store to a profile, use the following steps:

1. Open the Control Panel and double-click the Mail icon.

2. If you want to add Personal Folders to a profile other than the default profile, choose the Show Profiles button, select the profile you want to change, and then choose Properties.

3. Choose Add; then from the Add Service to Profile dialog box, select Personal Folders and choose OK.

4. The Create/Open Personal Folders File dialog box appears. If you are adding an existing file, locate and select the file in the dialog box; then choose Open. If you want to create a new file, enter a name for the file in the File name text box, and then choose Open.

5. If you are adding an existing Personal Folders file, skip to step 6. If you are creating a new file, Windows NT displays a dialog box similar to the one shown in figure 10.10. The Name and Password properties are the same as those explained in the preceding section. From the Encryption Setting group, choose one of the following options:

   - *No Encryption.* Choose this option if you don't want the file to be encrypted. If the file is not encrypted, other users can open the file and read its contents with another program, such as a word processor.

- *Compressible Encryption.* Choose this option if you want the file to be encrypted for security, but you also want to be able to compress (compact) the file to save disk space.

- *Best Encryption.* Choose this option if you want the most secure encryption. You will not be able to compress the file if you choose this option.

Fig. 10.10

The Create Microsoft Personal Folders dialog box enables you to set various properties for your information store.

6. If you are adding an existing Personal Folders file, adjust settings as explained previously.

7. Choose OK; then choose OK again to close the profile's property sheet.

Setting Delivery Options

Even though you can add multiple information stores to a profile, only one can be assigned to receive incoming messages. You can, however, assign an alternate information store to be used to store incoming messages if the primary store is unavailable for some reason.

To set these delivery options, follow these steps:

1. Open the Control Panel and double-click the Mail icon.

2. Click the Delivery tab to display the Delivery property page (see fig. 10.11).

3. Specify settings in the Delivery property page based on the following descriptions:

- *Deliver New Mail to the Following Location.* Select from the drop-down list the information store in which you want incoming mail to be placed.

Fig. 10.11
Specify which
store will receive
incoming mes-
sages.

- *Recipient Addresses are Processed by these Information Services in the Following Order.* This control lists the order in which mail providers distribute mail when you direct Messaging to deliver mail using all services. To move an item in the list, select it; then click either the up or the down arrow.

4. After specifying the desired settings, choose OK to save the changes.

Setting Up Address Books

Although you can send and receive mail without an address book, adding an address book to your profile makes it possible for you to store addresses and quickly select an address for a message. You can add addresses to the address book yourself, or let Messaging add originating addresses of received mail.

A profile can contain only one Personal Address Book. When you install Messaging, Windows NT automatically adds a Personal Address Book to your default profile. You can add a new, blank address book, or add an existing address book that already contains address entries.

If you want to add a Personal Address Book to a new profile or you have accidentally deleted your Personal Address Book from your default profile, follow these steps to add the address book:

1. Open the Control Panel and double-click the Mail icon.

2. If you want to add a Personal Address Book to a profile other than the default profile, choose the Show Profiles button, select the profile you want to change, and then choose Properties.

3. Choose the Add button; then from the Add Service to Profile dialog box, choose Personal Address Book and click OK. The Personal Address Book property sheet shown in figure 10.12 appears.

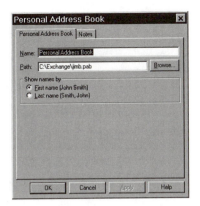

Fig. 10.12
Set properties for
your Personal
Address Book.

4. In the <u>N</u>ame text box, enter a name for the address book (or leave the name as-is, if you prefer).

5. In the <u>P</u>ath text box, enter the path and file name for the new address book file, or in the case of an existing address book, enter the path and file name of the existing file. If you prefer, you can choose the <u>B</u>rowse button to browse for the file.

6. From the control group Show Names By, choose how you want names to appear in the address book (sorted by first name or last name).

7. Choose OK; then choose OK again to save the changes.

Setting Addressing Options

Although you can have only one Personal Address Book in a profile, you can add other types of address books. For example, a CompuServe Address Book is included in the CompuServe Mail provider. Other service providers that you add might also include their own address books. For this reason, you need a way to specify which address book Messaging displays by default and other addressing options.

To set addressing options, open the Control Panel and double-click the Mail icon. Then click the Addressing tab to display the Addressing property page shown in figure 10.13.

The properties you can specify on the Addressing page are described in the following list:

■ *Show this Address List First.* Select from this drop-down list the address book you want Messaging to display when you click the <u>T</u>o button in the compose window, or choose <u>T</u>ools, <u>A</u>ddress Book. You'll have the option in Messaging of selecting a different address book if more than one is installed.

Fig. 10.13
Use the Addressing
page to specify
your default
address book.

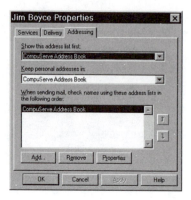

- *Keep Personal Addresses In.* Select from this drop-down list the address book in which you want a new address to be added unless you specifically choose a different address book.

- *When Sending Mail, Check Names Using these Address Lists in the Following Order.* Use this list to set the order in which Messaging checks addresses for validity when you send a message or click the Check Names button in the compose window toolbar.

After you specify the Addressing properties you want to use, choose OK to save the changes.

Troubleshooting

I'm trying to add a second Personal Address List, but Messaging displays an error that the service can't be added twice to the profile.

Only one copy of the Personal Address List service can be present in a profile. If you want to add a secondary address list, you'll have to create a new profile to contain it, then switch between profiles when you want to switch address books.

Setting General Messaging Options

It might sometimes seem like Messaging offers an overwhelming number of properties and options that you can set. This section helps you understand and set those properties and options. If you've read through the earlier parts of this chapter, you've already set some general Messaging options, including delivery and addressing options. The following sections explain the other options you can set. To reach the property pages referenced in the following sections, open Messaging; then choose Tools, Options.

Setting General Options

The General property page specifies a handful of properties that control how Messaging alerts you to new incoming messages and other common actions, such as deleting messages (see fig. 10.14).

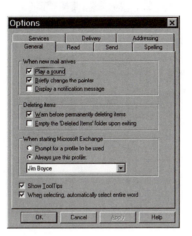

Fig. 10.14
Use the General property page to set general Messaging options.

The following list explains the properties you can set on the General property page:

- *When New Mail Arrives*. This group contains three options you can enable to control how Messaging notifies you of incoming messages.

- *Deleting Items*. Enable the option Warn Before Permanently Deleting Items if you want Messaging to warn you before you permanently delete a message (rather than deleting it to the Deleted Items folder). Enable the option named Empty the 'Deleted Items' Folder Upon Exiting if you want Messaging to permanently delete messages from the Deleted Items folder when you exit Messaging.

- *When Starting Microsoft Messaging*. Use the options in this group to either specify a default Messaging profile or cause Messaging to prompt you to select a profile each time Messaging starts.

- *Show ToolTips on Toolbars*. Enable this option if you want Messaging to display a ToolTip for a toolbar button when you rest the pointer on the button for a second.

- *When Selecting, Automatically Select Entire Word*. Enable this option if you want Messaging to automatically select entire words when you drag over the words with the pointer.

Setting Read Options

The properties on the Read property page control the way Messaging handles messages when you read, reply to, or forward the messages (see fig. 10.15).

Fig. 10.15

Set options for reading messages using the Read property page.

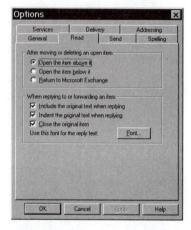

The properties you can set with the Read property page are explained in the following list:

- *After Moving or Deleting an Open Item.* The three options in this group control Messaging's actions when you read, move, or delete a message. The options are self-explanatory—select whichever option suits your preferences.

- *When Replying to or Forwarding an Item.* These properties control how Messaging handles messages when you reply to or forward a message. Enable the option labeled Include the Original Text when Replying if you want Messaging to include the text of the original message in your reply. If you want the original message text to be indented in the message, with your new text at the left margin, enable the checkbox labeled Indent the original text when replying. Enable the option labeled Close the Original Item if you want Messaging to automatically close the original e-mail message window after you start your reply. Choose the Font button to specify the font used for your reply text.

> **Tip**
>
> If you indent original message text or use a special font in a reply or a forwarded message, the recipient sees those message characteristics only if he or she is using Messaging and a service provider capable of sending and receiving messages in RTF (Rich Text Format). An example of such providers is the Microsoft Mail service provider.

Setting Send Options

You also can specify a few properties that control the way Messaging handles items you are sending. Click the Send tab to display the Send property page as shown in figure 10.16.

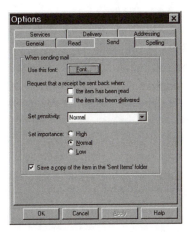

Fig. 10.16

Control outgoing message options with the Send property page.

You can click the Font button to choose the font Messaging will use by default for your outgoing messages. As with indented text, the recipient must also be using Messaging and a service provider that supports message transfer in RTF.

The two options in the group labeled Request That a Receipt Be Sent Back When control whether you will receive a return receipt from the recipient's mail system. The available options are as follows:

■ *The Item Has Been Read.* If you choose this option, you receive a return receipt only after the recipient reads the message, which could happen well after he receives the message.

■ *The Item Has Been Delivered*. Choose this option to receive a return receipt as soon as the message is delivered, regardless of whether the message has been read.

The Set Sensitivity and Set Importance options are self-explanatory. Choose the options you want to use by default. Note that you can override either of these settings when you create a message.

If you enable the option labeled Save a Copy of the Item in the Sent Items Folder, Messaging automatically places a copy of your outgoing message in the Sent Items folder. This is helpful if you need to review a message you previously sent. Just remember to periodically clean out the Sent Items folder to avoid having a huge message file filled with old messages.

Working with Microsoft Mail

If you are using Windows NT on a Microsoft-based network (Windows NT, Windows for Workgroups, or Windows 95), it's a good bet that you want to use the Microsoft Mail service provider—all of these Microsoft operating environments include a workgroup version of Microsoft Mail. Or, you might want to connect through Dial-Up Networking to a remote site, such as your district office, that uses Microsoft Mail. In either case, you need to create and configure a workgroup postoffice (WGPO) if your network does not yet include one. The following sections will help you do just that.

> **Tip**
>
> A *workgroup postoffice* is a special set of directories that Microsoft Mail clients and Microsoft Mail Messaging clients can use to send and receive e-mail. Before you can begin sending and receiving mail on your LAN using the Microsoft Mail provider, you must have a WGPO on your LAN. Fortunately, Windows NT makes it easy to create and manage a WGPO, as you will learn in the next section.

Setting Up a Workgroup Postoffice

The Control Panel contains an object specifically for creating and managing a workgroup postoffice. Open the Control Panel and double-click the Microsoft Mail Postoffice icon. Windows NT starts a wizard as shown in figure 10.17. This wizard lets you either create a new WGPO or administer an existing WGPO.

Note

When you create a WGPO, you also create an administrator's account. The administrator is responsible for creating and managing user mail accounts. Before you begin creating the WGPO, decide who will be administering the postoffice. In the following steps, you'll create an administrator account. You should be ready to provide the name of the person who will be administering the postoffice.

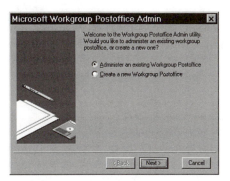

Fig. 10.17
You can create a new WGPO or administer an existing one.

To set up a new WGPO, follow these steps:

1. Start the Microsoft Workgroup Postoffice Admin wizard by opening the Control Panel and double-clicking the Microsoft Mail Postoffice icon.

2. Choose the Create a new Workgroup Postoffice option, then choose Next. Windows NT then prompts you for the name and location for your new postoffice (see fig. 10.18). Enter the name or choose Browse to browse for a folder for the WGPO.

Fig. 10.18
Enter the path and file name for your new postoffice.

Note

You must choose an existing folder in which to create the WGPO. The wizard will not create a folder for you, but instead creates the WGPO folder structure in the existing folder that you choose.

---

3. After you click Next, the wizard prompts you to verify the path and file name you entered. Choose Next if the path and file name are correct, or choose Back to change the path or file name. After you click Next, the wizard displays the Enter Your Administrator Account Details dialog box shown in figure 10.19.

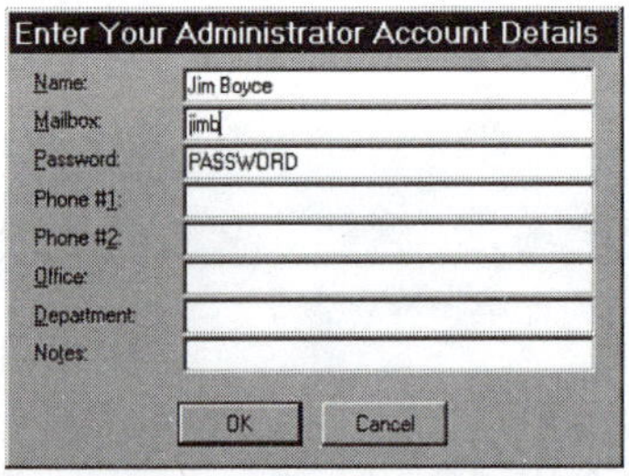

Fig. 10.19
You must specify details for an administrator account for your WGPO.

4. Fill out the fields in the account dialog box. You must provide entries for the following three items:

- *Name*. In this field, enter the first and last name of the person who will be administering the postoffice.

Tip

If you don't want to specify a particular user's name, use *Postmaster* as the Name and Mailbox entries for the account. When you or anyone else needs to log into the postoffice to administer it, simply log in using the Postmaster account.

- *Mailbox*. Enter in this field the name of the mailbox for the administrator's account. Windows NT suggests your Windows NT network name, but you should consider creating a general Post master account.

- *Password.* Although you can leave the password blank, it's a bad idea to leave your WGPO administrator's account unprotected. Windows NT uses PASSWORD as the default account password. You should enter a different password that others won't be able to guess.

> **Caution**
>
> Make sure you don't forget the account password. If you do, you won't be able to administer the WGPO without re-creating the entire WGPO (and losing all messages contained in it).

The remaining options in the account dialog box are optional and self-explanatory. They enable a system administrator to fine-tune individual user accounts and provide background information to others of your office information, such as a phone number. Choose OK after you have specified the information you want included with the account. The general information (not the password) will appear to other users when they browse the postoffice list of accounts.

Administering a Postoffice

After you create the administrator account, you can begin adding, removing, and modifying mail accounts for users. To administer mail accounts, follow these steps:

1. Open the Control Panel and double-click the Microsoft Mail Postoffice icon.

2. Choose Administer an existing Workgroup Postoffice, then choose Next.

3. Enter the path to your WGPO (or choose Browse to browse for the WGPO), then choose next.

4. Windows NT prompts you for the account name and password of the administrator's account. Enter the mailbox name and password, then choose Next. A Postoffice Manager dialog box similar to the one shown in figure 10.20 appears.

Fig. 10.20
The Postoffice Manager dialog box lets you manage user mail accounts.

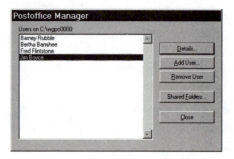

5. To view the account details for a user's account, select the account and choose the <u>D</u>etails button. A dialog box similar to the one shown in figure 10.21 appears. Modify any of the properties for the user, then choose OK.

Fig. 10.21
You can modify any mail account property, including the password.

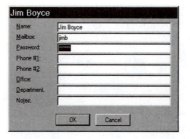

6. To add a user, click the <u>A</u>dd User button. Windows NT displays a dialog box nearly identical to the Details dialog box shown previously in figure 10.19. Enter the account details for the mail account, then choose OK.

7. To remove a user, select the user and choose <u>R</u>emove User. Windows NT will prompt you to verify that you want to remove the account. Choose <u>Y</u>es to delete the account, or choose <u>N</u>o to cancel the deletion.

8. When you are finished administering the WGPO, choose Close.

Changing Your Password

Your account in your Microsoft Mail WGPO is protected by a password to ensure that your messages are safe from snooping by others. To improve security, you should periodically change your mail account password. To do so, in Messaging choose <u>T</u>ools, Microsoft <u>M</u>ail Tools, and <u>C</u>hange Mailbox Password. Messaging displays a simple dialog box in which you enter your current password, then enter your new password in two separate boxes to confirm the new password. When you're satisfied with your new password, choose OK.

Using the Postoffice Address List

You probably will most often use a Personal Address Book (PAB) to store addresses. When you're working with Microsoft Mail, however, you have an additional address source available—the postoffice address list, which stores the addresses of all accounts in the WGPO. As new accounts are added and as accounts change, those changes are reflected in the postoffice address list. To make sure you have available the most current copy of the postoffice address list, you should periodically download the postoffice address list to your PC. To do so, choose Tools, Microsoft Mail Tools, and Download Address Lists. Messaging will connect to your WGPO and download the postoffice address list.

To work with addresses in the postoffice address list, begin composing a message. Click the To button to display the Address dialog box. Choose Postoffice Address List from the Show Names drop-down list. Messaging will display the postoffice address list, and you can choose addresses from it just as you do with other address sources, such as the PAB.

Using a Session Log

For the most part, Messaging should have no problems connecting to your e-mail account in the WGPO and sending and receiving your messages. If you run into problems, however, the Microsoft Mail provider offers a means for you to troubleshoot the problem—you can direct the Microsoft Mail provider to maintain a log of its connection sessions. You can view the log to identify connection or other problems.

To turn on logging, follow these steps:

1. In Messaging, choose Tools, Services. Or, open the Control Panel and double-click the Mail icon. Either of these two actions displays the property sheet for your message service(s).

2. Choose Microsoft Mail from the list of installed services, then click Properties.

3. When the Microsoft Mail property sheet appears, click the Log tab to display the Log property page (see fig. 10.22).

4. Place a check in the checkbox labeled Maintain a Log of Session Events.

5. If you want to specify a file other than the default (MSFSLOG.TXT) in which to store the file, enter the file name in the text box or click the Browse button to specify the file.

6. Choose OK to apply the change, then OK again to close the property sheet.

Fig. 10.22
Use the Log
property page to
turn on session
logging.

To view the log, simply locate it and double-click it. Windows NT will open
Notepad (or WordPad if the file is too large for Notepad) and display the file.

Setting Microsoft Mail Options

Like each Messaging service provider, the Microsoft Mail provider offers
many options that control how the provider sends and receives mail to
and from your WGPO. To set these options, use one of the following two
methods:

- From the Messaging window, choose Tools, Services.
- Open the Control Panel and double-click the Mail icon.

Either of these two methods displays the Services property page, although using the second method (through the Control Panel) displays the Delivery and
Addressing pages.

After the Services page appears, select Microsoft Mail from the information
services list, then click Properties to display the Microsoft Mail property sheet
shown in figure 10.23.

Fig. 10.23
The Microsoft Mail
provider's property
pages are similar to
those of other
service providers.

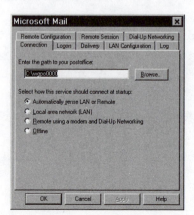

The following sections describe the settings found in each property page.

Connection

The following settings are found on the Connection page:

- *Enter the Path to Your Postoffice.* In this text box, enter the path to the shared directory containing your workgroup postoffice (WGPO). Or, click the Browse button to browse for the WGPO. If you are connecting to a WGPO on a remote system, you might map a local drive ID to the remote shared WGPO directory and specify the drive ID in this text box. Or, you can specify a UNC pathname to the postoffice.

- *Automatically Sense LAN or Remote.* Choose this option button if you want Messaging to automatically determine if you are connecting to the WGPO through a LAN or through a remote connection. If Microsoft Mail is unable to determine the type, it will prompt you to specify the connection.

▶ See "Configuring Messaging for Remote Mail," p. 452

- *Local Area Network (LAN).* Choose this option if you are connecting to the WGPO on your LAN.

- *Remote Using a Modem and Dial-Up Networking.* Choose this option if you are connecting to the WGPO through a Dial-Up Networking connection.

- *Offline.* Choose this option if you are not connecting to your WGPO, but instead want to work offline to compose and reply to messages. Incoming and outgoing mail will not be delivered until you reconnect to the WGPO. Outgoing mail will be stored in your Outbox, and incoming mail will remain in your WGPO mail box.

Logon

The following settings are found on the Logon page:

- *Enter the Name of Your Mailbox.* Enter the name of your WGPO mail account (mailbox) in this text box.

- *Enter Your Mailbox Password.* Enter your mailbox password in this text box. The password will appear as asterisks for security. If you prefer to enter your password each time you log on and not store your password on your system, leave this text box blank.

- *When Logging On, Automatically Enter Password.* Enable this checkbox if you want Microsoft Mail to automatically enter your password for logon when you start Messaging. Clear this checkbox if you want Microsoft Mail to prompt you for the password before logging on.

- *Change Mailbox Password.* Click this button to display a simple dialog box you can use to change your password. You must supply your old password in order to specify a new one. You should change your password periodically to ensure security.

Delivery

The following setttings are found on the Delivery page:

- *Enable Incoming Mail Delivery.* Enable this checkbox to allow messages to be delivered from your WGPO mailbox to your Messaging Inbox.

- *Enable Outgoing Mail Delivery.* Enable this checkbox to allow messages in your Inbox to be delivered to the WGPO.

- *Enable Deliver to…Address Types.* Click the Address Types button to specify address types to which you don't want messages delivered. A simple dialog box will appear that you can use to select the types of addresses to which you want messages to be delivered.

- *Check for New Mail Every nn Minutes.* Specify the frequency at which you want Microsoft Mail to check for new messages and send pending messages.

- *Immediate Notification.* Enable this checkbox if you want recipients of your messages to be notified when you send them messages. This option, when enabled, also causes you to receive notifications when others send you messages (if these other users have enabled this feature, also). This feature requires the use of a network protocol supporting NetBIOS.

- *Display Global Address List Only.* Enable this checkbox if you only want to work with the Global Address List (postoffice address list) and not your PAB.

LAN Configuration

The following settings are found on the LAN Configuration page:

- *Use Remote Mail.* Enable this checkbox if you want Microsoft Mail to retrieve message headers instead of messages, allowing you to preview your mail before retrieving it.

- *Use Local Copy.* Enable this checkbox to cause Microsoft Mail to use a local copy (stored on your computer) of the postoffice address list. To download the address list, choose Tools, Microsoft Mail Tools, and Download Address Lists.

- *Use External Delivery Agent.* Enable this checkbox if you want the EXTERNAL.EXE delivery agent to deliver your mail. EXTERNAL.EXE must be running on the server for you to make use of it.

Configuring the Internet Mail Provider

If you add the Internet Mail provider through the Control Panel, Windows NT automatically opens the property sheet shown in figure 10.24 as soon as you add the Internet Mail provider to a profile. You also can use this property sheet to configure the Internet Mail provider after you install it.

> **Note**
>
> Installing the latest version of Netscape installs the Netscape Internet Transport, a Windows Messaging service provider that performs essentially the same function as the Internet Mail provider included with Windows NT. If you already have Netscape installed, you shouldn't need the Microsoft Internet Mail service provider to send and retrieve Internet mail.

Setting Mail Properties

To set your Internet Mail properties, open the Control Panel and double-click the Mail icon. Select the Internet Mail provider, then choose Properties to display the General property page shown in figure 10.24.

Fig. 10.24
Use the General property page to set general Internet Mail properties.

The following list explains the settings on the General property page:

- *Full Name*. Type your first and last name as you want it to appear in the message headers.

- *E-mail Address*. Type your e-mail address in the form *user@domain*, where *user* is your e-mail account name and *domain* is the domain name of your Internet Mail server. Example: **jimb@nowhere.com**.

- *Internet Mail Server*. Type the domain name of your Internet mail server. Example: **nowhere.com**.

- *Account Name*. Type your e-mail account name (generally, the account you use to log on to the Internet server). Example: **jimb**.

- *Password*. Type the password for your Internet e-mail account.

- *Message Format*. Click this button to specify whether the Internet Mail service uses MIME encoding to send your e-mail messages and attachments.

- *Advanced Options*. Click this button to specify the name of a server to which you want all of your outbound mail forwarded. This is necessary if your default Internet Mail server doesn't process outbound mail.

Configuring the Connection

In addition to specifying mail properties, you also can specify how Internet Mail connects to the Internet. To do so, click the Connection tab of the Internet Mail property sheet to display the Connection page shown in figure 10.25.

Fig. 10.25
The Connection page determines how Internet Mail connects to the Internet.

The following list describes the properties on the Connection page:

- *Connect Using the Network*. Choose this option button if you connect to the Internet through your local area network.

- *Connect Using the Modem*. Choose this option button if you connect to the Internet using Dial-Up Networking.

■ *Dial Using the Following Connection.* If you selected the Connect using the <u>M</u>odem option, choose the correct Dial-Up Networking connection from this drop-down list. If you have not set up a Dial-Up Networking entry, click A<u>d</u>d Entry (explained next).

■ *A<u>d</u>d Entry.* Click this button to create a Dial-Up Networking connection to your Internet service provider. Refer to the *Windows NT Communications Handbook* (Que) for help creating the connection.

■ *Edit Entry.* Click this button to edit the selected Dial-Up Networking connection properties.

■ *<u>L</u>ogin As.* Click this button to display the dialog box shown in figure 10.26. Specify the user name and password required to log on to the remote Internet server.

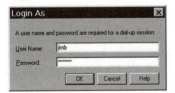

Fig. 10.26
Specify the log in name and password required by your Internet server.

■ *Work <u>O</u>ff-line and Use Remote Mail.* Enable this checkbox if you want to use remote mail and not send and receive Internet mail automatically.

■ *Schedule.* Click this button to display the dialog box shown in figure 10.27, which enables you to specify how often Messaging should check for new messages.

Fig. 10.27
Specify how often Messaging should check for new mail and send waiting mail.

■ *Log <u>F</u>ile.* Click this button if you want the Internet Mail provider to maintain a log of your Internet connection sessions. The Log File dialog box appears, enabling you to select the logging method and location of the log file.

IV

Communications

> ## Troubleshooting
>
> *Occasionally, a message comes through that Internet Mail can't decode properly and I end up with a lot of gibberish in the message.*
>
> It's really not gibberish—that's what a coded file looks like. In these situations you often can save the message and use an external coding program to convert the message to a binary file. To acquire a MIME encoder/decoder, connect via ftp to **ftp.andrew.cmu.edu:pub/mpack/**. You'll find versions of a MIME coder to suit most operating environments, including DOS. If you need more advanced MIME capability, check the site **ftp.thumper.bellcore.com:pub/nsb** for a program called MetaMail that provides advanced MIME coding.
>
> You also might need a program capable of UUEncoding and UUDecoding messages. One particularly good one is WinCode, which you can find in the WUGNET forum on CompuServe in Library 3.

On the Web

You also can find WinCode on the Internet at:

http://www.ccn.cs.dal.ca/Services/PDA/WindowsMisc.html

Installing and Configuring CompuServe Mail

You probably use a front-end application such as WinCIM, CompuServe Navigator, or GoCIS to send and receive mail on CompuServe. These programs all work well, but you might prefer to use Messaging for your CompuServe mail, bringing all your messages into Messaging's common Inbox.

The CompuServe Mail provider for Messaging enables you to do just that. With the CompuServe Mail provider, you can connect to CompuServe to send and receive messages through CompuServe's mail system. Although you can't send and retrieve forum messages through Messaging, at least you can handle your CompuServe mail. You can enjoy the advantages of remote mail preview, a common Inbox, automatic scheduled send/receive, and the other features supported by Messaging.

The CompuServe Mail provider is not included with Windows NT. You can download the CompuServe Mail provider from the CSMAIL and CISSOFT forums on CompuServe.

Installing CompuServe Mail

The CompuServe Mail provider includes its own Setup program to automate the installation process. To install the CompuServe Mail provider, follow these steps:

> **Note**
>
> This installation procedure assumes you are installing the CompuServe Mail provider from the Windows NT CD. If you have downloaded the CompuServe Mail provider from CompuServe, first create a folder to contain the CompuServe Mail files. Open a DOS session and change to that directory. Extract the CompuServe Mail files to the directory by running the compressed file. If you downloaded the file to \Wincim\ Download, for example, enter **\Wincim\Download\Csmail.exe**. If you renamed the file during the download, substitute the appropriate name in place of Csmail.exe. After extracting the files, proceed with step 3 (run the Setup program).

1. Create a folder to contain the CompuServe Mail for Microsoft Exchange source files.

2. Download the file CSMAIL.EXE from the CSMAIL or CISSOFT forums on CompuServe, placing the file in the folder created in step 1.

3. Run the CSMAIL.EXE file to extract its contents (it is a self-extracting archive).

4. Run the Setup program extracted from the CSMAIL.EXE archive. The Setup program will prompt you for a directory in which to store the CompuServe Mail files. The default is C:\Cserve.

The CompuServe Mail for Microsoft Exchange (version 1.1) was designed for Windows 95, but works with Windows NT. It does suffer, however, from one minor bug. You can't configure the location of your CompuServe files within the service provider's property sheet. Instead, you must manually edit the Registry to change the location. To do so, follow these steps:

1. Choose Start, Run, type **regedit** in the Open text box, then choose OK to start the Registry Editor.

2. In the Registry Editor, choose Edit, Find.

3. In the Find dialog box, type the string **001e661c** in the Find What text box, then click the Find Next button. Registry Editor should find the setting in HKEY_CURRENT_USER\Software\Microsoft\Windows NT\ Windows Messaging Subsystem\Profiles*your profile*, where *your profile* is the name of the Messaging profile containing the CompuServe Mail provider.

4. Double-click the 001e661c setting after Registry Editor locates it in the registry. This will open an Edit String dialog box you can use to change the setting's value.

5. In the Value data text box, type the path to your CompuServe directory, such as **C:\CSERVE**, then click OK.

6. Close the Registry Editor.

Configuring the CompuServe Mail Service

After you add the CompuServe Mail service to your Messaging profile, you need to configure various settings that define how Messaging connects to CompuServe and sends and receives your CompuServe mail. To configure your user account information in the CompuServe Mail service, follow these steps:

1. Open the Control Panel and double-click the Mail icon.

2. Select CompuServe Mail from the list of installed services, and then choose Properties.

3. In the Name text box on the General property page (see fig. 10.28), enter the name you want to appear in mail message address headers (not your CompuServe account name).

Fig. 10.28
Use the General page to specify your CompuServe account information.

4. In the CompuServe ID text box, enter your CompuServe account ID.

5. In the Password text box, enter your CompuServe account password.

In addition to configuring your account information, you also need to specify how the service will connect to CompuServe. To do so, use the Connection property page and the following steps:

1. Click the Connection tab to display the Connection property page (see fig. 10.29).

Fig. 10.29
Use the Connection page to specify how the connection to CompuServe is made.

IV

Communications

2. In the Phone Number text box, enter your CompuServe access number.

3. From the Preferred Tapi Line drop-down list, choose the modem you'll be using to connect to CompuServe.

4. From the Network drop-down list, choose the type of network connection provided by your CompuServe access number.

5. Choose the type of connection method you want to use from one of the following three options:

   - *Windows Modem Settings.* Choose this option to connect through one of CompuServe's access numbers using a modem (that you have already installed through the Modems object in the Control Panel).

   - *WinSock Connection.* Choose this option if you wish to connect to CompuServe through a WinSock Internet connection (such as through a Dial-Up Networking connection to your Internet service provider). Note that you must clear the Use CompuServe Dialer checkbox, because the CompuServe Dialer will not work properly under Windows NT.

   - *Direct Connection.* Choose this option if you have a direct connection to the Internet through one of your computer's serial ports.

At this point, you can choose OK, then OK again to begin using your CompuServe Mail service in Messaging. (Choosing the Apply button saves your current settings without exiting the property sheet.) You might, however, want to set a few advanced options. The Default Send Options page contains a selection of properties that define how messages are sent (see fig. 10.30).

Fig. 10.30
The Default Send
Options page
controls how
messages are sent.

The following list explains the properties on the Default Send Options page:

- *Send Using Microsoft Messaging Rich-Text Format.* Enable this checkbox if you want Messaging to include character (color, font, and so on) and paragraph formatting in your message. Only recipients who are using Microsoft Messaging will see the special formatting—other recipients will receive plain text.

- *Release Date.* If you enter a date in this field, messages will be held in your Inbox until the date specified, then forwarded on that date to the intended recipients. Leave this field blank if you want the messages to be sent as soon as the service connects to CompuServe.

- *Expiration Date.* If you enter a date in this field, the message will be deleted from the recipient's mail box when the date is reached.

- *Payment Method.* Select one of the three option buttons in this group to specify who pays for surcharged messages.

You can use the Advanced property page to schedule automatic connection to CompuServe and other advanced connection options (see fig. 10.31).

Fig. 10.31
Use the Advanced
page to control
advanced service
options.

The following list describes the controls on the Advanced page:

- *Create Event Log.* Enable this checkbox if you want the CompuServe Mail provider to place log messages describing the results of each connection attempt in your Inbox. These log messages are helpful for troubleshooting connection problems.

- *Delete Retrieved Messages.* Enable this checkbox if you want the CompuServe Mail provider to delete mail from your CompuServe mailbox after the mail is retrieved and stored in your Messaging Inbox.

- *Accept Surcharges.* Enable this checkbox if you are willing to pay for messages that carry a surcharge. Messages such as those from the Internet generally carry a nominal postage-due fee.

- *Change CompuServe Dir.* Click this button to change the folder in which the CompuServe Mail provider stores configuration and address book settings. If you are using another CompuServe product such as WinCIM, the CompuServe Mail provider can use the same address book and connection settings as your other CompuServe product.

- *Schedule Connect Times.* Click this button to display the Connection Times dialog box (see fig. 10.32) and schedule automatic connections to CompuServe. If you want, you can use a selection of different scheduled connection times.

Fig. 10.32
You can schedule the CompuServe Mail provider to connect automatically to CompuServe.

After you have specified all the settings and properties you want to change for the CompuServe Mail provider, choose OK, then OK again to save the changes. Restart Messaging to begin using the new settings.

Connecting on Time

Assume you configured the CompuServe Mail provider to check for messages at 8:00 AM and also every four hours, including times when you're away from your computer (like overnight). But, Messaging doesn't check at 8, 12, 4, and so on. It checks for mail at 8 AM, but the four-hour interval falls at odd times. You might be wondering why this happens.

continues

continued

The CompuServe Mail provider doesn't base its interval connection times on the explicit 8 AM setting you've specified. Instead, the provider checks at four hour intervals based on the last time it automatically checked for mail. Open Control Panel and choose the Mail icon. Select the CompuServe Mail provider and choose Properties. Choose the Advanced tab, then choose the Schedule Connect Times option to display the Connection Times dialog box. Clear the Every checkbox and close the dialog box, then close the Profile property sheets. Shortly before the time when you want one of your interval connections to be made, open the Control Panel, choose the Mail icon, then enable the Every checkbox in the Connection Times dialog box and specify the interval you want to use. Close the property sheets. Messaging should then connect close to the time you want.

Configuring Messaging for Remote Mail

Messaging's Remote Mail feature enables you to dial into your mail server to Messaging e-mail when you are working from home or out of town. It also enables you to preview your messages, downloading only those messages you feel are important. You can use Remote Mail with the Microsoft Mail, Internet Mail, and CompuServe Mail service providers. All of these service providers support Remote Mail through a dial-up connection, and the Internet Mail and Microsoft Mail providers also support Remote Mail through a LAN connection.

The Microsoft Mail and Internet Mail service providers rely on Windows NT's Dial-Up Networking to provide a connection to a remote mail server. If you have not yet configured Dial-Up Networking on your computer, see Chapter 12, "Using Remote Access Service and Dial-Up Networking," to set up remote access on your system.

The following sections will help you configure each service for Remote Mail.

Setting Up Microsoft Mail for Remote Mail

After you install the Microsoft Mail service provider, you can configure it for either LAN access or remote access. Microsoft Mail supports Remote Mail for message preview for both types of connections. In most cases, however, it isn't necessary to preview messages when connecting to the postoffice over a LAN because the connection is much faster than a remote connection. Nevertheless, the option is still available to you.

To configure Microsoft Mail for a remote connection, follow these steps:

1. First create a Dial-Up Networking connection to your LAN's dial-in server using the Dial-Up Networking icon in My Computer.

2. Open the Control Panel and double-click the Mail icon.

3. Select the Microsoft Mail service, then choose Properties to display the Connection property page shown in figure 10.33.

Fig. 10.33

Use the Connection page to configure Microsoft Mail for a remote connection.

4. Choose the option labeled Remote Using a Modem and Dial-Up Networking.

5. Click the Dial-Up Networking tab to display the Dial-Up Networking property page (see fig. 10.34).

Fig. 10.34

Use the Dial-Up Networking page to specify which connection to use for remote mail.

6. From the drop-down list, choose the Dial-Up Networking connection you want to use for the remote mail connection (the one that points to your Microsoft Mail server). You'll only see connections you have previously created.

7. In the Retry text box, enter the number of times you want the connection to be attempted if the initial attempt fails, then use the Times at Text box to specify the frequency of connection attempts.

8. Choose one of the three confirmation option buttons to specify whether Windows NT will confirm that the Dial-Up Networking connection is working before starting the remote Microsoft Mail session. Configuring Remote Mail not to confirm the connection can save a little connection time. The Confirm on first session and after errors option is the default.

9. Click the Remote Session tab to display the Remote Session page (see fig. 10.35).

Fig. 10.35
Use the Remote Session page to control when the Dial-Up Networking session is started.

10. If you want the Dial-Up Networking session to start as soon as you start Messaging, enable the checkbox labeled When This Service is Started. If you don't want the Dial-Up Networking session to start until you direct Messaging to send and retrieve your mail, leave this checkbox cleared.

11. Specify when you want the Dial-Up Networking session to be terminated using any combination of the following checkboxes (if you leave all checkboxes blank, the Dial-Up Networking connection won't terminate automatically):

- *After Retrieving Mail Headers.* Enable this checkbox if you want the Dial-Up Networking session to disconnect after Microsoft Mail retrieves your message headers.

- *After Sending and Receiving Mail.* Enable this checkbox if you want the Dial-Up Networking session to disconnect after Microsoft Mail sends and receives pending mail.

- *When You Exit.* Enable this checkbox if you want the Dial-Up Networking connection to disconnect when you exit Microsoft Messaging.

12. Choose OK, then OK again to save your configuration changes. Or, choose Apply to apply the changes without closing the property sheet.

If you want to use Remote Mail to preview messages when connecting to a WGPO on your LAN, follow these steps:

1. Open the Control Panel and double-click the Mail icon.

2. Select the Microsoft Mail service, then choose Properties to display the Connection page of the Microsoft Mail property sheet.

3. Select the Local Area Network (LAN) option button or the Automatically Sense LAN or remote option button.

4. Click the LAN Configuration tab to display the LAN Configuration page shown in figure 10.36.

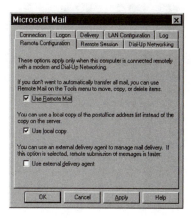

Fig. 10.36
Enable
Remote Mail
for a LAN
connection
through the
LAN Configu-
ration page.

5. Place a check in the checkbox labeled Use Remote Mail to enable Remote Mail.

Tip

Place a check in the Use local copy checkbox if you want to use a local copy of the post office address instead of checking addresses on the WGPO. When you're using Remote Mail through a Dial-Up Networking connection, you generally should check this box to enable Microsoft Mail to check addresses without connecting to the mail server. The Use external delivery agent checkbox controls whether or not Microsoft Mail uses the EXTERNAL.EXE program running on the server to expedite delivery. This checkbox does not apply specifically to Remote Mail.

6. Choose OK, then OK again to close the property sheets.

In the section "Working With Remote Mail" you learn how to preview messages, upload mail, and use other Remote Mail features. First, though, you need to decide how often Remote Mail will connect to your WGPO.

Setting Schedules

Although you can use Microsoft Mail interactively to check your mail, you also can configure the Microsoft Mail service to automatically connect at scheduled times to send and receive pending mail. This feature works with Remote Mail only if you're connecting to your WGPO over a Dial-Up Networking connection.

Tip

If your WGPO is located on the LAN, you can use Remote Mail to preview messages and control other message transfer options. But, you can't have Remote Mail automatically connect to the WGPO to update headers and perform other Remote Mail actions. Microsoft Mail's Remote Session property page, which enables you to specify a connection schedule (using the Schedule Mail Delivery button), only applies if you are connecting to the WGPO through a Dial-Up Networking connection. The Check for New Mail Every xx Minutes control on the Delivery page controls how often Microsoft Mail checks your WGPO for mail, but is ignored by Remote Mail.

To configure scheduled connection times for a Dial-Up Networking connection to your WGPO, follow these steps:

1. Open the Control Panel and double-click the Mail icon.

2. Select the Microsoft Mail item; then choose Properties.

3. Click the Remote Session tab, and then choose the Schedule Mail Delivery button to display the Remote Scheduled Sessions dialog box shown in figure 10.37.

Fig. 10.37
You can schedule
Microsoft Mail to
connect automati-
cally to check your
mail.

4. Click Add, then use the Add Scheduled Session dialog box to specify the
time at which you want Microsoft Mail to connect automatically. You
can schedule connections at period intervals, weekly on the same day
and time, or once only at a specific date and time. Choose OK after you
specify the desired connect time.

> **Note**
>
> Fixed-interval connections (such as every four hours) are not executed based
> on a specific time such as 8AM, 12PM, 4PM, and so on. The connection times
> are based on the last connection's completion time plus the specified fixed
> time interval.

5. Repeat step 4 to add as many other connect times as you like. Then,
continue to choose OK until you have closed the Messaging property
sheet and saved your new settings.

Setting Up CompuServe Mail for Remote Mail

If you prefer to preview your CompuServe mail before downloading it, you
can use Remote Mail. This is particularly useful if you routinely receive numerous messages or mail containing large binary attachments. When you install the CompuServe Mail provider, Remote Mail is enabled automatically.
There are no additional configuration tasks to perform.

Setting Up Internet Mail for Remote Mail

Whether you connect to your Internet mail provider through a LAN or Dial-
Up Networking connection, you can use Remote Mail to preview your mes-
sages and control message transfer. To configure Internet Mail for Remote
Mail, follow these steps:

1. Install the Internet Mail provider.

2. Open the Control Panel and double-click the Mail icon.

3. Select Internet Mail from the list of installed services, and then click

Properties to display the Internet Mail property sheet.

4. Click the Connection tab to display the Connection page (see fig. 10.38).

Fig. 10.38
Enable Remote
Mail for Internet
Mail through the
Connection
property page.

5. Place a check in the checkbox labeled Work Off-line and Use Remote Mail.

6. Choose OK, then OK again to close the property sheets.

CHAPTER 11

Using E-mail in Windows NT 4.0

by Kate Chase

Electronic messaging (e-mail) software has been an important concept in corporations for many years. Whether your company is located in one building, or is spread throughout the world, you can send messages to other company users without having to worry about their locations. The e-mail software distributes the mail because it has been configured to reach every electronic postoffice, every divisional headquarters, every part of the company. All you need to know is the e-mail name of the recipient you want to reach.

Individuals, working from home computers, discovered e-mail before most corporations did. For many years, computer users accessed Bulletin Board Systems (BBSes) to exchange messages with other users. Today, most of those users are using the Internet or a commercial service to communicate with each other. University personnel (students and faculty), and government workers have used the Internet for many years to exchange information and e-mail.

If you want to communicate electronically with people outside your company, you have to be able to reach out beyond the functions provided by the basic features of your internal e-mail application. You'll need the Internet or a commercial online service such as CompuServe. You can do this by using third party software that either runs in conjunction with your Windows Messaging software, or runs alone. In this chapter, we'll look at some of the things you can do to reach the information superhighway.

In this chapter, you learn to

- Obtain and use some of the popular software applications that give you access to Internet e-mail

- Use software that works in conjunction with your Windows Messaging Inbox to widen the e-mail features available

- Work efficiently and productively with e-mail

Understanding Electronic Messaging

Most of your internal (within the company) e-mail is handled by a system that's been installed specifically for that purpose. You might be using Microsoft Mail, Exchange Server, or another company-wide mail application.

However, when you want to send e-mail to someone outside your company, there are some additional functions needed and most of the time these needs are met by installing additional software.

> **Note**
>
> If your company is using Microsoft Exchange Server (the client/server back office software, not the standard Microsoft Exchange or Windows Messaging application that comes with Windows), or Lotus Notes, the system administrator can establish the software configuration needed to let you get to the Internet or to commercial services such as CompuServe. These system-wide applications have connectors built in for the exchange of e-mail with users outside your organization.

Within your company there are storage areas established for e-mail. Depending upon the software your company is using and the way it has been configured, the storage area may be called a Post Office, a Mailbox Directory, or something else. Within that storage area is your mailbox. Messages are placed in your mailbox when a sender enters your e-mail address in the TO: field of a message. Your e-mail address includes information that makes it possible to route the message to your mailbox. It all works just like snail mail—there has to be an address, not just a name, in order to deliver mail (e-mail users call the United States Postal Service version of mail "snail mail" because it is slower than the electronic method).

There is no way for your company's software to reach into the mailbox of any computer user outside your company in order to fetch mail addressed to you, or to deliver mail from you. In order to move e-mail between a foreign recipient (someone outside your company) and you, there has to be a middle man.

The same thing is true if you are working in Windows NT as an individual, running communications applications in standalone mode, keeping your own mailbox, and working independent of any network or corporate environment.

Using an ISP

If you and your correspondents have Internet addresses, an Internet Service Provider (ISP) acts as a middleman. An ISP is a service that provides access to the Internet, and there are many ISPs making this service available. They vary in their reliability and breadth of services, so you should do some homework before selecting one, by asking other Internet users about their experiences. Most ISPs charge a flat monthly rate for unlimited access. There may be some additional charges for extra services, for instance an 800 access number you can use when you travel (most ISPs are local services).

When you contact an ISP to sign up, the following information is exchanged:

- You will have to give the sales department a credit card number so the monthly charge can be collected automatically.

- You will be asked for your user name, which is the name that appears in message headers. This is usually your full name, such as Judy Bernardi.

- You will be asked to choose an e-mail name, which is usually some form of your user name, for instance judyb. Since there is some chance that this e-mail name may be duplicated somewhere on the Internet, you will probably be asked to supply at least two alternate names, which can be variations of your first choice (jbernardi or j_bernardi).

- The ISP's Internet address becomes the location part of your e-mail address. For instance, if judyb has an account at an ISP named myisp.com, the e-mail address for her becomes judyb@myisp.com.

- You may be given instructions for dialing in and downloading any software that's used for accessing the services available through the ISP. That may include a mail reader, a Web browser, and other Internet utility software.

Your connection to an ISP is established using Dial-Up Networking. The ISP instructions will include configuration information for the phonebook entry you create to connect to the ISP host computer. Once connected, you can use third party software applications to handle e-mail tasks. You can also link the Dial-Up connection to your Windows Messaging Inbox for delivering and receiving e-mail.

Using CompuServe

If you have a CompuServe account you can continue to use it with Windows NT 4.0, in fact you can use CompuServe Information Manager. However, you can't install CIM's Winsock because NT does not permit the installation of any Winsock services except its own.

You can also link CompuServe Information Manager software to your Windows Messaging Inbox.

Using Third Party Mail Software

There are several excellent applications available for Internet messaging. We'll discuss two of the most popular: Pegasus and Eudora. These applications are generally used with ISP services, and in fact are usually part of the software package offered when you sign up with an ISP. Most of the time you are given instructions to dial into the ISP and download them.

Using Pegasus

One of the most popular mail applications is Pegasus Mail, a freeware program that can be used either as a standalone or as a network application on Novell NetWare. Pegasus is free, and is available for download from CompuServe and the Internet. For more details check out the official U.S. Pegasus Mail World Wide Web site.

On the Web

Pegasus Mail's home page is at:

http://www.pegasus.usa.com

Installing Pegasus

Installing Pegasus is a breeze. Once you've downloaded the software, follow these steps:

1. In Explorer or My Computer find the file named W32-242.EXE in your download folder. This is a self-extracting file.

2. The install program selects a temporary location for the extracted files, offers an option to overwrite any existing files as the files are extracted, and also offers an option to begin the installation as soon as the extraction process is complete. You can change or deselect any of the choices (but there isn't any good reason to).

> **Tip**
>
> If you deselect the option to perform the installation automatically, you can do it later. Look for SETUP32.EXE in the folder where the temporary files are stored and double-click it to start the installation process. After you've finished installing and setting up Pegasus Mail, you can delete the temporary files to save disk space.

3. During installation you have an option to install the software as a Novell Netware application. Use this method if you want to install Pegasus to the NetWare server for other users to share. If you are on a network, but want to install the software on your local hard drive for your own use, that is a standalone installation.

> **Caution**
>
> You must be using the Novell client/32 requester to run Pegasus as a network application. The Microsoft 32-bit Netware client will not work.

4. Choose a folder for your Pegasus software. You can use the default folder or substitute another.

The files are copied to the Pegasus folder and the program group for Pegasus is on the Start menu. Click Pegasus Mail for Win32 to start the program.

Configuring Pegasus

The first time you launch the software, a configuration program is presented.

If the software is installed as a standalone program, indicate whether you are the only user or if multiple users will be accessing this standalone copy of the software (useful if you share your computer with other users, or if you want to have multiple e-mail accounts). If you are installing Pegasus to a NetWare server, choose the configuration options for the server directory.

Mail storage folders are created to match your responses. A mailbox folder is created for every user. Received mail is delivered to that folder.

Host Computer Configuration for Pegasus

The Configuration for Built-In Internet Mailer dialog box appears. Fill out the fields in the Configuration dialog box (see fig. 11.1), as follows:

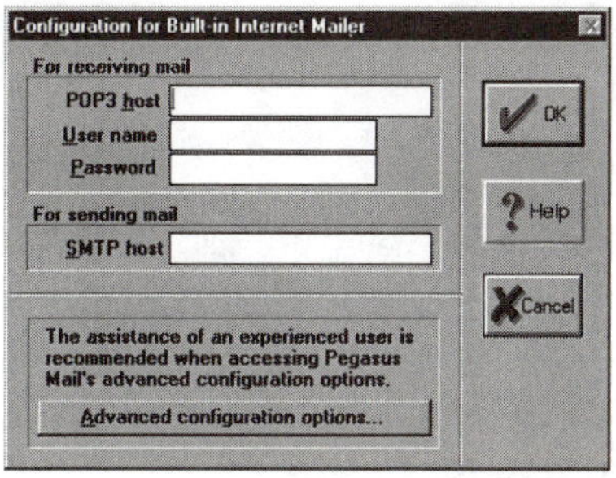

Fig. 11.1
The basic information for accessing your mailbox on the host computer has to be passed to Pegasus.

■ POP3 host is the name of the host computer on which your e-mail account resides.

■ User Name is the name of your POP account (this is not the same as your e-mail address), which is your account on the POP host.

■ Password allows you to log in to your mail account.

■ SMTP Host is the name of the host computer processing your outgoing mail.

If you are unsure of the answers, check with your network administrator or your service provider.

Advanced Settings for Pegasus

For your initial setup you should not have to adjust the Advanced settings (see fig. 11.2). Options such as how frequently you want Pegasus to check your mailbox for new mail, how deeply into a message Pegasus should search to ascertain whether or not there is an attachment with an e-mail message, and other specifications are preset to efficient defaults, and in most cases they will suffice.

Fig. 11.2
You can change Advanced settings if you're comfortable with the issues involved.

Caution

Be sure you don't inadvertently check the option to allow 8 bit MIME message encoding. It is not allowed in Internet mail and is included only for those few mailing systems (mostly outside the United States) that still use it. Enabling 8 bit encoding can potentially wreak havoc on your e-mail system if you are not equipped for it.

General Use Configuration for Pegasus

From the menu bar, choose File, Preferences, General settings to bring up the General Settings dialog box (see fig. 11.3) to tailor Pegasus to match the way you want to work.

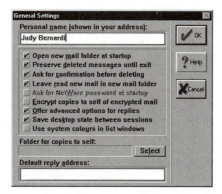

Fig. 11.3
Customize the setup and behavior for the way you want to use Pegasus.

The options available in this dialog box affect the way Pegasus manipulates messages. Use these guidelines to configure your software:

- *Personal Name*. It's a good idea to enter your full name to make it easy for recipients to recognize mail from you.

- *Open New Mail Folder at Startup*. If you are on a network with a company e-mail system, check this box to insure that any new mail will be displayed as soon as you launch the software.

- *Preserve Deleted Messages Until Exit*. Unless you never make a mistake select this box! It's easy to hit the delete key by mistake, but not so easy to remember that important phone number or detailed request from the boss after you've erased her message.

- *Ask for Confirmation Before Deleting*. Once again, it's better to be safe than sorry. Check this box to insure that you don't accidentally destroy an important message.

- *Leave Read New Mail in New Mail Folder*. While this is certainly a matter of choice, I prefer to check this box and decide when to move mail from the New Mail Folder myself. I often don't have time to respond to an important message as soon as it comes in. By leaving it in the New Mail Folder I'm sure to spot it the next time I check my mail.

- *Ask for NetWare Password at Startup*. This option is available only if you are in a NetWare environment. If you are, and you have any concerns about the security of your e-mail, check this box.

- *Encrypt Copies to Self of Encrypted Mail*. If you encrypt your messages and have a copy saved to a special file for future reference you can choose to have it saved encrypted or decrypted. Remember, in order to read the encrypted copy you will need the password. Once again, this depends on how secure your particular machine is and how sensitive the material.

- *Offer Advanced Options for Replies*. The advanced options offer some handy features such as custom headers and a choice of recipients. If you find that you don't use the extra options you can always deselect it later.

- *Save Desktop State Between Sessions*. Unless you have lots of free time on your hands, select this option. It will take you a while to figure out what desktop configuration suits you best. You certainly don't want to have to set it up each time you log on.

- *Use System Colours in List Windows*. Unless you have some particular need to make the display of list windows different for Pegasus than the rest of your system, leave this setting alone.

- *Folder for Copies to Self*. You can either choose a specific folder in which to save copies of outgoing messages or use the default Copies to self.

- *Default Reply Address*. If you want to receive replies to your mail at a different e-mail address enter the appropriate information, otherwise there is little reason to utilize this option.

Creating Address Books in Pegasus

Pegasus permits multiple address books, which can be handy for separating recipients according to a scheme that makes sense to you—perhaps business, personal, or even specific address books for projects.

Creating an address book is a simple process accomplished by choosing Addresses, Address books (see fig. 11.4).

Fig. 11.4
You can create as many address books as you need.

Enter an easily identifiable long name for this address book such as Business or Personal. You also have the option of choosing the filename at this time. Giving it a recognizable filename now will make it a lot easier to find later if you want to copy it. After assigning the names choose OK.

> **Tip**
>
> It's always a good idea to back up your address book. To find it, open Explorer and move to the subfolder Mail located in the Pegasus folder (default Pmail). If you don't remember the file name you can locate it by its extension (PMR).

Entering Addresses in Pegasus

To begin entering information in the address book, highlight the address book name and choose <u>O</u>pen to bring up the address book window. Then choose Add to access the address entry form (see fig. 11.5). This form offers you the option of including not only the contact name and e-mail information, but some more general data and even a picture. When you're finished entering data, choose OK and your entry is recorded.

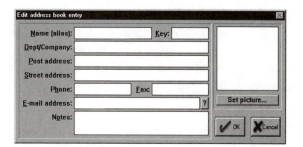

Fig. 11.5
Address entries have plenty of information fields available.

Sending Mail With Pegasus

Pegasus offers a robust set of features for handling your messaging. Distribution lists, lots of choices about the way e-mail is sent, and a fully customizable storage system for mail gives this software plenty of power.

To compose a message, click <u>F</u>ile, <u>N</u>ew message to open the new message window as shown in figure 11.6. Then choose <u>A</u>ddresses, <u>A</u>ddress books to open your address book and highlight the name or names of the those you wish to send this message to. When you're finished selecting, click the Paste button and your choices will be inserted in the recipient field of the new message.

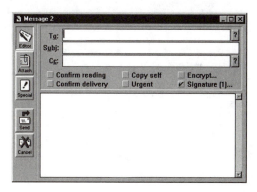

Fig. 11.6
Pegasus Mail offers sophisticated options when composing a new message.

IV

Communications

> ### Tip
>
> An easy way to start a new message is to keep your address book open in the Pegasus window. When you want to send an e-mail, double-click the name of the desired recipient. A new message box opens and the name is automatically inserted in the To: field.

Creating Signatures in Pegasus

When you send a message, chances are you will want to include some basic information, such as your full name, title, phone number, fax number, and so on. You can either type it in at the end of every message or you can work smart and create one or more signatures to do the job.

A *signature* is a small segment of text that can be appended to any message by checking the Signature option in the message editor. To create a signature, follow these steps:

1. Click File, Preferences, Signatures, Edit Signature Set1 (Pegasus allows up to nine different signatures).

2. In the signature editing dialog box (see fig. 11.7) enter a short, descriptive name for the signature.

Fig. 11.7
Create signatures
to save time and
keystrokes.

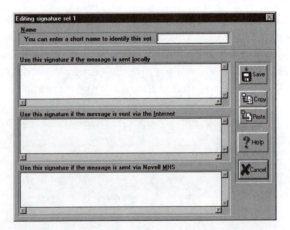

Using the Glossary in Pegasus

By taking advantage of Pegasus Mail's glossary you can input large text strings using small abbreviations. In the message editor you simply type in the abbreviation and expand it using the hot key combination Ctrl+/ or Ctrl+E.

To create abbreviations in the Glossary use the Glossary command in the Edit menu (see fig. 11.8)

Fig. 11.8
Creating an ab-
breviation in the
Glossary.

IV

Communications

Organizing and Managing Messages in Pegasus

The key to an efficient and productive e-mail system is knowing what to keep
and where to find it when you need it. You will undoubtedly want to keep
some mail for future reference. As a matter of fact, you will probably want to
keep too much. Before you save a piece of e-mail ask yourself "What's the
worst that will happen if I never see this again?" If the answer is nothing or
not much, get rid of it.

If, on the other hand, you decide that you can't live without it you'll need a
safe place to store it, some place that is easy to find when you need to find it.
Spending a little time establishing a well organized system of trays and folders will save you more than time in the long run.

> **Note**
>
> In Pegasus Mail terminology a folder is a storage container for messages, and a tray is
> a storage container for folders.

Since Pegasus Mail creates only the Main Folder during setup, you will have
to add trays and folders as one of your first tasks. How you design your folder
system depends a great deal on your job and the way you work. You might
want to create one tray for tasks, one for projects, and another for people.
Within those trays you could have individual folders for the specific tasks,
projects, and people you regularly deal with. And, you should probably create
a folder to hold deleted messages just in case you change your mind.

Using Advanced Features for Pegasus

Once you've mastered the basics you can increase your productivity even further by tackling Pegasus Mail's more advanced features. By automating mail
processing with filters and expanding functionality with third party plug-ins,
Pegasus Mail moves ahead of the pack.

Using Filters in Pegasus

One of Pegasus Mail's most powerful qualities is its ability to make your life easier by taking the drudgery out of some of e-mail's more tedious tasks.

Assuming you've set up a good, logical folder system, each time you read a piece of mail that you consider important you can drag it over to the appropriate folder to store it for future retrieval. Or, you can create a filtering rule that says each time I close my new mail folder, move any read mail from John Smith or Bill Smith into the folder marked Smith Brothers.

You can make your filters as simple or as sophisticated as your needs dictate. Actions can be performed on new mail at the time the new mail folder is opened, as new mail is received, or when the new mail folder is closed. You can also apply filtering rules to copies of mail you send to yourself. The range of actions that can be performed is quite extensive.

Teaching Pegasus to process your mail efficiently is accomplished by opening a Rules window for new mail (see fig. 11.9), which is accessed from the File menu.

Fig. 11.9
You can define filtering rules using triggers in the headers or the message itself.

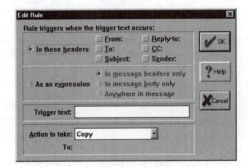

If you want to use header information to trigger an action choose In These Headers, then select the appropriate header.

If you want to use information contained elsewhere in the message, check As an Expression. Then, select where in the message the expression can be found.

> **Caution**
>
> Using either of the two options that search the message body (In Message Body Only or Anywhere in Message) can slow processing time down dramatically, especially if you receive a large volume of mail.

Now, enter the text that triggers the desired action. You can also use wild cards to expand or narrow the scope of the action.

- ■ *—Match any number of characters
- ■ ?—Match a single character
- ■ +—Match single or multiple occurrences of the last character
- ■ []—Literal match of characters enclosed within

Once you've established the criteria for the rule, choose the action the rule will invoke.

In addition to automatic filtering rules, you can establish general filtering rules that are applied only when you specifically activate them. A general rule can be created by choosing File, Mail Filtering Rules, Create/Edit General Rule Set, and following the same steps used in defining a new mail rule.

Using Pegasus Mail Extensions

Extensions, or plug-ins, are third party programs that can be loaded into Pegasus Mail to expand its functionality by adding features not available in the original application. Pegasus Mail version 2.42 (Win32) ships with several handy extensions.

The Pegasus Business Card Extension

This extension is a business card template (see fig. 11.10) that allows you to send the same information you include on your business card to any recipients you choose. Non Pegasus Mail users receive the card in graphical format. Pegasus Mail users will have the additional option of adding your information to their address book by simply clicking a button.

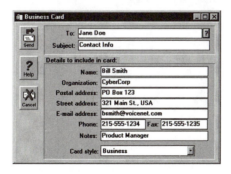

Fig. 11.10

Send your business card as a quick way to provide contact information.

The Pegasus Mail Merge Extension

The mail merge extension works just like your word processor's mail merge feature. You create two files, one containing the body text and the place-holder characters, and another containing the data to be merged. After you create the files, open the Mail Merge dialog box to generate the personalized e-mail messages (see fig. 11.11).

Fig. 11.11
Create personal-ized e-mail messages using the Mail Merge extension.

The Pegasus MultiPOP Extension

If you have more than one e-mail account that you access from within Pe-gasus Mail this extension will come in very handy. With it you create a list of different mail accounts which can be checked automatically or at your discre-tion. Other options include the ability to enable and disable each account with the click of a button, deleting retrieved mail on the host, performing a message count only and only retrieving unread mail (see fig 11.12).

Fig. 11.12
Managing multiple mail accounts is a breeze with MultiPOP.

For a list (updated monthly) of Pegasus Mail add-ons visit:

http://risc.ua.edu/pub/network/pegasus/0pmail.addons

Pegasus Mail has a lot to offer when it comes to managing e-mail, but there are a couple of missing ingredients (none of them fatal flaws):

- A two pane interface, one for folders and the other for messages.
- Right mouse button functions.
- A pop-up window in the message editor for an address book
- An address book that manages distribution lists as well as individual addresses.
- The ability to select fragments of message text, rather than whole lines only, for copying.

That being said, Pegasus Mail has a lot to offer and is certainly worth checking out.

Using Eudora

Another popular mailing software application, Eudora is found in many corporate environments as well as home computers. Eudora comes in two flavors, Eudora Light and Eudora Pro. Eudora Light is freeware and is distributed by many ISPs as part of their startup kits. It is designed to work with POP3 mail servers, and is available for download on the Internet.

On the Web

Eudora Light is available for downloading at:

http://www.eudora.com

At the time of this writing, the released version of Eudora Light is 1.5.4.

Eudora Light has all the basic features needed for messaging: full-featured reply and forwarding functions, signatures, good storage features, and all the ease of use of a well-designed application.

Installing Eudora Light

Eudora's installation is simply a matter of copying the executable file (EUDORA.EXE) and the help file (EUDORA.HLP) into a folder you create, and you'll probably name Eudora.

The help file, incidentally, is merely a guide to keystroke shortcuts (for instance, Ctrl+N opens a new message window). Full documentation is available for downloading at the Eudora Light Web site. You'll need Acrobat to read it (also available for downloading on the same site).

On the Web

Eudora Light documentation and the Acrobat reader are available for downloading at:

http://www.eudora.com/light.html

Double-click the icon for EUDORA.EXE to launch the software (it's a good idea to create a shortcut for this software so you don't have to browse Explorer or My Computer whenever you want to use it).

> **Tip**
>
> I found it better and more productive to create a desktop folder for my Internet meanderings. Into this folder I've place shortcuts to the Dial-Up Networking Connection for my ISP, and all the other Internet software I use. To begin an Internet session, I open the folder and double-click the Connection shortcut. Once I'm logged in, all the software shortcuts are displayed in the open folder and I have quick and easy access to any Internet software I need.

Configuring Eudora Light

Before you can begin to use Eudora, you must perform some configuration tasks. Choose Special, Settings to display the Settings dialog box (see fig 11.13).

Fig. 11.13
Set the configuration for Eudora before using it for messaging.

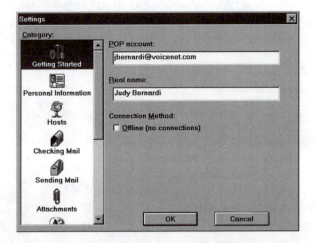

Go through each of the icons on the left pane and enter the appropriate information in the right pane:

- *Getting Started*. Enter the login name for your POP3 account and the full (domain) name of the host computer, separating them with an @.
- *Personal Information*. Enter your real name (which appears in the From field on messages you send) and your preferred return address (useful only if you have more than one Internet account).

■ *Hosts*. Enter the host names for your POP and SMTP accounts.

■ *Checking Mail*. Specify an interval for automatic checking of your mail-box on the host computer; you can also configure some mail tasks such as whether or not you want to leave mail in the host mailbox.

> ### Note
>
> Leaving mail in the host mailbox is useful if you check in from a variety of different computers—either because you travel with a portable computer, or because you're a roaming user in your company and use different workstations depending upon the work you're doing.
>
> The Leave mail on server option means that new messages are transferred from the POP server to the PC you are presently using and copies of those messages are kept on the server. The next time you check mail, Eudora Light transfers only new messages. However, all the messages are available on the server for copying to the computer you are presently using.

■ *Sending Mail*. Configure the options for creating and sending mail (see fig. 11.14).

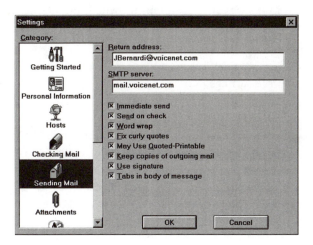

Fig. 11.14
The configuration options for creating and sending messages offer plenty of choices so you can create the environment most useful to you.

■ *Attachments*. Specify the encoding method for attachments you send (usually MIME); and choose a directory for holding attachments you receive.

■ *Fonts & Display*. Configure the Eudora Light software window, including the fonts, window size, toolbar, status bar, and other window prefer-ences.

- *Getting Attention.* Specify if you want to hear a sound, see a message, or both, when there is new mail in your mailbox.
- *Replying.* Set the configuration options for the message when you reply to a received message (see fig. 11.15).

Fig. 11.15
You can design some of the elements in a reply message.

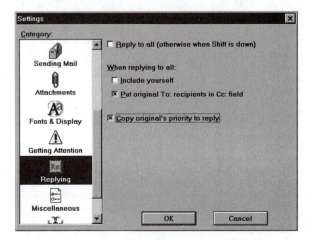

- *Miscellaneous.* Specify the conditions moving from message to message when you've opened your mailbox; and set the conditions for deleting messages.
- *Advanced Network.* Set Winsock options, network timeout options, and other advanced settings.

Creating Mailboxes in Eudora Light

By default, Eudora Light provides three mailboxes: In, Out, and Trash (which holds deleted messages). You can add as many new mailboxes as you wish. Then, you can move messages to those mailboxes to manage your mail. For example, you might want to create a mailbox container for each project you're working on; for personal mail; for business mail; or any other type of sorting of messages that makes sense to you.

To create a new mailbox, choose Mailbox, New. The New Mailbox dialog box appears and you can enter the Name for this new mailbox (see fig. 11.16).

Moving Messages in Eudora Light

Once you've created a new mailbox it is listed in the Mailbox menu and also in the Transfer menu. To move messages from any mailbox into another mailbox, select the messages, then choose the target mailbox from the Transfer menu.

Fig. 11.16
You can create a new mailbox whenever you have the need to store messages by category.

Selection of messages works with the normal Windows NT mouse and keystrokes. Click a message to select it; click while holding down the Ctrl key to select additional messages; click the beginning of a contiguous list, then hold down the Shift key and click the end of the list to select all the contiguous messages.

> **Tip**
>
> If you hold down the Shift key while you are performing a transfer, the message is copied instead of moved.

Creating Folders in Eudora Light

In some circumstances it is more productive to nest your mailboxes within folders in order to have categories and subcategories. For example, I keep a folder for types of messages (such as chapter documents), with mailboxes that subsort for me (each book I'm working on is a subsort). To create a folder, use the same dialog box as discussed previously, but select <u>M</u>ake it a folder.

You cannot transfer mail to a folder, so you must create mailboxes in the folder. As soon as you've created a folder, the dialog box returns, waiting for you to create a mailbox (see fig. 11.17).

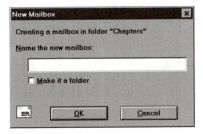

Fig. 11.17
When you create a mailbox in a folder, the dialog box shows the folder name.

Hereafter, when you use the Mailbox menu you will see your mailboxes and folders listed. The folders have an arrow and display a submenu of the mailboxes contained within them (see fig. 11.18). The same thing is true of the Transfer menu.

Fig. 11.18
Nested mailboxes are listed under the parent folder in the Mailbox menu.

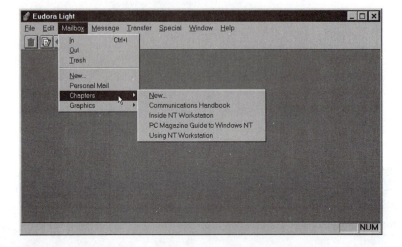

> **Tip**
>
> To keep the mailbox list short and efficient, you can nest folders under folders, then create mailboxes at every level. Depending upon the complexity of your category scheme, you might need a fairly elaborate set of folders and mailboxes.

Eudora Message Management Features

There are some other nifty features in the way Eudora Light handles the management of messages, such as:

- Create a new mailbox during a message transfer. This is handy if a message seems to belong in a totally new category. Just choose New for the mailbox during the transfer, create the mailbox, and move the message into it.

- If you have a brainstorm about a new mailbox name during a transfer procedure, but the message being transferred doesn't belong in this new mailbox (you just happened to have a thought about it, unrelated to this message) you don't have to transfer the message into the mailbox you're creating during a transfer. Just select Don't Transfer when you create the mailbox, then transfer the message to the mailbox it belongs in.

- To create multiple new mailboxes at the same time, use the choose Window, Mailboxes.

- Create new folders during a transfer procedure, and as soon as a new folder is created the new mailbox dialog box appears automatically. Once you've created the new mailbox in the new folder, you can complete the transfer of messages using the new mailbox as the target.

- Choose Windows,Mailbox to open a mailbox window and move mailboxes from one folder to another.

- After you have been deleting messages for a while you can compact the mailboxes to reclaim the disk space. Choose Special, Compact Mailboxes.

- Eudora Light automatically compacts mailboxes under certain conditions: If the amount of empty space in a mailbox is larger than the amount of space used by the messages in the mailbox; or if the amount of empty space in a mailbox exceeds 5 percent of the free space on the drive.

- The contents of mailboxes can be sorted by a variety of criteria (see fig. 11.19). You can create subsorts by sorting a second time on a different criteria. If you want to sort in descending order, hold down the Shift key when you select the sort category.

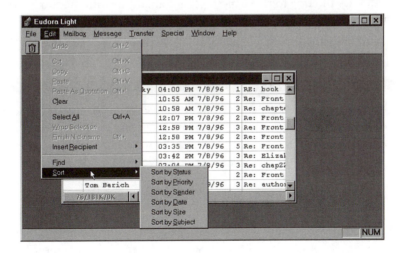

Fig. 11.19
Sorting messages can make it easier to find specific items.

- You can save messages as text files, including the header information.

- Eudora's Find function searches for text in a message, in multiple messages, or across multiple mailboxes.

Eudora Messaging Features

Composing, sending, receiving, replying, and forwarding messages are the tasks you'll perform most of the time when you work in Eudora Light. The software provides plenty of features to make these tasks easier, such as:

- Robust editing, with all the commands you're familiar with if you use a word processor—Cut, Copy, Paste, Select, and Undo.
- Multiple Nickname lists (mailing lists that use nicknames, or aliases) make it easy to find the recipients you need.
- MIME (Multipurpose Internet Mail Extensions) support for easy transfer of files and binary data.
- Attachments can be text, software files, videos or sound files.
- Signatures for automatically adding text to the end of your messages.

Moving Up to Eudora Pro

For extra features and power, you can purchase Eudora Pro (the pricing depends on the platform and number of copies). Some of the additional features available in this commercial version are:

- Spell checking with intelligence (it doesn't bother checking the original message if it's included in a reply).
- Message filtering to move messages automatically into the correct mailboxes.
- MAPI support to send e-mail from MAPI-compliant applications.

Using the Windows Messaging Inbox

For easy messaging services, you can combine your CompuServe or ISP activities with the Inbox on your Windows NT desktop. The Inbox, discussed more fully in Chapter 10, contains mailboxes, has a robust message composing feature, and can be used to collect your mail from your ISP or Compuserve.

Using Windows Messaging for CompuServe Mail

CompuServe has special software named CompuServe Mail for Microsoft Exchange, that you can use with Windows Messaging in Windows NT 4.0 to exchange messages with other CompuServe members and any Internet recipients with whom you correspond via CompuServe.

This provides an integrated e-mail environment that permits you to create, receive, and store messages all in one place, even if you have more than one mail service operating (perhaps the company e-mail service in addition to CompuServe access).

When you download CompuServe Mail for Microsoft Exchange, the software is free and so is your time online. The file is named CSMAIL.EXE and is a self-extracting compressed file. Follow these steps to install the software after it is downloaded:

1. Double-click the file to extract the files contained in CSMAIL.EXE.

2. Double-click SETUP.EXE to install the software.

3. The Install Wizard performs the installation with very little input from you (you will have to confirm the installation folder or enter a different path).

4. When you are asked if you wish to add this software to your default profile, answer Yes. This adds the software to the services provided in Windows Messaging.

The necessary files are copied to the software folder. When that is completed, open the Inbox for Windows Messaging and follow these steps to configure the application (there are some additional, optional configuration features you might want to examine, but we'll cover only the important ones):

1. Choose Tools, Services to open the Services dialog box.

2. Select CompuServe Mail and choose Properties to bring up the CompuServe Mail Settings dialog box with the General tab in the foreground. Enter your Name, your CompuServe ID, and your Password.

3. Move to the Connection tab and enter the access Phone Number and choose the modem you want to use.

4. Move to the Advanced tab to configure the behavior of CompuServe Mail (see fig. 11.20). Select options using these guidelines:

Fig. 11.20
The Advanced tab of the dialog box is where you configure the way the software works.

-   Choose Create Event log to have the software place a report of its activities in your Inbox. The report will indicate whether there were unread messages, how many messages were received, and how many messages were sent from your Outbox. It will also report any problems with the connection.

- Choose Delete Retrieved messages to delete messages from your CompuServe mailbox when they are retrieved and brought to your Inbox.

- Choose Schedule Connect Times to configure the software to connect to the CIS host on a regular basis (see fig. 11.21).

Fig. 11.21
You can schedule a connection at specific intervals to have your outbound mail sent and your CIS mailbox checked for new mail.

5. When you have finished making your selections, choose OK.

Your Windows Messaging menu bar now has additional choices in the Tools menu. The Deliver Now command has changed to Deliver Now Using and offers CompuServe Mail as a choice. An additional command, Remote Mail, has been added to the menu.

> **Note**
>
> In addition, a new address book, CompuServe Addresses, has been added to your Messaging system.

To launch a CompuServe session from the Inbox window, follow these steps:

1. Choose Tools, Remote Mail. The Remote Mail for CompuServe Mail window opens (see fig. 11.22).

Fig. 11.22
Launch a CompuServe session from the Remote Mail window.

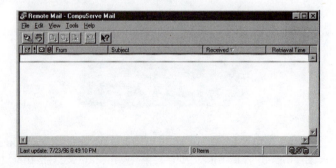

2. Click the Connect button on the toolbar to dial your CompuServe access number (or choose <u>T</u>ools, <u>C</u>onnect).

It's even faster to do this by choosing <u>T</u>ools, <u>D</u>eliver Now Using CompuServe Mail, because you don't have to wait for another window to open and choose Connect. As soon as you select this command the software starts. You don't have to have mail you want to deliver in your Outbox in order to use this menu command.

That's all you have to do—the software does the rest. It dials, logs on to CompuServe, checks your mailbox, collects the messages, brings back the messages, and deposits them in the Inbox of Windows Messaging (see fig. 11.23).

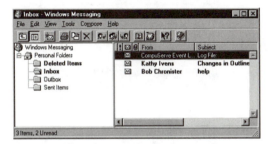

Fig. 11.23
The messages have been fetched from CompuServe and are in the Inbox, along with an Event Log.

> **Note**
>
> At the time of this writing, the Remote Mail choice on the Tools menu did not operate properly and the only way to collect CompuServe messages was to use Deliver Now. If you use the Remote Mail command and see dialog boxes indicating that mail has been found in your CompuServe mailbox, but no mail is returned, try Deliver Now Using before assuming you've done something wrong.

Using Windows Messaging for ISP Access

You can also set up Windows Messaging to dial out to your ISP through the Inbox. To establish this feature, follow these steps:

1. Choose <u>T</u>ools, <u>S</u>ervices from the Inbox menu bar.

2. Choose A<u>d</u>d to display the Add Service to Profile dialog box.

3. Select Internet Mail, then choose OK.

4. The Internet Mail dialog box appears with the General tab in the foreground. Fill in the Personal and Mailbox information (see fig. 11.24).

Fig. 11.24
Configure the
login information
for your ISP and
your mailbox.

5. Move to the Connection tab to establish the connection (see fig. 11.25).

Fig. 11.25
Select the settings
needed to use a
Dial-Up Network-
ing entry.

6. Choose Connect Using the Modem, since this is a Dial-Up Networking connection.

7. Enter the name of the Dial-Up Networking connection.

8. To make the connection manually (using Remote Mail or Deliver Now Using), select Work Off-line and use Remote Mail.

9. To schedule automatic dialing at an interval of your choice, deselect Work Off-line and choose Schedule. Then schedule the automatic dialing as described previously for CompuServe Mail.

10. Choose Log Eile if you want to enable logging. You can choose to log all basic events, troubleshooting events, or no logging at all. If you enable logging, enter the location for the log file.

11. Choose OK when you have finished configuring Internet Mail.

Internet Mail is now added to the submenu for Deliver Now Using and Remote Mail on the Tools menu.

Working Productively with E-Mail

There are a few tricks for getting the most productivity when you handle e-mail tasks:

- Set your system up properly, creating folders for downloaded messages and files. That makes it easier to find those items when you need them.

- Zip files whenever possible when you send attachments or binary files— ask the people you correspond with to do the same with the files they send you.

- Work offline as much as possible. This is particularly important if you use a commercial service such as CompuServe. The expression "time is money" is a literal statement with commercial services.

- Do your housekeeping—clean out your Inbox and Outbox so you don't have to scroll through a long list of messages to find the one you need. If you've finished working with a message, get rid of it.

CHAPTER 12

Using Remote Access Service and Dial-Up Networking

by Robert Bruce Thompson

Windows NT Workstation 4.0 provides two distinct facilities for Remote Access that are really two sides of the same coin. Both of these facilities use the Remote Access Service (RAS) as a foundation. RAS provides the core network, transport, and upper layer protocols used to establish and maintain the connection for these two services:

- *Dial-Up Networking (DUN)* allows Windows NT Workstation 4.0, using a modem or ISDN adapter, to connect to a remote network server and function as a LAN-connected client workstation, with the same access to shared disks, printers, and other resources that it would have if locally connected to the LAN.

- *RAS Server* service allows Windows NT Workstation 4.0 to act as a server for a Dial-Up Networking client. The RAS Server service is closely associated with RAS itself. Installing RAS also installs the RAS Server service.

In this chapter, you learn to

- Install, configure and manage Remote Access Service
- Secure your RAS server against unauthorized callers
- Install, configure, and manage Dial-Up Networking
- Connect using Dial-Up Networking

Understanding Remote Access and Dial-Up Networking

The term *remote access* is tacitly understood to mean using a computer system connected via a modem and telephone line to access local area network services on a remote server. Although using a standard asynchronous connection to access a bulletin board system or commercial online service can certainly be considered a form of remote access, the term is not used for this type of connection.

Remote access products fall into one of two categories, determined by which protocols are being used on the dial-up connection and where the network client software is running:

■ *Remote control* products, like pcANYWHERE and Carbon Copy, use proprietary asynchronous connection protocols. The network client software runs on a PC, called the *host*, that is connected directly to the LAN. The remote control software passes keystrokes from the remote computer to the host, and, in turn, passes screens from the host to the remote computer. Actual processing occurs on the host that is servicing the remote control connection. Remote control software simply enables you to control a locally connected network workstation from a distance. Remote control architecture is shown in figure 12.1.

■ *Remote node* products like Windows NT Workstation 4.0 RAS and DUN use industry-standard dial-up networking protocols like *Point-to-Point Protocol* (*PPP*) and *Serial Line Internet Protocol* (*SLIP*) to support standard Network and Transport Layer protocols like TCP/IP and IPX/SPX. The network client software runs on the remote computer system, which functions as a full-fledged network workstation. In essence, the only difference between a workstation running remote node software and a locally connected workstation is the Physical Layer and Data-Link Layer connection used—dial-up for the remote node workstation versus hardwired for the locally connected workstation. Remote node architecture is shown in figure 12.2.

Fig. 12.1

Remote control software sends keystrokes to, and receives screens from, a host computer that is connected directly to the LAN.

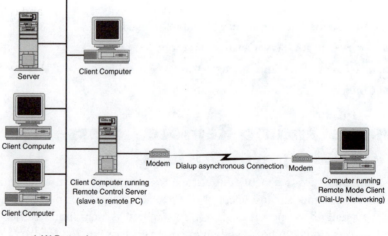

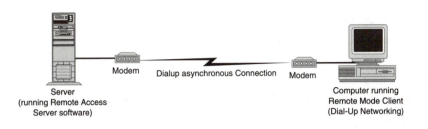

Fig. 12.2
Remote node
software
enables the
remote
computer
running it to
participate
directly as a full
network client.

Modem   Dialup asynchronous Connection   Modem

Server
(running Remote Access
Server software)

Computer running
Remote Mode Client
(Dial-Up Networking)

LAN Protocols

Choosing Between Remote Control and Remote Node

Remote control products have been around for several years, and have gradually improved both in features and in performance. Originally, remote control products were developed to address a crying need—users needed to access network services from a PC connected to the network by dial-up telephone lines. What we really wanted was a usable remote node product. What we got instead was remote control.

From the *beginning*, remote control has been a kludge. It originally required two computers—the remote workstation itself and the locally connected host workstation—to accomplish what should be done with a single computer. Although Windows multitasking may eliminate the need for a dedicated host workstation, remote control products architecturally still require a host, whether physical or virtual. Attempting to run these products as background processes on a non-dedicated host may cause performance and other problems for foreground processes.

Because it is the host workstation that actually accesses the network resources and does all the processing, problems often occur due to hardware and configuration differences between the host and the remote. For example, if the notebook computer you use for remote access supports only 640×480 screen resolution, you may find that some remote control products force you to run the same low resolution on the 17" monitor on your desktop system.

Both RAS and DUN as implemented in Windows NT Workstation 4.0 are remote node services.

Selecting Hardware for Remote Access Service and Dial-Up Networking

Because Windows NT Workstation 4.0 supports only a single concurrent RAS or DUN connection, no special hardware is required beyond a modem or ISDN adapter and an analog or ISDN telephone line, as appropriate for your communications hardware. As remote node products, both RAS and DUN typically transfer relatively large amounts of information across the connection, so there is a definite need for speed.

For best performance with RAS and DUN, do not consider using anything less than a v.34 modem running at 28.8kbps. By using a single B channel, ISDN doubles throughput to 56kbps or 64kbps, depending on the characteristics of the ISDN connection. When using both B channels, an ISDN connection quadruples the throughput of a v.34 modem, giving you 112kbps to 128kbps, depending on the ISDN hardware you are using and the throughput available on your ISDN connection.

Two factors may limit dual B channel ISDN throughput to less than the theoretical maximum of 128kbps. First, your provider may offer only 56kbps B channels rather than the standard 64 Kbps channels. Second, if you use an external ISDN adapter connected to your computer via a standard serial port, the inherent limitations of the serial port hardware will limit your throughput to 115kbps.

Relative to a LAN connection, almost all users will perceive the performance hit when using a v.34 connection. Conversely, when using ISDN, most users perceive performance comparable to that of a local connection. This seems to make little sense, because the ISDN connection offers only 128Kbps throughput, or about $1/80^{th}$ the throughput of a 10Mbps local Ethernet connection.

Two factors come into play to reduce the perceived performance differential:

- A heavily loaded local Ethernet connection in practice offers nowhere near the theoretical 10Mbps throughput. Under load, actual throughput may be only 25 to 40 percent of nominal, or 2.5mbps to 4.0mbps.

- The RAS or DUN connection can use compression to make the most of the available bandwidth. According to Microsoft, the compression algorithm used in RAS and DUN can compress suitable data by a factor as large as eight times, yielding effective throughput of about 1mbps on a nominal 128kbps connection. In the real world, you're likely to see compression ratios between two and four times on most data, but even these lower ratios result in perceptibly better performance than an uncompressed link.

Installing, Configuring, and Managing RAS

RAS runs as a system service on your Windows NT Workstation 4.0 computer. RAS provides gateway services to allow a remote computer using a modem and a telephone line to connect to your computer and to access network services on the Local Area Network (LAN) to which your computer is connected, including shared disks and printers, electronic mail, and WAN or Internet connections.

RAS Overview

Once a RAS connection is established, the remote computer system has access to all of the same network services it would have were it physically connected to your LAN cable, albeit at a substantially slower data rate. In essence, the telephone lines, modems, and RAS client and server software function together to provide a virtual network adapter card for the remote computer system, allowing it to behave as though it were physically connected to your LAN.

RAS as implemented in Windows NT Workstation 4.0 differs in only one major respect from the RAS version provided with Windows NT Server 4.0. While the NT Server version of RAS allows up to 256 concurrent connections, the NT Workstation version of RAS limits you to a single connection. So, although you probably wouldn't want to deploy Windows NT Workstation 4.0 RAS as a general purpose dial-up remote access server, it can be very useful for providing individual remote access.

For example, if RAS is running on your computer at work, you can dial in from home and access network services directly. Likewise, if you travel, you can use your notebook computer and modem to connect to your desktop system at work to access databases, check your e-mail, and so forth.

> **Tip**
>
> If you will be using RAS to access your Windows NT Workstation 4.0 via dialup, spend some time thinking about what you can do to minimize the amount of data that must be transferred across the relatively slow dial-up link. Mostly, this consists of loading all of your application programs on the remote system.
>
> For example, if you will use your notebook to retrieve Word documents stored on your desktop system, be sure to install the Word program itself locally on your notebook. Retrieving a document from the server might take a few seconds; loading Word across the dial-up connection might take an hour or more.

RAS Features

Windows NT Workstation 4.0 RAS provides all of the functionality and features you need to get the job done. These features include:

- *Client Support.* Windows NT Workstation 4.0 RAS supports any Microsoft RAS or DUN client, including those provided with Windows 3.1x, Windows 95, current and earlier versions of Windows NT Server and Workstation, and LAN Manager. Third-party dial-in clients, including UNIX, can connect using the standard PPP protocol.

- *Network API Support.* Windows NT Workstation 4.0 RAS supports numerous network API standards, including Winsock, NetBIOS, Named Pipes, Remote Procedure Calls, Mailslots, and the Windows NT Network and LAN Manager APIs.

- *Connection Type Support.* Windows NT Workstation 4.0 RAS supports client access via standard telephone lines, ISDN, and X.25.

- *Network Protocol Support.* Windows NT Workstation 4.0 RAS supports the industry standard Point-to-Point Protocol (PPP). The PPP RAS connection supports TCP/IP, IPX/SPX, and NetBEUI transport, each of which can be enabled and configured separately.

- *Software Compression.* Windows NT Workstation 4.0 RAS supports software compression of the data stream moving across the RAS connection. This compression is based on the DRVSPACE compression algorithm from MS-DOS 6.22, and can increase performance as much as eight times, relative to using a connection without compression, although most users will more likely experience compression ratios between two and four times.

- *Management.* Windows NT Workstation 4.0 RAS provides all of the tools you need to manage and control access to your RAS server.

RAS Security

Security is right at the top of most people's lists of concerns when they consider implementing remote access. Windows NT Workstation 4.0 RAS provides a full complement of security tools to ensure that unauthorized users cannot access your computer and your network. Properly configured, Windows NT Workstation 4.0 RAS is at least as secure as a locally connected workstation, and in some respects it is more so. The security tools provided with Windows NT Workstation 4.0 RAS include:

- *Encryption.* All authentication and logon information is encrypted using one of several robust algorithms. You may optionally choose to encrypt the entire data stream, if the client software in use supports it.

- *Integrated Domain Security*. Windows NT Workstation 4.0 RAS shares the same user account database used for general account management. This means that RAS is easy to administer because remote users log on with the same account information they use to log on locally. It also means that remote users can access only those network resources that they could access if they were locally connected.

- *Intermediate Security Hosts*. Windows NT Workstation 4.0 supports the use of intermediate security hosts, that provide a second line of challenge and authentication between the remote user and the RAS server, essentially providing a firewall function.

- *Callback Security*. Windows NT Workstation 4.0 RAS can be configured to require that the RAS server call back the remote user to establish the connection. In its most secure form, callback security can be set to return calls only to a specified telephone number for that user.

- *Audit Trails*. Windows NT Workstation 4.0 RAS allows you to enable auditing of remote connections. This function can log all attempts to access your RAS server, logons, and so forth.

- *Point-To-Point Tunneling Protocol (PPTP)*. Windows NT Workstation 4.0 will allow you to make secure calls across the Internet using PPTP protocol. The PPTP protocol encrypts your data as it is sent across the Internet to protect it from snoopers.

- *Login Security*. Windows NT Workstation 4.0 allows you to secure RAS logins using the same tools used to secure local logins. You can control access by time of day, lock out users who repeatedly fail to type the correct password, and more.

RAS Service

To install the Windows NT Workstation 4.0 RAS, proceed as follows:

1. Right-click the Network Neighborhood icon on your desktop to display the context-sensitive menu.

2. Choose Properties to display the Network property sheet, as shown in figure 12.3.

> **Note**
>
> You may also access the Network Properties property sheet from the Start button by choosing Settings, Control Panel to display the Control Panel and then clicking Network.

Fig. 12.3
Network property
sheet.

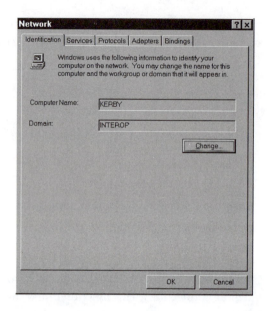

3. Click the Services tab to display the Services page, shown in figure 12.4. The Services page lists all installed services. If RAS is already installed, it is listed in the Network Services window. If RAS is not listed, choose Add to display the Select Network Service dialog box, shown in figure 12.5. Windows NT builds a list of available services, and displays them in the Network Service box.

Fig. 12.4
The Network
properties Services
page lists all
installed services.

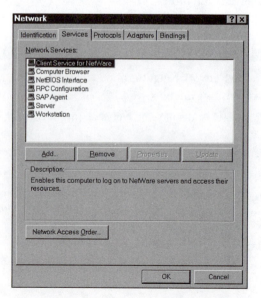

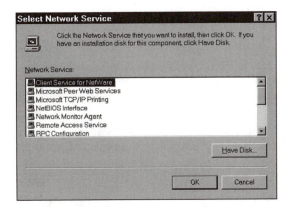

Fig. 12.5
The Select Network Service dialog box allows you to add services from a list of available services.

4. Click Remote Access Service to highlight it, and then choose OK to begin installing RAS. Windows Setup may prompt you for the location of the files to be installed. If so, enter the drive and path name where the setup files are located and choose Continue to continue installing RAS. Windows copies the RAS files to your hard drive, determines your current system configuration, and finally displays the Remote Access Setup dialog box, shown in figure 12.6.

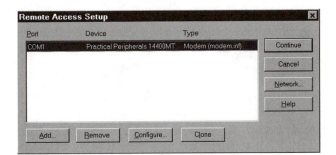

Fig. 12.6
The Remote Access Setup dialog box shows an installed legacy modem.inf RAS-compatible device.

Note

Figure 12.6 shows that an installed RAS-compatible modem exists from a previous installation, shown under Type as Modem (modem.inf). Windows NT 4.0 uses a newer type of modem driver, called Unimodem. For a cleaner installation, remove existing installed devices shown as (modem.inf) by clicking Remove. Before doing so, make sure to note the changes, if any, that you have made to the modem.inf for these devices. Once you have removed all legacy RAS-compatible devices, an empty Remote Access Setup dialog box appears, shown in figure 12.7.

Fig. 12.7

The Remote Access Setup dialog box allows you to install and configure RAS-compatible communications devices.

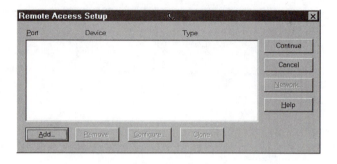

5. Click <u>A</u>dd to display the Remote Access Setup dialog box, shown in figure 12.8.

Fig. 12.8

The Remote Access Setup dialog box allows you to invoke the Modem installer to locate and install a RAS-compatible modem.

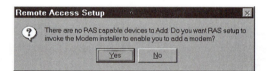

6. Click <u>Y</u>es to invoke the Install New Modem Wizard, shown in figure 12.9.

Fig. 12.9

The Install New Modem Wizard allows you to detect and install a modem automatically.

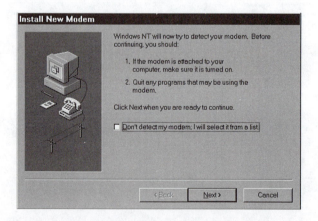

7. By default, Windows NT Workstation 4.0 will attempt to detect your modem and determine its type automatically. Click <u>N</u>ext to begin the detection phase. Windows NT scans each available serial port and queries the port to determine whether a modem is attached to that port. When it receives a response that indicates that a modem is attached to a port, it further queries the modem to attempt to determine its type.

> **Note**
>
> If you prefer to specify your modem's type and location yourself, mark the
> Don't Detect My Modem; I Will Select It from a List checkbox. Mark this
> checkbox only if you have good reason to believe that Windows NT will fail to
> detect your modem or will misidentify your modem.

8. When the detection process is complete, Windows NT displays the
Install New Modem dialog box, shown in figure 12.10, to inform you of
the type and location of the modem that it has detected. Verify that the
displayed modem type is correct. If Windows NT has misidentified your
modem, click Change to select the proper modem type from a list.
When the displayed modem type is correct, click Next to install the
modem. Windows NT displays the Install New Modem dialog box
shown in figure 12.11 to inform you that the modem has been installed
successfully.

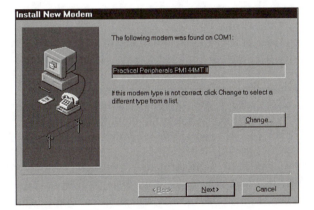

Fig. 12.10
The Install New
Modem dialog box
displays the
modem detected
by Windows NT.

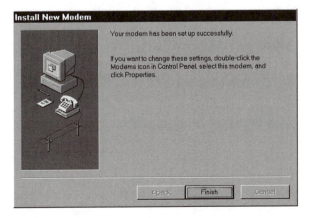

Fig. 12.11
The Install New
Modem dialog box
notifies you that
the modem has
been installed
successfully.

9. Click Finish to display the Add RAS Device dialog box, shown in figure 12.12. The modem you have just installed is displayed in the RAS Capable Devices list box. Click OK to install your modem as a RAS device and return to the Remote Access Setup dialog box, shown in figure 12.13. Note that the installed modem is now shown as a unimodem device.

Fig. 12.12

The Add RAS Device dialog box allows you to add an installed modem as a RAS device.

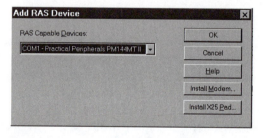

Fig. 12.13

The Remote Access Setup dialog box shows the modem installed as a unimodem device.

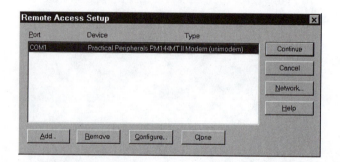

10. Click a RAS device to highlight it and then click Configure to display the Configure Port Usage dialog box, shown in figure 12.14. Specify how the RAS port is to be used by selecting Dial Out Only, Receive Calls Only, or Dial Out and Receive Calls. Choose Dial Out Only if this computer will use RAS only to place calls to another computer as a client; choose Receive calls only if this computer will function as a RAS server, but will not be used to place outgoing calls as a client; choose Dial Out and Receive Calls if this computer will be used for both purposes. By default, Windows NT Workstation 4.0 configures the RAS port for Dial Out Only.

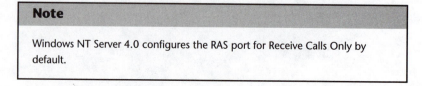

> **Note**
>
> Windows NT Server 4.0 configures the RAS port for Receive Calls Only by default.

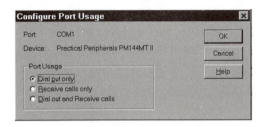

Fig. 12.14
The Configure Port Usage dialog box allows you to specify whether a RAS port will be used for outbound connections only, inbound connections only, or both.

11. Click Network to display the Network Configuration dialog box. Note that the contents of this dialog box vary, depending on how you configured the RAS port in the preceding step:

■ If you configured the port for Dial Out Only, the Network Configuration dialog box shown in figure 12.15 appears. This version of the dialog box allows you to specify only the transport protocols to be used for outbound calls.

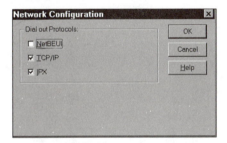

Fig. 12.15
The Network Configuration dialog box for a RAS port configured as Dial Out Only enables you to specify which transport protocols will be used by RAS.

■ If you configured the port for Receive Calls Only, the Network Configuration dialog box shown in figure 12.16 appears. This version of the dialog box allows you to configure only the transport protocols and encryption options for inbound calls.

■ If you configured the port for Dial Out and Receive Calls, the Network Configuration dialog box shown in figure 12.17 appears. This version of the dialog box allows you to specify transport protocol settings for outbound calls and to configure transport protocol settings and encryption options for inbound calls.

12. If your RAS port is configured to allow outbound calls, mark the protocols that you want to be available for placing the calls. You may select any combination of NetBEUI, TCP/IP, and IPX. Note that any protocol that is not marked here will not be available for use when you later configure a phonebook entry for outbound calling.

Fig. 12.16
The Network Configuration dialog box for a RAS port configured as Receive Calls Only allows you to configure transport protocols, authentication, and encryption options.

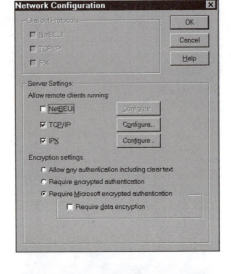

Fig. 12.17
The Network Configuration dialog box.

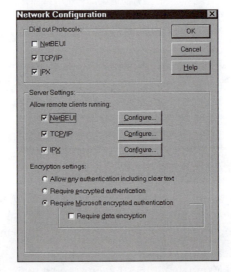

13. If your RAS port is configured to allow inbound calls, configure transport protocols and encryption settings for inbound calls under Server Settings. Begin by marking the checkbox for each transport protocol you want to enable for inbound traffic. You may select any combination of NetBEUI, TCP/IP, and IPX.

14. If you have enabled the NetBEUI protocol, click Configure to display the RAS Server NetBEUI Configuration dialog box shown in figure 12.18. Choose Entire Network to allow inbound NetBEUI callers to access resources on the network to which your computer is connected.

Choose This <u>C</u>omputer Only to limit inbound NetBEUI callers to accessing resources only on this computer.

> **Note**
>
> In Windows NT Server 4.0 there is another option called Enable MultiLink that allows two separate modems or ISDN channels to be aggregated and used as one larger channel. This means you can use two 28.8K modems to access the Internet as if there were one modem increasing the total throughput to 57.6K. The only problem is that the server must support multilink as well. Because Windows NT Workstation 4.0 can only receive one call at a time, this option does not appear.

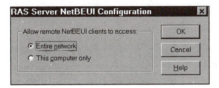

Fig. 12.18

The RAS Server NetBEUI Configuration dialog box allows you to specify which network resources are available to inbound NetBEUI callers.

15. If you have enabled the TCP/IP protocol, click <u>C</u>onfigure to display the RAS Server TCP/IP Configuration dialog box shown in figure 12.19. This dialog box allows you to specify which network resources are available to TCP/IP callers and to specify how IP addressing is handled. Specify the following items:

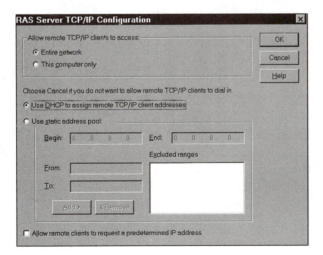

Fig. 12.19

The RAS Server TCP/IP Configuration dialog box allows you to specify IP address parameters and which network resources can be accessed by inbound TCP/IP callers.

- *Entire Network* allows inbound TCP/IP callers to access resources on the network to which your computer is connected.

- *This Computer Only* limits inbound TCP/IP callers to accessing resources only on this computer.

- *Use DHCP to Assign Remote TCP/IP Client Addresses* causes the RAS server to obtain an IP address for a remote client from a DHCP server on the network. Choose this option if a DHCP server is available on your network.

- *Use Static Address Pool* allows you to assign a pool of IP addresses to the RAS server, which it, in turn, assigns an IP address to a remote client. Click Begin to specify the first IP address in the pool. Click End to specify the final IP address assigned to the pool. The IP addresses you specify must be valid for the subnet of which this computer is a member.

  You must assign at least two IP addresses to the pool. One of these IP addresses will be used by the remote client, and the other is assigned to the network adapter on the RAS server. You may exclude Ranges within this pool by entering the first IP address of the range to be excluded in From and the ending IP address to be excluded in To. Use Add and Remove to modify the contents of the Excluded Ranges list box. In practice, there is little point to assigning more than two IP addresses to the RAS server, because Windows NT Workstation 4.0 supports only one concurrent dial-up user.

- *Allow Remote Clients to Request a Predetermined IP Address* allows the dial-up client to request a specific address by specifying the address in Dial-Up Networking.

When you have finished configuring the RAS Server TCP/IP Configuration dialog box, click OK to return to the Network Configuration dialog box.

16. If you have enabled the IPX protocol, click Configure to display the RAS Server IPX Configuration dialog box shown in figure 12.20. This dialog box allows you to specify which network resources are available to IPX callers and to specify how IPX network numbers and node numbers are assigned. Specify the following items:

    - *Entire Network* allows inbound IPX callers to access resources on the network to which your computer is connected.

    - *This Computer Only* limits inbound IPX callers to accessing resources only on this computer.

- *Allocate Network Numbers Automatically* causes the RAS server to locate an IPX network number that is not currently in use and assign it to the RAS client.

- *Allocate Network Numbers* allows you to assign a range of IPX network numbers to the RAS server, which it, in turn, assigns to RAS clients. Again, because Windows NT Workstation 4.0 RAS supports only one concurrent client, you may assign only a single IPX network number here.

- *Assign Same Network Number to All IPX* assigns the same IPX network number to all IPX RAS clients. This option is really useful only in the Windows NT Server environment, where many simultaneous IPX connections may exist. Enabling it reduces Novell RIP network traffic by adding only one entry to the routing table for all IPX RAS clients instead of adding a routing table entry for each IPX RAS client.

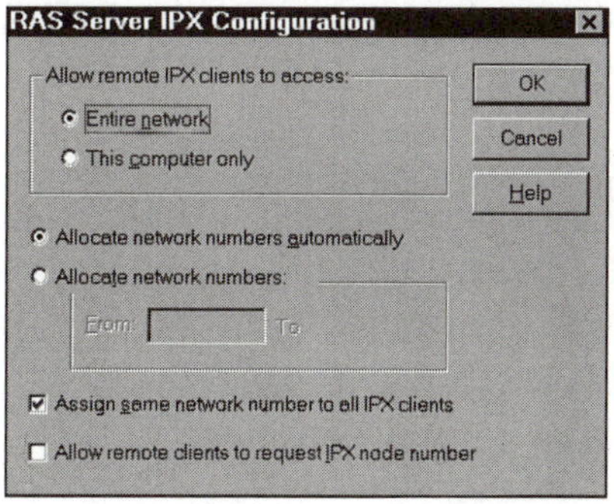

Fig. 12.20
The RAS Server IPX Configuration dialog box allows you to specify IPX network number and node number parameters and to control which network resources can be accessed by inbound IPX callers.

- *Allow Remote Clients to Request IPX Node Number* allows the remote IPX RAS client to request an IPX node number of its own choosing rather than accept a node number assigned by the RAS server.

> **Caution**
>
> You should leave the *Allow Remote Clients to Request IPX Node Number* checkbox unmarked unless you have very good reason for enabling it. Enabling this function creates a potential security threat, because a remote client may "spoof" or impersonate a previously connected IPX client and, by doing so, gain unauthorized access to network resources accessible to the legitimate prior IPX client.

IV

Communications

When you have finished configuring the RAS Server IPX Configuration dialog box, click OK to return to the Network Configuration dialog box.

17. Choose one of the three available encryption settings. Your choices are as follows:

- *Allow Any Authentication Including Clear* allows a RAS client to connect using any authentication method, including MS-CHAP, PAP, and SPAP. Choose this option if dial-up RAS clients accessing this computer may be running various types of client software, for example, Windows NT, Windows 95, and Windows 3.11 for Workgroups. This is the least restrictive (and least secure) encryption setting.

- *Require Encrypted Authentication* allows a RAS client to connect using any type of authentication except PAP. Choosing this option requires that all client passwords be encrypted.

- *Require Microsoft Encrypted Authentication* requires that any RAS client logging in do so using MS-CHAP authentication. If you choose this option, you can also mark the Require Data Encryption checkbox to ensure that all data being communicated between the RAS server and the RAS client is encrypted (rather than just the password). RAS uses the RSA Data Security, Inc. RC4 encryption algorithm. This is the most restrictive (and most secure) encryption setting.

  When you have selected an encryption setting, click OK to return to the Remote Access Setup dialog box.

> **Note**
>
> The Clone button allows you to configure a single port and then replicate that port's settings to additional ports. This feature is primarily useful in the Windows NT Server version of the operating system, because Windows NT Workstation is limited to a single concurrent connection. If for some reason you want to configure multiple ports to support RAS under Windows NT Workstation, configure one properly and then use Clone to replicate it as needed.

18. Click OK to finish installing RAS. Windows NT displays the Setup message shown in figure 12.21 to notify you that RAS has been installed successfully.

19. Click OK to acknowledge the message and return to the Network property sheet. Click Close to complete the installation. Windows NT

Fig. 12.21
The Windows NT
Setup Message box
informs you that
RAS has been
installed success-
fully.

configures, stores and reviews the bindings. When this process is complete, Windows NT displays the Network Settings Change dialog box.
Click Yes to re-start your computer immediately, or click No to return
to the Windows NT desktop. RAS will not be available until you re-start
your computer.

> **Note**
>
> You may modify these settings at any time. To do so, from Control Panel, double-
> click Network to display the Network property sheet. Click the Services tab to display
> the Services page. Highlight Remote Access Service and click Properties to display the
> Remote Access Setup dialog box.

Configuring RAS Startup Parameters

Once you have installed the RAS, you can configure it to start automatically
each time you boot your computer, or you can choose to have RAS start only
when you explicitly instruct it to do so. To configure RAS startup parameters,
take the following steps:

1. From Control Panel, double-click the Services icon to display the Services dialog box. Use the scroll bar to page through the list in the
Service box until the entries for remote access are visible, as shown in
figure 12.22.

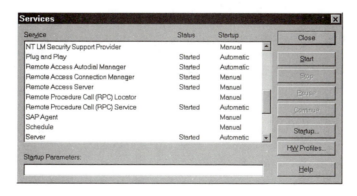

Fig. 12.22
The Services dialog
box allows you to
view and modify
startup parameters
for the RAS.

> **Note**
>
> The example shows the status for the Remote Access Autodial Manager, the Remote Access Connection Manager, and the Remote Access Server shows as started, which means that all of these services are currently running. Startup is shown as Automatic for the Remote Access Service Autodial Manager, which means that this service starts automatically when the system boots. Startup is shown as Manual for the other two services, which means that they must be explicitly started manually. If you configure RAS to require manual startup, start the service by highlighting it and clicking the Start button.
>
> When a service is running, you can use the Stop button to stop the service, or the Pause button to pause it. If you pause a service, you can use the Continue button to resume running it.

2. Highlight the service that you want to configure and click Startup to display the Service dialog box shown in figure 12.23.

Fig. 12.23

The Service dialog box allows you to modify the startup parameters for the selected service.

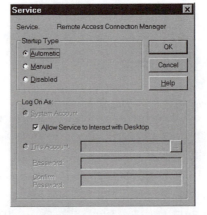

3. Select one of the option buttons for Startup Type. Selecting Automatic causes the service to start each time you boot the computer. Selecting Manual requires that you explicitly start the service manually when you want it to run. Selecting Disabled makes the service unavailable.

> **Note**
>
> Do not modify the parameters in the Log On As section of the Service dialog box. These parameters were set correctly by Windows NT when you installed RAS. Altering them can cause RAS to behave improperly or to fail.

4. Click OK to return to the Services dialog box. Figure 12.24 shows all three RAS services now configured to start automatically.

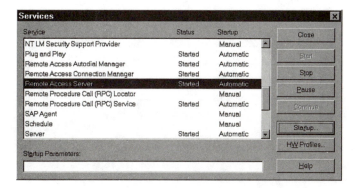

Fig. 12.24
The Services dialog box showing all RAS services configured to start automatically.

5. Click Close to save your changes and exit the Services dialog box.

Configuring User Permissions for Remote Access

When you have installed and configured RAS, the next step is to configure user permissions to determine who can use RAS. To configure a user for RAS access, take the following steps:

1. From the Start button, choose Programs, Administrative Tools (Common), User Manager to run Manager application, shown in figure 12.25.

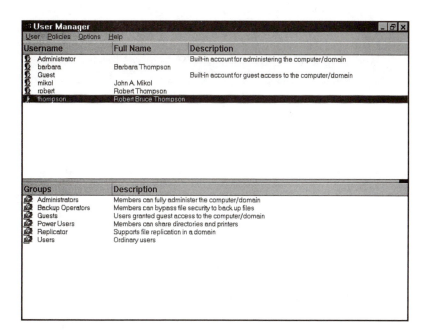

Fig. 12.25
Use User Manager to configure user accounts for RAS access.

2. Double-click a user name to display the User Properties property sheet, shown in figure 12.26.

Fig. 12.26
The User Proper-
ties property sheet
allows you to
configure an
individual user for
RAS access.

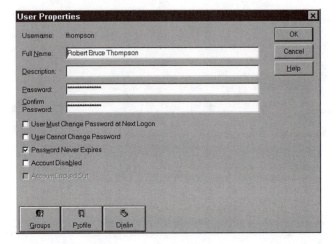

3. Click Dialin to display Dialin Information dialog box, shown in figure 12.27. Mark the Grant Dialin Permission to User checkbox if this user is to be permitted to dialin to this computer. Choose one of the Call Back option buttons in this dialog box as follows:

   ■ *No Call Back* disables call back and allows the user to connect directly to RAS with the original inbound telephone connection.

   ■ *Set By Caller* causes RAS to prompt the caller for a call back telephone number. RAS then disconnects and calls back the original caller to establish the connection. You might choose this option to allow the user to connect to RAS from any location while allocating long distance telephone charges for the RAS session to the RAS telephone line rather than to the caller's telephone line. Choosing this option also logs the call back telephone number, which allows you to review the log subsequently to determine the location from which a particular RAS call was placed.

   ■ *Preset To* causes RAS to drop the connection as soon as it is established and immediately call back the originator at the telephone number specified in the text box. Choose this option to enhance security by allowing a specified user to establish a RAS session only from a predetermined location. This option is also useful for a user who will be calling the RAS server from only one designated location, such as his home. Using it simplifies establishing the dial-up connection, because the user doesn't need to enter the call back telephone number.

4. When you complete the Dialin Information dialog box, click OK to return to the User Properties property sheet. Click OK again to accept your changes and return to the User Manager main screen. Close User Manager.

Fig. 12.27
The Dialin Information dialog box allows you to enable or disable access and specify call back parameters for the selected user.

Using Remote Access Admin

The Remote Access Admin application allows you to manage your RAS server. This application is essentially identical to the version provided with Windows NT 4.0 Server. Because Windows NT Workstation 4.0 supports only one concurrent RAS connection rather than the 255 concurrent RAS connections supported by Windows NT Server 4.0, this tool provides more functionality than you really need to manage RAS on Windows NT Workstation 4.0. This section describes how to use the most important features of Remote Access Admin to manage RAS in this environment.

Starting Remote Access Admin

To run the Remote Access Admin application, from the Start button, choose Programs, Administrative Tools (Common), Remote Access Admin to run Remote Access Admin, shown in figure 12.28.

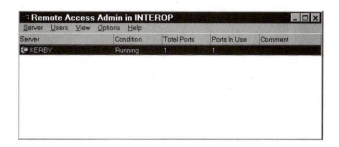

Fig. 12.28
Use Remote Access Admin to manage your RAS server.

Using Remote Access Admin to Manage the RAS Server

To use Remote Access Admin to manage the RAS server, take the following steps:

1. Start Remote Access Admin as described in the preceding section.

2. Choose <u>S</u>erver to display the <u>S</u>erver menu. This menu presents the following options:

   - *<u>C</u>ommunications Ports* allows you to manage the communications ports available to RAS. This option is described in more detail immediately following this section.

   - *<u>S</u>tart Remote Access Service* allows you to start RAS directly from Remote Access Admin.

   - *S<u>t</u>op Remote Access Service* allows you to stop RAS directly from Remote Access Admin.

   - *<u>P</u>ause Remote Access Service* allows you to temporarily make RAS unavailable to users.

   - *Co<u>n</u>tinue Remote Access Service* allows you to resume RAS after you have paused it. This option is grayed out and unavailable unless RAS is currently paused.

   - *Select <u>D</u>omain or Server* allows you to choose another domain or RAS server to manage.

   - *E<u>x</u>it* exits the Remote Access Admin application.

3. Choose <u>C</u>ommunications Ports to display the Communications Ports dialog box, shown in figure 12.29. This dialog box offers the following options:

   - *Port <u>S</u>tatus* displays the status of a RAS port, provides statistics on the port, and allows you to reset the port. This option is covered in more detail immediately following this section.

   - *Disconnect User* allows you to disconnect an active user.

   - *Send <u>M</u>essage* allows you send a broadcast message to the high-lighted user if the messenger service is running on the remote computer.

   - *Send To <u>A</u>ll* allows you to send a broadcast message to all users simultaneously, which, because Windows NT Workstation allows only one concurrent user, has the same effect as the Send <u>M</u>essage option.

4. Click Port <u>S</u>tatus to display the Port Status dialog box, shown in figure 12.30. Use the <u>P</u>ort drop-down list box to select a port for which to view statistics or to reset. Click <u>R</u>eset if you want to reset the selected port.

Resetting a port that is in use disconnects the user. When you are finished viewing statistics or resetting the RAS port, click OK to return to the Communication Ports dialog box. At the Communications Ports dialog box, click OK to return to the main Remote Access Admin screen.

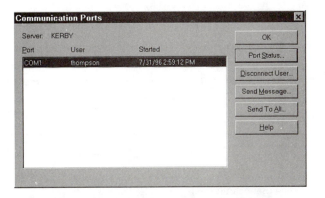

Fig. 12.29
The Remote Access Admin Communication Ports dialog box allows you to manage communications ports and view port status.

Fig. 12.30
The Remote Access Admin Port Status dialog box presents usage statistics and allows you to reset the port.

Using Remote Access Admin to Manage RAS Users

To use Remote Access Admin to manage RAS users, take the following steps:

1. Start Remote Access Admin as described in the section Starting Remote Access Admin.

2. Choose <u>U</u>sers to display the <u>U</u>sers menu. This menu presents the following options:

   ■ *Permissions* allows you to grant and revoke permissions for all users who may access your computer using RAS. You can also use this menu to control call back options for each user.

   ■ *Active Users* allows you to view and alter user account information, send messages to, and disconnect active users.

3. Choose <u>P</u>ermissions to display the Remote Access Permissions dialog box, shown in figure 12.31. The <u>U</u>sers list box displays all users who may have RAS permissions granted or revoked. This dialog box offers the following options:

Note

See the preceding section, "Configuring User Permissions for Remote Access" for more on user permissions.

   ■ *<u>G</u>rant All* grants permissions to all users in the <u>U</u>sers list.

   ■ *Re<u>v</u>oke All* revokes permissions from all users in the <u>U</u>sers list.

   ■ *Grant <u>D</u>ialin Permission to User* grants RAS dialin access rights for the selected user.

   ■ *Call Back* options allows you to specify how call back will be handled for the selected user. *<u>N</u>o Call Back* allows the user to originate the call and connect directly to the RAS server. *<u>S</u>et By Caller* allows the user to log in, prompts the user for a call back telephone number, disconnects the user, and then immediately places a call to the number provided by the user. *<u>P</u>reset To* allows the user to log in, disconnects the user, and then immediately places a call to the predetermined number entered in the list box.

Fig. 12.31

The Remote Access Permissions dialog box allows you to grant and revoke permissions and to control call back options for users.

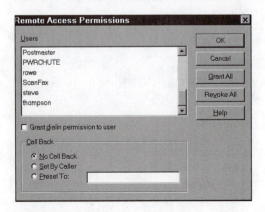

4. Make any necessary changes in the Remote Access Permissions dialog box, and then click OK to return to the Remote Access Admin main screen.

5. Choose Users and then Active Users to display the Remote Access Users dialog box, shown in figure 12.32. The list box displays the name of the active User, the Server to which he is attached, and the time at which the active session Started. This dialog box offers the following options:

■ *User Account* displays the User Account status box shown in figure 12.33. This status box lists details of the active user and his privileges.

■ *Disconnect User* allows you to disconnect the highlighted user.

■ *Send Message* allows you to send a broadcast message to the active user, if the messenger service is running on the remote computer.

■ *Send To All* allows you to send a broadcast message to all active users.

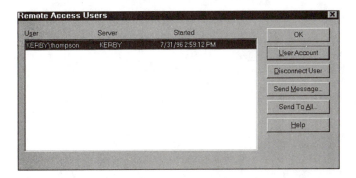

Fig. 12.32

The Remote Access Users dialog box allows you to modify user account information, send messages to users, and disconnect users.

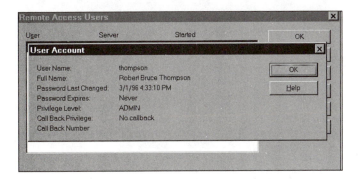

Fig. 12.33

The User Account status box lists details of the active user and his privileges.

6. Make any necessary changes in the Remote Access Users dialog box, and then click OK to return to the Remote Access Admin main screen. Choose Server and then Exit to exit the Remote Access Admin application.

Installing and Using Dial-Up Networking

Like the RAS Server service, Dial-Up Networking (DUN) depends on RAS to provide the core network, transport, and upper layer services necessary to establish and maintain a connection. While the RAS Server is designed to handle inbound calls, DUN is designed to let you dial out and connect to a remote server. You might use DUN, for example, to connect to a remote corporate RAS Server or to a remote Internet Service Provider.

Installing Dial-Up Networking

If you have already installed RAS, Dial-Up Networking was installed at the same time. If you have not yet installed RAS, you can either follow the steps described in the preceding section, "Installing, Configuring, and Managing Remote Access Service", or you can use the following procedure to install Dial-Up Networking and RAS at the same time.

To install Dial-Up Networking, take the following steps:

1. On your desktop, double-click the My Computer icon and then double-click Dial-Up Networking to display the Dial-Up Networking dialog box shown in figure 12.34.

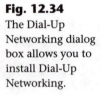

Fig. 12.34
The Dial-Up Networking dialog box allows you to install Dial-Up Networking.

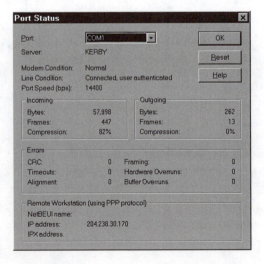

2. Click Install to display the Files Needed dialog box, shown in figure
  12.35. Enter the drive and path where the Windows NT Workstation
  4.0 distribution files are located, or click Browse to browse for the location of the files.

Note

If you are running Windows NT Workstation 4.0 on an Intel processor, the
distribution files are located in the \i386 directory of your CD-ROM drive.

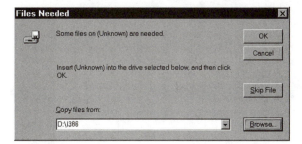

Fig. 12.35
The Files Needed
dialog box
prompts you to
specify the
location of the
Windows NT
Workstation 4.0
distribution files.

3. When you have specified the location of the Windows NT Workstation
  4.0 distribution files, click OK to begin copying files. The Dial-Up Networking setup procedure invokes the RAS Setup.

4. When all necessary files have been copied, Windows NT Workstation
  4.0 displays the Remote Access Setup dialog box shown in figure 12.36.
  Finish installing and configuring RAS as described beginning with step
  5 in the preceding section, "Installing Remote Access Service."

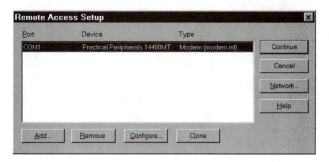

Fig. 12.36
The Remote Access
Setup dialog box
allows you to
install and
configure RAS.

IV

Communications

5. When you have finished installing and configuring RAS, the Dial-Up Networking dialog box appears. Click <u>R</u>estart to restart your computer immediately or click <u>D</u>o Not Restart to return to the desktop. RAS and DUN will not be available until you have restarted your computer (see fig. 12.37).

Fig. 12.37
The Dial-Up Networking dialog box informs you that Dial-Up Networking was installed successfully and prompts you to restart your computer so that the new settings can take effect.

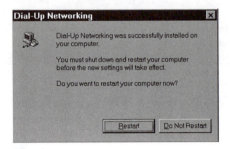

Using Dial-Up Networking

You can use Dial-Up Networking to connect to a variety of remote access servers, including Microsoft RAS servers, UNIX hosts, and Internet Service Providers. DUN supports TCP/IP, IPX/SPX, and NetBEUI at the network and transport layers.

All Dial-Up Networking functions are initiated from the Dial-Up Networking dialog box. To start using Dial-Up Networking, double-click the My Computer icon, and then double-click Dial-Up Networking to display the Dial-Up Networking dialog box, shown in figure 12.38.

Fig. 12.38
The Dial-Up Networking dialog box allows you to configure destinations and make connections to remote access servers.

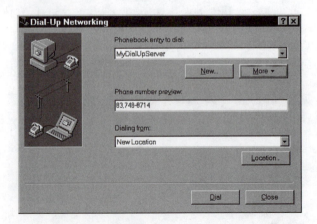

Creating a New Dial-Up Networking Phonebook Entry

Dial-Up Networking allows you to create and store multiple phonebook entries. Each of these entries contains the particulars about a specific remote access server, including its telephone number, the type of server, and more. To create and configure a new phonebook entry, take the following steps:

1. From the Dial-Up Networking dialog box, click Ne_w_ to display the New Phonebook Entry Wizard, shown in figure 12.39.

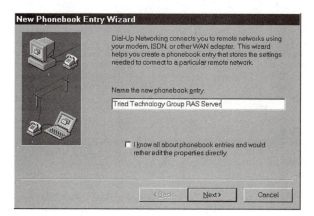

Fig. 12.39
The New Phonebook Entry Wizard leads you through the process of creating and configuring a new Dial-Up Networking phonebook entry.

2. Type a descriptive name for the new phonebook entry in the Name the New Phonebook _E_ntry text box. The I _K_now All About Phonebook Entries and Would Rather Edit the Properties Directly checkbox is unmarked by default. Leave this box unmarked if you want the wizard to lead you step-by-step through the process of adding and configuring the new entry. Mark the checkbox if you prefer to edit the properties directly. When you have completed these items, click Ne_x_t to display the Server dialog box, shown in figure 12.40.

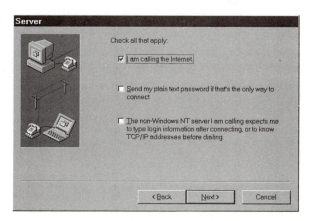

Fig. 12.40
The Server dialog box prompts you for information about the remote access server you are calling.

IV

Communications

3. The Server dialog box contains three checkboxes that control which protocols, authentication methods, and procedures are used to connect to this remote access server. These boxes include:

   ■ *I Am Calling the Internet* causes DUN to use TCP/IP protocols to establish and maintain the session. Mark this box if the destination remote access server is an Internet Service Provider, or if it is running UNIX.

   ■ *Send My Plain Text Password If That's the Only Way to Connect* allows the least restrictive form of authentication to be used. Mark this box only if you are unable to connect to the destination remote access server when the box is unmarked.

   ■ *The Non-Windows NT Server I Am Calling Expects Me to Type in Login Information After Connecting, or to Know TCP/IP Addresses Before Dialing* causes DUN to use manual login and IP address assignment procedures. Mark this box only if the remote access server you are calling is not running Windows NT, and only then if you are unable to connect to the server with the box unmarked.

> **Note**
>
> You may notice the conspicuous absence of any mention of the Point-to-Point Tunneling Protocol (PPTP). This is probably due to the limited number of ISPs currently offering PPTP as an option.
>
> PPTP is configured the same way as a normal connection except that one of the RASPPTPM modems must be used, and the IP address of the machine you are trying to reach is used instead of a real telephone number.

Mark one or more of the checkboxes, as appropriate, and click Next.

4. If you have more than one modem installed, or you have a modem and the Point-to-Point Protocol installed, you will be prompted to select the modem for the entry to use. In figure 12.41 you can see that I have a Courier Dual Standard v.34 modem installed, and 10 virtual private networks via the PPTP protocol. You cannot select Multilink in this dialog box. You will have to do this by manually editing the connection. The section "Modifying Properties for a DUN Phonebook Entry" later in this chapter contains information on how to do this.

5. Enter the main telephone number for the remote access server in the Phone Number text box as in figure 12.42. If you are using Telephony dialing properties, also enter the Country Code and Area Code as in figure 12.43.

IV

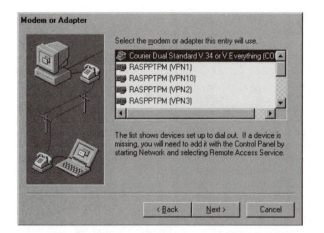

Fig. 12.41
Select the modem to use.

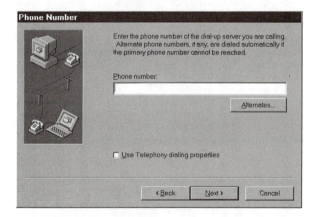

Fig. 12.42
The Phone Number dialog box prompts you to enter the main and alternate telephone numbers for the remote access server.

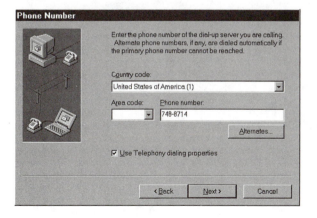

Fig. 12.43
The Phone Number dialog box using Telephony dialing properties.

> **Note**
>
> A large remote access server may have many telephone lines. These lines are usually combined into a *hunt group*, which allows you to dial a single main number and access the next available line in the hunt group. However, some servers may not have all of their lines in a single hunt group, so there may be two or more telephone numbers which can be used to call that server. Because it is expensive to combine telephone lines into hunt groups, some servers may not use hunt groups at all, but instead have many discrete telephone Numbers.

5. If this server has more than one telephone number, click Alternates to display the Phone Numbers dialog box shown in figure 12.44. The main telephone number you entered in the preceding step is highlighted in the Phone Numbers text box.

Fig. 12.44
The Phone Numbers dialog box allows you to enter alternate telephone numbers for the remote access server.

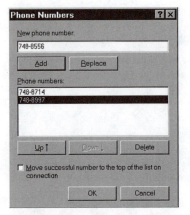

6. Enter an alternate phone number in the New Phone Number text box. Click Add to add this phone number to the list shown in the Phone Numbers text box, or click Replace to replace the phone number highlighted in the Phone Numbers text box.

7. When you have added all of the alternate phone numbers to the Phone Numbers text box, highlight a number and use the Up, Down, and Delete buttons to rearrange the list to your satisfaction. The first number on this list will be the first number that DUN attempts to use to make the connection. If that fails, DUN will then try succeeding numbers until it succeeds in making the connection or until it runs out of alternate numbers to try.

8. Mark the _Move successful number to the top of the list on connection_ checkbox if you want the last number successfully used to always be placed at the top of the list, so that this will be used for the first attempt on subsequent calls.

9. When you finish making changes to the Phone Numbers dialog box, click OK to return to the Phone Number dialog box. Click Next to display the New Phonebook Entry Wizard dialog box shown in figure 12.45. Click Finish to complete the entry. Windows NT displays the Dial-Up Networking dialog box shown in figure 12.46, with your new entry selected.

Fig. 12.45
The New Phonebook Entry Wizard informs you that you have completed the entry successfully.

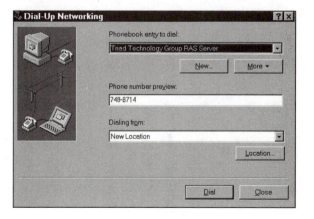

Fig. 12.46
The Dial-Up Networking dialog box displays the new DUN entry.

Entering DUN Location Information

DUN allows you to maintain information about each location from which you place calls. For example, you might need to first dial 9 to get an outgoing telephone line at the office, while at home you might simply dial the phone number. Entering this location information makes it easier to use your phonebook to place calls from various locations. To create or modify location information, take the following steps:

1. Double-click the My Computer icon, and then double-click Dial-Up Networking to display the Dial-Up Networking dialog box, shown earlier in figure 12.46.

2. Click Location to display the Location Settings dialog box, shown in figure 12.47.

Fig. 12.47

The Location Settings dialog box allows you to enter telephone prefixes and postfixes specific to different dialing locations.

3. Click Location list to display the Locations dialog box, shown in figure 12.48.

Fig. 12.48

The Locations dialog box allows you to enter and modify location information.

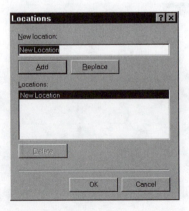

4. The New Location text box and the Locations text box display the default entry New Location. Type the name of the location you want to create in the New Location text box. Click Add to add your new location to those shown in the Locations text box, or click Replace to

replace the entry highlighted in the Locations text box. You may also click Delete to delete the location highlighted in the Locations text box. When you finish entering information, click OK to return to the Location Settings dialog box.

5. If you need to prepend a prefix to the telephone number at this location, use the Prefix drop-down list box to select a prefix from the list of defined prefixes. You may modify the list of defined prefixes by clicking Prefix list.

6. If you need to append a suffix to the telephone number at this location, use the Suffix drop-down list box to select a suffix from the list of defined suffixes. You may modify the list of defined suffixes by clicking Suffix list.

7. When you complete the Location Settings dialog box, click OK to return to the Dial-Up Networking dialog box.

Modifying Properties for a DUN Phonebook Entry

To modify the properties for an existing phonebook entry, take the following steps:

1. Double-click the My Computer icon, and then double-click Dial-Up Networking to display the Dial-Up Networking dialog box, shown in figure 12.49.

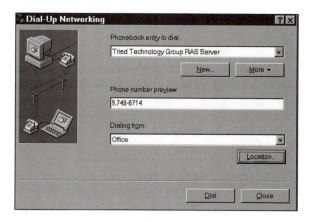

Fig. 12.49

The Dial-Up Networking dialog box allows you to modify DUN properties.

2. If you have more than one phonebook entry defined, use the Phonebook Entry to Dial drop-down list box to select the phonebook entry to be modified. If you have defined more than one location, use the Dialing From drop-down list box to select a location.

3. Click More to display the menu shown in figure 12.50. This menu has the following choices:

- *Edit Entry and Modem Properties* allows you to modify properties for the phonebook entry and the modem. This menu option is examined in more detail in the following section of the same name.

- *Clone Entry and Modem Properties* allows you duplicate the properties for the selected phonebook entry to a new entry, avoiding the necessity of re-entering the information that the two entries have in common.

- *Delete Entry* deletes the selected phonebook entry.

- *Create Shortcut To Entry* places a shortcut for the selected phonebook entry on your Windows NT Workstation 4.0 desktop.

- *Monitor Status* displays the Dial-Up Networking Monitor, which allows you to view connection statistics. This menu option is examined in more detail in the following section of the same name. (The Dial-Up Networking Monitor can also be accessed by double-clicking Dial-Up Monitor in Control Panel.)

- *Operator Assisted or Manual Dialing* is toggled off by default. You may toggle it on to place calls that require manual intervention, including operator assisted and credit card calls. DUN prompts you for intervention as required.

- *User Preferences* allows you set preferences for Dialing, Callback, Appearance, and Phonebook. This menu option is examined in more detail in the following section of the same name.

- *Logon Preferences* allows you to set preferences for the Login Using Dial-Up Networking selection when you login initially using Ctrl+Alt+Delete. Like User Preferences, this menu option allows you to set preferences for Dialing, Callback, Appearance and Phone book. This menu option is examined in more detail in the following section of the same name.

4. After you make the changes needed using any of these menu choices, click Close to save the changes and exit Dial-Up Networking, or click Dial to place a Dial-Up Networking call to the selected phonebook entry.

Edit Entry and Modem Properties. Choosing this menu option from the More menu of the Dial-Up Networking dialog box displays the Edit Phonebook Entry property sheet. The five pages of this property sheet, detailed in the following sections, allow you to configure the properties for the selected phonebook entry.

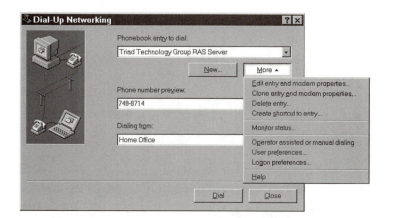

Fig. 12.50
The Dial-Up Networking dialog box More menu allows you to modify properties for DUN phonebook entries.

The Basic Page. The Basic page of the Edit Phonebook Entry property sheet, shown in figure 12.51, allows you to set basic properties for the phonebook entry.

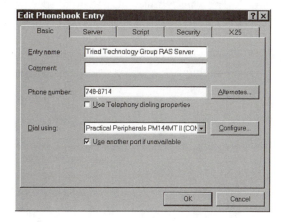

Fig. 12.51
The Basic page of the Edit Phonebook Entry property sheet allows you to modify the name, telephone number, and port for a phonebook entry.

The Basic page of the Edit Phonebook Entry property sheet allows you to add, modify, and delete basic information about the phonebook entry. It has the following elements:

■ *Entry Name* displays the name of the phonebook entry. You may modify this information as needed.

■ *Comment* allows you to enter or modify a description of the phonebook entry.

■ *Phone Number* displays the main telephone number associated with the phonebook entry. Click Alternates to add or modify alternate telephone numbers for this phonebook entry. Mark the Use Telephony Dialing Properties checkbox if you prefer to use them.

■ *Dial Using* displays the port currently assigned to this phonebook entry. You may select another port (if one is available) from the drop-down list box. Click Configure to modify the properties for the selected port. Mark the Use Another Port If Unavailable checkbox if you would like Windows NT to use a different port if this port is busy or not working.

The Server Page. Click the Server tab to display the Server page of the Edit Phonebook Entry property sheet, shown in figure 12.52. The Server page of the Edit Phonebook Entry property sheet allows you to specify the type of server and to enable and configure protocols. It has the following elements:

Fig. 12.52
The Server page of the Edit Phone book Entry property sheet allows you to modify parameters for the type of server, to enable and configure protocols, and to select protocol options.

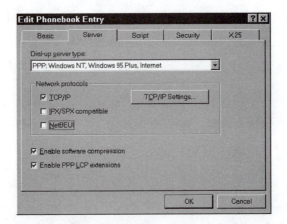

■ *Dial-up Server Type* allows you to select a type of server for this phonebook entry from a drop down list. You may select any of the following three server types: PPP: Windows NT, Windows 95 Plus, Internet; SLIP: Internet; and Windows NT 3.1, Windows for Workgroups 3.11.

■ *TCP/IP* enables the TCP/IP protocol. If this protocol is enabled, the TCP/IP Settings button is displayed. Click this button to configure the TCP/IP protocol.

- *IPX/SPX Compatible* enables the IPX/SPX compatible (NWLink) protocol. If this protocol is enabled, the IPX/SPX Settings button is displayed.
  Click this button to configure the IPX/SPX compatible protocol.

- *NetBEUI* enables the NetBEUI protocol. If this protocol is enabled, the
  NetBEUI Settings button is displayed. Click this button to configure the
  NetBEUI compatible protocol.

- *Enable Software Compression* causes Windows NT to use software compression on the data being transferred. According to Microsoft, using
  software compression can increase throughput by a factor of eight times
  relative to a link that does not use compression. This option is enabled
  by default. You should always enable software compression unless you
  are having difficulty establishing or maintaining a link.

- *Enable PPP LCP Extensions* enables PPP Link Control Protocol extensions. This option is also enabled by default. You should always enable
  LCP extensions unless you are having difficulty establishing or maintaining a link.

The Script Page. Click the Script tab to display the Script page of the Edit
Phonebook Entry property sheet, shown in figure 12.53. The Script page of
the Edit Phonebook Entry property sheet allows you to create and modify
scripts, which can be used to automate the process of dialing and logging
into a remote access server. It has the following elements:

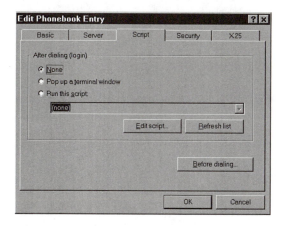

Fig. 12.53

The Script page
of the Edit
Phonebook Entry
property sheet
allows you to
modify the scripts
to be used before
dialing and after
login.

- *None* causes Windows NT to take no action after dialing the remote
  access server and logging into it.

- *Pop Up a Terminal Window* causes Windows NT to dial the remote access
  server, log in, and then display a terminal window and wait for your
  input.

■ *Run this Script* causes Windows NT to dial the remote access server, log in, and then run the script selected from the drop-down list box. Select a script from the drop-down list box and click Edit Script to make changes to an existing script. If (none) is displayed in the list box, clicking Edit Script displays a sample tutorial script that you may use as a basis for creating your own scripts. Click Refresh List to refresh the list of scripts available in the drop-down list box.

■ Click *Before Dialing* to display the Before Dialing Script dialog box. This dialog box offers the same options described in the three list items immediately preceding this one. However, these options affect what happens before dialing occurs rather than after the connection is made.

The Security Page. Click the Security tab to display the Security page of the Edit Phonebook Entry property sheet, shown in figure 12.54. The Security page of the Edit Phonebook Entry property sheet allows you to choose the level of authentication and encryption used for this connection. It has the following elements:

Fig. 12.54

The Security page of the Edit Phonebook Entry property sheet allows you to choose authentication and encryption options.

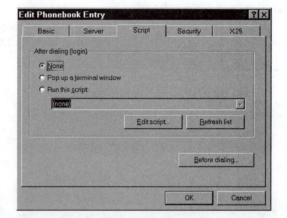

■ *Accept Any Authentication Including Clear Text* enables the least restrictive authentication available. Choose this option only if you cannot connect to the remote access server using one of the more restrictive authentication options.

■ *Accept Only Encrypted Authentication* enables more restrictive authentication than the preceding option. If the remote access server is running an operating system other than Windows NT, this may be the most restrictive authentication method that will work properly. If so, use it in preference to the Clear Text Authentication option.

■ *Accept Only Microsoft Encrypted Authentication* enables the most restrictive authentication method available with DUN. Choose this option if the remote access server is running Microsoft Windows NT RAS. When selected, this option enables the two checkboxes that appear immediately below it.

■ *Require Data Encryption* encrypts the entire data stream between the DUN client and the RAS server. If unmarked, only logon account information is encrypted, while subsequent exchanges of data occur in plain text form. While it may be unlikely that someone will intercept your data, choosing to encrypt the entire session incurs no performance or other penalties, so it makes sense to use Require Data Encryption if you are using Microsoft authentication.

■ *Use Current Username and Password* uses the username and password with which you logged on to Windows NT for the DUN session. You normally mark this checkbox if you are connecting to a RAS server owned by your company (that has your account information). You normally leave this box unmarked if you are connected to an external RAS server, for which your account information differs.

■ *Unsave Password* allows you to delete your stored password if you have saved it earlier. Although your password is stored in encrypted form, you may click this button if you are concerned about having your password stored.

The X.25 Page. Click the X.25 tab to display the X.25 page of the Edit Phonebook Entry property sheet, shown in figure 12.55. The X.25 page of the Edit Phonebook Entry property sheet allows you to select an X.25 network provider and specify the X.25 address of the remote access server. It has the following elements:

■ *Network* allows you to select a network provider from a drop-down list of providers.

■ *Address* allows you to enter the X.25 network address of the remote access server.

■ *User Data* and *Facilities* are optional items that may be used to enter information required by your X.25 provider.

Fig. 12.55
The X.25 page of the Edit Phonebook Entry property sheet allows you to specify X.25 settings.

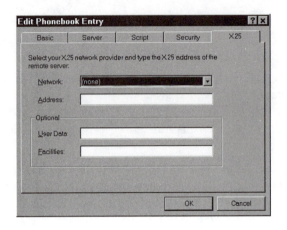

Note

X.25 is an obsolescent technology in developed countries, although in some parts of the world it remains the only alternative available for data communication. Chapter 2 describes more modern alternatives to X.25, such as ISDN and frame relay. These alternatives, if available, are almost always a less expensive and higher performance choice.

Monitor Status. Choosing this menu option from the More menu of the Dial-Up Networking dialog box displays the Dial-Up Networking Monitor property sheet. The three pages of this property sheet, detailed in the following sections, allow you to view the status of the connection, to view a summary of networks and users, or to set preferences for the DUN connection. You can also access the Dial-Up Networking Monitor property sheet from Control Panel by double-clicking Dial-Up Monitor.

The Status Page. Click the Status tab to display the Status page of the Dial-Up Networking Monitor property sheet, shown in figure 12.57. The Status page of the Dial-Up Networking Monitor property sheet allows you to select a port display status for. It has the following elements:

■ *Show the Status Of* allows you to select the port to be displayed from a drop-down list. For the selected port, Windows NT displays the Line Condition (for example, Inactive or Connected), the Line Speed (bps), and the Connect Time of the active call, if any. The Connect Response scrolling list box allows you to view messages exchanged by the DUN client and remote access server during and after the connection is established.

■ The *Incoming pane* displays the number of bytes, the number of frames, and the compression percentage for inbound data.

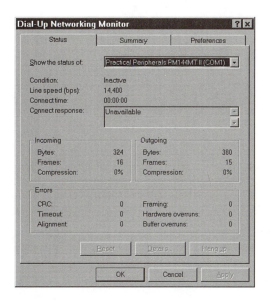

IV

Communications

Fig. 12.56
The Status page of the Dial-Up Networking Monitor property sheet displays connection parameters and statistics for the selected port.

- The *Outgoing pane* displays the number of bytes, the number of frames and the compression percentage for outbound data.

- The *Errors pane* displays errors of various types, including CRC, Timeout, Alignment, Framing, Hardware Overruns, and Buffer Overruns. On a clean connection, each of these error counters should remain at or near zero. An occasional error in any of these categories is not necessarily cause for concern, but the frequent occurrence of errors in any category is reason to drop the connection and re-establish it. If the errors persist, you probably have a hardware problem.

- Clicking the *Reset* button disconnects the active caller, if any, and resets the port.

- Clicking the *Details* button displays additional details about the port.

- Clicking the *Hang up* button disconnects the active caller.

The Summary Page. Click the Summary tab to display the Summary page of the Dial-Up Networking Monitor property sheet, shown in figure 12.57. The Summary page of the Dial-Up Networking Monitor property sheet allows you to view and manage the details of a multi-link connection. A *multi-link connection* uses more than one telephone line and modem to link to a remote access server. For example, if a single 28.8Kbps modem connection provides inadequate speed, you can use multi-link to use two telephone lines and two modems on each end to provide a combined 57.6Kbps link.

Fig. 12.57

The Summary
page of the Dial-
Up Networking
Monitor property
sheet displays
details of a multi-
link connection.

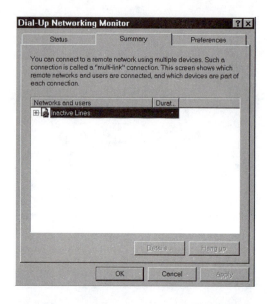

The Preferences Page. Click the Preferences tab to display the Preferences
page of the Dial-Up Networking Monitor property sheet, shown in figure
12.58.

Fig. 12.58
The Preferences
page of the Dial-
Up Networking
Monitor property
sheet allows you to
set audio and
video options for
DUN.

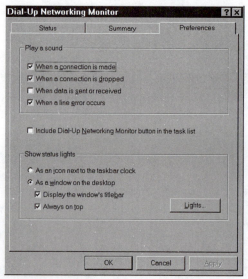

The Preferences page of the Dial-Up Networking Monitor property sheet allows you to specify which events cause a sound to be generated and how status lights are displayed.

The Play a Sound pane of the Preferences page has the following elements:

- *When a Connection Is Made* causes Windows NT to play a sound when the DUN connection is completed. This checkbox is enabled by default.

- *When a Connection Is Dropped* causes Windows NT to play a sound when the connection is dropped by the remote access server. This checkbox is enabled by default.

- *When Data Is Sent or Received* causes Windows NT to play a sound any time data is transferred in either direction between the DUN client and the remote access server. This checkbox is disabled by default. Enable it only under special circumstances, such as if you have a DUN connection minimized and want to monitor the connection for infrequent traffic. Enabling this checkbox for normal DUN connections results in almost continuous sounds being generated.

- *When a Line Error Occurs* causes Windows NT to play a sound any time a CRC, Timeout, Alignment, Framing, Hardware Overrun or Buffer Overrun error occurs. This checkbox is enabled by default, and should remain enabled for normal DUN connections. Disable it only under special circumstances, such as when you are forced to use a poor connection and want to eliminate the frequent sounds that would otherwise occur.

- *Include Dial-Up Networking Monitor Button in the Task List* causes Windows NT to display Dial-Up Networking Monitor as an active task when you use Ctrl+Alt+Delete to display the task list. This checkbox is disabled by default, causing Windows NT to hide the DUN Monitor process.

The Show status lights pane of the Preferences page has the following elements:

- *As an Icon Next to the Taskbar Clock* causes Windows NT to display DUN status lights in the taskbar tray. This option is not selected by default.

- *As a Window on the Desktop* causes Windows NT to display DUN status lights as a window. This option button is selected by default.

- *Display the Window's Titlebar* causes Windows NT to display the titlebar for the DUN status lights window. This checkbox is enabled by default. Disable it if you want to view only the window itself, with the titlebar hidden.

- *Always on Top* causes Windows NT to keep the DUN status lights window visible on top of a currently active maximized application. This checkbox is enabled by default. Disable it if you want the DUN status lights window to behave normally when it is not the active application.

■ *Lights* allows you to specify which devices will display DUN status lights. The default is all devices, but each RAS port and device can be set individually to determine whether it displays DUN status lights when in use.

User Preferences. Choosing this menu option from the More menu of the Dial-Up Networking dialog box displays the User Preferences property sheet. The four pages of this property sheet, detailed in the following sections, allow you to control Dialing and Callback parameters, determine the Appearance and functioning of the DUN application, and decide which phonebook to use.

The Dialing Page. Click the Dialing tab to display the Dialing page of the User Preferences property sheet, shown in figure 12.59.

Fig. 12.59

The Dialing page of the User Preferences property sheet allows you to set dialing parameters.

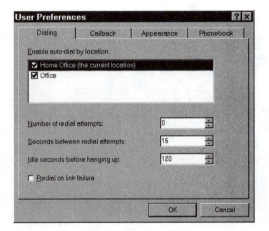

The Dialing page of the User Preferences property sheet allows you to enable or disable auto-dial by location, to determine how many redial attempts DUN will make, how long DUN will pause between attempts, how long DUN will keep an inactive link alive, and whether DUN will redial if the link is lost.

Auto-dial maps RAS phonebook entries to network addresses. A network address can be an IP address, a NetBIOS server name, or a DNS host name like **www.microsoft.com**. When a network address is referenced by an application, RAS automatically dials the phonebook entry associated with that network address and connects to the resource. RAS "remembers" network addresses that you have accessed via a RAS link. If an application subsequently references that network address, RAS will attempt to establish a connection to the resource.

The Callback Page. Click the Callback tab to display the Callback page of the User Preferences property sheet, shown in figure 12.60. The Callback page of the User Preferences property sheet allows you to specify how DUN responds to a callback offer made by a RAS server. You may select among the following three options:

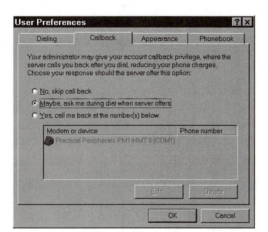

Fig. 12.60
The Callback page of the User Preferences property sheet allows you to specify how DUN handles a callback offer made by a RAS server.

- *No, Skip Callback* always refuses the RAS server's offer to place a callback, and connects directly to the RAS server with the initial inbound call to the server. Choose this option when your call to the RAS server is a local one, or if you prefer to have long distance charges billed to your telephone line rather than to the RAS telephone line.

- *Maybe, Ask Me During Dial When Server Offers* prompts you during the initial connection sequence to specify whether you prefer to have the RAS server call you back or to simply connect during the initial telephone call. Choose this option if you sometimes want to use the callback facility and other times you do not.

- *Yes, Call Me Back at the Number(s) Below* always accepts the RAS server's offer to place a callback, and does not offer you the option to refuse the callback. Choose this option when you are certain that you always want the RAS server to call you back.

If you select the final option button, the list box immediately below it is activated. Provide callback parameters for each Modem or Device listed which will be used to place DUN calls. Highlight the device to be configured and click Edit to display the Call Me Back At dialog box. Enter the Phone Number and click OK to accept your change. Highlight a device and click Delete to remove it.

The Appearance Page. Click the Appearance tab to display the Appearance page of the User Preferences property sheet, shown in figure 12.61. The Appearance page of the User Preferences property sheet allows you to set several options that control miscellaneous aspects of the appearance and functioning of DUN. You may enable or disable the following options, all of which are enabled by default:

Fig. 12.61

The Appearance page allows you to set options that control the appearance and functioning of DUN.

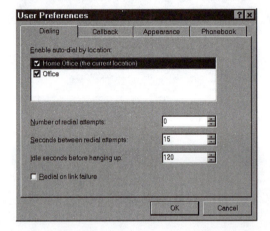

- *Preview Phone Numbers Before Dialing* displays—and allows you to change—the telephone number to be dialed before dialing occurs.

- *Show Location Setting Before Dialing* displays—and allows you to change—the location setting before dialing occurs.

- *Start Dial-Up Networking Monitor Before Dialing* activates the DUN Monitor automatically each time a DUN session is started. Unmark this checkbox if you prefer to run the DUN Monitor manually.

- *Show Connection Progress While Dialing* displays the progress of each DUN call step-by-step as the connection occurs and the session is established. Unmark this checkbox if you prefer not to see this information displayed.

- *Close on Dial* closes the Dial-Up Networking dialog box after dialing commences.

- *Use Wizard to Create New Phonebook Entries* uses the Dial-Up Networking Wizard to create new phonebook entries. You can unmark this checkbox if you prefer to edit DUN properties directly. Even if this wizard is enabled, the first screen always offers you the opportunity to bypass the wizard in favor of direct editing.

- *Always Prompt Before Auto-Dialing* prompts you before auto-dialing a RAS phonebook entry that is mapped to a network address.

The Phonebook Page. Click the Phonebook tab to display the Phonebook page of the User Preferences property sheet, shown in figure 12.62. The Phonebook page of the User Preferences property sheet allows you to select one of three option buttons that determine which phonebook will be used, as follows:

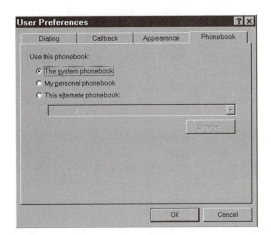

Fig. 12.62
The Phonebook page allows you to specify which phonebook will be used for DUN.

- *System Phone Book* causes DUN to use the system phone book.

- *My Personal Phone Book* causes DUN to use the personal phone book of the person logged on.

- *This Alternate Phone Book* causes DUN to use the phonebook selected in the list box immediately below the option button. Use the drop-down list box to select a phonebook, or click Browse to locate another phonebook.

Logon Preferences. Choosing this menu option from the More menu of the Dial-Up Networking dialog box displays the Logon Preferences property sheet. The four pages of this property sheet, detailed in the following sections, allow you to control Dialing and Callback parameters, determine the Appearance and functioning of the DUN application, and decide which phonebook to use. Logon preferences are very similar to User Preferences, described in the section immediately preceding this one. They differ in that Logon preferences effect only the Dial-Up Networking checkbox that appears when you initially log in to Windows NT Workstation 4.0 by pressing Ctrl+Alt+Delete and asks you if you want to log in using Dial-Up Networking.

The Dialing Page. Click the Dialing tab to display the Dialing page of the Logon Preferences property sheet, shown in figure 12.63. The Dialing page of the User Preferences property sheet allows you to specify how many redial attempts DUN will make, how long DUN will pause between attempts, and how long DUN will keep an inactive link alive.

Fig. 12.63
The Dialing page of the Logon Preferences property sheet allows you to set dialing parameters.

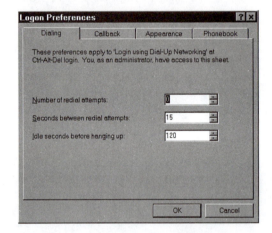

The Callback Page. Click the Callback tab to display the Callback page of the Logon Preferences property sheet, shown in figure 12.64. The Callback page of the Logon Preferences property sheet allows you to specify how DUN responds to a callback offer made by a RAS server. You may select among the following three options:

Fig. 12.64
The Callback page of the Logon Preferences property sheet allows you to specify how DUN handles a callback offer made by a RAS server.

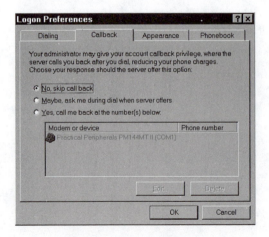

- <u>No</u>, *Skip Callback* always refuses the RAS server's offer to place a callback, and connects directly to the RAS server with the initial inbound call to the server. Choose this option when your call to the RAS server is a local one, or if you prefer to have long distance charges billed to your telephone line rather than to the RAS telephone line.

- *Maybe, Ask Me During Dial When Server Offers* prompts you during the initial connection sequence to specify whether you prefer to have the RAS server call you back or to simply connect during the initial telephone call. Choose this option if you sometimes want to use the callback facility and other times you do not.

- <u>Yes</u>, *Call Me Back at the Number(s) Below* always accepts the RAS server's offer to place a callback, and does not offer you the option to refuse the callback. Choose this option when you are certain that you always want the RAS server to call you back.

If you select the final option button, the list box immediately below it is activated. Provide callback parameters for each Modem or Device listed which will be used to place DUN calls. Highlight the device to be configured and click <u>E</u>dit to display the Call Me Back At dialog box. Enter the Phone Number and click OK to accept your change. Highlight a device and click De<u>l</u>ete to remove it.

The Appearance Page. Click the Appearance tab to display the Appearance page of the Logon Preferences property sheet, shown in figure 12.65. The Appearance page of the Logon Preferences property sheet allows you to set several options that control miscellaneous aspects of the appearance and functioning of DUN. You may enable or disable the following options, all of which are enabled by default:

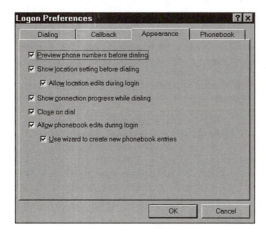

Fig. 12.65
The Appearance page allows you to set options that control the appearance and functioning of DUN.

- *Preview Phone Numbers Before Dialing* displays—and allows you to change—the telephone number to be dialed before dialing occurs.

- *Show Location Setting Before Dialing* displays the location setting before dialing occurs.

- *Allow Location Edits During Login* allows you to change the location setting when logging in. This checkbox is only activated if the Show Location Setting Before Dialing checkbox immediately above is enabled.

- *Show Connection Progress While Dialing* displays the progress of each DUN call step-by-step as the connection occurs and the session is established. Unmark this checkbox if you prefer not to see this information displayed.

- *Close on Dial* closes the Dial-Up Networking dialog box after dialing commences.

- *Allow Phonebook Edits During Login* allows you to edit phonebook entries during the login process.

- *Use Wizard to Create New Phonebook Entries* uses the Dial-Up Networking Wizard to create new phonebook entries. You can unmark this check box if you prefer to edit Dial-Up Networking properties directly. Even if this wizard is enabled, the first screen always offers you the opportunity to bypass the wizard in favor of direct editing. This checkbox is only activated if the Allow Phonebook Edits During Login checkbox immediately above is enabled.

The Phonebook Page. Click the Phonebook tab to display the Phonebook page of the Logon Preferences property sheet, shown in figure 12.66.The Phonebook page of the User Preferences property sheet allows you to choose between two options that determine which phonebook will be used, as follows:

- *The System Phone Book* causes DUN to use the system phonebook.

- *This Alternate Phone Book* causes DUN to use the phonebook selected in the list box immediately below the option button. Use the drop-down list box to select a phonebook, or click Browse to locate another phonebook.

Converting a DUN Entry to Use Multilink

Multilink allows you to use two modems, or ISDN channels as if they were a single channel. The new DUN Wizard does not allow you to select multilink when you are creating a new entry. You must create the new entry as described in the earlier section "Creating a New Dial-Up Networking Phonebook Entry," then modify the entry as follows:

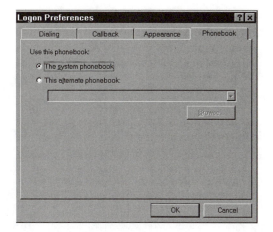

Fig. 12.66
The Phonebook page allows you to specify which phonebook will be used for DUN.

1. Double-click the My Computer icon, and then double-click Dial-Up Networking to display the Dial-Up Networking dialog box.

2. If you have more than one phonebook entry defined, use the Phonebook Entry to Dial drop-down list box to select the phonebook entry to be modified. If you have defined more than one location, use the Dialing From drop-down list box to select a location.

3. Click More. From the resulting menu, select the Edit Entry and Modem Properties option. The Basics tab appears.

4. Open the Dial Using drop-down list and select Multiple Lines.

5. Click the Configure button to display the Multiple Line Configuration dialog box as shown in figure 12.67.

6. Select the modems or ISDN channels that you wish to use together from the list.

7. Click the Phone Numbers button for each line to display the dialog box as shown in figure 12.68.

8. Enter the phone number or numbers for the system you are calling.

Fig. 12.67
The Multilink Configuration dialog box allows you to select the modems to use.

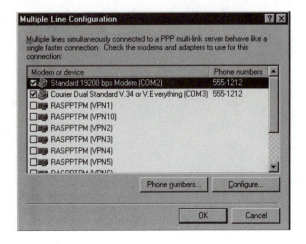

Fig. 12.68
Multilink requires that you specify a number or numbers for each modem.

Tip

If the system you are calling does not have phone line rollover setup with the phone company, do not enter the same phone number as the first number for all lines. This will cause one or the other of the modems to get a busy signal and it will take longer to connect.

9. Click OK to complete entering the phone numbers, and OK again to finish configuring Multilink options.

10. Click OK to close the DUN entry properties.

You can now make a call with your DUN entry using multiple lines. It works exactly as any other DUN entry except that you will hear or see two modems or channels dialing if you have an external modem or ISDN connection. The connection process itself, as described in the following section, is not changed.

> **Tip**
>
> If you have two lines at home—one for business and the other for the family—and you have two modems, you can use a standard connection during the day leaving the second line free for family use. But at night when everyone is asleep you can use both lines via a multilink DUN Entry and surf the Net, or communicate with the office at twice the speed.

Making a Call with DUN

Once you have all the entries for your DUN entry correct, you should test them. Dialing another computer is easy with Dial-Up Networking.

Dialing a Standard Connection. Dialing a standard connection is easy. All the parameters were set up when you created the entry. To connect, all you need to do is:

1. Double-click My Computer, and double-click Dial-Up Networking.

2. Select the correct entry from the Phonebook Entry to Dial drop-down list as shown in figure 12.69.

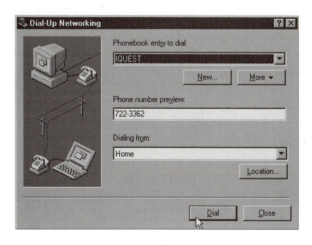

Fig. 12.69
Select the correct DUN phonebook entry and click the Dial button.

Tip

If you dial a particular RAS server frequently, you can create a shortcut on your desktop for that RAS server. To do so, select the entry as described in step 2. Click More to display the menu, and choose Create Shortcut to Entry. Windows NT creates a shortcut for that RAS server entry, allowing you to establish a session to that RAS server simply by double-clicking its icon on your desktop.

3. Verify the phone number and then click the Dial button.

4. If you did not check the Use Current Username and Password entry on the Security page, you are prompted for a password as shown in figure 12.70.

Fig. 12.70
You are prompted to enter security information, if necessary.

5. Wait for the connection to successfully complete. During the dialing you see a dialog box like the one in figure 12.71. When this dialog box disappears, you have connected successfully.

Fig. 12.71
Progress is reported during the connection process.

"Dialing" a Point-to-Point Tunneling Protocol (PPTP) Connection. Making a PPTP connection allows you to access your corporate network from the Internet, provided there is a server on your corporate network capable of understanding and accepting PPTP connections. PPTP was designed to answer concerns about corporate data being "eavesdropped" on while flowing across the Internet. It also addresses the problem of client CPU drain caused by encryption, by requiring that the ISP's systems encrypt the data. This frees the client from having to do the encryption; however, the server at the corporate network will still have the overhead of encrypting data.

To make a PPTP call, follow these steps:

1. Start an Internet connection with your ISP as described in the section "Dialing a Standard Connection." PPTP does not actually dial a phone. You must have an active connection to your ISP for PPTP to work.

> **Note**
>
> PPTP requires a PPP connection, and an ISP that supports PPTP. If your provider does not support PPTP or you are not connecting to your ISP via PPP, PPTP will not work.

2. Double-click My Computer, and then double-click Dial-Up Networking.

3. Select the PPTP entry from the Phonebook Entry to Dial drop-down list.

4. Verify the IP address of the corporate server with PPTP running, and then click the Dial button.

5. Wait for the connection to successfully complete. During the connection process, you see a dialog box like the one shown earlier in figure 12.71 (except it shows an IP address). When this dialog box disappears, you have connected successfully and can access your corporate network.

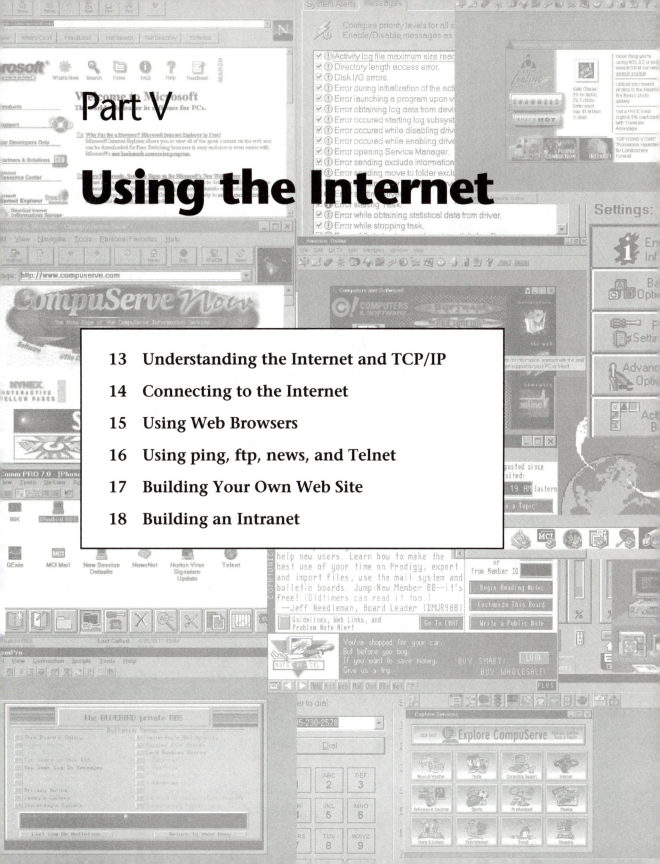

Part V

Using the Internet

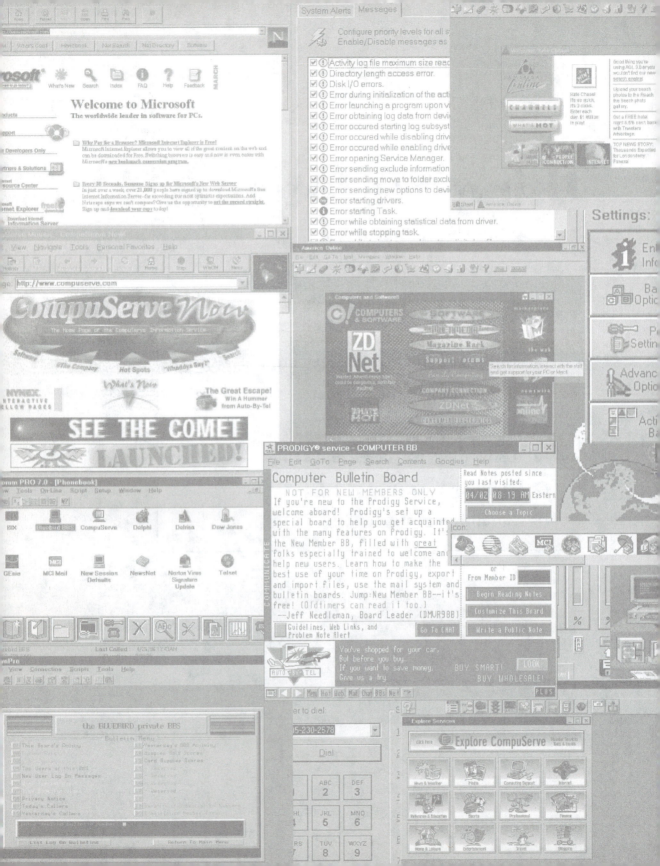

CHAPTER 13

Understanding the Internet and TCP/IP

by Robert Bruce Thompson

Just a couple of years ago, few people outside the computer and academic communities had even heard of the Internet. Even those that had largely regarded it as the province of super-technical types, researchers, and computer nerds. Three years ago, coverage of the Internet was rare even in computer trade publications. Things change fast. Today, it's hard to pick up the morning paper or watch the evening news without finding at least one story focusing on the Internet. The Internet has exploded into the mass consciousness of American life.

The Internet isn't just for techies anymore. Everyone uses the Internet: grandmothers and monks, schoolchildren and politicians, blue-collar workers and executives—there's something on the Internet for everyone today, and every day more becomes available.

The foundation for the Internet is a related group of many protocols called, logically enough, the Internet Protocol Suite. Of this group, two of the most important are Transmission Control Protocol, or TCP, and Internet Protocol, or IP. The names of these two protocols, TCP and IP, or TCP/IP, are often used as a sort of shorthand to refer to the entire Internet Protocol Suite.

In this chapter, we will examine:

- How the Internet came to be, how it has changed, and where it may be heading
- How to understand Internet Addressing, Network Classes, Subnetting, and Domain Naming Conventions
- What each major component of the Internet Protocol Suite provides, and how these protocols tie together

Understanding the Internet

The Internet is a vast interconnected network of networks, comprising millions of host computers located all over the world, connected by links ranging from ultra-high-speed fiber optic backbones to slow dial-up connections. These computers range in size from low-end personal computers to the largest supercomputers on earth. Each of these hosts is a peer, capable of participating fully in the activities of the Net.

Each connected host can both use services provided by other Internet hosts, and provide services to other users on the Internet. Whether you have lease line Internet access for your network, or use a dial-up connection to link your workstation to the Internet via an Internet Service Provider or commercial online service, you are actually "live" on the Internet as long as that connection remains in place.

A Brief History of the Internet

In order to understand the Internet as it exists today, it is useful to first understand something about how it originated and the forces that gradually altered its organization and emphasis. The story of the Internet begins, oddly enough, with the 1957 Soviet launch of the Sputnik satellite.

In the late 1950s, the people and government of the United States were complacent, secure in the belief that ours was the best and most advanced country in the world. Our factories supplied the world's consumers, our standard of living was the highest anywhere, and our technology stood head and shoulders above anyone else's, or so we believed. The Sputnik launch shattered our complacency literally overnight. The Soviets had not only done something we believed them incapable of doing. They had done something we couldn't do!

President Eisenhower was determined to regain the lead in science and technology that we had apparently allowed to slip away. One of the many steps he took was to recruit many of our most brilliant scientists and academics into a new organization called the Advanced Research Projects Agency, or ARPA. ARPA was first charged with matching the Soviet achievement by orbiting our own satellite, which they did within 18 months.

ARPA became the research and development arm of the military and the Department of Defense. The guiding forces behind ARPA realized that although evolutionary improvements in technology would continue to yield incremental improvements in the function of military hardware and technology, more was needed.

Making great leaps in science and technology requires revolutionary change, which in turn requires original creative thinking and experimentation. Although the payoff from such a process can be huge if it succeeds, so too are the associated costs and risks if it fails. For every blue-sky project that succeeds far beyond expectations, there may be many expensive projects that lead nowhere. Private industry had neither the budgets nor the inclination to risk large sums against the small chance of a major success. ARPA was therefore charged with the task of seeking these revolutionary leaps in technology, demonstrating their feasibility and carrying them through to the prototype stage.

By 1962, ARPA had begun to turn its attention to the military application of computer technology, and in particular to the possibility of connecting military computer systems to allow them to communicate with each other. ARPA began to shift its emphasis from contracting with private companies for basic research to subsidizing efforts by large universities to establish computer and data communications research departments.

By the late 1960s, the existence of the Cold War had become an increasingly major factor in military thinking. Many in the Department of Defense and the services believed that a full-scale nuclear exchange was not only possible, but even likely. One aspect of planning for such an eventuality was the need to guarantee that, after a Soviet first strike, military communications systems would be sufficiently survivable that they would allow coordination of a retaliatory strike. Many concluded that the existing military communications infrastructure was not sufficiently robust to provide such a guarantee.

In 1969, the Department of Defense contracted with ARPA to determine how military computer systems could be connected with sufficient redundancy to ensure that communications would not be severed by a Soviet nuclear strike.

Within the year, the first node of what was to become the Internet was brought up at the University of California Los Angeles Network Measurements Center on a large Xerox system. Shortly thereafter, additional nodes were activated at Stanford Research Institute, at the University of California Santa Barbara, and at the University of Utah, on systems ranging from IBM 360-series mainframes to Digital Equipment Corporation PDP-10 systems. Bolt, Beranek & Newman Inc. (BBN) under contract to ARPA, developed Information Message Processors based on Honeywell minicomputers to facilitate message exchange between the hosts.

The infant Internet-to-be continued its gradual growth for the next decade or so primarily as a research and development tool. In 1971, Stanford Research

Institute began to work on developing packet-switching technology as a means to increase the reliability of communications between remote computer systems. This research and development continued throughout the 1970s, with a functioning prototype packet-switching network finally being demonstrated in 1977. The protocols, methods, and technology used to create this prototype network were to provide the foundation of what was to become TCP/IP and the Internet Protocol Suite. Figure 13.1 shows the relationship of interconnnected networks that form an internetwork.

Fig. 13.1
Routers are used to connect networks to form an internetwork

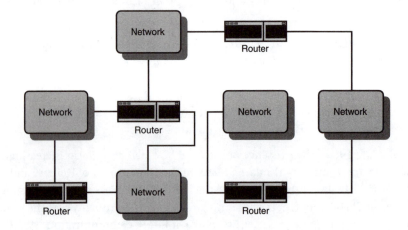

By the early 1980s, the number of connected systems was still numbered in the hundreds, but interest in the potential of a network of connected computer systems was quickly developing in the corporate and academic communities. In 1981, industry and academic leaders proposed to the National Science Foundation (NSF) that a network of computer science research bodies be established. The NSF accepted these proposals, and in 1981 created the Computer Science Network, or CSNET.

By 1982, ARPA had consolidated the research and development done to date into the Internet Protocol Suite and established it as the standard for ARPANET. Later that same year, the Department of Defense officially adopted TCP/IP as the *de jure* standard for communications between military computer systems, establishing the first TCP/IP-based internetwork and forming the foundation for today's Internet.

The early and mid 1980s saw the growth of what was to become the Internet increase by leaps and bounds in protocols and supporting standards, if it was not yet reflected in the number of connected systems. One key development occurred in 1983 when the University of Wisconsin developed a name server.

Until then, if you wanted to connect to another system on the net, you needed to know the numeric address of that system. People deal with words and names much better than they do with numbers. Today, if you want to access the Yahoo! search engine on the World Wide Web, you point your Web browser to **www.yahoo.com**. Imagine if, instead of using this relatively easy to remember site name, you needed to point your browser to 205.216.146.69, which is the corresponding IP address. Name servers allow you to use easily remembered English names rather than cryptic numeric addresses.

1984 was the biggest year yet for the fledgling Internet. In 1984, all of the following occurred:

- The name server developed at UW was expanded into a full-fledged Domain Name Service (DNS), which is one of the key elements of the Internet as we know it today.

- The ARPANET was divided into two separate networks, with MILNET carrying unclassified military traffic, and the remainder of the ARPANET dedicated to commercial and educational use.

- The NSF created the Office of Advanced Scientific Computing (OASC) and tasked it with advancing the development of supercomputers and developing means to ensure easy access to these supercomputers from throughout the country.

- The OASC in turn proposed the creation of NSFNET.

- The number of hosts connected to the Internet broke the magic 1,000 barrier. Nearly all of them were military and educational sites.

A need existed to provide high-speed links between the proposed supercomputer sites. ARPANET, for internal political and administrative reasons, was unable to meet this requirement. In 1985, the National Science Foundation accepted the OASC proposal to create the NSFNET, with the original intention to provide a link between each of the supercomputer sites using 1.544 Mbps T1 lines.

In 1986, at the instigation of OASC and with the backing of the Department of Energy and the National Aeronautics and Space Administration, the original NSFNET backbone was created. The newly created Supercomputing Centers were linked, and the network was extended to create a backbone to allow locations other than the Supercomputing sites to connect.

This first backbone was developed by expanding and consolidating existing regional networks and interconnecting them. The first backbone ran on 56

Kbps connections and made it possible for almost any university to connect to the network. This provided the critical mass needed for the first leap in what was to become the Internet.

By 1987, the NSF had determined that it really didn't want to be responsible for the day-to-day management of the NSFNET backbone, and so it contracted with the University of Michigan's Merit Network to take over these duties. The Merit Network in turn began working with MCI and IBM to manage the backbone. In 1987, the number of connected hosts exceeded 10,000.

The next few years showed dramatic increases in the number of connected hosts and the speed of the backbone used to support them. In 1989, the NSFNET backbone was upgraded to 1.544 Mbps T1 lines, and supported more than 100,000 hosts. By 1990, it had become obvious that NSFNET was the major network and that ARPANET had become increasingly less of a factor, so ARPANET was abandoned.

In 1990, Merit, IBM, and MCI formed a new non-profit corporation named Advanced Network and Services, Inc. (ANS), which would thereafter be responsible for managing the Internet backbone and administering the Internet infrastructure.

Up until 1990, the Internet was almost exclusively the domain of research, education, government, and non-profit. In fact, the NSF had established an Acceptable Use Policy that forbade use of the Internet for commercial purposes. This policy was strictly enforced, and attempting to use the Internet for commercial, for-profit activities was liable to result in the loss of your connection. As the 1990s dawned, the clamor from businesses wanting access to the Net was becoming too loud to ignore.

The NSF had always intended to withdraw its subsidization of the Internet backbone once it was firmly established, and had for years been telling the regional networks that comprised the backbone that they would eventually have to become self-supporting. In mid-1991, ANS formed ANS CO+RE Systems, Inc., which focused on providing commercial services using the existing ANS backbone infrastructure.

Inevitably, this need to support themselves combined with increasing demands from business and industry for access to the Internet led to the creation of commercial Internet Service Providers, or ISPs. In early 1991, three large regional networks combined to do something about it. Performance Systems International (PSI) had started life as the New York Educational Research Network and was subsequently spun off as a separate entity. PSI, in conjunction with UUNet Technologies' AlterNET and General Atomics'

CERFnet, founded the Commercial Internet Exchange, or CIX. CIX, pronounced "kicks," eliminated the NSF's Acceptable Use Policy prohibitions against commercial usage, and made it possible for the first time for commercial business entities to gain access to the Internet.

With the arrival of CIX came a transformation in the way new sites connected to the Internet. Before CIX, getting a connection was done in a casual fashion. If you needed a connection, you first found a site which was already connected, sweet-talked them into allowing you to connect your site to theirs, and had your connection. You provided the equipment needed at their end and paid for the line linking your location to theirs, but no money changed hands.

CIX changed all this. Because the NSF subsidy was disappearing, CIX needed to pay the costs of maintaining the network from revenues generated from usage. Accordingly, if a site wanted to provide you with Internet access, they first had to pay CIX for the privilege of becoming a service provider. CIX charged any site which wished to do so many thousands of dollars per year. The days of ad hoc Internet connections seemed to be gone forever.

In 1992, the NSFNET backbone was again upgraded, this time to 45 Mbps T3 lines, which by this time supported more than 1,000,000 hosts. It must have been synchronicity, because this backbone upgrade was made just in time to prepare for a tidal wave which was about to strike the Internet. That year, at CERN in Switzerland, development of a new technology first started in 1989 was nearing completion. Although it was originally developed to allow searching of Internet resources with a character mode front end, this technology would ultimately allow Internet users to instead use a graphical client interface to access resources provided by graphical servers linked by the Internet.

They named this new technology the World Wide Web. In and of itself, there was nothing new about a tool to allow searching. Archie, Veronica, Gopher, and other quaintly named tools had existed for quite some time to serve just that purpose. What was revolutionary about the Web concept was that it allowed the documents retrieved by the user to include hypertext links to other documents located at other sites. Merely clicking a highlighted hypertext link in one document immediately retrieved the document referenced by the hypertext link, allowing the user to jump from site to site, following a trail of related information.

On April 30, 1993, CERN placed the software developed by Tim Berners-Lee for the World Wide Web into public domain, and the Internet changed forever. Later in 1993, a group of graduate students at the University of Illinois

Champaign-Urbana led by Marc Andreesson released a graphical Web browser named Mosaic, and the gold rush began.

In the three years since Mosaic was released, the landscape of the Internet has been redefined. ANS and CIX have become much less important factors as responsibility for providing Internet backbone services has shifted to MCI. The backbone is being continually upgraded, and will eventually be wholly converted from 45 Mbps T3 service to multi-gigabit OC service. Internet Service Providers and wannabes are coming out of the woodwork. The major commercial online services are rushing to provide full Internet access to their subscribers, as are AT&T, MCI, and other telecommunications giants. Everyone believes that huge profits are to be made in this market, although there is little hard evidence yet that this will occur. Still, the smart money is on the Net to win, place, and show.

Like any hot new market, the Internet has too many competitors chasing too few dollars and too many would-be standards struggling for acceptance. Major players like Microsoft and Netscape are fighting to establish their products as the single standard, in the expectation that, having done so, they will reap large profits once the market settles. Marketers are attempting to devise new ways of selling all types of products to an audience they are not yet able to define.

As in any gold rush, confusion will reign until standardized ways of doing things are broadly accepted. The number of competitors in each market niche will continue to increase until market realities cause a retrenching and consolidation to occur. Also, a few will gain great wealth while many lose their shirts. In the past, all but the lucky few gold miners went broke. It was the purveyors of goods needed by the miners that made the real money.

The same is likely to occur with the Internet rush. Those who bring up new commercial Web sites in the hope that customers will come are engaging in a high-risk venture, albeit with a potentially high return. Those who instead focus on helping others establish a presence on the Internet will do well at little risk to themselves.

One thing is clear. The Internet in some form is here to stay. The Internet we all use in 1999 may be very different from the one we use today, but it will be the Internet nonetheless.

What's Out There Today

The development and proliferation of graphical Web browsers finally made it possible for ordinary mortals to search the Internet for information with some reasonable probability of finding what they were looking for. The problem was, at first there wasn't all that much to look for. Most of the content of the Internet was technically and academically oriented, but users of Web browsers arrived in droves anyhow, just to see what they could see.

If there aren't many mice, a mouse trap isn't likely to catch much. With the Web came the arrival of millions of mice to the Internet, in the form of new users from all walks of life and all levels of computer expertise. Marketing experts recognized very quickly that it was time to build a better mousetrap. Pretty soon there were new mousetraps all over the place, in the form of graphically rich Web servers, that catered to these millions of new Web users.

As you might expect, most of the earliest Web servers were brought up by companies that were involved in computer networking in one way or another. This quickly changed, however, with the emphasis rapidly shifting to general computer companies including direct marketers of hardware and software. Then the computer-oriented retailers started jumping in with both feet. From here, the computer-specific tenor of the Web started to shift toward high-technology in general. In the last year or so, companies whose business has nothing to do with computers or technology have begun establishing a major presence on the Web.

You can now find anything from purveyors of fine coffees and wines, to direct merchants like L. L. Bean and Lands' End on the Web. The demographics of the Web appeal to marketers. On average, a consumer who uses the World Wide Web is better educated and has higher disposable income than one who does not. Accordingly, most of the companies that market on the Web today provide products and services oriented toward these upper-income consumers. You are more likely, for example, to find a clothing boutique represented on the Web than you are to find K-Mart.

Even this is changing, however, as the demographics of the Web shift to being more representative of the makeup of the population as a whole. WalMart has recently announced plans to market on the Web, and its competitors won't be far behind. Eventually, the Web will resemble any other utility. Just like the power company or the phone company, it will provide service to anyone, regardless of income level or social group.

With the explosion of the number of Web sites available has come another problem. As any librarian can tell you, all of the information in the world is of little use unless it is properly cataloged and indexed to allow it to be searched. With thousands of new Web sites coming on stream each month, no one can keep track of what is available where. If the Web was not to collapse under its own weight, somebody needed to do something.

Someone did. The solution to the problem of too much information is called a search engine. Specialized Web sites like Yahoo! and Lycos exist solely for the purpose of collecting information about other Web sites, organizing this information, and then making it available in searchable form to Web users.

By starting at a Web site running such a search engine, you can search for documents that contain a term or terms relevant to your interest. Depending on how finely you specify what you are looking for, you may be presented with only a few matches, called *hits*, or with thousands. By refining your search—making it more and more specific—you can eventually winnow down a huge amount of information into a small, easily managed number of documents. Once you have isolated a reasonable number of pertinent documents, you can jump directly to those of interest by using the embedded hypertext links.

With all of the attention being paid to the World Wide Web, it's easy to forget that there really is much more to the Internet than just the Web. The Internet allows you to transfer files to and from your computer using file transfer protocol or ftp. Thousands of USENET newsgroups provide a forum for discussing almost any topic imaginable. Businesses use the Internet to link remote offices located across town or across oceans.

All of this and much more is covered in detail in the chapters immediately following this one. You will learn how to connect to the Internet, how to choose a Web browser, how to access resources on the Internet in general and the Web in particular, and even how to bring up a Web site of your own if you are so inclined.

But all of this is directed at the Internet as it exists today. Let's see if we can take a little bit longer view of things and predict where the Internet is heading in the near future.

The Future of the Internet

When all is said and done, the Internet as it exists today is simply an internetwork of computer systems running the TCP/IP Suite. We are now taking the first baby steps in exploring its potential. What we do with it will change with time, just as the Internet itself will change with time. Few of those who saw the first flickering efforts at television in the 1920s could have imagined Home Box Office and 500-channel satellite TV. Few today can predict how the Internet will be integrated with our daily lives in a few years' time.

We know that the Internet will continue to evolve. The current T3 45 Mbps backbone is clearly inadequate to serve even today's needs, and is in the process of being upgraded by MCI to gigabit-range speeds. We'll outgrow even those speeds soon enough, but something will always be on hand to replace technology that is becoming obsolescent.

Privatization is the best thing ever to hit the Internet. When the Internet was a creature of the U.S. government, what we could get was limited to what the government was willing to give us. We paid for the Internet indirectly through our taxes, but had effectively no say in how it was run or how quickly it was expanded to meet new demands. Now that the Internet is in the hands of private, profit-making companies, what we can get is whatever we're willing to pay for directly. In the long run, we'll end up paying less, and we'll be writing the checks to a provider that is much more responsive to our needs than the U.S. government ever could be.

Improvements in Infrastructure

At its foundation, the Internet depends on a data communications infrastructure, or backbone, adequate to transmit large and ever-increasing amounts of data. In just the past few years, the Internet backbone has progressed from running at 56 Kpbs to nearly 45 Mbps, an almost thousand-fold increase. Just a few years ago, if you had a 56 Kbps connection to the Internet backbone you were considered to have a fast link. Nowadays, a T1 link to the backbone running at 1.544 Mbps is common, and the shift to T3s running at nearly 45 Mbps is well underway at larger sites.

This is obviously going to become a problem sooner rather than later. If your pipe runs at 45 Mbps, my pipe runs at 45 Mbps, a lot of other peoples' pipes run at 45 Mbps, and all of us along with thousands of others are all connecting to a backbone that runs at that same 45 Mbps, something has to give. Unfortunately, that something is the backbone itself.

The Internet backbone is currently provided by MCI, and most of it runs on 45 Mbps T3 lines. MCI and other carriers have been scrambling over the past few years, spending billions of dollars to deploy a new technology called Synchronous Optical Network, or SONET. SONET promises multi-gigabit per second throughput, and its deployment is well under way now by MCI, AT&T, Sprint, and other carriers.

Unfortunately, demand is increasing even faster than is capacity. Network outages are, in general, increasing each year, and will continue to do so until SONET deployment is substantially complete in 1997 or 1998. What this means to Internet users is that slow-downs and outright network failures are going to be a fact of life for the next few years.

Bob Metcalfe, the inventor of Ethernet and a columnist for *Infoworld* magazine, has been trumpeting the imminent collapse of the Internet for some time now, and his predictions will almost certainly be realized sometime in 1996 or 1997. One of the design characteristics of a packet-switching network like the one used as the foundation of the Internet is that, as load increases, individual response times may suffer, but all requests are eventually serviced. This relationship remains reasonably linear within a wide range, but as design limits for the network are approached and in some recent cases exceeded, the theory breaks down. Because of the heavy traffic on the network, too many packets are lost and must be resent, which further increases the load on the network, which causes even more packets to be lost. This vicious circle will eventually cause the network to collapse unless the load is brought into closer equilibrium with the transport capacity of the network.

This equilibrium can be achieved either by reducing the amount of traffic carried or by increasing the size of the pipe that carries it, or by a combination of the two. Realistically, the amount of traffic is not going to be reduced, leaving the only alternative to avoid complete collapse as upgrading the network backbone.

If all of this presents a dim view of the future of the Internet, it isn't meant to. There is an old saying that because the government doesn't provide shoes doesn't mean that men go barefoot. Well, nowadays, the government does provide shoes, but the concept remains the same. The Internet is too useful a resource to be allowed to disappear. As sporadic outages and service slow-downs become even more common, and large-scale failures of the network begin to occur, they will serve as wake-up calls to those in whose hands the future of the Internet resides.

The already rapid transition to SONET and OC-48 level links will accelerate. We're in for a rough ride over the next few years, and planning for these outages and slow-downs will be essential if your business is to be able to weather them. Ultimately, the Internet is too useful to fail, and will be provided with the infrastructure it needs to succeed.

Internet Service Providers

Only a year or so ago, if you had Internet service, chances are it was provided by a small local company whose only business was to provide Internet Service. These companies bought a T1 or fractional T1 link to an upstream Internet provider like MCI, installed a router, put in some telephone lines and modems, and went into business selling Internet services to anyone they could interest. In structure and funding, most of these small Internet Service Providers (ISPs) resembled more of a hobbyist bulletin board system than they did a common carrier service provider like AT&T or MCI.

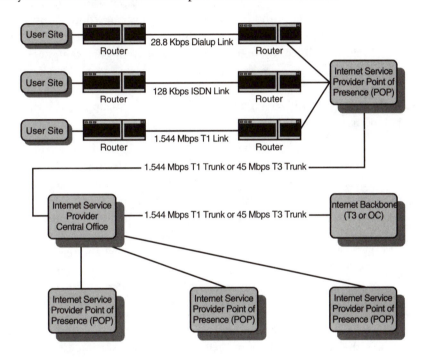

Fig. 13.2
A typical Internet Service Provider may have several points of presence, each of which serves hundreds of users, and all of which depend on a single connection to the Internet backbone.

V

Using the Internet

All of this has changed markedly in the last year. The small mom-and-pop ISPs no longer have the cost structure or the deep pockets needed to compete as ISPs. Their troubles began with increased marketing efforts by regional and national ISPs like PSInet. When CompuServe, America Online, Prodigy, and other commercial online services belatedly recognized the pent-up customer demand for Internet access, they took immediate steps to rectify their omission by integrating Internet access into their mainstream services. To make matters worse, the major commercial online services went into competition with themselves by introducing special Internet-only services for those with no interest in their other services.

The end result is that no one needs to depend on small local Internet Service Providers any longer for access to the Internet. The small providers are finding that the economies of scale enjoyed by the larger providers make it impossible for the mom-and-pop operations to continue to compete in the now commoditized business of delivering simple Internet access. As a result, many small ISP's have shifted their emphasis by attempting to provide value-added services like hosting Web sites for other companies. This effort, too, is doomed to fail.

Just as the advent of affordable and accessible desktop publishing software resulted in many newsletters and company publications being done in-house instead of being farmed out to a specialist as they had been in the past, the proliferation of simplified Internet software and technology into homes and businesses will eliminate any value-added aspect of the services offered by small ISPs. It is unlikely that small ISPs will succeed in adapting to the new market realities; they will soon go the way of the buggy whip and the vinyl record album.

As if things weren't gloomy enough already for small ISPs, looming on the horizon are the big guys—the telephone and cable television companies. These organizations see the huge potential profits to be gained by supplying Internet access to homes and businesses, and each intends to grab as much of that revenue stream as possible. The entry of these companies into the fray will likely doom small ISPs immediately, and eventually will probably do the same to the companies who are now the big fish—national and regional ISPs like PSInet and UUnet. Little fish are eaten by bigger fish, who are in turn eaten by even bigger fish. The phone and cable companies are the biggest fish of all.

In addition to the economies of scale enjoyed by the telephone and cable companies, they have one factor in their favor that almost guarantees that one or the other, if not both, will eventually become dominant in providing Internet services. They already have a wire that leads to your home or business. This advantage cannot be overstated. Essentially every home and business in the country already has one or more telephone lines connected to it. A majority of homes and many businesses are already wired for cable television, and even those that are not are usually within close proximity of a trunk line that makes connecting them inexpensive and straightforward.

The problem is, all of this existing cable was installed to provide specific functions, and high-speed data transmission wasn't one of them. As described in Chapter 2, "Understanding Communications Services and Hardware" large-scale efforts are underway by both the telephone and cable companies to allow them to make use of this existing cable to perform a function for which it was never intended. They will succeed in their efforts;. count on it. The potential payoff is too large to make failure an option.

The only reasons that telephone and cable companies are not already dominant as ISPs is that their fundamentally bureaucratic structure makes it difficult for them to adapt quickly to changing market conditions; and both were slow to recognize the market potential of providing Internet services. Both of these problems are being addressed. For example, in March, 1996, AT&T announced what will in the future probably be recognized as the harbinger of telephone and cable companies jumping into the market with both feet.

On March 1, 1996, AT&T announced the WorldNet pricing plan. In essence, this plan offers to provide any AT&T long distance customer with five free hours per month of Internet access for a full year, with extra hours billed at $2.50 per hour. Customers can also choose a flat-rate plan that allows unlimited Internet access for $20 per month. Even customers of other long distance companies were not overlooked. They can have similar service at somewhat higher rates. And by the way, AT&T guarantees no busy signals, the constant bane of users of other Internet access services.

Consumers greeted this announcement with joy, but only stunned silence resulted from other ISPs. They recognized immediately that AT&T WorldNet threatened their very existence. This realization was echoed immediately on Wall Street, where the stocks of competing ISPs plummeted. Nor is this effort likely to fail, as some observers of AT&T's earlier efforts at providing network services have predicted. If there is one thing that AT&T is good at, it's providing reliable service on a huge scale. AT&T has both the customer base to support this effort and the resources to provide Internet access to millions of customers. AT&T's existing Points of Presence (POPs) cover more than 80 percent of the United States, both geographically and in terms of customers.

With WorldNet, AT&T has also shown that they are worrying about the details. Each customer who signs up for WorldNet service receives an AT&T branded copy of the Netscape Navigator Web browser that provides the customer with a required best-of-breed software component, and standardizes the user environment to ease support problems. WorldNet will also provide home sites oriented toward both homes and businesses, along with a wealth of directories, search sites, and other Web services.

From the users' point of view, one of the most attractive benefits of WorldNet will be the absence of busy signals. Users of commercial online services, America Online in particular, have become used to constant busy signals which make it difficult or impossible to gain access to the service. If AT&T comes through on their promise, this will no longer be an issue.

V

Using the Internet

WorldNet also addresses the perceived problem of security for online financial transactions. In reality, of course, your credit card number is no more likely to be compromised by sending it to an online retailer via the Internet than it is by giving it to an anonymous salesman on the other end of an 800 number, or for that matter by giving it to a retail clerk at the mall. Still, the perception has been that there is a security risk involved in transmitting your credit card number via the Internet. From the other side, too, vendors have expressed some concern about accepting this information via the Internet and shipping goods on that basis. AT&T addresses these concerns with WorldNet by guaranteeing any online transaction made using the AT&T Universal Card.

MCI moved quickly to counter this marketing blitz by AT&T. On March 18, 1996, MCI announced its own competing service. Like AT&T, MCI offers its existing long distance customers five free hours of Internet access per month, and unlimited access for $20 per month. MCI also stated that they had been offering this service for some months before the announcement, but had not publicized it. In this same announcement, MCI said that they would be complete upgrading their portion of the Internet backbone from T3 lines running at 45 Mbps to ATM running at 155 Mbps by late April, 1996.

MCI's announcement puts another nail in the coffin of the small general purpose Internet Service Providers. Those that survive are likely to do so by focusing their efforts on niche markets rather than on the general dial-up Internet access market. As other major players enter the market and the resulting competition results in more diverse services being offered by the majors, even these niche players will be squeezed out.

Government and the Internet

With the explosion of the Internet has come increased interest from the government. Because the Internet at its present size and ubiquity is a new phenomenon, the government has not yet taken many measures to restrict it. This will change rapidly, and is in fact changing as these words are written. This government intervention will take three forms:

- *Control*. No government anywhere, regardless of how democratic or how benign, wants its citizens to have free, uncontrolled access to a means of communication that is not under the direct or indirect control of that government. The ability of ordinary citizens to exchange information freely threatens governments. Attempts by the U.S.

government to restrict encryption technology in the hands of private individuals to means easily decrypted by the NSA and other government agencies is an example of this concern.

■ *Censorship.* With the passage of the Communications Decency Act of 1996, the federal government has begun efforts on a large scale to censor the content of the Internet. As usual, this censorship initially takes the form of an attack on some aspect that nearly no one will defend, in this case pornography. It will proceed from there to an attack on the availability of information that no right-thinking person needs, for example how to make an ammonium nitrate/fuel oil bomb like the one used in the Oklahoma City bombing. From there, it is but a small step to forbidding discussion of issues that the government deems undesirable. Fortunately, a diverse coalition of organizations has filed a challenge to the Communications Decency Act, and has succeeded, at least temporarily, in eliminating enforcement of the more onerous restrictions of the CDA. Still, you can expect increased government efforts to control the Internet.

■ *Universal Access.* As might have been expected, the pleas for universal access are on the rise. Newspaper editorials and speeches by politicians decry the fact that the wealthier among us are more likely to enjoy the perceived advantages of Internet access, while the poor suffer its lack. We are heading for a stratified society, with information-haves and information-have-nots, or so they say. This "if everyone can't have it, no one can have it" attitude has been on the rise in this country for decades, and is likely to ultimately impact how you access the Internet and how much you have to pay to do so. Just as your health insurance subsidizes the use of hospital services by the poor, expect your monthly Internet access charge to have built in to it a subsidy to provide Internet access to the poor. Write your representative, making it clear to him that you believe that Internet access is neither a right nor a necessity, and that the government should keep its hands off. Otherwise, in a few years, you're likely to be depending for Internet access on the same folks who bring you the U.S. Postal Service.

New Services

Predicting what new services will become available on the Internet is a dangerous business. It is difficult to guess what can be done with millions of interconnected computer systems until you have those millions of systems linked, as we are just now doing. Improvements in the infrastructure have a great bearing on what is possible. What you can do practically with a T1 link running at 1.544 Mbps differs greatly from what is practical with a 28.8 Kbps dial-up link, just as it differs from what is possible with a 45 Mbps T3 link. As the speed of communications increases and the cost decreases, we may find revolutionary new applications that depend on widespread high-speed access.

Some of the possibilities are now beginning to appear. As we mentioned earlier, delivery of real-time audio and telephone service via the Internet is becoming a reality. Video on demand is a bit further out, but approaching. Ubiquitous home networking and control is still further in the future, as is truly usable mobile networking.

No one today can make even a reasonably accurate guess at exactly where the Internet will stand in five years, let alone 10 years. There are simply too many variables. What is clear is that, with so many companies devoting so many resources to developing the Internet, and so many people taking a serious interest in using the Internet, new services will be developed as new needs become clear.

By getting involved now, you are taking the first steps as an early adopter of Internet technology, which will ultimately benefit both you and your company. Those who stand by timidly awaiting things to settle down will find themselves left at the starting gate. Companies that fail to adopt the Internet will find themselves playing catch-up in order to be able to compete with companies that took an early stand in favor of the Internet. Don't be left out.

Understanding Internet Addressing

An *Internet address*, also called an *IP address*, is a four-byte or 32-bit value that is conventionally expressed as four decimal numbers separated by periods. This format is called *dotted decimal*. Here is an example of a dotted decimal IP address: 192.168.169.5

Because each decimal value represents one byte, it can assume only values between 0 and 255. This means that the lowest value possible for an IP address is 0.0.0.0 and the highest is 255.255.255.255. As we will see, these and other special values are reserved for specific purposes.

An IP address is subdivided into two parts, a *network number* and a *host number*. The network number designates the specific network to which the IP address belongs, and the host number designates a specific computer or other device attached to that network.

In the Internet community, workstations, servers, routers, and other devices that are assigned IP addresses are referred to as hosts. This confuses a lot of people new to the Internet, because they are used to thinking of a host as a large central computer. Not so with Internet terminology. Even the smallest component that needs to be discretely addressed must be assigned an IP address, and is then referred to as a host. For example, the IP address shown previously belongs to host "5" on network "192.168.169." Host "5" may be an old IBM XT, or it may be just a port on a router.

Internet Network Information Center (InterNIC)

Internet addresses must be unique. No two networks or hosts may have the same Internet address. If they did, the Internet would become hopelessly confused when trying to route a packet to the right destination. This means you can't just choose an Internet address for yourself at random. Some central authority is needed to allocate Internet addresses and make sure that they aren't duplicated.

This central authority is called the *Internet Network Information Center (InterNIC)*, and it is responsible for administering the IP address space, among other functions.

You can reach the InterNIC by pointing your World Wide Web browser to:
http://www.internic.net
or via anonymous ftp to:
ftp://ftp.internic.net

On the Web

The InterNIC was originally operated by Advanced Network & Services Inc. (ANS), a non-profit corporation established in 1990 by Merit, IBM, and MCI for the purpose of building and administering the Internet backbone. The National Science Foundation originally provided a full subsidy to cover the costs of operating the InterNIC, but this subsidy has recently been scaled back with the intent of eventually placing the InterNIC on a pay-as-you-go basis.

With the loss of government funding imminent, the structure and policies of the InterNIC have been changed to reflect this new reality. Although InterNIC continues to receive some money from the National Science Foundation, this too will disappear before long. The InterNIC has been reorganized into a cooperative effort between the NSF, AT&T, and Network Solutions, Inc. AT&T Corporation now provides Directory and Database Services, and Network Solutions, Inc. provides Registration Services.

V

Using the Internet

Network Address Classes

Internet addresses are divided into five classes, designated A through E. Of these, Class D is reserved for multicast use, and Class E is experimental. The only Internet Address classes you are likely to use on a regular basis are Classes A through C.

Remember that an Internet address comprises four bytes. The difference between Internet address Classes A through C is in how many of these four bytes are reserved for the network address and how many are therefore available to use for the host address.

- Internet Class A addresses allocate only the first byte to the network address, leaving three bytes available for host addresses within that network.

- Internet Class B addresses allocate the first two bytes to the network address, leaving two bytes available for host addresses within that network.

- Internet Class C addresses allocate the first three bytes to the network address, leaving only one byte available for host addresses within that network.

As we will see, the Internet address class assigned to your network has a great deal to do with how large your network will be, and how many sub-networks it will include. You may request that the InterNIC grant your network an address corresponding to any of these three Internet classes, but it is up to InterNIC to determine which class it is willing to grant.

Internet Class A Addresses

Because Internet Class A addresses use only the first byte of the Internet address to specify the network address, there can be very few Class A network addresses available—126 to be precise. However, because a Class A network address has three full bytes, or 24 bits, available to use for host addresses, each Class A network can have about 2^{24} or 16,777,214 host addresses contained within that network. Those readers who are quick with a calculator may have noticed that 2^{24} is really 16,777,216. The reason for the small discrepancy is that Internet host addresses comprised of all binary 0s or all binary 1s are reserved for special use. The allocation of bytes between the network address and the host address in an Internet Class A address is shown in figure 13.3.

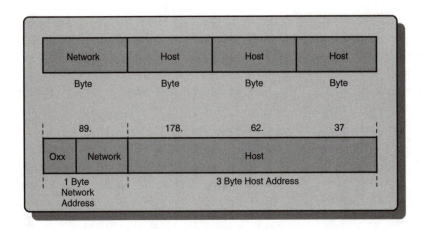

Once you have a little experience working with Internet addresses, it will be immediately obvious to you whether a given address represents a Class A, B, or C network, simply by looking at the first byte of the Internet address. If that first byte is between 1 and 126, you are looking at an Internet Class A address. Here's why.

Look at the first, or most significant, byte of an Internet address. The first, or most significant, three bits of this byte determine which class an Internet address belongs to. The first three bits—the 128-bit, the 64-bit, and the 32-bit—of a Class A address have the pattern 0xx. Because the value of the 128-bit must be zero, a Class A address can never begin with a decimal value larger than 128. Because the decimal values 0 and 255 are reserved for special purposes, a Class A Internet address always has a decimal value between 1 and 126 inclusive as the first byte.

Internet Class A addresses are reserved for the very largest corporations and government entities. Unless your corporate name is something like IBM or GM, don't bother to apply to InterNIC for a Class A address. All you'll accomplish is to give the folks at InterNIC a good laugh. Nearly all of the Class A network addresses have already been allocated. Getting one for your organization would almost literally take an act of Congress.

Internet Class A Addresses range from 1.0.0.0 through 126.0.0.0.

Internet Class B Addresses

Because Internet Class B addresses use the first two bytes of the Internet address to specify the network address, there can be about 2^{16}, or 65,534 Class B network addresses. Again, the actual count is reduced by two because addresses comprising all binary 0s or all binary 1s are reserved. Because a Class B network address has two full bytes, or 16 bits, remaining available to use for host addresses, each Class B network can have about 2^{16} or 65,534 host addresses contained within that network. The allocation of bytes between the network address and the host address in an Internet Class B address is shown in figure 13.4.

Fig. 13.4
Internet Class B networks use 2 bytes for the host address to allow more than 65 thousand hosts per network.

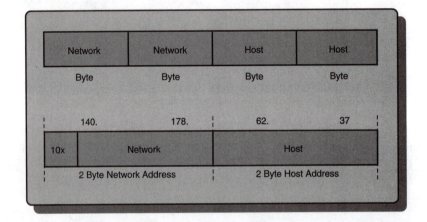

Again, you can identify a Class B network address simply by looking at the value of the first byte. If that first byte is between 128 and 191, you are looking at an Internet Class B address. Again, the first three bits of the Internet address determine the class of the network address. For a Class B network address, these first three bits have the pattern 10x. Because the first bit must be 1, this means that the first byte of a Class B network address must have a decimal value of at least 128. Because the second bit must be 0, this means that the first byte of a Class B network address can have a decimal value no greater than 191.

Internet Class B addresses are intended for large companies which operate moderate to large networks. For example, Microsoft has a Class B network address, as does Novell. A large Internet Service Provider may be granted a Class B network address with the intention of sharing those 65,534 network addresses among its subscribers. Multiple Class B network addresses are also now assigned in lieu of assigning a Class A network address to companies that would otherwise qualify for the Class A.

Up until the explosion of the Internet a couple of years ago, getting a Class B network assigned to you by InterNIC was pretty straightforward. They were pretty much passed out on request. Millions of new users and concern about remaining address space changed all that. Today, you must document and justify to InterNIC your need for a Class B network address. If you truly need a Class B, plan on spending at least a man-month of effort in collecting and presenting the required documentation. As this is written, about half of the available Class B network addresses have already been assigned.

Internet Class B addresses range from 128.1.0.0 through 191.254.0.0.

Internet Class C Addresses

Because Internet Class C addresses use the first three bytes of the Internet address to specify the network address, there can be about 2^{24}, or 16,777,214 Class C network addresses. Again, the actual count is reduced by two because addresses comprising all binary 0s or all binary 1s are reserved. Because a Class C network address has one full byte, or 8 bits, remaining available to use for host addresses, each Class C network can have about 2^8 or 254 host addresses contained within that network. The allocation of bytes between the network address and the host address in an Internet Class C address is shown in figure 13.5.

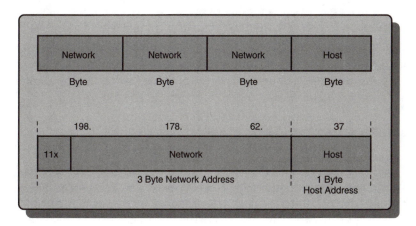

Fig. 13.5
Internet Class C networks use 1 byte for the host address to allow 256 hosts per network.

Again, you can identify a Class C network address simply by looking at the value of the first byte. If that first byte is between 192 and 223, you are look-ing at an Internet Class C address. Again, the first three bits of the Internet address determine the Class of the network address. For a Class C network ad-dress, these first three bits have the pattern 110. Because the first two bits must be 1, this means that the first byte of a Class C network address must have a decimal value of at least 128 + 64, or 192. Because the third bit must be 0, this means that the first byte of a Class C network address can have a decimal value no greater than 223.

Internet Class C addresses are intended for small and medium companies which operate small networks. With the intention of preserving the few remaining available Class B addresses for situations in which they are truly necessary, InterNIC now often assigns multiple Class C network addresses in lieu of assigning a single Class B network address to companies which would otherwise qualify for the Class B.

Again, until use of the Internet exploded a couple of years ago, getting a Class C network address assigned to you by InterNIC was almost automatic. Today, you must prove to InterNIC that you need a Class C network address. Rather than assigning a Class C address directly to a company, InterNIC prefers to allow Internet Service Providers to assign Class C blocks to companies which they serve. If you do decide to apply for your own Class C address, plan on spending at least an hour or two filling out the forms. As this is written, something less than half of the available Class C network addresses have already been assigned.

Internet Class C addresses range from 192.0.1.0 through 223.255.254.0.

Internet Class D and Class E Addresses

Although we mention Internet Class D and Class E addresses for completeness, you are unlikely to have occasion to deal with either of them. Internet Class D addresses are reserved for Multicast use, and range from 224..0.0.0 through 239.255.255.255. Internet Class E addresses are reserved for experimental use, and range from 240.0.0.0 through 255.255.255.255.

Host Addressing, Subnets and Netmasks

When you apply to the InterNIC for a block of addresses, what they provide is only the network address portion of the address. It is then up to you to assign Host Addresses to each of your systems and to otherwise manage your IP Addresses. For instance, let's say you have applied for and been granted an Internet Class C network address, otherwise called a C Block. Let's take a look at how you might assign addresses to your systems and otherwise manage your new C Block.

Assigning Host Addresses

The network address assigned to you by InterNIC may, for example, be 192.168.169.0. Because all hosts must be assigned a non-zero host number, the lowest address you can assign to one of your systems is 192.168.169.1. Because an address of 255 (all binary 1s) is reserved for broadcasts, the highest address you can assign is 192.168.169.254. This means that you have a total of 254 addresses that you can assign to systems in your network.

It is completely up to you how these host addresses are assigned within your network. InterNIC doesn't care, as long as you use the network address they assigned to your network. By convention, the first available address, in this case 192.168.169.1, is assigned to the boundary router which connects you to the Internet. Your Internet Service Provider may require you to assign your router to the first available host address, but if it does, this is due simply to an internal policy of the ISP rather than to any hard requirement enforced by InterNIC or anyone else. Servers are also often assigned low addresses.

You may assign IP addresses to devices by one of two methods:

- *Static IP address assignment* means that you manually "hard code" a specific IP address to each device, and that this IP address, once assigned, never changes. How you assign an IP address manually varies from device to device. With some computer systems, you may edit a configuration file. With routers and other active network components, you may physically toggle DIP switches or use a terminal to program the device. With Windows NT and Windows 95, you manually assign an IP address from the Control Panel Network icon.

- *Dynamic IP address assignment* means that you create a pool of available IP addresses, which are then assigned to devices on an as-needed basis. Dynamic IP address assignment is done using the Dynamic Host Configuration Protocol (DHCP) supported by Windows NT Workstation 4.0, and covered later in this chapter.

Before the development of DHCP (and an earlier, less capable protocol named BOOTP), Static IP address assignment was the only alternative. Although using this method is workable in a small network, as the number of devices grows, it becomes almost impossible to manage them manually. Also, the proliferation of notebook computers and the increasing demands that a computer be able to plug in anywhere has made Dynamic IP address assignment almost mandatory. Most network managers today prefer to use DHCP to manage most of their IP devices by assigning IP addresses from a pool.

There are, however, exceptions to the desirability of using Dynamic IP address assignments, even in very large networks. Active network components like routers need to have a static IP address so that they can be found reliably, not only by workstations on the local network, but by routers on other networks. Similarly, you don't want your servers having one address today and a different one tomorrow or next week. Accordingly, DHCP makes provision for reserving static IP addresses for such components.

V

Using the Internet

Subnets

With the boom in the Internet, network addresses, once thought to be inexhaustible, suddenly became a scarce commodity. Only a few years ago, if you told InterNIC that you had offices in three physical locations, they would have granted you three Class C network addresses almost automatically. Although you might have had only, say, 10 computers in each location, wasting 244 IP addresses at each location was of little import, because there were so many IP addresses available and such a relatively small demand for them. Nowadays, InterNIC will assign you a single C Block—if you're lucky—and tell you to make do with it.

This obviously presents a problem. You have three separate locations, each with its own separate network, and you would like to link all of these networks to the Internet while paying for only one Internet connection at one of the locations. You would like to treat these three networks as components of your entire network, but you have only a single network number.

Your first thought might be to simply divide the available IP addresses between the offices, assigning 192.168.169.1 through 192.168.169.85 to the first office; 192.168.169.86 through 192.168.169.170 to the second office, and 192.168.169.171 through 192.168.169.254 to the third office. Nice try, but it won't work. Here's why.

Remember that IP addresses, both network addresses and host addresses, must be unique to prevent confusion in delivering packets. Imagine a remote router that needs to deliver a packet to your network. It looks in its routing table and finds that your network address is 192.168.169.0 and forwards the packet to that address. But wait, the network address of your first office is 192.168.169.0. The network address of your second office is also 192.168.169.0. The network address of your third office is—you guessed it—also 192.168.169.0. Which office gets the packet? The real answer is that none of them will, because the infrastructure of the Internet does not allow for such an arrangement.

The real problem here is that we have three separate networks and we therefore need three separate network addresses. The way that we take the single network address granted to us by InterNIC and turn it into three separate network addresses is called *subnetting*. Subnets are assigned by the local IP administrator to extend the network portion of the address.

Remember that InterNIC has assigned us a network address that requires the full first three bytes of the four-byte Internet address, but has left us the final byte to do with as we please. The solution to our problem is to use some of those eight available bits to create our own sub-network address scheme. For example, rather than using all eight bits to designate the host address, we might use only 5 bits, and add the remaining 3 bits to the 3-byte network address provided by InterNIC. Like network addresses and host addresses, the subnet portion cannot be all binary 0's or all binary 1's. Figure 13.6 illustrates using a 3-bit subnet mask to subnet a single Class C block into six sub-networks.

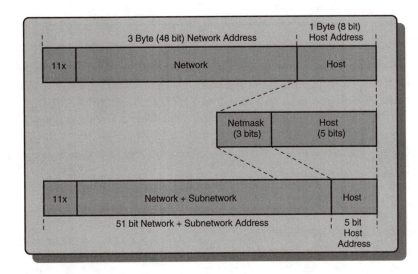

Fig. 13.6

Subnetting an Internet Class C address using a 3-bit subnet mask creates six sub-networks, each with 30 host addresses.

This means that by using 3 bits of the host address to subnet, we now have (2^3-2) or six network addresses to use as sub-network addresses. The disadvantage is that each sub-network can have only (2^5-2) or 30 devices assigned to it, rather than the (2^8-2) or 254 devices available when using the entire 8 bits for a host address (see Table 13.1.) Still, this is a small price to pay because we can now give each of our offices a separate network address, and each has only 10 systems anyway.

Table 13.1   Using Subnet Masks of Various Sizes

Subnet Bits	Host Bits	Subnet Mask	Number of Subnets	Hosts per Subnet	Total Hosts
1	7	128	0	126	0
2	6	192	2	62	124
3	5	224	6	30	180

(continues)

Subnet Bits	Host Bits	Subnet Mask	Number of Subnets	Hosts per Subnet	Total Hosts
4	4	240	14	14	196
5	3	248	30	6	180
6	2	252	62	2	124
7	1	254	126	0	0

Table 13.1 Continued

Subnetting is useful for larger networks as well. In fact, although subnetting a Class C network address preserves the network address, it so limits the number of hosts available that subnetting a Class C network address is sometimes unworkable, and you have no alternative but to convince InterNIC that you need additional Class C network addresses. With Class A and Class B network addresses, on the other hand, you have three full bytes or two full bytes, respectively, available for the subnet portion and the host address portion, which gives you plenty of room to operate. Class A network addresses are almost always subnetted at the byte level. Class B network addresses are typically subnetted at the byte level, but may be subnetted at the bit level.

Subnet Masks or Netmasks

The subnet mask is the decimal value of that portion of your host address space that you have assigned to use for subnetting. For example, to subnet your Class C network address to yield six subnets each with room for 30 hosts, you use the three most significant bits of the full byte available to you. These three bits are the 128-bit, the 64-bit and the 32-bit. Totaling these values yields 224, which is the subnet mask for your 3-bit subnetwork. A subnetted network using a 3-bit subnet mask is shown in figure 13.7.

Similarly, if you elect to subnet using 4 bits to yield 14 subnets, each with 14 hosts, your subnet mask includes the most significant 4 bits—the 128-bit, the 64-bit, the 32-bit and the 16-bit—to give a 4-bit subnet mask of 240. A subnetted network using a 4-bit subnet mask is shown in figure 13.8.

The default subnet mask for an Internet Class A network address is 255.0.0.0. The default subnet mask for an Internet Class B network address is 255.255.0.0. The default subnet mask for an Internet Class C network address is 255.255.255.0. In each case, this means that the default is to have no subnetting at all, instead allocating all available bits to the Host Address portion.

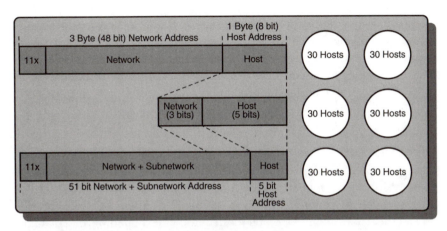

Fig. 13.7
Using a 3-bit subnet mask allows you to subnet a Class C network address into six sub-networks, each with 30 host addresses.

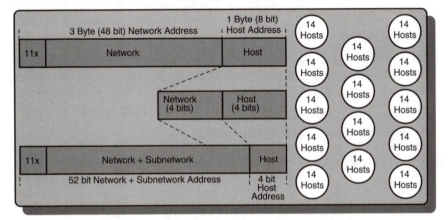

Fig. 13.8
Using a 4-bit subnet mask allows you to subnet a Class C network address into 14 sub-networks, each with 14 host addresses.

Some routers accept the subnet mask value in dotted decimal format. Others require that this information be entered as a binary string.

Default Router

An IP device uses the subnet mask to determine if the destination address is on the same network as the source address, or if the packet instead needs to be forwarded to a different network. If the source and destination addresses are on different networks, the source IP device forwards the packet to its designated *default router*, also called the *default gateway*.

Each IP host must know its default router. If you are using Static IP address assignment, you will specify this information as well as the IP address itself when you are configuring a host. If you are instead using Dynamic IP address assignment, the default router is specified on the DHCP server or BooTP server and is then assigned automatically to a host.

All packets whose destination address is not on the local subnet, as determined by applying the netmask, are forwarded to the default router. A Layer 2 packet, or frame—created by Ethernet, Token Ring, FDDI, and so on—which is destined for a remote network is sent to the hardware address (or MAC address) of the local default router for subsequent forwarding. A Layer 3, or IP, packet which is destined for a remote network is sent to the software address, also called the network address, of that remote network.

The router compares the destination network address to entries in its *routing tables*. If the destination network address is found, the router forwards that packet using the appropriate interface, as specified in the routing table. An interface may, for example, be a leased T1 line to an Internet Service Provider, an Ethernet connection to a router located in the next building, or a dial-up connection to a router located at a branch office. The routing table entries are entered in the following ways:

- *Connected*. An automatic entry that exists for each installed interface.
- *Static*. An entry assigned manually by the network administrator.
- *Protocol*. An entry assigned by the router itself using information received from other routers to which it is directly or indirectly connected. This information is exchanged between routers using routing protocols, which are covered later in this chapter.

Internet Protocol Version 6, IPv6 or IPng

The perceived shortage of address space and other issues that became apparent with the explosion of the Internet have led to increasingly vocal demands for changes to the basic structure of the Internet Protocol Suite, beginning with improvements to the core IP protocol itself. These demands have resulted in the creation of a new version of the Internet Protocol called *IPng*, for *Internet Protocol Next Generation*. More formally known as *Internet Protocol Version 6*, or *IPv6*, it is intended to solve many of the problems which exist with the current version of IP, designated IP Version 4, and in particular to eliminate the address space issues that have plagued IPv4 for the last two years or so.

IPv6 Design Considerations

The fact that government and corporations throughout the world depend on IPv4 for mission critical applications means that a radical departure from existing methods is unacceptable, and that the upgraded IP has to offer backwards compatibility with existing IPv4 networks. Accordingly, IPv6 is an evolutionary step up from IPv4, rather than being revolutionary. The experts examined IPv4. What didn't work was fixed; what wasn't needed was removed; what was needed but wasn't there was added. Throughout the process, the need to maintain backwards compatibility and to ensure a clear transition path was always foremost in the designers' minds.

Although backwards compatibility and transition concerns are overwhelmingly important design considerations for IPv6, they are not the only such issue. One design consideration that has some subtle implications is that of growth.

Taking growth into account would seem to be an obvious design consideration for the development of IPv6, because, after all, the growth of the Internet and the resulting shortage of address space were the reasons for the creation of IPv6 in the first place. What may not be so obvious is that the nature of the Internet market will change over the next few years.

Right now, the Internet and TCP/IP are phenomena that are almost exclusively related to computers and networks. Today, a significant percentage of the existing computer systems are already connected to networks using IP. Even if one considers the large percentage of home computer systems that are not currently connected, factors in compound growth in installed computers in businesses, and projects a large increase in networked computer systems in third world countries, the potential for growth of the Internet is not overwhelmingly large—perhaps 10 times the number of systems currently connected to perhaps 50 times the current number. Although nothing to sneeze at, this growth could probably have been accommodated even without IPv6. The real need for expanded addressing has little to do with computers and networks as we think of them today.

How many computers do you have in your home? I have eight, counting workstations and servers. No, wait a minute. The microwave ovens in my kitchens each have a computer of sorts in them. So do all the TVs, the audio systems, the VCRs, the security system, the printers, the modems, the dishwasher, the home automation system controls, the clock radios, the telephones, and the telephone system controller. The microprocessor power just in a modern automobile is greater than the computing power used to manage the first moon shots. After thinking about it for only a couple of minutes, I count at least 50, and probably more than 100 microprocessors in my home. Yours probably has a similar number.

Right now, at least in most homes, few of these microprocessors connect to anything but the equipment they are a part of. That is destined to change. From the first faltering steps with X10 technology, home automation alternatives have expanded to include SmartHouse®, the Consumer Electronics Bus (CEBus®), and Echelon LonWorks® technology. It is likely that within the next 10 to 20 years, your home will be networked far more thoroughly than your computer system is today.

The lamp on your end table will have its own microprocessor, as will your refrigerator and probably even the lock on your front door. Even the individual items you bring home from the grocery store may well have their own microprocessors, and each will connect to the refrigerator and to your central computerized home controller to aid in menu planning and reduce food wastage. The thought of your broccoli chatting with your milk, and the two of them negotiating with the oven may seem bizarre, but the potential benefits are great. This may sound like science fiction, but it is not. The first steps are already underway, with companies the size of Motorola and Texas Instruments investing heavily in the future of home automation.

Because many of these devices will be designed to communicate with each other, the need for a networking schema is clear. The only thing on the horizon that will accommodate networking on such a scale is an extended version of the Internet Protocol, which is just what IPv6 will accommodate.

In addition to the home-automation market, the mobility market will continue to explode. Consider that only 10 years ago it was common for an entire family to share one, or perhaps two, personal telephone numbers, with each employed adult perhaps having another telephone number at work. Now, it is common for an individual to have 10 or more telephone numbers allocated to his personal use. You might have a voice number and a fax number at work, a business cellular number, a pager number, one or two personal telephone numbers at home, a personal cellular number, or perhaps one for each spouse, a data line at home, a fax line at home, and so on.

When you consider the explosion in the number of individually addressable communications devices, in combination with the shift from analog communications to digital, it is likely that hundreds of millions or billions of such mobile devices will need network addresses in the not too distant future. These mobile devices will all be networked, and they will use a variety of means to do so, including traditional wired networks, wireless networks, the cellular system and its follow-ons, and so forth.

A particular device may use different means of networking depending on its current location. For example, a Personal Data Assistant (PDA) may use the cellular telephone network to communicate while you are driving to work, a traditional cabled network while it is docked at home or at the office, and a wireless network as you wander around the building at work or at home. The demands on the networking infrastructure to support huge numbers of these nomadic systems will be gigantic. Again, IP is the only workable technology visible on the horizon, and again IPv6 will be used to accommodate this growth in mobile devices.

One potential market that may dwarf the others in terms of traffic generated is delivering entertainment across the network. The pay-per-view systems currently offered by most cable television companies will prove to be a dead-end technology. As the use of VCRs for time shifting and the explosion of video rental stores has proven beyond all possible doubt, what people want is to be able to watch exactly what they choose, exactly when they choose to do so.

The answer is called Video on Demand, and the technology to provide it isn't quite here yet. Within the next 10 years or so, it will be. With Video on Demand, if you decide that you'd like to watch the 1964 movie "Father Goose," starring Cary Grant at 4:17 a.m. on a Friday morning, you simply make your request to a centralized video server, which retrieves the movie from disk and starts sending you packets. Your video IP host, otherwise known as your television set, reassembles these packets and displays the movie for you in whatever resolution, aspect ratio, and sound quality you prefer. If you'd prefer to hear the soundtrack in Spanish, German, or Russian, you simply so indicate.

Video on Demand won't be limited to old movies, however. New movies, news, sports, live theatre—all of these and more will be available at the press of your remote button. In a few years, the network infrastructure to support this technology will be in place, and Sony won't be selling many VCRs. They will, however, be selling a lot of new television sets, or Video IP Hosts, if you prefer. The monstrous quantity of packets generated by this service would overwhelm IPv4. IPv6 will handle it easily.

These new markets have in common that they are consumer, or mass markets with huge audiences. Also, each of these new markets is now poised near critical mass. When they explode, it will likely be simultaneously, or at least with a high degree of overlap. Thus, we will have not just one new technology attempting to swamp the IP network, but several simultaneously.

IPv6 Improvements

Most of the problems with IPv4 are related to limited address space and to routing problems. Accordingly, most of the effort in designing IPv6 was devoted to making sure that address space limitations never again would become an issue, and that routing capabilities were expanded and enhanced. IPv6 makes many important changes from Ipv4, each discussed in the following sections.

Address Space Expansion. IPv6 expands the IP Address from 4 bytes (or 32 bits,) to 16 bytes (or 128 bits). This has two immediate benefits, one obvious and one not so obvious. First, the expansion from 4-byte addressing to 16-byte addressing increases the number of available IP Addresses. Using 4-byte, 32-bit, addresses gives us 2^{32}, or about 4,000,000,000, discrete addresses. This sounds like a lot, but we are starting to run out now. Using 16-byte, 128-bit, addressing, on the other hand, gives us about 3.4 x 10^{38}, or 300,000,000,000,000,000,000,000,000,000,000,000,000 discrete addresses. This number of addresses should suffice, at least until intergalactic settlement becomes a reality.

The second, and not so obvious, benefit to using a 16-byte address is that it allows us to add additional hierarchical levels of addressing. As IPv6 is widely adopted, the old differentiation between Class A, B, and C addresses will disappear, and we will again be able to design our network address hierarchies without concern about limited address space.

Routing Enhancements. Routing in IPv6 is nearly identical to IPv4 routing except that the addresses are 128 bit. IPv6 also has extensions which support new routing functionality, including Provider Selection, Host Mobility, and Auto-Readdressing.

- *Provider Selection* allows for routes to be based on policy, performance, or cost.

- *Host Mobility* accommodates the nearly impossible task (with IPv4) of routing to roaming wireless devices and portable computers.

- *Auto-Readdressing* also aids in the deployment of roaming devices by allowing the network to automatically route packets to the newly changed address of the device.

Multicast Addressing. IPv6 adds a *Scope* field to Multicast Addresses to allow the delivery of a packet to all members of a Multicast Group. For example, this feature could be used in video and audio broadcast servers. Instead of requiring the server to transmit the same data packet repeatedly to each receiver of the broadcast, it would simply transmit the packet once and leave it to the network routers to disseminate the traffic to all receivers. Unlike IPv4, IPv6 does not support broadcast addresses. Instead, IPv6 will send a multicast packet to the Multicast Group that is automatically created for each local subnet.

IPv6 also adds a new address type called an *Anycast Address*, which will deliver a packet to any one member of an Anycast Group. An Anycast Group could be multiple NICs on a host, or a group of load-sharing Web servers.

IP Header Formatting Additions and Changes. An IPv4 header contains the IP address and other information, some of which was seldom or never used. Because the IPv6 address is four times the size of the IPv4 address, keeping these unused fields would have done little but increase the size of the IPv6 header, with essentially no benefit to the user. This larger header size would also have increased the overhead involved in moving IP traffic through the Internet. Accordingly, several IPv4 header fields were either made optional, or eliminated entirely in the interests of keeping the number of bits that needed to be moved to a minimum. The resulting IPv6 header is only twice the size of the IPv4 header, although the address sizes have quadrupled.

At the same time, it had become obvious that new IP header fields were needed to cover options and eventualities that had not been considered when the IPv4 header format was designed. Accordingly, the IPv6 header format is designed to provide several new options or extensions, along with the ability to easily add others as needed. Two of the most important of these new options pertain to defining types of service and supporting native security.

The first of these extensions allows packets to be flagged by the sender to request a special type of service. For example, IP as it exists now is not a real-time service, and is therefore not appropriate for communicating audio, video, and other applications that cannot tolerate delay. With IPv6, such real-time data can be flagged to indicate its nature and request that it be routed via a path that uses ATM or another technology suitable to real-time requirements.

The second extension provides built-in support for security and authentication. With IP as it exists now, security was an afterthought. With the increasing use of TCP/IP for sensitive data and critical applications, two problems have become apparent. First, IPv4 packets are transferred across the network in unencrypted form, accessible to anyone with a few technical smarts and the desire to intercept your data. Second, with IP, you are who you say you are. No provision is made for user authentication, and a technically knowledgeable eavesdropper can use *IP Spoofing* to imitate an authorized sender or recipient by assuming that station's IP address.

Currently, the best defenses against this kind of activity are encryption and firewalls, neither of which is a completely satisfactory answer. Two means of encryption are used.

First, data can be encrypted at the application level before being assembled into packets. This method can work in tightly defined applications where it can be made transparent to users, such as using a custom database application with built-in encryption. It is largely ineffective when it requires manual user intervention, such as expecting users to manually encrypt each e-mail message they send.

The second method of encryption is done at the packet level, typically by the router, although sometimes by specialized encryption hardware. This method is secure and transparent, but has several drawbacks. It requires expensive equipment to implement, and adds a level of management complexity to the network. Perhaps more important, it operates only between defined points, typically remote locations within a single company where the necessary hardware has been installed. Traffic to and from general destinations remains unencrypted.

Firewalls are used to filter inbound and outbound traffic to restrict the sources from which packets will be accepted and the destinations to which they may be sent. A well-implemented firewall can add substantially to the level of security enjoyed by a network, but at the price of requiring additional expensive equipment, demanding scarce staff time to install and maintain it, and limiting the flexibility of the network that it serves. Firewalls are covered in much more detail in Chapter 18, "Building an Intranet."

The IPv6 header format addresses these security and authentication concerns by providing standardized support for them.

IPv6 Transition

Because IPv6 is designed to coexist with IPv4, we will see a period of several years during which both versions will be used. Routers will likely be the first devices to be upgraded to IPv6, because router vendors are in fierce competition with each other to include the newest features in their products. The only prerequisite for IPv6 implementation is to upgrade your name server to support the new IPv6 addressing format.

Internet Naming Conventions

With millions of connected systems on the Internet, nobody wants to try to remember a site as 192.168.169.8. It's much easier for most people to remember a site name of something like **ftp.nasa.gov** or **www.yahoo.com**. If you're going to assign English-like names to sites, it makes sense to develop a hierarchical naming system. That way, just knowing the name of a site may also tell you something about what type of site it is, where it might be located, and so forth. Two methods are used to name Internet sites.

Organizational Hierarchy

The first and older of these hierarchical naming methods is called the *Organizational Hierarchy*, and assigns sites to one of several types of enterprise, such as commercial, education, government, and so on. When the Internet was young, nearly all connected systems were located in the United States, and nearly all of them were either civilian government, military, or university sites. It made sense to group them by type, and the Organizational Hierarchy came into use. Here are the site category abbreviations and their corresponding types:

- com is used for commercial for-profit businesses, (**ibm.com**, **microsoft.com**)
- edu is used for universities and other educational institutions, (**harvard.edu**, **princeton.edu**)
- gov is used for civilian government at the federal and state level, (**nasa.gov**, **senate.gov**)
- int is used for international organizations, (**nato.int**)
- mil is used for military organizations, (**army.mil**, **navy.mil**)
- net is used for organizations which provide network services to other user organizations, (**att.net**, **mci.net**, **ans.net**)
- org is used for non-profit and charitable organizations, and for educational organizations that do not fit within the edu domain, (**eff.org**, **nra.org**, **democrat.org**, **republican.org**)

These categories are called *Top Level Domains* because they are used to group sites in the most general terms. The most generalized portion of an Internet domain name is farthest right. As you move to the left, using periods to separate the segments of the name, the components become more and more specific to a particular site and system.

For example, consider the wholly imaginary Internet domain name **athena.cs.wfu.edu**. The **edu** portion tells us that this is a university or educational institution. The **wfu** portion probably refers to Wake Forest University, although this is not immediately evident just from the domain name. The **cs** portion most likely refers to the Computer Science Department, although again this is simply an educated guess. The left-most portion of the domain name, **athena,** is a specific host located at **cs.wfu.edu**.

As we proceed even farther to the left, the information gets more specific still. For example, we may have a friend named John Smith who works at the Computer Science department of Wake Forest University, and whose logon name is John_Smith. To send e-mail to our friend, we would enter the following address into our e-mail package as the recipient:

john_smith@athena.cs.wfu.edu

Notice that the farther you proceed to the left, the less clear and the less "guessable" the information becomes. The **edu** portion is both clear and certain—we know for sure just looking at it, that this site is an educational institution. The **wfu** portion is less clear because unless we just happen to know that it refers to Wake Forest University we might not guess it. It is just as certain as the top level domain information, however, in that you can look up the meaning of **wfu** and find that, without ambiguity, it refers to Wake Forest University. Once you pass this point heading left, all of the information becomes both less clear and less guessable, short of contacting the site and asking.

To understand why, let's return to our old friends at the InterNIC. In addition to assigning IP addresses, InterNIC assigns *domain names*, again ensuring that each is unique. Just as the InterNIC assigns only the network address portion of your address block and leaves the host address portion up to you to assign, InterNIC also assigns only the top and second levels of the full domain name and leaves the rest up to you. In the case given above, InterNIC assigned the **wfu.edu** portion of the domain name to Wake Forest University. Wake Forest University in turn themselves created a sub-domain named **cs** and assigned the machine named **athena** to that sub-domain, without having to ask InterNIC to approve any of these actions. Similarly, the system administrator on **athena** created the username **john_smith** without having to tell anyone, let alone ask for approval.

That said, there are certain unofficial, yet closely followed practices for assigning names to domains and to certain systems within those domains. For example, many users may want to connect to both the ftp server and the World Wide Web server provided by a company. As a matter of courtesy to, and convenience for those users, it is common practice to name the ftp server **ftp.[domain name]** and the World Wide Web server **www.[domain name]**. For example, if you wanted to connect to the ftp server provided by Microsoft, you might guess, correctly as it turns out, that the system would be named **ftp.microsoft.com**. Similarly, if you were trying to connect to the World Wide Web server provided by Conner Peripherals, you might try **www.conner.com**, and you would again be successful.

> **Note**
>
> *Aliasing* allows more than one name to point to the same physical machine. For example, the names www.acme.com and ftp.acme.com may both point to the same physical machine and IP address. This allows you to run more than one service on a single computer, and still have each addressable by a discrete name.
>
> Conversely, one name may point to more than one physical machine and IP address. For example, ftp.netscape.com points to an array of many ftp servers, each with its own IP address. Which server you actually access when you ftp to ftp.netscape.com doesn't matter, since the contents are replicated across all of the servers. However, this arrangement allows the huge volume of ftp requests at this site to be serviced efficiently.

This method is not guaranteed to work, both because domain names aren't always what you might guess, and because not all administrators name their systems this way. For example, the domain name for Western Digital Corporation is not **westerndigital.com** as you might guess, but instead **wdc.com**. Similarly, there are many ftp sites that are not named **ftp** and some World Wide Web sites that are not named **www**. Still, it works most of the time, and avoids having to look something up first.

Geographical Hierarchy

The second and newer of these hierarchical naming methods is called the *Geographical Hierarchy*, and assigns domain names based on the two-letter country abbreviation for the physical location of that site. For example, using the Geographical Hierarchy, sites located in the United States have a top level domain of **us**, sites located in the United Kingdom use **uk**, those in France use **fr**, and so forth. A complete list of these country codes appears in Appendix A.

Because the Internet has become a world-wide phenomenon, this is now the preferred domain naming method. Before long, you may be unable to get a domain name using the older organizational hierarchy, and may instead be required to use the newer method. It is unclear at this point if existing domain names assigned under the organizational hierarchy will be required to change to the newer naming method. If this change is mandated, the imaginary Wake Forest University system located in Winston-Salem, North Carolina, U.S.A and used as an example above might instead have the Domain Name **athena.cs.wfu.ws.nc.us**

The only problem with geographic hierarchy domain names is that they are usually long, ugly and "uncool." Right now, the ultimate in prestige on the

Internet is to have an e-mail address that combines the shortest possible domain name with only either your full first name or your full surname. For example, I can be reached at **thompson@ttgnet.com**, a very prestigious address because it is short and sweet. If instead, for example, I had an account named **thompsrb@athena.cs.wfu.ws.nc.us**, that would be a considerably less prestigious account name—an obviously assigned username combined with a domain name that is too long, too ugly, and too institutional.

To be really cool, the domain name has to obviously belong to you rather than to some large corporation. For example, the domain name **aol.com** may be short, but it just isn't cool, no matter what username is in front of it. It immediately places you among the Internet masses and marks you, fairly or unfairly, as a "newbie" who will be granted little or no respect.

One of my partners, John Mikol, has the ultimate in cool domain names. He is simply **john@mikol.com**. It just doesn't get any better than this. If all of this seems trivial, it is, at least in some respects. Mail gets to you just as well at a long, ugly domain name as it does at a short, pretty one. Your file transfers don't run any slower, and you can access just as many Web sites.

Still, some people will go a long way to make sure they get a good domain name. And, to be fair, there are some real commercial advantages to a short and sweet domain name. If you work for Acme Inc., would you rather have people sending you mail as **smith@acme.com** or as **smith@acme.podunk.ut.us**? The first is short, elegant, and easy to remember. The second is long, much less elegant, and much more difficult to remember. In the next chapter, we'll examine in detail how to register your domain name.

Domain names are assigned on a first-come, first-served basis. Get the domain name you want now, before someone else gets it first. Ask Coca-Cola Corporation about what happens when you fail to register your domain name in a timely manner. A California college student originally registered **coke.com**, and Coca-Cola has spent a considerable amount of time and money attempting to get it back from him.

The Internet Protocol Suite

The foundation of everything we've been talking about so far is a collection of related protocols and standards called the Internet Protocol Suite. Nearly everyone calls it TCP/IP for short. In this section we will examine the major components of TCP/IP in some detail.

TCP/IP is the transport mechanism used by the Internet to move information from point to point within the network. TCP/IP is only one of many transports that are available. Windows NT Workstation 4.0 in fact supports two other transports:

- *IPX/SPX*, called NWLink by Windows NT, is the transport mechanism developed by Novell for NetWare. IPX/SPX is fast, reliable, simple to configure, and well-suited for local area networks. Although it is a routable protocol, it was not originally designed for wide area networks and internetworks, and is not the best choice for them. IPX/SPX can be considered obsolescent. It is still heavily used and will continue to be so at sites that use Novell NetWare. Even Novell, however, plans to introduce soon a version of their network operating system that will use native TCP/IP transport. As the years pass, IPX/SPX is likely to increasingly become a niche product, running only on small networks that are not internetworked.

- *NetBEUI*, or Net BIOS Extended User Interface, was used primarily by earlier versions of Microsoft peer networking, and is included in Windows NT Workstation 4.0 only for backwards compatibility with existing networks that run this protocol. NetBEUI is fast, reliable, and simple to configure. In the past, these benefits made it a good choice for a small-scale peer network. However, NetBEUI does not provide the Network Layer packet header information needed to route packets. Accordingly, NetBEUI networks can only use bridging and not routing, making NetBEUI totally inappropriate for any kind of internetworking.

TCP/IP has all of the advantages of IPX/SPX and of NetBEUI, and more. It does, however, have one drawback relative to these other transport protocols. Both IPX/SPX and NetBEUI were plug- and-play before that term became capitalized. Neither requires any setup or configuration to speak of. You just plug them together and they work.

TCP/IP is about as far from plug-and-play as you can get. It requires a great deal of setup and configuration to work at all, and a great deal more to work efficiently. Few organizations have anyone on staff who is paid to be an IPX/SPX expert or a NetBEUI expert. On the other hand, many organizations who depend on TCP/IP for internetworking have one or more highly skilled individuals who pretty much deal with TCP/IP all day long, every day. With the added complexity of TCP/IP, however, comes added capabilities and flexibility.

V

Using the Internet

Don't let this scare you off. If you are a user, your network administrator can arrange things so that you receive the benefits of TCP/IP without being aware of any of the underlying complexity. If you are the administrator, you may not need to learn as much about TCP/IP as you might fear. If all you need to do is run TCP/IP transport on your local area network and connect that network to the Internet, you can get away with just knowing some fundamentals and depend on your Internet Service Provider to take care of the really complicated things.

The Internet Activities Board (IAB) and Requests for Comment (RFC)

The Internet is often described as an anarchy, which it is in the true sense of the word. However, many people believe the words anarchy and chaos to be synonyms, which they are not. The Internet is anything but chaotic. For any data communications to occur, let alone for a world-wide network like the Internet to exist, rigidly defined rules must be in place to govern the communications between systems and networks. With the Internet, the difference is that all of these rules are arrived at cooperatively and are adhered to voluntarily. If you don't play by the rules, no one comes to haul you off to jail. You simply can't communicate with anyone else.

The governing body of the Internet is called the Internet Activities Board, or IAB. It sponsors two major committees. The Internet Research Task Force (IRTF) explores new technologies and evaluates their possible application to the Internet. The Internet Engineering Task Force (IETF) is charged with developing specifications and standards for new components of the IP Suite and for extensions to and improvements of existing components.

The Internet Protocol Suite is constantly evolving in response to new requirements and to improvements in technology. The mechanism used for this process is called the Request for Comment, or RFC. When a new protocol or a modification to an existing protocol is proposed, a detailed description of that protocol is issued to the Internet community as a numbered Request for Comment. As comments, suggestions, and criticisms are received in response to the RFC, they are incorporated and again circulated. After this iterative process has continued until everything has been worked out, the RFC is adopted by the IAB as a formal standard and is then promulgated. Even after being formally adopted, it retains the same number and is still referred to as an RFC.

You can view and download any and all RFCs that may interest you from **www.internic.net**. These documents are usually extremely technical in nature, and are of little practical interest to network administrators, even those who work with TCP/IP internetworking on a daily basis. Their real use, other than in the abstract as the codified body of standards that forms the foundation of the Internet, is as a checklist item when purchasing equipment.

For example, if you intend to purchase a router that will be used to link networks running Windows NT Server, you may want to be sure that it is RFC-1542 compliant. You don't need to read RFC-1542 or even know very much about it. All you need to know is that you need a particular feature or capability that is detailed in a particular RFC.

The DoD Model versus the OSI Reference Model

In Chapter 7, "Building a Network Infrastructure," we examined the OSI Reference Model in some detail, using it as a framework to understand networking issues. TCP/IP was designed around an earlier, but similar, model called the DARPA Model or the Department of Defense (DoD) Model. Because the layers of the DoD Model correspond so closely to those of the OSI Reference Model, albeit not necessarily on a one-to-one mapping, it has become the norm to apply the OSI Model to TCP/IP. In short, although the DoD Model has itself become obsolescent, the child of that model, TCP/IP, is anything but, so we use the new model to describe the older protocol. Figure 13.9 shows how the layers of these two models relate.

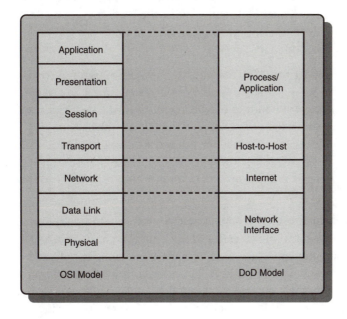

Fig. 13.9
The OSI Reference Model and the DoD Model.

Major IP Suite Components

In order to understand the place that each component of the Internet Protocol Suite has in communicating data, it is first necessary to understand something of how data flows through the network. Using the OSI Reference Model as a framework, data originates at the top layer, called the Application Layer. It is then passed in turn to each lower layer, much like a bucket brigade. Operations may be performed at each of these lower layers, and additional administrative information may be added in the form of headers and/or trailers specific to the layer in question.

When the data reaches the lowest, or Physical Layer, it is placed on the network cable to be transmitted to the destination device. At the destination device, the whole process is reversed. The destination device receives the data at the lowest, or Physical Layer, and then passes it up through each succeeding layer until it reaches the layer that corresponds with the layer on the source device where the data originated. As the data is passed through each higher layer, administrative information contained in headers and trailers specific to that layer is stripped out and acted upon.

For the purposes of this section, we will treat the upper three layers of the OSI Reference Model—the Application, Presentation, and Session Layers—as a single entity, and refer to them as the Upper Layers. This corresponds well to the DoD Model treatment of these three OSI Layers as a single Process/Application Layer. Similarly, we will treat the lower two layers, the Physical and Data Link Layers, as a single entity called the Lower Layers. Again, this corresponds well with the DoD Model treatment of these two OSI Layers as a single Network Interface Layer.

We will examine the OSI Network Layer, which corresponds to the DoD Internet Layer, as a separate issue. We will also examine the OSI Transport Layer, which corresponds to the DoD Host-to-Host Layer, separately. Note that all protocols do not necessarily fit neatly into the arbitrary layers defined by these models. For example, the Address Resolution Protocol (ARP) and Reverse Address Resolution Protocol (RARP) described later in this section are nominally Network Layer protocols. In fact, both belong at least partially in the Data Link Layer.

Deciding which protocols belong exactly where isn't important to most of us. What is important is to understand the general concept of how data flows through the network. Each layer communicates directly only with the layers immediately above and below it. Upper Layers provide data to, and request services from, the layer immediately below them, which processes that data and in turn passes it down another layer. Each layer does its job and depends upon the other layers to do theirs.

We will not examine the Internet Protocol Suite protocols that operate at the two lowest Layers of the OSI Model, because doing so would be of little help in gaining a working understanding of TCP/IP, and would be of interest only to the super-technical types. Let it suffice to say that the Internet Protocol Suite provides full support for nearly any Physical Layer or Data Link Layer function imaginable, including dial-up protocols like SLIP and PPP; LAN protocols like Ethernet, Token Ring, FDDI and ARCnet; MAN/WAN protocols like x.25, SMDS/802.6, and so forth. Instead, we will begin at the third, or Network Layer of the OSI Model, and work our way up. Figure 13.10 shows how these protocols relate to the layers of the OSI Reference Model and the DoD Model.

OSI Model							DoD Model
Application	Electronic Mail	Terminal Emulation	File Transfer	File Transfer	Client/ Server	Management	
Presentation	Simple Mail Transfer Protocol (SMTP)	TELNET	File Transfer Protocol (FTP)	Trivial FileTransfer Protocol (TFTP)	Sun Network File System (NFS)	Simple Network Management Protocol (SNMP)	Process/ Application
Session							
Transport	Transmission Control Protocol (TCP)			User Datagram Protocol (UDP)			Host-to-Host
Network	Address Resolution Protocol (ARP)		Internet Protocol (IP)		Internet Control Message Protocol (ICMP)		Internet
Data Link	Network Interface Cards (Ethernet, Token Ring, ARCnet, FDDI, etc.)						Network Interface
Physical	Physical Media (UTP, Coax, Fiber Optic, etc.)						

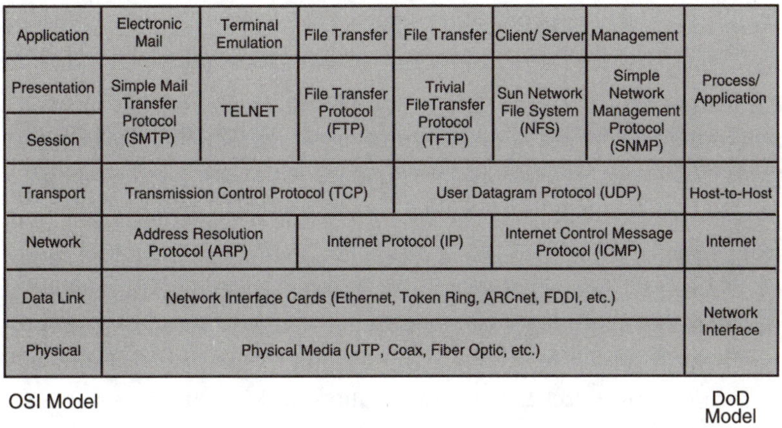

Fig. 13.10
Internet Protocols in Relation to the OSI Reference Model and the DoD Model.

Internet Protocol (IP)

The Internet Protocol (IP) operates at the Network Layer of the OSI Reference Model, which corresponds to the Internet Layer of the DoD Model.

IP is a connectionless protocol, which offers best-effort delivery of routed datagrams. This means that no physical or virtual connection exists between two devices that communicate with IP. Instead, the source device simply inserts the address of the destination device and places the packet on the network. It is then up to the network and to other supporting protocols to ensure that the packet is delivered to its ultimate destination.

IP processing begins when IP receives a segment of data from the Transport Layer above. If necessary, IP fragments that segment of data into blocks of usable size. Although IP can handle data in blocks of up to 64K, it is more common to use blocks of 1,460 bytes in order to avoid the performance penalty of IP fragmentation. Once the data has been fragmented into blocks of the appropriate size, IP appends software addresses—also called network addresses—for the source and destination to that block, along with a header checksum and other administrative information.

Once the data segment has been processed by IP, the resulting collection of data is called a packet. IP then passes the packet down to the Data Link Layer, where additional information is appended to create a *frame*. Frames are specific to the Data Link Layer, and are media dependent. For example, if you are running an Ethernet network, the IP packet will be encapsulated in an Ethernet frame. The Data Link Layer then passes the packet to the Physical Layer where it is placed on the network physical media.

Address Resolution Protocol (ARP)

Address Resolution Protocol (ARP) operates at the Network Layer of the OSI Reference Model, which corresponds to the Internet Layer of the DoD Model.

ARP is used to determine the Data Link Layer Hardware Address, which is also known as the MAC Address, of a known IP Address, which is also called the Network Address or Software Address. The process of discovering an unknown address of one type by using a known address of another type is known as address resolution.

When an IP host sends packets to another host on the same subnet, including the default router, it uses the Address Resolution Protocol to map IP Addresses to MAC Addresses. ARP entries are maintained in a table on the host. These entries expire after a short time to allow for MAC and IP changes on a host. For example, if you change the Ethernet card in a system, you change that system's MAC address at the same time.

The host broadcasts a message at both the MAC and IP level, something like "Whoever has x.x.x.x, please tell y.y.y.y." When x.x.x.x receives this broadcast, it makes a directed reply to y.y.y.y to inform y.y.y.y.

Reverse Address Resolution Protocol (RARP)

Reverse Address Resolution Protocol (RARP) operates at the Network Layer of the OSI Reference Model, which corresponds to the Internet Layer of the DoD Model.

RARP is used to resolve an unknown IP Address from a known MAC address. RARP was designed before BOOTP and DHCP for hosts to automatically obtain their IP Address. An RARP server would be programmed with a table of MAC addresses and their corresponding IP addresses, and then listen for and respond to RARP packets. The severe limitation to RARP is that it can only supply IP addresses, and the client would have to obtain the other required information (Default Gateway, subnet mask, and so on) by other means.

Internet Control Message Protocol (ICMP)

The Internet Control Message Protocol (ICMP) operates at the Network Layer of the OSI Reference Model, which corresponds to the Internet Layer of the DoD Model.

ICMP provides control and messaging services that allow hosts and routers to communicate with each other concerning problems they are having in routing IP datagrams, for example, no route being available. One of the most common uses of ICMP is the ping utility used to verify that a path exists between hosts.

Transmission Control Protocol (TCP)

The Transmission Control Protocol (TCP) operates at the Transport Layer of the OSI Reference Model, which corresponds to the Host-to-Host Layer of the DoD Model.

TCP is one of two major protocols at the Transport Layer. TCP guarantees that packets will arrive in order and intact, and therefore incurs overhead which slows its performance. TCP is used for applications that need a reliable streaming connection oriented transport. For example, Telnet, SMTP, and HTTP use TCP transport.

User Datagram Protocol (UDP)

The User Datagram Protocol (UDP) operates at the Transport Layer of the OSI Reference Model, which corresponds to the Host-to-Host Layer of the DoD Model.

UDP is the second major Transport Layer protocol in the Internet Protocol Suite, and is used as an alternative to TCP. When compared with TCP, UDP offers faster performance and higher throughput at the expense of reliability. UDP simply blasts connectionless datagrams out of the interface. It makes no attempt to verify delivery, and therefore incurs much lower overhead than does TCP. UDP is used for applications that exchange short messages, often locally, or those that require the highest possible throughput. For example, BOOTP, DHCP, and WINS use UDP transport.

File Transfer Protocol (ftp)

File Transfer Protocol (ftp) is an upper-layer client/server protocol that allows you to transfer text or binary files to and from a remote host. The software running on that host is called an ftp server. The software you run to access that ftp server is called an ftp client. ftp server software is available for most operating systems likely to be running on systems connected to the Internet, including Windows NT. ftp client software is available for almost any workstation operating system imaginable. ftp client software is covered in detail in Chapter 16, "Using ping, ftp, news, and Telnet."

At the option of the system administrator, an ftp server can be configured either to require that a user have a valid account name and password, or to allow anyone to access the files on the ftp server anonymously. The latter, and more common case, is called anonymous ftp, and is used by many computer companies to allow any caller to download program updates, drivers, and so forth. To access an anonymous ftp server, you simply enter the account name **anonymous** when prompted and supply your full e-mail address as the password.

ftp uses the Transmission Control Protocol (TCP) Transport Layer protocol described earlier in this section to ensure reliable file transfers.

Next to your Web browser, a good ftp client is the most useful tool you can have. Although your Web browser will allow you to ftp files, it is best suited for casual use. When you have a lot of files to transfer, a purpose-built ftp client is faster and more convenient. Two of the best available ftp clients are WS_FTP and Cute FTP, both of which are included with *Windows NT Workstation 4.0 Internet and Networking* CD-ROM and are discussed further in Chapter 16, "Using ping, ftp, news, and Telnet."

Trivial File Transfer Protocol (TFTP)

The Trivial File Transfer Protocol (TFTP) is an upper-layer protocol similar in name to ftp, and is also used to transfer files, but is intended for a completely different purpose. TFTP allows files to be transferred to a destination that has not provided a username or password to the TFTP server—in other words, you don't have to log in to a host before using TFTP.

Because of the wide-open nature of TFTP, the information that it is allowed to access is limited. Only files that are accessible to anyone on the host can be transferred. Because TFTP does not allow listing filenames and directories, you must specify the exact name and path of the file to be transferred.

Unlike ftp, which uses TCP at the Transport Layer, TFTP uses the User Datagram Protocol (UDP) for transport.

You might wonder of what use such a limited protocol might be, particularly on a host that also has ftp available. One common use for TFTP is to allow network components like routers to boot from a boot image file located on the TFTP host. A router using this method has just enough of the bootstrap program stored in local ROM to allow it to begin the boot process and then make a request to the TFTP host to transfer the remainder of the startup files needed to boot.

Simple Mail Transfer Protocol (SMTP)

Simple Mail Transfer Protocol (SMTP), like ftp, is an upper-layer client/server protocol used to transfer data between hosts. SMTP provides the foundation for Internet mail services. SMTP is intended to provide a reliable message delivery mechanism, and uses TCP rather than UDP toward that end. It does not, however, absolutely guarantee delivery of a message to the intended recipient, as any Internet mail user will have observed for himself.

SMTP is based upon a store-and-forward model, in which an entire mail message is communicated as a single unit from the source host to the destination host, possibly being stored and subsequently forwarded via intermediate hosts. When the message arrives at the destination host, it is moved to a storage location—usually called a mailbox—for subsequent retrieval by the user.

Telnet

Telnet is an upper-layer terminal emulation protocol that allows a user on one system to log into and establish a terminal session on a remote host. Most Telnet implementations emulate a DEC VT100 series or VT200 series terminal, although TN3270 versions are available that emulate an IBM 3270 series mainframe terminal.

Like ftp and SMTP, Telnet uses TCP at the Transport Layer.

After your Web browser and ftp client, a good Telnet client is the next tool you should acquire. One of the best available Telnet clients is a shareware product called QVTnet, which is included with the bundled CD and discussed in detail in Chapter 16.

Network File System (NFS)

The Network File System (NFS), originally developed by Sun Microsystems, Inc. in 1985, is now a standard part of the Internet Protocol Suite. NFS is an upper-layer protocol that uses a client/server architecture to allow clients to transparently access files, directories, and applications located on an NFS server. NFS allows you to mount a remote file system so that it appears as a network drive. Any host may act as either an NFS client or an NFS server, or as both simultaneously.

NFS places no restrictions on the locations of the client and server. You can, for example, use a workstation running NFS client software to access files located on an NFS server on the other side of the planet. The only indication you might have that the files do not reside on a local server would be if a low-speed connection made transfers to and from the NFS server slower than local transfers.

One major advantage to using NFS is that it automatically handles the logical formatting conversions needed between hosts running different operating systems. If, for example, you are running an NFS client on a Windows computer, the data files you access via NFS on a UNIX or VAX/VMS host will be transparently reformatted into a form usable by your operating system as you access them.

NFS uses IP at the Network Layer and UDP at the Transport Layer. Because this provides a connectionless, unreliable link between the NFS client and the NFS server, NFS makes no assumption that data has been delivered correctly. It instead uses *stateless* protocols to ensure the integrity of data and transactions. In simple terms, under a stateless model, when the client makes a request to the server, it does not assume that the request has been received and acted upon by the server until it receives a response. If no response is received after a specified time, the client re-transmits the request. This way, if the server crashes or the network link goes down, no data is corrupted. The client simply continues to re-transmit the request until it is acted upon.

The NFS Suite comprises three major components, each of which uses the underlying IP/UDP network transport services:

■ The *Remote Procedure Call (RPC)* protocol operates at the Session Layer of the OSI Model. RPC is used to establish the connection between the NFS client and the NFS server.

■ The *External Data Representation (XDR)* protocol operates at the Presentation Layer of the OSI Model. XDR performs the data format conversions described above that allow dissimilar hosts to exchange information with transparent reformatting of the data into the form required by each.

■ The *Network File System (NFS)* protocol, for which the suite is named, operates at the Application Layer of the OSI Model. NFS defines the file and directory structures and procedures used between the client and the server.

Simple Network Management Protocol (SNMP)

Simple Network Management Protocol (SNMP) is an upper-layer protocol that is designed to allow network administrators to monitor and manage active network components from a remote management workstation. SNMP uses an agent/manager model similar to the client/server model used by other components of the Internet Protocol Suite.

SNMP Agents are entities that exist on devices that are to be monitored. For example, a manageable network hub, router, or workstation. Agents maintain statistics about the machine they are running on, (total number of IP packets transmitted, the IP address of an interface, and so on).

SNMP Proxy Agents are entities that reside on a manageable component, but are intended to observe and report on unmanaged devices, for example, a T1 CSU/DSU that has an SNMP serial port for out-of-band management.

SNMP Managers poll SNMP Agents periodically to ensure that they are up and functioning. SNMP Managers may also send commands to query or set fields in the Agent database, which is known as a Management Information Base, or MIB. Some Agents have the ability to send or trap important notifications to a Manager. Traps are usually reserved for critical events, such as a WAN link going down, that need to be communicated to a network manager as soon as possible.

Domain Name Service (DNS)

The Domain Name Service (DNS), shown in figure 13.11, is a world-wide distributed database of machine names and their corresponding IP Addresses. It is the availability of DNS that allows you, for example, to point your Web browser to **www.microsoft.com** rather than to 198.105.232.4.

In operation, using the example given above, an IP client makes a request to its local DNS server to resolve **www.microsoft.com** into its IP Address. The local DNS first searches its own cache. If the information is found there, the server returns it to the requesting client. If the information is not found, the local DNS queries other DNS servers until the information is located, or resolved, and then returns the resolved IP Address to the client. There are four types of DNS servers:

- *Root Domain Name Servers* have primary responsibility for a root of the DNS tree.

- *Primary Domain Name Servers* are those that have been delegated authority for a specified second-level domain, such as microsoft.com. If you connect to the Internet, you must have a Primary DNS. It may be a computer located at your site, or it may be located at your Internet Service Provider's site.

- *Secondary Domain Name Servers* are redundant backups of a Primary DNS. They continually replicate the contents of the Primary DNS, and take its place if it fails.

- *Forwarder Domain Name Servers* forward all unknown requests and then cache the result.

A DNS server can function simultaneously as a Primary DNS and as a Secondary DNS for multiple domains. Larger organizations usually have both a Primary DNS and a Secondary DNS physically located at their sites. Smaller organizations may have a Primary DNS sited locally and depend upon their Internet Service Provider to maintain the Secondary DNS off-site. Very small companies may have no DNS locally at all, but depend upon the ISP to provide both Primary DNS and Secondary DNS.

The Root Name Servers are maintained by InterNIC. Each DNS Server needs a periodically updated file that lists these Root Name Servers. This file can be downloaded via anonymous ftp from InterNIC registration services as /DOMAIN/NAMED.ROOT.

Fig. 13.11
Domain Name Services Organization.

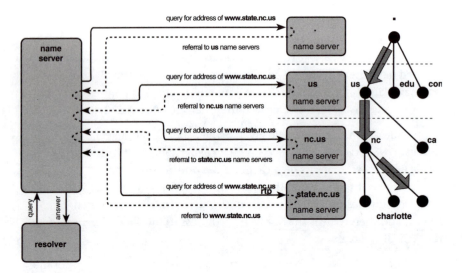

InterNIC delegates responsibility for the top-level domains —.COM, .EDU, and so forth—to other DNS Servers. These other DNS Servers then delegate authority to other downstream name servers, for example, to the Primary Domain Name Server located at **microsoft.com**.

The system administrator of the **micrsoft.com** Primary Domain Name Server then adds host names and their corresponding IP address entries in his name server. He may then optionally delegate subdomains to other name servers within Microsoft, that is **sales.microsoft.com**, **programming.microsoft.com**.

When you request the IP address of **www.microsoft.com**, your DNS server first determines if the required information is stored in its cache. If not, your

DNS queries the Root Name Servers for the address of the .COM Name Server. Once this information is returned, your DNS Server then queries the COM Name Server for the address of the MICROSOFT.COM Name Server. Once this information is received, your DNS Server then queries the MICROSOFT.COM Name Server for the address of WWW.MICROSOFT.COM.

Because your DNS Server has cached this incoming information, if you subsequently ask for the address of **ftp.microsoft.com**, your DNS Server still knows the address of the DNS Server at MICROSOFT.COM. Rather than starting at the beginning, it can instead just directly ask the DNS Server at MICROSOFT.COM for the address of **ftp.microsoft.com**. Similarly, if you then ask for the address of **www.yahoo.com**, your DNS Server starts the query at the COM Name Server because it has that cached as well.

The MICROSOFT.COM DNS administrator determines how long an entry will be cached in your DNS Server. This allows, for example, the MICROSOFT.COM DNS Administrator to shorten the expiration time prior to a planned major change to a well-known host, guaranteeing that the change is propagated throughout the network quickly.

Dynamic Host Configuration Protocol (DHCP)

Dynamic Host Configuration Protocol (DHCP) is an extension of BOOTP, which automatically assigns IP addresses to clients that are running DHCP client software. Windows NT Workstation 4.0 includes a DHCP client. The server grants the address for a predetermined lease period, which may range from 1 minute to "infinity and beyond." The client periodically checks with the server to make sure that the lease is still valid. If so, it renews the lease. This lease renewal always occurs when the client boots.

With DHCP you do not have to worry about gathering and maintaining key IP information for each client. Drastic changes to the network can be made easily at the DHCP server and automatically implemented by the clients.

DHCP is a broadcast protocol. You need to have either a DHCP server on each local subnet or else use routers that are RFC-1542 compliant. RFC-1542 compliant routers forward DHCP requests to a specific destination, eliminating the need to have a DHCP server on each subnet, and instead allowing you to use a single DHCP server to service all of your subnets.

Windows Internet Naming Service (WINS)

Microsoft Networking is a NetBIOS- based, upper-layer protocol. NetBIOS Extended User Interface, or NetBEUI, is a superset of NetBIOS. Both IPX and, to a lesser extent, IP support NetBIOS. WINS allows Microsoft Networking hosts to map NetBIOS machine names to IP addresses. A client registers its name with the WINS server and then queries the WINS server for the IP addresses that correspond to other client names. Most network administrators employ several WINS servers for redundancy. WINS servers can be configured to replicate with each other to propagate their databases among themselves.

There are two alternatives to using one or more WINS servers on your network. The first is to use a DNS server, which limits machine names to the same domain. The second is to manually maintain a list of machine names and their corresponding IP Addresses in an lmhosts file. This lmhosts file must be present—and kept individually updated—on every workstation that uses Microsoft Networking.

The DNS server supplied with Windows NT Server 4.0 can create a subdomain and automatically integrate the WINS database into DNS. This feature will be welcomed by network administrators, because the older method required that you reserve an address in the DHCP server for a particular client and then manually add it to the DNS. This newer method makes it easy, for example, for a notebook user to move around within the enterprise and still have a DNS entry, which is often required for security purposes on ftp and Web servers.

Routing Protocols

In order to do their jobs, routers need to talk to each other "on the side." That is, routers must obviously transmit packets containing user data from point to point, but beyond this, they also need to communicate administrative data among themselves. For example, routers need to know which paths are congested, when an existing path disappears, when a new path is added, and so forth.

Routers also need to trade *routing tables* with their peers. Each router maintains a dynamic database, called a routing table, that lists all other routers to which that router has direct links, along with destinations that can be reached indirectly through these other "neighbor" routers.

When a packet arrives at a router, the router first determines if it can deliver that packet directly to the destination. In other words, the router determines whether or not the destination address is located on the same network as that router. If it is, the router delivers the packet to the destination address. If not, the router then checks to see if it can forward the packet to a neighbor router "closer" to the destination. These packet transfers between routers are referred to as *hops*.

Once this second router receives the packet, it also checks to see if it can deliver the packet to its destination. If not, it again forwards the packet to one of its neighbor routers "closer" to the destination. This process continues until the packet arrives at a router connected to the same network as the destination address, where it is finally delivered to the addressee.

The status of a router changes constantly. Connection paths may be added or removed, a given link at a particular time may be heavily loaded or lightly used, the cost associated with using a particular link may change, etc. As these changes occur, the "best" path for a packet that needs to get from Point A to Point B may also change. "Best" may be defined in a variety of ways. It may mean the shortest route, or the one that requires the fewest hops. It may mean the fastest route, or the one that uses the highest throughput links available. Finally, it may mean the least costly route, or the one that uses a less expensive transmission path. Routers maintain all of this information in their routing tables, and must have some means of communicating these changes to the other routers on the internetwork so that the best path can be chosen.

Routers do this administrative chatting using Routing Protocols, which operate at the upper Layers of the OSI Model. Broadly speaking, two types of Routing Protocols exist, *Distance Vector Routing* Protocols and *Link State Routing* Protocols.

Distance Vector Routing Protocols. The Distance Vector Routing (DVR) protocol contained in the Internet Protocol Suite is called *Routing Information Protocol*, or RIP, not to be confused with Novell RIP. Distance Vector Routing protocols are also referred to as Ford-Fulkerson protocols, after the originators of this algorithm.

Routers based on DVR protocols like RIP use information supplied by neighbor routers to build their own routing tables. For example, if a neighbor router indicates that it can reach a particular destination in two hops, then our DVR router adds this destination to its own routing table with an associated distance of three hops—the two hops required by the neighbor router to reach the destination, plus the one hop it takes to get from our DVR router to the neighbor router. It then broadcasts its updated routing table to all of the other neighbor routers on the internetwork, including the router from which it received the information just described. These routers then update their own routing tables to take this new information into account.

Therein lies a serious problem with DVR routing. Let's call our DVR router in the example above ROUTER 1 and the neighbor router ROUTER 2. Let's further assume for simplicity that ROUTER 1, and therefore NETWORK 1, is connected only to ROUTER 2 on NETWORK 2, which also connects to the world via its link to ROUTER 3. All traffic from NETWORK 1 destined for the outside world must first be forwarded to ROUTER 2 and then to ROUTER 3. ROUTER 2 advertises the existence of its link to its neighbor routers, including ROUTER 3, and the associated cost of 1 hop. ROUTER 1 receives this information and updates its own routing table to indicate that NETWORK 3 is accessible using two hops—the one hop advertised by ROUTER 2, plus the one hop it takes to get from ROUTER 1 to ROUTER 2. ROUTER 1 then broadcasts its updated routing table to the neighbor routers.

Here's where the problem occurs. When ROUTER 2 receives the updated routing table from ROUTER 1, it discovers a "new" route to ROUTER 3. Because ROUTER 1 advertised that it could reach ROUTER 3 in two hops, ROUTER 2 adds a new route to its routing table indicating that it can now reach ROUTER 3 by a new route via ROUTER 1, at a cost of three hops—the two hops advertised by ROUTER 1, plus the one hop it takes to get to ROUTER 1. In reality, of course, there is still only one way to get to ROUTER 3, and that is by the link between ROUTER 2 and ROUTER 3. This doesn't cause any immediate problem, however, because ROUTER 2 will always choose the direct 1-hop path to ROUTER 3 in preference to the three-hop path required by the route that goes through ROUTER 1.

Let's assume, however, that for some reason the link between ROUTER 2 and ROUTER 3 goes down, leaving NETWORK 1 and NETWORK 2 connected to each other, but isolated from the world. ROUTER 2 notices that it no longer has a direct link to ROUTER 3, and so falls back on the alternate route via ROUTER 1 that requires three hops. ROUTER 2 recalculates its routing table and forwards the updated routing table to its neighbor routers, which in this case means only to ROUTER 1.

ROUTER 1 notices that the original two-hop route to ROUTER 3 is no longer available, and that sending packets to ROUTER 3 now costs four hops—the three hops advertised by ROUTER 2, plus the one hop required to get to ROUTER 2. ROUTER 1 updates its routing table and broadcasts the new routing table to the internetwork, including its new route to ROUTER 3, which now costs four hops. ROUTER 2 examines this new routing table and finds that its cost to reach ROUTER 3 via ROUTER 1 is now four hops, so it adds the one hop required to reach ROUTER 1 and advertises that it can now reach ROUTER 3 in five hops. Because neither router is aware that this loop exists, each router continues to increment its hop count by one and advertise the resulting new route.

This vicious circle is inherent in the DVR model, but can be addressed by limiting the number of hops before a process times out. For example, if you use a Ping or Traceroute utility program to access a remote host, you will notice a parameter named "max hops" or something similar. This parameter typically defaults to a value of 30 or thereabouts, meaning that, if a loop occurs, the program will time out after 30 hops and inform you that the destination is unreachable. Similarly, the routers themselves can be configured by the system administrator to have a maximum allowable hop count. When this maximum is reached, the router assumes that the destination network is unreachable.

Against this single disadvantage, RIP has several advantages, and is still widely used. First, RIP, as the original routing protocol in the TCP/IP suite, is well-developed, mature, and widely supported. Second, RIP makes minimal demands on processor power, which is to say it runs on relatively inexpensive routers. Third, when properly configured, RIP requires little network bandwidth for overhead administrative traffic. Fourth, although managing routing in general is a non-trivial task, RIP is relatively easy to implement compared with the alternatives.

RIP is particularly appropriate for small internetworks, offering good performance and easy manageability. If, however, your internetwork comprises 20 or more subnetworks, you will find that RIP begins to break down under the geometric growth in the number of routes which such a large internetwork implies. At some point on the close order of 20 subnets, you will add another subnet only to find that RIP has ceased working altogether.

Link State Routing Protocols. The Link State Routing (LSR) Protocol contained in the Internet Protocol Suite is called *Open Shortest Path First*, or *OSPF*.

DVR routers build their routing tables based on hearsay—what other routers have told them. DVR routers also recalculate their route tables before broadcasting routes. In contrast, LSR routers build their routing tables based on direct investigation of their environments. Also, LSR routers can pass on routing changes before they recalculate their routing tables. Let's look at what happens when an LSR router is first connected to a network and switched on.

The LSR router begins the process by advertising itself using a "hello world" protocol. Each neighbor router responds with information about itself and its environment. Once the LSR router has detected its neighbor routers, it has complete information about its local environment and can begin discovering how it fits into the larger internetwork environment.

It begins by assembling the information it has received about its local environment into a special message, called a link state packet or LSP. The only information contained in this LSP is the direct connections available to that router and their associated costs. Information concerning indirect routes to remote routers, that is those that have one or more intervening routers, is not included.

Each neighbor router receives this LSP, stores a copy of it, and then forwards the LSP to all other routers to which it is connected except to the router from which it originally received the LSP. As this process continues, each router eventually has a stored copy of the LSP provided by each of the other routers on the internetwork. Because a router can pass on route changes before recalculating its routing table, the looping problem peculiar to DVR routers does not occur.

LSR/OSPF routers have several advantages over DVR/RIP routers. First, because each LSR router maintains a copy of all LSPs, accurate current information about the internetwork can be obtained by querying any router. Second, because LSR routers are always current on the exact present state of the internetwork, routing errors are much less common. Third, and most significant, LSR routers converge much faster than do DVR routers, meaning that changes to the internetwork are propagated much more quickly.

Against these advantages must be weighed a couple of disadvantages. First, LSR routers generate more overhead administrative traffic than do DVR routers. In fact, if one or more LSR routers is configured incorrectly, the resulting flood of LSP traffic can degrade network performance. Second, LSR routers must do much more processing than do DVR routers, and therefore require faster processors and more memory. Accordingly, LSR routers are typically more expensive than DVR routers.

If you have a large internetwork, comprising many subnets, you have no real alternative but to use LSR routers. Even on smaller internetworks, LSR routers can be a good choice, particularly if you expect significant growth to occur. If your internetwork is small and likely to remain so, instead choose DVR routers.

The Growth of TCP/IP as a Wide Area Networking Standard

In the struggle between competing internetworking protocol suites to establish dominance, the war is over. TCP/IP won. Other internetworking protocol suites like OSI, DECnet, and SAA each have various theoretical advantages in performance or features over TCP/IP, but the fact remains that TCP/IP is ubiquitous, standardized, and inexpensive. It simply works.

Virtually every computer system can run TCP/IP. TCP/IP, often by default, is the common denominator in heterogeneous environments. TCP/IP allows disparate systems, which would otherwise have no protocol in common, to interoperate. Organizations large and small have deployed TCP/IP as the backbone of their internetworks, using the Internet as a model. Of the three transports provided by Windows NT, only TCP/IP is appropriate for internetworking. Although IPX is routeable, it was not designed for WAN links. IPX SAP and RIP updates can overwhelm a slow WAN link. Also, a TCP/IP link can be used to tunnel other protocols, encapsulating, for example, IPX/SPX packets within the TCP/IP packet.

For nearly any network, including those that are not yet internetworked, there is little reason to choose any transport other than TCP/IP. The availability of DHCP, WINS, and other TCP/IP services provided by Windows NT has reduced or eliminated the additional support burden of running TCP/IP. You should use TCP/IP for transport on your network unless you have very good reason to do otherwise. Even then, forget the good reason and run TCP/IP anyway. ❖

V

Using the Internet

CHAPTER 14

Connecting to the Internet

by Robert Bruce Thompson

If you work in a corporate environment, you may already have Internet access and not even know it. Some companies, fearful of lost employee productivity, keep the fact that Internet access is available as a closely held secret from most of their staff. Others restrict access to the Internet because they are concerned about security. It's worth talking to your IS department to find out what, if any, Internet access services may be available to you. If it's available, chances are good that you can talk your way into a connection. If it's not, this chapter can help you lead the charge to get Internet access up and running.

If you work at home or in a small business, you may be your own IS department. If so, this chapter is for you, too. Just a few years ago, if you needed Internet access, there weren't a lot of choices. You found someone who already had access, usually a university or hospital, and convinced them to allow you to piggy-back onto their connection. Today, things are a lot different. Hundreds of businesses exist solely to provide Internet access to other businesses and to individuals. Internet access is available from commercial online services like America Online and CompuServe. Sorting out the alternatives and making the best choice isn't easy.

Once you've decided that you want access to the Internet, the next obvious problem is how to go about getting connected. You'll want the best performance possible. You'll also want the lowest price available for the service level you select, along with easy installation and good technical support. Getting the best deal from your own point of view requires that you know a little bit about the Internet access market. After reading this chapter, you'll have all the tools you need to talk intelligently to Internet Service Providers and to negotiate the deal you want for the service you need.

In this chapter, you learn to

- Understand the various connection types available for Internet access, including asynchronous, proprietary, and network connections
- Decide which connection type is appropriate for you
- Choose the best carrier facility—analog dialup, ISDN, or leased line—and what to watch out for when working with ISDN
- Evaluate Internet access services and select the Internet Service Provider that is best for your needs

Choosing the Connection Type

There are many ways to connect to the Internet, varying in cost, level of service available, and number of users supported. The method you ultimately choose will depend upon your needs and your budget.

Asynchronous, Proprietary, and Network Connections

The first distinction in connection types is the asynchronous connection versus the proprietary connection versus the network connection.

- *Asynchronous connection* was a very popular Internet access method a few years ago, but has declined in popularity due to its limited capabilities.
- *Proprietary connection* is a nonstandards-based method still in use by some commercial online services and Internet Access Providers. A proprietary connection offers greater access to the array of Internet services than does the Asynchronous connection, but does so at the expense of locking you into a single access provider and to using whatever tools are specified by that provider.
- *Network connection* is the method of choice today. It offers full standards-based access to the Internet. The word network refers to the Internet itself, and not to a local area network. You can use a network connection to connect a single machine to the Internet.

Asynchronous Connection

The asynchronous connection, shown in figure 14.1, provides a terminal mode asynchronous link to a system that is connected to the Internet. The distinguishing characteristic of an asynchronous connection is that no TCP/IP link exists directly between your computer system and the Internet, meaning that you are not connected to the Internet in any real sense. Because you do not have a TCP/IP link to the Internet, you cannot run programs locally like Web Browsers, ftp clients, and so on.

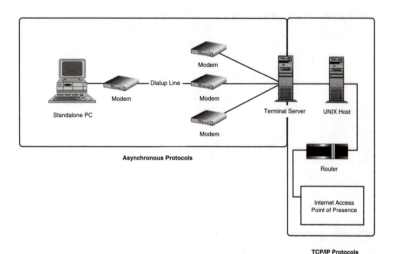

Fig. 14.1
An asynchronous (non-network) connection offers limited Internet connectivity.

Any programs that use Internet services must run on the central host, which does have a TCP/IP link to the Internet. The asynchronous connection is conceptually similar to dialing a bulletin board system, where all programs run on the central host and your PC provides only a terminal window to those services. This limitation has two major implications:

■ *You are limited to running the Internet utilities available on the host.* You can't simply choose to run Netscape Navigator as your browser or CuteFTP as your ftp client. The utilities available on the host are relatively primitive character mode applications like the Lynx Web browser. They're functional, but limited and not very pretty.

■ *Because it is the central host that is connected to the Internet, any files you transfer end up on the central host.* For example, if you ftp a new driver from Microsoft, that driver ends up on a hard disk on the central host. You must then use the file transfer function of your communications software to download the file as a separate step.

Asynchronous connections were commonly offered a couple of years ago, but have become relatively uncommon as users demand full Internet access. Today, the most likely places to find asynchronous connections offered are community Freenets and Public Access UNIX systems.

If all you care about is e-mail, an asynchronous connection may be all you need, and you can probably get one for free, because in this day and age an asynchronous connection isn't worth paying for. If you want more complete access to Internet resources, look elsewhere for your connection.

> **Tip**
>
> If for some reason you find that an asynchronous connection is your only option for Internet access, you need to know about a product named SlipKnot. SlipKnot is a $30 shareware Windows-based graphical Web browser designed for users of UNIX shell accounts, like those available on many Freenets, to work on an asynchronous connection.
>
> For more information about SlipKnot, e-mail **slipknot@micromind.com** or connect to their Web page at **www.interport.net/slipknot/slipknot.html.**

Proprietary Connection

Neither fish nor fowl, a *proprietary connection,* shown in figure 14.2, gives you access to more Internet services than an asynchronous connection, but limits you in terms of what you can do with that link. What distinguishes a proprietary connection is that it uses nonstandards-based protocols to establish the link between your computer system and the service provider. This limits you both to using that provider and to using the Internet access programs supported by that provider.

At the same time, the proprietary link provides reasonably full access to Internet services, including Web browsing, transferring files with ftp, reading USENET news, and so on. The limitations are not so much in the services available as in the tools that you may use to access them.

Fig. 14.2
A proprietary connection offers full Internet access, but limits your choice of client programs.

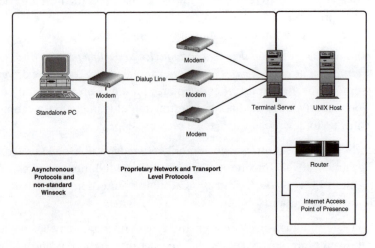

Choosing the Connection Type

Proprietary connections are offered by many commercial online services and by some general *Internet Service Providers (ISP)*. They use these proprietary methods in the interests of standardization and supportability. It's much easier to support thousands of users with greatly varying levels of experience if you know exactly what software they're using—if your connection method is proprietary you have this information. If instead you offer a standards-based connection, a user calling for technical support may be using any of dozens of Web browsers and any of hundreds of other Internet access utilities.

Caution

The proprietary aspect of the connection is usually simply a result of using a non-standard *Winsock*. WINSOCK.DLL provides the low-level interface between TCP/IP services and Windows programs. Installing the access kit for a service that uses a proprietary connection method usually installs a nonstandard Winsock over the top of your existing Winsock. This normally isn't a problem if you will be using only the Web browser and other utilities bundled with the access kit offered by the service provider. However, installing a nonstandard Winsock usually breaks other installed software that uses Winsock services.

You are sometimes offered a choice between installing a new Winsock or using your existing Winsock when you install an access kit. If given the choice, always choose to keep your existing (standard) Winsock instead of overwriting it with the proprietary Winsock included with the kit.

If you are satisfied with the services available from a particular provider and their costs, and if the proprietary tools used with that service satisfy your needs, there are no particular technical drawbacks to using a proprietary connection.

Note

Even if your commercial online service or Internet Service Provider uses a proprietary access method, you may be able to reconfigure their access software to use standard protocols. Doing so usually requires a substantial amount of work on your part and several calls to the provider technical support line. It's usually not worth the trouble. Often it's both easier and cheaper to simply switch to an Internet Service Provider that uses standard protocols

---

A proprietary connection from a commercial online service or Internet Service Provider provides service to a single user, and typically costs somewhere in the range of $8 to $20 per month for anywhere from five hours of Internet access up to an unlimited number of hours. Hours beyond the bundled number are typically charged at $1 to $2.50 additional. AT&T WorldNet service effectively places a ceiling on Internet access costs, with five hours per month free and unlimited hours for $20 per month.

Network Connection

The third method used to connect to the Internet is the *network connection*, shown in figure 14.3. When a network connection is established, for the duration of that connection, your computer system is actually live on the Internet. Given the appropriate client software, you can access any and all services available anywhere on the Internet.

Fig. 14.3

A network connection provides complete Internet access and allows you to choose any client software.

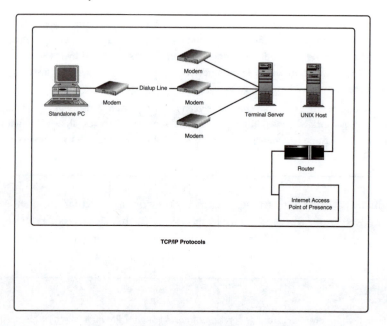

At the same time, other computers on the Internet can access any Internet services that are running on your computer. For example, with a network connection, you can install Web server software and bring up your own personal Web site. This Web site can serve your Web pages to someone in Tokyo while at the same time you are browsing the Web or reading USENET news. With a network connection, your computer is a full peer on the Internet, capable both of using and providing services.

The only limitation to what you can do with a network connection is how fast your connection is. An individual single-user network connection may typically range from 14.4 Kbps or 28.8 Kbps dialup to 128 Kbps ISDN. A network connection for a typical corporate local area network runs at 1.544 Mbps T1 speed, although 45 Mbps T3 links are becoming more common.

What distinguishes a network connection is that it uses the standard TCP/IP protocol suite to support the connection. Because the connection is standards-based, you can select among the great variety of software available on the Internet itself and elsewhere to access Internet services.

Relative to a proprietary connection, the sole drawback of using a network connection is that it requires more work on your part. Proprietary connections are designed to be turn-key. You install the software and it works. Little or no configuration is needed, other than perhaps entering the local access telephone number.

A network connection is typically a little bit more complicated to set up. You may have to set up your dialer to access the ISP. In addition to the local access telephone number, you may have to enter TCP/IP configuration information like the assigned IP address of your computer, a subnet mask, the names or addresses of the Domain Name Servers and Gateway at your ISP, and so on. Usually, this is just a matter of following directions, or perhaps making a short telephone call to tech support when you first set up your computer for Internet access. Sometimes, the ISP sends you software preconfigured, eliminating most of this extra work.

Network connections are available from a variety of sources. Internet Service Providers (ISPs) range from those with a national or international presence like AT&T, MCI, and PSInet, to regional ISPs that cover a state or a region to local ISPs that cover only one city. These ISPs provide connections ranging in speed from 14.4 Kbps dialup to 45 Mbps T3 leased lines, and sometimes even faster.

The cost of a network connection from different ISPs varies widely. It depends on the type of connection, its speed, the number of users supported, and how competitive the local Internet access market is. In general, an individual account using dialup should run about $20 per month for unlimited access. Many ISPs provide ISDN access at the same rate as dialup, or slightly more. A multiuser network connection for your local area network may cost from $250 per month to $10,000 per month or more, depending on the speed of the link.

V

Using the Internet

Individual versus Multiuser Connections

The second distinction in connection types is the individual or single-user connection versus the multiuser connection. You may connect a single computer system for an individual user to the Internet using an asynchronous, proprietary, or network connection. For all practical purposes, connecting multiple users on a local area network to the Internet must be done using a network connection.

Confusingly enough, a multiuser connection is also commonly referred to as a *network connection*, referring to the fact that a local area network is being connected to the Internet. Properly, any connection that provides a full TCP/IP link, whether to a single computer or an entire network, is termed a network connection. Using a network connection to connect an entire local area network to the Internet is referred to as a multiuser connection.

Individual Connections

The distinguishing feature of an individual connection, shown in figure 14.4, is that the account exists on a remote computer system rather than on a local computer system. Each user of an individual connection must establish a separate dial-up connection to the Internet Service Provider in order to use Internet services. Using individual connections, if more than one person in your company requires an Internet connection, you must establish a separate account for each.

Fig. 14.4

An individual network connection provides Internet access for only one person.

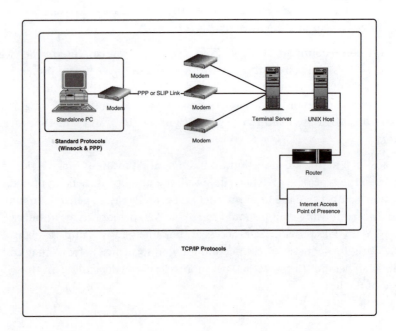

An individual connection that uses the network access method offers access to Internet services while that connection is active. Using individual connections may make sense, particularly if you are a small company or have few people who need Internet access. There are two main drawbacks to an individual connection, however:

- *Using an individual connection means that your computer system is "live" on the Internet only while you are actually dialed in and connected.* This means that an individual connection is not appropriate for systems that need a permanent, full-time presence on the Internet, such as a Web server. It also means that Internet services are not instantly available when you need them. For example, you have to dial in each time you want to check your mail or browse the Web.

- *Because your account exists on the remote host rather than locally, your username is in the host domain rather than your own.* For example, using an individual connection, you might be SMITH11@SOMEBODY.NET or XYZ123@SOMEBODY.NET, when what you really want to be is SMITH@YOURCOMPANY.COM. Except in special circumstances, an individual connection makes you a member of the collective domain of the ISP.

Using Your Own Domain Name with an Individual Connection

Even if you have only an individual connection to the Internet, you'd probably prefer that your e-mail address use your own company domain name instead of the domain name of your ISP. JOHN_SMITH@ACME.COM is more identifiable, easier to remember, and far more prestigious than something like 123456.765@COMPUSERVE.COM or JSMITH9@SOMEISP.NET.

Internet e-mail relies heavily on Domain Name Servers (DNS), which form an Internet-wide distributed database that maps host names to their corresponding IP addresses. When an e-mail message is sent to AUSER@SOMEHOST.ACME.COM, the sender's mailer first uses DNS to look up the IP address of SOMEHOST.ACME.COM. It then makes a connection to the IP address corresponding to SOMEHOST.ACME.COM and delivers the mail message to the AUSER mailbox located on SOMEHOST.ACME.COM.

Although Acme Corporation may have several hosts on its network, it may want all e-mail to be addressed to USERNAME@ACME.COM. DNS accommodates this with a special *Mail Exchange* (*MX*) record. Aside from adding the MX records to the DNS, the host(s) that will be handling all the incoming mail for ACME.COM must be configured to receive and disseminate the mail to the proper mailboxes on the corresponding hosts.

(continues)

(continued)

The vast majority of e-mail servers on the Internet are UNIX hosts running sendmail. *Sendmail* is an incredibly complex system that uses very cryptic and unintuitive commands in its configuration file. An experienced and competent sendmail administrator can make the required changes to the sendmail configuration file in just a few minutes, but a novice attempting to do so will require days or weeks of reading reference manuals, and will most probably "break" sendmail beyond repair several times.

An MX record can also be used to redirect e-mail from one domain to another, so an ISP can have e-mail redirected from ACME.COM to an e-mail server on its own network. If you would like your ISP, or for that matter anyone else with an e-mail server that is directly connected to the Internet, to redirect your mail in this fashion, take the following steps:

First, contact your ISP or another ISP and tell them that you would like them to host your domain name and MX your mail. Some small ISPs may not have the technical expertise to delve into sendmail, and may refuse your request. This may be a good reason to consider changing ISPs. Setting up the MX record is a one-time job and should be charged accordingly. Don't let them con you into paying a monthly fee for this service. They may argue that they deserve a monthly fee for the mailbox on their server. Don't buy into this argument. The ISP business is a buyers' market, and the ISP knows you can always go elsewhere. A one-time charge of $25 or $50 might be about right. Some ISPs will MX your mail at no charge, so negotiate for whatever you consider reasonable.

Second, if you don't already have a domain name, now is the time to apply for one. Get the ISP to cut as much of the red tape as possible when dealing with *InterNIC*. Expect to pay the ISP a setup charge of at least $100. InterNIC charges $50 per year to register and maintain your domain name, and requires that you pay for the first two years up front. Thus, the first $100 of whatever ISP charges you incurred is passed through directly to InterNIC.

Next, you need to come up with a list of candidates for your domain name. Domain names are granted by InterNIC on a first-come-first-served basis, and most of the good ones are already taken. While you may want to use ACME.COM, you will probably find that it is in use and that you have to settle instead for a domain name that combines your company name with some other identifying information, such as ACMEMFG.COM. After you have made your list, use either a WHOIS client or Telnet to RS.INTERNIC.NET and run WHOIS online to see if your desired domain name is in use or available.

An individual connection can use any method to connect to the Internet Service Provider, although 14.4 Kbps or 28.8 Kbps dialup and 64/128 Kbps ISDN network connections are most common.

Multiuser Connections

A *multiuser network connection*, shown in figure 14.5, puts you in the big leagues on the Internet, providing full Internet connectivity to all the computers attached to your local area network. What distinguishes a multiuser connection is that a network component called a *router* sits between your local area network and the Internet.

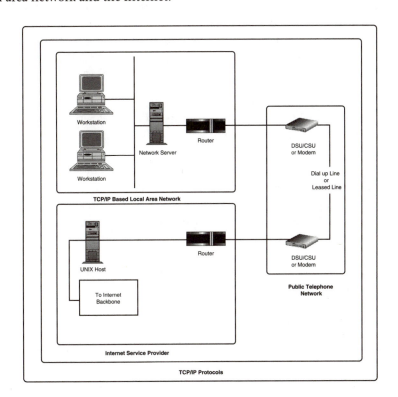

Fig. 14.5

A multiuser or shared network connection links an entire LAN to the Internet, and allows all LAN users to access Internet services.

The function of the router is two-fold. First, it examines each packet that originates on your local area network and directs those addressed to remote destinations out over the Internet. Second, it examines inbound packets and directs them to the proper computer on your local area network.

Two other characteristics are common to a multiuser network connection:

- *Because it uses a router to connect to the Internet, your local area network becomes a connected network on the Internet, with its own domain name.* Accounts on a multiuser network connection are created locally rather than by the ISP, so a user automatically becomes username@yourcompany.com.

- *Usually, although not always, a multiuser network connection implies that the network is connected to the Internet full-time.* This means that Internet services are immediately available when needed, without waiting for a dial-up connection to be established. The sole exception is on low-end multiuser network connections that depend on dial-up connections. These can be configured for dial-on-demand. If the connection goes unused for anything from a few minutes to an hour or so, the connection is dropped and must be re-established the next time an Internet service is invoked.

Multiuser network connections vary widely in cost, depending on the speed of the link and the means used to connect to the Internet Service Provider. As of mid-1996, a low-end multiuser network connection using dialup or ISDN might cost from $250 to $500 per month. A mid-range connection using a 1.544 Mbps T1 line might cost from $1,500 to $3,500 per month. A high-end connection using a 45 Mbps T3 line might cost from $10,000 to $20,000 per month. If you are located far from your Internet Service Provider, the additional costs of running a high speed line to your location can mount quickly.

Access Facilities

The third distinction in connection types is the type of telephone company facility used to access the Internet Service Provider. Three methods are commonly used:

- *Standard telephone lines* are commonly used for any individual access method, and may be used for a low-speed, low-cost multiuser network connection to serve smaller sites like remote offices. This method ordinarily provides at most a 28.8 Kbps v.34 connection, although in special cases—typically when one phone line is just too slow but ISDN is not available—you connect two or more standard telephone lines to your router, combining their throughput to yield 56 Kbps or more.

- *ISDN lines* are commonly used for individual network connections and for low-end to mid-range multiuser network connections. Throughput with ISDN varies with the individual telephone company, the ISP, and the capabilities of your router. A *Basic Rate Interface (BRI)* ISDN line provides two 64 Kbps B channels and a D channel for call setup and control. Your actual available throughput on a BRI may be 56 Kbps, 64 Kbps, or 128 Kbps.

- *High-speed Leased Lines,* typically 1.544 Mbps T1 and 45 Mbps T3, are used to deliver high-end multiuser network connections. Depending on your locale, high-speed Internet service may also be delivered via ATM, Frame Relay, or SONET, as covered in Chapter 2 "Understanding Communications Services and Hardware."

Of these three methods, the inexpensive standard telephone line and the high-speed leased line both present few problems in installation and configuration, although for different reasons. Installing a standard telephone line and using it for Internet access presents few problems for anyone who has ever used a modem.

At the other extreme, the high-speed leased line presents few problems simply because all the work on both ends is done for you by the telephone company and the Internet Service Provider. T-carrier technology is well-understood both by the telephone company and by the ISP. You simply place the order for service and perhaps order some hardware specified by the ISP as to the make and model. After that, you just pay the bills and let them worry about the details.

With ISDN, it's often a different story. It's usually up to you to get the ISDN line installed at your site and to make it work with your equipment. Although getting ISDN working is easier than it was just a year ago, it's still more of a black art than a science. Let's take a closer look at what it takes to get ISDN installed and working.

> **Caution**
>
> If you install an ISDN line, and particularly if you do so for a multiuser network connection that will be up 24 hours a day, seven days a week (24X7), make sure it is billed on a pure flat-rate basis. ISDN lines are often charged at a low monthly cost—perhaps $25 to $50. This charge includes some number of minutes of service, with additional minutes billed at a seemingly very low cost, typically a cent or two per minute per B Channel. This looks reasonable until you start calculating. Assuming 1,440 minutes per day and 30 days per month yields 43,200 minutes per month. Multiplying by two B Channels yields 86,400 channel minutes. If you pay for excess minutes at 2 cents per minute per B Channel, you could easily incur a charge of $1,500 a month or more in per minute charges. Make sure you get flat-rate billing.

Understanding ISDN

Although many telephone companies have made ISDN deployment a high priority in the past few years, ISDN is still nowhere near universally available. It is generally offered only in major metropolitan areas. Even if you live in an area where ISDN is offered, it may not be available at your site.

The first problem is that ISDN is generally limited to being run a maximum of 18,000 feet from the Central Office switch. This distance limitation is due to cross talk and attenuation of digital signals, and is inherent in the ISDN technology itself when it is run on cabling of the quality provided by the typical local loop.

Even if the proposed installation falls within the 18,000 foot limit, there are other factors, most notably the presence of Subscriber Loop Circuits (SLCs), that can determine whether an ISDN line can be successfully installed. SLCs are a mixed blessing, depending on the individual SLC. Older SLCs may be incompatible with an ISDN, but if your site is connected via a compatible SLC, you may be able to have an ISDN line without paying for a repeater even if you are located miles from the central office.

Traditionally, if you were located beyond the 18,000 foot limit, the telephone company might offer to install an ISDN repeater, either charging you the $5,000 that the repeater costs or amortizing the cost over several years by adding it to your monthly bill. In either event, the cost of the BRI could become astronomical. Recently, Adtran, a leading telecommunications equipment manufacturer, announced an ISDN line extender called Total Reach. Instead of placing a $5000 repeater in the middle of the line, the Total Reach equipment goes on both ends of the line, extending the distance limitation to 30,500 feet at a cost of about $1,000.

Ordering ISDN

Simply placing an order for ISDN service can be incredibly time consuming and frustrating. If you decide to install an ISDN line, follow the steps in this section to avoid headaches.

First, find the toll-free ISDN information number for your telephone company. Don't bother calling the local business office. They are almost always clueless. There are several good ISDN locator services on the Web that can help you find this information.

On the Web

As a good starting point, direct your Web broswer to:

www.microsoft.com/windows/getisdn

Second, once you have located a phone number for someone within your phone company who understands ISDN, ask them to do a facilities check to determine if they can install ISDN at your site. If not, ask them why and when will it become available, and then keep calling every few weeks to find out what progress is being made. If ISDN is available at your site, ask the telephone company representative what type of switch you will be connecting to. This will usually be a Nortel DMS or an AT&T 5ESS. Once you have determined the type of switch, ask them if they offer *National ISDN*.

Third, with this information in hand, decide what type of ISDN terminating hardware you will purchase, and verify that it is compatible with what you are trying to connect to. Most people will connect either to an ISP or to their corporate network, or possibly both. Make sure to talk to your ISP and/or your network administrator to ensure that the equipment you select is compatible with the equipment on the far end. You may find that the remote end is expecting a proprietary method to combine the B channels, or worse, that it demands a user authentication scheme that your equipment does not provide. Make sure the equipment you choose is compatible with the Central Office switch. Also, make sure it is compatible with *National ISDN-1 (NI1)*.

Fourth, get your *provisioning* information lined up. There are literally hundreds of parameters for ISDN lines, and each of them needs to be set exactly right if your hardware is to function properly. These parameters are collectively known as provisioning. Most vendors now supply a standard provisioning code for you to relay to the telephone company. There are two standard configurations that make things easier. Most hardware vendors conform to the set of options that Intel has dubbed Intel Blue. Also, most central offices can run National ISDN 1 (NI1) software that eliminates most of the confusion by using standard values for most ISDN parameters.

Fifth, actually place the order for the ISDN line. If you received provisioning information from your hardware vendor, as you should have, relay that information to the telephone company. The telephone company is going to ask you what equipment you plan to install on the line. If you do not have specific provisioning information, they will make their best guess as to what options they think will work with your equipment. Chances are, their best guess will be wrong.

Now is also the time to specify which features you want on your line. Some options, such as voice service, are often free or very low cost. Others, such as *Calling Line Identifier* (*CLID* or *Caller ID*), may add a few dollars a month to your bill. Consider carefully which services you choose to add and at what cost. For example, CLID may be useful for authentication purposes and voice service may be useful simply as an extra phone line.

Some people believe that it is always a good idea to put voice service on both channels for testing purposes, but as mentioned later in this section, *Q.931 debugging* is a far more useful tool. If you do not specify all the options you

V

Using the Internet

want during the initial order, you may have to pay a substantial order processing charge to add the feature later.

Caution

If you are handy at wiring, you may be inclined to do the inside wiring yourself instead of paying the telephone company to do it. Think long and hard before you decide to do the wiring yourself. If you decide to do so, think again. While the telephone company charges a very high price for installing inside wiring, it may be worth the extra expense to have them terminate the ISDN line near your equipment. You may save $100, $200, or more by doing the wiring yourself, but you will probably be shooting yourself in the foot by doing so.

If you have problems with the line, as you probably will, and the inside wiring was installed by the telephone company and under maintenance, they will resolve the problem for you. If instead you install your own inside wiring, the technician will only test the line from the central office to the demarcation point. After that, you're on your own in a place that you really, *really* don't want to be.

Having inside wiring installed by the telephone company avoids finger pointing and delays when problems occur with the ISDN line, which are very likely to occur.

Once the ISDN line is actually installed, the technician will test it before he leaves. This test is usually just a 10-minute *Bit Error Rate Test* (*BERT*) of both B Channels when dialed in to a special ISDN test number. The technician relays the pertinent information to you, including switch type and *SPIDs*.

Your next step is to program the switch type and possibly the SPIDs and the phone numbers into your hardware and give it a try. If you've followed all these steps, chances are it works. Make sure that you can dial out and accept calls. If you can, congratulations. It will probably continue working.

If it doesn't work, you may have more of a problem than you realize. If you call repair service, they will send a technician who will do a BERT test, tell you the line is fine, shake your hand and say goodbye. Your next step is to try to coordinate between the telephone company repair service and the tech support staff of your hardware vendor. After perhaps hours or days spent on numerous conference calls, blindly trying different things to get it working and running into numerous dead ends, you may succeed in fixing the problem and you may not.

There is a better way. Make sure that your ISDN line provides *Q.931 debugging*. If a problem occurs, you can simply capture the Q.931 and possibly the Q.921 debugging information and relay this information to the hardware vendor technical support department. They can use this information to determine exactly what the problem is, explain the situation to you, and tell you exactly what you need to tell the telephone company to get the problem resolved.

ISDN Standardization

The need for standardization of ISDN is obvious even to the most obtuse observer. As this chapter is written, it appears that such standardization may soon become a reality. In March, 1996, the National ISDN Council announced that several carriers, including Ameritech, Bell Atlantic, BellSouth, Cincinnati Bell, GTE, NYNEX, Pacific Bell, Southern New England Telecommunications Corporation, Southwestern Bell, and U.S. West had agreed to standard parameters for ISDN service.

Under this plan, participating carriers use the same SPID format for new installations of National ISDN lines. Originally, each carrier used its own proprietary SPID format, based on the capabilities of the switch it was using and the services it offered. The current versions of software available for the ISDN capable switches made by various manufacturers now have enough features in common to allow the use of a generic SPID, which specifies features available on any supported switch.

This new generic SPID format comprises 14 characters. The first 10 represent the telephone number of the ISDN terminal, while the final four characters specify the number of connected devices and the services available on them. Although the telephone companies will continue to provide SPIDs when an ISDN line is ordered, the use of a generic SPID will greatly simplify installation and troubleshooting of new ISDN installations. The generic SPID is also backwardly compatible with existing SPIDs.

SLIP and PPP Dial-Up Connections

A dial-up connection to the Internet is similar to any other asynchronous dial-up connection, with a single exception. If you want to be on the Internet, you have to be running TCP/IP, and a dial-up Internet connection accommodates this requirement by running one of two protocols—*Serial Line Internet Protocol (SLIP)* or *Point-to-Point Protocol (PPP)*. Either of these protocols allows TCP/IP packets to be transferred across an asynchronous dial-up connection, supplying the IP connectivity you need to be live on the Internet.

SLIP is the older and less desirable of the two protocols, although you may have no choice but to use it, depending on the requirements of the ISP you select. If you are given the choice, choose a PPP connection.

Installing and Configuring a Router

Now here's a topic that deserves a book of its own, if not an entire library. The first rule of configuring routers is to avoid the job entirely. If you work with routers every day and can be found at parties off in the corner debating the merits of OSPF versus RIP with other techies, you don't need any advice—except perhaps regarding your social skills. If you don't, don't attempt to configure your own router unless you're the type of person who would be willing to make an attempt at performing neurosurgery at home. Setting up and configuring a router is a job best left to the pros.

> **Tip**
>
> If you want your multiuser ISDN or leased line network connection to the Internet to be up and running sometime this century, bite the bullet and hire a consultant to install and configure the router. Assuming you have the line installed, all hardware present and all the information required at hand, a good consultant can probably get your router up and running in a few hours, although it may well require more than one on-site visit. Competent network consultants charge from $100 per hour to $250 per hour, depending on qualifications and where you live, so the cost of getting the router installed and configured properly will probably range from $300 to $2,000. If you have never installed and configured a router but are otherwise technically competent and insist on doing the job yourself, plan on making dozens of calls to tech support and spending at least 20 to 40 hours of your time on the job. Seriously.

The reality is that a multiuser network connection requires a router to link your network to the upstream provider. Recognizing the problem, many national and regional ISPs have begun providing turnkey solutions. Rather than simply buying the service from them, you buy an entire package, including the DSU/CSU needed to terminate the line and a router guaranteed to work with their equipment.

On high-speed, high-price links, this turnkey package may include having the equipment delivered, installed and configured on-site by a technician. On lower-priced ISDN connections, a preconfigured router will probably show up via UPS, and it will be up to you to physically connect the components and test them. In this situation, again consider hiring a consultant to complete the installation and setup of the router. If it is truly preconfigured, the consultant won't need to be on-site for long. If, as is often the case, when you hook things up according to directions nothing works, at least you'll have a competent professional right there to help.

Selecting an Internet Service Provider

Just a couple of years ago, picking an Internet Service Provider (ISP) was straightforward. If you had one that provided local service you were lucky. If you had two, you were blessed. The explosion of the Internet in general and the Web in particular has resulted in an equally explosive growth in the number of companies offering Internet access.

At last count, there are more than 1,500 companies that specialize in providing Internet connectivity services in the U.S. These companies range in size from multi-billion dollar corporations like AT&T and MCI down through smaller regional providers and eventually to garage shops with a dozen phone lines and a fractional T1. When you consider that the commercial online services like CompuServe and America Online have also recognized, if belatedly, the demand for Internet access and begun to provide these services, your choices are broader than they have ever been.

Your choices now are also broader than they are likely to be in the near future, as shake outs and consolidation hit this industry. In a business school sense, there has been a lack of equilibrium in the market. Ordinarily, markets with low barriers to entry are also low in profitability. Markets with high profitability have correspondingly high barriers to entry. This only makes economic sense, because if the barriers weren't high, everyone would be going where the money is.

The business of providing Internet access has, over the last couple of years, been out of sync with these market realities. It was both highly profitable and had low barriers to entry. Anyone with a modicum of data communications knowledge and a small amount of capital could buy a T1 or fractional T1 Internet link, install a few modems and phone lines, place a few ads and be off and running as an ISP.

The proliferation of providers is evidenced by rapidly dropping prices for Internet access, as too many competing providers vie for a huge, but nonetheless finite, number of prospective users. The small local providers will be first to feel the squeeze, as many are doing right now. Eventually, even the larger regional providers will likely fall prey to the economies of scale enjoyed by the national providers. Yet another nail in the coffins of the smaller providers is the looming presence of the as-yet uncommitted giants—the cable television companies and the local telephone companies. Neither has made any serious penetration into the Internet access market, but both are poised to do so in the near future.

Another change that has resulted from the explosion of the Internet is the altering focus of the ISP marketers. The emphasis has moved from selling services to techies to selling solutions to consumers. A few years ago, if you wanted to connect to the Internet, you had to be fully conversant with TCP/IP, communications facilities, and the alphabet soup of communications protocols. This is still largely true today if you plan to install a multiuser network connection, but if all you're looking for is an individual network connection, you can get one up and running about as easily as ordering a new telephone line.

In general terms, there are three ways to get access to the Internet. If you need an individual connection, you can get one from a commercial online service, from a local or regional ISP, or from a national ISP. If you need a multiuser connection, you are limited to the latter two. Each of these methods has advantages and drawbacks, depending on your personal requirements and your budget.

Let's look at your choices as they exist today, and where they may lead in the near term.

Access via Commercial Online Services

The situation with commercial online services and Internet access is an odd one. The majority of individual Internet users—as opposed to users accessing the Internet via a corporate network—use the commercial online services to do so. In particular, they use America Online and CompuServe. These services have profited greatly from the explosion of the Internet. Each has added hundreds of thousands or millions of new users for whom a commercial online service seemed to offer the quickest, easiest, and least expensive way to sample the joys of the Internet.

The commercial online services hope that although these millions of new users may have been motivated to join by the lure of Internet access, they will stay to sample the proprietary content offered by the online service. The commercial online services regard Internet access as just one aspect of their attractiveness to users. By and large, they're wrong. Most of these new users are motivated solely by the desire for Internet access, and look upon the commercial online services as just the mechanism that gets them there. After all, how often do you see headlines in the newspaper or stories on CNN about the latest proprietary offering from CompuServe or AOL?

What users want is flat-rate unlimited access to the Internet. What commercial online services need in order to stay in business is per-minute charges for usage. These two fundamentally incompatible requirements do not bode well for the future of commercial online services in their current form.

Things were easier a couple of years ago for the commercial online services. They could point to their proprietary content as a drawing card. Although their content is good and getting better, the incredible variety of material available on the Web is beginning to challenge all but the premium content of the commercial online services. As Web sites gain advertisers to support even better content, the gap is likely to narrow even further.

A year ago, commercial online services could make a valid argument that, for light Internet access at least, their services were economical. This argument is also disappearing fast, as competition among specialized ISPs reduces costs to very low levels. After all, AT&T and MCI now offer up to five hours a month of free Internet access to anyone who uses their long distance services. How do you compete with that? The next step may be to pay people to use your service. Seriously.

Another argument put forward by the commercial online services has been the availability of universal access. A business traveler can connect to CompuServe and other commercial online services via a local access number from nearly anywhere in the U.S. and from many places abroad. This argument, too, is losing credibility as national and international service providers like AT&T and MCI come on stream. After all, it's pretty hard to argue that you have a better network than AT&T or MCI.

The last argument, and one that is still gaining users for the commercial online services, is that they are easily accessible to ordinary mortals. The necessary access software comes to your snail mail box on a regular basis. All you have to do is insert the disk in your drive, type **setup** and have your credit card ready. If you have problems, there's help on the other end of an 800 number. You don't need to worry about IP addresses, DNS, and gateways. You just log on and go to work. All true, and all becoming increasingly immaterial. The commercial online services aren't the only ones with 800 numbers, and the national ISPs, like AT&T WorldNet, are bundling preconfigured access software and taking other steps to make their services easy to use.

Most of the commercial online services have recognized the importance of Internet access, and in the old business tradition have gone into competition with themselves. If America Online can't get your Internet access business, they hope that instead you'll sign up with their Global Network Navigator (GNN) subsidiary, which provides dedicated Internet access. Prodigy, CompuServe, and other commercial online services have similar dedicated Internet access services in the works or available. Evaluate these specialized Internet Access Provider offshoots of the commercial online services just as you would any other national level provider.

For most people, using a commercial online service for dedicated Internet access is the worst possible choice. It costs more than the alternatives, offers less flexibility, and is usually the slowest performing alternative. You are often locked into using only the Internet utilities supported by the provider, and per-minute connect time charges add up quickly. Consider using a commercial online service only as a last resort.

That said, there are times when using a commercial online service to provide Internet access does make sense. For example, if you travel frequently, particularly overseas, you will find that CompuServe has points of presence (POPs) in some places that barely have running water. Also, if your primary online activity is focused on the use of a commercial online service and you have need of accessing the Internet only infrequently, using the commercial online service to do so can be the simplest and least expensive alternative.

All of the Big Four commercial online services—America Online, CompuServe, The Microsoft Network, and Prodigy—now offer at least some level of Internet access. Prodigy was first out of the gate with a Web browser, but CompuServe, America Online and The Microsoft Network have countered with similar features. All offer the ability to send and receive Internet e-mail and read USENET newsgroups, although with varying degrees of power and ease. All of them also offer tutorials and other features oriented to Net newbies and family-oriented features like parental controls on what may be viewed.

Let's take a brief look at what the commercial online services offer in terms of Internet access.

America Online (AOL)

America Online (AOL) was the first of the major commercial online services to realize both that the Internet was important to users and that it wasn't going to go away. The AOL 2.5 access software offers a decent if unexciting Web browser, and the Internet connection area of AOL provides access to most major Internet services.

There are, however, two major problems with using AOL for Internet access:

First, because your dial-up connection to AOL does not use standard PPP, you are limited to using the tools provided by AOL itself to access the Internet. If, for example, you would prefer to use Netscape Navigator instead of the standard AOL Web browser, you're out of luck. Although AOL does offer a free replacement WINSOCK.DLL to allow use of standard Internet utilities with an AOL connection, this product is not intended for Windows NT. Even using it with Windows 95 is aggravating, since it must replace the standard WINSOCK.DLL rather than simply coexisting with it.

The second problem with depending on AOL for Internet access is that AOL is notorious for busy signals, dropped connections, and slow throughput. AOL has grown too rapidly for its own good. It seems that every time AOL adds 10,000 new modems and phone lines for access, they also add about half a million new users to compete for those resources.

AOL is demonstrating an ongoing commitment to providing Internet services, as exemplified by their 1995 acquisition of ANS (the former Internet backbone people) and by their roll-out of the GNN dedicated Internet access service. Still, for most businesses, AOL is not the best choice.

CompuServe

Of the commercial online services, CompuServe (CIS) is probably the best choice for business use and Internet access. Although it lagged AOL in providing a Web browser, WinCIM 2.0.1 now includes Spry Mosaic, arguably the best browser provided by any of the commercial online services. CIS has also led the other services in providing access to such Internet services as USENET newsgroups, ftp, and Telnet.

Because CIS uses a standard PPP link for dial-up connections, you can establish a connection to CIS and then use Netscape Navigator or any other standards-based Internet utility to access Internet services. CIS also has fewer problems with busy signals, lost connections, and slow throughput than most of the other commercial online services, and is available almost anywhere on planet Earth.

One of the main objections to using CIS historically has been their relatively high connect time charges. CIS has attempted to address this with their Super Value Plan, which offers 20 hours of access for $25 per month, with an additional charge of $2 per hour for hours beyond 20. Although this is certainly less costly than earlier plans, CIS still has a long way to go to match the now-standard $20 per month for unlimited access. Like other commercial online services, CIS has drawn a line in the dirt concerning flat rate access. They apparently believe that they cannot survive with flat-rate charges for unlimited connect time. The market will leave them little choice but to learn to do so or disappear.

Like AOL, CompuServe is demonstrating an ongoing commitment to the Internet. In May, 1996, CompuServe announced a $40 million network upgrade that will substantially alter the way CIS provides Internet services. Until now, CIS has been buying Internet access from MCI and UUnet Technologies. The completion of this network upgrade will give CIS its own 45 Mbps T3 backbone and speed Internet access for CIS users.

V

Using the Internet

Prodigy

Prodigy is, in many respects, the Rodney Dangerfield of the commercial online services. They've almost-but-not-quite gotten it right several times. As of now, it appears that their chances have about run out.

Throughout its history, Prodigy has suffered bad press. First, early users were annoyed by the intrusive advertisements that appeared on each screen and slow performance that resulted from transferring graphics. Then, although Prodigy was initially marketed as a completely flat-rate service, some subscribers began abusing this privilege, at least in Prodigy's opinion, by sending too many mail messages. Prodigy began charging extra for sending e-mail messages beyond 30 per month, annoying a lot of normal subscribers by doing so. Then the STAGE.DAT scandal arose, and Prodigy was unjustifiably but very publicly charged by some know-nothings with surreptitiously attempting to gather information from users' hard drives. On the heels of the STAGE.DAT tempest came numerous charges of censorship when Prodigy attempted to regulate the content of messages posted to public areas. At times it seemed as though Prodigy couldn't do anything right.

Although Prodigy led the charge to provide Web access among the commercial online services, their current offerings are limited both in features and in scope as compared with other commercial online services. One of the most significant problems with Prodigy over the years has been its generally slow performance, which has been exacerbated by Prodigy's continuing dependence on 14,400 bps modems for dial-up access. Using the Web is painful enough at 28,800 bps. Using it on Prodigy at 14,400 bps is fit only for a masochist.

Prodigy appears to be on a downhill slide, and is now a distant third in size to AOL and CompuServe. While AOL in its latest quarter added 905,000 new members, for a total of more than 5.5 million subscribers, Prodigy has actually lost subscribers, declining in the six months prior to this writing from about 1.6 million members to about 1.1 million.

Although Prodigy flirted with profitability in early 1995, its seven-year history has been one of continuing losses. For a long time, the deep pockets of IBM and Sears Roebuck, equal partners in the Prodigy service, isolated Prodigy from market realities. Between them, IBM and Sears are reputed to have sunk close to $1 billion into Prodigy over the years. As this is written in early July, 1996, Prodigy has just been sold to a group of outside investors. It seems likely that Prodigy will continue to exist, if at all, as simply a premium Web site.

Many industry experts believe that only one or two of the Big Four commercial online services will survive the coming shake out, and Prodigy is on almost nobody's list of those that are likely to remain standing. Commercial online services in general are usually a poor choice for Internet access, and for many users Prodigy will be the worst of the commercial online services.

The Microsoft Network

The Microsoft Network (MSN) is a chameleon, showing that, if nothing else, Bill Gates is fast on his feet. When first announced, MSN was to be a full-featured commercial online service, competing directly with the likes of AOL and CIS. Many of the other commercial online services immediately cried foul, fearing that the stated plans of Microsoft to bundle MSN with Windows 95 would give MSN an unfair advantage in competing for new users.

As it turns out, the fears of AOL and CIS were apparently groundless. Although MSN quickly garnered several hundred thousand subscribers, the other commercial online services continued to grow by leaps and bounds as well.

In the last few months, it has become increasingly apparent that MSN is being recast in the role of a general Internet Service Provider instead of the original concept of a commercial online service. The MSN development team departed all together to form a company devoted to developing Internet utilities. While the other commercial online services, particularly AOL and CIS, devoted significant resources to developing new content, MSN appeared to be content to add new users and continue to develop as an ISP.

On the plus side of the ledger, MSN uses standard PPP connections, allowing you to use industry standard products like Netscape Navigator if you choose to do so. MSN also provides a top-notch browser in Internet Explorer. There is a downside to MSN, however. Although MSN POPs are all equipped with v.34 28,800 bps modems, the service as a whole is slow. Some of this may be attributable to start-up pains, but it appears that at least some of the problems may be systemic, including Microsoft's reliance on PC-based servers running Windows NT to back-end the service.

Part of the announced rationale behind developing MSN was as a technology demonstrator to prove that Windows NT Server was scaleable to support very large environments. In contrast to other commercial online services that use a mix of PC servers and heavy iron, Microsoft runs MSN on hundreds of quad-processor Compaq ProLiant 4000 servers running Windows NT. Based on frequent complaints about performance by many MSN users, it appears that Windows NT may not be quite as scaleable as Microsoft had hoped.

Although you have to admire the effort made by Microsoft in going from nothing to a full-blown service in a very short time, most users will find that there are better alternatives available for accessing the Internet.

National Internet Service Providers

Another choice for Internet access is to sign up with an ISP with a national presence. Some of these have been around for years, almost since the birth of the Internet. Others are relatively recent arrivals.

Strangely enough, most of the old hands at providing Internet access—companies like UUnet Technologies and PSInet—are relatively young in an absolute sense, having been born with the Internet and grown up with it. The more recent arrivals as national ISPs are the communications behemoths, companies like AT&T and MCI. Many of these older companies have had a major background presence in the Internet all along, but have just recently begun to market Internet services directly to consumers and small businesses.

National ISPs have a reputation for providing reliable, high performance service at bargain basement prices. From a reliability standpoint, each has long experience in maintaining large network infrastructures, and this experience is exhibited in increased up-time relative to the commercial online services and smaller local providers. From the performance side, each has a staff expert in managing large data communications networks. Network designers, planners, and traffic managers don't come cheaply, and each of these organizations is large enough and has the resources needed to put such specialized talent on board. On the pricing side, each is used to dealing in data communications as a commodity business, and has the cost structure in place to do so successfully.

The consolidation and shake out of ISPs exists even at this level. In May 1996, MFS Communications announced the planned $2 billion acquisition of UUNet Technologies, one of the national ISP giants. Ultimately, like any new and vigorous industry, ISPs are likely to consolidate into a handful of very large national and international corporations. The major players in a few years will likely be AT&T and MCI, with perhaps one or two of the cable television giants like Time Warner and TCI providing additional competition. Whatever the results of the shake out, the long-term news will be good. Internet facilities will continue to be upgraded, and the cost of service will continue to drop precipitously.

Caution

Don't sign a long term contract in a buyers' market. If you are signing up for individual Internet access with a national ISP, you have little choice but to accept the standard terms and conditions of the provider. If instead you are contracting for a multiuser network connection delivered via leased-line service, take care. A more-or-less standard contract from a national ISP will waive installation and setup charges in return for a contract of one year's duration. That part is fine. What they will also try to do is get you to commit to service for three or even five years. In return, they will offer discounts of perhaps 25 percent. Don't fall for it, or before long you'll find yourself paying more for service than you would on a short term contract. Ever increasing competition means that the cost of Internet access is declining, and most likely will continue to do so for the foreseeable future. Negotiate accordingly.

Until recently, national ISPs focused their marketing efforts primarily on experienced users and corporate customers, not deigning to go after the individual Internet access market. The explosion of the Internet, however, means that millions of new prospective customers are out there, and the national ISPs have finally decided that this is simply too large of a market to ignore. Accordingly, they have shifted both their marketing efforts and their support structures toward this huge new pool of prospects.

Tip

The subject of performance guarantees for Internet access is beginning to get more attention. Historically, the contract you signed with your ISP promised absolutely nothing about level of service, available throughput, time to correct outages, and so on. Your ISP couldn't make these promises to you simply because the upstream ISP made no such commitments to him. This is now changing, as the Internet begins to be used for mission-critical business applications and hit-or-miss network availability is no longer acceptable.

When you negotiate your contract with the ISP you select, make sure to bring up the subject of performance guarantees, and get any promises made in writing. If the ISP won't talk about performance guarantees, look for a different ISP. These guarantees are a recent phenomenon, so you may not find an ISP that will commit to the terms you want, but it's at least worth a try.

V

Using the Internet

In entering this new market, the national ISPs are making life harder for the commercial online services and almost unbearable for the local and smaller regional ISPs. The smaller fry see their competitive advantages disappearing one by one, as the national ISPs uncover new needs and develop programs to address them. In short, now and for the foreseeable future, a national ISP is likely to offer you both the best service and the best price.

Let's take a look at three of the likely contenders. Each of these companies has different programs for individual network Internet access and multiuser network Internet access. Most of them have two or more programs in each category targeted at different market niches.

AT&T WorldNet

In early March 1996, AT&T stunned the ISP community with the announcement of WorldNet Internet access service, shown in figure 14.6. Although most of the local and regional ISPs tried to put on a brave face, the fact is that the entry of AT&T into the fray dramatically changed the rules overnight.

Fig. 14.6
AT&T WorldNet.

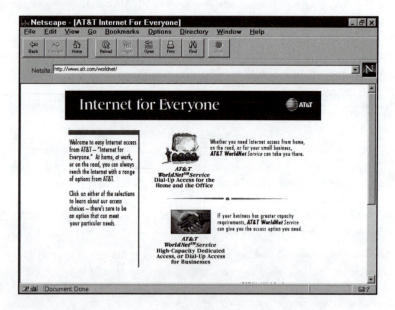

That a company the size of AT&T had decided to enter the competition for individual Internet access accounts was bad enough news for other ISPs. That AT&T offered unlimited Internet access for $20 a month set a lower ceiling than most ISPs were used to operating under. That AT&T was willing to provide five free hours a month of Internet access to any existing AT&T long distance customer was truly frightening. Obviously, AT&T is seriously committed to becoming a major provider of individual Internet access accounts.

The AT&T WorldNet individual Internet access service is available to both residential and business users, although in slightly different forms. Residential users may elect five free hours per month for one year, with the only requirement being that they must use the service for at least one hour per month. Hours beyond five are charged at $2.50 per hour. Residential users may also choose unlimited access for $20 per month. Those who are not AT&T long distance customers pay $5 per month for 3 hours and $25 per month for unlimited access. Business customers aren't offered the free option, but can elect unlimited access for $20 a month if they use AT&T long distance services or $25 per month if they do not.

AT&T provides a sign-up kit that contains an AT&T branded copy of Netscape Navigator, although the service uses standard PPP connections and is therefore browser independent. As some indication of the likely popularity of WorldNet, AT&T received nearly 500,000 requests for the sign-up kit within 30 days of the announcement.

One of the most attractive features of WorldNet to those used to constant busy signals when attempting to dial a commercial online service or local ISP is that AT&T guarantees no busy signals. They are in a unique position to make this guarantee because of the size and redundancy of their network. If you dial your local POP and all lines are busy, AT&T simply shifts your call to another POP with available resources. The transfer is completely transparent to you. As far as you can tell, your local POP simply never rings busy. It remains to be seen whether even a company with the resources of AT&T can truly fulfill this goal, given the level of customer demand likely to occur.

Generally overlooked in all the excitement about the terms for individual accounts was the fact that the AT&T announcement was not limited to individual accounts. AT&T plans to offer multiuser network connections to businesses on a turnkey basis, providing transmission facilities, hardware, and on-site support as a packaged Internet access service. For further information about AT&T WorldNet services, both individual and multiuser, call 1-800-WORLDNET or point your Web browser to **www.att.com/worldnet**.

MCI InternetMCI

As a major Internet provider, MCI couldn't let the AT&T WorldNet announcement go unchallenged for long, and they didn't. Within a week, MCI announced a competing plan to provide individual Internet access accounts to their long distance customers, and on terms almost identical to those announced by AT&T.

For individual Internet access customers, MCI offers InternetMCI Dial Access, shown in figure 14.7, on one of two plans. Unlimited Access offers just that, at $20 per month. Preferential Access offers 5 free hours per month, with additional hours billed at $2.50 per hour. On either plan, toll free 800 number access costs $6 per hour.

As might be expected from the relative sizes of the corporations, MCI offers access in fewer cities than does AT&T. By the time you read this, MCI should offer access in most cities in the top 100 markets. You can check to see if your city is one by pointing your Web browser to **www.mci.com/resources/ forhome/content/local.shtml**.

Like AT&T WorldNet, InternetMCI Dial Access uses standard PPP connections and supports dial-up access at speeds to 28.8 Kbps. Unlike AT&T WorldNet, InternetMCI Dial Access also supports BRI ISDN connections, although only at single channel 56 Kbps/64 Kbps rates. AT&T says that it also plans to provide ISDN connections, although it has not made specific commitments as to when and at which POPs it will do so.

MCI also has a major presence in providing Internet access for businesses. As one of the key providers of backbone services to the Internet itself, MCI is well placed to provide direct access services for businesses.

Fig. 14.7
MCI InternetMCI.

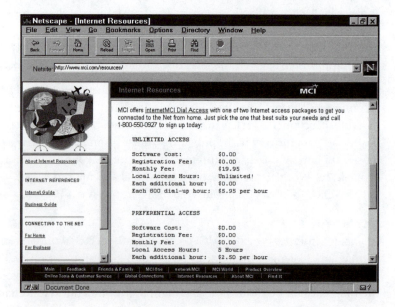

> **Tip**
>
> Many businesses are initially put off by the apparently higher prices for MCI services compared with those offered by local ISPs. For example, MCI may quote $2,800 a month for a T1 Internet connection, while the local ISP may quote $1,500 a month.
>
> On the face of it, this seems like a no-brainer. It isn't. What you actually get for your money from the local ISP is often a connection that shares limited bandwidth with dozens or even hundreds of other users. What you get from MCI is a clear-channel connection that guarantees you the full nominal bandwidth all the way from your site to the Internet backbone. In this example, find out what MCI can provide for the same $1,500 a month. A nominally slower connection provided by MCI often provides much higher actual throughput than the supposedly faster connection provided by the local ISP.

You can contact MCI directly for further information at 1-800-550-0927 or by setting your Web browser to **www.mci.com**.

Performance Systems International (PSI)

Until the AT&T WorldNet announcement, PSI offered two plans for individual network access. Pipeline was intended primarily for novice and casual Internet users, and offered unlimited access for $20 per month. Initially, Pipeline used proprietary access methods rather than a standard Winsock/PPP connection, and therefore mandated the use of the bundled software. It was later upgraded to use standards-based connection methods. InterRamp was always a standards-based service, and offered either nine hours for $9 per month or 29 hours of prime-time usage plus unlimited off-prime access for $29 per month.

The introduction of WorldNet prompted PSI to announce WorldLink Remote Access Service at the end of April, 1996. WorldLink, shown in figure 14.8, is positioned as a volume purchase program for small businesses and corporations and will replace the InterRamp for Business bulk purchase program. As of this writing, WorldLink was scheduled for roll-out in early June.

At first glance, it is difficult to tell how PSI plans to position WorldLink against the similar competing offerings from AT&T and MCI. Like the others, WorldLink offers unlimited Internet access at a flat rate, but that rate is 50 percent higher than that charged by AT&T and MCI. WorldLink costs $30 per month for a 28.8 Kbps dial-up connection or a 56/64 Kbps single channel ISDN link. A 128 Kbps 2 B channel ISDN link is available for $50 per month. Like AT&T and MCI, PSI offers toll free 800 number access at $6 per hour.

Fig. 14.8

Performance
Systems Interna-
tional (PSI).

Tip

If you want a multiuser Internet connection for your small business, but can't justify
the $1,000 per month or more that this service normally costs, check into the PSI
LAN-on-Demand service.

Available both as LAN-Dial using a standard dial-up telephone line and as LAN-ISDN
using an ISDN link, LAN-on-Demand is an entry-level multiuser solution appropriate
for small businesses and branch offices of larger businesses.

LAN-Dial currently costs $295 for setup and $145 per month. LAN-ISDN costs $495
for setup and $245 per month. In addition to these costs, you pay for installation and
monthly charges for the phone line at your site. You also have to purchase and install
a dial-up router, which may run $1,000 to $1,500 for the router itself and another
$500 to $1,500 to have it installed and configured for you. Not cheap, but certainly
a lot less expensive than traditional methods.

The "on demand" part of the name comes from the fact that the connection doesn't
stay up all the time. It is established automatically when anyone on your LAN uses a
service that requires Internet access (or if you have incoming traffic from the
Internet). If the connection isn't used for a certain period, it is automatically dropped
and then re-established when it is again needed.

> **Caution**
>
> PSI LAN-ISDN service is good, but not perfect. I found that getting a connection to stay up was a problem, and that even once the service was supposedly working properly it regularly dropped connections, seeming to time out every few hours whether or not the connection was in use. This occurred on a newly established POP. PSI claimed that the problems were not representative of the service in general but were merely startup glitches. Maybe so. We have no basis to judge other than our own experiences with the Winston-Salem, North Carolina PSI POP.
>
> Also, if you do decide to sign up for the LAN-ISDN service, make sure to buy your router from PSI, or at least buy a model that appears on their supported equipment list. PSI remarkets Ascend Pipeline routers, an excellent choice for small businesses, and will preconfigure the router for you if you wish.

PSI also offers several other multiuser network access plans for businesses, including high-speed dedicated line connections and frame relay services. You can contact PSI at 800-827-7482 or point your Web browser to **www.psi.net**.

Local Internet Service Providers

There are few barriers to starting up a small local ISP business, and the number of them out there proves it. All it takes is a few thousand dollars to install a T1 or Fractional T1 link to the Internet, buy a router and a UNIX box to run DNS, and put in a few phone lines and modems. You're in business as an ISP, probably serving a single city, or perhaps a lightly populated region.

Some of these local ISPs are wonderfully good and others are unspeakably awful. Even the best of them, however, are unlikely to survive the onslaught of the national ISPs. Local ISPs do not have the cost structure, the staff diversity, the technical expertise, or the deep pockets that the national ISPs do. Those local ISPs in the top 100 markets are under siege right now. As the national ISPs extend the reach of their networks by adding POPs in the top 250 markets and eventually covering the top 1000, local ISPs will become an endangered species.

If you live in a market served by the national ISPs, don't even consider using a local ISP. The local ISP will most likely have inferior service at a higher price. If a local ISP prices its service to compete with the nationals, it is simply spending itself into bankruptcy by providing service at a price lower than its costs.

V

Using the Internet

If you live in a small town, your only choice for a multiuser network connection may be a local ISP. In fact, sometimes you have to use a local ISP for an individual connection because the nearest POP for a national ISP is a long distance call for you. Interestingly, small towns are often served by not one but two competing ISPs, probably because of the low barriers to entry and the perception a year or two ago that providing Internet service would be a very profitable business. The profits are no longer there, if they ever were, and price competition in small towns can approach the ferocity evident in larger markets.

> ### Tip
>
> If two or more competing local ISPs serve your city, make sure everything is on the table when you negotiate for Internet service. The ISPs will try to portray the market as being similar to tariffed phone company services, with standard terms and pricing and no room for individual bargaining. Don't believe it. The market is more like that for used cars. Everything is negotiable, except perhaps service guarantees and the cost of the leased line you use to connect to the ISP POP.
>
> Play one ISP against the other as you negotiate. When the ISP actually walks away from the table, you know that's really the best deal you can strike. Keep in mind that you're not the only customer pushing for a good deal, so the long term stability of the ISP with whom you finally negotiate an agreement may be tenuous.

If you find yourself with a choice between competing local ISPs, there are a few things to be on the lookout for, all based on the fact that the back-end Internet connection costs the ISP money while the front-end dial-up and leased-line customer links generate revenue.

First, ask the ISP about his link to the Internet. He'll probably tell you proudly that he has a T1 link, but this doesn't really mean much. T1 is a telephone company carrier facility that provides 1.544 Mbps of throughput, but this doesn't necessarily mean that the ISP actually has this amount of bandwidth to the Internet. It is quite possible, and in fact commonly done, to use a full T1 link to transfer data at a slower rate. So, while the ISP may use a 1.544 Mbps link to his upstream provider, he may have contracted with that provider for only 512 Kbps, 384 Kbps, or even less actual throughput to the Internet. Also, what the ISP calls a "T1" may actually be only a fractional T1. Ask the ISP specifically what throughput to the Internet he has with his upstream provider.

Second, ask the ISP if his link provides clear-channel throughput to the Internet backbone. His upstream service provider has the same motivations he does insofar as back-end costs for his own Internet link versus revenue generated from his customers, of whom your ISP is one. It is common for a service provider to sell T1 Internet service to two or more ISPs and then fulfill that commitment using a single T1 Internet link There's nothing dishonest going on here. It's simply a matter of getting what you pay for. A T1 Internet Link provided on this resource sharing basis might cost your ISP $1,500 a month. A true clear channel T1 link might cost him $2,500 or more.

Third, ask the ISP how many dial-up and leased-line customer links are supported by his Internet link. Simple division of data rates, ignoring data compression and other factors, says that a single 1.544 Mbps T1 link will provide full bandwidth simultaneously to either about 50 28.8 Kbps dial-up links or to about 25 56 Kbps leased-line links. It's not uncommon to find that an ISP has 50 or 75 28.8 Kbps dial-up lines, a dozen 56 Kbps leased-lines to customer sites, and perhaps several customer T1 links, all contending for the bandwidth provided by the ISP's single T1 or even fractional T1 link to the Internet.

There are a couple of other issues you need to keep in mind when evaluating ISPs. Because most local ISPs operate on a shoestring, they are unlikely to have much in the way of equipment spares. If their router fails, they (and you) are out of service until it can be repaired. Similarly, they are likely to depend on a single link to their upstream provider rather than having backup links in place. If a backhoe severs a line, service may be interrupted for hours or even days.

Perhaps the biggest weakness of small local ISPs is in staffing. Good networking people don't come cheap, and small ISPs are hard-pressed to hire and pay the kind of staff it takes to keep an internetwork up and running. Many different skills are needed, and a larger ISP can hire a diverse staff with all of these skills represented. A smaller ISP can usually afford to hire only one or two people, and hope that they can do at least an adequate job of meeting these diverse demands. Many small ISPs do a very good job, considering the constraints they operate under, but the reality is that a larger ISP will almost always provide more responsive and reliable service.

All of this said, small local ISPs do have some things going for them:

- *Cost*. Although on average a local ISP will charge as much or more as a national ISP, some local ISPs have incredible bargains available—while they last. Unlimited access individual accounts may be available from some ISPs for as little as $10 per month.

- *Value Added Service.* If all you're looking for is an Internet connection, local ISPs usually can't compete with the nationals. If you want someone to provide Internet training and consulting, design Web pages, or even host your Web site, a local ISP can often provide more responsive service than a larger ISP.

- *Local Content.* Many local ISPs provide a significant amount of local content—links to local weather, news, public affairs, online library catalogs, and so on. Although much of this information can be accessed by other means, some people find it useful to have it available in one place.

CHAPTER 15
Using Web Browsers

by Robert Bruce Thompson

The World Wide Web, also called the WWW or simply the Web, is by far the fastest growing segment of the Internet, and with good reason. Older Internet services like Gopher, Archie, and ftp are primarily text-based, and are often accessed with character-mode client software. Functional, perhaps, but certainly unattractive. The Web, on the other hand, presents a much more compelling multimedia environment which includes graphics, video, sound, and animation.

A less obvious advantage—but perhaps just as important—is the suitability of the Web for browsing. With most of the older services, you had to have a pretty good idea in advance of what you were looking for and where it might be located. The Web, on the other hand, allows you to follow active links related to your topic. You can jump from server to server until you locate the information you need. In the process, you may well come across other valuable information that you didn't even know existed. The pretty face of the Web is its most obvious advantage. The fact that, by encouraging browsing, the Web converts a search for information from a sequential process to a matrix process is likely to be more valuable in the long run.

The concept of browsing is so central to the Web that the client software used to access the information on the Web is called a *Web browser*. If you use the Web often, you owe it to yourself to spend an hour or so to choose the best Web browser for your needs. A good Web browser can make the time you spend on the Web productive and enjoyable. A bad one can limit your options considerably.

In this chapter, you learn to

- Recognize the fundamental building blocks of the Web, including hypertext documents, Hypertext Markup Language (HTML), Hypertext Transfer Protocol (HTTP), and Uniform Resource Locators (URLs)

- Use the important features of Web browsers and recognize what these features might mean for you

- Install and configure Microsoft Internet Explorer and Netscape Navigator, the two products which, between them, hold the vast majority of the market share for Web Browsers

- Locate information using four of the largest and most popular Web search engines

Understanding the World Wide Web

The *World Wide Web*, also called the *WWW* or simply the *Web*, is a network of servers running specialized Web server software. These servers communicate with each other and with users via the Internet using the TCP/IP protocol suite. A *Web server* is essentially a document server. The Web server stores documents in a structured fashion and delivers them upon request to users. Users access the Web server through a Web client software package, also referred to as a *Web browser*.

Hypertext

The foundation of the Web is hypertext documents. An ordinary document is intended to be read sequentially. Although you can jump from place to place within an ordinary document to locate other information, doing so is a manual process. A hypertext document, on the other hand, is "live." Portions of a hypertext document—words or short phrases—are highlighted. These highlighted portions, called *links*, are pointers that enable the reader, simply by clicking the link, to immediately jump to another location (see fig. 15.1). The link can point to another location within that same document, to another document stored on the same Web server, or to another document stored on a different Web server, which may be located on the other side of the planet.

HyperText Markup Language (HTML)

The hypertext documents stored on Web servers are created using a special format called *HyperText Markup Language*, or *HTML*. An HTML document comprises ASCII text with embedded special tags, also in the form of ASCII text (see fig. 15.2). These special tags indicate how text is to be formatted and where the resources referred to by links are located. HTML originated as a very limited subset of the industry-standard *Standard Generalized Markup Language* (SGML). With the addition of numerous enhancements, HTML has diverged from SGML to take on a life of its own.

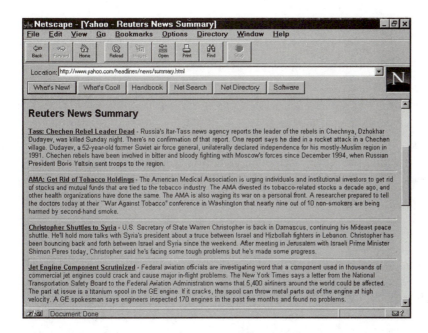

Fig. 15.1
Web page showing
hypertext links.

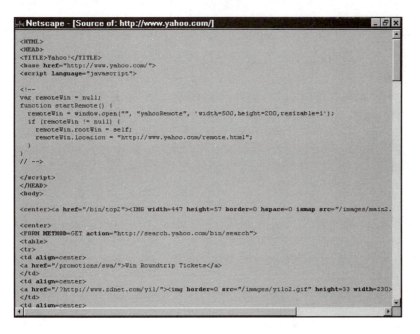

Fig. 15.2
A fragment of
HTML code.

The tags used by HTML to organize documents fall into five categories:

■ *Structural commands*. Define the structure of the HTML document, including the beginning and end of the header and body information to be displayed to users.

■ *Character formatting commands*. Emphasize portions of the displayed text by applying such characteristics as boldface, italic, and underline.

■ *Paragraph formatting commands*. Control the appearance of paragraphs within the HTML document, including indenting, line breaks, text flow-around, heading level, and the use of monospaced versus proportional fonts.

■ *List commands*. Display bulleted, numbered, and annotated lists, tables, and so forth.

■ *Anchor commands*. Define the hypertext links within the document, specifying the appearance of these links to the user, and the action to be taken when a user clicks a link.

Fortunately, you don't need to understand HTML in order to use the Web. The HTML commands within a hypertext document provide generalized information about how that document is to be displayed. Your Web browser is aware of the hardware capabilities of your computer, and uses these embedded HTML commands to display the hypertext document to its best advantage.

The generalized nature of hypertext documents makes the Web universally accessible, because any HTML document can be displayed on any system, regardless of its hardware configuration or which operating system it is running. As long as the system has a graphical Web browser available for it, any HTML document can be displayed in essentially the same way as it appears on any other system.

Due to display resolutions, available fonts, and other minor variations between systems, there are often some minor differences in the exact way the hypertext document is displayed. For example, say that you have two computer systems, each of which runs Windows NT, and the same Web browser software. The systems are identical except that one of them is running 640×480 resolution, and the other 800×600. If you use these two systems to display the same HTML hypertext document, you will notice some minor variations (see figs. 15.3 and 15.4).

Fig. 15.3
Web page displayed at 640×480 resolution.

Fig. 15.4
Web page displayed at 800×600 resolution.

The system with the higher resolution (refer to fig. 15.4) shows you more of the HTML document onscreen at any one time, simply because it gives you a larger window on the document. Likewise, text paragraphs flow a little differently, with line breaks occurring at different points. You may notice minor differences in the fonts used, simply because the Web browser is doing the best it can with the fonts available, which may vary between the two systems. Although the displays vary in minor particulars, the overall impression is the same.

HyperText Transfer Protocol (HTTP)

Hypertext Transfer Protocol (*HTTP*) is a client-server protocol that is used between Web servers and Web browsers. HTTP operates at the OSI Session Layer and above to establish sessions, perform user validation, and so forth.

Uniform Resource Locator (URL)

Every page on the World Wide Web has a unique address, specified by its *Uniform Resource Locator*, or *URL*. The URL specifies both the server upon which the page is located and the protocol or service needed to access it. Not only does each page have a unique URL, but each element of that page—graphic, link, or frame—also has its own unique URL. You can access any page or any element of a page directly by using its associated URL.

A URL has two required sections and two optional sections. The first two sections are required, and specify the type of protocol to be used to access the service, and the site name:

[*protocol-type*]://[*site-name*]

For example, the URL

http://www.microsoft.com

specifies that the HTTP protocol should connect to the site **www.microsoft. com**. All Web browsers support the HTTP protocol used to connect to Web sites. Most browsers also support the ftp protocol used to connect to ftp servers, and many support News, Gopher, and other protocols.

> ### Tip
>
> Web browsers assume that they will access World Wide Web sites using the HTTP protocol unless otherwise specified, so you can usually omit the `http://` portion of the URL and simply type the site name, for example, **www.microsoft.com**.

The third section of the URL, the *path name*, is optional. It contains the directory location and, optionally, the file name of a particular Web page or page element. Loading a URL that contains only the first two elements brings you to the home page of the site in question. Including a path name enables you to directly access a page further down in the tree. For example, if you frequently access the Windows NT Workstation area on Microsoft's Web server, rather than connecting to **http://www.microsoft.com** and then navigating down the tree to reach the Windows NT Workstation home page, you might instead simply set a bookmark to

> **http://198.105.232.4:80/NTWorkstation**

and jump directly there.

Note two things about this URL:

- The site location is specified as an IP address, rather than as a name. You can always use a numeric identifier if you prefer to do so.

- This URL illustrates the fourth and final element of a URL. The `:80` following the IP address specifies a port number to be used. *Port numbers* are software "sockets" that are assigned to various services like HTTP. Although these port assignments are standardized, nothing prevents the administrator of a Web site from assigning nonstandard port numbers to services. This is not done frequently, and when it is, it is usually done as an *ad hoc* security measure.

Choosing Browser Software

Two years ago, Web browsers were a tiny product category. Few people had even heard of the Internet, and fewer still were using it. Those who were mostly used character-based ftp, Telnet, and News clients, along with some services that today are largely historical footnotes—Gopher, Archie, and Veronica. The World Wide Web was in its infancy, and if you used a Web browser, it was almost certainly NCSA Mosaic. There wasn't much to browse on the Web, either. The few Web servers were mostly found at academic sites, and provided little of interest to the general public. What was available was mostly text pages with a few hyperlinks to other documents and sites.

Things change fast. As far as many people are concerned now, the Web *is* the Internet. The Web is responsible for most of the traffic on the Internet today, and its share is increasing. Today there are tens of thousands, even hundreds of thousands, of Web servers, operated by everyone from major corporations in their computer centers to college students in their dormitory rooms. The content has changed, too, and not only quantitatively, but qualitatively. University sites, with their dry collections of academic documents, are no longer the dominant content providers on the Web. You can find almost any conceivable type of information on the Web today.

To access the Web, you need a client software package called a *Web browser*. Although people continue to use dedicated standalone clients for ftp, Telnet, and news, all of these functions can also be provided by a good Web browser. Choosing a good Web browser doesn't rank up there with choosing your spouse or even your next car, but it determines how effectively and how efficiently you can surf the web.

Everything started with a graphical Web browser called *NCSA Mosaic*. Looking back now, Mosaic seems rather primitive, but it single-handedly created a new software product category and spawned the dozens of Web browsers now competing for attention in this exploding market. A quick check of the Net locates dozens of free or inexpensive standalone Web browsers, and this doesn't even count the many commercial browsers and those that are bundled as a part of Internet suites.

The incredible growth rate in this product segment means that standards lag the actual products. Vendors with a major presence in this market—such as Netscape and Microsoft—are trailblazers, constantly pushing the envelope to add new capabilities, while standards bodies like the Internet Engineering Task Force (IETF) attempt to keep up with these proprietary innovations.

For users, the upside is that the products are constantly being improved, often by quantum leaps. The ultra-competitive environment of browser development ensures that this situation is likely to continue for the foreseeable future. Anyone who questions that users benefit from this free-market competition need only compare one of today's typical Web pages with one from a year or so ago. We have migrated from "thin" text-oriented content to pages that compare favorably in content, graphics, and layout with the best available printed documents. The best Web pages now far exceed the capabilities of printed content by including audio, video, and animation.

For all of the advantages to this unrestrained browser development, there is one downside. Because standards lag products by so much in this market, the continuing enhancements are, by their nature, proprietary.

Enhancements to HTML made by Netscape for its Navigator Web browser are incorporated only in a later version, if at all, in Microsoft Internet Explorer. In the same way, improvements made by Microsoft and incorporated into Internet Explorer show up only much later, if at all, in Navigator. The increasing presence on Web sites of notices informing the user that the site "Looks Best When Viewed with Netscape Navigator," or "Looks Best When Viewed with Microsoft Internet Explorer" are a symptom of this lack of standards.

In the early days of telephones, competing telephone companies often served customers within the same city, and no interconnection between the telephone companies existed. This meant that in order to talk to everyone, you had to install separate telephone lines and telephones from each company. Telephone companies regarded this exclusivity as a marketing advantage—"Only subscribers to our telephone service can call the hospital or the Mayor's office"—and actually competed to sign exclusive service agreements with popular destinations for telephone calls. Eventually, users revolted, and the phone companies realized that it was in their best interests to provide interoperability.

For the user, all of this means that choosing a Web browser is more complex than it really needs to be. Fortunately, market forces are beginning to take effect, and even arch-rivals Netscape and Microsoft are beginning to merge their product capabilities. The best of the Web browsers are very good indeed, and are getting better with each passing month.

Other software product categories are consolidating, too. A few years ago, computer magazines ran articles comparing 30 word processors, 20 spreadsheets, or a dozen databases. Today, only two or three viable products exist in each of these categories, and they typically share 90 percent or more of the market among them. Tightly focused niche products compete for the small remaining share.

Web browsers, too, are consolidating, although this may not be immediately evident at first glance. Everything about the Web browser product segment has been accelerated when compared with traditional product categories. Two years ago, the category didn't even exist. Product life cycles, which in traditional segments started at 18 months and gradually declined to perhaps 12 months, in Web browsers are on a three-month cycle. Given this rapid development pace, it is not surprising that consolidation has also hit the Web browser segment early. Netscape Navigator now owns a huge share of the market. Microsoft Internet Explorer is chipping away at that share. All of the other Web browsers have become minor players in this Duel of the Titans.

In practical terms, all the innovations in Web browsers come from Netscape and Microsoft. Other vendors have good ideas, certainly, but unless their innovations are adopted by one of the two major players, they have little chance of becoming standardized. In isolation, the best of ideas will die an unsupported death.

For all intents and purposes, then, for many users, choosing a standalone Web browser may devolve to one of only two alternatives—either Netscape Navigator or Microsoft Internet Explorer. Any other choice may ultimately be pointless. Let's take a look first at what is important in a Web browser and then at the specifics of Navigator and Internet Explorer.

Web Browser Features

A good browser must provide both a high degree of compatibility with the rapid changing standards on the Web and a full complement of convenience and usability features. Both Netscape Navigator and Microsoft Internet Explorer do well in this regard, with the balance between them leap-frogging with every update of each product. Let's take a look at some of the more important features to consider when choosing a browser.

HTML Support

The most important aspect of any browser is the level of support it provides for HTML. At a minimum, the browser must support the current HTML 2.0 standard. Because various elements of the proposed HTML 3.0 standard—for example, tables and frames—are commonly implemented on Web sites, support for these is very desirable. Navigator and Internet Explorer both provide full support for HTML 2.0. Each provides support for some elements, but not all, of HTML 3.0. Some of these elements, such as tables, are supported by both products. Others, like frames, are currently supported by Navigator but not by Internet Explorer. Still others, such as moving marquees, are supported by Internet Explorer but not by Navigator.

Convenience Features

Even a browser with the best technical features must take usability into account. If you spend a great deal of time using your browser, foreground features such as easy navigation and fast performance will be less important to you than background issues such as exactly which HTML features are supported. Using hypertext links to jump from place to place is at the heart of the Web, and anything that makes this task easier and faster is a worthwhile feature.

One such feature is *bookmarking*, which enables you to automatically capture and store the addresses of Web sites you visit. For maximum usability, the Bookmark feature should enable you to edit and rearrange the entries, preferably in a hierarchical folder structure. It is also useful to be able to create category headings to which individual site addresses can be assigned. Both Navigator and Internet Explorer provide strong bookmarking features.

Another useful feature that contributes greatly to performance is *caching*. By storing recently accessed pages in a local cache, the browser can eliminate the need to reload these pages directly from the remote server each time they are accessed. Both Navigator and Internet Explorer enable you to set the amount of disk space to be used for caching. Navigator enables you to specify the amount of disk space in absolute terms, and Internet Explorer enables you to specify the percentage of available disk space to be used for caching. Navigator goes a step further by allowing you to also specify how much RAM is to be used for session-level caching.

Image Support, Multimedia Features, and Extensibility

During its short first phase, the Web was primarily text-based, with an occasional small image used to break up the tedium. Images were mostly used as window dressing, often bearing little relation to the text with which they were associated. As the Web moved into its second phase, inline images were used more frequently and in much greater numbers, becoming an integral part of the presentation.

Today, a good browser must provide, at the very least, native support for the raster graphics imaging formats commonly used on the Web, and in particular for the Joint Photographic Experts Group (JPEG) and Graphics Interchange Format (GIF) graphics formats. Developing standards such as Progressive JPEG and Progressive GIF, which display a "quick and dirty" image initially and then use background data transfer to fill out the image as you are viewing the rest of the page, are also increasingly important, although not yet widely used.

One of the hottest developing areas on the Web is in multimedia content. *Multipurpose Internet Mail Extensions*, or *MIME*, allows audio and video information to be transferred in a variety of formats, with new formats and extensions to existing ones, seemingly appearing on almost a weekly basis.

This rapid rate of change makes it impossible for any browser to include the capability to decode and present all of these formats. The solution to this problem has been to make the browsers themselves extensible via add-ons from the browser vendors and from third parties, allowing new multimedia formats to be accommodated via additional software. Today, a good browser serves only as the initial framework upon which the entire Web client is built. The browser provides the core capabilities needed to surf the Web, while add-on products are used to keep it up-to-date with changes as they occur.

Netscape started this process by supporting so-called *helper applications*, which are small programs devoted to decoding and presenting one particular type of multimedia format, such as RealAudio files. The browser is configured to specify which helper application is to be used for each specific type of multimedia file. When your browser accesses a page with that type of multimedia file embedded, the helper application is automatically invoked and used to present the data. This is one area where Internet Explorer betters Netscape. While Netscape requires you to manually configure helper applications, Internet Explorer uses the association information stored in the Registry to automatically associate helper applications with media types.

The next step beyond helper applications is already being pioneered by Netscape, in the form of *plug-ins*. Unlike helper applications, which are external programs invoked by the browser, plug-ins are tightly integrated with the browser itself, much like DLLs within Windows. A particular helper application can be used with any browser that allows the use of helper applications. A plug-in, on the other hand, is written to an application programming interface (API) of a particular browser, and is specific to that browser. Because it operates as a part of the browser rather than as a separate program, it can be tied more tightly to the browser. This means, for example, that multimedia files supported by the plug-in can be displayed within the browser itself rather than as a separate application window, and that audio files can be decoded and played in real time while you continue to use the browser to read text.

Although each subsequent release of the major browsers increases the number and types of multimedia files that are supported natively, updating your helper applications and plug-ins frequently will continue to be necessary as standards evolve.

Java Support

Extensibility is all well and good. It allows your browser to support media types that it was not originally designed to recognize. However, extensibility does not address one major problem. As anyone who uses the Web regularly will immediately notice, new media types pop up very frequently, and if your browser is not already configured with a helper application or plug-in specific to that data type, you can't decode it.

The solution to this problem is called *Java*, and it's one of the hottest topics on the Web. Because Java is a new technology, there appears to be a lot of confusion about it. Many people use the terms Java, JavaScript, and HotJava interchangeably. Here's the real story:

■ Java itself is a complex, full-featured programming language developed by Sun Microsystems, Inc., based on the object-oriented programming language C++.

■ HotJava is a Web browser, developed by Sun Microsystems as a technology demonstrator for the Java language. HotJava is itself written in Java.

■ JavaScript is a scripting language which is a subset of the full Java language, and currently implemented only in Netscape Navigator 2.0 and higher. As it is now implemented, JavaScript is simply a relabeled version of the earlier LiveScript scripting language co-developed by Netscape and Sun Microsystems. When someone talks about accessing a Web site that uses Java, what he probably really means is that the site uses JavaScript.

Java is designed to make Web pages interactive. When you use a Java-enabled Web browser to access a Web page that has Java code embedded, you download not only the multimedia data contained on the page, but the program (written in Java) needed to decode and present that data. Your browser can deal with any type of multimedia content, including types not previously known to it, because both the lock and the key are transferred in the same message.

By using Java, the browser running on your local PC includes a Java interpreter. The Web site you access sends machine-independent Java code to your computer, which then decodes and presents it using the built-in Java interpreter. Because the code residing on the Web server is machine-independent, it can be accessed by any Java-enabled browser running on any type of hardware. Because the Java interpreter running within the local browser is aware of the capabilities of your computer, it can run the received Java applet and customize the presentation to best use the capabilities of your computer.

In April, 1996, Netscape announced that it had licensed AppAccelerator compiler technology from Borland International, Inc., and would incorporate it in future releases of Navigator. According to Netscape, the use of this technology will speed up execution of Java applications by a factor of five to ten times when compared with the same applications running via interpreter. AppAccelerator works by doing an on-the-fly compile of the Java source code as it is being received, and then passing the resulting machine-executable code to the browser to be run. Netscape made no promises about the release date of a browser using this technology, but did announce that it would first be implemented in Windows 95 and Windows NT versions of Navigator.

As things stand, Java is not yet widely implemented, nor is it guaranteed to succeed as an industry standard. Microsoft is attempting to put forward Visual Basic as an alternative to Java, but recently they seem to be falling into line with the rest of the world. They are not happy about the apparent strength of Java as a developing standard. They will continue to promote Visual Basic as an alternative, but at least they will support Java, if only as one alternative. Netscape Navigator is the only full-featured Web browser now available that provides Java support, although Microsoft has promised Java support in a future release of Internet Explorer.

Microsoft is nothing if not opportunistic. There is an old Russian proverb which says that success has many fathers but failure is an orphan. If Java succeeds in the market, you may be sure that Microsoft will provide full support for it. If the past is any guide, Microsoft will attempt to build Java in its own image, extending it with its own proprietary enhancements.

Web Browsing on Commercial Online Services

If you plan to use the Web only occasionally, or if you'd just like to see what all the excitement is about before you dive in, accessing the Web via one of the commercial online services may be your best bet. It's certainly easier than getting a live Internet connection set up and working, and it may even be less expensive than going through an Internet service provider if you are a very light user.

The big four commercial online services—America Online (AOL), CompuServe (CIS), Prodigy, and the Microsoft Network (MSN)—all provide Web access in one form or another. All of them are beginning to realize that Web access is an important feature for many or most of their subscribers, and all are taking steps to improve the access they provide to the Web. America Online and CompuServe held discussions with both Netscape and Microsoft concerning bundling Navigator and Internet Explorer as front-ends to their services. Let's take a look at what each of these commercial online services can provide.

America Online

Although in many ways AOL has been a leader among the commercial online services in providing Internet access, their browser falls short of those provided by the other services. In its current incarnation, the AOL browser lacks support even for tables, let alone frames. The good news is that AOL enables you to use any standard Winsock, including that provided with Windows NT Workstation, so it is possible to establish a connection to AOL and then use your choice of browser. Doing so is not simple, however, and requires that you first download and install special software.

AOL recently acquired ANS, the original Internet backbone service provider, and has also been involved recently in negotiations with both Microsoft and Netscape to use their respective browsers as front-ends to the AOL service. Both of these facts indicate that AOL has a serious commitment to providing their customers with Internet services in general, and with Web access in particular. It seems likely that AOL will improve these services in the very near future.

CompuServe

CompuServe bundles a Spyglass, Inc., implementation of NCSA Mosaic with its WinCIM access software. Although not the most modern or feature-laden of browsers, Mosaic is at least finally integrated with the remainder of the access software in WinCIM version 2.0.1. Because CompuServe uses PPP by default on dial-up connections, and because WinCIM can use the standard Winsock implementation provided by NT Workstation, you can use any standard Web browser once the connection is established.

Prodigy

The future of Prodigy is unclear. In early 1996, Sears announced its intention to abandon its stake in Prodigy. Its partner in this joint venture, IBM, also seems to be unenthusiastic about continuing the effort.

The Web access services provided by Prodigy are second only to MSN among the four major commercial online services. The Web browser provided by Prodigy is a step behind the major standalone Web browsers, but a recent agreement between Prodigy and Netscape means that Prodigy's browser will soon support many of Netscape's enhancements, including tables and frames.

The Microsoft Network

The Microsoft Network offers by far the best Web access of any of the four major commercial online services. It uses both the standard Winsock stack provided with Windows NT and PPP connections, meaning that once a connection is established, you can use any standard Web browser or other Winsock utility on that connection. Because it uses Internet Explorer—one of the two best Web browsers available—as its standard interface, you will probably have little reason to switch browsers.

There have been many changes at MSN recently. The emphasis seems to have changed from competing directly with CompuServe and the other commercial online services to providing general Internet services.

Microsoft Internet Explorer 3.0

If it weren't for Netscape Navigator, Microsoft's Internet Explorer would be considered the stellar performer in the world of Web browsers (see fig. 15.5). As it is, Internet Explorer stands head and shoulders above every other Web Browser except Netscape Navigator.

Fig. 15.5

Microsoft Internet Explorer 3.0.

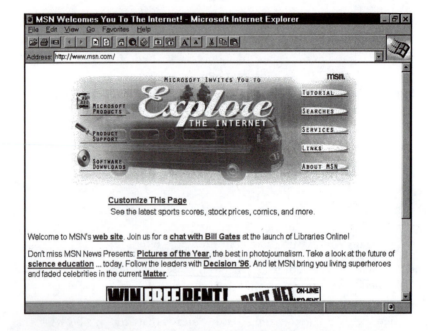

Microsoft's problem at this point is that Netscape is the *de facto* industry leader in establishing standards for the Web in general, and for extensions to the HTML language in particular. Going head to head against Navigator on a feature basis, Internet Explorer usually turns up a day late and a dollar short, simply because Microsoft finds itself playing a perpetual game of catch-up with Netscape as the latter establishes and implements new standards, sometimes on what seems like a weekly basis.

Microsoft has done a lot with Internet Explorer, particularly considering that it started out less than two years ago as a derivative product of the original NCSA Mosaic, a product that was showing its age even then. Since then, Microsoft has built Internet Explorer into a competitive product, albeit usually a step or two behind Netscape Navigator.

Don't get the idea that everything goes Netscape's way, however. Internet Explorer has several things going for it, even in comparison to Navigator:

- *Ease of installation.* Installation and setup couldn't be much easier. The Setup Wizard leads you through the installation step-by-step, including connecting to the Internet via LAN or dial-up service provider. If you have neither a LAN connection nor a current dial-up provider, Setup enables you to establish an account with the Microsoft Network simply by providing your name and billing information.

- *Tight integration with Windows.* Internet Explorer is completely integrated with the Windows NT Workstation 4.0 interface and with the underlying Windows NT services. It supports the right mouse button, OLE, and drag and drop. You can create shortcuts to favorite Web sites simply by dragging them to the desktop and dropping them. Internet Explorer provides full Internet e-mail services with MIME support. E-mail is integrated with the Exchange Inbox, enabling you to maintain a single address book. Internet Explorer uses file associations stored in the Registry to configure multimedia helper applications, eliminating the need to do so manually.

- *Speed.* Although it is difficult to make valid performance comparisons between browsers, Internet Explorer feels fast. Microsoft uses several methods, including multithreading, a persistent page cache, and progressive rendering to increase performance. Place Holder Mode inserts a temporary placeholder for graphics while allowing the text content of a Web page to be rendered immediately. While the graphics download in the background, you are able to scroll through the text content. HTTP Keep Alive allows Internet Explorer to open and transfer multiple Web page elements on a single connection instead of opening a separate connection for each element. The overall result is a fast and responsive browser.

- *HTML extensions.* Although historically Netscape has been the leader and Microsoft the follower in extending HTML, Internet Explorer can teach Navigator a few tricks. In addition to full HTML 3.0 table support, Internet Explorer adds fixed backgrounds, moving marquees, inline AVI support, and background audio support to the mix. On the virtual reality front, Microsoft has included support via a VRML add-in using the Reality Lab engine for 3D objects.

- *Security.* Internet Explorer provides full support for the existing Secure Sockets Layer (SSL) version 2.0 encryption technology pioneered by Netscape, and will support version 3.0 when it is released. Internet Explorer was also designed with hooks for the joint Microsoft/VISA Secure Transaction Technology (STT), which should be available by the time you read this.

■ *Cost.* Internet Explorer has one unquestionable advantage over Netscape Navigator. You have to pay for Navigator, but Internet Explorer is free.

Installing Internet Explorer

Microsoft Internet Explorer is supplied in the form of a single large self-extracting archive file named MSIE20.EXE. Copy this file to a temporary folder and run it by either choosing Start, Run, Browse or by highlighting the file and double-clicking it from within Windows NT Explorer.

When executed, the program first warns you that it is about to install Internet Explorer. If you tell it to continue, you are then given the opportunity to read the licensing agreement. If you accept the terms, you are then given the opportunity to browse the directory tree to select a folder into which Internet Explorer will be installed.

> **Tip**
>
> Strangely enough, although the Internet Explorer installation routine allows you to browse for and select an installation directory, it does not enable you to create a directory on-the-fly. If you want to install Internet Explorer to a particular directory, create that directory before beginning the installation.

Once you have specified a destination directory, the Setup program unpacks and installs Internet Explorer into that directory and creates a shortcut named The Internet on your desktop. The program is then ready to be configured.

The first time you run Internet Explorer, the Internet Setup Wizard is invoked. It automatically leads you through the process of connecting to the Internet and configuring the program.

The Internet Setup Wizard first prompts you for the method you want to use to connect to the Internet, either via dial-up connection to an Internet Service Provider (ISP) or via your local area network. If you choose the dialup connection, you are prompted to enter information about your current ISP. If you don't already have an ISP, the Internet Setup Wizard kindly offers to connect you via The Microsoft Network. You need provide only the information needed to create an account on The Microsoft Network, along with your credit card information for billing of course.

No matter which connection method you choose, you are then prompted as to whether you want to use Exchange for Internet e-mail. If you elect to do so and you do not already have Exchange installed, you are prompted to insert the distribution CD so that the necessary files can be copied to your hard drive.

If you select the LAN connection method, you are then asked how your work-station obtains its IP address. If your network includes a DHCP server, your IP address can be automatically assigned by that server. Otherwise, you must enter your IP address and subnet mask manually. If TCP/IP is already set up on your system, this information is already filled in for you.

You are next prompted for the IP addresses of your primary and secondary domain name servers. Again, if you are already set up for TCP/IP, this information is filled in for you.

Finally, you are prompted to enter the IP Address of your Internet Gateway. Again, if your system is already set up for TCP/IP, simply accept the address that is supplied. Once you have supplied this last piece of information, Setup is complete and the program terminates. When next you run Internet Explorer, you are automatically connected to the Microsoft Network.

Configuring Internet Explorer

Although the default configuration of Microsoft Internet Explorer is fine for most users, you may reconfigure these default settings as needed to suit your preferences. Internet Explorer offers fewer configuration options than does Netscape Navigator, making it both easier to configure and somewhat less flexible.

Internet Explorer 2.0 stores all of its configuration information in the Registry. Although you may use the Registry Editor to edit this information directly, there is no real reason to do so. Internet Explorer enables you to change your preferences directly. Choosing View, Options opens a tabbed screen with six pages devoted to setting the operation of Internet Explorer.

Appearance. The Appearance tab enables you to specify whether pictures and animations are used and if sounds are played (see fig. 15.6). You can also choose custom colors for text and background and select fonts for proportional and monospaced text. You may also select colors for new and followed links, specify whether or not links are to be underlined, and determine whether and how addresses are to be displayed.

Fig. 15.6
You can configure
the appearance of
Internet Explorer
in this tab.

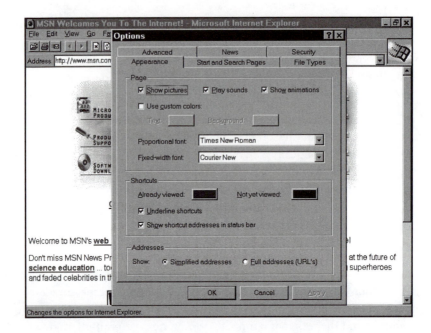

Start and Search Pages. The Start and Search Pages tab enables you to specify a URL as your start page, to be invoked when you run Internet Explorer, and a second URL as your search page, invoked when you choose Go, Search the Internet (see fig. 15.7). You may redefine your start page or your search page at any time, simply by loading the desired page, selecting either Start Page or Search Page under the Your pick list, and clicking the Use Current button.

File Types. The File Types tab enables you to map file extensions to the executable programs used to view them (see fig. 15.8). Unlike Netscape Navigator, which requires you to manually enter this information, Internet Explorer uses the file associations stored in the Registry. You may use the File Types screen to add, remove, or edit associations. Any changes you make here are reflected immediately in the Registry, and apply to all programs. Similarly, any changes you make to the Registry outside of Internet Explorer that affect file associations are also used by Internet Explorer.

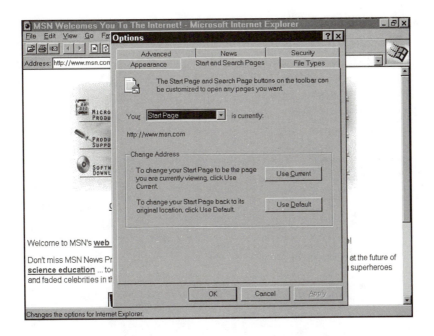

Fig. 15.7
You can configure
Internet Explorer
via the Start and
Search Pages
options.

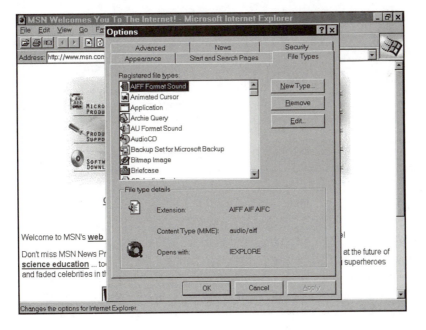

Fig. 15.8
You can also
configure Internet
Explorer by using
the File Types tab.

Advanced. The Advanced tab enables you to specify how many of your most recently accessed pages will be stored in the history list, with a default of 300 (see fig. 15.9). You may also specify the size of the disk cache, as a percentage of disk space, to be used for storing recently accessed pages. You may change the location for either of these items by clicking the Change button. You may delete the history list or flush the cache by clicking the Empty button. Unlike Netscape Navigator, the size of the RAM cache is not settable.

Fig. 15.9
Configure Internet Explorer features in the Advanced tab.

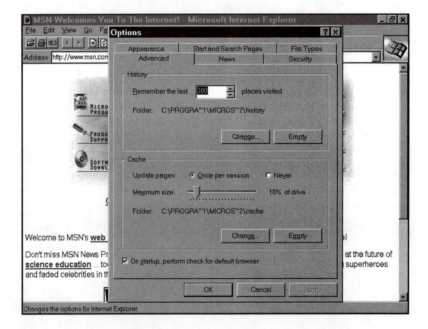

News. The News tab allows you to specify whether or not you will use Internet Explorer to read USENET newsgroups (see fig. 15.10). If so, you may enter the name of your news server and, if necessary, a username and password for it. You may also specify the name and e-mail address you would like to appear in articles you post to the USENET.

Security. The Security tab enables you to set the level of security to be used while sending and receiving data on the Web (see fig. 15.11). The default settings, Medium for sending data and Low for receiving it, are probably a good compromise for most people. If you never send your credit card number or other sensitive information over the Web, you can safely set both of these values to Low. This will minimize the intrusive notifications that you are about to send data to a nonsecure site.

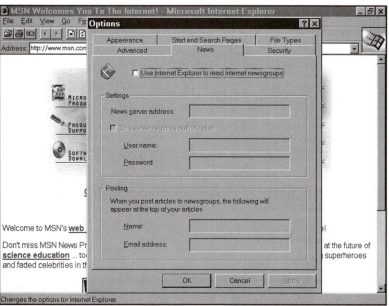

Fig. 15.10
Configure Internet
Explorer by using
the News tab.

Fig. 15.11
Configure Internet
Explorer via the
Security tab.

V

Using the Internet

Netscape Navigator 3.0

A shark must swim constantly to keep forcing water through its gills in order to breathe. If it stops swimming, it dies. Like the shark, Netscape has little choice but to continue moving forward with its Navigator Web browser, adding features and extending the HTML standard. If Netscape stops advancing for even a moment, both the browser and the company itself will become casualties of the incredibly intense browser war. The only thing standing between Netscape and annihilation by Microsoft is Netscape's technology, and what is new technology today is old news tomorrow (see fig. 15.12).

Fig. 15.12

Netscape Navigator 3.0.

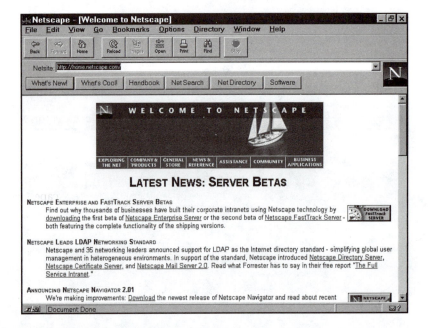

Microsoft and Netscape are the super powers of the browser war. Both of them know it. Everyone else knows it. They both believe that the battle for domination of the Internet will be won or lost on the browser front. Netscape competes with its technology. Microsoft, realizing that it is perpetually a step or two behind Netscape's technology, competes instead primarily with its marketing.

Regardless of Microsoft's efforts, Netscape Navigator remains the standalone browser of choice for most power users. Because Netscape continues to play a leadership role in the on-going development of HTML, most new features arrive first in Navigator and only later in Internet Explorer. Netscape has pioneered HTML 3.0 enhancements like tables and frames, developed the plug-in concept to keep their browser current with changing multimedia file formats, and introduced enhancements such as client-side image maps and progressive JPEG display. Netscape has also championed Java, a language and environment that has the potential to change the entire face of the World Wide Web.

In simple terms, Internet Explorer is always about one version behind Navigator, and this is likely to remain true for the foreseeable future. Let's take a closer look at Netscape Navigator.

Installing Netscape Navigator

The Netscape installation procedure assumes that you already have a connection to the Internet via LAN or a dialup service provider. Netscape is supplied as a large self-extracting EXE file which, when run, automatically invokes the InstallShield Wizard to perform the actual installation. Although the Setup program defaults to installing Navigator in the C:\PROGRAM FILES\ NETSCAPE\NAVIGATOR directory, you can browse your disk drives to locate and specify another installation directory. You can create a new directory if desired.

After prompting you as to whether to install the optional CoolTalk support, the Setup program extracts and installs the files, adds a Netscape folder to your Programs menu, and then prompts you to connect to the Netscape Web site to complete installation. If you elect to do so, you are given the opportunity to register Navigator online, purchase a license for the product, and download the latest versions of Netscape plug-ins, which add support for various multimedia file formats.

Early versions of Netscape Navigator stored configuration information in a NETSCAPE.INI file. Later versions store their configuration information in the Registry. When you upgrade from any previous version of Netscape, the Setup program automatically reads and uses stored preference information to configure the new installation based on existing preferences.

Configuring Netscape Navigator

Although the default configuration of Netscape Navigator is fine for most users, you may reconfigure these default settings as needed to suit your preferences. Navigator offers many more configuration options than does Internet Explorer, enabling you to modify the program to function exactly as you want.

Navigator 3.0 stores all of its configuration information in the Registry. Although you may use the Registry Editor to edit this information directly, there is no real reason to do so. Netscape allows you to change your preferences directly from the Options menu within Navigator.

General Preferences. Choosing <u>O</u>ptions, <u>G</u>eneral Preferences brings up a tabbed Preferences screen with seven pages devoted to setting the general operation of the program, as follows:

- *Appearance.* Allows you to specify whether toolbars are displayed as pictures, text, or both (see fig. 15.13). It also allows you to specify whether the Web browser, the Mail client, or the Newsreader is displayed at program startup, to enter your default home Web page, and to determine whether or not you are automatically connected to your home page when you start the program. This section also allows you to specify how links are displayed and when they expire.

Fig. 15.13
Configure Netscape Navigator's General Preferences options in the Appearance tab.

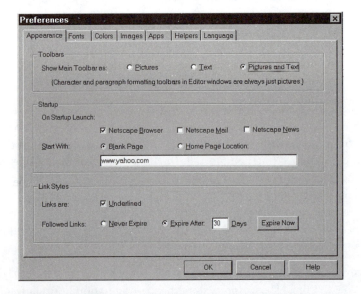

Tip

Most people find that they frequently begin their Web sessions from the same Web page. It may be a search engine like Yahoo! or AltaVista, or it may be the home page on your company Intranet. To jump immediately to your preferred Web page each time you start Navigator, enter the URL for the page in the Start With field of the Appearance page.

- *Fonts.* Allows you to specify which proportional and monospaced fonts should be used, and which encoding method you prefer. This enables Navigator to be used, for example, with various nonWestern languages (see fig. 15.14).

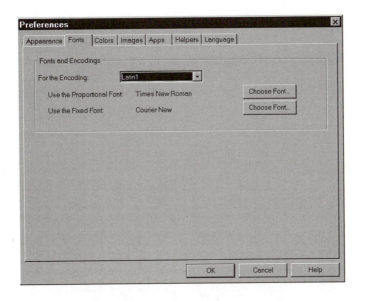

Fig. 15.14
Configure
Netscape
Navigator's
General Prefer-
ences in the Fonts
tab.

- *Colors*. Allows you to specify the colors that will be used for links, followed links, text, and backgrounds. You can choose to use default colors, or to specify your own colors. You can also specify that your own
  color choices are to override colors specified in displayed Web pages
  (see fig. 15.15). You can, if you want, specify an image file to be used as
  a background.

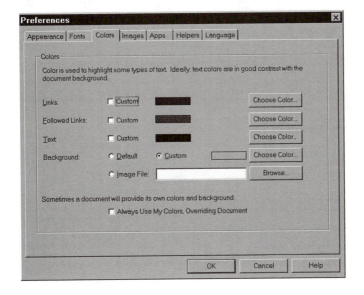

Fig. 15.15
Configure
Netscape
Navigator's
General Prefer-
ences options in
the Colors tab.

V

Using the Internet

■ *Images.* Allows you to specify how colors will be handled in displaying images (see fig. 15.16). You may also specify whether images should be displayed while loading or after loading.

Fig. 15.16
Configure
Netscape
Navigator's
General Prefer-
ences options
using the Images
tab.

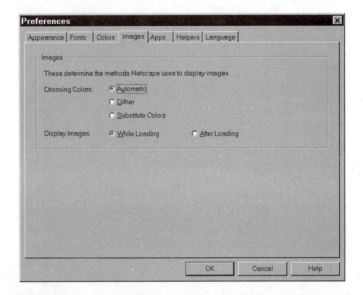

■ *Apps.* Allows you to specify where supporting applications, including Telnet, Telnet 3270, and a Source Viewer are located (see fig. 15.17). You also specify the location of a temp directory within this page.

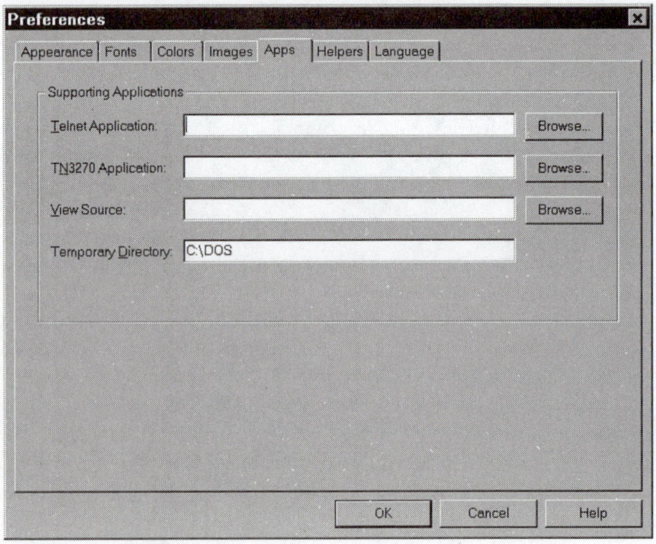

Fig. 15.17
Configure
Netscape
Navigator's
General Prefer-
ences options
using the Apps
tab.

> **Caution**
>
> Don't confuse supporting applications with helper applications. *Supporting applications* add connection and page formatting support to Navigator, while *helper applications* add support for multimedia file types.

■ *Helpers.* Allows you to specify how to map specific file extensions to the helper applications needed to render them (see fig. 15.18). Navigator can use helper applications to handle files that it retrieves but is unable to render.

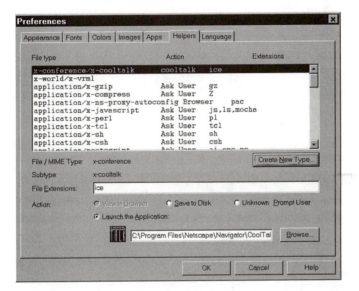

Fig. 15.18
Configure Netscape Navigator's General Preferences options using the Helpers tab.

■ *Language.* Allows you to tell remote Web servers which languages your copy of Navigator is configured to accept (see fig. 15.19). You can select standard languages displayed under Language/Region, or you can enter your own language code and regional code using ISO conventions.

Mail and News Preferences. Choosing Options, Mail and News Preferences brings up a tabbed Preferences screen with five pages devoted to setting options for the built-in Newsreader and Mail clients included in Navigator, as follows:

■ *Appearance.* Allows you to determine whether to use a proportional or monospaced font to display e-mail messages and news articles, to specify how quoted text will be handled, whether to use the built-in mail and news clients or Exchange, and how to layout the mail and news windows (see fig. 15.20).

Fig. 15.19

Configure Netscape Navigator's General Preferences options using the Language tab.

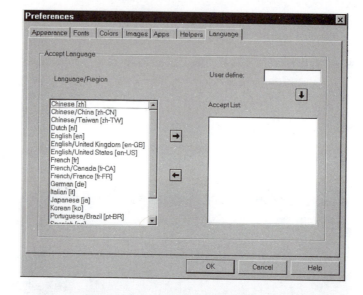

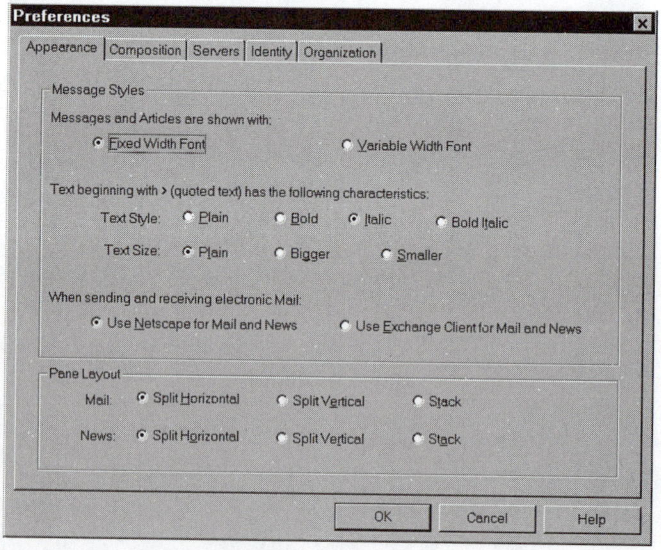

Fig. 15.20

Configure Netscape Navigator's Mail and News Preferences options using the Appearance tab.

■ *Composition.* Allows you to set options for creating, sending, and managing outgoing e-mail and news messages (see fig. 15.21).

Preferences
Appearance
Composition
Servers
Identity
Organization
Mail
When Composing Mail and News Messages:
Send and Post
Allow 8-bit
Mime Compliant (Quoted Printable)
By default, email a copy of outgoing message to:
Mail Messages:
News Messages:
By default, copy outgoing message to the file:
Mail File:
C:\Program Files\Netscape\Navigator\Mail\Sent
News File:
Automatically quote original message when replying
OK
Cancel
Help

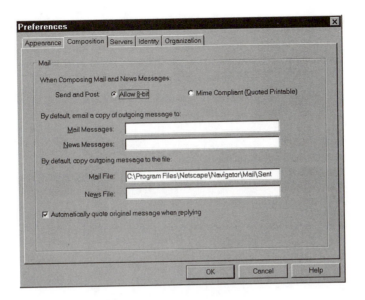

Fig. 15.21
Configuring Netscape Navigator—Mail and News Preferences—Composition.

■ *Servers*. Allows you to specify the identity of your mail and news servers and to configure various operational settings (see fig. 15.22).

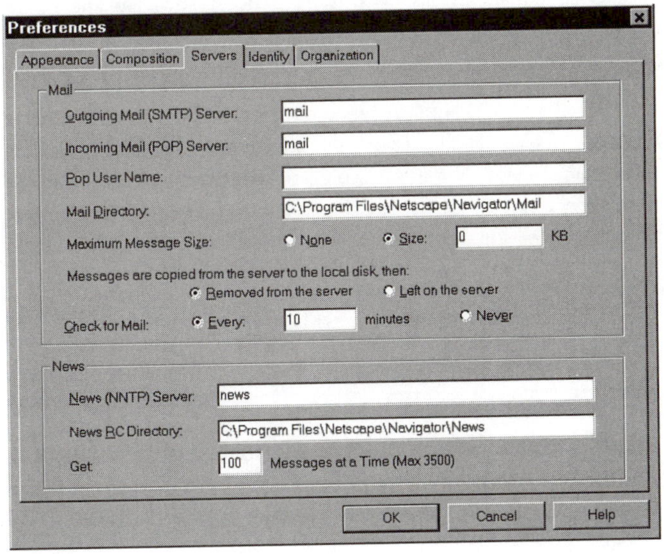

Preferences
Appearance
Composition
Servers
Identity
Organization
Mail
Outgoing Mail (SMTP) Server:
mail
Incoming Mail (POP) Server:
mail
Pop User Name:
Mail Directory:
C:\Program Files\Netscape\Navigator\Mail
Maximum Message Size:
None
Size:
0
KB
Messages are copied from the server to the local disk, then:
Removed from the server
Left on the server
Check for Mail:
Every
10
minutes
Never
News
News (NNTP) Server:
news
News RC Directory:
C:\Program Files\Netscape\Navigator\News
Get
100
Messages at a Time (Max 3500)
OK
Cancel
Help

Fig. 15.22
Configure Netscape Navigator's Mail and News Preferences options using the Servers tab.

■ *Identity*. Allows you to enter your name, e-mail address, and other particulars to be used in outbound e-mail messages and news articles (see fig. 15.23).

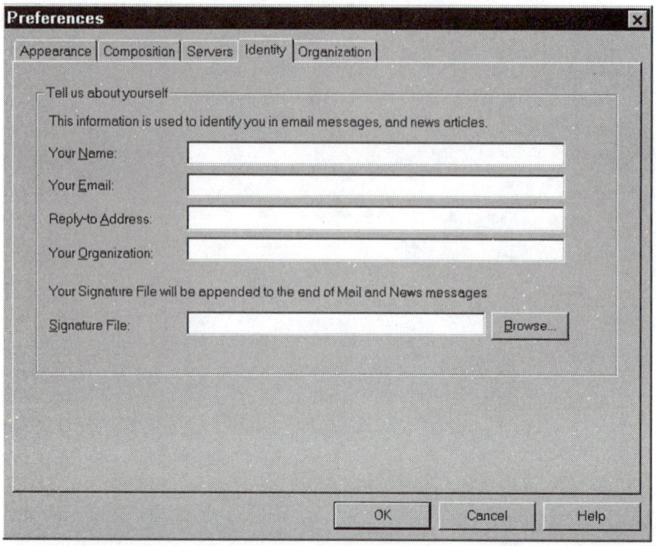

Fig. 15.23

Configure
Netscape
Navigator's Mail
and News
Preferences
options using the
Identity tab.

Caution

Junk e-mail is becoming an increasing problem. By using only a few lines of Java, it is possible for any server you access to download and store the information you enter in this section.

If you want to use Java but do not use Navigator for e-mail or news, help keep yourself off junk e-mail mailing lists by leaving this section blank. If you want to use Navigator's e-mail or news clients, but don't care about Java, you can disable Java and JavaScript processing by choosing Options, Security, and selecting the General tab. You can then safely enter the information in this section.

If you want to use both Java and Netscape's e-mail and News, resign yourself to knowing that whatever information you enter here will probably be made available on numerous junk e-mail lists.

■ *Organization.* Allows you to indicate whether or not Navigator should save your password, and to specify options for sorting and threading e-mail messages and news articles (see fig. 15.24).

Network Preferences. Choosing Options, Network Preferences brings up a tabbed Preferences screen with three pages devoted to setting options for Cache, Connections and Proxies, as follows:

■ *Cache*. Allows you to specify how much RAM will be used to cache recently accessed Web pages, how much disk space will be used for the same purpose, and where the disk cache file is to be located (see fig. 15.25). Caching allows Navigator to retrieve Web pages more quickly by doing so from the local cache rather than reloading the page each time from the remote Web server. You can also specify how often Navigator checks pages for revisions.

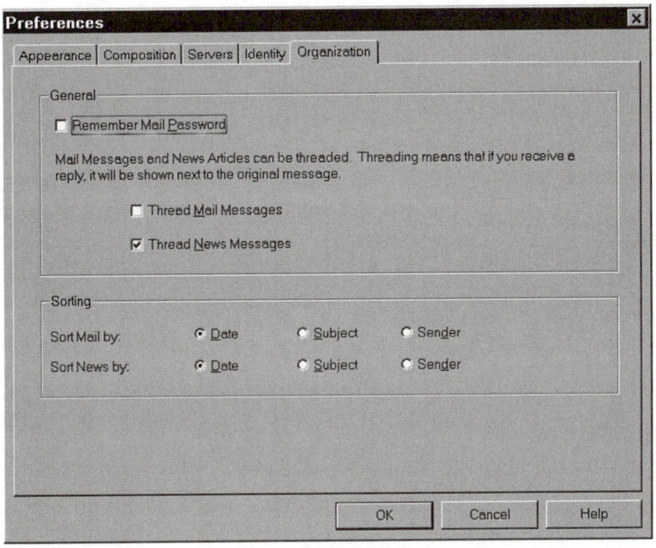

Fig. 15.24
Configure Netscape Navigator's Mail and News Preferences options using the Organization tab.

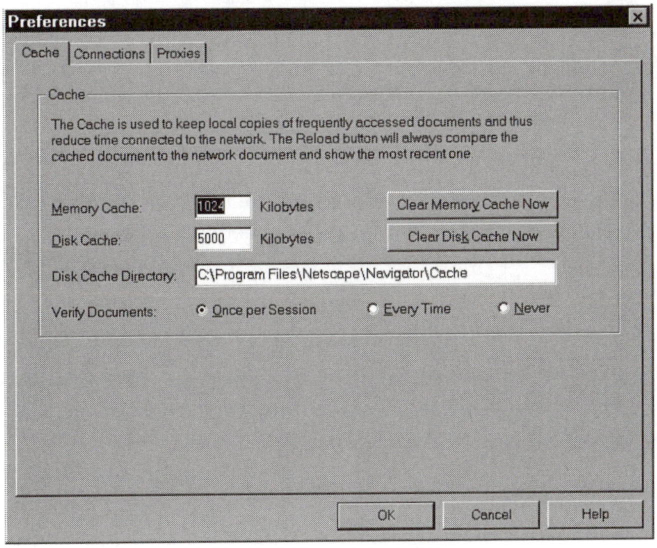

Fig. 15.25
Configure Netscape Navigator's Network Preferences options using the Cache tab.

V

Using the Internet

Tip

The default cache sizes for Navigator are 600K for the RAM cache and 5M for the disk cache. You can increase performance by boosting either or both of these numbers. I set the RAM cache to 1,024K on my 40M system and use a 5M disk cache.

The trade-off for faster performance in retrieving frequently accessed pages is the consumption of RAM and disk resources dedicated to the cache, and the fact that it takes somewhat longer to exit Navigator because cache maintenance is performed as you exit. If you are very short of resources—for example, running NT Workstation on a system with 16M of RAM—turning off the RAM cache will actually improve performance, even though the system must then actually retrieve documents from either disk or the remote server rather than from RAM.

Tip

For better performance, save the HTML code of your favorite Web pages to your hard disk using the Save As function of your Web browser, and access the information locally. If the HTML code for a page references links with absolute path names, you will be able to jump directly to those links from your stored page.

There are two drawbacks to this method. First, graphics don't appear unless you download them. Having done so, you may also have to edit the HTML code to point to your local hard disk instead of the original location on the Web site. Second, and more important, many web pages are updated frequently, and using this method gives you only a static snapshot of the Web page as it was when you downloaded the HTML code for it.

Still, this method can be very useful for sites that are relatively static and that you access very frequently, such as a search form on a Web search site.

■ *Connections.* Allows you to specify the maximum number of simultaneous network connections and to set the network buffer size (see fig. 15.26). HTTP establishes connections to transfer elements from the Web page on the remote server. For example, if a Web page contains both text and an image, Navigator can open one connection and use it to transfer text, while at the same time opening a second connection and using it to transfer the graphic. The default value for connections is 4. Network buffer size specifies how much memory will be allocated to buffering incoming data, with a default setting of 1K.

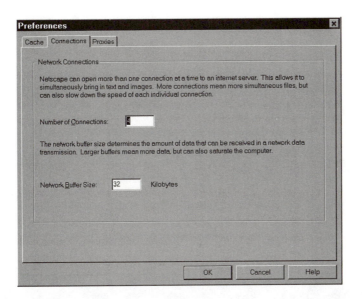

Fig. 15.26
Configure
Netscape
Navigator's
Network Prefer-
ences options
using the Connec-
tions tab.

Tip

Setting the number of connections higher than the default value of 4 allows Navigator to download more than four Web page elements simultaneously, at a cost of
lowering the data transfer rate for each connection. If you are using a slow connection to the Internet, such as 28.8Kbps dial-up, leave this value at 4. If you have a
higher speed connection, such as a T1, set this value to 8 or even 16. Setting it much
higher accomplishes nothing, because few Web pages require more than this number of simultaneous connections.

Similarly, increasing the network buffer size can improve performance, but setting it
too high can swamp a slow computer. You can experiment with the buffer size to see
what works best for you. I use 32K.

■ *Proxies.* Allows you to specify proxy servers and port assignments for
various protocols, including ftp, HTTP, SSL, and others (see fig. 15.27).
A *proxy* is a conduit that allows workstations located behind IP firewalls
to access servers in the outside world. If you have a direct or dial-up
connection to the Internet, leave this page at default. If you are behind
a firewall, see your network administrator for information about the
names and port assignments of proxy servers for services available to
the world.

Fig. 15.27
Configure Netscape Navigator's Network Preferences options using the Proxies tab.

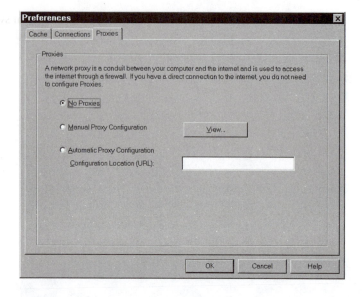

Security Preferences. Choosing Options, Security Preferences brings up a tabbed Preferences screen with four pages devoted to setting options for alerting passwords and security certificate information, as follows:

- *General.* Allows you to enable or disable Java and JavaScript processing, and to specify what warnings, if any, will be provided when you enter and leave secure server space, submit documents to an insecure server, and so forth (see fig. 15.28).

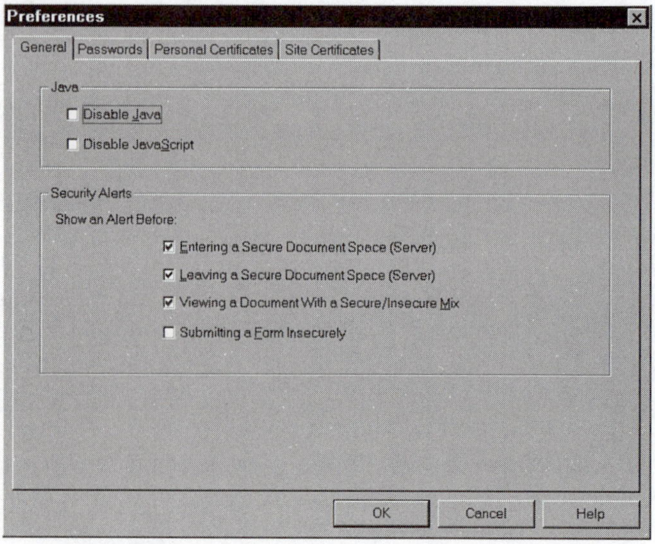

Fig. 15.28
Configure Netscape Navigator's Security Preferences options using the General tab.

■ *Passwords*. Allows you to specify a password to protect your local system when running Navigator and to determine how often and under what circumstances entering that password will be required (see fig. 15.29). Note that this section refers only to securing your local system, and has nothing to do with security on the Web.

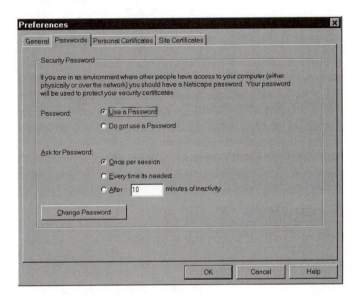

Fig. 15.29
Configure Netscape Navigator's Security Preferences options using the Passwords tab.

■ *Personal certificates and site certificates*. Allow you to enter information about security certificates owned by you or by your site. Using a security certificate essentially guarantees other users on the Internet that you are in fact you (see figs. 15.30 and 15.31). Certificates are issued for a fee by various certificate authorities, once they are satisfied as to your *bona fides*. Unless you plan to establish a site which will engage in commerce over the Web, you probably have no need of a certificate of any sort.

Plug-Ins

Netscape plug-ins are the follow-up to helper applications, and are used to add support for multimedia file types not supported by the base Navigator package. Helper applications are actually external executable programs usable by any browser that supports calling external applications. Plug-ins are instead written to an API specific to the browser in question, and when loaded actually become a part of the browser in much the same way that DLLs and VxDs become a part of Windows.

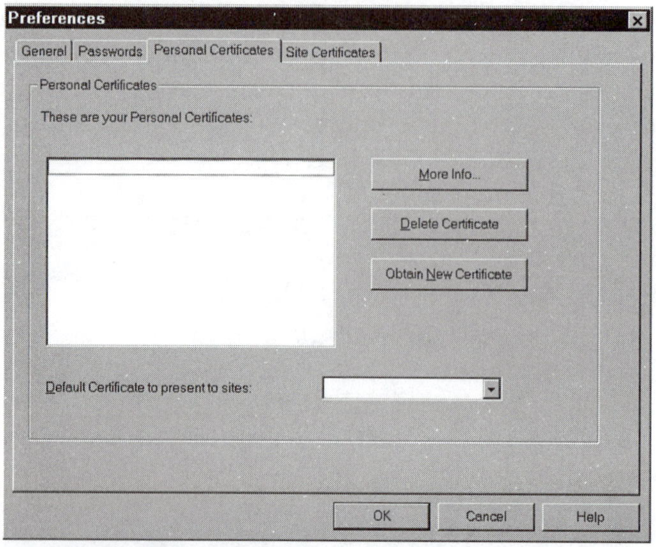

Fig. 15.30
Configure
Netscape
Navigator's
Security Prefer-
ences options
using the Personal
Certificates tab.

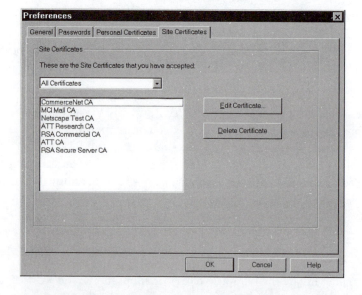

Fig. 15.31
Configure
Netscape
Navigator's
Security Prefer-
ences options
using the Site
Certificates tab.

Compared with helper applications, the main advantage of plug-ins is that
they are so closely integrated to the browser itself. Using a helper application
to display an unsupported media type results in a separate program being invoked and the file being displayed in the window of that application. Using a
plug-in instead to display the same unsupported media file results in it being
rendered within the main Navigator window.

Plug-ins are new and in a state of flux. For the latest information about plug-ins in general and about specific plug-ins available for Navigator, start Navigator and choose <u>H</u>elp, About <u>P</u>lug-ins. You are transported to the Netscape Plug-In page, where you find up-to-date information.

Netscape Power Pack 2.0

The Netscape Power Pack 2.0 provides a collection of companion utilities for power users of Netscape Navigator. These utilities include:

- *SmartMarks 2.0.* Downloads and stores Web pages for offline browsing, automatically refreshing the stored local copy of a page when you connect to the Web server upon which that page originated. You can easily create a local copy of any bookmarked page, and download one or two levels of linked pages, including image data. SmartMarks uses agent technology to monitor the remote Web site for changes, allowing you to automatically poll sites that change frequently and update these changes to your local copy.

- *INSO CyberSpell for Netscape Mail.* An add-on spell checker designed specifically for the Internet mail environment. It integrates directly with the Navigator mail module, and adds a menu choice for spell checking to all of the edit screens within mail. CyberSpell goes beyond simple spell checking to correct errors in spacing, capitalization, punctuation, and formatting. Because it is Internet-aware, CyberSpell avoids the problem common to most spell checkers of highlighting URLs, Internet addresses, and so forth as misspellings.

- *Norton AntiVirus Internet Scanner.* Applies Norton's antivirus scanning technology to the Internet. This product integrates directly into Navigator, and then scans all files received over the Internet from within Navigator, including e-mail attachments and files downloaded with ftp. This is a Windows 95 product, and at this point is not clear when (or whether) an NT version will be made available.

- *Netscape Chat 2.0.* An Internet Relay Chat (IRC) client that allows you to participate in public or private IRC sessions from within Navigator.

In addition to these products, Netscape Power Pack 2.0 includes a full complement of plug-ins. You can download an evaluation copy of the product from the Netscape Web site at HOME.NETSCAPE.COM, or purchase a CD-ROM version from your favorite retailer.

Netscape Navigator Gold 3.0

Netscape Navigator Gold 3.0 extends the traditional functionality of a Web client to include WYSIWIG HTML editing and Web publishing capabilities. If you're thinking about bringing up a Web site but are concerned about the complexities of doing so, Navigator Gold may be for you. If you already have a Web site being managed remotely by your Internet service provider, you can use Navigator Gold to maintain your Web pages and then upload changed pages automatically to your ISP using the Publish feature.

Although the built-in HTML editor in Navigator Gold isn't a threat to the best standalone HTML editors, it does allow you to create Web pages by simple drag and drop, without worrying about the intricacies of coding HTML. You can use it to lift graphics from existing Web pages, whether local or on the Net, and drop them into your new Web page. You can also drag files from NT Explorer or the desktop into your Web page, and allow Navigator Gold to handle the links.

Navigator Gold makes it easy to start creating your first Web page by providing numerous templates, graphics, backgrounds, and other elements needed to create a good looking home page. The Page Wizard is a forms-based tool that creates a Web page from scratch using information you provide.

Navigator Gold is certainly not the consummate tool for developing a professional Web site, but if you're new to the subject and perhaps looking to dip your toe in, it can at least get you started. You can download an evaluation copy of Netscape Navigator Gold 3.0 from **home.netscape.com** or purchase a commercial version from your favorite software vendor.

Are Web Transactions Secure?

There has been a great deal of discussion as of late in both trade journals and the general media about security on the Web. On a monthly basis, it seems, we hear stories about Internet security being cracked. People who think nothing of giving a credit card number to an anonymous voice on an 800 line, or of seeing their waiter disappear for 20 minutes with their credit card, seem convinced that using the Web to purchase something via credit card will hopelessly compromise security. So how safe is the Web anyway?

The answer is, pretty safe. If thieves had their own Ten Commandments, one of them would be:

Thou shalt not spend more to steal something than that thing is worth.

The *Secure Sockets Layer* (*SSL*) technology used both by Navigator and by Internet Explorer make it very expensive indeed to steal a transaction by breaking the encryption used to protect transactions between the Web browser and the secure Web site.

The issue is complicated somewhat by the insistence of the U.S. government on controlling export of encryption tools in the same manner as munitions. Because of this, both Netscape and Microsoft must provide two versions of their products. One, the so-called *export* version, uses only a 40-bit encryption key, the maximum allowable by the government for exported encryption technology. The *domestic* versions of both products use a 128-bit encryption key, making their transactions 2^{88} more difficult to crack. Put another way, using a computer that enables you to crack a transaction from the export version in one second would require billions of years to crack a single transaction from the domestic version.

However, even the encryption used in the export version is nothing to sneeze at. The widely reported cracking of Netscape Navigator's encryption was done in France by a researcher who used two supercomputers and many workstations working for a solid week to crack a single transaction, and that was one that used only a 40-bit key. Cracking a single 40-bit encrypted transaction today requires something on the order of a week and $50,000 worth of computer time. As processors get faster, the time and associated costs to do so will decrease, and even now, 40-bit encryption is not regarded as secure for anything beyond commercial purposes.

The encryption methods used by these products depend upon the fact that it is currently impossible to factor large prime numbers other than by brute force. It is conceivable although unlikely that somewhere deep within the recesses of the National Security Agency someone has come up with a revolutionary method of doing so, rendering most current encryption methodologies useless.

Unless you have good reason to suspect that someone in the National Security Agency desperately wants your credit card number, you can feel safe using even export-level encryption. Incidentally, because they are available worldwide via the Internet, downloadable versions of products which provide encryption—including both Navigator and Internet Explorer—are the export version. Contact Microsoft or Netscape on their Web pages to find out how to upgrade your encryption to the domestic-only level.

V

Using the Internet

Tip

The Web can be slow, particularly if you're using a dial-up Internet link. Most of the performance hit is caused by the time needed to download graphics and other supplemental information. If you're using the Web purely to seek out information, do what the pros do. Turn off inline image autoloading. You're session will run much faster, and as a side benefit, you'll avoid all the ads.

Locating Information on the Web

Once you've chosen and installed a browser and hooked up your system to the Web, the next step is to find what you are looking for, which can be a non trivial problem to say the least. There are hundreds of thousands of Web sites out there now, and thousands of new ones come online every month. Some smaller number disappears just as regularly. Like a living organism, the Web is in a constant state of flux.

You can never be sure that the Web site you hit yesterday will still be there tomorrow. Even if it is, there may be a better site for your purposes that you won't access simply because you don't know about it. Fortunately, although the vast diversity of the Web creates the problem, it also provides the solution, in the form of Web search engines.

Web search engines are specialized Web sites whose only purpose is to cruise the Web looking for other Web sites, collect and index information about them, and provide it to users like you. Search engines vary greatly in size and content. Vast monoliths like Carnegie-Mellon's Lycos and Digital Equipment Corporation's AltaVista cruise the Web 24 hours a day almost without human intervention, sucking in data and indexing it. Smaller (but still huge) search engines like Yahoo! trade comprehensiveness for more human attention to the subset of information that they do index. Still smaller search engines may index only a few thousand Web sites, but provide reviews or other value-added material about these few sites.

> **Tip**
>
> If you find yourself searching the Web frequently, save yourself some time and make one of the search engines your startup page so that when you start up your Web browser, you are automatically connected to the site. Four of the sites we look at here are particularly appropriate for this. Check each of them, set your favorite as the startup Web page in your browser, and bookmark the others.

> **Tip**
>
> If you'd like one place with a variety of search engines, set your Web browser to **www.search.com** from CINet. Search.com offers more than 250 Internet search engines. You find all of the search engines we cover here, along with many others, devoted to everything from finding people to finding software to finding movie reviews.

You can invoke major search engines like AltaVista, Infoseek, Lycos, and Yahoo! directly from the Search.com main screen. You can also choose by category to display search engines related to that category. If you're using either Netscape Navigator or Microsoft Internet Explorer, you can even create your own personal page that displays only your favorite search engines.

The major drawback to Search.com is that for sites which offer both a simple query and an advanced query, Search.com limits you initially to doing the simple query. Still, if you search for information on a broad array of topics, this site can be a valuable control center for your searching.

Let's take a little more detailed look at several of the best of these search engines.

AltaVista

Digital Equipment Corporation's AltaVista provides a huge database, excellent search tools, and results which are usually very pertinent to your search. Set your browser to **www.AltaVista.digital.com**. AltaVista is probably the best search engine for serious work on the Web.

AltaVista roared into the consciousness of Web users in late 1995, springing seemingly full grown from nothing at all (see fig. 15.32). In the short time since Digital Equipment Corporation brought up this site, it has become a favorite of many people whose jobs involve searching the Web for information. Many people find that AltaVista returns not only a large number of hits on their searches, but that these hits are very pertinent overall to what they are searching for. The comprehensiveness and speed of AltaVista is chiefly a result of the powerful hardware and software that DEC has allocated to this service.

The Hardware Behind AltaVista

AltaVista originated as a research project and technology demonstrator at Digital's Research Labs in Palo Alto, Calif. in the summer of 1995. Those responsible for it combined a fast Web crawler to gather content with a fast indexing and search engine. By the end of 1995, AltaVista sprang full-blown on the Web scene, and grew within two months to include a full text index of more than 10 billion words in more than 20 million documents. By February, 1996, AltaVista was servicing more than four million HTTP requests per day. No other search engine service has grown as fast or done as good a job at scaling itself to such growth.

Fig. 15.32
AltaVista main
screen.

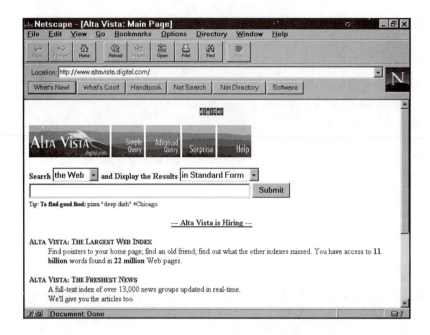

AltaVista communicates with users on a pair of AlphaStation 250 4/266 systems with 256M RAM and 4G of hard disk space, sending HTTP queries to the
Web indexer and News indexer servers. The Web indexer runs on a pair of
AlphaServer 8400 5/300 systems, each with 10 processors, 6G of RAM, and a
210G RAID storage subsystem. These systems, the most powerful built by
DEC, are responsible not only for servicing queries, but also for building the
index based on information received from the Web crawler called Scooter.

Scooter is a DEC 3000/900 Alpha Workstation running 1G of RAM and a 30G
RAID storage subsystem. Scooter spends all of its time retrieving 2.5 million
Web pages a day and forwarding the information to the Web indexers for
processing.

The News Indexer runs on a DEC AlphaStation 250 4/266 with 196M of RAM
and 13G of hard disk. It continually updates the index of the news spool. The
News Server runs on a DEC AlphaStation 400 4/233 with 160M of RAM and a
24G RAID disk array, both maintaining the news spool for the News Indexer
and providing a general HTTP News server.

Searching with AltaVista

AltaVista offers two databases, one containing information gleaned from Web
sites, and the other information from USENET newsgroups. You may search
either of these databases using either the **Simple Query** (see fig. 15.33) or
the **Advanced Query** keywords (see fig. 15.34).

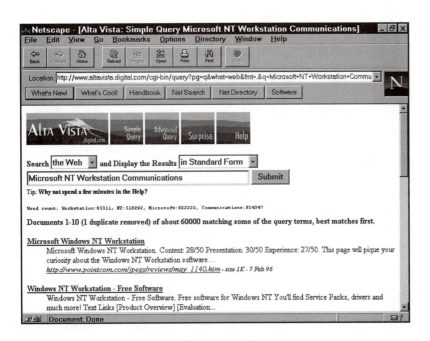

Fig. 15.33
AltaVista—Simple
Query.

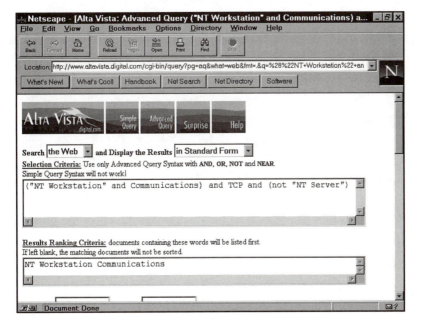

Fig. 15.34
AltaVista—
Advanced Query.

Using the Simple Query is very straightforward. You first choose the database to be searched, either the Web or the USENET, with the default being the Web. You then specify the level of detail to be displayed, either Standard, Compact, or Detailed Format, with Standard Format as the default. Then simply enter a word or words to search for and click the Submit button. AltaVista returns a ranked list of Web sites that meet your query specification, weighted by relevance.

If you'd like more control over your search, the Advanced Query enables you to use the Boolean operators AND, OR, NOT and the proximity operator NEAR in the Selection Criteria field to filter matching records. Once again, you first specify the database to be searched and the level of detail to be provided in the results. Here the Advanced Query parts company from the Simple Query.

Enter the words or phrases you are searching for in the Selection Criteria field, using Boolean operators to connect and filter search terms. You can submit your query without further ado, but if you do, all documents that meet your search criteria are returned without sorting. You can instead complete three more fields to further refine your query.

The Results Ranking Criteria field enables you to enter one or more words. Documents that meet the search criteria and contain this word or words are sorted toward the top of the results list. The words you enter in this field may be, but are not required to be, the same as those you entered in the Selection Criteria field.

For example, say you are looking for information about Web server software, and are particularly interested in such software from Netscape. You could enter something like:

> Netscape and "Web server"

in the Selection Criteria field and leave the Results Ranking Criteria field blank, but many of the returned documents would refer to the Netscape Navigator browser rather than to Netscape Web server software.

If instead you enter

> "Web server"

in the Selection Criteria field and

> Netscape

in the Results Ranking Criteria field, AltaVista first filters the documents, re-turning only those which contain the phrase `"Web server."` It then sorts the returned documents, placing those which also contain the term `"Netscape"` near the top of the returned list of documents.

> **Tip**
>
> Each time you access the AltaVista site, you are presented with the default set of options. Instead of changing options each time to reflect how you work, you may store your own preferences as follows.
>
> First, access AltaVista and change the options to suit your preferences. Once you have done so, submit a null search. That is, click the Submit button without first entering anything to search for. When the results are returned, bookmark that page.
>
> The next time you want to do an AltaVista search, simply retrieve the page you bookmarked and your options will already be set to your preferences. You can use this method with other search engines as well.

Infoseek

Infoseek Corporation's *Infoseek Guide* is another one of the early search en-gines, and offers a large database with good search tools. Many users find that Infoseek returns fewer hits than either AltaVista or Lycos, but that these hits are of high quality. Infoseek goes beyond AltaVista and Lycos in that it pro-vides not only a searchable index of the Web and USENET newsgroups, but also includes links to other sites that provide such services as e-mail address locators. Set your Web browser to **www.infoseek.com** to try it.

Infoseek Corporation offers two services. The first, Infoseek Guide (see fig. 15.35), is a free service that provides a searchable index of Web sites, USENET newsgroups, and other data available on the Internet. The second service is called *Infoseek Professional*, and adds information derived from wire services, business publications, and commercial databases. Infoseek Professional costs $4.95 per month for up to 50 searches and $.10 per search thereafter. Some of the databases included in Infoseek Professional are charged separately as pre-mium services.

V

Using the Internet

Fig. 15.35
Infoseek Guide.

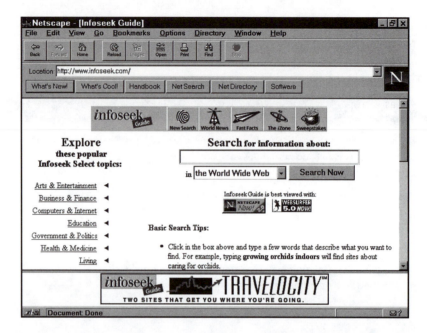

Note

A persistent urban legend about Infoseek is that the free Infoseek Guide returns only 10 hits and that if you want more, you have to pay for the premium service. This misinformation is published regularly in magazines which should know better. Although it was true at one time, it hasn't been for years.

Infoseek Guide returns up to 100 hits, grouped 10 at a time. If your search returns more than 100 hits, don't bother signing up for the premium service just so that you can view more hits. Instead, focus your search string more tightly to reduce the number of hits to a manageable number.

That said, Infoseek Professional is still worth paying for because of the greatly increased amount of information available with it.

Searching with Infoseek

In its simplest form, an Infoseek search can be simply words and phrases in plain text. For example, the search phrase

What inexpensive laser printers have high resolution

will locate Web pages that mention laser printers and resolution information. However, Infoseek also offers a sophisticated and powerful searching syntax that allows you to further refine your search. Let's look at these.

Finding Proper Names. Infoseek makes it very easy to isolate your search to Web pages containing a specific proper name or names. Keep the following rules in mind when searching:

- Infoseek searches are case-sensitive. If you capitalize a word, it is treated as a proper name. Otherwise, it is treated as any other search term. For example, using the search phrase **gates** returns hits on Bill Gates as well as on numerous other topics containing the word gates. Searching instead on **Gates**, with the initial letter capitalized, returns only hits in which the proper name Gates appears.

- If two or more adjacent words are capitalized, they are treated as a single proper name. For example, searching on **bill gates** returns many articles on Bill Gates, but also returns many unrelated pages which happen to contain the words bill" or gates or both. Searching instead on **Bill Gates** returns only pages in which the proper name Bill Gates appears.

- If a search phrase contains two or more proper names, they must be separated by commas. For example, searching for **Bill Gates, Microsoft** returns numerous hits with information about the company and its founder. Searching instead on **Bill Gates Microsoft** returns nothing, because Infoseek treats the entire three words as a single proper name.

Finding Phrases. You can use two methods to require an exact match with a phrase that forms part or all of a search string. First, you may enclose the phrase in double quotation marks, such as

"Microsoft Windows NT Workstation"

to limit your search to only pages which contain this exact phrase. Alternatively, you may use hyphens to concatenate words which must appear as a single phrase, such as

Microsoft-Windows-NT-Workstation

Either of these methods has exactly the same effect. Use the one you prefer.

Finding Words in Close Proximity. You can use square brackets to enclose two or more search terms that must appear within 100 words of each other, but are not necessarily adjacent to each other. For example, you might be interested in Web pages in which both Intranets and Virtual Private Networks (VPNs) are mentioned. You can enter the search phrase:

[intranet vpn]

You can also combine phrase searching with the proximity operator. For example, you might be interested in learning about the use of RAID disk arrays with Windows NT Workstation, while eliminating pages that refer only to RAID with NT Server. Searching for the following:

> ["NT Workstation" RAID]

would locate pages which include both the exact phrase NT Workstation and the term RAID in close proximity.

Specifying Required Search Terms. You can specify that one or more search terms must appear in the document by prepending a plus sign to the search term. For example, to find documents that refer to intranets and virtual private networks (VPNs), but to limit your search to only documents that include both the words Cisco and encryption, you might use the following search phrase:

> intranet "virtual private network" vpn +Cisco +encryption

Note that the required search term must immediately follow the plus sign and not include a space. Note also that a space must separate the plus sign from the preceding search term.

Specifying Excluded Search Terms. You can specify that one or more search terms must not appear in a document by prepending a minus sign to the search term. For example, you might want to search for documents concerning the artist Michelangelo but exclude those referring to the Michelangelo virus. To do so, use the search phrase:

> Michelangelo -virus

Tip

Most of the time, getting enough hits on your searches isn't the problem. The problem is winnowing down the hits you do get to a usably small number. As a general precept of searching, use uncommon words that are unique to exactly what you are looking for. For example, searching for Michelangelo returns a huge number of documents, some focused tightly on the artist, some on the computer virus, and some which are totally extraneous. If you happen to know that the artist's full name was Michelangelo Buonarotti, you can use both of these relatively uncommon words in the search phrase to isolate your search to the artist himself.

As an interesting test, and perhaps as an indication of the relative value of these search engines, searching on the phrase **"Michelangelo Buonarotti"** returned the following number of hits with both terms included:

AltaVista	30
Infoseek Guide	1
Lycos	10
Yahoo!	0

Lycos

Carnegie-Mellon's *Lycos* engine was one of the original search engines, and offers a huge database with decent search tools (see fig. 15.36). Many people find that although Lycos returns a large number of hits, the results are not as likely to be quite as pertinent to their searches as those provided by AltaVista. For some users, however, Lycos proves to be the best site available. To try it, set your Web browser to **www.lycos.com**.

Lycos combines a huge database with a rather inflexible search engine. Lycos treats search terms as discrete items, and returns hits ranked on how many of the search terms appear in a given document, how many times the search terms occur in a document, and how close to the beginning of the document the search terms appear. That said, although Lycos gives you little choice as to exactly how your search is performed, a typical Lycos search returns a large number of documents, often surprisingly relevant to what you intended.

If you are skilled at searching and fully comfortable with using Boolean logic, you will probably find that AltaVista and Infoseek provide better and more tightly focused results. If you are a novice at searching, give Lycos a try. You may be surprised by just how good the built-in search algorithms really are.

Searching with Lycos

The Lycos search engine is easy to use simply because you don't have many options when using it. The default search simply allows you to enter one or more words, and returns documents that contain some or all of those terms, weighted as described previously.

The Enhance Your Search option enables you to focus your search strategy somewhat more tightly, although it does not allow you to perform full Boolean searches, to match exact text strings within the database, or to or exclude terms from your search. It does, however, allow limited Boolean searching.

The Boolean AND operator is full supported by the Match All Terms selection under Search Options. The Boolean OR operator is supported by the Match Any Term selection under Search Options. Unfortunately, this is strictly an either-or choice, because the Boolean AND and OR operators cannot be combined in a single search. Unique to Lycos is the Match *X* Terms operator, which allows you to specify how many, but not which, of your search terms must be matched for a document to be returned as a hit. You can specify from that any number of terms from 2 to 7 must appear in a document, giving you some but not all of the flexibility of full Boolean searching.

Fig. 15.36

Lycos.

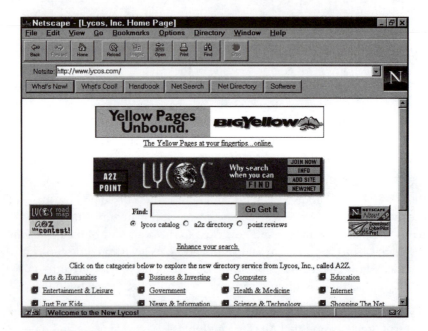

Lycos treats the plus sign as a special character, and makes no other provision for requiring that a term appear, unless you have used the AND operator to encompass it. You can exclude a term after a fashion by prepending it with a minus sign. This does not truly exclude pages in which that term appears, but reduces the weighting given to that page, causing it to appear further down in the listing of hits.

In short, Lycos is an impressive database which is somewhat hampered by a less than ideal search engine. Lycos in theory shouldn't be a good choice for searching the Web. In practice, for many users, Lycos works quite well.

Yahoo!

Yahoo! is in a class by itself. Unlike AltaVista, Lycos, and Infoseek, which are primarily or exclusively search engines, Yahoo! attempts to be a nexus for Web users. Yahoo! provides a carefully structured list of Web sites that enable you to choose sites by category or to search for them based on plain-text search criteria (see fig. 15.37). Search results are often quirky and less comprehensive than those returned by other search engines. However, Yahoo! automatically links your query to other search engines on the Web, allowing you to jump to each of them and review results there without re-entering the query. To check out Yahoo!, set your Web browser to **www.yahoo.com**.

Yahoo! has neither the largest database nor the most powerful search engine. What it does have is an eclectic selection of some of the best Web resources available, cross-indexed and categorized by type. A lot of effort goes into maintaining Yahoo!, and it shows. Yahoo! is just fun to use.

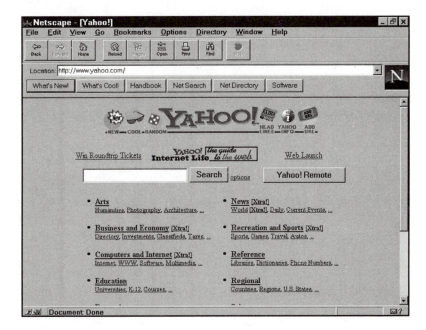

Fig. 15.37
Yahoo!

V

Using the Internet

Searching with Yahoo!

Like Lycos, Yahoo! offers limited searching flexibility. You can specify whether to search Yahoo! or USENET. You can also search e-mail addresses provided by the Four11 database. You can specify whether to require all terms (Boolean AND) or require only that one of the search terms be matched (Boolean OR). As with Lycos, you can't mix and match Boolean operators within a single search string. One nice thing about doing a Yahoo! search is that Yahoo! automatically passes your search string to other engines, including Lycos and AltaVista. ❖

CHAPTER 16

Using ping, ftp, news, and Telnet

by Robert Bruce Thompson

For most people, a Web browser and an e-mail client are their most important Internet utilities. The Internet has more to offer, however, than just surfing Web sites and using e-mail.

Thousands of File Transfer Protocol (ftp) sites offer millions of shareware and public domain files—everything from updated drivers and utility programs to the latest version of *Doom*. The USENET has more than 10,000 conferences, or *newsgroups*, each focusing on a narrowly defined special interest. Thousands of other sites allow you to log in remotely using Telnet and access databases and other resources.

Some of these services can be accessed on at least a minimal level by using your Web browser, but using them properly requires software designed for the purpose. Your Web browser may serve to download an occasional file using ftp, but if you need to transfer files frequently, a dedicated ftp client will be much better for the job. Your Web browser may also allow you to read newsgroups, but again, a dedicated newsreader client offers more features and more convenience. There are two ways to get the client software you need.

First, the recent surge in popularity of the Internet has resulted in many commercial collections of programs designed to perform all of these functions— the so-called Internet Suites. These suites provide, at a minimum, a Web Browser, an e-mail client, an ftp utility, and a newsreader. Most also provide a Telnet client and various other utilities. This chapter looks at three of the best of these commercial Internet Suites.

The second method is to choose best-of-breed clients individually for each of these purposes. Contrary to what you might think, the freeware and inexpensive shareware products often equal, and sometimes exceed, the quality of the best commercial products. Just as the best Web browsers are from companies that specialize in Web browsers, the best client for a particular Internet service is often written by people who specialize in writing clients for that service. What you gain by selecting individual components for your Internet tool kit is the ability to choose the absolute best clients as defined by your particular needs. What you lose is integration between the components of your Internet tool kit. This chapter looks at one or two of the best clients in each category.

In this chapter, you learn to:

- Use ping and Trace Route to verify that TCP/IP connectivity is functioning properly on your workstation, and determine the cause of network outages

- Select an ftp client, and use ftp to transfer files to and from remote servers

- Choose a news client, and use the news Newsreader to access information on the USENET

- Select and use other Internet utilities to establish a terminal mode connection to remote hosts, set the time on your computer accurately, and map your network graphically

Internet Suites versus Best-of-Breed

You can take one of two routes to develop a tool kit of Internet utilities. The easy route is to purchase a commercial bundle of utilities, usually called an Internet Suite. The difficult route is to pick individual commercial or shareware components for each purpose. It's more work, but you end up with the best-of-breed in each product category.

If you decide to purchase a packaged Internet Suite, tread carefully. The best of the suites are very good. They offer well-integrated collections of usable, if not always top-notch, utilities. The worst of the suites appear to be random assortments of mediocre utilities thrown together purely for marketing purposes, with little or no integration between the components. Attempting to use one of these suites can quickly sour anyone on using the Internet.

A good Internet Suite can be the best choice for beginners, for corporate environments, and for those who want the comfort of technical support provided by a single company. Purchasing a packaged Internet Suite can even be less expensive than choosing individual components. The street price of most commercial suites ranges from $75 to $200, an amount you can easily exceed when paying shareware registration fees. The section "Internet Suites" later in this chapter takes a look at three of the best Internet Suites.

Sometimes the best things in life really are free, or at least pretty cheap. This is nowhere more true than on the Internet. Looking for a good ftp client, Telnet utility, or newsreader? You can find many free or low-cost shareware versions of these products on the Internet, and the best of them will be at least as good as and usually better than the commercial alternatives. If you want a best-of-breed Internet tool kit, and you're not concerned about using different products from different vendors, rolling your own is the way to go.

There are a few drawbacks to putting together your own tool kit from free utilities. First, you give up single-source technical support. In some cases, you give up technical support completely. Many of these public domain and shareware products have limited or non-existent formal technical support, which forces you to depend on your own resources and those available on the Internet to resolve problems. Second, you give up the level of integration present in the best of the Internet Suites, although many of these free utilities (notably John Junod's WS series), are beginning to coalesce as pseudo-suites. Third, depending on the products you select, you can end up paying more than you would for an integrated Internet Suite. Still, on balance, most advanced users will find the trade-offs worthwhile and elect to go the *a la carte* route.

> ### Tip
>
> Keeping up with all of the Internet utilities available is no easy job. Many are updated frequently, and worthwhile new applications appear frequently. One easy way to keep current with what's out there is to point your Web browser to **http://www.cwsapps.com/** and check out Stroud's Consummate Winsock Applications List. CWSApps is updated frequently, and includes ratings and more detailed reviews of individual products. You can locate software by name or by product category. Bookmark this site on your Web browser and visit it every month or so.

Checking Connections with ping and tracert

When you connect your Windows NT Workstation to a TCP/IP network, whether internal or the Internet, the first thing you should do is verify that TCP/IP is properly configured and working correctly. When working with TCP/IP and the Internet on a day-to-day basis, there will be times when, for one reason or another, you cannot connect to a host that you know you should be able to connect to.

When you do have problems connecting, it isn't always immediately clear where the difficulty lies. It may be the site you're trying to connect to. It may be your own workstation or your router. It may be your Internet Service Provider. It may even be the Internet. The way to find out is to use either or both of two utilities called ping and tracert. These tools can help you quickly diagnose where the communications breakdown has occurred.

It's important to note that, although ping and tracert are essential tools for checking connectivity, all they establish is whether the target computer system is accessible on the network and is running TCP/IP. If, for example, you cannot access a particular Web server, use ping or tracert to verify whether the machine running the Web server is running TCP/IP and is reachable. Neither program will tell you, other than by inference, if the machine is up but the Web server software is not running on it.

ping

The *Internet Control Message Protocol*, or ICMP, is a standard part of the Internet Protocol Suite. ICMP allows testing and monitoring of an IP network. One of the functions of ICMP is to respond to an *echo_request* datagram with an *echo_response* datagram. The ping utility sends echo_request messages to a specified host, and displays echo_response messages that are in turn received from that host. Ping also displays the elapsed time required for each message to be received, which gives you some idea of how the network is responding.

A ping utility is easy to come by. Windows NT Workstation bundles a rather spartan character-mode version of ping, located in the windows\system32 folder as ping.exe. To use it, simply type **ping [IP address] or ping [host name]** at the command prompt, substituting the appropriate IP address or host name. For example, typing **ping www.microsoft.com** pings the Microsoft Web site.

tracert

Tracert, also known as *trace route*, *traceroute*, and *hopcheck*, uses a rather ingenious method to determine the route used to connect to a specified host. One of the fields contained in the IP header is named *time to live*, or *ttl*. Tracert uses the ttl field to determine the exact route used to connect to a remote host. Here's how.

For example, if you issue the command **tracert www.microsoft.com**, the tracert utility sends an ICMP echo_request datagram with the ttl field set to 0. The first router that receives this packet replies to your computer that the ttl has expired, and that the packet therefore could not be forwarded. The tracert utility displays the address and optionally the DNS name of that router, and marks it as the first hop on the path to **www.microsoft.com**. After incrementing the ttl field by one, tracert repeats this action until it finally receives an ICMP echo_response from the target host, **www.microsoft.com**.

Windows NT Workstation bundles a character-mode version of tracert, located in the windows\system32 directory as tracert.exe.

ICMP Ping for Windows

For casual use, the ping and tracert utilities bundled with Windows NT Workstation may serve the purpose. If you want something a lot prettier and more functional, take a look at ICMP Ping for Windows, also called WSPing32, and written by John A. Junod. In addition to ping and tracert functions, WSPing32 provides *nslookup* and *Winsock lookup* functions.

WSPing32 has no automated installation procedure, but installing it is simple. Create a directory with a name of your own choosing and extract the WSPing32 archive to that directory. Add it to your menu or create a shortcut on your desktop and you're done.

Using WSPing32, shown in figure 16.1, to ping another host is also easy. Type the name of the host, or its IP address, in the Host field or select a host from the drop-down list. Click the Ping button. By default, the ping function sends 10 echo_request packets and displays the responses and elapsed time as they arrive. After all echo_request packets have been sent and a suitable time-out period has elapsed, WSPing32 displays summary statistics, including the number of packets lost, if any, and the minimum, average, and maximum time required for the echo_response packets to arrive.

Most of the time, if the pinged host responds at all, there will be no lost packets. If the host is unreachable, you'll have 100 percent packet loss. Something in-between indicates that the network is extremely busy or has other problems. The elapsed time varies depending on the location of the host you're pinging and the path used to reach it. For a host located on your LAN, ping response times should be well under 100 ms. For a host located across the country, ping responses may take 500 ms (half a second) or more. It is not unusual for the first packet or two to take significantly longer than the others to make the trip.

Fig. 16.1
Using WSPing32 to ping a remote host.

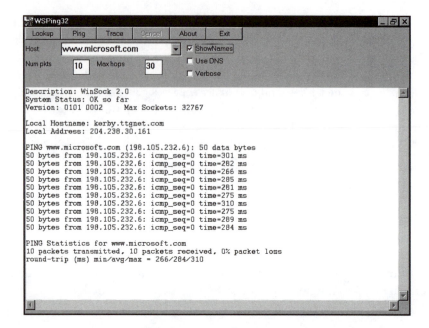

Using the tracert function of WSPing32, shown in figure 16.2, works in much the same way. Enter the host name or its IP address in the Host field and click the Trace button. WSPing32 displays each intermediate hop on the way to the destination machine, up to the limit of the number of hops specified in the Max Hops field.

Fig. 16.2
Using WSPing32 to tracert a remote host.

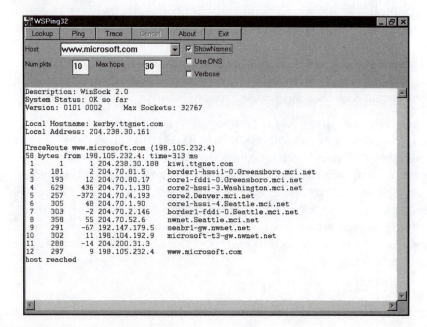

If you have an IP address and want to learn the host name that corresponds to it, enter the address in the Host field and click the Lookup button, as shown in figure 16.3. Similarly, if you enter a host name in the Host field and click the Lookup button, WSPing32 displays the IP address corresponding to that host name, as shown in figure 16.4.

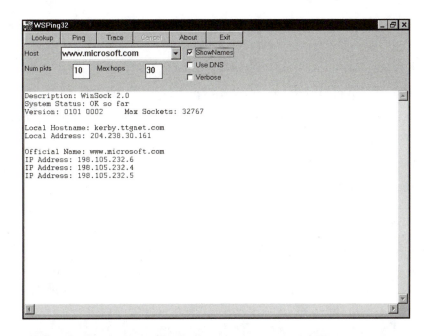

Fig. 16.3

Using WSPing32 NSLookup to resolve an IP address.

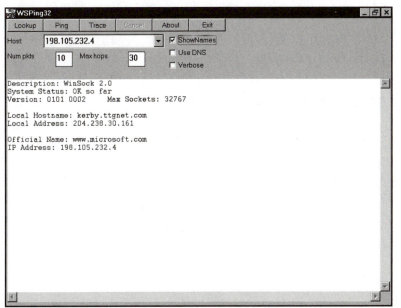

Fig. 16.4

Using WSPing32 Winsock Lookup to resolve a host name.

V

Using the Internet

Like all of Mr. Junod's TCP/IP utilities, WSPing32 can be used freely by any
U.S. government organization, by individuals for non-commercial home use,
and by students, faculty, and staff of academic institutions. Corporate and
other business users can license the product by contacting Ipswitch, Inc. at 81
Hartwell Avenue, Lexington, MA 02173 (617-676-5700) or via Internet mail
at **info@ipswitch.com**.

On the Web

The latest release version of WSPing32 can be downloaded from CompuServe
in WINCON Library 11 or via anonymous ftp from the following sites:

ftp://ftp.coast.net/SimTel/win3/winsock

ftp://winftp.cica.indiana.edu/pub/pc/win3/winsock

Test versions and beta versions are available via anonymous ftp from the following sites:

ftp://ftp.usma.edu/pub/msdos/winsock.files

http://www.csra.net/junodj

Windows Sockets Net Watch (Watch95)

Another of John Junod's utilities, Watch95, is the latest in the series of
WS_Watch utilities for different versions of Windows. Watch95, shown in
figure 16.5, uses ping and tracert to serve as a kind of poor man's SNMP.
Watch95 allows you to create a graphical representation of your local IP network and any remote sites of interest to you. It then polls each of these sites
on demand or at a specified interval and displays a color-coded map listing
the status of each site. Watch95 can also alert you by visual or audible
prompts or by sending a message to your pager. Development on the
WS_Watch series has ceased, with efforts being shifted to IWatch, the commercial version of this product available from Ipswitch.

Transferring Files with ftp

ftp is a client-server protocol that allows files to be transferred from one system to another. The host computer runs ftp server software, and is called the
ftp server. The ftp server software running on the host can send files to and
receive files from the remote computer, which runs ftp client software. The
ftp server and the ftp client between them take care of establishing a session,
negotiating transfer parameters, checking for errors, and re-transmitting damaged blocks of data. After their e-mail client software and their Web browser,
the Internet utility most people would find it hardest to live without is their
ftp client.

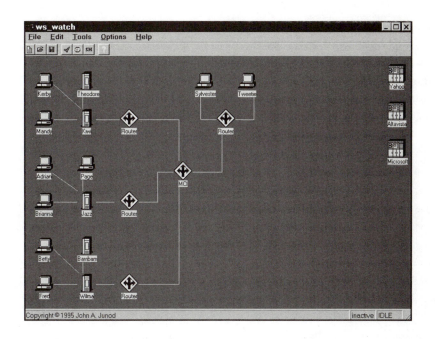

Fig. 16.5
Using Watch95 to display a network configuration.

In the bad old days before Windows, using ftp meant using a character-mode ftp client package with few amenities. When you connected to an ftp server with one of these old character-mode clients, you were presented with a spartan command prompt. You needed to have at least a basic understanding of UNIX file and directory structures and command syntax because the server was almost certainly running UNIX. Neither the server nor the client software did much to make your life easier, because the implicit assumption was that anyone who used ftp knew exactly what he was doing and exactly what files he wanted to get.

The advent of Windows ftp clients has changed all of this for the better. The underlying ftp protocols haven't changed much, but nowadays a graphical front end hides the ugliness and gets on with the business of transferring files. Using ftp has become a simple matter of pointing and clicking. Still, it's useful to have a basic understanding of how ftp works, if only to appreciate how much easier life is in a Windows world.

ftp Basics

Although ftp was originally designed for and used on computers running the UNIX operating system, it has since been enhanced and ported to nearly any operating system imaginable. ftp server software is available for any multi-user computer system that runs TCP/IP, and is installed by default on most. ftp client software of one sort or another is available for any workstation operating system, including long obsolete ones like CP/M.

Logical File Format Translations

ftp is designed to eliminate problems due to differences in the logical file format used to store files on different operating systems. For example, you might use an ftp client running under Windows NT to retrieve a text file stored on an ftp server running UNIX. Windows uses a carriage return character followed by a line feed character to indicate the end of each line of text. UNIX uses only the line feed character for the same purpose. If you simply copied the text file from the UNIX system to the Windows NT system, you would find that this difference in logical file format would make the UNIX text file unreadable on the Windows NT system.

Using a modern ftp client to do the transfer solves the problem. The client recognizes that it is running on Windows NT and that it is transferring a file from a UNIX ftp server. Because the client is aware of the logical file format differences between UNIX and Windows NT, it can take the necessary action to correct the problem. It does so, in this case, simply by inserting a carriage return character before the line feed character at the end of each line sent by the UNIX ftp server.

Note that this capability to translate between incompatible logical file formats is not an absolute guarantee that all differences can be resolved. Many advanced operating systems designed to run on large computer systems, such as DEC VAX/VMS and IBM MVS, have complex file structures that are not easily transferable to computers running other operating systems. Even as common an operating system as that used on the Apple Macintosh stores files in a fundamentally different way, using two forks, each of which contains some information about the file in question.

Note also that the conversion performed by ftp is only that of converting one logical file storage format to another. Although you can, for example, use ftp to transfer a UNIX executable program file to a Windows client, that file will not then run.

All of this aside, ftp is a valuable addition to your Internet tool kit. You will use it to download driver updates and program patches from manufacturer ftp sites, without worrying about what type of computer the ftp server runs on. You may also use it to transfer program files, text files, and archive files among members of your workgroup, again without concern about the underlying platform.

ASCII versus Binary Mode

All ftp clients and servers support ASCII mode (or Text mode) transfers and Binary mode (or Image mode) transfers. Although there are additional types of transfers available on different clients and servers, you will use either ASCII mode or Binary mode for nearly all file transfers.

An ASCII mode transfer is designed to move a text file from one system to another, storing that file on the destination computer system in that system's native format. Using ASCII mode transfer, the ftp protocol automatically translates the different text file formats, making the file usable on both computer systems.

Binary mode transfers the file byte by byte with no conversion. Because changing even a single bit can render a binary file useless, Binary mode is used to transfer all files other than pure ASCII text files. Because it can be problematic to exchange complex files like databases between machines with disparate operating systems, it is common practice to encode the file with a common utility available across both operating systems. ZIP files are becoming the most popular format, and have the added benefit of superior compression.

ftp Commands

Using ftp requires that you know only half a dozen or so basic commands to navigate the remote ftp server and to send and receive files. Depending on the ftp client software you are using, even these commands may be hidden from you, invoked instead by a simple point and click operation.

- ls is the UNIX equivalent of the MS-DOS dir command, and is used to display a directory listing of the current directory on the ftp server.

- cd is the UNIX equivalent of the MS-DOS cd or chdir command, and is used to navigate the ftp server directory tree.

- pwd, or print working directory, is the UNIX command to display the current default directory, equivalent to using the MS-DOS command cd with no argument.

- lcd, or local change directory, is used to change the local directory on the ftp client machine while an ftp session is in progress.

- get is used to retrieve a file from the remote ftp server to your local machine. get allows you to rename the file by specifying the new name as the second parameter. mget, or multiple get, retrieves a list of files or specifies a wildcard template for retrieving multiple files.

- put is used to upload a file from your local ftp client to the remote ftp server. You must have write privileges in the target directory of the ftp server to do so. mput is used to specify a list of files to be uploaded or to specify a wildcard template for uploading multiple files.

V

Using the Internet

> **Tip**
>
> Locating the exact file or files you want to download on an ftp server can be difficult. On many ftp servers, you will find a file in the root directory (usually /pub) called `ls-1R`. This file is in ASCII text format, and contains a raw UNIX directory listing of every file on the ftp server that is available to you for download. `ls-1R` is the UNIX command to list the directory in long format and to recurse the directory tree.
>
> Because the `ls-1R` command can be run automatically to update the `ls-1R` file, many ftp administrators use it as an easy means to provide a current listing of all files available on the server. Because it contains only the raw directory information and not file descriptions, however, it may be of limited use to you unless you know the exact name of the file you're trying to locate.
>
> For just this reason, many ftp sites also post file and directory listings with descriptions appended, often with the file name `00dir`, `00index`, or a similar name.

Using Anonymous ftp

Many organizations set up ftp servers to allow anyone to access a particular set of files. For example, many hardware and software companies have supplemented or entirely replaced their BBSes with ftp servers to distribute updated drivers and software patches.

Setting up such an ftp server introduces two conflicting demands. On the one hand, it is obviously impractical to expect the ftp administrator to set up an individual account for each person who wants to use the server, so a publicly known shared account name is needed. On the other hand, no company wants just anyone who logs in to be able to delete files, upload files contaminated with viruses, or otherwise damage the ftp server.

The solution to this dilemma is to set up an *anonymous ftp server*. Instead of having to create an account for each user, the ftp administrator creates a special account called *ftp*. The ftp account grants limited access to a specified part of the ftp server directory tree to anyone who logs in with the username *anonymous*. Anonymous users can see only those directories on the ftp server that have been specifically authorized for anonymous access, and usually then only to download files from the ftp server rather than upload them.

Some ftp servers are configured to allow anonymous users to upload files, but usually only to a specified directory, typically called /PUB/UPLOADS. Files uploaded to the /PUB/UPLOADS directory are normally invisible to users logged in anonymously, meaning that the ftp administrator can review all uploaded files before posting them to a publicly accessible directory for download. This is done to protect other anonymous ftp users against the possibility of a malicious file being uploaded and being available for general download before it has been reviewed.

> **Caution**
>
> A certain body of etiquette has developed for anonymous ftp use, and you disregard these conventions at your own peril. Although you may be logging on as anonymous, the ftp administrator still has some information about you, including your IP address. If you abuse an ftp site, it is quite possible that you will find your privileges at that site revoked. Even worse, other users at your company or your Internet Service Provider may also find their privileges revoked.
>
> First, when you log in as anonymous, you are expected to enter your full e-mail address as the password. Although some ftp sites allow you to enter anything—or even nothing at all—as the password, it's common courtesy to provide your e-mail address. Identify yourself properly. It's little enough to ask in return for the service being provided.
>
> Second, pay close attention to the policies of the ftp server you're using, which will be displayed when you first log on. ftp servers at businesses and universities may run on hosts that are used for other purposes during the working day. If you plan to download a large number of files, do so after hours—this is calculated as local time at the ftp server location.

Choosing an ftp client program

ftp clients aren't hard to find. As a matter of fact, there's probably one on your hard drive right now, put there when you installed Windows NT Workstation. The command-line interface ftp client bundled with Windows NT is certainly functional, but that's about all to say for it. The best thing to do with it is to use it to download one or more of the ftp clients covered in this section, and then delete it.

Feature bloat has begun to hit the market for Internet utilities. Because ftp is a relatively simple protocol, it's easy for programmers to implement correctly. Not very long ago, your Web browser provided only Web browsing functions, your newsreader was only useful for retrieving UseNet news, and you used your Telnet program only when you wanted to establish a terminal session on a remote server. Today, chances are that each of these programs also has an ftp client built in. For example, in figure 16.6, Netscape Navigator is being used as an ftp client.

Fig. 16.6

Using Netscape
Navigator as an ftp
client.

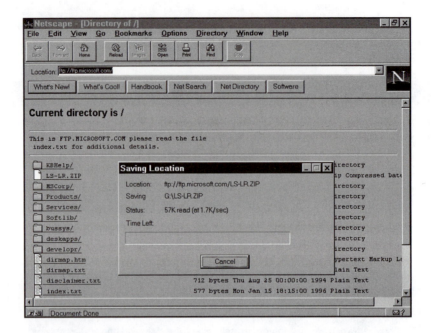

The secondary ftp clients included in browsers and other TCP/IP utility suites
often appear to have been tacked on as afterthoughts, perhaps simply as a
check box item to satisfy purchasing departments. Although they're functional in an absolute sense, they usually lack most of the features of a full-
blown ftp client package, and they're nearly always slower at transferring
files. If you plan to use ftp only occasionally, consider using one of these
built-in ftp clients. It's already there, you've already paid for it, and it keeps
things simple.

If, on the other hand, you will be using ftp heavily, you owe it to yourself to
get a better ftp client. In the course of several years working on the Internet, I
have seen dozens of ftp clients, and tried many of them. Two of the best are
available as free or inexpensive shareware. One or the other of them should
provide everything you need in a full-featured ftp client. Try both, choose
one, and don't forget to send in the registration fee for the one you select.

WS_FTP32

With WS_FTP32, shown in figure 16.7, John Junod has done it again.
WS_FTP32 is a simple, fast, elegant, and full-featured Windows ftp client.
Most users need look no further than this product as an ideal ftp client.

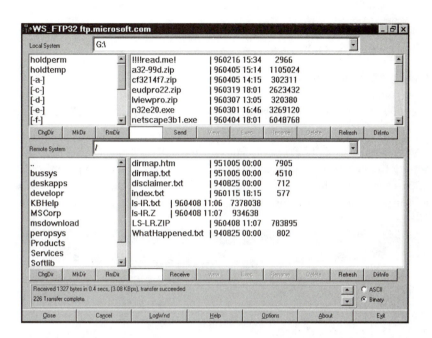

Fig. 16.7
WS_FTP32 main
screen.

WS_FTP32 supports batch downloads, transaction logging, and a variety of transfer filtering options. It supports ftp servers running on almost any operating system, either by explicit choice or via an auto-select mode. You can run multiple instances of WS_FTP32 to allow simultaneous downloading of files from more than one ftp site. The program comes with an extensive list of useful ftp sites to get you started. Although the default settings will work well for most users, you can reconfigure almost any aspect of the program to your requirements. About the only thing missing from WS_FTP32 is drag-and-drop file transfers.

Installing WS_FTP32. Like Mr. Junod's other TCP/IP utilities, WS_FTP32 has no automated installation procedure. To install it, you simply create a directory with a name of your own choosing and extract the WS_FTP32 archive to that directory. Add it to your menu or create a shortcut on your desktop, and you're ready to start transferring files. I find it useful to keep all of my Internet utilities grouped under the \TCP directory, with WS_FTP32 installed in \TCP\WSFTP.

All WS_FTP32 files are installed to the directory you specify. No files are added to the Windows or Windows System directories, and no changes are made to the Registry. The `wsftp.ini` file is stored in the application directory, and contains program settings and your list of recently accessed ftp sites. Be careful not to overwrite your `wsftp.ini` file when upgrading WS_FTP.

V

Using the Internet

Not only will you overwrite your program preferences, but you will wipe out your personal ftp site list.

Configuring WS_FTP32. The default settings of WS_FTP32 work well for most users. You do need to make a few minor settings when you first install the program (for example, to store your e-mail address, which will be used as your password for anonymous ftp sites).

Configuring WS_FTP32 Program Options. Begin to configure WS_FTP32 by setting the Program Options, shown in figure 16.8. These options control the appearance and general functioning of the program. Settings made here affect all connections you make using WS_FTP32.

Fig. 16.8
WS_FTP32
Options screen.

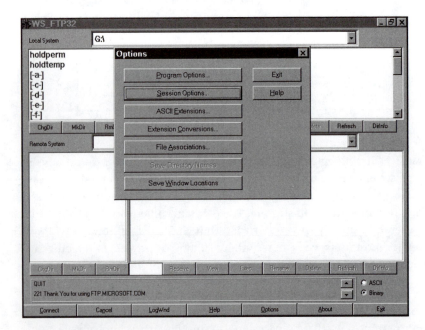

1. At the main WS_FTP32 screen, click the Options button.

2. At the Options screen, click Program Options.

3. In the Program Options dialog box, shown in figure 16.9, select the following check boxes to configure WS_FTP32 display and other parameters:

   - *Alternate Screen Layout.* If selected, tiles the local and remote directory listings vertically rather than the default horizontal tiling.

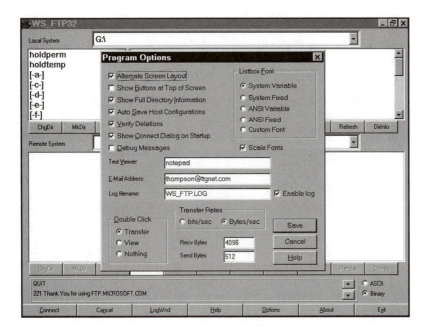

Fig. 16.9
WS_FTP32
Program Options
dialog box.

- *Show Buttons at Top of Screen*. If selected, moves the button bar from its default location at the bottom of the screen to the top.

- *Show Full Directory Information*. If checked, causes WS_FTP to display all available file and directory information. Depending on the host type of the ftp server, more information may be available than is displayed by default.

- *Auto Save Host Configurations*. If checked, causes WS_FPT32 to automatically save the Session Profile.

- *Verify Deletions*. If checked, causes WS_FTP32 to prompt you before allowing you to delete a file.

- *Show Connect Dialog on Startup*. If checked, causes WS_FTP32 to display the connect dialog when the program is started.

- *Debug Messages*. If checked, causes WS_FTP32 to display verbose debugging information in the message window. For most users, this information is useless, and therefore this option is deselected by default. Note that even with this option deselected, all error messages continue to be displayed.

4. In the Text Viewer text box, enter the program you want to use to display text files you download, such as index files. This text box defaults to NOTEPAD.EXE, but you can use any editor that can load and display ASCII text files. I prefer Programmers' File Editor (PFE).

5. In the E-Mail Address text box, enter your full e-mail address. This is used as your password when you connect to an anonymous ftp site.

6. In the Log Filename field, enter the name of the file you want to use for logging ftp file transfers. When a transfer is completed, WS_FTP32 creates a file of this name in the directory where the file is located. Logging only occurs if you select the Enable Log check box.

7. In the Double Click section, choose one of the radio buttons to determine what happens when you double-click a file name. Your choices are to Transfer the file, View the file, or do Nothing. Most people leave this set at Transfer.

8. In the Transfer Rates section, choose one of the radio buttons to determine whether WS_FTP32 will display transfer rates in bits per second (bps) or bytes per second (Bps). This setting has nothing to do with the way the program functions. It determines only how it reports transfer efficiency to you. In general, if you connect to ftp servers on a slow link, like a dial-up connection, choose bits/sec. If you are on a fast link, like a LAN or a T1, choose Bytes/sec.

9. Set the Recv Bytes text box to your preference. This value determines how many bytes WS_FTP reads from the network in each read. It can be set from 80 bytes to 4,096 bytes, and should generally be left at the default value of 4,096. The actual number of bytes read per read will be determined by the TCP/IP stack, so leaving this value set high will do no harm. Setting it to a value lower than the block size of the underlying TCP/IP stack can reduce efficiency and slow throughput, sometimes dramatically.

10. Set the Send Bytes text box to your preference. This value determines how many bytes WS_FTP blocks into each send. Again, this parameter can be set to values between 80 and 4,096 inclusive. The proper value for this parameter is determined by your TCP/IP stack. Generally, if you have a direct (network) connection, use 4,096. If you are using a SLIP or PPP dial up connection, set this value to the same number as the MTU. Setting this number either too low or too high can adversely effect performance.

11. In the Listbox Font section, choose a radio button to determine which font will be used for file and directory listings. The default, System Variable, is an attractive proportional font. System Fixed is a monospaced font that you can choose to improve the alignment of columns separated by spaces. The ANSI Variable and ANSI Fixed fonts are similar, but somewhat narrower. You can also choose Custom Font, which allows you to use any TrueType font installed on your system.

12. WS_FTP uses ANSI Variable for all text outside the list boxes. Select or deselect the Scale Fonts check box to determine whether or not to reduce the size of this font as the Window size is reduced.

13. When you have the Program Options parameters set as you want them, click the Save button.

Configuring WS_FTP32 Session Options. Continue to configure WS_FTP32 by setting the Session Options. These options control the program function for connecting to a particular ftp site. Different Session Options can be stored for each site on your list. You can also save a group of Session Option settings as a default template, which will be used when you create a new session for a new site.

> **Caution**
>
> Be careful when changing Session Options defaults. When you save Session Options for a particular session, only those that differ from the default options are saved for that session. If you subsequently alter the Session Options defaults, the setting for your individual stored sessions will also change.

1. At the main WS_FTP32 screen, click the Options button.

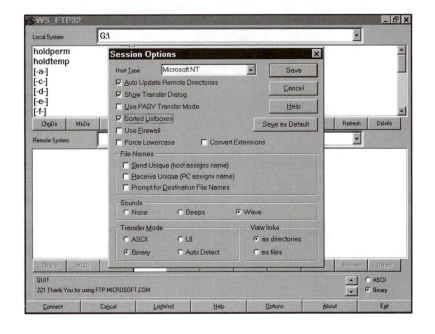

Fig. 16.10
WS_FTP32 Session Options dialog box.

V

Using the Internet

2. At the Options screen, click Session Options.

3. In the Session Options dialog box, shown in figure 16.10, first choose Host Type from the list box. The Automatic Detect selection nearly always works correctly, and should be left as the default selection.

> ### Tip
>
> If you can connect to a remote ftp server but have trouble getting a directory listing, try changing the Host Type within the Session Options for that particular site. Check the message window for further information about the operating system the remote host is running, which it normally provides as you log in.

4. Use the check boxes to configure WS_FTP32 display and other parameters, as follows:

   ■ *Auto Update Remote Directories.* If checked, causes WS_FTP32 to automatically refresh the directory listing on the remote server when any change is made to it, such as uploading a file, deleting a file, creating or deleting a directory. If this box is unchecked, you must click the Refresh button to manually update the remote server directory listing.

   ■ *Show Transfer Dialog.* If checked, causes WS_FTP32 to display a dialog box during transfers that shows progress and allows you to abort the transfer if necessary.

   ■ *Use PASV Transfer Mode.* If checked, forces data connections to be established by the client rather than by the server. You may need to use PASV mode if there is a firewall between you and the remote ftp server.

   ■ *Sorted Listboxes.* If checked, causes the directory listing from the remote ftp server to be sorted alphabetically. If unchecked, the directory listing is displayed in the order received from the remote server.

   ■ *Use Firewall.* If checked, enables WS_FTP32 to work with various methods of firewalling.

   ■ *Force Lowercase.* If checked, causes WS_FTP32 to convert all file names to lowercase.

   ■ *Convert Extensions.* If checked, converts the file name extension of received files according to a stored map. For example, you may have HTML mapped to HTM. When you download a file that has an HTML extension on the remote server, it will automatically be renamed and stored locally as an HTM extension.

Tip

If you're consistently unable to connect successfully to outside ftp sites using WS_FTP32, and in particular if when attempting to list the directory of a remote ftp server you see the message `Dirlist returned 0`, the problem may be caused by your Internet Service Provider rather than by a bug in WS_FTP32.

To correct the problem, click the Options button at the main WS_FTP32 screen. In the Options dialog box, click the Session Options button. In the Session Options dialog box, select the Use PASV Transfer Mode check box. The problem should disappear.

---

5. In the File Names section, use the check boxes to specify how to handle file names, as follows:

- *Send Unique (Host Assigns Name).* If checked, verifies that the file name you are sending does not conflict with an existing file name on the remote ftp server. If that server supports the ftp STOU command, it renames the received file so that it is unique.

- *Receive Unique (PC Assigns Name).* If checked, verifies that the file name you are receiving does not conflict with an existing file name on your local computer. If a file of the same name already exists, WS_FTP assigns a number between 000 and 999 as the file extension, making the file name unique.

- *Prompt for Destination File Names.* If checked, enables local and remote file name prompting. Each time you transfer a file, you will be prompted whether to accept the proposed destination file name or to change it.

6. In the Sounds section, choose one of the radio buttons to determine how WS_FTP32 will use sound to notify you of events. The choices are None for no notification, Beeps for using the PC speaker, and Wave for using your sound card.

7. In the Transfer Mode section, select a radio button to determine the method used to transfer files. Your choices are:

- *ASCII,* which is used to transfer only text files. If the line end convention used on the remote ftp server is different from your local machine, ASCII mode automatically corrects for this difference during the transfer, allowing the received text file to be displayed correctly.

V

Using the Internet

- *Binary*, which does a bit-by-bit transfer with absolutely no conversion. The received file will be an exact duplicate of the file on the other machine. You must use Binary mode to transfer any file that contains anything other than pure ASCII text.

- *L8*, which is used in transferring some files to and from a DEC VAX/VMS host.

- *Auto Detect*, which transfers all files in binary mode, unless the extension is found in a lookup table, in which case WS_FTP32 uses ASCII mode.

8. In the View Links section, choose one of the radio buttons to determine how links are displayed. Your choices are to display them as directories or as files.

After you configure the options as you want them, you can save these settings for either the active session (by clicking the Save button) or as the default for newly created sessions (by clicking the Save As Default button).

Configuring Other WS_FTP32 Options. From the Options window, you can configure several of the choices referred to in the preceding section.

- *ASCII Extensions*. Allows you to specify which file extensions will cause the Auto Detect Transfer mode to use ASCII rather than Binary.

- *Extension Conversions*. Allows you to specify mapping for converting extensions during transfer, such as from HTML to HTM.

- *File Associations*. Allows you to specify which executable programs are invoked by which extensions when you use the Exec button.

- *Save Directory Names*. Allows you to save the local and/or remote directory names associated with each session. For example, you might want to be placed by default in the /PUB directory of a particular remote server every time you log in. You might also want to have the \DATA\FTP directory set as the default on your local drive so that downloaded files are placed there automatically. This option allows you to do so, on a session-by-session basis.

- *Save Window Locations*. Allows you to save the size and location of the main WS_FTP32 window.

Creating and Using Session Profiles with WS_FTP. After you install and configure WS_FTP32, you can create and store session profiles for ftp sites you want to use. A *session profile* stores information about a particular ftp site. To connect to that site, you simply highlight that session profile and click the OK button.

1. When the WS_FTP32 main screen is displayed, by default you see the Connect Dialog displayed as the Session Profile dialog box, shown in figure 16.11. If you have turned off automatic display of the Connection Dialog in Program Options, click the Connect button to display it.

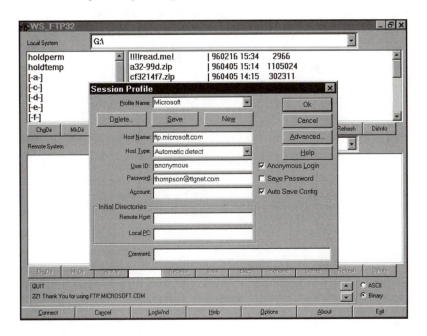

Fig. 16.11
WS_FTP32 Session Profile dialog box.

2. To create a new Session Profile, click the New button, and enter the information for the new site, as follows:

   ■ *Profile Name*. Enter a descriptive name for the ftp site in this text box.

   ■ *Host Name*. Enter the fully qualified machine name, including the domain, of the ftp server.

   ■ *Host Type*. This is the operating system being run by the remote ftp server. Automatic detect usually works here, but if you have problems, you can choose a specific host type manually, as noted previously in the section, "Configuring WS_FTP32 Session Options."

   ■ *User ID*. This is the login name to be used on the remote ftp server. Selecting the Anonymous Login check box automatically inserts **anonymous** in this text box, as well as inserting your e-mail address in the Password text box. If you want to log in to a non-anonymous ftp server, you need an existing account on that server before you can do so. Enter that account name here.

■ *Password*. This is the password required by the account on the re-mote ftp server. With anonymous login, always send your full e-mail address as the password. On a non-anonymous ftp server, you must enter the real password associated with your account here. Select the Save Password check box if you want to store your password. For better security, you may want to leave this box un-checked.

■ *Account*. This is used to record information needed by hosts with multiple step login processes, for example, those that require a user ID, an account, and a password as three separate items.

■ *Initial Directories*. Allows you to specify the default directories on both the remote ftp host and the local PC at login time.

■ *Comment*. You can enter any information or notes you might want to keep about this site in this text box.

3. To connect to an ftp site, choose an existing Session Profile from the Profile Name list box.

Note

You can use the Advanced button in the Session Profile dialog box to set advanced options for a profile, including Network Timeout, port selections, passive transfer options, and firewall parameters. You will almost never need to alter any of these parameters from their default values. If you have trouble connecting to a site, contact the site administrator (usually **ftpadmin@sitename.domain**) or your local ftp administrator and explain the difficulty. You may be told to alter one or more of the parameters in the Advanced dialog box. Otherwise, don't touch them.

Transferring Files with WS_FTP32. After you configure WS_FTP32 and create one or more session profiles, transferring files is simplicity itself. Pro-ceed as follows:

1. Start WS_FTP32.

2. In the Session Profile dialog box, highlight the ftp site to which you want to connect and click the OK button. After the connection is estab-lished, you will see directory listings of your own PC in the Local Sys-tem window and of the ftp server in the Remote System window.

3. Navigate on both systems simply by pointing to a directory name and double-clicking. You can go up a directory level by double-clicking the ".." entry in a directory listing. After you're in the correct directories on both the local and remote system, you may begin transferring files.

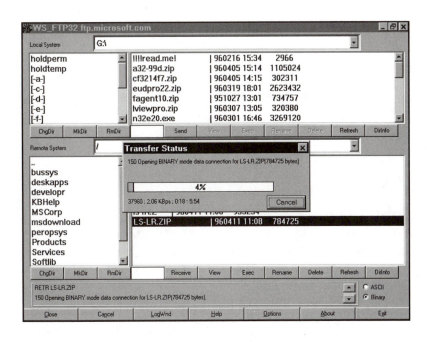

Fig. 16.12
WS_FTP32 transfer
status.

4. To receive a file or files from a remote system, highlight the file name
or file names on the remote ftp server and click the Receive button in
the Remote System window. To send a file or files from your PC to the
remote ftp server, highlight the file name or file names in the Local
System directory listing and click the Send button in the Local System
window. In either case, the Transfer Status dialog box, shown in figure
16.12, appears and displays the progress of the transfer.

Tip

You can highlight multiple files simultaneously in either window. To select multiple
files that are not contiguous in the directory listing, click the first file to highlight it,
press the Ctrl key, and then click to highlight additional files. To highlight a contiguous group of files, click to highlight the first file, press the Shift key, and then click the
last file name to highlight the entire list.

Getting WS_FTP32. Like WSPing32, WS_FTP32 can be used freely by U.S.
government organizations, by individuals for non-commercial home use, and
by students, faculty, and staff of academic institutions. Corporate and other
business users can license the product by contacting Ipswitch, Inc. at 81
Hartwell Avenue, Lexington, MA 02173 (617-676-5700) or via Internet mail
at **info@ipswitch.com**.

On the Web

The latest release version of WS_FTP32 can be downloaded from CompuServe in WINCON Library 11 or via anonymous ftp from the following sites:

ftp://ftp.coast.net/SimTel/win3/winsock

ftp://winftp.cica.indiana.edu/pub/pc/win3/winsock

Test versions and beta versions are available via anonymous ftp from the following sites:

ftp://ftp.usma.edu/pub/msdos/winsock.files

http://www.csra.net/junodj

CuteFTP

CuteFTP, shown in figure 16.13, vies with WS_FTP32 for the laurels as best standalone ftp client. With v1.4, CuteFTP has incorporated many of the features of WS_FTP32, and surpassed it in several respects. If you're willing to pay a $30 shareware registration fee, you can use an ftp client that many now consider to be even better than WS_FTP32.

One of the best features of CuteFTP is that it uses the index files provided by most ftp sites to integrate file listings with descriptions. Other ftp clients simply display a raw listing of the files in a directory on the remote ftp server. File descriptions are contained in a file typically named OOINDEX.TXT, or something similar. Unless you already know the exact file name you want to download, you must first download the index file, search the descriptions to locate the file you need, and then download it. CuteFTP shortens this process by automatically finding the index file, parsing it, and displaying the associated description next to the file name in the directory listing.

Another nice feature of CuteFTP is the ftp Site Manager, shown in figure 16.14, which allows you to group your frequently visited ftp sites into a hierarchical folder structure. Although WS_FTP32 and most other ftp clients store a list of previously accessed ftp site information, they keep all of these entries in a single list, usually alphabetized. If you work with dozens or hundreds of ftp sites, this single list can become cumbersome. The ftp Site Manager in CuteFTP allows you to organize ftp sites in a hierarchical folder structure. You can group related sites, such as Hardware Vendors, in a folder. Because folders can contain other folders, you can extend this hierarchical organization to any extent you want.

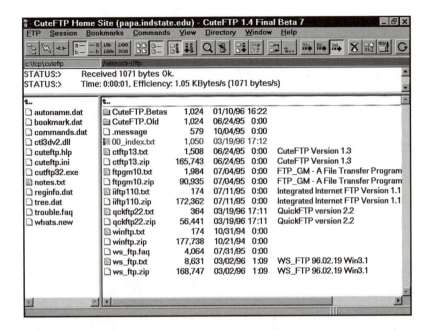

Fig. 16.13
CuteFTP main screen (showing Integrated Index Descriptions).

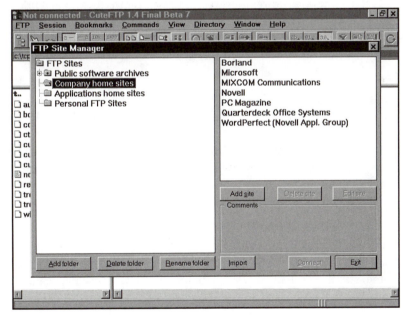

Fig. 16.14
CuteFTP ftp Site Manager.

V

Using the Internet

CuteFTP is modeled on the Windows File Manager interface, and provides toolbars and context-sensitive help. Because it caches recently visited directories and their associated index files, you need only transfer a directory listing once until it changes, instead of doing so each time you visit the site. CuteFTP allows you to download an entire directory tree as a single transfer, and includes the capability to recurse the tree. CuteFTP also has a "stop" command that works as you would expect it to. With most ftp clients, attempting to abort a transfer in progress results in a dropped connection. CuteFTP just stops the transfer and allows you to continue working with the connection.

There are several features that are implemented only in the registered version of the product. The most important of these for most people is the Bookmark feature. Other features limited to the registered version include the capability to resume interrupted downloads, support for non-standard ftp commands, direct server-to-server transfers, and a full ftp server built in to the CuteFTP product.

About the only drawback to CuteFTP other than the registration fee is the fact that it is somewhat slower than WS_FTP32 at transferring files. While reviewing it, I noticed that CuteFTP "felt" slower than WS_FTP32. To verify this, I used both CuteFTP v1.4 Final Beta 7 and WS_FTP32 version 96.03.02 on a very lightly loaded Ethernet connection to a local ftp server to transfer a single large file and to transfer several smaller files.

In both cases, I found that CuteFTP typically takes about twice as long to transfer files than does WS_FTP32. For example, transferring a 2.6M file with CuteFTP yielded throughput of 196.67 KBps, while the same file transferred with WS_FTP yielded throughput of 387.01 KBps. I then used both ftp clients to transfer a 302,311 byte file across a v.34 28,800 bps dial up link. Again, both the ftp server and the link were dedicated to the test. WS_FTP32 transferred the file in 1:48 at 2.72 KBps, and CuteFTP in 1:55 at 2.57 KBps.

When I contacted the author of CuteFTP, he was unaware of the problem, but immediately took steps to correct it. Within days, I received a fixed version. My informal benchmarks on the fixed version still showed that CuteFTP was somewhat slower than WS_FTP32, but the difference was much smaller. On large files and LAN transfers, CuteFTP went from taking twice as long to make transfers to only about 25 percent longer. On small transfers and those across dial-up lines, the difference was only about 10 percent in favor of WS_FTP32.

Don't make too much of these speed differences, however. For practical purposes, the delays inherent in using the Internet to connect to remote ftp servers will usually subsume any minor differences in speed between the two products.

Installing CuteFTP. Like WS_FTP32, CuteFTP has no formal installation procedure. Simply create a directory named as you choose and copy the CuteFTP distribution files to that directory. Add CuteFTP to your menu or create a shortcut on your desktop.

Configuring CuteFTP. Configuring CuteFTP is conceptually very similar to configuring WS_FTP, and most of the same options need to be set in the same way. CuteFTP is configured from the FTP-Settings dialog, with most user options set in the Options dialog.

Unlike WS_FTP32, CuteFTP uses Windows 95-style tabbed dialog boxes. You can change some options in CuteFTP, particularly display options, that are fixed in WS_FPT32. Conversely, some options are fixed in CuteFTP that are configurable in WS_FTP. Overall, however, after you configure either of these products, you should have no trouble configuring the other.

Using CuteFTP. Again, using CuteFTP to connect to remote ftp servers and to transfer files is quite similar to using WS_FTP32 for the same purposes. The two major differences, noted previously, are that the ftp Site Manager in CuteFTP allows you to organize your ftp sites in a hierarchical manner and that CuteFTP displays index file descriptions alongside the file names on the remote server directory. To connect to a site using CuteFTP, use ftp Site Manager to highlight the remote ftp server, and click the Connect button.

After you're connected, CuteFTP displays the local system directory on the left pane of the main display and the remote system directory on the right pane. To transfer files with CuteFTP, simply navigate to the proper directories on the remote and local machines, highlight the file you want to transfer, and double-click it.

Getting CuteFTP. The office ftp Site for CuteFTP is **papa.indstate.edu**. The directory /winsock-l/ftp contains the latest non-beta version. The directory /winsock-l/ftp/CuteFTP.Beta contains beta versions. The latest version of CuteFTP can usually be found in this directory.

The official CuteFTP Web site home page is **http://papa.indstate.edu: 8888/CuteFTP/**, which posts news about CuteFTP and contains a Frequently Asked Questions (FAQ) list.

V

Using the Internet

Announcements of new versions are posted regularly to the alt.winsock USENET newsgroup, and to the CuteFTP-L mailing-list and WINSOCK-L mailing-list. Set your Web browser to **http://papa.indstate.edu:8888/** for information about how to subscribe to this listserv.

Archiving Utilities

In the early days of BBSes, downloading files made two needs immediately clear. First, a utility was needed to combine related groups of files into a single file for ease of downloading. Second, a means of compressing files was needed to minimize transmission time. Both of these needs were met by archiving programs, the best known early example of which was System Enhancement Associates ARC.

Phil Katz released a competing product called PKARC and was promptly sued by SEA, which claimed that PKARC infringed their file storage format, their file extension name, and some of their algorithms. Mr. Katz settled with SEA and then released a modified version of his program called PKZIP. The BBS community in general had sympathized with Mr. Katz's position during the lawsuit. Many BBS sysops stopped using the SEA product and switched, literally overnight, to using PKZIP. PKZIP became the dominant file archiver, and ARC was relegated to a historical footnote.

Compression utilities like PKZIP are able to create their archive files in one of two formats:

- *Native Archive Format* files are indicated by a file extension peculiar to that program. For example, PKZIP creates archive files with a ZIP extension, Robert Jung's ARJ compressor creates ARJ files, and so on. In their native compressed format, the files are useless to you. You need to use an archive utility to expand these archives to their original form.

- *Self-Extracting Executable Format* files are simply compressed files that have had a program stub added to allow them to run as EXE program files. When the EXE file is run, it expands and uncompresses the encapsulated archive file automatically, eliminating the need to use a special archive utility to retrieve the original contents of the compressed file.

Today, most of the archived files you download from ftp sites will be either ZIP files or self-extracting executables. You'll also run into an ARJ or LZH archive occasionally. If you work with UNIX files, you'll see TAR, GZIP, ZOO, Z, and GZ files, as well as some more esoteric extensions.

To handle this variety of compression types, you need an archiving utility specific to each type of file. The problem is, the native compression utilities are DOS programs, many of which will not run under Windows NT. Fortunately, archive utilities that are designed to run under Windows are available. The following sections look at a couple of these products.

PKZIP for Windows 2.0

The long-awaited Windows version of PKWare's popular PKZIP utility finally began shipping in February, 1996. PKZIP for Windows, shown in figure 16.15, is essentially a 16-bit Windows 3.*x* port of the original DOS PKZIP v2.06g. As you might expect from a program from PKWare, PKZIP for Windows is designed to handle only the ZIP compression format.

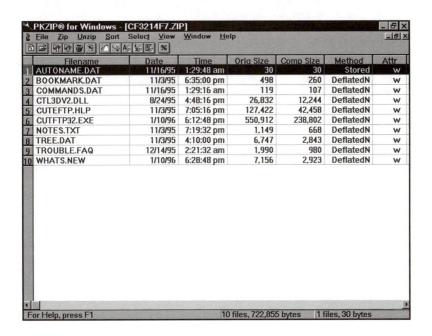

Fig. 16.15
PKZIP for Windows main screen.

Although PKZIP for Windows has had some enhancements made to it with the goal of providing at least nominal support for Windows 95, it is not the best primary choice of archiver for use with Windows NT. It has several problems, most notably the fact that the long file name support implemented for Windows 95 does not work properly under Windows NT.

V

Using the Internet

For all its faults, PKZIP for Windows is still worth installing on your hard drive because it is the only Windows-based ZIP archive utility that provides full support for all ZIP compression features. If, for example, you need to process a ZIP file that has been encrypted or spans multiple floppies, PKZIP for Windows is your best choice.

You can get the shareware version of PKZIP for Windows via anonymous ftp from **ftp.pkware.com** in the /PUB/PKWARE directory, or by setting your Web browser to **www.pkware.com**.

Caution

PKWare products, perhaps because they're updated infrequently, have unfortunately been a target for malicious mischief.

For the last year or more, a Trojan Horse version of PKZip has been in circulation on BBSes and the Internet. This version, variously named PKZ300.ZIP and PKZ300B.ZIP, will destroy the contents of your hard drive if you run it.

Most BBS syops and all of the commercial online services take great care to avoid posting programs like this for public download. However, to play it safe, download the latest version of PKWare utilities directly from their Web site, at **www.pkware.com**.

On the CD

WinZIP 6.0a for Windows

Once in a while, you run across a product that is so clearly superior to its competitors that it becomes a must-have for your tool kit. WinZIP from Nico Mak Computing, shown in figure 16.16, falls in this category. It integrates seamlessly with Windows NT Explorer, and allows you to view archives, add and remove files, create new archives, and so on by simply pointing, clicking, and dragging.

You can add a file to an existing archive simply by dragging it to the open archive within WinZIP and dropping it. You can create new archives simply by dragging a file or a group of files to the WinZIP icon and dropping them. Opening archives is just as easy. You can extract a file from an existing archive simply by highlighting it and dragging. If it is a program file, it will be launched. If it is a data file, WinZIP will invoke the application program associated with it in the Registry.

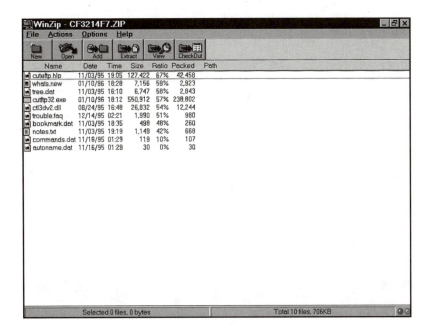

Fig. 16.16
WinZIP for
Windows main
screen.

One of the nicest features of WinZIP, particularly if you download a lot of
shareware, is its capability to do a "trial run" by temporarily installing a program using the Checkout and Install feature. You can try the new program
from within WinZIP. If you like it, you keep it. If you don't, you can uninstall
it automatically, because it was never really installed to start with.

You can always get the latest version of WinZIP on the Web from **http://
www.winzip.com**. You can also call 800-242-4775 to order it directly. The
cost is $29. It may be the best $29 you'll ever spend.

Accessing the USENET with news

Although the Web gets most of the attention nowadays, there's an older service on the Internet with millions of users that accounts for a significant
amount of the total traffic on the Internet. The USENET isn't technically a
part of the Internet, but because it uses the Internet to deliver its traffic, most
people still think of it as being an Internet service.

The USENET is difficult to describe until you've actually seen it. Imagine
every conference area on every BBS in the world combined into a single gigantic entity. Then throw in every SIG, Conference, and Roundtable area on
every commercial service for good measure. You still don't have anything approaching the USENET in size or diversity.

The USENET comprises thousands of individual conferences, called *newsgroups*. Each newsgroup is devoted to a particular topic. If you're looking for home improvement tips, you can find them in a newsgroup called misc.consumer.house. If you're trying to fix your car, or want to talk about gay rights, you can find newsgroups devoted to these topics. Almost any imaginable topic—and some unimaginable ones—has a newsgroup devoted to discussing it. At last count, there were about 15,000 newsgroups available, although your service provider may not carry all of them.

Messages can be posted to any of these groups by anyone who has access to the newsgroup on the USENET. In turn, anyone with access can read any message in any group to which he subscribes. A very active general interest newsgroup may have hundreds of new messages added every day. A less active newsgroup, or one focused on a more obscure topic, may have only a few messages posted each month.

Using listservs

An alternative to the USENET exists in the form of Internet mail-based mailing lists called *listservs*. Thousands of listservs exist, with topics generally paralleling USENET newsgroups. In fact, some USENET newsgroups are available in digest form on listservs.

A listserv is an automated mailing list. When you post a message to the listserv, it sends a copy of that message to all other subscribers to the listserv. You, in turn, receive copies of all other messages posted to the listserv.

Listservs typically have two e-mail addresses. The first, usually in a form something like `subscribe-list@something.someplace.edu`, is intended for administrative messages, such as requests to subscribe to or be removed from the list. The second, something like `listserv@something.someplace.edu`, is the address you use to post new messages and replies.

Some people love listservs and some hate them. There is a key difference between the USENET and listservs. With the USENET, you choose when to read new articles by running your newsreader. With listservs, new articles arrive in your e-mail box as they're posted.

Like USENET newsgroups, some listservs are moderated and others are wide open. Consider carefully before subscribing to a listserv. A busy one can generate several hundred messages a day, and every one of these ends up in your e-mail in-box. Many listservs offer you the option of getting each article as an individual mail message or having an entire day's articles sent to you as a single message in digest form.

If you do subscribe, make sure you don't lose the address for administrative correspondence in case you want to drop the listserv. Everyone hates to see "get me off this list" messages in the general flow of articles.

If you want to explore using listservs, set your Web browser to **http://tile.net/listserv/** for a searchable list of Internet listservs.

To keep things manageable, the USENET is set up on a hierarchical basis. Each of the top level USENET groups may include hundreds or thousands of individual newsgroups organized hierarchically beneath it. There are many major top-level groups, most of which will probably be available from your provider. There are other minor top-level groups with limited distribution that may not be available to you. Here are the major top-level groups:

- *alt.* Includes groups devoted to almost anything imaginable. The other top-level groups have a formalized process for creating a new group within that domain. Anyone can create an alt. group, and it seems that most people have. Most of these groups are simply noise, and contain few if any messages. Some, however, are very active groups with useful content. The alt. domain allows those who feel unduly constrained by the formal USENET process for creating new groups to create their own. Sometimes the results are interesting.

- *biz.* Includes commercially oriented groups. Here, for example, you find groups actively sponsored by industry leaders, such as Digital Equipment Corporation and Telebit. Here also are paid-subscription groups, such as Clarinet.

- *comp.* Includes hundreds of groups devoted to all aspects of computers, networking, and related topics.

- *misc.* Includes groups that don't fit anywhere else in the hierarchy. Many of the most interesting groups are in this domain.

- *news.* Includes groups that focus on USENET specific news. Newly created newsgroups are announced here, as are votes on whether a new group should be created. Information for new users is also posted here periodically.

- *rec.* Includes groups devoted to recreational pursuits. If you play bridge, for example, you'll find a group where you can discuss your bidding and dummy play with others of similar bent. If you engage in sports, listen to music, or do just about anything at all with your spare time that someone else on earth also does, you'll find a newsgroup here devoted to discussing it.

V

Using the Internet

- *sci*. Includes groups devoted to hard science; it's populated mainly by professional scientists.

- *soc*. Includes groups devoted to the world of sociology. If you're interested in learning about the lifestyles of the rich and famous—or those of the poor and unknown, for that matter—you'll find it here. Discussions of everything from British culture to Australian Aborigines find a home here.

- *talk*. Includes groups for those who like to debate the unresolvable. More flaming (exchanges of pointed personal comments) goes on here than anywhere else on the USENET. If you're pro-life and looking for an argument, you'll find it here. Neo-Nazis duke it out with communists, and gay rights advocates with skinheads. Nothing ever gets done in these groups, and no one ever changes his mind. If you're actively looking for a place to waste some time, this is it.

Newsgroups come in two varieties. Unmoderated newsgroups allow anyone to post an article directly to the group. As a result, the signal-to-noise ratio is often pretty low. You'll find scads of "me-too" messages, blatant advertisements, money-for-nothing deals, mindless flames, and so on.

Moderated newsgroups, on the other hand, do not allow direct posting. Instead, you submit your article to the moderator, who decides whether it should be posted. If so, he posts it to the newsgroup. If not, he sends you a rejection notice. A moderated group stays very much on-point, because the moderator eliminates the garbage messages before you see them.

Newsgroup moderators are volunteers for one of the worst jobs on earth. No one ever thanks them for the not-insignificant effort they make on behalf of the group. There is no shortage of complaints, however, particularly from those who have had articles rejected for publication. If you've been formally diagnosed as masochistic, consider a career as a newsgroup moderator. It doesn't pay anything, but you'll get all the abuse you could possibly ask for.

Caution

It's easy to make a name for yourself on the USENET. All you need to do is engage in *flaming* or *spamming*.

A *flame* is USENET jargon for a personal attack on another poster. No one objects to your taking exception to statements made by another poster, but the anonymity of the USENET makes it very easy for otherwise polite people to exceed the bounds of decency. It's fine to say "I disagree with your statement." It's even marginally acceptable to simply say, "you're wrong," if you're really sure that's the case. What's not fine is to say, "you're a complete moron and your mother wears Army boots." Unfortunately, that or even worse equivalents are frequently seen on the USENET.

When you flame someone, they'll flame you back—count on it. Others will join in, and pretty soon there's a flame war between a few participants, who generally ignore the protests of the other users of the group. Some flame wars are so long-lived and become so intense that they render the group essentially useless for its original purpose. Other users give up in disgust and go elsewhere. Don't get involved in a flame war. Use common sense and you'll do fine.

The other no-no is called a *spam*, which consists of cross-posting an article to numerous newsgroups whose topics are completely unrelated to the content of the article. Some notable spams, including the notorious Green Card spam, are posted to hundreds or even thousands of newsgroups. No one in these groups wants to read these messages, but they clutter up the group anyway.

Curiously, many spams are accidental. It happens this way: You see a message that is clearly inappropriate in the group you are reading, and so you post a reply to the message protesting it being posted in your group. What you don't notice is that yours is only one of hundreds or thousands of groups that the original article was posted to. When you click the Send button, your well-intentioned article of protest is posted to all of those same newsgroups, creating Son of Spam, which is just as annoying as was the original post. Be careful. This can happen even to experienced USENET users because good news software makes it easy—sometimes too easy—to cross post to multiple groups.

The USENET has caught a lot of heat recently. Most of the public outcry about pornography on the Internet results from USENET newsgroups devoted to some pretty tasteless topics. The Bavarian State Prosecutor Office forced CompuServe to eliminate access worldwide to scores of newsgroups it regarded as pornographic. The recent passage of the Communications Decency Act was motivated mainly by sexual content on the USENET. The Oklahoma City bombing and the Unabomber cases have focused attention on the availability of bomb-making instructions in USENET groups. Right now, it's pretty popular to bash the USENET. All of this doesn't change the fact that the USENET is an invaluable and unique forum for those with specialized interests. To get the most benefit from the USENET you need to install a good newsreader package, also called a news client.

Choosing a newsreader

To explore the USENET, you will need a newsreader or news client. More than with any of the other Internet utilities discussed in this chapter, the choice of newsreader is a very personal one. A newsreader that one user raves about may be the worst available so far as another user is concerned. Everyone uses the USENET differently, and everyone values different newsreader features. A feature that is critical to me may be unimportant to you and vice versa. For me, ease of use may be paramount, while for you robust threading capability may be all that matters.

Fortunately, there are many newsreaders available, and one of them probably has the right mix of features for you. Newsreaders come in three varieties:

- Look first to your Web browser. Packages like Netscape Navigator come standard with built-in newsreaders. Although these newsreaders are simple applications that lack the bells and whistles of serious newsreaders, they may be all you need if you plan to use the USENET only casually.

- The second source for a newsreader is an Internet Suite. Products like Wollongong Emissary, Delrina Cyberjack, Quarterdeck InternetSuite2, and the shareware product QVT all have built-in newsreaders. These products typically offer a much more complete feature set than the readers built in to Web browsers. If you choose to buy an Internet Suite product, chances are the newsreader will be more than sufficient for your needs.

- The third category is standalone newsreaders, such as Forté Agent and Free Agent, News Xpress and WinVM. If you use the USENET on a daily basis and monitor many groups, one of these packages is probably for you.

Newsreaders vary greatly in how well they support the basic functions needed to use the USENET efficiently. For most users, the most important aspects of a newsreader are how easily it handles discussion threads and how easily it handles posting new articles and follow-ups to existing articles.

USENET discussions comprise threads of related articles. Because a follow-up article may be posted at any time by someone anywhere on earth, and because it takes a while for articles to propagate throughout the USENET, discussions are non-linear with respect to time. You may in fact see a follow-up article before the original article appears on your news host. Because of this, as well as because of the sheer volume of unrelated articles posted in many newsgroups, it is essential that your newsreader provide good threading capabilities. A good newsreader will organize the mass of inbound articles into clearly delineated threads, allowing you to read and respond to those threads of interest to you and ignore the rest. A bad newsreader can make you sort through a lot of articles that are meaningless to you just so you can get to the ones you care about.

Although you may, like many new USENET users, *lurk* for quite a while—reading articles but not responding to any of them—you'll probably decide at some point to jump in and get your feet wet by posting a new or follow-up article. When you do, you will appreciate a newsreader that makes posting easy.

A third issue, important to some users and of no concern to others, is how easily the newsreader handles file attachments. Many newsgroups, particularly those dedicated to computer graphics and programming, have many articles that include binary file attachments.

The USENET is designed to operate over 7-bit links, so attempting to transfer a binary file directly would trash it beyond usability. One solution to this is a method called *uuencoding*, which translates 8-bit binary files into a form that can be transmitted as 7-bit symbols. These 7-bit symbols are then reassembled at the destination using the inverse process, called uudecoding.

Another solution is called *Multipurpose Internet Mail Extensions*, or *MIME*. MIME defines many standard object types, including text formatting enhancements, audio data, and graphics. A MIME-encoded message encapsulates these data as separate elements and includes headers that describe the number of enclosures and their types. This header information enables the receiving client to separate the enclosures properly and process them accordingly.

Note

Supplementary files can be included with an Internet mail message (or a USENET message) in one of two ways. The older method is called a *file attachment*, and sends each supplementary file as a separate mail message. The newer method is called a *file enclosure*, and combines all supplementary files with the original mail message.

Using enclosures simplifies mail handling and enables enhanced functionality, like MIME. However, some old e-mail clients—and a few poorly designed newsreaders—become confused when attempting to process enclosures. If someone to whom you are sending messages with enclosures is unable to decode them, simply reconfigure your e-mail software to use attachments instead.

Newsreaders vary greatly in their capability to handle MIME and uuencoded attachments and enclosures. The best of them automatically recognize the attachment or enclosure, decode it, and store it on your disk, all of this transparently. Mediocre newsreaders may require you to highlight the attachment or enclosure portion of the message and manually decode it and store it to disk. The worst newsreaders make no provision at all for handling attachments or enclosures. Using one of these, you must highlight the attachment or enclosure portion, save it to the Clipboard, manually write it to a disk file, and then finally run a separate decode utility to retrieve the binary file.

Forté Free Agent and Forté Agent

Forté Agent 1.0, shown in figure 16.17, is one of the few commercial standalone news clients available. It offers a robust feature set, including excellent threading capabilities and transparent decoding of file attachments. Its newsgroup views allow you to create a subset of groups of interest to you, and to watch or ignore specific threads within those groups. Agent is extremely customizable, allowing you to modify screen layout and program functioning to suit your needs. Agent is widely considered to be the best available newsreader for power users. Its only drawback is that the sheer number of features and options can be confusing for novice users.

Fig. 16.17
Forté Agent main screen.

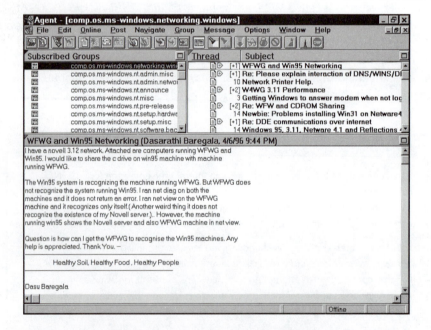

Forté also makes available a freeware version of Agent, called Free Agent. Free Agent trims some of the more advanced features of Agent, but the result is still a more powerful newsreader than most of its competitors. Both Agent and Free Agent can be used as offline readers, allowing you to log on, retrieve new articles in groups to which you are subscribed, log off, and read and reply to those articles at your leisure. When you again log on, the Forté software gets new articles and sends any replies you have written.

If you find that the newsreader included in your Web browser is inadequate for your needs, try Free Agent first. You may find that it does everything you need to do. If not, Agent is an easy and inexpensive upgrade.

You can download Agent and Free Agent from:

http://www.forteinc.com

On the Web

Agent costs $29 for the downloaded version or $40 plus shipping and handling for the full version with disks and manual. Free Agent is free for non-commercial use. You can reach Forté at 619-431-6496.

News Xpress for Windows 95

News Xpress, shown in figure 16.18, contains most of the features required in a good newsreader. It includes inline image viewing and built-in support for uuencode, uudecode, and Base64, along with myriad other features. One aspect in which it betters the Forté product is in its handling of articles cross-posted to several groups, allowing you to avoid re-reading the same article in different groups. Two features it lacks are robust threading and the capability to conveniently work offline. It is available in 16-bit and 32-bit versions, both of which are fast.

Unfortunately, the product is difficult to recommend for most users because

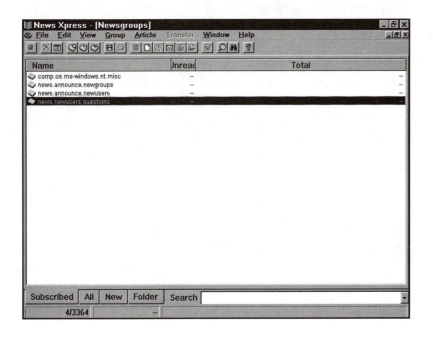

Fig. 16.18
News Xpress main screen.

V

Using the Internet

it is buggy, at least in the beta version I reviewed, and because the documentation is poor. However, earlier versions of News Xpress have been well thought of by many users, so it may be worth your time to check out the final version when it ships.

On the Web

You can get the latest information about News Xpress, including a FAQ, and download it from:

http://www.malch.com

Connecting to Remote Hosts Using Telnet

Telnet allows you to connect in terminal mode to a remote host. Telnet initiates a connection to the remote host's login program. You are always challenged to supply a valid username and a password, if required for the account. Remote login (*rlogin*) allows for "trusted hosts" to login to a host without going through the login process. Because the risk to system integrity is great with rlogin, the remote host's system administrator has to configure his system to allow you to connect via rlogin.

The explosion of the Web and the rich graphics content of today's Internet has made character mode products like Telnet much less important than they were formerly, but there are still times when a Telnet client is the only product that will do the job. You should have a good one in your grab bag. There are scores of shareware and freeware Telnet clients available, varying greatly in their feature sets and in how well they implement terminal emulation.

One of the best Telnet packages I've found is a part of a shareware Internet Suite called QVTNet. QVTNet provides an excellent Telnet client called Terminal, shown in figure 16.19. It also bundles a comprehensive set of clients for ftp, gopher, mail, news, and lpr. It provides servers for ftp, RCP, and SMTP.

All of the various clients and servers are quite good, and are worth installing to check them out. About the only product QVTNet doesn't put in the box is a Web browser. Because many people who choose to use an Internet Suite will elect to substitute their own Web browser for that contained in the suite, QVTNet provides a viable alternative to commercial Internet Suites. License QVTNet, add a copy of Netscape Navigator or another Web browser, and you have all the tools you'll need to access almost any service on the Internet.

Fig. 16.19

QVTNet terminal
screen.

As competent as are the other components of QVTNet, the jewel in the
crown is the Terminal program, which is itself worth more than the cost of
the entire QVTNet suite. Terminal outperforms the most expensive commercial Telnet packages at a fraction of their cost. Terminal is very flexible,
customizable, and easy to use. Most important, it is an excellent DEC VT200
Series terminal emulator. Although many products claim to provide DEC VT
terminal emulation, most such emulations are seriously deficient, including
those in many of the expensive commercial products. QVTNet gets DEC emulation right.

QVTNet uses a formal Windows installation process. If you download
QVTNet via the Web or an ftp server, you will receive it in the form of a ZIP
file. Decompress the ZIP file and run SETUP.EXE. QVTNet installs itself via a
wizard by default to the C:\PROGRAM FILES\QVTNET40 directory and creates a Programs-QVTNet group on your Start menu. You are given the opportunity to select which components to install via a series of check boxes, all of
which are checked by default.

QVTNet is available from numerous ftp sites including **ftp://OAK.
Oakland.edu**. Look in the /SimTel/win95/winsock/ directory for the latest
version of QVTNet, which, at the time of this writing, is QVTNET402.ZIP.

The registration fee for QVTNet 4.0 is $40 U.S. plus $5 for shipping and handling, with volume discounts and site licenses available. You can contact

QPC Software at P. O. Box 226, Penfield, NY 14526, or at 716-381-4610 (voice) or 716-381-1215 (fax). You can also contact QPC Software via Internet mail. Direct sales questions to **robin@qpc.com** and technical questions to **chloe@qpc.com**.

Internet Suites

Although many will prefer to select among best-of-breed applications to fill out their Internet tool kits, an alternative exists in the form of commercial Internet Suites. These suites typically include a Web browser, clients for ftp, news, and Telnet, and a mail package. Many include other utilities, and some throw in everything but the kitchen sink. There are good arguments to be made for selecting an integrated Internet Suite product that provides all or many of these same tools in a single box.

- The single source issue can be compelling in corporate environments. The fact that you can depend on formal technical support from a single vendor rather than using hit-or-miss support from several shareware authors can make the difference between an installation that is supportable and one that is not.

- If you will be installing Internet utilities on many workstations, the ease of installation and administration of the suites makes them almost an automatic choice. Even if the alternative is using completely free software, the staff time and associated costs required to install the "free" software will probably make it ultimately much more costly than the commercial suites.

- The integration of the better suites makes them much easier to learn and to use than an eclectic collection of shareware. Particularly if you are installing Internet utilities for casual users, you will find that using a suite results in reduced demands for training and support, with costs reduced accordingly.

- Even in terms of absolute cost, suites can offer a good deal. The days of $500 commercial Internet suites are long gone. With street prices now ranging from less than $50 to something over $100, the suites provide a lot of bang for the buck. The cost to license even a few standalone shareware Internet utilities can rapidly exceed the cost of a commercial suite.

Commercial Internet Suites vary in quality from very good to almost unusable. The worst of them are simply thrown-together collections of unrelated programs, with little or no effort made to integrate the disparate elements. The best of them offer competent utilities with a high degree of integration.

Even the best of them, however, have some weak components. When compared to the best of the standalone Internet utilities, a typical high quality suite has one or two strong components, several mediocre ones, and perhaps one or two that are truly awful. The weakest component is often the Web browser. Most suites base their browsers on modified versions of Mosaic, which was a wonderful browser in its day but was long ago overtaken in features and functionality by more modern browsers, like Microsoft Internet Explorer and, in particular, Netscape Navigator.

If you're putting together an Internet tool kit for only yourself, you will almost certainly be better off assembling best of breed individual components. That way, you get the best in each category, and personal preferences can take free reign. You may end up paying more for your tool kit, but you'll have exactly the tools you want to do the job.

If you are selecting utilities for your company as a whole, give strong preference to buying a suite. If the suite you would otherwise choose has one component you just can't live with, don't overlook the possibility of using the suite to provide most of your Internet tool kit and adding a single component to fill it out. Many organizations which have standardized on Netscape Navigator or Microsoft Internet Explorer continue to use them, simply replacing the suite browser with their preferred browser.

The following sections take a closer look at three of the best Internet Suites.

Delrina Cyberjack

The recent acquisition of Delrina by Symantec might have been expected to cause a few problems with integrating product lines and shipping new releases, but if Cyberjack 7.0 is an example to go by, the merger seems to have gone smoothly. With Cyberjack 7.0, Delrina has shipped one of the best Internet Suites on the market.

Cyberjack is a full-featured product, allowing users to access almost any content type available on the Internet. It includes a Web browser, clients for ftp, news, Gopher, Archie, and Internet Relay Chat (IRC). Cyberjack installs easily and requires very little tinkering to get it set up, automating much of the process. After it's installed, users will find it well-integrated with an intuitive user interface.

One of the nicest features of Cyberjack, and one that should be imitated by other software vendors, is its patch update feature. The increasing ubiquity of Internet access to the desktop means that Internet enabled applications like Cyberjack have easy access to vendor Web and ftp sites. Cyberjack makes the most of this fact by allowing you to update your copy of Cyberjack simply by making a menu choice. Cyberjack does the rest, automatically connecting to the Symantec server, determining if a patch or an updated version of the software exists, downloading any such patches, and applying them. All of this is done without user intervention after the Update selection is made. Pretty slick.

The individual components of the Cyberjack suite vary from mediocre to very good. All of the various clients are at least competent, although none is as good as the best standalone products in that category.

Perhaps the weakest component is the rather pedestrian Web browser. Although competent enough if not compared too closely to state of the art browsers, like Netscape Navigator, the Cyberjack browser, shown in figure 16.20, lacks support for functions that are almost taken for granted in more competent browsers. For example, the Cyberjack browser supports neither tables nor inline JPEG decoding. Perhaps the most puzzling omission is the lack of a Home button. Although you can specify an URL as your home page and have that page invoked at startup, there is no way to return to that page during a session short of seeking it out and reloading it manually.

Fig. 16.20
Cyberjack browser.

Cyberjack is built around the Guidebook, shown in figure 16.21, which allows you to create and organize a personal list of favorite Internet resources. Guidebook is reminiscent of NT Explorer, using a hierarchical folder structure to organize your favorite Internet sites. The default Guidebook setup includes hundreds of Web pages, UseNet newsgroups, and ftp sites to get you started—and updates are available automatically from the Symantec server. You can add your own sites easily with a single click.

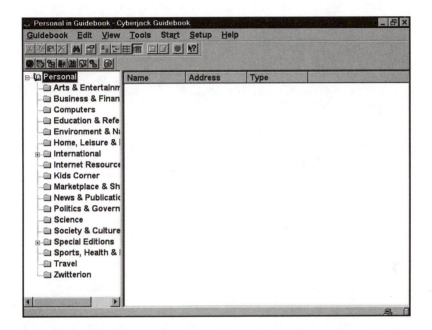

Fig. 16.21
Cyberjack
Guidebook.

Cyberjack uses OLE 2.0 to integrate all of its individual applications, including the Web browser, the ftp client, the newsreader, e-mail, and the Guidebook itself. For example, if a friend sends you e-mail that mentions a particular Web site, simply clicking the URL for that site invokes the Web browser and loads the home page. Similarly, right-clicking an Internet address invokes the Windows Messaging System mail client to send a mail message to that address.

If you can live with the rather quirky and feature-poor Web browser, Cyberjack is an excellent choice. New users will find using it intuitive, making access to various Internet resources almost transparent. Even power users will be happy with most of its features. The MIS department will be happy with its ease of installation, configuration, and management. At a street price of under $100, Cyberjack has a lot to offer.

Quarterdeck InternetSuite2

Quarterdeck InternetSuite2, shown in figure 16.22, is an interesting product. Of the three Internet Suites I examined, Quarterdeck's product is notable for consistency. Installation and configuration goes quickly, aided by a wizard that automates much of the process. InternetSuite2 offers a full selection of high quality clients that are well integrated. Relative to the best-of-breed standalone client products, the components of InternetSuite2 lose, but in many cases not by much.

Fig. 16.22

InternetSuite2 Quarterdeck Message Center (QMC).

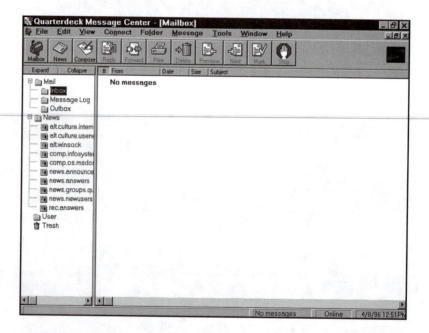

The weakest point of most Internet Suites is their Web browser. Both Netscape and Microsoft believe that owning the standard for Web browsers is the key to succeeding in the Internet market, and both are striving to gain the lead. Netscape has succeeded in maintaining the lead, but must continually advance the state of the art in Web browsers in order to prevent Microsoft from overtaking it. Accordingly, the Web browser market is on a very short development cycle, with major new releases occurring every three to six months. None of the vendors of Internet Suites have been able to keep up with this frenetic pace, and the Web browsers they bundle are typically a year or more out-of-date in function.

Fig. 16.23
InternetSuite2
QMosaic.

Quarterdeck's entry, QMosaic, shown in figure 16.23, is no exception to this rule, but it at least runs a close third to the two major competitors. In addition to the Web browser features you would expect, Quarterdeck integrates support for e-mail, ftp, and Telnet into QMosaic. It supports most advanced HTML features, and includes integrated helper applications like Adobe Acrobat, QuickTime, and RealAudio. For those concerned about smut on the Internet, Quarterdeck also includes CyberSitter to restrict access to pornography. About the only thing missing in QMosaic is support for frames and Java.

If you're looking for a commercial Internet Suite, Quarterdeck InternetSuite2 may be your best choice. It offers a full complement of high quality clients, including a Web browser that doesn't give much away to Netscape. Novices will find it easy to use, and power users will be satisfied with its feature set. Again, MIS will find it easy to install, configure, and support. At a street price of about $50, InternetSuite2 offers more than any other Internet Suite product out there for the price, commercial or shareware.

Wollongong Emissary

If integration is your top priority in choosing an Internet Suite, take a close look at Wollongong Emissary, shown in figure 16.24. Emissary 1.1 includes clients for Web browsing, e-mail, ftp, and news. Of the three Internet Suites I examined, Emissary is the most tightly integrated, and perhaps the most powerful. Like the other products I looked at, Emissary installs and configures easily, making it an excellent choice for company-wide deployment.

Fig. 16.24

Wollongong
Emissary 1.1 main
screen.

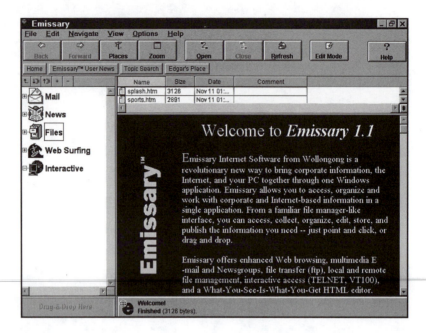

Proving its corporate orientation, Emissary is available in two versions. The $99 retail Desktop version provides a set of utilities comparable to the other Internet Suites discussed in the previous sections. The $499 retail Office version is intended to serve as the foundation of a corporate Intranet, and adds extended terminal emulation, an ftp server, and ipr/lpr print utilities.

As is usually the case with Internet Suites, the Emissary Web browser, shown in figure 16.25, is the weakest component, lacking support even for tables. This weakness, however, is offset by many strengths. Emissary provides strong clients for ftp, news (shown in fig. 16.26), and mail. Its greatest strength is that it organizes all of your personal Internet resources using an interface reminiscent of NT Explorer, with the left pane listing remote files and the right pane displaying them with Emissary's built-in viewers. Emissary automatically selects the correct viewer for the document type.

Emissary provides bookmarks that allow you to organize your personal Internet sites using a folder metaphor. You can create folders for related groups of sites and organize these folders on any basis you choose. Because a folder can contain any content type supported by Emissary, you can mix and match Web sites, ftp sites, newsgroups, and e-mail messages in a single folder. All documents are "live," so you can, for example, click an URL in a mail message and automatically invoke the Web browser to load that site. Any document of any content type, including HTML Web pages, can be edited at any time.

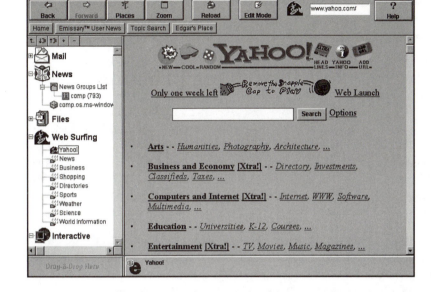

Fig. 16.25
Wollongong
Emissary 1.1 Web
Browser.

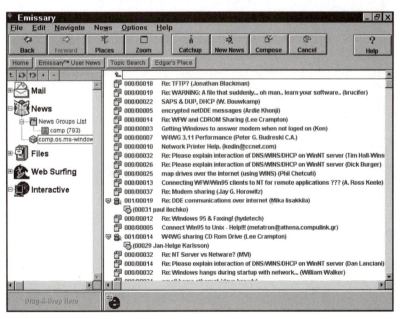

Fig. 16.26
Wollongong
Emissary 1.1
newsreader.

V

Using the Internet

The high level of integration provided by Emissary is at once its greatest
strength and its greatest weakness. Although, as with the other products, you
can always substitute a more competent Web browser, doing so with
Emissary gives up many of the benefits of using the product. More Web sites

every day are implementing the HTML extensions and other enhancements driven by Netscape Navigator and Microsoft Internet Explorer. Until Wollongong enhances the Web browser in Emissary to support at least the more popular of these extensions, using it limits your options.

Simple Network Time Protocol (SNTP)

One of the minor aggravations of working with PC's is that their clock/calendars frequently fail to keep time accurately. In the past, if you needed accurate time on your PC clock, the best alternative was to pay several hundred dollars for the special radio and interface board needed to receive accurate time information and set your PC according to the time tick received on the radio.

If you need extremely accurate time, the radio method is still the best alternative. However, if getting the time right to within a few tenths of a second is close enough for your purposes, consider using one of the utilities described in the following sections. Both are implementations of the Simple Network Time Protocol (SNTP) described in RFC 1361, which is itself a subset of the Network Time Protocol (NTP) described in RFC 1305. You can use either of these SNTP products to synchronize your PC clock to a time server running the Network Time Protocol (NTP).

WinSNTP

The WinSNTP SNTP client, shown in figure 16.27, is available in two 32-bit NT versions, one of which runs as an application and the other as an NT service. WinSNTP can maintain your PC clock to within 200 milliseconds of the time information provided by the time server, automatically correcting for time zones and daylight savings time changes.

WinSNTP can be invoked manually whenever desired, or it can be set to poll a timeserver on a regular basis. If set for single-shot use, the program runs, sets the PC clock to the correct time and then exits. If it is set to poll, both the initial polling frequency and the allowable time differential can be set. The program "learns" by observing the results of each poll and comparing them to the allowable time differential set by the user. If the disparity is wide, the poll frequency is increased. If there is little difference between the PC time and the actual time, the polling frequency is reduced to limit network traffic and the load on the timeserver.

Fig. 16.27
WinSNTP.

SNTP Server functions are built into WinSNTP, which means that you can designate one computer on your LAN as a time server and have all other workstations on the network synchronize their clocks to that of the master computer. You can use this feature to keep the clock/calendars of all of your computers synchronized even if you don't have a full-time Internet connection.

The application version of SNTP can be run as a hidden window by invoking it with the -h argument. Running it in this manner allows it to continue polling in the background without occupying space on your taskbar. Alternatively, you can install WinSNTP as an NT Service set to load at system startup.

About the only downside to WinSNTP is the $25 shareware registration fee and the fact that it requires somewhat more effort to configure initially than do some of its competitors. It is, however, a rock-solid product. After you load it, you can forget about it, secure in the knowledge that your PC time will always be correct, give or take a few milliseconds.

On the Web

You can always download the latest version of WinSNTP from
www.solaris.com

Fourth Dimension

Fourth Dimension, shown in figure 16.28, is a somewhat less ambitious product than WinSNTP, but its very simplicity may appeal to many users. It makes no attempt to implement the server functions or the variable polling rates of WinSNTP, and simply allows you to do one-shot polls or to set a specified polling frequency.

Fig. 16.28
Fourth Dimension.

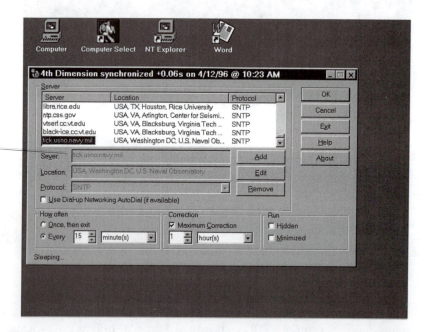

Fourth Dimension is freeware. The author, Rob Chambers, requests no payment and encourages free distribution. If you decide to use it, he requests that you mail him your comments at **robc@thinkman.com**.

On the Web

You can always get the latest version of Fourth Dimension from:

http://www.thinkman.com/~thinkman

CHAPTER 17

Building Your Own Web Site

by John Mikol and Michael Marchuk

Although building your own Web site may seem like an arduous task, the advent of Windows NT Web server software and HTML authoring tools have made the process much easier. This chapter takes you through the process of selecting the right Web server software for your application and then explores the HTML authoring tools needed to get your Web site up and running.

In this chapter, you'll learn about

- Web server software for Windows 3.1, Windows 95, and Windows NT
- Web page editors, from simple to complex
- Web page-checking tools

Overview of WWW Server Software

As the growth of the Internet progresses, so does the number of companies producing software applications for Internet implementation. Nowhere is this more evident than in the market for Windows NT- and 95-based WWW server software. A little more than a year ago there were no (that's right, none!) professional windows-based Web server software packages. Today, there are more than 20 and there are quite a few more on the horizon. This mirrors the situation in the software markets for Web browsers and browser add-on packages.

For both the corporate level publishing site and the home hobbyist, the availability of professional server software is clearly good news. The progression of the Internet from a domain of UNIX gurus and hackers to one that is accessible to Microsoft Windows users for both browsing and publishing is a significant breakthrough. The barrier for entry to publishing and communicating via the Web has fallen.

This cornucopia of server software leaves you with the dilemma of deciding which software will fit your site's needs. There are many issues to consider including:

- Costs
- Features
- Standards implementations

The original standard for Web servers comes from the NCSA (National Center for Supercomputing Applications) server software originally developed for the UNIX operating system.

You can read more about NCSA and its server platform at:

On the Web

http://hoohoo.ncsa.uiuc.edu.
Many Web servers are little more than this server ported to a different platform. However, most commercial servers now seek to differentiate themselves from the pack and often endeavor to set a new standard for others to follow. Our task is to decide which features are the most valuable to your organization as well as which features are likely to become irrelevant as development of Web servers progresses.

There are a number of excellent lists of available server software. At the Yahoo Internet Directory you will find links to commercial server software packages that are registered. You will also find terrific links to additional utilities and services that will help speed you on your way to running a perfect Web site.

On the Web

http://www.yahoo.com/Computers_and_Internet/Internet/ World_Wide_Web/HTTP/   At the World Wide Web Consortium (W3C) you will find in-depth information, white papers, and links to additional resources regarding all facets of the Web.

http://www.w3.org/pub/WWW

Survey of Server Software

As the demand for 32-bit Web servers has exploded, so has the dividing list of features. Here is a list of many of the top packages in terms of both market presence and popularity.

Microsoft Internet Information Server

The Microsoft Internet Information Server (IIS) for NT Server is a powerful and flexible tool for serving up Web pages. The IIS is actually three servers: World Wide Web, File Transfer Protocol (ftp), and Gopher. While the IIS is relatively new, it does have some fairly robust features such as a built-in database connectivity tool and advanced logging features. Additionally, IIS is a free add-on for Windows NT Server 3.51 and is included with Windows NT Server 4.0. Windows NT Workstation 4.0 includes a peer Internet server that provides a somewhat less robust feature set. Microsoft will be introducing an even more robust new Web server, code name Tarantula, which will provide more site management features and will run under Windows 95, Windows NT Workstation, and Windows NT Server. Some of Tarantula's features include:

- GUI administration tool
- Remote server management
- ODBC Database access
- Advanced server API set

You can find more information on the IIS server on the Web at:

http://www.microsoft.com/InfoServ/IISInfo.htm

On the Web

WebSite

WebSite, from O'Reilly & Associates, was one of the first commercial NT Web servers to be released. WebSite (see fig. 17.1) was written by Bob Denny who wrote an extremely popular Web server for 16-bit Windows.

> **Note**
>
> If you need to implement a Web server on a Windows 3.1 system, there is a server available. However, due to some of the serious architectural limitations of 16-bit Windows, your server performance and feature set will be limited. The Windows 3.1 Web server was written by Bob Denny, who later authored the popular WebSite server. The server is no longer enhanced or supported, but you can still get this Survey of Server Software at:
>
> **http://www.city.net/win-httpd/**

Fig. 17.1
O'Reilly WebSite software provides a very well-rounded environment for developing and running a Web site.

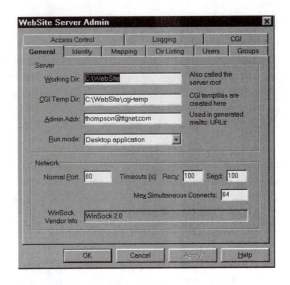

WebSite is a 32-bit multi-threaded server that allows you to use standard Windows programming languages to access Excel, FoxPro, and other data from within a Web document. Additional features include:

- WebSite 1.1 supports a Visual Basic 4 framework (CGI32.BAS) with sample applications as well as server-push applications.

- A graphical interface for creating virtual servers and it supports remote administration, password authentication, and access control.

- WebSite Pro features SSL for encrypted transactions.

- A GUI tool, Webview, that provides a tree-like display of the documents and links on your server.

- Wizards that automatically create common Web documents.

- Indexing and search tools to locate items anywhere on your site.

- Server Side Includes (SSI) so you can combine static and programmed documents on-the-fly, and common document components are easier to maintain.

On the Web

For more information on O'Reilly's Website software, see:

http://website.ora.com

EMWACs HTTPS for NT

The only freeware server on our list, it has been available for over a year courtesy of the European Microsoft Windows Academic Center. This server has been used widely across the Internet, and the Purveyor Server is a commercial adaptation of the HTTPS server.

The EMWACS server is well-suited to the simple serving of Web pages. It lacks any administration utilities and has only the most basic of features. If you are running a simple low-volume site and don't mind editing a few configuration files, then be sure and take a look. Features include:

- MAP file support
- Automatic Directory indexing
- CGI support
- Runs as a Windows Service
- Links to the WAIS toolkit for text searching and retrieval

To find more information about the EMWAC Web server or to download the server software, see: **http://emwac.ed.ac.uk**

On the Web

Purveyor for Windows NT and 95

The Purveyor Web server from Process Software has its origins in the EMWACs server listed above, but has quickly grown to become a full-featured server with advanced administration tools. Purveyor was one of the earliest commercial-strength NT Web servers and is highly regarded. One of the three servers to offer Proxy services, Purveyor also features advanced database publishing capabilities. The Purveyor product line spans Windows NT, Windows 95, NetWare, and VMS. An SSL enhanced server for secure transactions is in the works as well. Features include:

- Data Wizard simplifies integration of ODBC/SQL databases
- Internet Server API
- Advanced Proxy Services
- Advanced Logging features
- Remote Server Management
- Security implemented via Microsoft File Manager

For more information about the Purveyor Web server software, see:

http://www.process.com

On the Web

Netscape Communication/Commerce/FastTrack Servers for NT

Netscape, the company that publishes the popular Netscape browser also publishes a line of Web servers and related products. While Netscape was founded fewer than two years ago, the Netscape server development team includes many of the original members of the NCSA team.

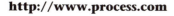

The Netscape server family is split into three components. The Communication server is a high-performance server for Windows NT. The Commerce server includes the features of the Communication server and also supplies the means for secure data transmission. The Netscape servers are cutting edge and have been priced accordingly. The FastTrack server (see fig. 17.2) is an entry-level, low cost server that includes configuration and authoring tools to enable a novice to bring up a Web site in short order. FastTrack includes new technologies that Netscape is integrating into the Commerce and Communications servers. Features include:

- Virtual Server hosting

- Remote graphical management via HTML forms

- Netscape Server Application Programming Interface (NSAPI) for programmable access to a suite of server application functions and a dynamic loading interface

- Integrated security using SSL, which incorporates public key cryptographic technology from RSA Data Security

- Remote administration using a Web browser

- Easy setup via Web forms-based tools

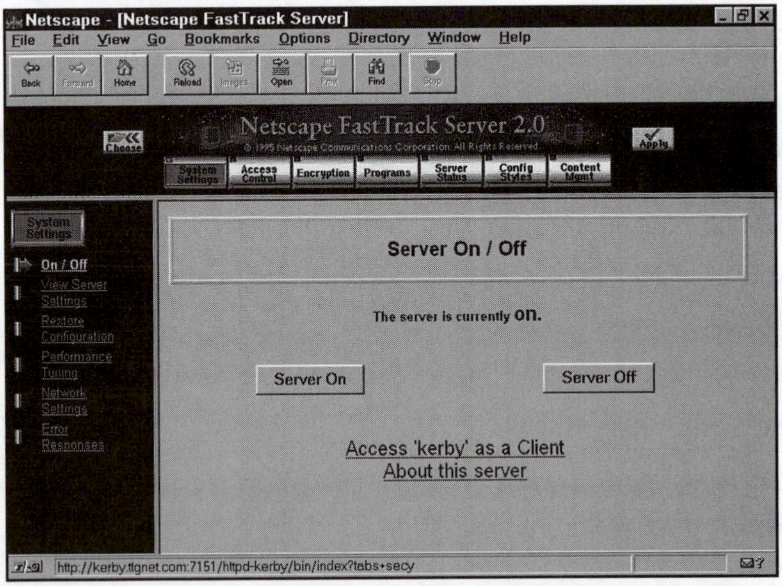

Fig. 17.2
Netscape FastTrack
Web Server
provides a high-
performance
server with an
entry-level feature
set.

You can find more information about Netscape's Web server line at:
http://www.netscape.com/comprod/netscape_commun.html

On the Web

Oracle WEB System

The Oracle Web system is from renowned database software developer Oracle Corporation. The Web System is from the newly evolving group of servers that are not based on static documents, but rather on dynamically created documents served up by a database. The Oracle 7 RDBMS is queried by the Web server and responds with pages created on-the-fly. Features include:

- Database driven Web pages
- Graphical Web and Database administration

See **http://www.oracle.com/products/websystem/webserver/** for more information about Oracle's Web server.

On the Web

CompuServe Spry Web Server and Safety Web Server for Windows NT

A robust Web server from the Spry Internet division of CompuServe, the Safety Web Server (see figs. 17.3 and 17.4) adds support for SSL and includes Spry's Internet Office, a suite of TCP/IP clients and servers including e-mail, NFS, telnet, and Spry's Mosaic Web browser. Features include:

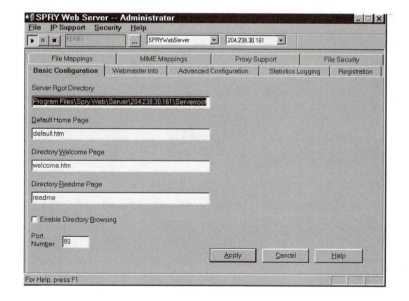

Fig. 17.3
Spry Web Server provides a good feature set for entry-level Web sites.

V

Using the Internet

Fig. 17.4
Spry's Safety Web
Server provides
services for larger
and more
complex Internet
sites.

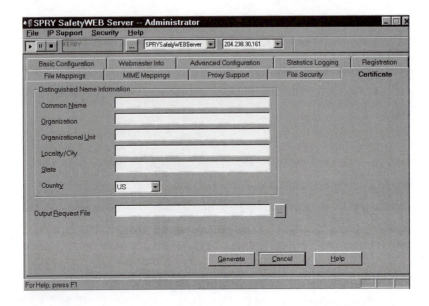

- Remote Administration from NT or Windows 95
- Virtual Server Hosting
- Extended logging to ASCII files and ODBC databases
- Direct Database Access to ODBC Compliant databases
- Caching Proxy Server to facilitate use with a firewall
- Supports compiled Windows DLLs for salability and high performance

On the Web

For more information on Spry's Web servers, see:

http://support.spry.com/public/iosws

Key Considerations for Server Selection

Selecting your NT-based Web server is (for the most part) a simple matter of selecting the features you need and matching them up with a reputable company. Cost is also a factor, but should be one to consider after you define your needs.

Features

First and foremost, define the features you need in a Web server. You should start this process by declaring the main purpose of the Web server. Will your site focus on document publishing, database access, financial transactions, or custom programming? Next, consider the overall environment in which your server will be running. Will you need to service large numbers of users? You will need a server that can handle the load. Will you need to manage and administer these users extensively? You will want a server with extensive administration tools.

When evaluating the type of Web server you will need:

- Examine your goals.
- Determine what features your software will need.
- Align your needs with the server software available.

Administration

The new generation of Windows-based Web servers now offer graphical administration tools. These tools make it much easier for you to set up and administer your server. If you are a non-technical shop, consider this a high priority. It will help you avoid wasted time and consultant fees.

Cost

The broad selection of NT- and 95-based servers run the gamut from free of charge for the EMWACs and IIS server, to several thousand dollars for the Netscape Commerce Server. Generally, the more features there are the more expensive the server is. Fortunately, as the market has matured, prices have dropped.

Company Strength and Commitment

In a rapidly maturing software market there will be many winners and losers. If your project requires a large resource commitment. take a close look at the vendor of your software. Do they have the financial wherewithal to ride out the storm? Or are they a one-product company in a crowded market? Building and maintaining a large Web site is a complicated process in and of itself. Access to bug fixes, upgrades, and technical support can prove to be extremely vital.

Extending Web Server Capabilities

A relatively new group of products is now available for use in extending the power and capabilities of your Web server. These products can be divided into roughly three categories.

Database

Large amounts of corporate data are stored in databases. The latest trend in Web services is to provide access to corporate data either directly from your Web server or via a database that you have imported this information into. The direction of NT and 95 database add-ons is to implement a direct connection to an already existing ODBC compliant database.

> **Note**
>
> ODBC is an acronym for Open Database Connectivity, a Microsoft strategy to pro-vide a standard interface for accessing heterogeneous databases. ODBC uses Struc-tured Query Language (SQL) as a standard for accessing data. This interface provides maximum interoperability; a single application can access different database man-agement systems through a common set of code. This allows a developer to build and distribute a client-server application without targeting a specific database man-agement system.

On the Web

You can learn more about ODBC and other Microsoft development strategies at **http://www.microsoft.com/DEVONLY/strategy/.** The value of Web services often rises dramatically when a company realizes that this is a terrific new tool for deploying a client-server database system.

Programming/Scripting

A new selection of products on the market allows you to provide sophisti-cated interaction with users via the Web. Instead of merely serving up pages and forms, you can build entire systems that bear little resemblance to their HTML forefathers. For several years scripting has been accommodated through a standard known as the Common Gateway Interface (CGI). This is a powerful means of providing a way to send data from a browser to a program that runs on the Web server.

Because the original Web servers existed solely in the UNIX environment, most of the tools used are foreign to our NT environment. Most of the cur-rently existing CGI programs were written using Perl and run on UNIX serv-ers. Fortunately for us, there are now more options that utilize languages more common to the Windows and Windows NT world.

> ### Note
>
> Perl is an acronym for Practical Extraction and Report Language and has achieved high popularity for ease of use in creating CGI programs. Perl has been ported to Windows NT, so you can now make use of the many Perl programs that are in the public domain. You can pick up the latest version of Windows NT Perl on Beverly Hills Software's Web site at **http://www/bhs.com/**.

> ### Tip
>
> The Windows NT Resource Center at **http://www.bhs.com/** contains a great wealth of information for anyone using or considering using Windows NT. The software library contains many great freeware, shareware, and evaluation programs for use with Windows NT and Windows 95.

Interestingly, CGI evolved as a superior method of enhancing Web servers instead of the method commonly referred to as a Server Include. The Server Include method is a powerful means of enhancing your server, but also has a number of potential security holes. Server Includes are now offered in many of the servers discussed here. The WebQuest server offers an enhanced specification referred to as SSI+. You can read more about this at **http://www. questar.com/ssiplus.htm**.

Development Aids

Now there are a number of products that conform to the CGI specification and provide a framework for programmers to utilize the languages they are most comfortable in. If your needs include extensive scripting, be sure to contact your programming software vendor to explore the available options. An excellent example of this type of product is the WebHub framework for Borland's Delphi language. Learn more at **http://www.href.com**.

HTML Editors and Tools

It's easy to write an HTML document. After all, the main document is nothing but ASCII text, and much of that is often the plain-language text that you're trying to communicate on the page. The tricky part is getting the proper tags in the right place to make your text and images come out looking like you want them to. Browser programs are very literal in the way that they interpret HTML, so errors in your HTML syntax make your page look very unusual. You need to take extra care to ensure that your page comes out looking like you planned.

Because HTML documents are all ASCII code, originally Web documents were written with simple text editors, such as the Windows Notepad. As people began writing longer and more complex documents, many turned to their favorite word-processing programs (which can save documents in plain ASCII text) and wrote macros and tools to help them.

As the Web expanded, dedicated HTML editing programs (similar to word processing programs, but designed to produce results for the screen and not the printed page) began to appear. These programs allow Web page creators to more quickly format their text into proper HTML format by allowing authors to have codes placed automatically around text at the click of a toolbar button. Stand-alone HTML editors have since evolved into very advanced HTML authoring systems which provide end-to-end support for the Web page creation process.

In addition to editors and authoring systems, special filters and utilities that convert existing documents to HTML format have also cropped up. These applications save authors an immense amount of time as they can take information formatted for other programs and mark it up with HTML to produce the same formatting on a Web page.

As you can see, there are many ways you can write your HTML documents; you can use your favorite line editor, a word processor, or a dedicated HTML tool. The choice of which system to use depends on personal preference and your confidence in your use of HTML.

Because many HTML-specific tools have checking routines or filters to verify that your documents are correctly laid out and formatted, they appeal to new writers of Web documents. They also tend to be friendlier and more graphically based than non-HTML editors.

On the other hand, if you're a veteran programmer or writer, you may want to stick with your favorite editor and use a filter or syntax checker afterwards. Luckily, there are ample tools available for whichever approach you take.

This section looks at five types of applications that are useful in developing HTML documents:

- Plain text editors and word processors
- Stand-alone HTML editing tools
- Advanced HTML authoring systems

- Converters and filters for importing other types of documents into HTML

- Analyzers and other tools that check the syntax of your HTML documents

Since new HTML authoring tools have become available all the time, you should check one of the following Web sites for the most up-to-date information. The World Wide Web Consortium maintains a list of HTML editing tools at **http://www.w3.org/hypertext/WWW/Tools/**.

On the Web

You can read Mag's Big List of HTML Editors by pointing your browser to:

http://union.ncsa.uiuc.edu/HyperNews/get/www/html/editors.html

And of course, Yahoo provides an extensive list of editing tools at:

http://www.yahoo.com/Computers_and_Internet/Internet/World_Wide_Web/HTML_Editors.

MS-DOS Editor

You may not have used it in a very long time, but the MS-DOS Editor is a perfectly good tool for composing or making quick changes to an HTML document. The Editor provides menu options for all of the basic editing operations like Cut, Copy, and Paste. It also has Find and Replace options to make it fairly easy to make global changes to your documents. The Editor automatically saves documents in ASCII format, so there's no need to do any special conversions.

The big drawback, of course, is that you have to open an MS-DOS window to get to the Editor. If you're not adverse to this, you can open up a window and type **edit** at the DOS prompt to fire up the Editor.

Windows Notepad

If you can't bring yourself to leave the Windows environment, you can use the Windows Notepad. Notepad is a fine way to edit HTML documents, as long as the documents are not too long. Notepad has a file size limit; any particularly complex HTML document probably exceeds its capacity.

Like the MS-DOS Editor, Notepad saves files in ASCII format. It also provides menu options to Cut, Copy, Paste and Find text, but it does not have a Find and Replace feature.

Notepad proves most useful if you just need to make a quick tweak on a document that's already mostly edited. You may be able to open the HTML document in Notepad and make the minor adjustment without having to go through the hassle of opening your word processor and activating the proper template.

> **Tip**
>
> If you use Notepad to edit HTML, choose Edit, WordWrap. Otherwise your HTML code can run off the edge of the window, and you'll have to scroll to see parts of it.

Windows WordPad

If the document you want to edit is too big for Notepad, Windows will give you the ability to open the document in WordPad—a document editor that occupies the middle-ground between a simple editor like Notepad and a full-featured word processor like Microsoft Word.

WordPad offers full-editing support through menu options to Cut, Copy, Paste, and Find and Replace. When saving a document in WordPad, you have a choice of several formats. Be sure to choose the Text Document option.

> **Tip**
>
> You'll need to turn word wrap on in WordPad as well when you work with plain text documents. You can do this by choosing View, Options. The Word Wrap radio buttons are on the Text tab of the Options dialog box.

> **Note**
>
> No plain text editor will check the syntax of your HTML for you. If you do most of your HTML authoring in a plain text editor, it's a good idea to check the HTML syntax in your documents before putting them on your server. See the "Analyzers" section at the end of this chapter for programs that will do HTML syntax checks.

Word Processing Programs

Because many people are already familiar with the editing features of their favorite word processor, a number of HTML authors have turned to creating specialized macros and tools that take advantage of the properties of the word processing programs to make editing HTML easier. Now, even developers are getting into the act, producing programs designed explicitly as add-ons for commercial word processors.

For whatever reason, be it the strong use of styles or an easy, powerful macro language, Microsoft's Word seems to be the word processor of choice for those writing HTML editing tools; the vast majority of these types of tools are written expressly for Word for Macintosh or Windows. The first two discussed in this section are simple shareware templates that add helpful toolbars and HTML-specific pull-down menu options to those already available in Word. Quarterdeck's WebAuthor 2.0 is a commercial package that not only provides assistance for HTML authoring, but for syntax checking as well. And naturally, Microsoft has an offering to enhance Word: Microsoft Internet Assistant turns Word into a fully functional Web browser, while also adding support for HTML editing.

CU_HTML

CU_HTML, named after the Chinese University of Hong Kong where it was created by Kenneth Wong and Anton Lam, is a template-based add-on for Word 2 and Word 6.

The information in this section is based on CU_HTML.DOT, version 1.5.3. You can acquire the template and its related files by directing your browser to: **http://www.cuhk.hk/csc/cu_html/cu_html.htm**

On the Web

This document provides information on the current release of CU_HTML and provides a link to the file cu_html.zip, which is the file you want to download.

CU_HTML comes with installation instructions in an HTML format. Use your browser to open the file CU_HTML.HTM. If your browser's not working, just open the Word document CU_HTML.DOC. After you install CU_HTML's files, you can select the CU_HTML template when you open a new document in Word.

If you choose this template, several new styles equivalent to HTML tags are loaded. By choosing Format, Style, you can apply formatting to produce the six heading levels, addresses, preformatted text, ordered and unordered lists, and horizontal rule. You can apply bold, italic, and underline styles using Word's usual formatting toolbar. When you instruct CU_HTML to write your final HTML document, it will convert these formats into the appropriate HTML tags.

There's also an extra pull-down menu, called HTML, and a new toolbar (see fig. 17.5). The HTML menu provides you with some options for tagging text, mostly for linking text in the document to other files (such as graphics or other hypertext links). Buttons on the toolbar replicate the choices found under the HTML menu, giving you quick access to these functions.

Fig. 17.5
Loading the
CU_HTML
template gives you
an HTML pull-
down menu and
extra toolbar to
assist you in your
editing.

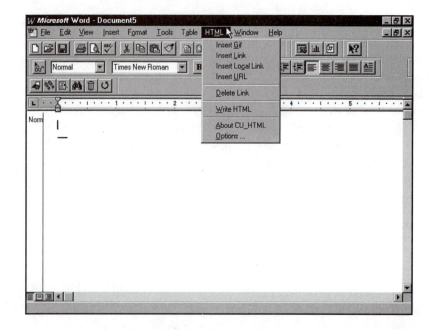

After you open a new document, you should save it. CU_HTML requires that you save a copy of the file before formatting text, placing graphics, and writing the final HTML file.

When you've entered text, you can use the options under the HTML menu to format links to other files. You can link to a graphics file with the Insert GIF option, or another locally stored HTML file with Insert Link. You can create a link to another section of your Web document with Insert Local link, or link to another document on the Web with Insert URL. The Delete Link option lets you remove any type of link you've inserted.

Like most of the templates for Word, CU_HTML creates files in Word format. You must be sure to save the completed document in HTML format before you try to use it on the Web. To do this using CU_HTML, choose HTML, Write HTML. This instructs CU_HTML to create an ASCII file in which all Word formatting codes are converted to HTML. The file will have the same name as your Word document, but it will end with the extension HTM.

GT_HTML

GT_HTML is a template add-on for Word developed at Georgia Tech. It is as easy to install as CU_HTML, but it provides many more editing support features.

The following section is based on GT_HTML, version 6.0d. You can download GT_HTML by pointing your browser to:

On the Web

http://www.gatech.edu/word_html/

Look for the download link to the file GT_HTML.ZIP.

Installation of GT_HTML is simple; just copy the template file gt_html.dot into your templates subdirectory for Word. If you activate the template when you open a new document in Word, you have the ability to add the two new toolbars shown in figure 17.6. To activate the toolbars, put a check in the boxes next to Toolbar 1 (Gt_html) and Toolbar 2 (Gt_html) by choosing View, Toolbars.

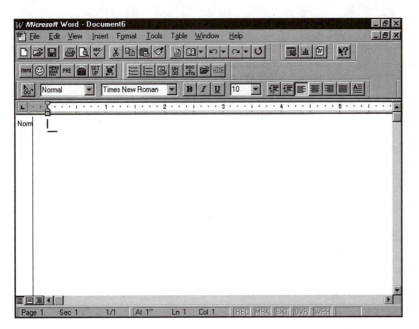

Fig. 17.6

When you install GT_HTML, you have the option of turning on two toolbars to help you edit HTML.

In addition to the two toolbars, GT_HTML adds HTML-related options to most of Word's pull-down menus. The new options appear at the bottom of each pull-down menu and start with HTML. Because GT_HTML doesn't load a lot of styles into Word like CU_HTML does, most of your special formatting will be done using the new menu options.

One of the more helpful menu options is the HTML Browser option under the File menu. Selecting this option opens the browser you configure to work with GT_HTML. Having quick access to a browser while you edit makes it easier to test your documents as you develop them.

Another helpful menu option is the HTML Toolbox under the Tools menu. You can quickly insert tags for rule, titles, comments, centering and blinking text, and line breaks using selections from the Toolbox. The Toolbox also gives you a way to launch GT_HTML's handy HTML Form Creator and HTML Table Converter. The Form Creator launches a second dialog box where you can configure your form input fields, while the Table Converter will convert a simple (no cell in the table spans more than one row or one column) Word table to HTML format. Toolbox items are shown in figure 17.7.

Fig. 17.7
GT_HTML's HTML Toolbox makes it easy to insert many types of HTML tags.

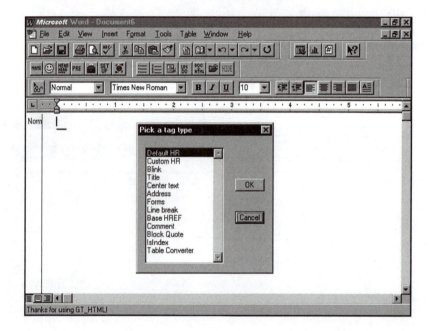

The Format menu includes options for formatting highlighted text as a heading, preformatted text, or an ordered or unordered list. To apply bold, italics, and underline styles, you can use Word's normal formatting toolbar. GT_HTML converts these formats to HTML tags when it saves the HTML version of your document.

Microsoft Internet Assistant for Word

Given the surge of HTML authoring add-ons for Word, it's no surprise that Microsoft itself has produced one. Internet Assistant for Word is a no-cost add-on that turns Word into a Web browser and includes styles, toolbars, and tools for authoring HTML.

In addition to the Internet Assistant for Word, Microsoft also produces assistants for Excel, Access, and Powerpoint.

For the latest release of the Internet Assistants and links to the downloadable files, direct your browser to:

On the Web

http://www.microsoft.com/msdownload/

Microsoft will also ship a copy on floppy disk to registered owners of Word for a shipping and handling charge of $5. Call (800) 426-9400.

After downloading the file, the installation of the Internet Assistant is fairly easy. If you have installed a Microsoft program yourself, this process should be familiar. During the installation, you are given the option to make Internet Assistant your default HTML browser. If you choose to do this, the Internet Assistant add-on will be placed in your Word Startup directory. This causes Internet Assistant's functionality to be loaded each time you start Word.

> **Caution**
>
> Be sure to close all open Windows applications, especially Word, before you install Internet Assistant.

The Internet Assistant Web Browser

When you start Word with Internet Assistant installed, the only difference you'll notice at first is that addition of the Switch to Web Browse View button shown in figure 17.8. Clicking this button takes you to the browser side of Word that Internet Assistant creates. As you can see in figure 17.9, the Word browser has most of the usual features found in other popular browsers including forward and backward navigation buttons, reload and stop buttons, and the ability to store the URLs of your favorite sites (Favorites). To return to the Word editing window, you can click the Switch to Edit View button.

Loading and Editing Documents

When you start a new document, you will find that you have access to a new template called HTML.DOT. This template provides an extensive set of HTML styles and additional menu options and toolbars to support HTML authoring. Figure 17.10 illustrates the modified toolbars. If you want to edit an existing HTML document, Word will automatically open the HTML template when you select a document with an htm extension.

Fig. 17.8
The Switch to Web Browse View button activates the Web browser features included as part of Internet Assistant.

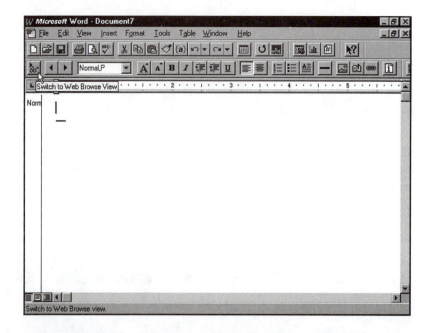

Fig. 17.9
The Word Web browser supports most popular browser features for navigation and bookmarking.

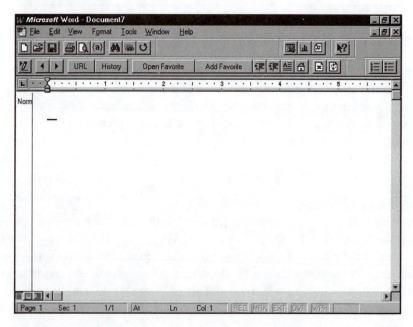

> **Note**
>
> In the figure, both the Standard and Formatting toolbars are open. Keep in mind that you can customize these toolbars, like all of the toolbars in Word. You can add buttons and rearrange their order; your toolbars may look different than those shown in figure 17.10.

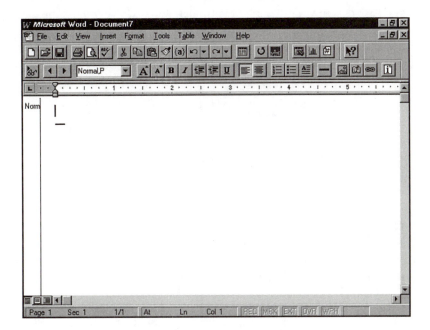

Fig. 17.10

Starting a new document with Internet Assistant's HTML template modifies Word's Standard and Formatting toolbars.

As you type in the text of your Web page, you can mark it for specific text effects such as bold or italic using the standard Word tools. Word automatically translates those effects into HTML tags. You can also format text in HTML modes, such as Strong or Preformatted, by using the styles available under the HTML template. You can select a style using the Styles tool in the formatting toolbar, or you can choose Format, Style or Format, Style Gallery.

Internet Assistant also provides a way to place special codes such as diacritical marks, copyright and trademark symbols, or other special punctuation. To access these special characters, choose Insert, Symbol. A dialog box with listings of special characters appears. Double-clicking a specific character places it in the text where the I-beam cursor is located.

V

Using the Internet

Handling HTML Codes Not Supported by Internet Assistant

There are also several HTML tags and effects that Internet Assistant does not accommodate through styles or tools. To enter these additional tags (or any extra HTML code), choose Insert, HTML Markup. A dialog box with a large window for entering direct HTML code appears (see fig. 17.11). The entered text is handled and displayed as HTML code without ever being translated into Word format. This feature is nice because it lets you include newly introduced HTML tags in your document, although you do have to type the tags out yourself.

Fig. 17.11

Internet Assistant's Insert HTML Markup dialog box lets you enter unsupported HTML tags.

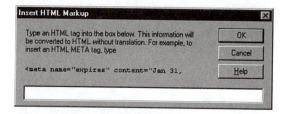

Creating Forms Using Internet Assistant

Internet Assistant has some fairly extensive features for creating HTML forms. You can begin a form by choosing Insert, Form Field. This causes Internet Assistant to enter the HTML tags that surround a form. The Forms dialog box and floating tool palette are shown in figure 17.12.

If you've created forms in Microsoft Access, you may recognize the look of some of these form tools. The Forms tool palette gives you point-and-click access to creating checkboxes, pull-down list boxes, radio buttons, and text boxes. This palette also provides standard Submit and Reset buttons. When you place a field in the form area, additional dialog boxes open up to help you create the necessary choices for a pull-down list box or other controls to help make the form work.

Saving Documents in HTML Format

Internet Assistant for Word saves documents in HTML format by default. The resulting document is then ready to be used on your Web server. This is a contrast to many of the third-party templates discussed in this chapter, which require a special File menu option to save your document in ASCII format.

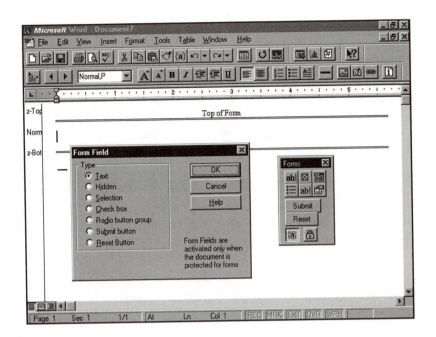

Fig. 17.12
Internet Assistant
provides extensive
support for
creating HTML
forms.

HTML Editors

Beyond the templates for word processors, some stand-alone editors are designed completely for the purpose of authoring HTML documents. Many of the initial versions of these products have been re-released in "professional" versions, which offer souped-up editing capabilities for people who do large amounts of commercial HTML editing. This section covers some of the more popular stand-alone HTML editors available.

Netscape Navigator Gold

After setting the standard for browser software, Netscape has taken its browser a step further by adding document-editing features. Packaged under the name Netscape Navigator Gold, the browser/editor combination provides a What-You-See-Is-What-You-Get (WYSIWYG) editing environment. What's more, with Navigator Gold you can create a Web document *without ever seeing an HTML tag!*

Getting Started

There are two ways to get started editing a document in Navigator Gold. The first is to load a document into the browser and then switch to the editor. What you see in the editor window will look exactly like what's in the browser window, except that you can make changes to the version in the editor window. Figures 17.13 and 17.14 show the same document in the browser and editor windows, respectively. Note how little difference there is between them.

Fig. 17.13

A sample document loaded into the Navigator Gold browser.

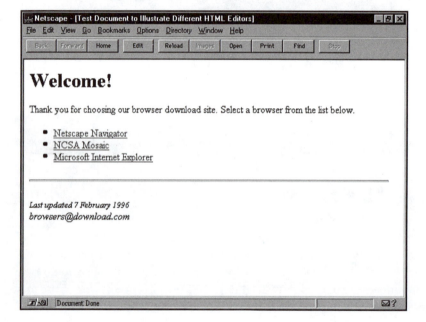

Navigator Gold Toolbars

One thing that is fundamentally different in the editor window is the presence of three toolbars to assist you with your authoring tasks. Most of the buttons in the top toolbar are for formatting text at the font level. You can increase or decrease font size, set the font color, and apply bold, italic, and fixed-width styles. Other buttons let you set up links, place an image, or insert horizontal rule. The Properties button calls up a dialog box that details the attributes of a selected item and lets you apply multiple attributes if needed.

The middle toolbar handles common file and editing operations. It also provides buttons to open a new browser window, print the edited document, search for a specific text string, and access the Netscape Web Page Starter—a new feature on Netscape's Web site with links to several HTML authoring resources.

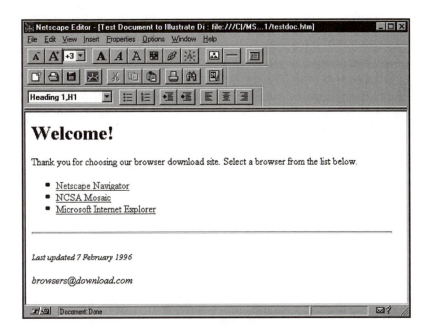

Fig. 17.14
The same sample document loaded into the Navigator Gold editor.

The bottom toolbar returns to the purpose of formatting text. A pull-down menu lists several styles you can apply to highlighted text. Other buttons let you format ordered and unordered lists, increase or decrease indent levels, and specify left, right, and center alignments.

> **Note**
>
> Depending on your screen width, Navigator Gold's toolbar buttons may arrange themselves differently from how you see them in figure 17.14.

Opening and Editing a Document

Once you've opened a document by either loading what's in your browser window into the editor, or by starting a new one, editing the document becomes almost like using a word processor. Applying a style is just a matter of highlighting the text to be formatted and choosing a style from the pull-down menu or from a toolbar button. You can move images, links, and rule around by simply clicking and holding on them, dragging them to where you want them to be, and then releasing your mouse button. This drag-and-drop feature of Navigator Gold makes it easy to place these items exactly where you want them.

Along with the toolbars you get in the editor window, you also pick up two new menus in your menu bar. The Insert menu lets you place new links, images, rule, line breaks, and non-breaking space into your document. Many of these options call up a dialog box where you can specify the different attributes of the item you're placing. Figure 17.15 shows the dialog box for inserting an image. Note how the information you're asked for in the dialog box directly corresponds to the different attributes of the image tag.

Fig. 17.15

When inserting a new image into a Navigator Gold document, you can specify the attributes of the image in this dialog box.

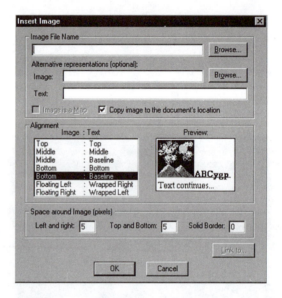

The other new menu is the Properties menu. The different options under Properties let you review and change properties at the font, character, list, paragraph, and document levels.

Perhaps the most curious thing about the Navigator Gold editor is that there is no sign of any HTML tags. You don't see them on the screen, and there are no menu options or toolbar buttons that explicitly refer to them. As you read on about other HTML editors, you'll see that many of them make explicit mention of tags. Because they do this, the people who use them have to know at least *some* HTML. With Navigator Gold, you could theoretically *not know a single HTML tag* and still be able to author a Web document! The upshot of this is that Navigator Gold will make Web publishing accessible to a much larger group of people. Whether this is beneficial or not remains to be seen.

Publishing Your Documents

With Navigator Gold, you are able to publish your finished document right to a Web server with the press of a single button. Navigator Gold writes the HTML file and then transfers it and any necessary image files to the destination server. This saves you from having to save and ftp all of the files by yourself.

Microsoft FrontPage

Microsoft, not wanting to be out done by Netscape, has released FrontPage, another WYSIWYG HTML tool. FrontPage goes beyond Navigator Gold in that it is designed to manage a Web site. FrontPage is a client-server environment, where the server is actually a set of CGI programs that Microsoft calls Server Extensions. FrontPage supports the NCSA, CERN, Apache, Netscape, Open Market Web servers running various flavors of UNIX, WebSite, and IIS under Windows NT.

FrontPage is supplied with many wizards (see fig. 17.16) that allow the user to generate fairly sophisticated HTML documents in just a few minutes. But the real advantage of FrontPage is its ability to manage an entire Web site. FrontPage allows multiple users to develop a Web site simultaneously, and will keep track of work in progress with a ToDo list. FrontPage provides a Link, Outline, and Summary view of the entire set of HTML documents that comprise the Web site. It also will check the validity of all hypertext links within the Web site, and automatically fix referring links to moved or deleted Web pages.

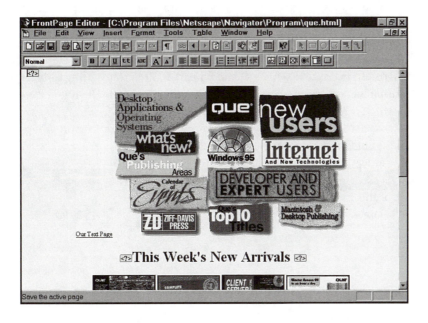

Fig. 17.16
Microsoft FrontPage Editor uses Wizards to assist you in creating Web pages.

HoTMetaL 2.0

If your objective is to write near-perfect HTML on the first try, you should look into HoTMetaL 2.0 from Soft Quad. There are two versions of HoTMetaL 2.0 available. HoTMetaL FREE 2.0 is intended for use in academe and for internal business purposes. Commercial users are required to purchase HoTMetaL PRO 2.0. In paying for a license, you also get technical support and some features that are not active in the freeware version including a spell checker, a thesaurus, and a user-defined macro capability.

On the Web

This review of HoTMetaL 2.0 is based on HoTMetaL FREE 2.0, which you can download by visiting:

http://www.sq.com/

The features discussed here are also available in the PRO version, along with the added functionality noted above.

Getting Started

When you open a new document in HoTMetaL, you see the window shown in figure 17.17. The figure shows HoTMetaL's standard document template. Note that the tags in the template are easy to pick out, with starting and ending tags both pointing inward toward the text they contain. Note also that the template is very complete. All of the tags that are technically required are present, including <HTML>, <HEAD>, <TITLE>, <BODY>, and their corresponding closing tags. The cursor is initially between the <TITLE> and </TITLE> tags in an effort to compel you to put a title in right away.

The completeness of HoTMetaL's default template points to one of the program's strengths: it forces you to use good HTML. HoTMetaL's Rules Checking feature makes it almost impossible to insert an inappropriate tag into your document. When Rules Checking is on, the tag insert features of HoTMetaL are context-sensitive, and you are limited to inserting only those tags that are legal at the current cursor position. For example, if you were inside the <DL> and </DL> tags, you could only insert <DT> and </DT> tags or <DD> and </DD> tags. HoTMetaL prevents you from inserting other tags by graying them out or by just not presenting them.

> **Tip**
>
> Rules Checking can be annoying if you're a seasoned pro who has developed a particular authoring style. You can turn Rules Checking off by pressing Ctrl+K.

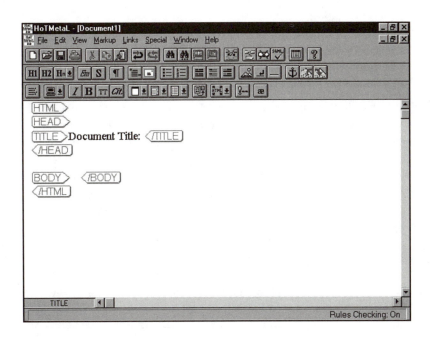

Fig. 17.17
HoTMetaL's
standard docu-
ment template is
in proper HTML
form and encour-
ages you to title
your document
immediately.

In addition to Rules Checking, HoTMetaL also comes with an SGML validator that will test your document for conformance to the rules of proper HTML. These features make HoTMetaL a great choice for the HTML beginner because they encourage good authoring habits right from the start.

The HoTMetaL Toolbars

HoTMetaL provides three toolbars to assist with typical editing tasks. The Standard Toolbar is at the top and provides buttons for frequently used file (New, Open, Save) and editing (Cut, Copy, Paste) operations. Other buttons support searching the document (Find, Find Next), showing, hiding, inserting and removing HTML tags, and activating the SGML validator. In the freeware version of HoTMetaL, the buttons to activate the Spell Checker and Thesaurus are grayed out.

The Common HTML Toolbar is below the Standard Toolbar and lets you quickly tag markup text with heading styles, frequently used logical styles (Emphasis, Strong, Block Quote, Address), and list tags. Buttons toward the end of the toolbar are not style-related and let you place images, horizontal rule, line breaks, and hyperlinks.

At the bottom, you'll find the Other Toolbar. The Other Toolbar is something of a concession on HoTMetaL's part because it allows for the use of the extensions to standard HTML. This becomes significant when you consider that earlier versions of HoTMetaL refused to recognize these tags and wouldn't even *open* documents that contained them! The HTML extensions are accessible on a pull-down menu that you see when clicking and holding on the HTML Extensions button.

Other such pull-down menus give you quick access to tags for the document head, computer-related logical styles (Code, Keyboard, Variable, Sample), compact list tags, and form tags. You can also markup text with physical styles using buttons in the Other Toolbar. Pressing the Special Characters button produces the floating palette you see in figure 17.18. This palette is handy when coding multilingual pages as it lets you place special characters by pointing to and clicking them, rather than having to remember the escape sequence of the character.

> **Note**
>
> You can suppress the display of any of the HoTMetaL toolbars by choosing View, Toolbars.

Fig. 17.18

The floating Special Characters palette makes placing foreign language characters as easy as point-and-click.

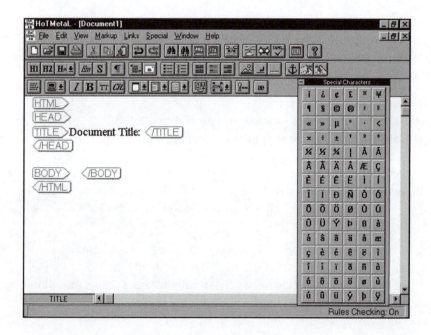

Opening and Editing a Document

Figure 17.19 shows an HTML document open in the HoTMetaL window.
Note how *all* tags—even those like <HR> and <BR> which ordinarily occur by
themselves—have a closing tag. You can also get a greater sense of
HoTMetaL's tolerance for non-standard HTML tags because it let us load a
document that contained <FONT SIZE=-2> and </FONT> tags.

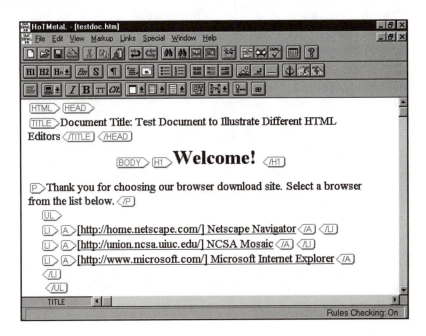

Fig. 17.19
Unlike its prede-
cessors, HoTMetaL
2.0 lets you load
documents with
non-standard
HTML tags.

As you edit the document, you'll notice that HoTMetaL treats tag pairs as a
single unit. If you delete one tag in the pair, its companion tag and all of the
text between them is deleted as well. This is helpful in that it saves you some
keystrokes and provides an almost iron-clad guarantee that there will be no
stray tags floating around in your document.

When it's time to insert a tag, choose <u>M</u>arkup, <u>I</u>nsert Element. You can then
choose the tag you want to insert from the dialog box that appears. Remember that if rules checking is on, you'll be restricted to inserting only those tags
that are legal at that point of the document.

Publishing Your Documents

The <u>P</u>ublish option under the <u>L</u>inks menu is handy if you've developed the
pages for a site with all hyperlinks pointing to files on your local hard drive,
and you need to change those URLs once you place the documents on your
server. Once you've validated and saved your documents, you can use the

Publish option to prepare your documents for life on the Web server. The Publish dialog box lets you do a search for all URLs that start with the file:/// protocol and replace them with URLs that start with http:. This dialog box is shown in figure 17.20.

Fig. 17.20
HoTMetaL's Publish feature allows you to quickly convert the local URLs in your documents to URLs appropriate to being on a Web server.

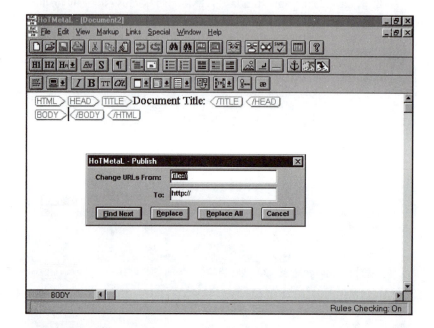

HTMLed Pro

Hailing from Canada, HTMLed Pro is the commercial version of the HTMLEd editor, which has been around for a few years. Both programs are produced by Internet Software Technologies.

The information about HTMLed Pro presented here is based on the demo copy of version 1.1.

On the Web

You can download the most recent version from Internet Software Technologies by visiting :

http://www.ist.ca/htmledpro/

If you choose to buy HTMLed Pro, the license will set you back U.S.$99.95 plus U.S.$10 for shipping and handling.

Getting Started

Just starting up HTMLed Pro leaves you with an empty editing window. You need to start a new document to activate most of the program's toolbars

(which HTMLed Pro calls *speedbars*) and menu options. When you choose
File, New you are presented with a dialog box that lets you set up a basic template for your new document. Checkboxes in the dialog box let you include
<HTML>, <HEAD>, <BODY>, and corresponding closing tags. You can also
specify your document's title and include comments to indicate that you
wrote the document and the date you started it. Once you've filled in the dialog box and clicked OK, you'll see a screen much like the one in figure 17.21.
Note that once the new document is open, HTMLed Pro's speedbars are no
longer grayed out, and many new items appear in the menu bar.

Note

You can also choose to create a new document with a custom template of your own
design. Just choose File, New with Document Template.

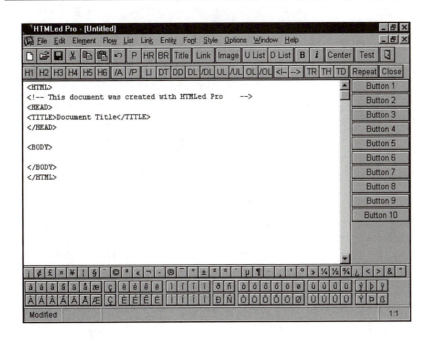

Fig. 17.21
Starting a new
document in
HTMLed Pro
activates the
program's
speedbars and
menu options.

HTMLed Pro Speedbars

One of the first things you notice about HTMLed Pro is all of its speedbars.
There are five across the width of the screen and one down the right hand
side.

When all speedbars are displayed, the topmost one is the Standard Speedbar.
Buttons on this speedbar handle the most frequently used options like file

and editing operations, paragraph and line breaks, horizontal rule, placing images, setting up hyperlinks, formatting unordered and definition lists, centering text, and applying bold and italics styles.

Just below the Standards Speedbar is the Common Tags Speedbar. Here you'll find many of the tags you use most, like heading styles, list and table tags, and tags for creating comments. The closing tags of many popular tag pairs are also available.

The first of the three speedbars at the bottom of the window is the Extended Characters speedbar. Placing any of the characters in this speedbar is as easy as clicking its button. This relieves you from having to remember or look up the escape sequences to produce these characters.

The other two speedbars along the bottom are the Special Characters speedbars. The two are essentially identical with the upper bar supporting the lowercase versions of characters in the lower bar. If you're editing HTML in another language, you'll want to have these two speedbars active.

The speedbar down the right-hand side of the screen is the Custom Speedbar. Each button in this bar is custom designed by you. To place a button on the bar, right click your mouse while it is pointing to an empty spot on the bar and choose New Button. Once you've placed the button, you can right-click again and choose Modify to get the custom button editing dialog box shown in figure 17.22. Custom buttons are great for tag combinations like bold and italics that would otherwise require the application of two or more separate styles.

Opening and Editing Documents

Once you have a document open, HTMLed Pro provides extensive support for inserting tags and marking up text through a large number of pull-down menus. HTMLed Pro supports all of the tags proposed in HTML 3.0 and many of the Netscape extensions to HTML.

Most of the text-formatting styles are found under the Font or Style menus. Specifically, the Font menu lets you apply any of the physical text styles and gives you access to the <FONT> and <BASEFONT> tags. The Style menu is home to the heading styles and the logical text styles.

Under the Element menu, you'll find options to activate HTMLed Pro's Table Designer and Form Designer. The Table Designer makes it easy to set up a simple table of any number of rows or columns and to place headers and data in each of the table's cells. The Form Designer, shown in figure 17.23, is

particularly nice as it lets you drag and drop form elements around on a
blank worksheet. Clicking <u>O</u>K when you're done places the appropriate
HTML in your document.

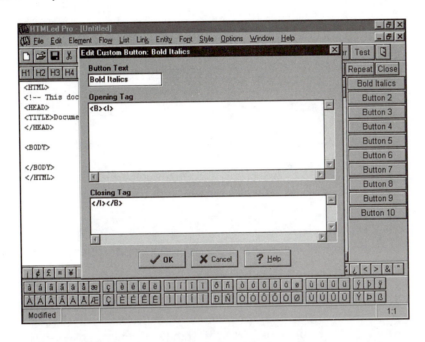

Fig. 17.22
You can customize
buttons on
HTMLed Pro's
Custom Speedbar.

V

Using the Internet

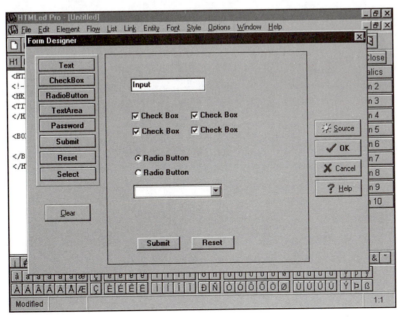

Fig. 17.23
HTMLed Pro's
Form Designer
lets you drag
and drop form
elements on a
blank page.

Fig. 17.24

The HTMLed Pro HTML Page Builder "interviews" you and creates a personal home page based on your responses.

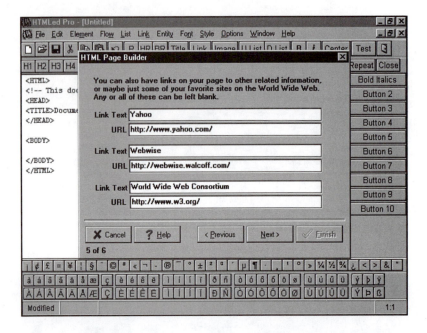

If you or a friend needs to get a home page up quickly, the HTML Page Builder option under the Options menu is probably the way to go. The Page Builder "interviews" you over a series of several dialog boxes and composes a home page based on your responses. One of the Page Builder's dialog boxes appears in figure 17.24.

You can further customize the editing environment by defining your own Quick Keys under the Quick Keys tab of the Preferences dialog box. Rather than type the same text in over and over, you can store frequently repeated text under one of the Quick Keys and save your fingers the extra effort.

Publishing Your Documents

When you save your documents, you can choose a DOS or UNIX (no carriage returns) file format. If your documents need to end up on a remote server, you can choose File, Save Remote to save directly to that server using the ftp protocol.

HotDog Pro

HotDog Pro is a popular new HTML editor from Sausage Software in Australia. You have to pay to license the commercial version, but there is a freeware version (just called HotDog) available as well.

The following information on HotDog Pro is based on the fully functional demo that you can download from Sausage Software's Web site. The URL is: **http://www.sausage.com/**

On the Web

You have 30 days to review the demo. After that, you can pay US$99.95 to license HotDog Pro or let the demo expire. If you choose to pay for a license, Sausage Software will send you a registration number by e-mail, saving you shipping and handling charges.

Getting Started

When you first start HotDog Pro, you see the screen shown in figure 17.25. Note that HotDog Pro gives you a standard document template, complete with <HTML>, <HEAD>, <TITLE>, and <BODY> tags, without having to start a new document. You can create and save your own custom templates in HotDog Pro, but you'll need to choose File, New to load them.

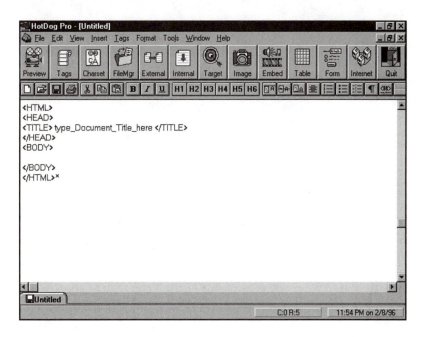

Fig. 17.25
When you start HotDog Pro, the standard document template loads automatically.

HotDog Pro Toolbars

HotDog Pro has two toolbars at the top of the editing window and two informational bars at the bottom of the window. The topmost toolbar, shown in figure 17.25 with buttons containing both text and icons, is called the Button Bar. The buttons on the Button Bar are pre-configured to perform the tasks you will probably do most often when editing HTML. However, it is very easy to customize the Button Bar to your own editing habits. Choosing Tools, Customize Button Bar opens the dialog box you see in figure 17.26. Inside the dialog box, you can remove buttons from the bar by dragging them into the trash or add a new button to the bar by specifying the text label, icon, tool tip, and function of the new button.

> **Tip**
>
> You can reduce the amount of space the Button Bar takes up by changing the buttons to display only text. This is done under the Display tab in the Options dialog box. You can shut off the Button Bar, as well as any other toolbar or informational bar by selecting or deselecting the menu options under the View menu.

Fig. 17.26
You can remove buttons from the Button Bar or add your own custom buttons.

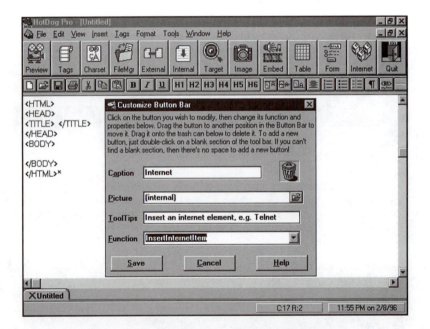

Immediately below the Button Bar is the Elements Bar. This toolbar has significantly smaller buttons than the Button Bar, but it provides you with single-click access to a large number of program options. Buttons on the Element bar let you do common file and editing operations, apply physical or heading styles, align text after an image, create a list, insert a paragraph or line break, or place a horizontal rule very quickly.

The first informational bar is immediately below the horizontal scrollbar in figure 17.25. This bar is called the Documents Bar. A different tab, much like the tabs you see at the bottom of an Excel workspace to denote the different spreadsheets in the space, shows up on the bar for each document you have open. HotDog Pro lets you save multiple files together in what's called a *project*. Opening or saving a project opens or saves each file contained in the project. This is a handy feature because the sites you develop are not likely to be comprised of just one page. You'll author many pages in creating a site, and HotDog Pro's project capability is a great way to keep track of them all. The Project Manager, accessible under the File menu, lets you perform different tests on documents in a project and prints a report for you when the testing is complete.

Directly below the Documents Bar is the Status Bar. The Status Bar lets you know what the program is doing at any point and provides time and date information as well.

Opening and Editing Documents

You open documents in HotDog Pro by choosing File, Open. A new twist is that you can open multiple files at once from the Open File dialog box.

Once you're editing, HotDog Pro supplies you with a lot of helpful editing tools. The Tags and Entity palettes are shown in figure 17.27. You can select and insert just about any piece of HTML markup you'll ever need from these two palettes. If a palette with the complete list of HTML tags is too much to scroll through, you can use Options under the Tags menu to call up smaller versions of the palette that have similar tags grouped together. For example, the Graphics palette contains the <IMG> and <FIG> tags, along with standard and extended attributes for each. The Entity palette is useful when you have a lot of special characters in your document.

> **Tip**
>
> You can activate the Tags or Entity palettes quickly by pressing the F6 or F7 keys, respectively.

Options under the Insert menu use easy-to-follow dialog boxes to guide you through the insertion of complicated tags and tag sequences. The Insert List dialog box is shown in figure 17.28. Note the options to create unordered, ordered, definition, and plain lists as well as fields for entering a heading, specifying the bullet character, and making the list compact. Other options under the Insert menu let you insert embedded program items and marquees (a Microsoft Internet Explorer extension to HTML).

Fig. 17.27
The Tags and
Entity palettes list
all HTML tags and
entities.

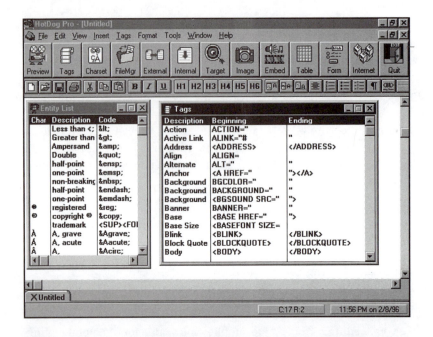

Fig. 17.28
Dialog boxes
accessible from the
Insert menu guide
you through the
placement of
complex HTML
tags.

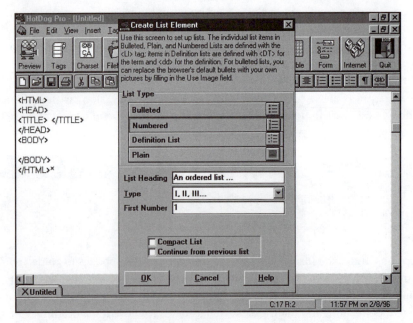

If you find you're performing a certain operation frequently and there is no shortcut key for that operation, you can define your own shortcut key in the Shortcut Keys dialog box under the Tools menu.

> **Caution**
>
> If you define a shortcut key that HotDog Pro assigns to another operation at startup, your definition will override the startup definition. However, the shortcut key will continue to appear next to the operation to which it was originally assigned.

Publishing Your Documents

Once you're done editing, you should spell check your document and validate the HTML. HotDog Pro can do both with the Spell Check and Validate options under the Tools menu.

After you make these checks on your document, you'll next want to look at them in a browser to see how they appear on-screen. If you don't want to open a separate browser program to do this, you can try HotDog Pro's Real-time Output ViewER (ROVER) to test your document. Figure 17.29 shows the HotDog Pro editing window with a ROVER window open below it. The ROVER window provides a near-WYSIWYG display of how your document will look.

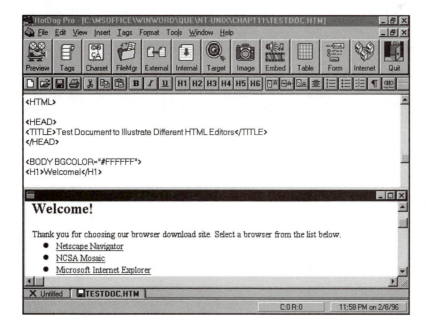

Fig. 17.29
HotDog Pro's Real-time Output ViewER (ROVER) supports a near-WYSIWYG display of your document's online appearance.

Advanced Editing Systems

There may be times when your document editing and conversion will go beyond simply authoring single Web pages. In these cases, you may need document conversion tools that can translate your word processing or other files to HTML. This section explores some of these utilities.

Document Conversion Tools

HTML filters are useful tools that let you convert a document produced with any kind of editor (including ASCII text editors) to HTML. Filters are useful when you work in an editor that has its own proprietary format, such as Word, WordPerfect, or Rich Text Format (RTF).

HTML filters are attractive if you want a utility to convert your document with tags to HTML as you continue to work in your favorite editor. Filters tend to be fast and easy to work with because they take a file name as input and generate an HTML output file.

On the Web

The World Wide Web Consortium maintains a good list of HTML filters and converters. Check it out at:

http://www.w3.org/hypertext/WWW/Tools/Filters.html

Converting Word Documents

Word for Windows and Word for DOS documents can be converted to HTML using the CU_HTML and GT_HTML add-ons mentioned earlier. A few standalone conversion utilities have also begun to appear. Because Word can read other word processor formats (including WordPerfect and RTF), you can use these filters when error checking is required or when a dedicated filter for your word processor is not available.

Converting WordPerfect

The utility WPTOHTML converts WordPerfect documents to HTML. WPTOHTML is a set of macros for WordPerfect versions 5.1 and 6.0. You can also use the WordPerfect filter with other word processor formats that WordPerfect can import.

On the Web

WPTOHTML is available through anonymous ftp from **oak.oakland.edu** in the directory SimTel/msdos/wordperf as the file WPTXXD10.ZIP, where XX is the version number of WordPerfect (either 51 for 5.1 or 60 for 6.0).

Converting FrameMaker

FrameMaker release 5 includes a filter to translate FrameMaker documents to HTML. This release also lets you export your document in RTF format, in which case you can use the RTF converter, RTFTOHTML, discussed next.

To learn more about FrameMaker 5, consult the Adobe site:

http://www.adobe.com/prodindex/framemaker/main.html

On the Web

Converting Rich Text Format (RTF)

RTFTOHTML is a common utility that converts RTF documents to HTML. While most versions are available for UNIX and Macintosh systems, there is a version for DOS as well.

The DOS binary file for RTFTOHTML can be downloaded from:

http://www.georgetown.edu/acc/software/rtftohtm.zip

On the Web

Note the abbreviated name, owing to DOS's eight character limit on file names.

Because many word processors handle RTF formats, you can import an RTF document into your favorite word processor, and then run one of the word processor specific filters. However, RTFTOHTML seems to be faster at performing this conversion.

Converting TeX and LaTeX

Because you're using Windows NT, your best bet here is to convert TeX and LaTeX files to RTF with TEX2RTF. You can convert the file further using one of the other tools that have already been mentioned.

TEX2RTF is available in a 32-bit version for Windows NT by anonymous ftp at:

ftp://ftp.aiai.ed.ac.uk/pub/packages/text2rtf/ tex2rtf1.52_win32.zip

On the Web

Converting PageMaker

EDCO produces the PM2HTML converter in both freeware and production versions. The production version costs $49 and can handle a greater number of conversions.

The freeware version of PM2HTML is available by anonymous ftp at:

ftp://ftp.gate.net/pub/users/edco

On the Web

V

Using the Internet

The World Wide Web Consortium's list of filters reports that Adobe has released an HTML authoring plug-in for PageMaker 6.0, but a search of Adobe's Web and ftp sites yielded no information about this add-on.

Converting Excel Spreadsheets

There are a couple of good options for converting Excel spreadsheets into HTML table format. XL2HTML.XLS contains a Visual Basic macro for Excel 5.0 that allows you to specify a range of cells and then generate the HTML that converts data in the cells to a table form. XTML is an add-on for Excel 5.0 that can do this conversion as well.

On the Web

You can learn more about XL2HTML.XLS at:

http://www710.gsfc.nasa.gov/704/dgd/xl2html.html

XTML lives under Ken Sayward's directory at:

http://users.aol.com/ksayward/xtml

Additionally, you can use Microsoft's Internet Assistant for Excel to convert your spreadsheets. Check out Microsoft's Web site at:

http://www.microsoft.com/msdownload

Converting Lotus Notes

Lotus Notes users can now convert their documents to HTML format with Lotus InterNotes Web Publisher. Lotus Notes databases can be converted to HTML by using the program TILE from Walter Shelby Group, Ltd.

On the Web

Lotus has online information about Lotus InterNotes Web Publisher at :

http://www.lotus.com/inotes

You can get information on how to order TILE at:

http://tile.net/info/about.html

Converting Interleaf

Interleaf users can use Cyberleaf 2.0 to not only convert Interleaf documents to HTML, but Framemaker, RTF, WordPerfect, and ASCII documents as well. Additionally, Cyberleaf converts graphics to either GIF or Postscript formats and it converts tables to GIF images, Postscript files, or HTML 3.0 markup.

On the Web

Information related to Cyberleaf for Windows NT is available on Interleaf's Web site at:

http://www.ileaf.com

HTML Analyzers

When you have completed the creation of your Web pages, it makes sense to run them through an application that will verify the syntax of the tags you have used. This is especially necessary if you have used one of the "simple" editors like Notepad or DOS Edit.

Doctor HTML

Doctor HTML is a nifty Web-based HTML analyzer that lets you perform up to eight different tests on your documents, including:

- Spell checking.
- An analysis of the document structure that looks for unclosed or extraneous tags.
- An image analysis that loads each image and measures how much bandwidth each consumes.
- An image syntax check that makes sure you've used WIDTH, HEIGHT, and ALT attributes in your <IMG> tags.
- Proper table and form structure tests.
- A check on hyperlinks that reports all links that time-out after ten seconds.
- A command hierarchy analysis displaying all HTML commands in the document.

The command hierarchy analysis also indents nested tags, making them easier to read. The hierarchy test is best used in combination with one or more of the other tests.

To check your documents with Doctor HTML, direct your browser to:

http://www.sai.msu.su/admin/drhtml.html

On the Web

The form-based interface lets you specify which tests you want done and the URL of the document to test.

HTML Check Toolkit

The HTML Check Toolkit measures how well your documents conform to the rules of standard HTML. You can choose Strict, HTML 2.0, HTML 3.0, Mozilla (recognizes Netscape extensions to HTML), and HotJava (recognizes HTML used to embed Java applets) conformance tests. The report you get back can include a display of the input, the parser output, and the formatted output. In addition to being able to supply a URL to test, you can also submit a smaller chunk of HTML code for testing.

On the Web

You can open the HTML Check Toolkit at:

http://www.webtechs.com/html-val-svc/.

WWWeblint

WWWeblint "picks the lint" off your HTML documents by performing an extensive number of tests. Some highlights of WWWeblint's analysis include checking for:

- Proper document structure
- Unknown tags or attributes
- Overlapping tags
- The presence of a title in the document head
- The use of ALT in <IMG> tags
- Inappropriate nesting of tags
- Unmatched quotation marks
- Existence of local anchors

WWWeblint supports elements proposed in HTML 3.0 including table and math tags. You can ask WWWeblint to check a URL, or you can supply a chunk of code for it to test.

On the Web

You can clean the lint of your documents by checking out:

http://www.unipress.com/cgi-bin/WWWeblint

HTML_ANALYZER

A popular hyperlink analyzer is HTML_ANALYZER. It examines each hyperlink and the contents of the hyperlink to ensure that they are consistent. HTML_ANALYZER functions by examining a document links, and then creating a text file that has a list of those links. HTML_ANALYZER uses the text files to compare the actual link content to what it should be.

HTML_ANALYZER actually does three tests. It validates the availability of the documents pointed to by hyperlinks (called *validation*). It looks for hyperlink contents that occur in the database but are not, themselves, hyperlinks (called *completeness*). And it looks for a one-to-one relation between hyperlinks and the contents of the hyperlink (called *consistency*). Any deviations are listed for the user.

On the Web

You can download the compressed archive that contains the HTML_ANALYZER files from:

http://www.gatech.edu/pitkow/html_analyzer/README.html

CHAPTER 18

Building an Intranet

by Michael Marchuk

One of today's hottest buzzwords, *intranets* are redefining the computer industry and making traditional groupware vendors fight for their very existence. An intranet is quite simply one or more servers that employ Internet, and especially Web technology, and are only accessible to people within their own organization. The appeal of sharing enterprise data with a universal client, a Web browser, has organizations that are currently using legacy products thinking twice about upgrading. More importantly, smaller enterprises that could not cost justify products like Lotus Notes or Novell's GroupWise are finding out that they can employ an intranet for much less money.

To date, commercial intranet packages are few and far between, but are being developed at a frantic place. Most organizations will end up writing their own Web-based applications that will bridge their corporate databases with their Web servers. Luckily, this is relatively easy to do with the CGI, Server Side Includes, and other standards that exist.

In this chapter, you learn to

- Make informed decisions about some of the intranet products available today
- Protect information assets in a client/server computing environment
- Control access to your intranet resources
- Utilize CGI, SSI, and NSAPI to build Web-based applications and front ends

Commercial Intranet Products

The very new market of commercial intranet products is just beginning to define itself. There are only a few products available today, but the vendors are racing with each other to get their products out. Most of the existing intranet products are either front ends to existing legacy applications, or browser plug-ins that allow the user to seamlessly run the legacy application from his Web browser.

Microsoft Peer Web Services and Internet Information Server

Windows NT comes with an integrated Web, ftp, and Gopher server that is bundled under the title of Peer Web Services. These services allow your Windows NT workstation to publish Web data and transfer files on your intranet easily and securely.

The Web server portion of the Peer Web Services is a pared down version of Microsoft's popular Internet Information Server (IIS). The features within the Peer Web Services are similar to the IIS version, except that the number of simultaneous connections is limited to 10 users.

Microsoft IIS provides integrated security and virtual directory hosting (see fig. 18.1) to enable your intranet site to provide data to your users quickly and securely. Microsoft has also included the Database Connector software that allows the server to access databases through Open Database Connectivity drivers (ODBC). This allows your intranet to access Oracle or Sybase databases that contain customer information or order processing data. Additionally, the IIS can log the intranet access to an ODBC file to allow administrators the ability to remotely query access statistics.

Fig. 18.1
Microsoft's Peer Web Services and Internet Information Server provide an easy and secure way to publish data on your intranet.

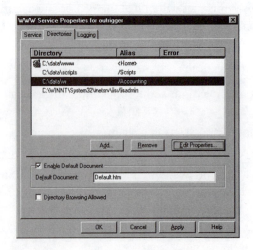

WebBoard

WebBoard (**http://webboard.ora.com**), a $250 Web-based bulletin board system from O'Reilly & Associates (see fig. 18.2), works with any Win-CGI compliant Web server. WebBoard supports many traditional bulletin board features, including threaded discussions, user profiles, searching, automatic message archiving, and activity logs. WebBoard allows an unlimited number of conferences, and supports up to 255 individual bulletin boards per server with remote administration.

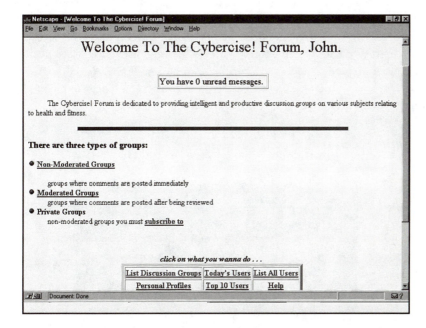

Fig. 18.2
WebBoard provides the means to setup discussion groups on any subject.

Action Workflow

Action Workflow Metro (**http://www.actiontech.com**) is a $995 Web-based workflow package that includes 20 applications. Metro requires Windows NT, Microsoft SQL Server, and Netscape Commerce Server or Communications Server. An additional $3,995 will be required for the Metro Development Center, for any customization of the included 20 applications. As a native Web solution, it allows your customers and employees to access workflow applications using any standard Web browser.

InterNotes Web Publisher

InterNotes Web Publisher, (**http://www.internotes.lotus.com**) is a bundled component of Lotus Notes 4. InterNotes converts Notes databases and documents into HTML 2.0 pages. It also allows browsers to perform full-text searches of Notes databases and enter data directly into a Notes database. InterNotes does not provide real-time access but rather converts documents at configurable intervals (from every second to once per day) in batch mode. Of course, using InterNotes requires using Notes, which defeats the purpose of building an intranet.

World Group

Galacticomm's World Group, starting at about $500, is a client/server bulletin board system, with all of the features of an advanced BBS: e-mail, group discussion forums, polls and questionnaires, file libraries, and live-chat features. The World Group Server functions both as the BBS server and Web Server. The client software, World Group Manager, a freely distributable application, is required to access the server. Galacticomm has made the World Group Manager a Netscape plug-in (see fig. 18.3), allowing Web pages to have HTML links to World Group applications.

Galacticomm's World Group:

http://www.gcomm.com

On the Web

Fig. 18.3
Galacticomm
World Group
makes it easy to
setup a BBS on
your Intranet.

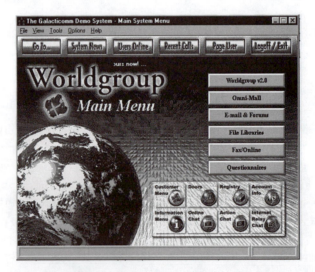

Aspects of Security

Everyone knows it's a jungle *out there*, but isn't security a much smaller concern on webs entirely within company walls? Smaller, perhaps, but not by much. One reason is that the employees of any company are drawn from the general population, with its small but significant fraction of hackers, vandals, and opportunists. Another is that a large organization's intranet may span offices around the country or the globe, using the public Internet as a wide area network to keep costs low. Finally, even without malice aforethought, an intranet without proper access controls invites accidental erasure or overwriting of documents.

Intranets make many aspects of computing simpler, but security policy isn't one of them. This section presents a basic approach to protecting your company's information assets in a Web-based network environment.

Protecting Information Assets

There are three types of hazards to consider when planning your secure intranet:

- *Exposure of confidential or private data to unauthorized personnel.* The latter might be employees without a legitimate need to know, temporary workers with login privileges, or outside agents, if your intranet connects to the Internet or other public network.

- *Corruption or deletion of valuable files.* This hazard exists whenever multiple users have the ability to update shared information.

- *Illegitimate access to shared resources.* This includes files, applications, and network peripherals such as printers or modems.

Note

When deciding which documents and data on your intranet need protecting, remember that well-meaning users with inappropriate access privileges can do almost as much damage as the bad guys. Each of the hazards listed above can happen purely by accident, as well as by purposeful intrusion. For example, salary data stored in a publicly accessible area might be viewed by an unauthorized user during a legitimate hunt for sales data. As a rule it's better to limit access initially and loosen it on demand than to leave the vault door open.

Protecting your company's information from these hazards is a matter of controlling who can do what with which resources and services on the network.

The process of verifying that a user is who she says she is called *User Authentication.* Most networks, including intranets, can be set up to authenticate the user through a challenge/response dialog box. Often this takes the form of a username/password exchange. Stronger authentication is possible with "public key" technology, which is the basis for securing commercial transactions on the WWW. User authentication techniques are discussed later in this chapter.

Once the server trusts the client, it grants or denies access to given resources based on each resource's Access Control List (ACL). How you set up access control depends on your choice of server and network operating system. For instance, on a UNIX-based intranet, access control is mostly a matter of file permissions. Web pages in a Netware-shared directory can be accessed according to "trustee rights." (See the following sidebar entitled "File Permissions and Security" for more information.) Access Control is discussed later in the section "Controlling Access to Intranet Resources."

File Permissions and Security

The first line of defense in every network comes from file permissions. Network operating systems enable administrators to assign access rights for a specific resource—file, printer, or Internet service—on a user-by-user basis.

If you're running a UNIX-based Web server, for instance, you can assign read, write, and execute permissions by owner (the user who created the file), group (the group to which the owner belongs), or world (all users). A world-readable file is visible to everyone, while a world-writeable file can be changed (or deleted) by anyone. Furthermore, because in UNIX everything is a file, intranet services such as ftp and script execution can be similarly controlled.

Windows NT, Novell Netware, and Banyan Vines each have their own capabilities and nomenclature for controlling access.

Client/Server Security

As the phrase suggests, there are two sides to any client/server story. Often there is a third element as well: the network connecting clients to servers. Security is an issue at each of these.

Server security protects the back-end resources of your network, including Web servers and databases. It is mainly of concern to system administrators. *Network security* is concerned with the secure transport of data from point A to point B, for which encryption is the technology of record. Network and server security are discussed at greater length below. Important *client security* issues are mentioned in this section.

The number one security risk for clients on an intranet is careless setup of so-called Helper Applications, also called *viewers*. (Netscape 2.0 plug-ins are in this category, as well.) Viewers pose a risk by associating downloaded file types with client-resident applications, which is tantamount to inviting strangers to run code on your computer. When setting up browsers on your intranet, don't assign viewer associations that can launch applications before you've had a chance to virus scan any downloaded files.

Three additional steps required to secure clients on an intranet are listed in the table that follows.

What You Should Do	Reason
Always log off before leaving a client computer unattended.	Anyone can masquerade as the active user once the login has been completed.
Be conservative when sharing disk drives over the network.	Clients can easily expose more than what is intended when sharing directories via file://localhost/.
Consider encrypting sensitive files, including copies on tape backup and floppy disk.	Even when your computer is turned off, tapes and floppy disks can compromise security if openly readable.

Legal Considerations

The ease with which Web servers can be set up heightens the risk that confidential data will be casually replicated across an organization. A corollary is that some of this material may be legally protected by the Privacy Act or other entitlements. Distributing protected material on an intranet could carry severe legal penalties for a business.

As an example, consider the value of making a central repository of personnel data available to managers via an intranet. With a form allowing keyword searches as a front end, such a repository would doubtless be a powerful staffing tool. But the allowable search criteria would have to be restricted by design, to preclude queries specifying discriminatory attributes such as age or sex. Not doing so would invite lawsuits. This is equally true of traditional databases, of course. The difference is that setting up a database server typically involves Information Systems (IS) professionals and perhaps auditors in addition to users, while an Intranet application can be assembled by a lone power user in a weekend, without IS knowledge. Moreover, if the Human Resources department runs Windows 95, users can launch the application on a home-grown 32-bit Web server, as well.

The point of this cautionary tale is not to say that user empowerment is dangerous. On the contrary, lowering barriers to information flow is what intranets are all about. But as our hypothetical situation makes clear, security awareness has a crucial role to play in the way Intranets are deployed and operated.

Controlling Access to Intranet Resources

You can restrict access to documents or whole directories on a Web server in three ways:

- *By IP address or domain name.* This is the weakest form of restriction, because it takes on faith that the visitor's IP address is accurate.

- *By user authentication (name and password).* This method provides moderate security and is recommended for most applications.

- *Using public key cryptography.* This, the strongest method, is recommended for applications where absolute confidentiality must be assured.

Controlling access using public keys requires digital certification of the server and issuance of public and private keys by a "certification authority." These topics are discussed in the section on encryption later in this chapter in the section titled, "Encryption: The 'Key' to Secure Communications."

Controlling Access by IP Address, Segment, or Domain Name

Virtually all Web servers offer a global access control mechanism for administrators and a local, directory-level mechanism for users. The weakest form of controlled access, restrictions based on IP addresses, can easily be defeated by someone within an organization changing their IP address.

An intranet server's network is usually connected to the Internet as well. If no precautions, such as access lists and firewalling, have been taken on the border router or firewall, it is a trivial matter for hackers to spoof an IP address.

Controlling Access by User/Group Authentication

Most Web servers support username and password authentication. Often usernames can belong to one or more groups of users. The server administrator can then assign access to any portion of the Web server to individual users or groups of users. When an area of a server is restricted, that area is referred to as a *Realm*.

When a browser requests a file from the server that is part of a Realm, the server demands that the browser authenticate itself by supplying a valid username and password. If the browser hasn't authenticated with that specific Realm since it was started, it will pop up a dialog box asking for the username and password. After a successful authentication, the browser will retain the username and password in memory and authenticate without user intervention for any further requests within that Realm.

> **Note**
>
> Most browsers do not have an option to clear their cache of Realm authentications. If you access a protected area of a Web server and leave your browser running when you leave your computer, any one who may use your computer while you are gone will have access to those Realms. The only way to prevent this is to exit your browser.

Figures 18.4 and 18.5 illustrate browser authentication. Cisco Systems Home Page offers general and marketing information to the public. Cisco also offers an intranet with extensive technical information and customer support to its customers. Cisco requires authentication to access their intranet, and offers differing level of services to its intranet users.

Cisco Systems:

On the Web

http://www.cisco.com

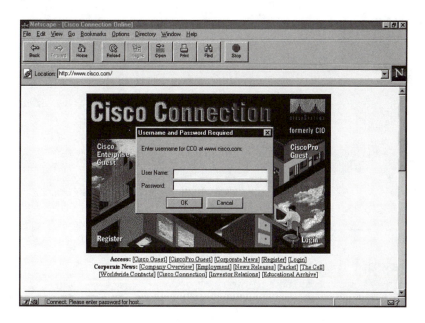

Fig. 18.4
Browser Authentication—selecting a realm.

Fig. 18.5
Browser Authentication—after
authentication.

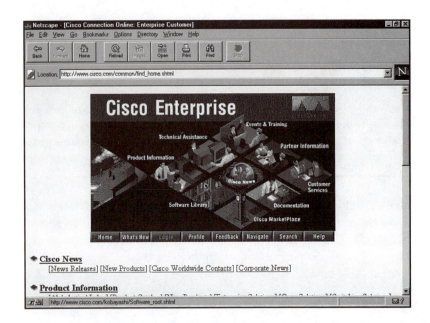

> **Note**
>
> Often, an intranet acts as a presentation layer for data gathered from many sources, such as Web servers, databases, and legacy systems. Each of these servers may well repeat the user authentication process, in fulfillment of its own security plan.
>
> It *is* possible to pass authentication data securely from server to server, making multiple logins unnecessary. In practice, however, few networks have implemented "single login" designs, because doing so requires resource coordination at the enterprise level. Secure frameworks like Open Software Foundation's Distributed Computing Environment address this problem.
>
> For now, try not to get too frustrated if you're challenged more than once on the way to crucial information.

Firewalls and Proxies

Intranets put corporate data within reach of your Web browser, but what happens when you need to access information outside the company? Standard security practice is to isolate internal systems from the Internet with a firewall.

A *firewall* is a system that enforces an access control policy between two networks, such as your intranet and the global Internet. Network-level firewalls are routers that either pass or block packets, depending on their source and destination addresses. Application-level firewalls block all traffic, inspect it against a set of access rules, and forward legitimate packets.

A *proxy* is a server that allows intranet users to access the World Wide Web and other Internet services through a firewall. It's like a one-way mirror; you can see out through it, but the bad guys can't see in. Proxies enable administrators to set up fine-grained access rules, such as allowing inbound ftp but blocking outbound transfers.

Ask your network administrator if your organization offers one or more proxy services. If it does, you'll need to configure your Web browser accordingly. Here's how to do it for Netscape Navigator:

1. Choose Options, Network Preferences.
2. Select the Proxies tab.
3. Click the Manual radio button and then click View.
4. Enter the names and port numbers of the various proxies on your network. Often, one proxy will provide all the services shown; such as, WWW-Relay:8080 (see fig. 18.6).
5. Enter the host names or IP addresses of servers within your firewall in the No Proxy For text box.
6. Choose OK to save your settings.

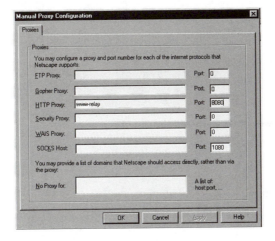

Fig. 18.6
Setting up a Proxy Server with Netscape.

Remote Intranet Access

Connecting mobile users to an internal Web poses special security problems. There are two fundamentally different approaches. One is to provide authenticated dial-up access to the intranet via a modem pool. In effect, the company acts as an ISP (Internet Service Provider) for its own employees, but provides access to the company intranet, rather than the World Wide Web. This method is about as secure as the public telephone network (good enough to carry credit card and automatic teller machine transactions). If additional security is wanted, the channel can be encrypted.

The other approach is to leverage the Internet as a *wide area intranet*. While less secure on its face than dialup, this method offers other advantages. Where remote users have access to high-speed Internet connections—for instance, at a client's site—they can access the headquarter's intranet at speeds much greater than the dialup maximum of 28.8 Kbps. Moreover, Internet access costs are flat. Mobile users can connect locally to the Internet in the city where they're staxù° via any of several thousand points of presence. The savings in line charges (or 800 numbers) can be great for business travelers accessing the intranet from across the globe.

In either scheme, authentication can be strengthened by using one-time passwords (such as Bellcore's S/KEY system) or a password generator such as the CRYPTOCard.

The two approaches are compared in the table that follows.

Remote Access Method	Pros/Cons
Direct dialup	*Pros:* inherently as secure as the public telephone network; easy to administer
	Cons: data rates limited to 28.8 Kbps; long-distance access costly
via Internet	*Pros:* can support higher data rates than dialup; access charges aren't usage-based
	Cons: less secure than dialup

Encryption: The "Key" to Secure Communications

Encryption is the controlled process that takes usable data and makes it unusable for purposes of securing that data. The actual processing varies greatly, but the intention is always the same: to scramble every piece of the data so that no part can be used. In this section, cryptographic technology is discussed as it pertains to intranets.

Encryption works by encoding the text of a message with a *key*, which is just a very long number. Typical keys are 40, 64, 80 or 128 digits long, with the longer keys affording stronger encryption.

Secure Web servers like Netscape Commerce Server use public key technology to provide encryption, authentication, and digital signature services. In a public key system, everyone owns a unique pair of keys. One is called the *public key*, and is widely distributed to anyone who wants a copy. The other, called the *private key*, is kept secret.

Under this system, a person who needs to send a message to a recipient encrypts the message with the recipient's *public* key. So encrypted, the message can only be read by decrypting it with—you guessed it—the recipient's *private* key. This way, anyone can send a secure message, but only the intended party can read it.

In order to set up a server capable of secure communications, you will need a *digital certificate*. Certificates attest that the person holding a public key is who he claims to be. The details of obtaining a public key and certificate depend on the particular server you run. For both the Netscape Commerce Server and Microsoft Internet Information Server, for instance, the Certifying Authority is VeriSign, Inc. VeriSign's Web site gives a six-step procedure for obtaining a certificate.

On the Web

VeriSign:

http://www.verisign.com

Once you have your certificate and key pair, you'll be able to add security to your intranet by setting up an HTTP-over-SSL, or HTTPS, server. Documents, forms, and e-mail sent through this server will be fully encrypted.

> ### Tip
>
> There may be no free lunch, but you can set up HTTP and HTTPS on the same server! The two protocols are independent and use different ports (80 and 443, respectively). Hence, you can design a single server to handle secure and non-secure information. The Netscape and Microsoft browsers will accommodate both protocols gracefully.

Administrative Concerns

Creating a secure network requires planning, and maintaining it demands vigilance. In this section you will learn the basics of secure server administration.

Setting and Enforcing a Security Policy

One of the simplest guidelines for securing a server is also one of the most effective: Less is more. Here are some steps you can take to put this into practice.

- Limit the number of login accounts on the host, and periodically scan for, and delete, inactive users.

- Don't activate TCP/IP services you don't intend to use. Common culprits include ftp (physically remove the ftp server program if possible), TFTP, NFS, and finger. On a UNIX host, check the file /ETC/INETD .CONF for daemons you don't need and comment them out.

- Use the Password option in Web fields to mask sensitive entries like your password as you type.

- Make sure user passwords are strong enough to withstand at least cursory attempts at cracking. User education is your best hope here, followed by password-testing programs like *crack* (for UNIX, available at **ftp://info.cert.org/pub/tools/crack**).

Passwords to Pass On

They may seem obvious, but the following list of passwords to avoid bears repeating, especially to your users. When choosing a password, NEVER use:

- Words found in the dictionary of any language (such as, gesundheit).

- Proper nouns, including names of real or fictitious characters (such as, Bullwinkle).

- Acronyms commonly used by computer professionals (such as, WYSIWYG).

- Simple variations of first, last, or login names, pets' names, your birthday, and so on (such as, Snookums).

CGI Scripting Risks

CGI scripting and the easy programming interface it provides are among intranetworking's most attractive features. Unfortunately, they're also the greatest contributors of security risk in a Web-based network.

The problem lies not with the Common Gateway Interface itself, but with the power it gives to CGI script authors and, potentially, to users. The burden of establishing secure CGI guidelines falls on the server administrator. This section tells you what to look out for.

> **Tip**
>
> Remove shells and interpreters from the server that you don't intend to use. For example, if you don't run Perl-based CGI scripts, remove the Perl interpreter.

There are two types of risk associated with scripts. One is inadvertent disclosure of server information, such as password or Registry files, that could be used to further subvert security measures. The other is the potential that users can spoof the script into doing something perverse, like executing system commands.

You can take several precautions to lower the risk of running CGI scripts on your Web server:

1. Keep all CGI scripts in a single directory (such as, /CGI-BIN) that only the Web administrator can write to.

2. If possible, use compiled executables rather than Perl scripts, and avoid shell scripts altogether for CGI processing. (This includes *.BAT programs on NT-based servers.)

3. Never trust input data. In Perl, for instance, use the following routine to "untaint" insecure user-input data:

   ```
   $SCARY =~ /^([\w.]*$/;
   $COOL =~ $1;
   ```

   If you must allow non-alphanumeric characters, here's a filter to escape potential metacharacters:

   s/([;<>*\|'&\$!#\(\)\[\]\{\}:'"])/\\$1/g

> **Tip**
>
> If you're using Perl 5, test your scripts using perl -T to invoke the "taint" checking option.

4. Check out the following Web sites for additional detail on safe scripting.

Safe CGI Programming	**\<http://www.cerf.net/~paulp/cgi-security/safe-cgi.txt\>**
CGI Security Tutorial	**\<http://csclub.uwaterloo.ca/u/mlvanbie/cge c/\>**

CGI is the most common means of adding functionality to a Web page, but there are others.

■ *Server Side Includes* are directives embedded in HTML code itself, making possible inline execution of scripts or operating system commands. Quite a few Web servers support SSI. Some, such as WebQuest NT™ by Questar Microsystems Inc., offer an extended set of directives (such as, ODBC database access).

■ *Proprietary APIs* have begun to appear in commercial servers such as Netscape. These trade the portability of CGI for enhanced performance and functionality.

The caveats given in this section concerning CGI administration apply to these tools as well, and to any means of launching processes remotely on network computers.

Using Server Access Logs

Over and above their value for market research and server capacity planning, access logs can alert you to certain types of security violation.

Check your server access and error logs periodically for suspicious activity. On UNIX systems, look for accesses involving system commands such as rm, login, /bin/sh, or perl. On NT servers, look for cmd, ntperl, or del. These may indicate an attempt to trick a CGI script into invoking a system command. Also look for very long lines (greater than 256 characters) in URL requests. This could be an attempt to overrun a program's input buffer and sneak commands to the server. Look as well for multiple unsuccessful attempts to access password-protected documents, particularly configuration files like /etc/passwd (UNIX) or the Windows Registry (NT).

Caution

While server logs can be a powerful tool for enhancing security, distributing them casually can be a security risk. The reason is simple: access logs reveal a lot about the usage patterns and interests of your users. Outside the firewall, this gives rise to privacy concerns that have led many Internet providers to restrict the visibility of logs.

On an intranet, privacy may still be a concern, particularly if the intranet has a social dimension that includes things like the Alcoholics Anonymous meeting schedule. Another concern is that analysis of logs can indicate the location of confidential data. The files most accessed by payroll personnel, for instance, might contain sensitive salary or budgetary data.

As with other files on the Web server, take a conservative approach to access and error logs. Make them available on a need-to-know basis.

CGI Scripts, Server Side Includes, and Server APIs

It's time to talk about creating dynamic documents on your server. One of the earliest means of creating documents on-the-fly is through the use of the Common Gateway Interface (CGI). Using CGI scripts, your server can interact with third-party applications which can execute document searches, query databases, or return a dynamically-created HTML page. You can give your intranet users that customized and professional feel to your server.

There are other means of creating interactive services on your Web servers. Server Side Includes are customized capabilities offered by Web server applications that allow you to produce dynamic documents but without the resource overhead of CGI script processing. In addition, some servers offer access to dynamically-linked code libraries known as Application Programming Interfaces (APIs).

Introduction to CGI

Normally, Web servers respond to requests from Web browsers in the form of HTML documents and images. The browsers send a URL to the server, and the server sends the file—whether it's an HTML document, GIF or JPEG graphic, sound file, or movie—to the browser via an HTTP connection. Sometimes, the browser sends a URL that does not point to a document but instead it points to an application. The server activates this application which then responds to the browser with the requisite information. This application is a CGI script and in this section, we'll discuss how this script interacts with the Web server and browser.

One of the most important features of HTML 2.0 was the ability for Web designers to create interactive forms. These forms collect data entered by the user; this data is processed by the Web browser and sent via an HTTP request to a Web server. Usually, the Web server will receive requests for HTML documents or graphic images. However, the HTML form implies that a specific action is requested of the server. With this type of request, the server knows to ignore the content of the form data and redirect the information to a CGI script specified in the HTML form page.

The CGI script is actually a third-party application developed in a language like C, C++, Perl, Visual Basic, or really any language supported by the operating system in which the server is running. However, some languages lend themselves to CGI scripting more than others and we'll discuss those later in this chapter in the section titled, "CGI Scripting."

How the CGI Works

The process through which the Common Gateway Interface works is quite simple. The following lists the step-by-step process:

- The browser accumulates data from an HTML form and prepares it for transmission to the server.
- The server reads the URL enclosed in the browser request and activates the application.
- The server relays the information from the HTML form to the CGI application.
- The CGI script processes the form data and prepares a response. This processing can include a database query, a numerical calculation, or an imagemap request. The response is usually in the form of an HTML document. However, the response is cleverly phrased by the CGI application to convince the Web browser that it originated from the server.
- The CGI application passes the response to the server which immediately redirects it to the Web client. The server does not process the response in any way.

> **Note**
>
> Note that the server merely passes information to the script. The script receives the data from the Web server through some mechanism unique to the language in which the script was developed. As long as this mechanism is in place, any programming language can be used to implement a CGI script.

Client/Server HTTP Header Formats

Web browsers communicate with Web servers via the HTTP protocol. Not only does this protocol specify the physical packet structure of the protocol, but it also defines the manner in which the server and browser exchange information. For example, a Netscape Navigator client might send the following text to a Web server for a simple file request:

```
GET /article1.html HTTP/1.0
Accept: www/source
Accept: text/html
Accept: image/gif
Accept: image/jpeg
User-Agent: Mozilla/2.0b5 (Windows; I; 32bit)
     ...a blank line...
```

This message header informs the server that the browser is looking for the file "article1.html" and intends to use version 1.0 of the HTTP specification. The browser then informs the server as to which file formats it can interpret. In the above message, this list is truncated from what browsers usually express, but the server is informed that the client can interpret several text and graphics MIME types. The browser then informs the server as to its brand of client; in this example, the browser is defined as Netscape Navigator. Finally, the browser passes a blank line to complete the request.

The server will respond with a message generally like the following:

```
HTTP/1.0 200 OK
Date: Thursday, 01-Feb-96 19:15:32 GMT
Server: WebQuest 1.0
MIME-version: 1.0
Last-modified: Friday, 15-Dec-95 17:54:01 GMT
Content-type: text/html
Content-length: 7562
    ...a blank line...
<HTML><HEAD><TITLE>Article....
```

In this response, the server provides enough information to allow the browser to process the requested data. The server denotes that it, too, is providing data using the HTTP v.1.0 protocol. Furthermore, it returns an HTTP code of 200 OK which tells the browser that the requested file was not only found but is being returned in this message. The date and server type are described in the header. The server type is included as the browser may interpret certain features not described in other servers. The server tells the Web client which version of MIME encoding is being used so that the browser can re-process the data. The browser is also informed as to the MIME type of the data and the size of the file; this last datum is important because it allows the browser to inform the user as to the progress of the data transfer.

The server needs to be flexible enough to provide the file in a format that is accessible to the client. For example, the server would need to provide a GIF file if a browser, which could only process GIF files, requests a file that is offered in JPEG.

Tip

The client and server header formats are defined in RFC 822.

As mentioned previously, the HTTP server does not process output from a CGI application; the response is merely funneled through the server back at the browser. The message, however, must be configured so as to conform to the HTTP message header specifications. Later in this chapter in the section titled, "The CGI Data File", we will discuss ways that you can program your CGI script to insert an HTTP header at the beginning of your response to ensure correct processing by a Web browser.

HTML Forms and CGI

By using an HTML form page, you can allow users to enter data which is processed by a CGI script. As discussed earlier in this book, users can enter text and specify options using forms developed with HTML. The types of data input options are as follows:

- Multi-line text entry fields
- Pop-up selection menus
- Radio buttons
- Checkboxes

Figure 18.7 shows an example of an HTML form that can be used to transfer data to a CGI application. Note that this sample page contains text, checkboxes, and radio buttons. The HTML code for this page follows:

```
<HTML>
<HEAD>
<TITLE>
Forms Test
</TITLE>
</HEAD>
<BODY>
<FORM ACTION="http://hoohoo.ncsa.uiuc.edu/cgi-bin/post-query"
➥METHOD=POST>
A normal text field:
<TEXTAREA NAME="comments1"></TEXTAREA><p>
<HR>
<DL>Please indicate your favorite holiday:
<DD>
<INPUT TYPE="radio" NAME="holiday" VALUE="Christmas">Christmas
<DD>
<INPUT TYPE="radio" NAME="holiday"
➥VALUE="Thanksgiving">Thanksgiving
<DD>
<INPUT TYPE="radio" NAME="holiday" VALUE="Easter">Easter
<DD>
<INPUT TYPE="radio" NAME="holiday" VALUE="NYDay">New Year's Day
</DL>
<DL>Please put a check next to the applications you own:
<DD>
<INPUT TYPE="checkbox" NAME="msword" VALUE="No" CHECKED>Microsoft
➥Word
<DD>
<INPUT TYPE="checkbox" NAME="photoshop" VALUE="No">Adobe Photoshop
<DD>
```

```
<INPUT TYPE="checkbox" NAME="netscape" VALUE="No">Netscape
<DD>
<INPUT TYPE="checkbox" NAME="excel" VALUE="No">Microsoft Excel
</DL>
<INPUT TYPE="submit" VALUE="Submit This Form">
</FORM>
</BODY>
</HTML>
```

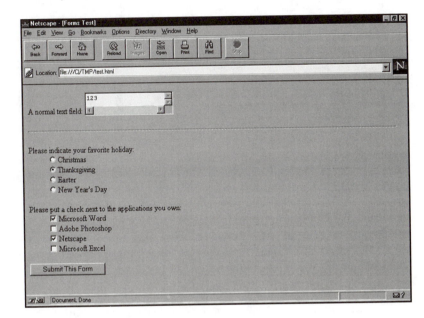

Fig. 18.7
There are several types of HTML forms you can use to retrieve information from Web users.

Note that all of the form elements in the above code use the NAME attribute. The idea is that the user enters text in a field or checks a radio button; this data is assigned a variable corresponding to the value of the NAME attribute. The CGI script uses this data by referencing the corresponding variable name. For example, the response from a post-query script to the above example is shown in figure 18.8.

> **Note**
>
> A post-query script is a generic term for any script that merely echoes back the results of an HTML form submission. In the nominal NCSA httpd software distribution, a simple CGI script entitled post-query reflects the values of the entered text data. Post-query scripts are one of the simplest implementations of CGI scripting and are useful for debugging HTML form pages.

Fig. 18.8

A post-query script is useful for displaying the values of an HTML form.

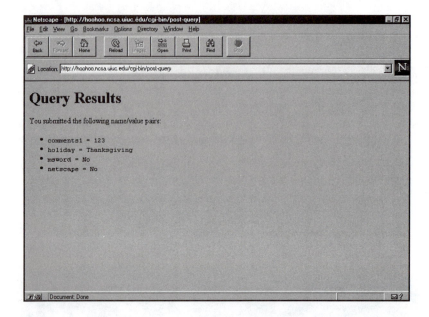

Two alternative methods of transferring form data to a CGI script are POST and GET. These are the possible values of the METHOD attribute in the opening <FORM> tag. The GET method of transferring data is somewhat antiquated dating back to the old Gopher days. You are limited to passing no more than 24K of data back to the server using GET.

POST, however, allows the transfer of much more data. This results from the fact that a request made through the GET method assembles all the HTML form variables into a single string; this string is appended to the URL in the HTTP message that identifies the CGI script. Requests made through the POST method combine all the form parameters into an internal variable that is passed to the script.

The CGI Data File

In order to get the CGI application to run on any operating system, there needs to be some mechanism to convey the form data from the HTTP server to the CGI application. With UNIX, this is done through the use of environment variables, standard input, and output. With Web servers running under the MacOS, AppleEvents are used to convey data to and from the CGI script and Web server. With Windows 3.1, Windows 95, and Windows NT, CGI variables are exchanged using a Windows "private profile" file in key-value format. The CGI script can then use standard Windows APIs for differentiating and retrieving the key-value pairs from the file.

CGI Variables

The variables described in this section are passed from the browser to the server; they pertain to information about the browser. These variables can be used by your CGI application to display information about the server, the user, the user's browser, or the user's connection to the server. The DOS CGI environment variable is included in parentheses where applicable.

- *Server Software* (SERVER_SOFTWARE)

  The name and software version of the Web server answering the request and launching the CGI application.

  Example: `WebQuest/V1.0`

- *Server Name* (SERVER_NAME)

  The server's host name or IP address.

  Example: `www.mcp.com`

- *Server Port* (SERVER_PORT)

  The port number that received the request.

  Example: `80`

- *CGI Version* (GATEWAY_INTERFACE)

  The version of the CGI standard to which the server replies.

  Example: `CGI/1.2 Win`

- *Request Protocol* (SERVER_PROTOCOL)

  The name and version of the protocol used by the client for this request.

  Example: `HTTP/1.0`

- *Request Method* (REQUEST_METHOD)

  The HTTP method specified in the request.

  Examples: `GET`, `HEAD`, `POST`

- *Referrer* (REFERRER)

  The URL of the document from which the CGI script was referred.

  Example: `http://www.anywhere.com/cgi-test.html`

- *From* (FROM)

  The e-mail address of the Web browser user.

> **Note**
>
> The *From* variable is not used by every browser because of privacy concerns although it is included in the HTTP specification.

■ *User Agent* (HTTP_USER_AGENT)

This variable contains the description of the browser software. Your CGI scripts may react differently depending on the particular browser which is accessing your site.

Example: Mozilla/2.0b6 (Windows; I; 32bit)

■ *Logical Path* (PATH_INFO)

Sometimes, a request may specify a logical path to a needed resource. This path may be in a logical path name This variable can be used as an alternative to repeatedly referring to an excessively long path name.

Example: Instead of `http://myweb/cgi-bin/myscript/homepage`, use `"homepage"`

> ### Tip
>
> As of this writing, the WebQuest server does not support the Logical Path variable.

■ *Physical Path* (PATH_TRANSLATED)

If a logical path is specified in the client message, that path can be referenced to a physical location on the WWW server.

Example: `http://myweb/cgi-bin/myscript/homepage` is equivalent to `"C:\WEBQUEST\USER\HOME"`

■ *Executable Path* (SCRIPT_NAME)

The logical path of the CGI script specified by the request. This is referenced to the server URL.

Example: `cgi-dos/test-cgi.bat`

■ *Query String* (QUERY_STRING)

The encoded version of the query data. This data follows the ? in the URL and is usually the result of a query from an HTML form.

Example: `Joe%20Smith+5551321`

■ *Remote Host* (REMOTE_HOST)

The IP host name of the Web browser making the request.

Example: `s115.slipper.net`

■ *Remote Address* (REMOTE_ADDRESS)

The IP address of the Web browser making the request.

Example: `167.142.100.115`

■ *Authentication Method* (AUTH_TYPE)

The protocol-specific method of authentication used to validate the user if the document is protected and the server supports authentication.

> **Note**
>
> This corresponds to the `AuthType` directive in NCSA's HTTPd.

■ *Authenticated User Name* (REMOTE_USER)

The name of the authenticated user if the document is protected and the server supports authentication.

> **Note**
>
> This corresponds to the `AuthUser` directive in NCSA's HTTPd.

■ *Authentication Realm*

The authentication realm used if the document is protected and the server supports authentication. The list of members of a particular realm are checked upon requested access of a particular document.

■ *Authenticated Username*

The authenticated username if the document is protected and the server supports authentication.

■ *Content Type* (CONTENT_TYPE)

The MIME type/subtype of the HTML form data contained in a PUT or POST request.

Example: `text/plain`

■ *Content Length* (CONTENT_LENGTH)

The number of bytes of data contained in a PUT or POST request. This allows the browser to display the progress of a lengthy transmission to the user.

Example: `42`

■ *Content File*

The path to the server-created temporary file that contains the content (query string) sent by the client in a PUT or POST request. This is used when a file is included in the HTTP request.

The Accept Section

This section contains the MIME types that can be processed by the Web client making the connection.

- *Accept* (HTTP_ACCEPT)

  The list of MIME types accepted by the client. You can pass parameters for some of the MIME type/subtype combinations.

  Example: `text/plain, text/html, image/gif`

The System Section

This section contains information relevant only to the Windows implementation of CGI.

- *Output File* (OUTPUT_FILE)

  The full name and location of the file from which the server is told to look for the CGI script output. The server sets this variable and makes it available to the script.

  Example: `C:\DOS\HS063D62.ACC`

- *GMT Offset* (DATE_GMT)

  The number of seconds to be added to Greenwich Mean Time (GMT) to reach local time. Note that this value changes if your server resides in an area of the U.S. that uses Daylight Savings Time.

- *Debug Mode*

  This variable can be used to provide conditional tracing within the CGI program.

  Example: `Yes¦No`

The Extra Headers Section

This section contains additional headers that were included in the request. These headers must be implemented in the "key=value" format in the browser request. The server needs to parse the key-value pair before writing them to the CGI data file.

The Form Literal Section

If the Web browser request is made using the POST method from an HTML form, the server will decode the data and put it in the Form Literal section of the CGI data file. If the MIME type of the encoded data is application/x-www-form-urlencoded, then the input will be in the form of "key=value&key=value&..." with the latter parts of the pair in URL-encoded format. The server processes this input by differentiating between the different pairs and then again by key and value. The key and decoded value are installed in key-value pairs in this section. If the encoded data is of MIME multipart format (MIME type is multipart/form-data), then the input is delivered to the server in a MIME-style multipart format with separated fields. The server extracts this information and installs it in key-value pairs in this section.

Several HTML form types (checkboxes, radio buttons, and pop-up menus) allow the user to select multiple options. In this case, there will be multiple occurrences of the identical key value passed to the server. In this instance, the server generates a key-value pair for the first selection and it appends a sequence number for the following occurrences.

The Form External Section

This section contains the path name of a temporary file written by the server when a decoded value string is longer than a certain amount (usually 254 characters). This temporary file is also written if the string contains special characters such as double-quotes or non-standard ASCII characters. The server writes the decoded string to a temporary file and inserts the path name and length of the string in this section.

The Form Huge Section

In instances where a value string is longer than a large amount, usually 65,535 bytes, it is not decoded but instead stored in a temporary file. The server notes the size of the file and its offset position in the content file in this section. A value string this large usually is not a string but a binary file sent with the browser request, so that the CGI application must note this accordingly.

The Form File Section

If the browser request is transmitted using the multipart/form-data format, then the browser request consists of several file uploads. In this case, each file upload is stored in an external file. The server takes note of the location of the uploaded file, the transfer MIME type, and the original name of the uploaded file and stores this information in this section.

Sample CGI Data File

The following example details part of a hypothetical CGI data file. Note that in the Form Literal section, the results of a multiple selection are displayed with the field name followed by a sequence number. Also note the expression of a large field and a field with quote characters in the Form Large section. A file is stored in a temporary file, and its location and size are denoted in the Form Huge section.

V

Using the Internet

Note

Note that the CGI data file sections are denoted with left and right brackets ([ ]). These aid in processing by the CGI script.

```
[CGI]
Request Protocol: HTTP/1.0
Request Method: Post
...
[Accept]
Accept: text/html
Accept: image/gif
Accept: image/jpeg
[Form Literal]
streetaddress=234 Elm St
phonenumber_1=5552323
phonenumber_2=5553434
phonenumber_3=5551234
[Form External]
largefield=C:\TEMP\FG18AF6C.000 300
fieldwithquotes=C:\TEMP\FG18AF6C.001 56
[Form Huge]
hugefield=C:\TEMP\ FG18AF6C.002 30345
```

Choosing a CGI Platform

Now that we have a good idea of how CGI applications work, we can talk about the environment in which to develop your scripts. Your main options are DOS and Windows. In this section, we will examine the strengths and weaknesses of each system as a platform for developing CGI applications. There are several tasks that you will want your script to perform.

Note

In reality, you can utilize CGI applications that reside on different computers. Your NT server can access a CGI application which resides on a UNIX computer or even a Macintosh Web server. The Web server will communicate with a remote script with only a nominal communication delay. This technique is advisable if the script you wish to execute is sizable, and the remote computer is a faster machine that the one on which your NT server resides.

Text Manipulation and Searching

You will find text-processing CGI scripts written in DOS provide superior performance to those written in Windows 3.x. One reason for this is that DOS provides a native file search command (FIND) and other file redirection utilities. Windows NT provides a command shell interface similar to DOS to allow you to write similar text-manipulation applications in native 32-bit code.

Binary Data Manipulation

There may be instances where you will want to access information stored in spreadsheets or databases. In these instances, it may be more advantageous to work with Windows CGI scripts. You will be able to take advantage of OLE and DDE to exchange data between your scripts and sophisticated applications such as Microsoft Excel or Oracle databases. Furthermore, you will find it much easier and faster to open these applications within Windows than from a DOS batch file.

Many of the sophisticated Windows applications also maintain powerful macro languages. You can utilize these macros within a Windows script file to further customize your CGI application. Using these macros in conjunction with the powerful OLE and DDE capabilities of a language such as Visual Basic affords you many scripting opportunities.

> **Tip**
>
> Although launching Windows applications such as word processors and spreadsheets as scripts is possible, the time required to load these programs for each request is significant. A better way is to run the desired applications continually in the background and to communicate with them via small Visual Basic executables that utilize DDE or OLE.

Miscellaneous Trade-offs

Running a DOS CGI under Windows NT will, in most instances, provide slower performance than a script written entirely with NT applications. There is a great deal of overhead involved in launching a DOS script within Windows NT, as the DOS session must be launched as well. Furthermore, the DOS CGI environment is designed for 16-bit DOS programs so you will be able to inherit neither standard input and output handles, nor the environment variables from a 32-bit NT server. Instead, the DOS CGI interface stores these variables in a BAT file containing SET statements for all of the environment variables and explicit command line redirection for the input and output files.

> **Note**
>
> The latest version of DOS (version 7.0) uses a 32-bit architecture but has not been extensively tested as a CGI interface as of this writing.

> **Tip**
>
> Examination of DOS CGI files provides an excellent means of debugging your scripts. All of the environment variables, input, and output files are available for your perusal. Using the WebSite server, you can easily swap your CGI applications from the Windows to the DOS interface by moving the executable from the **\cgi-shl** directory to the **\cgi-dos** directory. Simply change the URL in the HTML document and you have an effective means of debugging your scripts.

Except for very simple scripts, such as text searches or simple HTML document creation, you will want to develop your CGI scripts using the Windows interface. While there is sufficient overhead in developing and utilizing a Windows CGI script, the exchange protocols inherent in the 32-bit operating system make it a powerful scripting environment.

CGI Scripting

Under Windows NT, you have several environments to choose from in developing your CGI scripts. Just as certain operating systems lend themselves to certain tasks, certain scripting languages are better suited for various CGI applications. There is nothing requiring you to develop all of your CGI applications in only one language. You can develop text-processing CGIs in DOS batch files, search CGIs in Perl, and spreadsheet and database manipulation scripts using Visual Basic or Delphi. In this section, we will look at the various languages and scripting environments at your disposal.

DOS Shell Scripts

You can take advantage of the DOS CGI interface using the default MS-DOS shell, COMMAND.COM. This shell environment allows you to create rudimentary scripts which return files and simple text. The biggest disadvantage of this shell is that the left and right brackets (<>) used to develop HTML formatting tags imply special file redirection commands. To get around this shortcoming, you can insert files containing pre-formatted HTML commands. As an alternative to the MS-DOS shell, you can use more robust DOS environments such as those offered by Norton Utilities—NDOS, IBMs PC-DOS, or DR-DOS. Except for scripts that perform the most rudimentary functions, you should avoid developing scripts using DOS shell commands.

C/C++

Many people write CGI applications using C or C++ under all major operating systems. Compiled 32-bit code will run extremely quickly, and it would be difficult to see a script run more quickly using a different application environment. However, C is extremely difficult to learn and C++ is slightly less so. Furthermore, there is no freeware/shareware C/C++ compiler so you have to acquire a compiler from a commercial vendor such as Borland or Microsoft.

Whereas the difficulty of using the languages is a drawback, there are many libraries of C/C++ CGI scripts available, so many of the mundane tasks you wish to script may have already been done so. CGIs written in these languages will provide superior performance for complicated text processing. However, if you wish to develop a script that works with other NT applications, these languages may not be for you as such an interface would be clumsy and complicated.

Visual Basic

Microsoft's Visual Basic (VB) is a visually-oriented programming tool designed to aid you in creating applications under the Windows environment. Using VB, you can develop CGI applications that read and interpret the CGI data file and process the key/value pairs. Visual Basic scripts execute considerably faster than DOS shell scripts. Furthermore, the language has seen a rise in popularity as a CGI platform so there are many libraries of VB CGI applications available on the Internet.

> **Note**
>
> If you're looking for a good reference for Visual Basic uses with OLE and DDE, you can find thorough coverage of Visual Basic along with OLE and DDE in Que's *Using Visual Basic for Applications Excel Edition*.

Delphi

Similar to Visual Basic and PowerBuilder, Borland's Delphi is an extremely popular programming language which uses a compiler optimized to create very fast applications. Like these other languages, Delphi applications are self-contained and do not need to run with dynamically linked libraries as is the case with Visual Basic. Delphi incorporates the Borland Database Engine (BDE), providing direct access to data stored in dBASE, Paradox, the Local InterBase Server, and to other data formats via ODBC. Therefore, Delphi would be an easy means of developing very nimble CGI applications that work with external databases.

Perl

The Practical Extraction and Report Language (PERL or most commonly, Perl) is a popular text-processing language with origins in the UNIX operating system. Perl offers much of the utility of C and C++ but with easier syntax rules. As a result, Perl is wildly popular as a CGI platform in the UNIX environment and has been ported to the major OS platforms such as OS/2, MacOS, DOS, and Windows NT.

Perl is a compiled language and provides one of the fastest compilers of any high-level language. However, Perl scripts are compiled at runtime, so using Perl scripts as CGI applications will give them that interpreted feel. The ubiquity of Perl throughout the major operating systems ensures that you will find a vast resource of CGI scripts available for your perusal. With minor modifications, you can incorporate these Perl scripts into your server.

Perl has been ported to the 32-bit Windows environments. This version of Perl for Win32 is available at Hip Communication's WWW site (**http:// www.perl.hip.com**). Binaries are available for the MIPS, Alpha, PowerPC, and Intel architectures. You will need a copy of WinZip, rather than PKZIP, to decrypt the file (as Perl for Win32 uses long filenames).

When unzipping the distribution, make sure that you preserve directory structure as well. This will prevent errors when compiling the source code. In order to compile the source code, you will also need a Win32 compiler such as MSVC2.0 or the Win32 Software Developer Kit. The makefiles require the utility **nmake** to build the tree.

While the hooks are in Perl for Win32 to access applications like databases through OLE Automation extensions, you will not be able to interact with other Windows 32-bit applications with the ease offered by Visual Basic or Delphi CGI scripts. For this reason, you will want to use Perl for Win32 to develop large scripts that do not require sophisticated interaction between Windows applications. Examples of scripting applications useful for Perl would be guestbooks, document access counters, and mail forwarding.

Server Side Includes with WebQuest

You may have portions of your Web site that are actually documents within documents. For example, you may want to include on your home page, a "news of the day" file that you edit separately from your HTML document. One way that you can do this is to create a CGI script that creates your home page by creating an HTML document and processing the updated file. However, the disadvantage of this is that your home page, which is no doubt accessed frequently, will now be a script instead of a simple HTML file. Regardless of your scripting language and your skills as a programmer, your server will always execute the script more slowly than it will display the HTML file.

Another alternative is to use Server Side Includes (SSIs) to display the file within your HTML document. An SSI allows you to serve a file on-the-fly without the use of CGI scripting. Some possible uses of SSIs include:

- Send e-mail via HTML form input
- Include output from a CGI script
- Display current date and time
- Display file modification dates
- Conditional execution of external applications

Questar has developed an extension to the SSI concept known as SSI+ for use with the WebQuest server. While you can still run SSIs and CGI scripts as with other servers; with SSI+, you can add additional functionality to your server.

How SSIs Work

When a Web server responds to a document request from a Web browser, it sends the file as it's stored in the file system. When the document contains SSI commands, the server scans the file looking for the commands to instruct it to include various files. The server knows that a file contains SSI information by the extension; while normal HTML documents contain HTML suffices, documents containing SSI commands have suffices of SHTML. The MIME type for these documents is *text/x-server-parsed-html*.

> **Note**
>
> You are not required to assign a special suffix for HTML files. You could assign the MIME type *text/x-server-parsed-html* to files with the HTML suffix. However, this would significantly degrade performance because the server would have to read every file, even those without SSI commands, before sending it.

SSI Specifications

SSI statements in HTML documents have the general format:

```
<!--#command tag1="value1" tag2="value2" -->
```

Note that SSI statements begin with the same formatting characters as HTML comments. This is so that browsers will ignore include statements as if they were comments. Normally, the server replaces the include statements with the items to be included, but if SSI support were turned off on the server, the statements are passed along intact. This also allows you to port your code, with minimal impact, if you are forced to move your documents to a server that does not support SSI statements.

Including Files

To include another file in an HTML document, the format is:

```
<!--#include virtual="virtual_path"-->
```

or

```
<!--#include file="relative_path"-->
```

The virtual option specifies a URL-style virtual path to any document on your server. This virtual path is referenced to the server URL. The file option specifies a path relative to the current directory.

Any normal document, or even a document containing SSI commands, can be included using the Include command.

Including CGI and SSI Variables

The ECHO command can be used to display the contents of any DOS CGI environment variable discussed earlier in this chapter or one of the special variables defined for include statements. The general format is:

```
<!--#echo var="variable_name"-->
```

Besides the DOS CGI environment variables, variable_name can be one of the following SSI variables:

- DOCUMENT_NAME. The document file name.
- DOCUMENT_URI. The virtual path to the document.
- DATE_LOCAL. The current date and time in the local time zone.
- DATE_GMT. The current Greenwich Mean Time.
- LAST_MODIFIED. The last modification date of the document.
- QUERY_STRING_UNESCAPED. The text of any query string sent by the client.

Including Information About Other Files

Two commands can be used to include information about files other than the current document. These are FSIZE, which prints the size of any file, and FLASTMOD, which prints the last modification date of any file. The format for these commands is:

```
<!--#fsize file_spec-->
```

and

```
<!--#flastmod file_spec-->
```

The *file_spec* is either file="*relative_path*" or virtual="*virtual_path*" as in the include command.

Including Script and Command Output

You can include the output of any command or CGI script in a parsed document. The general format for this is:

```
<!--#exec cmd="command_string"-->
```

or

```
<!--#exec cgi="virtual_path"-->
```

where command_string denotes a DOS command file and virtual_path denotes a path to a CGI executable relative to the base directory of the Web server.

Caution

The EXEC option is the most dangerous Server Side Include command because it can be used to run any command or program on the server. Among other things, this could rapidly crash your server if a particularly large program were executed every time a certain document was accessed.

Customizing Output

The CONFIG command is used to control the output format of other include commands. The format is:

```
<!--#config [errmsg="error_message"] [sizefmt="{bytes¦abbrev}"]
[timefmt="format_string"]-->
```

The following tags are used with the CONFIG command:

errmsg   Specifies error message to be sent to client if error occurs during document parsing.

sizefmt   Specifies whether file size information will appear in bytes (251,335) or in abbreviated format (251K).

timefmt   Specifies the format to be used for all time and date information.

SSI+ Specifications

SSI+ extends the functionality of SSI by adding such capabilities as database access, comparison statements, e-mail, and other capabilities. Furthermore, you can use DLL and ODBC calls to run in the code space of your server, which is much more efficient than using external CGI scripts. The SSI+ specifications, as defined by Questar, call for an interface to the new CScript language; CScript is a C-like programming language with object-oriented extensions customized for HTTP service. CScript allows you to develop applications that integrate seamlessly with your server.

Output Configuration

In the SSI+ specification, the config statement is further extended with the following options:

cmdecho=[ON|OFF]   When a command is executed using exec, this tag determines whether any output is issued with the HTML document. The default is OFF.

cmdprefix="string"   Determines "string" that is used to prefix any command output.

cmdpostfix="string" Determines "string" that is used to postfix any command output.

onerr=<action>   Performs some action upon error. The action is equivalent to the action described in the if command below.

Updating ODBC Databases

The obdc command is used to query and update ODBC databases. The syntax for the command is similar to the SSI commands discussed above. There are four types of obdc tags listed below:

debug   Turns on advanced diagnostic messages to be used during application development.

connect   Defines data source name, username, and password.

format   Defines format and appearance of query result.

statement Describes the SQL statement to be performed.

Sending E-mail

When included in an HTML file accessed by the server, the e-mail command sends a message via SMTP according to certain parameters. These parameters are listed below:

debug	Enables advanced diagnostics for use during application development.
fromaddress	Defines the e-mail From field.
toaddress	Defines the e-mail address to which the message will be directed.
message	Defines the content of the mail message.
subject	Describes the subject of the message.
sender	Defines a sender e-mail address.
replyto	Describes the e-mail address to which replies should be sent.
cc	Defines the carbon copy address.
inreplyto	Contains the in-reply-to field of the message.
id	Defines the ID field of the message.

Conditional Statements

Using the if command, you can execute conditional statements in your HTML documents. With this statement, you can evaluate numerical, alphabetic, or CGI or SSI+ variable conditions. For example, you may wish to display a certain message if your browser is using a non-Netscape Web client warning them that there are Netscape extensions used in the page.

```
<!--if {logical expression #1}{operator}{logical expression #2}
➥{action}-->
```

The expressions, logical expression #1 and logical expression #2 are evaluated using the logical operator. The operator consists of one of the following:

==	Equal
!=	Not Equal
<	Less Than
>	Greater Than
!<	Not Less Than
!>	Not Greater Than
hasstring	Returns true if string in logical operator #1 contains logical operator #2.

V

Using the Internet

If the if statement is evaluated as false, nothing happens. If the comparison is evaluated as true, then one of the following operations can take place as defined in the action tag.

goto "label"	Causes a jump to a pre-defined SSI label.
print "string"	Prints "string" to the HTML document.
error	Prints the error message defined in config.
break	Terminates HTML transmission to the client.
errorbreak	Prints the config error message, then suspends the HTML transmission.
printbreak "string"	Prints "string," then suspends the HTML transmission.

For example, you may wish to notify non-Netscape users that your page contains Netscape HTML extensions. This could be done with the following script:

```
<!--#if"&&HTTP_USER_AGENT&&" hasstring "Mozilla" goto nscplabel-->
<P>You will need Netscape Navigator to view the features on this
page.
<!--#break-->
<!--#label="nscplabel"-->
...next SSI commands
```

> **Note**
>
> The DOS CGI environment variable was accessed by enveloping it with double ampersands (&&). All environment and HTML form variables are accessed in SSI+ scripts in this manner.

Be Careful with SSIs

Use Server Side Includes sparingly. Users can imbed SSI statements into CGI script requests that could download sensitive data such as password files. Make sure that your SSIs do not have access to your script directories. Some server administrators even disable the exec command to prevent users from bogging the system down with execution of large files.

Server Side Includes Summary

The advantages of Server Side Includes is that they offer a sophisticated means of processing data without the overhead or complication of developing CGI scripts. These commands are built in to the server architecture, and the server performs the processing. The disadvantage is that your Web pages are no longer portable and must be served by the WebQuest server or some server that supports SSI or SSI+.

As the Web is a very volatile environment, you cannot say for sure that you will be using a server application 12 months from now or even six months from now. While SSI+ offers many sophisticated capabilities, it is still not widely supported by Windows NT servers other than WebQuest at this time. You will need to evaluate your commitment to WebQuest or other servers before making extensive use of SSI.

Other Scripting Additions

Besides the CGI and SSI specifications, there are other means with which you can add functionality to your server. The two methods discussed in this section pertain to the Netscape browser and server, but may be eventually extended to other servers as well.

The Netscape Server API

The Netscape Server API (NSAPI) is an extension that allows you to customize the capabilities of the Netscape server. Using the NSAPI, you can provide a scaleable and high-performance mechanism for building interfaces between the server and external applications.

Your external applications are executed as if they were part of the HTTP server application itself. The applications are stored as code libraries to which the Netscape server can dynamically link. You will need to spend time adjusting your applications to take advantage of the NSAPI, and you will also need to modify the server configuration files to include your software libraries. This means that you will need to use higher-level languages such as C/C++ or Delphi over simpler scripting environments such as Perl or DOS Shell. However, data will transfer much more quickly as the applications will be linked into the server as if they were part of the Netscape server application.

The NSAPI specification is available at:

http://www.netscape.com/newsref/std/server_api.html

Using HTTP Cookies

Cookies are a new CGI add-on mechanism proposed by Netscape Communications, but as of this writing, are also supported by the Microsoft Internet Explorer. Cookies are designed to communicate state information to the browser from the server. This is in contrast to the standard HTTP process where server information outside of the HTTP response is not communicated to the browser.

When a browser accesses a CGI script containing a cookie header, that cookie type is transferred back to the browser along with the CGI response. Each time the browser accesses that CGI script, it will send the cookie value in the environment variable HTTP_COOKIE. Possible applications include client preferences, such as user accounts and personal information, for online shopping services.

The syntax for a cookie header is as follows:

```
Set-Cookie:  name=Value; expires=Date;
path=Path; domain=Domain_Name; secure
```

The cookie name is the only required attribute that identifies the cookie. You can set an expiration date with the expires tag; after that date, the cookie becomes invalid. The domain keyword is used by the server to validate the cookie; while searching the cookie list for valid entries, the domain keyword is matched against the domain of the requesting host. This enables the server to match the cookie from many other browsers making similar requests. Similarly, the path keyword is used to validate the cookie request. The cookie is transferred if the path defined by the requesting browser matches the cookie path attribute. The secure keyword alerts the server to transfer the cookie only if the connection is made using the Secure Sockets Layer protocol.

The Cookie specifications are available at:

On the Web

http://www.netscape.com/newsref/std/cookie_spec.html

As of this writing, the implementation of the cookie mechanism has not been finalized, so the specifications should be consulted before attempting to utilize cookies. ❖

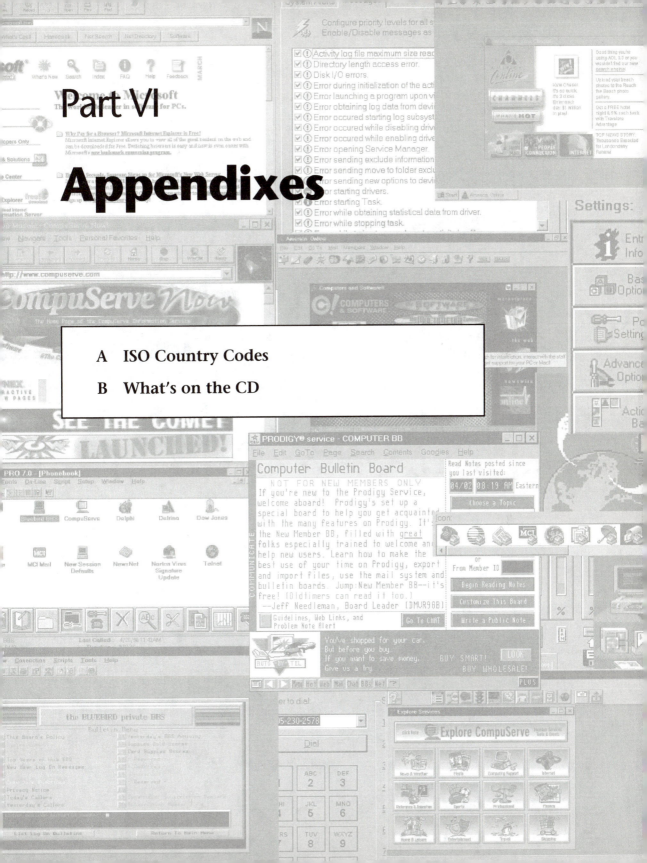

Part VI

Appendixes

ISO Country Codes

The International Organization for Standardization (ISO) publishes a standard two-letter country code abbreviation table that includes the code for each country. This table, reproduced below, allows you to determine the geographic location of Internet sites and Internet e-mail addresses.

Country	ISO Code
AFGHANISTAN	AF
ALBANIA	AL
ALGERIA	DZ
AMERICAN SAMOA	AS
ANDORRA	AD
ANGOLA	AO
ANGUILLA	AI
ANTARCTICA	AQ
ANTIGUA AND BARBUDA	AG
ARGENTINA	AR
ARMENIA	AM
ARUBA	AW
AUSTRALIA	AU
AUSTRIA	AT
AZERBAIJAN	AZ
BAHAMAS	BS
BAHRAIN	BH

(continues)

(continued)

Country	ISO Code
BANGLADESH	BD
BARBADOS	BB
BELARUS	BY
BELGIUM	BE
BELIZE	BZ
BENIN	BJ
BERMUDA	BM
BHUTAN	BT
BOLIVIA	BO
BOSNIA AND HERZEGOWINA	BA
BOTSWANA	BW
BOUVET ISLAND	BV
BRAZIL	BR
BRITISH INDIAN OCEAN TERRITORY	IO
BRUNEI DARUSSALAM	BN
BULGARIA	BG
BURKINA FASO	BF
BURUNDI	BI
CAMBODIA	KH
CAMEROON	CM
CANADA	CA
CAPE VERDE	CV
CAYMAN ISLANDS	KY
CENTRAL AFRICAN REPUBLIC	CF
CHAD	TD
CHILE	CL
CHINA	CN
CHRISTMAS ISLAND	CX
COCOS (KEELING) ISLANDS	CC
COLOMBIA	CO
COMOROS	KM
CONGO	CG
COOK ISLANDS	CK
COSTA RICA	CR

Country	ISO Code
COTE D'IVOIRE	CI
CROATIA (local name: Hrvatska)	HR
CUBA	CU
CYPRUS	CY
CZECH REPUBLIC	CZ
DENMARK	DK
DJIBOUTI	DJ
DOMINICA	DM
DOMINICAN REPUBLIC	DO
EAST TIMOR	TP
ECUADOR	EC
EGYPT	EG
EL SALVADOR	SV
EQUATORIAL GUINEA	GQ
ERITREA	ER
ESTONIA	EE
ETHIOPIA	ET
FALKLAND ISLANDS (MALVINAS)	FK
FAROE ISLANDS	FO
FIJI	FJ
FINLAND	FI
FRANCE	FR
FRANCE, METROPOLITAN	FX
FRENCH GUIANA	GF
FRENCH POLYNESIA	PF
FRENCH SOUTHERN TERRITORIES	TF
GABON	GA
GAMBIA	GM
GEORGIA	GE
GERMANY	DE
GHANA	GH
GIBRALTAR	GI
GREECE	GR

VI

Appendixes

(continues)

(continued)

Country	ISO Code
GREENLAND	GL
GRENADA	GD
GUADELOUPE	GP
GUAM	GU
GUATEMALA	GT
GUINEA	GN
GUINEA-BISSAU	GW
GUYANA	GY
HAITI	HT
HEARD AND MCDONALD ISLANDS	HM
HONDURAS	HN
HONG KONG	HK
HUNGARY	HU
ICELAND	IS
INDIA	IN
INDONESIA	ID
IRAN (ISLAMIC REPUBLIC OF)	IR
IRAQ	IQ
IRELAND	IE
ISRAEL	IL
ITALY	IT
JAMAICA	JM
JAPAN	JP
JORDAN	JO
KAZAKHSTAN	KZ
KENYA	KE
KIRIBATI	KI
KOREA, DEMOCRATIC PEOPLE'S REPUBLIC OF	KP
KOREA, REPUBLIC OF	KR
KUWAIT	KW
KYRGYZSTAN	KG
LAO PEOPLE'S DEMOCRATIC REPUBLIC	LA

Country	ISO Code
LATVIA	LV
LEBANON	LB
LESOTHO	LS
LIBERIA	LR
LIBYAN ARAB JAMAHIRIYA	LY
LIECHTENSTEIN	LI
LITHUANIA	LT
LUXEMBOURG	LU
MACAU	MO
MACEDONIA, THE FORMER YUGOSLAV REPUBLIC OF	MK
MADAGASCAR	MG
MALAWI	MW
MALAYSIA	MY
MALDIVES	MV
MALI	ML
MALTA	MT
MARSHALL ISLANDS	MH
MARTINIQUE	MQ
MAURITANIA	MR
MAURITIUS	MU
MAYOTTE	YT
MEXICO	MX
MICRONESIA, FEDERATED STATES OF	FM
MOLDOVA, REPUBLIC OF	MD
MONACO	MC
MONGOLIA	MN
MONTSERRAT	MS
MOROCCO	MA
MOZAMBIQUE	MZ
MYANMAR	MM
NAMIBIA	NA
NAURU	NR

(continues)

VI

Appendixes

(continued)

Country	ISO Code
NEPAL	NP
NETHERLANDS	NL
NETHERLANDS ANTILLES	AN
NEW CALEDONIA	NC
NEW ZEALAND	NZ
NICARAGUA	NI
NIGER	NE
NIGERIA	NG
NIUE	NU
NORFOLK ISLAND	NF
NORTHERN MARIANA ISLANDS	MP
NORWAY	NO
OMAN	OM
PAKISTAN	PK
PALAU	PW
PANAMA	PA
PAPUA NEW GUINEA	PG
PARAGUAY	PY
PERU	PE
PHILIPPINES	PH
PITCAIRN	PN
POLAND	PL
PORTUGAL	PT
PUERTO RICO	PR
QATAR	QA
REUNION	RE
ROMANIA	RO
RUSSIAN FEDERATION	RU
RWANDA	RW
SAINT KITTS AND NEVIS	KN
SAINT LUCIA	LC
SAINT VINCENT AND THE GRENADINES	VC

Country	ISO Code
SAMOA	WS
SAN MARINO	SM
SAO TOME AND PRINCIPE	ST
SAUDI ARABIA	SA
SENEGAL	SN
SEYCHELLES	SC
SIERRA LEONE	SL
SINGAPORE	SG
SLOVAKIA (Slovak Republic)	SK
SLOVENIA	SI
SOLOMON ISLANDS	SB
SOMALIA	SO
SOUTH AFRICA	ZA
SOUTH GEORGIA AND THE SOUTH SANDWICH ISLANDS	GS
SPAIN	ES
SRI LANKA	LK
ST. HELENA	SH
ST. PIERRE AND MIQUELON	PM
SUDAN	SD
SURINAME	SR
SVALBARD AND JAN MAYEN ISLANDS	SJ
SWAZILAND	SZ
SWEDEN	SE
SWITZERLAND	CH
SYRIAN ARAB REPUBLIC	SY
TAIWAN, PROVINCE OF CHINA	TW
TAJIKISTAN	TJ
TANZANIA, UNITED REPUBLIC OF	TZ
THAILAND	TH
TOGO	TG
TOKELAU	TK
TONGA	TO
TRINIDAD AND TOBAGO	TT

(continues)

VI

Appendixes

(continued)

Country	ISO Code
TUNISIA	TN
TURKEY	TR
TURKMENISTAN	TM
TURKS AND CAICOS ISLANDS	TC
TUVALU	TV
UGANDA	UG
UKRAINE	UA
UNITED ARAB EMIRATES	AE
UNITED KINGDOM	GB
UNITED STATES	US
UNITED STATES MINOR OUTLYING ISLANDS	UM
URUGUAY	UY
UZBEKISTAN	UZ
VANUATU	VU
VATICAN CITY STATE (HOLY SEE)	VA
VENEZUELA	VE
VIETNAM	VN
VIRGIN ISLANDS (BRITISH)	VG
VIRGIN ISLANDS (U.S.)	VI
WALLIS AND FUTUNA ISLANDS	WF
WESTERN SAHARA	EH
YEMEN	YE
YUGOSLAVIA	YU
ZAIRE	ZR
ZAMBIA	ZM
ZIMBABWE	ZW

What's on the CD

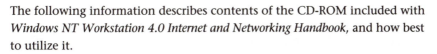

by Rob Tidrow

The following information describes contents of the CD-ROM included with *Windows NT Workstation 4.0 Internet and Networking Handbook*, and how best to utilize it.

Specifically, you learn about

- What type of software you will find on *WINDOWS Magazine*'s Fall 1996 CD-ROM
- System requirements to run the CD
- How to install the *WINDOWS Magazine* CD-ROM
- Where to go for help

Quick Overview of Contents

Que has included the best that *WINDOWS Magazine* has to offer. This CD-ROM is loaded with original, exclusive material you can't find anywhere else.

WINDOWS Magazine CD Exclusives!

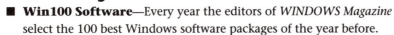

- **Win100 Software**—Every year the editors of *WINDOWS Magazine* select the 100 best Windows software packages of the year before.
- **IMA CD Match**—The Interactive Multimedia Association (IMA) CD Match system enables you to quickly match your computer's multi-media capabilities with that of multimedia CD-ROMs on the market. This way you avoid purchasing CD-ROMs that cannot run on your system.
- **Windows NT Extras**—Here are *WINDOWS Magazine* editor-at-large John Ruley's answers to the most frequently asked Windows NT questions.

- **Windows NT's Future**—Take a peek at the future of Windows 95 and Windows NT. Will Windows 95 be around after 1999, or does Microsoft want the world to migrate to Windows NT exclusively? Find out here. Also, take a peek at Microsoft's Web browser strategy and see what Internet Explore 4.0 looks like.

- **Web Publishing Secrets**—Find Web design and publishing secrets and tips on the *WINDOWS Magazine* CD-ROM. You also can find out about Web site security and virtually everything you want to know about the Internet.

Hardware/Software Buying Tips

- **All The Products**—If you've ever been frustrated trying to find the vendor for a product, or the products in a particular category, you'll appreciate the return of All The Products, a listing of every product that has been mentioned in the editorial pages of *WINDOWS Magazine* since its relaunch in February 1992.

- **WinMag Lab Comparisons**—All the notebook computers and desktop systems reviewed in the last year are placed side-by-side in multiple formats so you can search, order and compare using your own criteria.

- **DecideRight Files**—Until February of 1996, *WINDOWS Magazine* typically did one or two comparative reviews, one of software and one of hardware. Each review had a report card and a feature table associated with it. Now, that information is on the CD-ROM.

Software You Can Run Right Now!

- **Demonstrations**—Included in this issue: Kai's Power Tools 3 demo (you must have PhotoShop 3, Painter 4.0, PhotoPaint 6, or Picture Publisher 6.0 to run this demo) and Visio.

- **Wintune 95**—The industry's only Test and Tuneup Kit—now for Windows 95! If you have Windows 95 clients on your Windows NT network and want to tune them up, use WinTune 95. There are a lot of programs out there that tell you how fast your computer is, but only one that tells you how to make it faster: Wintune from *WINDOWS Magazine*.

- **Superior Shareware**—Normally, you'd need a modem to get these shareware packages from an online service—and you'd pay for the connect time, and run the risk of getting a bad download—but now you can pick from among the 120 best software packages of the last year...and unzip them in an instant.

- **Browsers**—Internet Explorer 2.0 and 3.0 (beta 2) for Windows are available on this CD-ROM.

WINDOWS Magazine **Back Issues**

■ Over a year's worth of searchable, printable *WINDOWS Magazine* back issues.

About *WINDOWS Magazine*

■ *WINDOWS Magazine* **Staff**—Electronic contact information for the editors and sales staff of *WINDOWS Magazine*.

■ **Subscription Information**—How to subscribe to the paper or CD-ROM versions of *WINDOWS Magazine*.

■ **About This CD-ROM**—Find out the technical aspects of the *WINDOWS Magazine* CD-ROM, as well as copyright and conditions of use.

■ **Setup Instructions**—If you have problems setting up the *WINDOWS Magazine* CD-ROM using the instructions shown in this appendix, look for additional instructions on the WELCOME.HTM file.

System Requirements

The minimum recommended hardware configuration should include a 486SX 25MHZ class processor, 4M RAM or more, 256-color video card, color monitor, CD-ROM drive—MPC Level 1 or better—hard disk, sound card, and speakers.

Minimum software should include Microsoft Windows NT 4.0 Server or Workstation (beta 2 or later). You also need a World Wide Web browser designed for Windows NT 4.0, such as Microsoft Internet Explorer 3.0 or Netscape Navigator 3.0. If you already have a Web browser installed then you need only 1K of free disk space (you only set up a shortcut to the CD-ROM). If not, Microsoft's Internet Explorer (versions 2 and 3) is included on the CD, and requires about 4M of free disk space.

> **Note**
>
> Shareware and demonstration programs on this disc may require additional memory or hardware.

Installation

The basic purpose of the install routine is to set up an icon for your current browser to view the contents of the CD, and set up the full-text search engine to work with your browser. To do this, the CD copies a few small files to your hard disk and registers file associations, if they have not been set already.

Installing a Web Browser

If you don't have a browser currently installed, you need to install one now. Internet Explorer 2.0 and 3.0 (beta 2) are included on the WINDOWS Magazine CD-ROM, which you can install by following these steps:

1. Open Control Panel in Windows NT and double-click the Add/Remove Programs icon.

2. Click the Install button on the Install/Uninstall tab.

> **Tip**
>
> The Windows NT 4.0 distribution CD contains the Internet Jumpstart Kit, which includes a copy of Internet Explorer 2.0. You can install Internet Explorer from the distribution CD by clicking the Windows NT Setup tab in step 2 and selecting Accessories, Details, and clicking the Internet Jumpstart Kit option. You need to have your Windows NT 4.0 distribution CD handy when you do this.

3. On the Install Program From Floppy Disk or CD-ROM Wizard screen, click Next.

4. When the Run Installation Program screen appears, click the Browse button and locate the Internet Explorer folders on the *WINDOWS Magazine* CD. These include IEXPLORE, IEXPLORE.30, IEXPLORE.31, and IEXPLORE.NT. For best results under Windows NT 4.0, you should use Internet Explorer 2.0 or Internet Explorer 3.0 (beta 2). For the latest beta version of Internet Explorer 3.0, double-click the IEXPLORE.30 folder and select the MSIE30B2.EXE file. If you want to use Internet Explorer 2.0, select IEXPLORE and select the MSIE20 file.

5. Click Open after you select the specific MSIE file, to display the Run Installation Program screen.

6. Click Finish to install Internet Explorer on your system. Follow the installation messages on-screen to finish installing the Web browser.

Installing the WinMag CD On Windows NT 4.0

After you install a Web browser, just run the install program (INSTALL.EXE) in the root of the CD. You can do this in Windows NT by following these steps:

1. Place the *WINDOWS Magazine* CD in your CD-ROM drive.

> **Note**
>
> If you have turned off Windows NT's AutoStart feature, use the following procedure to install the *WINDOWS Magazine* CD:
>
> Click the Start button. Select Run from the pop up menu and type **D:\ install.exe** (with **D:** as the drive letter of your CD-ROM drive, yours may be different) in the Run dialog box. Choose OK. Continue with step 2.
>
> Alternatively, you can run the Add/Remove Programs applet found in the Control Panel.

2. Windows NT automatically starts the *WINDOWS Magazine* CD installation program, but does not fully install the CD. Because the *WINDOWS Magazine* CD is designed to install automatically only under Windows 95, you must perform manual installation procedures for Windows NT. You are presented with a text file explaining how to continue with the installation process. You can skip to step 26 in the text file to read how to install a Web browser in Windows NT. Skip to step 32 in the text file to review how to install the *WINDOWS Magazine* CD under Windows NT 4.0. Or, follow along in this appendix.

3. Double-click the My Computer icon or launch the Windows NT Explorer application.

4. Choose View, Options. You need to add an association for the *WINDOWS Magazine* CD files, so select the File Types tab.

5. Click the New Type button to display the Add New File Type dialog box.

6. In the Description of type field, type **WinMag CD File**.

7. In the Association extension field, type **WM**.

8. Click the New button to display the New Action dialog box.

9. In the Action field, type Open.

10. Click the Browse button and locate the WMLAUNCH.EXE file on the *WINDOWS Magazine* CD. You may need to insert the CD in your system and change folders in the Open With dialog box to locate WMLAUNCH.EXE. The full name of the *WINDOWS Magazine* CD is CMP Publications Win Mag Fall.

11. Click OK in the Open With dialog box to return to the New Action dialog box. Notice that WMLAUNCH.EXE is inserted in the Application Used to Perform Action field. This tells Windows NT which application to launch when you open files of type WM.

12. Click OK to return to the Add New File Type dialog box.

13. Uncheck the Confirm Open After Download checkbox. If you leave this box checked, each time you open a file of WM type you will be asked by Internet Explorer if it is OK to do so.

14. Click the Close button. In the Registered File Types list on the File Types tab you should see a setting for WinMag CD File that lists WM as its extension and WMLAUNCH as the application with which to open it.

15. Click Close.

16. Right-click the Start button and select Explore All Users. This displays the Windows NT Explorer with the Start Menu folder open.

17. In the right pane of the Explorer window, double-click the Programs folder to open it.

18. Create a new folder called WinMag CD (Common) and open it.

19. In the WinMag CD (Common) folder, create a shortcut to the DEFAULT.HTM file in the \LIBRARY folder on the *WINDOWS Magazine* CD. To do this, choose File, New, Shortcut and click the Browse button on the Create Shortcut dialog box to locate the DEFAULT.HTM file on the CD-ROM. You need to select the All Files option from the File of Type drop-down list to display all the files in the Library folder. By default, only applications display.

    When the Select a Title for the Program dialog box appears, change the name from Default to **WinMag CD Home Page**.

20. Close the Explorer or My Computer window.

The WinMag CD (Common) item is now listed on the Programs folder, which you can see by clicking the Start button. You can activate the *WINDOWS Magazine* CD by selecting Start, Programs, WinMag CD (Common), WinMag CD Home Page.

Uninstall

The *Windows Magazine* CD-ROM is a low-impact product. To uninstall it, simply perform the following steps:

1. Right-click the Start button and select Explore All Users. This displays Windows NT Explorer with the Start Menu folder open.

2. In the right pane of the Explorer window, double-click the Programs folder to open it.

3. Delete the WinMag CD (Common) folder.

If you uninstall the CD-ROM, you must reinstall it before you can properly browse and operate it again.

> **Note**
>
> If you use this CD to install another program —DecideRight, for example, or one of the shareware programs—you must follow their own, separate uninstallation instructions.

Technical Support

If you have a question, check out the listing of frequently asked questions—WMCDFAQ.TXT—in the root folder of the *WINDOWS Magazine* CD. You can view this by opening Windows NT Explorer or My Computer and double-clicking the WMCDFAQ.TXT file. *WINDOWS Magazine* cannot provide one-on-one technical support via e-mail, telephone, or mail for this CD.

A combination FAQ for the WinMag CD and Wintune® 2.0 is available by Internet e-mail answerback. Send a message to **wmcdfaq@dnai.com** and the latest version will be sent back automatically.

> **Note**
>
> The system sends only one copy per day to the same e-mail address.

WINDOWS Magazine currently provides direct technical support only through their forums on CompuServe—**GO WINMAG**, message section 14—and America Online—keyword **WinMag**, then choose Message Exchange, then look in the folder CD_TIPS.

Damaged Discs

CDs are occasionally damaged at the factory or in shipment. Depending on the extent and nature of the damage, you may encounter a wide variety of error messages, or the disc may be completely unreadable.

If you think your CD might be damaged, here's an easy way to tell for sure.

1. Open My Computer.

2. Right-click the CD-ROM drive icon.

3. Select Find from the context menu.

4. Type *.* in the Named field and click Find Now.

If you get error messages during the search, it's a bad disc, and you should call customer support at 800-829-9831 or 904-445-4662 for a replacement.

If the search completes normally without an error message, then the disc is probably good and something else is causing the problems. ❖

Index

C

Y-Z

Complete and Return this Card for a *FREE* Computer Book Catalog

Thank you for purchasing this book! You have purchased a superior computer book written expressly for your needs. To continue to provide the kind of up-to-date, pertinent coverage you've come to expect from us, we need to hear from you. Please take a minute to complete and return this self-addressed, postage-paid form. In return, we'll send you a free catalog of all our computer books on topics ranging from word processing to programming and the internet.

Mr. ☐   Mrs. ☐   Ms. ☐   Dr. ☐

Name (first) ☐☐☐☐☐☐☐☐☐☐☐   (M.I.) ☐   (last) ☐☐☐☐☐☐☐☐☐☐☐☐☐☐☐☐☐☐

Address ☐☐☐☐☐☐☐☐☐☐☐☐☐☐☐☐☐☐☐☐☐☐☐☐☐☐☐☐☐☐☐☐☐

☐☐☐☐☐☐☐☐☐☐☐☐☐☐☐☐☐☐☐☐☐☐☐☐☐☐☐☐☐☐☐☐☐

City ☐☐☐☐☐☐☐☐☐☐☐☐☐☐☐☐☐☐   State ☐☐   Zip ☐☐☐☐☐☐☐☐☐☐

Phone ☐☐☐ ☐☐☐☐☐☐☐   Fax ☐☐☐ ☐☐☐☐☐☐☐

Company Name ☐☐☐☐☐☐☐☐☐☐☐☐☐☐☐☐☐☐☐☐☐☐☐☐☐☐☐☐☐☐

E-mail address ☐☐☐☐☐☐☐☐☐☐☐☐☐☐☐☐☐☐☐☐☐☐☐☐☐☐☐☐☐☐

1. Please check at least (3) influencing factors for purchasing this book.

Front or back cover information on book .... ☐
Special approach to the content .... ☐
Completeness of content .... ☐
Author's reputation .... ☐
Publisher's reputation .... ☐
Book cover design or layout .... ☐
Index or table of contents of book .... ☐
Price of book .... ☐
Special effects, graphics, illustrations .... ☐
Other (Please specify): _____

2. How did you first learn about this book?

Saw in Macmillan Computer Publishing catalog .... ☐
Recommended by store personnel .... ☐
Saw the book on bookshelf at store .... ☐
Recommended by a friend .... ☐
Received advertisement in the mail .... ☐
Saw an advertisement in: _____ ☐
Read book review in: _____ ☐
Other (Please specify): _____ ☐

3. How many computer books have you purchased in the last six months?

This book only .... ☐   3 to 5 books .... ☐
2 books .... ☐   More than 5 .... ☐

4. Where did you purchase this book?

Bookstore .... ☐
Computer Store .... ☐
Consumer Electronics Store .... ☐
Department Store .... ☐
Office Club .... ☐
Warehouse Club .... ☐
Mail Order .... ☐
Direct from Publisher .... ☐
Internet site .... ☐
Other (Please specify): _____

5. How long have you been using a computer?

☐ Less than 6 months   ☐ 6 months to a year
☐ 1 to 3 years   ☐ More than 3 years

6. What is your level of experience with personal computers and with the subject of this book?

	With PCs	With subject of book
New	☐	☐
Casual	☐	☐
Accomplished	☐	☐
Expert	☐	☐

Source Code ISBN: 0-7897-0817-5

7. Which of the following best describes your job title?

Administrative Assistant .... ☐
Coordinator .... ☐
Manager/Supervisor .... ☐
Director .... ☐
Vice President .... ☐
President/CEO/COO .... ☐
Lawyer/Doctor/Medical Professional .... ☐
Teacher/Educator/Trainer .... ☐
Engineer/Technician .... ☐
Consultant .... ☐
Not employed/Student/Retired .... ☐
Other (Please specify): _____ ☐

8. Which of the following best describes the area of the company your job title falls under?

Accounting .... ☐
Engineering .... ☐
Manufacturing .... ☐
Operations .... ☐
Marketing .... ☐
Sales .... ☐
Other (Please specify): _____ ☐

9. What is your age?

Under 20 .... ☐
21-29 .... ☐
30-39 .... ☐
40-49 .... ☐
50-59 .... ☐
60-over .... ☐

10. Are you:

Male .... ☐
Female .... ☐

11. Which computer publications do you read regularly? (Please list)

_____
_____
_____
_____
_____
_____
_____
_____
_____

Comments: _____
_____
_____

Fold here and scotch-tape to mail.

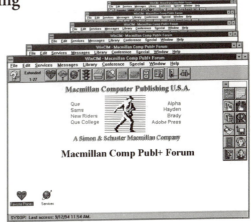

Check out Que® Books on the World Wide Web
http://www.mcp.com/que

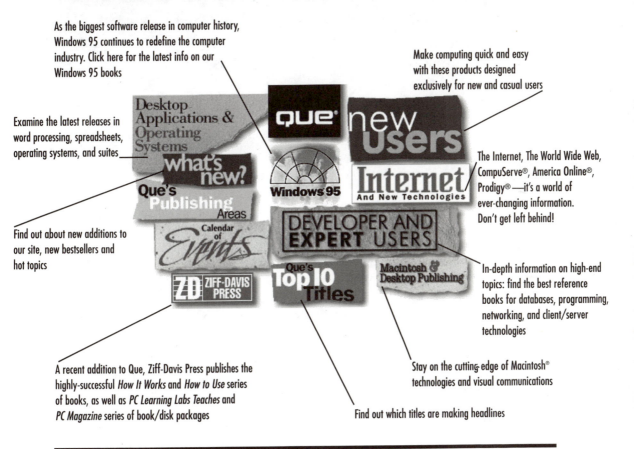

As the biggest software release in computer history, Windows 95 continues to redefine the computer industry. Click here for the latest info on our Windows 95 books

Make computing quick and easy with these products designed exclusively for new and casual users

Examine the latest releases in word processing, spreadsheets, operating systems, and suites

The Internet, The World Wide Web, CompuServe®, America Online®, Prodigy®—it's a world of ever-changing information. Don't get left behind!

Find out about new additions to our site, new bestsellers and hot topics

In-depth information on high-end topics: find the best reference books for databases, programming, networking, and client/server technologies

A recent addition to Que, Ziff-Davis Press publishes the highly-successful *How It Works* and *How to Use* series of books, as well as *PC Learning Labs Teaches* and *PC Magazine* series of book/disk packages

Stay on the cutting-edge of Macintosh® technologies and visual communications

Find out which titles are making headlines

With 6 separate publishing groups, Que develops products for many specific market segments and areas of computer technology. Explore our Web Site and you'll find information on best-selling titles, newly published titles, upcoming products, authors, and much more.

- Stay informed on the latest industry trends and products available
- Visit our online bookstore for the latest information and editions
- Download software from Que's library of the best shareware and freeware

Before using this disc, please read Appendix B "What's on the CD," for information on how to install the disc and what programs are included on the disc. If you have problems with this disk, please contact Macmillan Technical Support at (317) 581-3833. We can be reached by e-mail at **support@mcp.com** or on CompuServe at **GO QUEBOOKS**.

License Agreement

By opening this package you are agreeing to be bound by the following:

This software is copyrighted and all rights are reserved by the publisher and its licensers. You are licensed to use this software on a single computer. You may copy the software for backup or archival purposes only. Making copies of the software for any other purpose is a violation of United States copyright laws. THIS SOFTWARE IS SOLD AS IS, WITHOUT WARRANTY OF ANY KIND, EITHER EXPRESSED OR IMPLIED, INCLUDING BUT NOT LIMITED TO THE IMPLIED WARRANTIES OF MERCHANTABILITY AND FITNESS FOR A PARTICULAR PURPOSE. Neither the publisher nor its licensers, dealers, or distributors assumes any liability for any alleged or actual damages arising from the use of this software. (Some states do not allow exclusion of implied warranties, so the exclusion may not apply to you.)

The entire contents of the disc and the compilation of the software are copyrighted and protected by United States copyright laws. The individual programs on these discs are copyrighted by the authors or owners of each program. Each program has its own use permissions and limitations. To use each program, you must follow the individual requirements and restrictions detailed for each. Do not use a program if you do not agree to follow its licensing agreement.